"Poythress does a masterful job of showing how our ability to think rationally is grounded in the very nature of God himself. I heartily recommend this book to every student of the subject."

Douglas Wilson, Senior Minister, Christ Church Moscow, Idaho; coauthor, *Introductory Logic*

"Each of Vern Poythress's books has been, in my judgment, the best book on its particular subject."

John Frame, Professor of Systematic Theology and Philosophy, Reformed Theological Seminary, Orlando

"Every new item that Vern Poythress writes is thoughtful, creative, and worth reading."

C. John Collins, Professor of Old Testament, Covenant Theological Seminary

Logic

Logic

———

A God-Centered
Approach to the
Foundation of
Western Thought

———

Vern Sheridan
Poythress

CROSSWAY

WHEATON, ILLINOIS

Trade paperback ISBN: 978-1-4335-3229-0
PDF ISBN: 978-1-4335-3230-6
Mobipocket ISBN: 978-1-4335-3231-3
ePub ISBN: 978-1-4335-3232-0

Library of Congress Cataloging-in-Publication Data

Poythress, Vern S.
   Logic : a god-centered approach to the foundation of
western thought / Vern Sheridan Poythress.
      p. cm.
   Includes bibliographical references and index.
   ISBN 978-1-4335-3229-0
   1. Logic. 2. Faith and reason. I. Title.
BC101.P69   2013
160—dc23   2012035512

Crossway is a publishing ministry of Good News Publishers.

SH		22	21	20	19	18	17	16	15	14	13
15	14	13	12	11	10	9	8	7	6	5	4	3	2	1

Contents

Part III.E: Special Logics and More Enriched Logics

Part IV: Supplements

Part IV.A: Supplements to Elementary Logic

Part IV.B: Supplementary Proofs for Propositional Logic

Part IV.C: Proofs for Quantification

Tables and Illustrations

Tables

Illustrations

Symbols Used in Parts II–IV

(Listed in the order in which they are introduced; the symbols ⊢, ∨, ∧, and |
each have two different usages.)

Symbol	Stands for	Introduced on page
⊢	"it is the case"	230
∨	logical "or" (disjunction)	235
~ (or ¬)	logical "not" (negation)	236
∧	logical "and" (conjunction)	237
⊃ (or → or ⇒)	logical ("material") implication	238
{ $a, b, c, \ldots$ }	the set with members $a, b, c, \ldots$	261
∪	union of two sets	262
∈	"is a member of" (for a member of a set)	262
∩	intersection of two sets	262
$'$	complement of a set	263
⊆	set inclusion	264
∨	join (in the context of a lattice or a partially ordered set)	267
∧	meet (in the context of a lattice or a partially ordered set)	267
∗	a binary operation (in the context of abstract algebra)	272
⊕	an addition-like operation (in the context of Boolean algebra)	274
⊗	a multiplication-like operation (in the context of Boolean algebra)	275
⊖	a negation-like operation (in the context of Boolean algebra)	276
≡ or ↔	truth-functional ("material") equivalence	281
|	Sheffer stroke (logical incompatibility)	322
∀	all	376

∃	existential quantifier ("there exists")	378
φ	an arbitrary propositional function	396
=	equality	404
⊨	satisfies (in model theory)	458
◊	possibility (in modal logic)	494
□	necessity (in modal logic)	494
|	"such that" (in the context of defining members of a set)	526
⊢	in proof theory, "it is provable that" (on the basis of the propositions that *precede* the symbol ⊢)	600

Preface

In this book we explore elementary parts of logic and neighboring fields. Part I of the book lays the foundation. In parts II and III we look at further developments in the nineteenth and twentieth centuries. These later developments have affected people's views of logic as a whole. But not all readers will be equally interested in them. I have placed the discussion of Christian foundations for logic at an early point, in part I, so that people may access it without worrying about technical details. Some readers may content themselves just with part I. Parts I.A–I.C provide the basic discussion of Christian foundations. Part I.D illustrates how these Christian foundations influence our view of Aristotelian syllogisms, which were the earliest and longest lasting form of formal logic.

Logic can be studied without considering the history of philosophy and its interaction with logic. But, for those interested, I have included in appendices F1–F5 some indications of how the nature of logic affects philosophy.

Fully appreciating modern logic involves understanding its interfaces with neighboring fields of study: rhetoric, analytic philosophy, set theory, proof theory, computation theory, abstract algebra, model theory. These fields have experienced extensive development in the twentieth century. One book or even several books cannot begin to cover them. So we have made only a beginning. In addition, logic has a rich and fascinating history.[1] I regret that I can mention only a few pieces of history in passing.

I have received help from many sources, both direct and indirect. I thank the Lord, the almighty God, the Creator of heaven and earth, who has given me life and breath and every truth and insight that I have received. He has redeemed me from the pit through Christ my Savior, and set me on the path of eternal life. To him I give all the glory.

I owe a debt also to many human beings, living and dead, to whom God has given truth and insight through his common grace or special grace. I thank my wife, who has borne with the production of this book and has

---

[1] "Logic, History of," *Encyclopedia of Philosophy*, 2nd ed., ed. Donald M. Borchert, 10 vols. (Detroit/New York/San Francisco/ . . . : Thomson Gale, 2006), 5:397–484.

helped in editing it. I want to recognize Kenneth Pike, Edmund P. Clowney, and John Frame, whose insights gave me many of the tools that I have used in undertaking a Christian analysis of logic. I appreciate Cornelius Van Til, who boldly stressed the distinctiveness of a Christian approach to logic, and D. H. Th. Vollenhoven, who wrote about the necessity for a Christian logic.[2] These two men built upon Augustine, who understood the radical absoluteness of God; John Calvin, who vigorously articulated the Creator-creature distinction; and Abraham Kuyper, who proclaimed the lordship of Christ over every sector of life and over every field of academic study.

Then there are those who have worked on logic and neighboring areas: the Sophists, Socrates, Plato, Aristotle, Euclid; and in modern times János Bolyai, Nikolai Lobachevsky, George Boole, Gottlob Frege, Charles S. Peirce, Alfred North Whitehead, Bertrand Russell, Kurt Gödel, David Hilbert, Alan Turing, Alonzo Church, Stephen Kleene, and Alfred Tarski, to name a few. Among them I may also list Hilary Putnam and Saul Kripke, who were my teachers in logic, and Garrett Birkhoff, my advisor and mentor in abstract algebra. I have not always agreed with them, but the world has been blessed by the positive insights that they have contributed through common grace.

---

[2] Dirk Hendrik Theodoor Vollenhoven, *De noodzakelijkheid eener christelijke logica* (Amsterdam: H. J. Paris, 1932); see also Vollenhoven, "Hoofdlijnen der logica," *Philosophia Reformata* 13 (1948): 59–118.

Part I
Elementary Logic

We develop a Christian approach to logic. In part I, where we consider elementary logic, no special symbols are needed. Our discussion focuses on traditional classical logic, leaving until parts II and III developments in the nineteenth and twentieth centuries.

Part I.A

Introducing Logic and Argument

Chapter 1

Logic in Tension

In the original *Star Trek* TV series, the characters Spock and Leonard McCoy are opposites. Spock is logical; McCoy is passionate. Spock is cold; McCoy is hot. The contrast raises lots of questions. How does logic fit in with our humanity? Is logic opposite to emotion? What should we be like as human beings—logical or emotional or both?

Logic and Humanity

The *Star Trek* series gained popularity not only because it had entertaining plots but also because it laid out in narrative form some of the big questions about man and his relation to the cosmos. Who are we? What is the meaning of life? What is the cosmic purpose of humanity? Why do logic and emotion struggle within us?

Viewers' reactions to Spock reveal different attitudes toward logic. To some people, Spock's logic is an ideal. To others, he may be either admirable or pitiable, but he lacks something. The creators of the show make their own comment by revealing that, while McCoy is human, Spock is the offspring from a Vulcan father and a human mother. He is only half human. A deeper look at Spock reveals further complexity: though Spock endeavors to follow logic, he sometimes struggles with inner emotions because of his human side. Does this fictional portrayal hint that logic is not enough?

What about us? How do we relate to logic? Does it appeal to us? Or do we feel that by itself it is too "cold"?

Some people are more logical, some more emotional. Some people think that we have problems because we are not logical enough. Others think that we are much too logical. In their view, devotion to logic creates difficulties, and we ought to move beyond logic to something else—to nature or mysticism or art. Science, in the minds of some, is driven by logic and by a tightly defined, cold rationality. Human beings in their full personality are driven by warmth: they have desires and emotions and imagination, which are aptly expressed in the arts, in leisure, in entertainment, and in the humanities. Science, according to this view, is at odds with the humanities and with what is most precious to us.

So what is logic? Is it important? How do we understand its relation to emotion, intuition, and other aspects of human life? How do we use it? Does it have limits?

Christian Logic?

I believe that common conceptions about logic do not provide healthy answers to these questions. We need a new approach to the subject—we need a distinctively *Christian* approach.

Is there such a thing as a *Christian* view of logic? We would not be surprised to find a distinctively Christian approach to theology or ethics, because the Bible has much to say about God and ethics. But could there be a distinctively Christian approach to logic? Many people would say no. They would say that logic is what it is, irrespective of religious belief. I think that the reality is more complicated. There *is* a Christian view of logic. But it will take some time to see why.[1]

Readers may, if they wish, treat this book as a general introduction to logic. Our discussion does not assume any previous acquaintance with the subject. We try to make the ideas accessible by including simple explanations with each new concept. But the discussion also has pertinence for experts, because we do not take a conventional approach. We develop a distinctively Christian approach. Human thinking about logic needs redeeming. As a result, it will take us some time to come to the point of discussing details that typically become the focus of logic textbooks.

---

[1] I appreciate the inspiration I have received from Abraham Kuyper, *Lectures on Calvinism* (Grand Rapids, MI: Eerdmans, 1931), and from Cornelius Van Til, who continued Kuyper's legacy. Both men counsel us to think and act in all our lives as committed followers of Christ, and to bring our distinctive Christian commitments to bear on every area of life. In principle, Christian distinctiveness applies to logic. But Kuyper says at one point that logic does not need a distinctly Christian reading, and for this concession Cornelius Van Til rightly criticizes him (Abraham Kuyper, *Principles of Sacred Theology* [Grand Rapids, MI: Eerdmans, 1968], 159–160; Cornelius Van Til, *Common Grace and the Gospel* [n.l.: Presbyterian & Reformed, 1973], 42–44; Van Til, *The Defense of the Faith*, 2nd ed. [Philadelphia: Presbyterian & Reformed, 1963], 287–288).

For Further Reflection

1. What makes the difference between Spock and McCoy so fascinating?
2. What different reactions are there to Spock as a character, and what do they say about people's views about logic?
3. When people think about an ideal for humanity, what role do they assign to logic?
4. How might human beings deal with the apparent tension between logic and emotion? What implications are there for the nature of our humanity?
5. Why might some people think that a distinctively Christian approach to logic makes no sense?

Chapter 2

Why Study Logic?

Why should we bother to study logic? Spock exemplifies one part of its importance. On the one hand, Spock's rational analysis gives the *Star Trek* crew valuable advice. On the other hand, we struggle with an apparent conflict between logic and emotion, or even between logic and humanness. We need a remedy.

We can find other reasons for studying logic. Some people find logic intrinsically interesting. For them, it is fun. Others study it for practical purposes. They hope that studying logic can help them sharpen their ability to reason carefully. Practice in logic can help us detect logical errors in reasoning, which have been called *logical fallacies*.

The Influence of Logic

Logic is important for another, historical reason. Logic has had a profound influence on the whole history of Western thought. In the Western world, the formal study of logic began largely with the Greek philosopher Aristotle—though Aristotle built to some extent on his philosophical predecessors, Socrates and Plato.[1] Plato and Aristotle hoped to find deep truths about the nature of the world by careful reasoning. Aristotle's study of logic tried to codify the most basic forms of reasoning. This codification could then serve as a solid foundation for philosophical investigations trying to answer the big questions about the nature of reality and the meaning of life.

Western philosophy ever since Aristotle's time has followed in the steps of Plato and Aristotle. Philosophers have *reasoned*. They have used logic. Up until the nineteenth century, with few exceptions, they built on the foundation of Aristotle's logic. The nineteenth and twentieth centuries have seen further, more technical developments in logic, which have gone well beyond what Aristotle achieved. But for the most part these developments have

---

[1] Susanne Bobzien, "Logic, History of: Ancient Logic," *Encyclopedia of Philosophy*, 2nd ed., ed. Donald M. Borchert, 10 vols. (Detroit/New York/San Francisco/ . . . : Thomson Gale, 2006), 5:397–401.

enhanced rather than overthrown the classical logic developed by Aristotle. (For more detailed discussion of logic and philosophy, see part IV.F, especially appendix F2. For some alternatives to classical logic, see chapters 63 and 64.)

Logic and philosophy have had a broad influence on intellectual culture in the West. Philosophy has directly influenced intellectual life, because it has seemed to many people to offer the most profound and far-reaching kind of knowledge. Science has taken a leading role in more recent times, but for centuries reasoning in intellectual centers was influenced and guided by ideas from philosophy.

In addition, logic has had indirect influence. People engage in reasoning in every area of serious study, not just in philosophy. In almost every sphere, universities today rely on reasoning—in natural sciences, medicine, historical studies, law, economics, political science, language study, literary analysis, mathematics. Academic work aspires to conduct its reasoning *rigorously*. And logic is a model for rigor. Reasoning in universities today still has underneath it the foundation for logic that Aristotle laid.

Though Aristotle's logic functions as a foundation for Western thought, we should not exaggerate its role. In both the past and the present, much influential reasoning takes the form of informal reasoning and does not explicitly invoke Aristotelian logic or any kind of formally organized logic. Appropriately, logicians themselves distinguish between the *formal logic* that Aristotle developed and the *informal logic* involved in more ordinary instances of reasoning.[2] Yet rigorous formal logic offers an ideal that can still influence what people expect and how people evaluate informal reasoning. Logic has an influence far wider than its core.

Logic has also influenced perceptions about the contrast between rationality on the one hand and emotion, desire, and imagination on the other. The historical movement called the Enlightenment championed *reason*. But soon people became restless. They sensed that reason was not enough. Reason gave us only half of humanity—or less. The Enlightenment stimulated a reaction, the Romantic movement, which depreciated reason and championed the imaginative, the spontaneous, the natural, and the pre-rational aspects of humanity. Like the opposition between sciences and humanities, the opposition between the Enlightenment and the Romantic movement expresses the contrast between logic and emotion, or between

---

[2] On the distinction between formal and informal logic, see chapter 4.

Spock and McCoy. Thus, the contrast between Spock and McCoy has ana-logues that play out in culture and history.

At the foundation of this cultural opposition lies logic. It feeds into the Enlightenment's conception of reason, and it shapes the Romantic opposi-tion to the Enlightenment as well, because the opposition defines itself in reaction to reason.

This foundation for Western thought in logic needs to be redone. And that means that the whole of Western thought has to be redone. It is a most serious issue.

Arguments

What do we mean by logic? One textbook on logic defines it as "the analysis and appraisal of arguments."[3] When we hear the word *argument*, we may picture a situation where two people are having a dispute with each other—perhaps a bitter, heated dispute. They are fighting verbally, each person vig-orously defending his own view. But the word *argument* can be used not only to describe quarrels but to describe any reasoning in support of a conclusion.

Arguments of this kind may crop up in friendly settings. An advertise-ment for a car may present arguments to persuade you to buy one. The advertisement tells you that its car gives you good gas mileage. It is durable. It has special computerized features to play your favorite songs. It has a luxurious interior. It looks cool. And so on. These are informal arguments in favor of buying the car.

We meet arguments not only when someone else is trying to lay out the desirable features of a product, but when we are quietly trying to decide something for ourselves. For example, Irene may be "arguing with herself" about which college to attend. College A is closer to home. College B has lower tuition. College A is reputed to have a better program in economics. College B has a beautiful rural campus. College A is right in the middle of exciting city life. College B has a larger student body. Irene formulates argu-ments in her own mind in favor of each of the options. Arguments are useful not only for small purchases, but also for major decisions like choosing a college or deciding what kind of job to pursue.

---

[3] Harold J. Gensler, *Introduction to Logic* (London/New York: Routledge, 2002), 1. This definition is picked up in Wikipedia: http://en.wikipedia.org/wiki/Logic, accessed September 11, 2010. Isaac Watts's book *Logic*, widely used in an older era, defines logic more broadly: "Logic is the art of using reason well in our enquiries after truth, and the communication of it to others" (*Logic; or, the Right Use of Reason in the Enquiry after Truth: With a Variety of Rules to Guard against Error, in the Affairs of Religion and Human Life, as Well as in the Sciences* [many editions] [London: Tegg, 1811], 1).

We also meet arguments in academic settings. A university class may lay out reasoning to reach conclusions in chemistry or in the history of World War I. When a class considers disputed ideas, the class members may study arguments both for and against the ideas. Underneath the particular arguments lies a foundation in logic, which analyzes general principles of argument.

Arguments can help to lead us to a wise conclusion. But they can also lead us astray. For example, a student says, "Either you get an A in the course or you show that you are an idiot." But might there be a third alternative? The presentation of two extreme alternatives as if they were the *only* alternatives is called the *fallacy of bifurcation*. There are other forms of fallacy as well. A fallacy is a kind of argument that may sound plausible but that uses tricks rather than solid reasoning.[4] Logic includes the study of various kinds of fallacies. People hope that by studying fallacies they may more easily detect them in the future.

Arguments in the Bible

Arguments occur in the Bible. We should not be surprised, because the Bible describes human life in all its ups and downs. For example, a major argument takes place in 2 Samuel 17:1–14. Absalom, the son of David, has just mounted a rebellion against the kingship of his father David. He has forced David out of Jerusalem, the capital city. But as long as David is alive, Absalom's own position in power remains in jeopardy. Absalom asks for advice from Ahithophel, who has a reputation for giving shrewd counsel (2 Sam. 16:23). Absalom also consults Hushai, who gives opposite advice. Ahithophel says Absalom should attack David right away with a small force of select troops (17:1). Hushai advises Absalom to wait in order to assemble a large army. Both Ahithophel and Hushai give supporting reasons in favor of their stratagems.

Absalom and his supporters think that Hushai's advice is better. Hushai's arguments are convincing; but they lead to disaster. Absalom is killed in the battle that eventually takes place (2 Sam. 18:15). Clearly an argument can be a major turning point in a person's life, and even in the life of a whole kingdom—in this case, the kingdom of Israel.

The arguments from Ahithophel and Hushai are even more striking

---

[4] A fallacy is "an often plausible argument using false or invalid inference" (*Webster's Ninth New Collegiate Dictionary*). See S. Morris Engel, *With Good Reason: An Introduction to Informal Fallacies* (New York: St. Martin's, 1982).

because the reader of 2 Samuel receives some information that Absalom and Ahithophel did not know. Hushai is pretending to serve Absalom, but secretly he is loyal to David. In fact, David has earlier told Hushai to go to Absalom and to try to interfere by dissuading Absalom from following Ahithophel's advice (2 Sam. 15:34). Hushai appears to Absalom to give his advice sincerely, and the arguments that he offers are plausible and attractive. But the reader can infer that Hushai does not believe in these arguments himself. He is acting out a role. Hushai's arguments therefore have two layers: what he intends Absalom to understand and what he himself understands and intends. In fact, the arguments have a third layer, because God the Lord is active behind the scenes: "For the LORD had ordained to defeat the good counsel of Ahithophel, so that the LORD might bring harm upon Absalom" (17:14).

Arguments can be used to deceive and manipulate. But they can also become part of wise counsel. At one point David has decided to order his men to attack Nabal and kill him. Abigail, Nabal's wife, comes out and dissuades him with her arguments (1 Sam. 25:23–31). David is persuaded, and blesses Abigail for having kept him back from sin (v. 33). The story has a further happy ending because after Nabal dies—by God's act rather than David's—David and Abigail marry (v. 42). Abigail's arguments have steered David toward righteous action and away from sin.

We meet still further arguments within the Bible, including arguments that address all-important religious decisions. The serpent in Genesis 3 gives arguments to try to induce Adam and Eve to sin. Elijah in 1 Kings 18 gives arguments (and a demonstration) to try to turn the people of Israel away from worshiping Baal and toward worshiping the Lord, the true God of Israel. Since Elijah presents himself as a prophet of God, his arguments claim to be not merely human but also divine. Elijah claims that God is presenting the arguments to Israel through him.

The New Testament indicates that God continues to speak, and it includes arguments to call people to come to Christ for salvation. The apostle Peter presents arguments in his sermon in Acts 2:14–36. Since Peter is an apostle, commissioned by Christ, these arguments also present themselves as divine arguments. The apostle Paul presents arguments in his sermons here and there in Acts. Acts 13:16–41; 14:15–17; and 17:22–31 give examples. In addition, some of the summaries of Paul's preaching mention argument and reasoning:

> And Paul went in, *as was his custom*, and on three Sabbath days he *reasoned* with them from the Scriptures, explaining and *proving* that it was necessary for the Christ to suffer and to rise from the dead, and saying, "This Jesus, whom I proclaim to you, is the Christ." (Acts 17:3)

> So he [Paul] *reasoned* in the synagogue with the Jews and the devout persons, and in the marketplace every day with those who happened to be there. (Acts 17:17)

> And he [Paul] *reasoned* in the synagogue every Sabbath, and tried to *persuade* Jews and Greeks. (Acts 18:4)

> And he [Paul] entered the synagogue and for three months spoke boldly, *reasoning and persuading* them about the kingdom of God. (Acts 19:8)

We also hear of arguments within the church when controversies arose:

> And after Paul and Barnabas had no small *dissension and debate* with them, Paul and Barnabas and some of the others were appointed to go up to Jerusalem to the apostles and the elders about this question. (Acts 15:2)

> The apostles and the elders were gathered together to consider this matter. And after there had been *much debate*, Peter stood up . . . (Acts 15:6–7)

In 1 Corinthians 15 Paul presents an extended argument to try to correct wavering in the Corinthian church over the question of whether there will be a future resurrection of the body.

The Bible contains many other types of communication in addition to arguments. It has songs, historical reports, prophecies, and so on. But we can use the idea of argument and persuasion as a perspective on everything the Bible does. In a looser sense, we can say that the whole of the Bible functions as an argument to induce us to change ourselves, our beliefs, and our behavior.[5]

Clearly, arguments play an important role within the Bible. They also have important roles in modern life. Arguments are important, and so logic as the analysis of argument also has an important role.

---

[5] I owe to John Frame this idea of using argument as a perspective on the whole of the Bible.

For Further Reflection

1. Is logic important? Why or why not?
2. How has logic influenced Western thought?
3. How does logic function in universities?
4. What kinds of arguments take place in Genesis 18:23–33; 27:5–13; 41:33–40; Exodus 4:1–17; 18:13–27; 2 Samuel 12:1–15; 14:1–24; Job; Acts 2:14–36; 3:12–26; 4:8–12; 7:2–53; 13:16–41; 14:15–17; 15:6–21; 17:22–31; 1 Corinthians 15; Galatians; Colossians; Hebrews; James?
5. What do you think are the most crucial arguments for human well-being?
6. Why do good arguments sometimes fail to persuade people?

Chapter 3

What Do We Trust?

In the discussion above we have introduced the Bible into our thinking about argument. What status does the Bible have?

The Status of the Bible

People have different opinions about the Bible. I believe that the Bible is God's word, his own speech in written form. What the Bible says, God says. But not everyone agrees.

So on this question we have the opportunity to examine arguments and analyze them. Jesus himself testifies to the authority of the Old Testament (Matt. 5:17–18; John 10:35; Luke 24:44–47). Other parts of the Bible and evidence from outside of the Bible can be drawn into the arguments. The arguments about the Bible have already been presented many times in extended form.[1] We do not have space to repeat them here. Rather, we are going to use the Bible to try to understand more deeply the character of arguments and logic.

An approach using the Bible may leave many people uneasy. Why? People may have many reasons, but one reason is that, in the modern world, we are accustomed to examining all claims critically. We use reasoning to sift through claims, and we do not trust anything—including statements within the Bible—until they are sifted.

People have attempted to sift through the Bible in many ways, and as a result we have a lot of disagreement about ideas in the Bible. In the modern world, people do not agree about whether God exists. There are other questions as well, a whole list of them. Is Jesus Christ really the Messiah and Savior promised in the Old Testament? Did Jesus Christ really rise from the dead? Is he the only Savior? Does the Bible give us an accurate picture

---

[1] There could be an extended list. As a beginning, we might mention John M. Frame, *The Doctrine of the Word of God* (Phillipsburg, NJ: Presbyterian & Reformed, 2010); and Benjamin B. Warfield, *The Inspiration and Authority of the Bible* (reprint; Philadelphia: Presbyterian & Reformed, 1967). For arguments about the truth of the Christian faith as a whole, see Timothy J. Keller, *The Reason for God: Belief in an Age of Skepticism* (New York: Dutton, 2008).

of who Jesus is and what he did? Does following him lead to trusting in the Bible? Is the Bible God's word?

Foundations: Divine Instruction versus Autonomy

These questions are all important, and they have led to books full of arguments, both pro and con. Any inquirer may examine them for himself. We could repeat some of these arguments, or add further arguments. But such arguments are for other books. In this book, we are focusing on logic. That is, we are focusing on the very process of analyzing arguments. When an inquirer undertakes to analyze a specific argument, whether about God or about some other issue, he inevitably has in the background of his thought some general principles or ideas about evaluating arguments. In effect, he is relying on logic, even if he is not consciously aware of it.

Now a difficulty arises. There are two radically different ways of understanding logic, not just one. There is the Christian way, and there is the usual modern way, which has also been the dominant way within the history of Western philosophy.[2] The Christian way is to listen submissively to the instruction of Jesus Christ, who is the Lord of the universe. The modern way is the way of *autonomy*, where we treat our own human powers as ultimate when we engage in the process of evaluation.

We can illustrate the difference using an incident from the philosopher Socrates, as recorded in Plato's dialogue *Euthyphro*. At a key point Socrates requests, "Tell me what holiness is, no matter whether it is loved by the gods or anything else happens to it."[3] The gods in question are the Greek gods, each of whom is limited in relation to the others, and all of whom are finite. They quarrel with one another; they are not reliable. Given that context, it seems eminently reasonable for Socrates to try to find out the real nature of holiness, independent of what the gods may say. He will *reason* it through. In the context of later philosophical developments in the Western world, Socrates becomes an emblem for using one's mind and one's reasoning powers *autonomously*. The word *autonomy* in its etymology means "self-law." Autonomy means making human judgment and human standards for judgment an ultimate touchstone in one's life.

In contrast to the way of autonomy we have the way of submitting to

---

[2] See John Frame, "Greeks Bearing Gifts," in *Revolutions in Worldview: Understanding the Flow of Western Thought*, ed. W. Andrew Hoffecker (Phillipsburg, NJ: Presbyterian & Reformed, 2007), 6–7.
[3] Plato, *Euthyphro*, trans. Harold N. Fowler (London: Heinemann; Cambridge, MA: Harvard University Press, 1966), 13B. See the further discussion in appendix F2.

divine revelation. But is this way really open to us? The situation with the Greek gods shows the difficulty. So-called revelations from so-called gods may be unreliable. They may be worse—they may be manipulative. Human beings may falsely claim to have revelations in order to gain power and prestige. According to the Bible, evil spirits may come to people and give them deceitful "revelations" (Acts 16:16–18; 2 Thess. 2:9–12).

The reality of such counterfeit revelations does not show that genuine revelation is impossible. The counterfeit is the counterfeit of the genuine. The Bible's claim is precisely that it is the genuine revelation from the one true God. Is that claim true?

Each person has to decide. He has to decide what he thinks about God, about Jesus Christ, about the resurrection of Jesus Christ, and about the status in the Bible. He may find himself weighing arguments pro and con.

Each person has his own personal history. But in some cases, people start with the account of Jesus Christ given in the Bible in the four Gospels—Matthew, Mark, Luke, John. They find out who Jesus is. They read about what he has done. They see the evidence within the Bible for believing that he rose from the dead. Maybe they hear arguments from others. Somewhere along the line, they may become convinced that Jesus really did rise from the dead, and that this miracle proves his claims. They may also become convicted concerning their own rebellion against God and their need for Christ to save them. They commit themselves to become followers or disciples of Christ.

As part of this process, they see that Christ testifies to the divine authority of the Old Testament, and indirectly to the New Testament, because Christ authoritatively commissioned the apostles as witnesses (Acts 1:8). So their view of the Bible changes. They begin to use the Bible's instruction rather than autonomous judgment as their ultimate guide. Whether the process is long or short, we can see a marked difference between the beginning and the end: they were formerly in rebellion, and now they have been reconciled to God through Christ.

But according to the Bible no one is neutral in the process. We are all by nature rebels against God and we do not want to submit. The Bible itself indicates that the heart of the difficulty is not in the alleged doubtful character of the evidence presented in the Bible (the evidence for the resurrection of Christ is particularly pertinent), but in the doubtful or rather sinful character of us who read it. Moreover, our sinfulness infects our reasoning, so that we come to the evidence with corrupted standards for judging it. Even if the Bible is genuine, we want to judge it rather than submit to God. We want to remain in charge of our life (autonomy), including the life of reasoning. Our desire for autonomy, and the conception of reasoning that goes with it, need changing. We need to be redeemed by God from our rebellion.

"But," someone may ask, "if an unbeliever is interacting with the Bible and with the evidence for the resurrection of Christ, is he not engaging in autonomous reasoning? Are you not endorsing autonomy at the beginning, when an unbeliever starts his investigation, only to move beyond it at the end?" No, we are not endorsing autonomous reasoning, either at the beginning or at the end. The Bible makes it clear that such reasoning constitutes a form of rebellion against God. It is sinful.

The Bible indicates that God comes to sinners and *changes them*, through the power of Christ and the power of his resurrection. Christ was raised to new life physically. People who come to Christ receive new life *spiritually*. They are "born again," to use the expression in John 3. Such is the only way to overcome sinful rebellion: "Truly, truly I say to you, unless one is *born again* he cannot see the kingdom of God" (John 3:3).[4]

This new birth from God is mysterious, because it happens inside people, and no human being is fully aware of all that is going on (John 3:8). On the level of spiritual reality, any particular individual is either for God or against him. But on the level of conscious perception, the situation can often appear to be mixed. People may find themselves attracted to Jesus and yet unwilling to believe his claims or submit to him. God uses his own word in the process of change (1 Pet. 1:23). God's power and God's truth in Jesus overcome and change the autonomous dispositions in a person's heart. A positive result comes about in spite of autonomous desires, not because of them.

If our thinking about reasoning needs redeeming, we are not going to be able confidently to use reasoning in the way that it has often been understood in the Western tradition. We must have a more reliable foundation. God himself is that foundation. We come to know God through Christ. God instructs us about his ways in the Bible. By loving him and absorbing his instruction, we have hope of coming to a sound understanding of reasoning and logic.

---

[4] The underlying expression in Greek can mean either "born again" or "born from above." Both meanings are probably intended. New spiritual life is new, like being born a second time, and it is from above, that is, from God.

But immediately we confront objections to this kind of approach. Objectors might say that they do not accept the Bible as a trustworthy source of truth. They might present arguments. And we in turn may respond with further arguments. But in this process, we differ not only in the conclusions but in our means for evaluating arguments, because there is more than one possible understanding of reasoning and logic.

Reasoning in a Circle?

Are we engaged in circular reasoning? We are already relying on a particular conception of reasoning and logic when we use arguments to establish our conception of logic. But there is no other way of arguing when the nature of logic itself is at stake. We start with instruction in the Bible, and we use it in order to reform logic. And after our reform, we find that logic is in harmony with the God who is described in the Bible. So what have we really accomplished?

The process is really a spiral rather than a circle, because, by the grace of God, we can learn in the process. But it is also worthwhile to point out that when we come to consider the ultimate foundations for thought and the ultimate foundations for human life, everyone is moving in a circle of some kind.[5]

Autonomy is a circle. Socratic reasoning assumes autonomy at the beginning, and in the end it will develop an autonomously shaped idea of holiness—or justice or goodness or whatever else is the topic of discussion. The typical university program of instruction assumes autonomy at the beginning, and naturally it ends there as well. It appeals to autonomy to establish autonomy. But autonomy is a fruitless circle. In actuality, we are human beings and not gods. We have to rely on other people and on a lot of assumptions, but we typically do not notice it. We do not worry about it.

Should we worry? If we were all naturally good and naturally healthy in our reasoning and in our assumptions, we might conclude that we have no cause for worry. We might also conclude that we can confidently accept the common assumptions made by the people around us, and we can confidently accept what they take to be true. Thoughtful people know better. Why do we grow suspicious?

Are we naturally good? Are we naturally rational in a healthy way? The Bible says we are not. We are corrupted by sin and by sinful desires:

---

[5] On circularity, see John M. Frame, *The Doctrine of the Knowledge of God* (Phillipsburg, NJ: Presbyterian & Reformed, 1987), 130–133.

. . . you must no longer walk as the Gentiles do, in the futility of their minds. They are darkened in their understanding, alienated from the life of God because of the ignorance that is in them, due to their hardness of heart. They have become callous and have given themselves up to sensuality, greedy to practice every kind of impurity (Eph. 4:17–19).

> None is righteous, no, not one;
>> no one understands;
>> no one seeks for God.
> All have turned aside; together they have become worthless;
>> no one does good,
>> not even one. (Rom. 3:10–12)

People could present arguments back and forth, arguing for and against the proposition that human beings are naturally good. But when we undertake to evaluate the arguments, we already have implicit assumptions or presuppositions about whether we are naturally good and sound in our ability to evaluate. The dispositions of our hearts, whether toward sin or toward righteousness, affect our evaluations.[6]

As we shall see, we covertly rely on God all along, but we suppress the truth about our reliance. The modern university aspires to be radically critical, but it is not at all critical of the widespread assumption of autonomy, nor is it critical of its own rational foundations.

Biblical Teaching

As a background for our work, we need to take into account the overall message of the Bible. The Bible says that there is one God. This God created the whole world and human beings within it (Gen. 1:1–31). Originally, as it came from God's hand, this world was good (Gen. 1:31). The human beings whom God created were good, and enjoyed his love and his presence. But human beings rebelled against God—they sinned. Ever since, the human race has suffered under the reign of sin, and human sin has had indirect effects on the rest of the world, which human beings were appointed to care for and rule over (Gen. 1:28–30).

God sent the definitive and perfect remedy for sin in the person of his Son, Jesus Christ, who died for our sins and rose to make us right with God. We are to "believe in him who raised from the dead Jesus our Lord,

---

[6] See chapter 8, and the discussion of reason in K. Scott Oliphint, *Reasons for Faith: Philosophy in the Service of Theology* (Phillipsburg, NJ: Presbyterian & Reformed, 2006), chapters 1 and 2.

who was delivered up for our trespasses and raised for our justification" (Rom. 4:24–25). By believing in him, we are saved (John 3:16; Acts 10:43; 13:38–39; 16:31; Rom. 10:9–10). Christ was raised from the dead, and now reigns over the whole universe (Eph. 1:20–22). We wait for the full restoration of human beings and the cosmos when Christ returns (Rom. 8:18–23). Thus we have a sequence of core events: creation, fall into sin, redemption through Christ, and future consummation.

What do these events have to do with arguments? The coming of sin contaminates and distorts arguments. Absalom sinned in trying to murder his father David. Hushai used his arguments deceitfully to try to block the consequences of Absalom's sin. Abigail had to try to persuade David with arguments because David had undertaken a sinful course of action. The arguments in the sermons in Acts try to persuade people to turn from their sins. Arguments can be used for good, but they can also be used for ill. In Acts 13:8, "Elymas the magician . . . opposed them [Paul and Barnabas], seeking to turn the proconsul *away from* the faith."

Christ came to redeem us from sin, not merely to redeem us from bad arguments. The overall picture of the effects of sin is large in scope and deep in its implications. But bad arguments are clearly part of the picture. So the central realities of redemption, and the hope for the consummation of redemption in the future, are pertinent to our understanding of argument.

Moreover, Christ's reign over the universe implies that he is Lord and judge over all, including being Lord over arguments and over logic. It is beneficial for us to submit to him, because he is infinitely wise with the wisdom of God himself (Col. 2:3). But we also have an ethical obligation to submit to him. Our submission should be thorough, and so it should include submitting our thoughts to him in the area of logic. The apostle Paul talks about taking "every thought captive to obey Christ" (2 Cor. 10:5), and in principle this includes thoughts about logic. But does allegiance to Christ actually make a difference in logic, and if so, what difference? That is the remaining question.

Apologetics

The Bible indicates that in our time the human race is divided in two. We all have sinned (Rom. 3:23); we have all rebelled against God. But some people—not all—have had their rebellious hearts changed and renewed, because God has worked in them to save them. They have trusted in Christ to save them from their sin, and have been united to him as their Savior. Within this life, they are not totally free from sin, but in their hearts they have turned to God and have begun to follow Christ (1 Thess. 1:9). Their minds are being renewed (Rom. 12:1–2).

As a result of this renewing work of God, there are two modes of thinking among human beings. There is rebellious thinking, and there is thinking in communion with God, that is, thinking that endeavors to have fellowship with God, to listen to him, and to submit to his instruction, relying on the power of the Holy Spirit. We might call these two kinds of thinking non-Christian thinking and Christian thinking. But the word *Christian* needs attention. Many people today may think of themselves as Christian because their parents were, or because they have feelings of admiration for Jesus, or because they attend services in a church building whose roots were Christian. All this is merely superficial. If Christianity is nothing more than this, it is fake Christianity. True Christianity is a matter of the heart, not a matter of a name.

We should also say that, historically, much evil has been done by people who claimed to be Christians. Some of them were only fake Christians. Others were genuine Christians but they nevertheless acted in accordance with sin that was still in them. Christians are not necessarily morally better than anyone else. In fact, they may be worse. But through the Holy Spirit they have recognized that they are worse and that they need help. They have come to Christ, and they have begun to change. But they may still have a long way to go. They may still commit terrible sins. Following the way of Christ does not imply that we condone evil deeds done in his name.

In short, even genuine Christians are not perfect in their deeds. Likewise, they are not perfect in their thoughts. Nevertheless, in principle there are two kinds of thinking, the Christian way and the non-Christian way. In terms of fundamental assumptions and commitments, these two ways are at odds with each other. They are *antithetical* to each other.

Because there are two kinds of thinking, rather than one, communication is a challenge. It is a challenge even when we study logic, because there are two ways of studying logic, the Christian way and the non-Christian way. The Christian way submits to God's instruction through Christ. We can receive Christ's instruction because God has caused it to be written down in the Bible. The non-Christian way follows other standards. Those standards may be the standards within some other religion. But most commonly they are standards of *autonomy*. Everyone simply judges for himself.[7]

As a result, we need to reckon with people's allegiances and heart commitments. Within the twentieth century, some Christians have grappled with this difficulty, and *presuppositional apologetics* has arisen as a result.[8] Because presuppositional apologetics aspires to be based on the Bible's teaching, it disclaims any independent authority. It intends that its ideas and principles be based on the Bible. Presuppositional apologetics articulates how Christians may be fully loyal to Christ and to the Bible's teaching when they engage in dialogue with non-Christians. We cannot expound presuppositional apologetics at length, so we will be content to summarize.

Simply put, we who are followers of Christ must be consistent with our basic commitment to him. We submit to his instruction in the Bible. We sift human ideas using God as our standard. We know that God is the source of all truth. We know that even those in rebellion against him know him (Rom. 1:20–21) and rely on him (Acts 14:17). We can communicate with them because they are created in the image of God and live in his world. We can talk about any subject we choose, because every area of life reflects God's presence in the world. We may speak about what the Bible says, because the Bible as God's word has spiritual power to convict listeners, even when they do not yet agree that it is God's word (1 Cor. 2:1–5).[9]

But in our communication with non-Christians we try to make it clear that we do not agree with their fundamental assumptions and fundamental commitments against God. We have *presuppositions* different from theirs.

---

[7] We have phrased the issue of autonomy in black and white terms, because it is more easily explained if we present the opposing alternatives in their purest form. But many people, Christian and non-Christian alike, have endeavored to find compromise routes. For example, some people have tried having autonomy in some respects, and listening to God's revelation in some respects. Or they have fallen into inconsistencies. The compromises, as well as "purer" forms of intellectual life, are also part of the history of the West. Since the Enlightenment the Western intelligentsia has become more and more secularized. But prior to the Enlightenment Christian faith had a major influence. What about this history of Christian thought? Without minimizing its influence, we may still observe that theologians in the ancient church were influenced by Platonism, and that medieval theology critically sifted Aristotle's legacy without achieving a fundamental revision of Aristotle's logic or his system of categories. Christian thought in the West, like non-Christian thought, is a mixed legacy. If we revise Aristotle's logic, we must also reinspect the history of Christian thought, with an awareness of how Aristotle's logic may have had a damaging influence (as well as positive influence because of insights from common grace).

[8] For a simple introduction, see Richard L. Pratt, *Every Thought Captive: A Study Manual for the Defense of Christian Truth* (Phillipsburg, NJ: Presbyterian & Reformed, 1979); more advanced are Cornelius Van Til, *Christian Apologetics* (Phillipsburg, NJ: Presbyterian & Reformed, 2003); John M. Frame, *Apologetics to the Glory of God: An Introduction* (Phillipsburg, NJ: Presbyterian & Reformed, 1994); Cornelius Van Til, *Defense of the Faith*, 2nd ed. (Philadelphia: Presbyterian & Reformed, 1963); John M. Frame, *Cornelius Van Til: An Analysis of His Thought* (Phillipsburg, NJ: Presbyterian & Reformed, 1995).

[9] See K. Scott Oliphint, *The Battle Belongs to the Lord: The Power of Scripture for Defending Our Faith* (Phillipsburg, NJ: Presbyterian & Reformed, 2003).

Because of God's mercy, non-Christians can know and do know many bits of truth. In fact, they know God (Rom. 1:20–21). But Christians and non-Christians see truth differently, because non-Christians suppress the fact that they are receiving truth from God, and that what they know is found first of all in the mind of God.

These principles apply to the study of logic. We will try to study logic as followers of Christ. In the process, we need to acknowledge that our thinking is distinct from the thinking of non-Christians. We may still invite non-Christians to listen to our thinking. But the issues are clearer if they are aware that Christians and non-Christians have differing presuppositions.

Are Arguments Unspiritual?

Some Christians have imagined that engaging in argument is innately unspiritual. Argument is indeed unspiritual when it is carried out in an unloving or contentious spirit (2 Tim. 2:24–26; Titus 3:10–11). But what about the apostles' sermons in Acts or the argument that the Bible presents in 1 Corinthians 15? Are they unspiritual? We cannot draw that conclusion without criticizing the apostles and by implication criticizing God himself. No, in these cases argument clearly has a positive, spiritual role. When Peter and Paul spoke as apostles, they acted out of love for God, zeal for God's truth, and out of love for people who did not know the truth or who were in danger of rejecting it. In addition, God himself empowered them to speak, so that what they spoke was God's own word (1 Thess. 2:13; 1 Cor. 2:13; 2 Pet. 1:21).

We should note, however, that if people are stubborn, they may reject an argument even when they should be convinced. Even when an apostle is the preacher, it takes the Holy Spirit to soften the hearts of the hearers (Acts 16:14; 2 Cor. 2:15–16; 2 Cor. 4:4–6).

The resistance to God's message is serious. It is not merely that people may defiantly stop their ears to argument (Acts 7:57). First Corinthians 1:18–31 indicates that the gospel seems "folly" to those who consider themselves wise. How can a criminal death on a cross, which looks like an ignominious defeat, really mean salvation? People also consider the Christian message foolish because it threatens their pride and position. They already have their own standards for evaluating claims; they have their own views of what is wrong with the world and what a reasonable remedy would be like. They have their autonomous standards for evaluating the Christian message.

In sum, argument has an important role not only in human communication but in God's own speech to us through agents like the apostles Peter and Paul. God himself uses arguments in religious persuasion. But God is also present through the Holy Spirit to bring about inward readiness in a person's heart, and to bring subjective conviction in response to arguments and other explanations of the truth. Until God changes people's hearts, they resist the truth of the gospel.[10]

For Further Reflection

1. What are the two antithetical basic stances in human life and in human reasoning?
2. Does the antithesis between two stances in human life make argument between the two impossible? Why or why not?
3. What answer can be given to the objection that the Bible must first be sifted before it can be used in support of an argument?
4. How is the Bible's message of redemption relevant for the treatment of arguments?
5. How can people come to know the truth when they are resisting the message of the Bible?
6. How could you reply to someone who claims that all arguments are unspiritual?

---

[10] On the work of the Holy Spirit in bringing conviction concerning God's word, see John Murray, "The Attestation of Scripture," in *The Infallible Word: A Symposium by the Members of the Faculty of Westminster Theological Seminary*, 3rd rev. printing (Philadelphia: Presbyterian & Reformed, 1967), 42–54.

Chapter 4

Formal Logic

The arguments we encountered in chapter 2 were arguments from everyday life. They were what we might call *informal* arguments. But we can also consider more *formal* arguments. Formal arguments have been carefully pruned and arranged to follow one step after another. Consider an example:

> Premise 1: All men[1] are mortal.
> Premise 2: Socrates is a man.
> Conclusion: Therefore, Socrates is mortal.

The first two lines are called *premises*. The argument treats them as assumptions that are supplied at the start. The final line is called a *conclusion* because it is not given beforehand. Rather, it follows from what is given in the premises. Each of the three sentences on the three lines is called a *proposition*. A proposition is simply the content of a declarative statement.[2] The three propositions together form what has been called a *syllogism*. (The term *syllogism* is derived from a Greek word for *reasoning* or *inference*.) Ever since Aristotle inaugurated the study of syllogisms, they have been an important part of logic.[3]

Formal and Informal Logic

In a broad sense, logic includes the study of both the *informal* arguments in chapter 2 and *formal* arguments like Aristotle's syllogisms. We can therefore divide logic into two parts. *Informal logic* studies informal arguments; *formal logic* studies formal arguments. In the nature of the case, informal logic

---

[1] This piece of reasoning has often been used as a classic example within the literature on logic and syllogisms. "Men" and "a man" were used in this example before the rise of gender issues in the last half of the twentieth century.

[2] More precisely, a *proposition* in the context of logic is usually viewed as the content of a statement, *independent of the language* used to express the content. For more on propositions, see chapter 21. The focus on content depends on the distinction between form and meaning (since "meaning" is similar to "content"; see chapter 20).

[3] Susanne Bobzien, "Logic, History of: Ancient Logic," *Encyclopedia of Philosophy*, 2nd ed., ed. Donald M. Borchert, 10 vols. (Detroit/New York/San Francisco/ . . . : Thomson Gale, 2006), 5:398–401.

is a fairly diffuse field, because informal arguments come in many forms and have many purposes. Informal logic overlaps with the study of rhetoric and persuasion, and more broadly with the field of communication and even the whole field of human knowledge.

Formal logic is more focused. It has devoted special attention to the general conditions for valid argumentation, conditions that hold no matter what is the subject matter. Informal logic may have a more significant role in ordinary life. But formal logic has greater prestige, because of its greater precision. Historically, it has been viewed as an ideal to which we ought to aspire, and informal arguments have been evaluated by how well they approximate to the rigor of formal logic.

The Influence of God in Informal Arguments

What difference does God make in arguments and in logic? First, consider informal arguments. Informal arguments are obviously shaped by human motivations, human beliefs, and heart commitments. For example, Absalom's desires, his pride, and his fears had a role in swaying him to prefer the advice of Hushai to the advice of Ahithophel. According to the Bible, the most fundamental issue of all is the commitment of the heart. Are you for God or against him (see Josh. 24:14–15; 2 Cor. 2:15–17; 4:1–6)? Do you rely on Christ for salvation or do you direct your hopes in other directions (Acts 4:12)? Do you follow Christ as Lord or do you serve some other lord—perhaps the lordship of some strong desire? Our hearts clearly influence which arguments we will be inclined to accept.

The Bible indicates that unbelievers who reject the message of salvation in the gospel, the good news about Christ, have their eyes blinded by Satan:

> And even if our gospel is veiled, it is veiled to those who are perishing. In their case the god of this world [Satan] has *blinded the minds* of the unbelievers, to keep them from seeing the light of the gospel of the glory of Christ, who is the image of God. (2 Cor. 4:3–4)

This statement about the reception of the gospel indicates that the gospel deserves to be welcomed and believed. There is plenty of evidence, including the divine witness of the Holy Spirit that accompanies it (1 Thess. 1:5). But unbelievers are not persuaded by this evidence. They are blind to it. At some crucial points they do not accept the arguments, no matter how convincing these arguments may be in their own right.

Our hearts can easily deceive us. Even if we pride ourselves on our ability to criticize bad arguments, we are more likely to undertake a critique if our heart inclines us to dislike the argument's conclusion or to be suspicious of it. On the other hand, in practice we are more likely to neglect the task of critical analysis and to swallow a flawed or fallacious argument if our hearts tell us that the conclusion is pleasing.

God is involved in our use of informal arguments in everyday affairs and in the big issues of life. He is of course especially involved when it comes to the proclamation of the gospel and human response to the proclamation. But he is involved also in more mundane affairs. He can allow people's sinful desires to trap them into foolish beliefs and foolish decisions, as happened in the case of Absalom (2 Sam. 17:14). He can also give wisdom to people (Prov. 2:6; Job 32:8; 28:20–28). Then they become skilled in evaluating arguments.

We can already begin to see ways in which logic and emotion relate to each other. On the one hand, emotion or commitments in the heart can sway people to reject good arguments, arguments in accord with sound logic. On the other hand, God can change human hearts, and he can give wisdom to people who love him. Rightly understood, love and logic go together. We will explore the connection more fully later on.

The Influence of God in Formal Arguments

What about formal arguments and formal logic? We will focus a lot of our attention on this narrower arena, because many people have thought that formalization and rigor in logic eliminate the need for God. Formal arguments appear to people to lead to conclusions *in and of themselves*, independent of any religious interference. Apparently, God is absent. Or if he is present, in some vague sense, people think that his presence makes no difference. Formal logic, according to this view, is cold, impersonal, and Spockian.

Consider again the syllogism about Socrates.

Premise 1: All men are mortal.
Premise 2: Socrates is a man.
Conclusion: Therefore, Socrates is mortal.

It is a *valid* argument. The conclusion, namely, that Socrates is mortal, is true if both premises are true. The same pattern of reasoning remains true if we use different content:

All cats are carnivores.
Felix is a cat.
Therefore, Felix is a carnivore.

Aristotle studied general patterns of reasoning like these, which display valid argumentation.

There are several kinds of syllogisms. For simplicity we confine ourselves in part I of this book to *categorical syllogisms*, the most well-known form. A categorical syllogism consists of two premises and a conclusion, such that both premises and conclusion are simple propositions about categories or classes. "All cats are carnivores" is a simple proposition relating the category of cats to the category of carnivores. By contrast, the proposition "All cats are carnivores or some cats are not carnivores" is a compound proposition.

(Technically, "Felix is a cat" is called a *singular* proposition because it makes a statement about a single individual, Felix, in relation to a single class, "cats," rather than making a statement about two classes ["All cats are carnivores"; "No dogs are cats"]. For convenience we have included such cases along with cases that make assertions about two classes, such as the class of cats and the class of carnivores.)

We can illustrate a syllogism with a more fanciful case:

All horses are green.
George is a horse.
Therefore, George is green.

In this case, if George in fact is a human being, both premises are false. But the form or argumentation is still *valid*. "Validity," in a technical sense, has to do with whether the conclusion follows from the premises, not with whether the premises are true. Whether the premises are true must often be determined from various sources of information about the world. By contrast, the *validity* of the overall argument does not depend on observations about horses or about George, but only on the logical form. Valid reasoning always results in true conclusions whenever the premises are true.[4] But it does not explicitly *claim* that the premises are true; it only claims that the conclusion follows *if* the premises are true.

Logicians have tried to distinguish consistently among three concepts:

---

[4] Part I.C indicates how summaries about formal logic must be qualified.

truth, validity, and soundness. A *valid* argument is an argument whose conclusion follows from the premises. But in using the word *valid* we do not indicate whether the premises are actually true. A *sound* argument is an argument that is valid and whose premises are all true. The argument about the mortality of Socrates is both valid and sound.[5] The argument that George is green is valid but unsound, because neither of its premises are true. We can also give examples of arguments that are invalid but whose premises and conclusions are true:

> All mammals are animals.
> All cats are animals.
> Therefore, all cats are mammals.

The argument is *invalid* because the conclusion, though true, does not follow from the premises. We can see the invalidity of this form of argument by providing another case of the same form that results in an untrue conclusion:

> Premise 1: All dogs are animals.
> Premise 2: All cats are animals.
> Conclusion: Therefore, all cats are dogs.

Whether or not various premises are true usually depends on particular facts about the world. Logic focuses not on whether the premises are true, but on whether a conclusion follows from the premises. It focuses, in other words, on the question of which arguments are *valid*.

---

[5] There are complexities about being "mortal." Human beings in the new heaven and the new earth are free from the threat of death. Human beings within the present world are mortal, that is, capable of dying, but Enoch and Elijah did not die; they were taken up to heaven alive (Gen. 5:24; 2 Kings 2:11; Heb. 11:5). After his death and resurrection Jesus was no longer subject to death (Rom. 6:9) and was taken up to heaven (Acts 1:9).

For Further Reflection

1. What is the difference between an *informal* and a *formal* argument?
2. What is a *premise*? What is a *conclusion*?
3. Identify which of the following arguments are valid, sound, and/or have true premises and conclusions.

Everything made of green cheese is edible.
The moon is made of green cheese.
Therefore the moon is edible.

No dogs are fish.
All collies are dogs.
Therefore no collies are fish.

All fish are vertebrates.
All salmon are vertebrates.
Therefore all salmon are fish.

No books are intelligible.
All ads are intelligible.
Therefore no ads are books.

If Socrates is a Greek, Socrates speaks the Greek language.
Socrates is Greek.
Therefore, Socrates speaks the Greek language.

If Socrates is a Greek, Socrates speaks the Greek language.
Socrates speaks the Greek language.
Therefore, Socrates is a Greek.

All dogs are invisible.
All cats are dogs.
Therefore all cats are invisible.

Chapter 5

Inductive Logic

Syllogisms are a form of *deductive* argument, because the conclusion is *deduced* from the premises. We may also say that the conclusion *follows* from the premises, or that the conclusion is *implied* by the premises, or that the conclusion is *inferred* from the premises. All these formulations are meant to be equivalent. If we know that the premises are true, we can also be certain that the conclusion is true. The valid formal arguments in the previous chapter are all examples of deductive argument.

Examples of Inductive Argument

A second kind of argument, called an *inductive* argument, generalizes from individual cases.[1] Consider the following reasoning:

> Premise 1: Swan #1 is white.
> Premise 2: Swan #2 is white.
> Premise 3: Swan #3 is white.
> . . .
> Premise 1001: Swan #1001 is white.
> Conclusion: Therefore, all swans are white.

Is the conclusion valid? If the premises are true, do we know that the conclusion is true? We might still entertain a nagging doubt, that sometime, somewhere, we might find a swan that turns out not to be white.

Inductive arguments are used all the time in scientific experiments. For example, a scientist may drop a ball one, two, three, or a hundred times, and each time measure the time it takes to fall to the ground. He then concludes that the ball *always* drops at the rate that he has measured.

---

[1] Some authors use the word *inductive* in a broader sense, such that it includes several kinds of arguments by analogy (Maria Carla Galavotti, *Philosophical Introduction to Probability* [Stanford, CA: Center for the Study of Language and Information, 2005], 29–31). For simplicity, we confine ourselves to the most typical form of induction.

Differences between Deductive and Inductive Arguments

What is the difference between a deductive argument and an inductive argument? They differ with respect to the certainty of the conclusion. A deductive argument implies its conclusion with certainty; an inductive argument does not.

When we consider a valid deductive argument, if we know that the premises are true, we know for certain that the conclusion is true. In particular, if "All cats are mammals" and "Felix is a cat," we know for certain that "Felix is a mammal."

By contrast, inductive reasoning results in conclusions that are merely possible or probable, given the truth of the premises. The conclusion does not follow without fail merely from the truth of the premises. After a scientist performs his experiments with balls, he still does not know for certain that the next drop of the ball will have the same result. For example, unknown to him, some trickster may have concealed a piece of iron inside the ball. As the scientist is preparing for the next drop, the trickster turns on an electromagnet in the vicinity, and the magnetic force affects the ball. All of the scientist's previous experiments cannot absolutely guarantee that the next experiment will involve nothing new or unexpected. Thus, in the case of inductive arguments, the conclusions always fall short of certainty.

A second difference lies in the kinds of propositions used in the premises. A deductive argument moves from general propositions in the premises to a general proposition in the conclusion. Or it may use a general proposition plus a singular proposition to deduce a second singular proposition:

> Premise 1: All cats are mammals. [general proposition]
> Premise 2: Felix is a cat. [singular proposition]
> Conclusion: Felix is a mammal. [singular proposition]

By contrast, an inductive argument moves from singular propositions like "Swan #1 is white" in the premises to a general proposition like "All swans are white" in the conclusion.

God's Involvement in Inductive Reasoning

We have observed that even after repeating an experiment many times, a scientist cannot draw a generalizing conclusion with complete certainty. But we may explore another type of question, namely, why the scientist has any degree of confidence at all. Why should a scientist have *any* positive expectation that the ball will behave as it did before? If we lived in a world of complete chaos, nothing would be in the least predictable. It would hardly be a world at all. And we ourselves could not count on the reliability of our memories or the regularity of our heartbeat, or anything else. Why, most of the time, do we find that regularities that we have observed continue to be observed?

Philosophers have puzzled over these conundrums, but they have not reached a consensus. If we listen to what the Bible says, we have the beginning of an answer. God has created a world that has regularities in it. He has created a world using his wisdom, and he has made a world suitable for human habitation. Inductive arguments about balls work because God has seen to it that balls behave in a regular fashion. In addition, he has made human beings in his image, so that our minds are in some ways in tune with his.[2] So our expectations about regularities frequently (though not always) match God's own plans for the world. Inductive arguments work because God made the world with regularities that harmonize with our sense of what to expect.

On the other hand, God is God and is superior to us. So we should not be shocked if sometimes our inductive conclusions turn out to have exceptions. Our uncertainty about conclusions is an expression of our finite knowledge and our dependence on God.

Retroduction

Students of logic have also identified another form of logical argument, called *retroduction*. In retroduction, an analyst infers a probable cause or causes or a deeper explanation on the basis of observable phenomena. For example, in a jury trial the jury tries to determine, on the basis of the evidence, who committed the crime. In chemistry, even before individual atoms had ever been observed, chemists inferred that chemical reactions could be explained by recombinations of atoms.

Retroduction is similar to induction, in that the inferences are not completely certain. Usually the inferences involve more complicated assumptions and an understanding of circumstances, so that the reasoning is not fully formalized. Thus, typical cases of retroduction belong to *informal logic*.

---

[2] For further discussion of regularity as a presupposition for science, see Vern S. Poythress, *Redeeming Science: A God-Centered Approach* (Wheaton, IL: Crossway, 2006), especially chapter 1.

For Further Reflection

1. What are the differences between deductive and inductive arguments?
2. Why do inductive arguments tend to "work" a good deal of the time?
3. What do the limitations in inductive arguments imply about the nature of science?
4. Classify the following arguments as deductive or inductive.
   a. All fish are vertebrates.
      All trout are fish.
      Therefore, all trout are vertebrates.
   b. All 100 trout that I have caught in this stream are fish.
      Therefore, all trout are fish.
   c. Galileo's experiments with falling objects show that the rate of fall does not depend on the weight of the object.
   d. The measurement of deflection of starlight by the sun conforms to Einstein's general theory of relativity. Therefore, Einstein's general theory of relativity is true.
   e. Biochemical analysis shows that all living cells contain DNA.
   f. No birds are fish.
      All robins are birds.
      Therefore, no robins are fish.

Chapter 6:

The Importance of Formal Logic

Inductive logic can be useful in ordinary life and in sciences, but its results fall short of certainty. Deductive logic is in some ways more prestigious, because its results are certain. Deductive logic has also undergone more formalization. For the most part, we will now concentrate on formal deductive logic. For convenience, we will speak of *formal logic* or just *logic* when we mean *formal deductive logic*. (Most, but not all, inductive logic is conducted informally.)

Exploring Assumptions by Formalization

Formal logic is useful because it can illumine debates about important issues. For example, people have debated for centuries whether capital punishment (the death penalty) is an appropriate punishment for murder. The debates have often used informal arguments. But we can also try to produce a formal argument:

> Premise 1: All murderers deserve death.
> Premise 2: Tom is a murderer.
> Conclusion: Therefore, Tom deserves death.

This argument matters vitally to Tom, as well as to a courtroom and to the prosecutor. It is a *valid* argument. But some people would dispute the first premise, that "All murderers deserve death." So we could construct a more complex argument that leads to the first premise given above:

> Anyone who destroys the image of God deserves to be destroyed.
> Anyone who destroys a human being destroys the image of God. [See Gen. 9:6.]
> Anyone who is a murderer destroys a human being.
> Tom is a murderer.
> Therefore, Tom deserves to be destroyed.

Pacifists might still dispute the propriety of capital punishment. They might dispute one or more of the premises in the argument above. Or they might say that Tom deserves to be destroyed, but that the new ethics of Jesus forbids us from giving Tom what he deserves:

Everyone who loves people does not kill them.
Everyone who truly follows Jesus loves people. [Matt. 5:44–45]
We truly follow Jesus.
Therefore, we do not kill people.

Advocates of capital punishment might reply to this argument by disputing the first premise. They might argue that an agent of the government who puts a murderer to death may be doing so out of love for God's justice and love for the people who are protected from the possibility of the murderer carrying out a second murder. Or they might dispute the second premise, by arguing that Jesus's broad command to love has exceptions. The arguments can become more and more complex. Whether simple or complex, all these arguments use logic.

Most of the time, people use informal arguments. They do not write out explicitly all their assumptions. In many practical cases, writing out all the premises and making an argument conform to a strict formal pattern might be pedantic. But sometimes we may clarify issues by adopting a strict formal pattern. If we force ourselves to write out explicit premises and explicit conclusions, we can help to make clear some of the assumptions that people are making.

Consider still another argument:

Everything that began to exist has a cause.
The universe began to exist.
Therefore, the universe has a cause.

This argument is part of the so-called "kalam cosmological argument" for the existence of God. More steps are needed to arrive at the conclusion that God exists. But the above argument is an important step. Formal logic, then, can play a significant role in argument.

Fallacies

Logic is also important because people can make mistakes in reasoning. They can commit *fallacies*. Consider the following argument:

Every murderer has killed a human being.
Tom has killed a human being.
Therefore, Tom is a murderer.

The argument may sound plausible at first glance. But suppose Tom killed someone *accidentally* rather than intentionally. We have a name for such an accident, namely, "involuntary manslaughter." Tom is a manslaughterer but *not* a murderer. And of course that fact will make a decided difference to a jury and a judge.

So what is wrong with the argument above, which concludes that Tom is a murderer? It moves backwards from the broader category, "killing a human being," to the narrower category, "murder." All murder is killing, but not all killing is murder. The argument is an example of a fallacy. This particular fallacy, of arguing backward from the broader category, crops up so frequently that it has been given a name: "false conversion." It has this name because "All murder is killing" is falsely converted to "All killing is murder."

The Independence of Logic

Neither validity nor invalidity depend on the particular content of the propositions used in the argument. We do not first need to check out whether all cats are carnivores or whether all horses are green, in order to judge whether the form of the argument is valid. Logical validity in this way seems to be independent of the nature of the world.

Formal logic seems to be special because we could not imagine it otherwise. We can imagine a world in which all horses are green, or in which all human beings live forever and are not subject to mortality. We *cannot* imagine a world in which all cats are carnivores, in which Felix is a cat, and yet in which it turns out that Felix is not a carnivore.

Works of science fiction or fantasy can help us imagine very strange kinds of beings and strange kinds of worlds. But we would not put up with a writer of fantasy who affirmed the premises and yet denied the conclusion that Felix was a carnivore. We would say it did not make sense. We would suspect that the writer had had a mental lapse. He would have failed to give us a *consistent* imaginary world, and that tends to destroy its charm.

Logic seems not only to be independent of the particular facts of the world, but independent of the people who use logic in their arguments. Logical validity holds in any language of the world, in any culture of the world, for any person in the world. No matter what language you use, the conclusion that Socrates is mortal follows from the premises. Logical validity of this kind is truly universal. That is one implication of its being impossible to imagine otherwise.

People cannot with integrity deny logic or argue against it, because any such denial or argumentation would already be relying on logic and on general principles for judging validity *in the very process of setting forth a counterargument*. An opponent of logic would be using logic to deny logic, and that is self-defeating.

A person might try to find a way around this dilemma by saying that he is using logic only as a temporary tactic. He himself does not believe in what he is doing, but he uses logic temporarily as a therapeutic method to help those who still have a confidence in logic. Yet even in formulating this tactical use, the person who desires to destroy logic relies in one sense on a logical principle, namely, that if an assumption leads to a false conclusion, the assumption must be wrong. In this case the alleged erroneous assumption is the assumption that logic itself is sound. The logical principle for disproving erroneous assumptions is called the principle of *reductio ad absurdum* (Latin for "reduction to absurdity"). That logical principle is the fundamental principle that has to be used in order for an argument against logic to have any hope of succeeding.

Silence or illogicality in communication would seem to be the only route that could be used with full sincerity by a person who would destroy logic, and he would be unlikely to convince many—because we tend only to be convinced by arguments that *do* in some way have the appearance of relying on logic rather than overtly flouting it.

The Need for Logic

The person who undertakes to oppose logic has even more severe difficulties. He is not likely to live long. Consider some practical reasoning:

> All pedestrians can be killed by rapidly moving buses.
> I am a pedestrian.
> Therefore I can be killed by rapidly moving buses.

Of course, typically we do not self-consciously think through this process of reasoning, using explicit premises. But we tacitly rely on it. I know that I could be killed, even though I have no previous accumulated experience of being killed many times already by speeding buses.

There are a thousand ways to die by ignoring elementary logic. Each person is free to pick his or her own method. In fact, no one abandons logic, except perhaps in some selective, "safer" cases, where he thinks he can get away with it. People who do abandon logic in more extended or severe ways die as a result of their foolishness, or else end up behind locked doors in psychiatric institutions, for their own protection.

It appears, then, that deductive logic simply is what it is—necessarily. If it is independent of particular people and particular cultures, it is also independent of their religions. It is independent of God or gods. So the reasoning might go. In particular, it is independent of the Christian faith.

I do not completely agree with this reasoning. But to see why, we must first make a distinction between logic and human use of logic. Human reasoning can be flawed. Someone may actually be convinced by a fallacious argument that involves false conversion. Human use of logic, whether flawed or not, is clearly dependent on the human beings who are engaged in reasoning.

Moreover, human beings may adhere to various religions of the world. The religions may even color their attitudes toward logic and toward reasoning. In fact, certain forms of mysticism have advocated seeking union with "the divine" by abandoning or suppressing normal forms of reasoning, with the idea of traveling "beyond" reason or logic into an immediate experience of oneness.

We may conclude, then, that the actual practical use or disuse of logic in human affairs has a certain entanglement with and dependence on human beings. If we say that logic is independent of mankind, this independence belongs to logic as it should be, or logic as it really is, not to its flawed use. The reasoning about Socrates holds true *in reality*, whether or not you or I acknowledge the truth or see the validity of the reasoning. But then what is this thing that we call "logic as it really is"? Is it a kind of absolute, a sort of heavenly original to which proper human reasoning conforms?

For Further Reflection

1. How can formal logic be useful in analyzing practical arguments?
2. How is logic "independent" of the world?
3. How do people tacitly rely on logic in everyday life?
4. Try to fill in extra premises, in order to tighten up the following not-completely-formalized arguments.
    a. All human beings need exercise.
       Therefore, I need exercise.
    b. Only fish can survive under water.
       Human beings cannot survive under water.
    c. A person who takes items out of a store without paying for them is shoplifting.
       Dottie engaged in shoplifting.

Part I.B

God in Logic

Chapter 7:

Logic Revealing God

Is logic independent of God? Care is needed here. Logic is independent of any particular human being and of humanity as a whole. If all human beings were to die, and Felix the cat were to survive, it would still be the case that Felix is a carnivore. The logic leading to this conclusion would still be valid. An angel examining the argument could still acknowledge its validity. This hypothetical situation shows that logic is independent of humanity. But, if God exists, God is still there. So it does not necessarily follow that logic is independent of God. What is the relation of God to logic?

Is Logic Just "There"?

Through the ages, philosophers are the ones who have done most of the reflection on logic. And philosophers have mostly thought that logic is just "there." According to their thinking, it is an impersonal something. Their thinking then says that, if a personal God exists, or if multiple gods exist, as the Greek and Roman polytheists believed, these personal beings are subject to the laws of logic, as is everything else in the world. Logic is a kind of cold, Spockian ideal.

For example, the law of noncontradiction says that something cannot both have a property and not have the same property at the same time and in the same way. If God is righteous, then he must not be unrighteous. More precisely, it is impossible for him to be righteous and not to be righteous at the same time and in the same way. According to this view, God is then *subject to* the law of noncontradiction.

This view has the effect of making logic an absolute *above* God, to which God himself is subjected. This view in fact is radically antagonistic to the biblical idea that God is absolute and that everything else is radically subject to him: "The LORD has established his throne in the heavens, and his kingdom rules over *all*" (Ps. 103:19). A Bible reader may try to escape the implications of this verse by interpreting the word *all* in a limited sense. He might say that God rules over all things that have been created. But logic is not created. Philosophers have maintained that it just "is."

But if logic is not created, and it just "is," we have to return to the question of whether God is subject to the laws of logic. If he is, he is not truly absolute. Logic rules over him. Logic appears to be a kind of ruling "god" above God, making us question who or what is the final controller. But what is the alternative to the assumption that God is subject to the laws of logic? If God is *not* subject to the laws of logic, should we conclude that he is illogical? Then we cannot depend on him.

We seem to be on the horns of a dilemma.

Biblical Resources

The Bible provides resources for moving beyond this apparent dilemma. It has three important teachings that are relevant. First, God is dependable and faithful in his character:

> The LORD passed before him and proclaimed, "The LORD, the LORD, a God merciful and gracious, slow to anger, and abounding in steadfast love and *faithfulness*, . . . (Ex. 34:6)

The constancy of God's character provides an absolute basis for us to trust in his faithfulness to us. And this faithfulness includes logical consistency rather than illogicality. God "cannot deny himself" (2 Tim. 2:13). He always acts in accordance with who he is.

Second, the Bible teaches the distinction between Creator and creature. God alone is Creator and Sovereign and Absolute.[1] We are not. Everything God created is distinct from him. It is all subject to him. Therefore, logic is not a second absolute, over God or beside him. There is only one Absolute, God himself. Logic is in fact an aspect of his character, because it expresses the *consistency* of God and the *faithfulness* of God. Consistency and faithfulness belong to the character of God. We can say that they are *attributes* of God. God is who he is (Ex. 3:14), and what he is includes his consistency and faithfulness. There is nothing more ultimate than God. So God is the source for logic. The character of God includes his logicality.

---

[1] Scott Oliphint perceptively observes that the word *Creator* implies a relationship with creation, and such a relationship would not have existed if God had not decided to create the world. Thus the word *Creator* is not ideal for describing God in his absoluteness and eternal character. Oliphint therefore prefers to describe God's absoluteness with the word *Eimi*, which is Greek for "I am" (K. Scott Oliphint, *Reasons for Faith: Philosophy in the Service of Theology* [Phillipsburg, NJ: Presbyterian & Reformed, 2006], 178). In this book we use the more common term *Creator*, with the understanding that it is intended to express God's absoluteness.

Third, we as human beings are made in the image of God (Gen. 1:26–27). We are like God, though we are creatures and not divine. We are like God in many ways, and many verses of the Bible beyond Genesis 1:26–27 invite us to notice many of the ways in which we imitate God.

God has plans and purposes (Isa. 46:10–11). So do we, on our human level (James 4:13; Prov. 16:1). God has thoughts infinitely above ours (Isa. 55:8–9), but we may also have access to his thoughts when he reveals them: "How precious to me are *your thoughts*, O God!" (Ps. 139:17). We are privileged to *think God's thoughts after him*.[2] Our experience of thinking, reasoning, and forming arguments imitates God and reflects the mind of God. Our logic reflects God's logic. Logic, then, is an aspect of God's mind. Logic is universal among all human beings in all cultures, because there is only one God, and we are all made in the image of God.

None of us escapes God. Whenever we reason, we are imitating God, whether we recognize it or not. The only alternative is insanity, which means the disintegration of the image of God in us.

Logic Revealing God's Attributes

We may see the close relation of logic to God by reflecting on the ways in which logic reveals God. We can begin with the form of argument that we have already discussed:

> All men are mortal.
> Socrates is a man.
> Therefore, Socrates is mortal.

The general scheme is like this:

> All Bs are As.
> C is a B.
> Therefore C is an A.

Or we may generalize to include all Cs:

> All Bs are As.

---

[2] More precisely, as Van Til indicates, we "think God's thoughts after Him *analogically*" (Cornelius Van Til, *Common Grace and the Gospel* [n.l.: Presbyterian & Reformed, 1973], 37). With the word *analogically* we guard the Creator-creature distinction. God is the original Father, while human fatherhood is derivative. God is the original king, while human kings are derivative. Human fathers and kings are *analogous* to God. Likewise, God's thoughts are the original. Ours are derivative. At the same time, by saying that we "think God's thoughts," we indicate that we have genuine knowledge.

All Cs are Bs.
Therefore all Cs are As.

Here is an example:

All dogs are animals.
All collies are dogs.
Therefore all collies are animals.

This form of argumentation, which is one of the syllogisms that Aristotle studied, is valid.

Attributes of God

We can now proceed to consider how this general validity in argument reflects the character of God. We proceed in a manner analogous to arguments already in print as to how scientific laws and all truths reveal attributes of God.[3]

If an argument is indeed valid, its validity holds for all times and all places. That is, its validity is omnipresent (in all places) and eternal (for all times). Logical validity has these two attributes that are classically attributed to God. Technically, God's eternity is usually conceived of as being "above" or "beyond" time. But words like "above" and "beyond" are metaphorical and point to mysteries. There is, in fact, an analogous mystery with respect to laws of logic. We may call the validity of a syllogism a "law" of logic because it is universal. If the law is universal, is it not in some sense "beyond" the particularities of any one place or time? Moreover, within a biblical worldview, God is not only "above" time in the sense of not being subject to the limitations of finite creaturely experience of time, but he is "in" time in the sense of acting in time and interacting with his creatures.[4] Similarly, the law is "above" time in its universality, but "in" time through its applicability to each particular piece of human reasoning.

Divine Attributes of Law

The attributes of omnipresence and eternality are only the beginning. On close examination, other divine attributes seem to belong to laws of logic.

---

[3] See Vern S. Poythress, *Redeeming Science: A God-Centered Approach* (Wheaton, IL: Crossway, 2006), chapters 1 and 14. Some of the wording from those chapters is adopted in the following reasoning about logic.
[4] John M. Frame, *The Doctrine of God* (Phillipsburg, NJ: Presbyterian & Reformed, 2002), 543–575.

Consider. If a law for the validity of a syllogism holds for all times, we presuppose that it is the *same* law through all times. Of course human analysis of logic has a history. Later logicians sometimes correct or improve what they consider to be flawed formulations from their predecessors. But we are not focusing on human formulations. We are rather focusing on logical laws themselves. Are there norms for good reasoning? If a syllogism really does display valid reasoning, does it continue to be valid over time? The law—the law governing reasoning—does not change with time. It is immutable. Validity is unchangeable. Immutability is an attribute of God.

Next, logic is at bottom ideational in character. We do not literally see logic, but only the effects of logic on particular cases of reasoning in language. Logic is essentially immaterial and invisible but is known through its effects. Likewise, God is essentially immaterial and invisible but he is known through his acts in the world.

If we are talking about the real laws, rather than possibly flawed human formulations, the laws of logic are also absolutely, infallibly true. Truthfulness is also an attribute of God.

The Power of Logic

Next consider the attribute of power. Human formulations of logic offer *descriptions* of valid reasoning. Valid reasoning has to be there in the world first, before the logicians make their formulations. The human formulation follows the facts, and is dependent on them. Standards for validity must exist even before the logician formulates a description. A law of logic must hold for a whole series of cases. A student of logic cannot force the issue by inventing a law and then forcing reasoning to conform to the law. Reasoning rather conforms to laws already there, laws that are discovered rather than invented.

The laws must already be there. They must actually hold. They must "have teeth." If they are truly universal, they are not violated. Human beings may of course engage in fallacious reasoning, but even their failure is measured by reference to standards for validity that always hold. No reasoning escapes the "hold" or dominion of these logical principles. The power of these real laws is absolute, in fact, infinite. In classical language, the law is omnipotent ("all powerful").

But what about paradoxes or mysteries found in the Bible? The Bible indicates that God is sovereign over all of history, including human actions

(Acts 2:23; 4:25–28). It also says that human beings are morally responsible for their actions (Acts 2:23; Matt. 12:36–37). How does human moral responsibility fit together with God's sovereignty? It is a mystery.

The Bible also teaches that God is one God, in three persons. How do we understand how these things can be? Do these mysteries violate the laws of logic? Though there is mystery here for us as creatures, there is no mystery for God the Creator. If logic is ultimately an aspect of God's mind; what for us is a mystery is in full harmony with the logic that is in God.

Logic is both transcendent and immanent. It transcends the creatures of the world by exercising power over them, conforming them to its dictates. It is immanent in that it touches and holds in its dominion even the smallest bits of this world.[5] Logic transcends the galactic clusters and is immanently present in the way in which it governs the truths about a single proton. Transcendence and immanence are characteristics of God.

For Further Reflection

1. What difficulty arises if people say that God is *subject* to the laws of logic? What difficulty may arise if people say that he is above logic?
2. Why is it important to distinguish between logic as it should be and human use of logic?
3. What attributes of God are reflected in the laws of logic?
4. Reflect on how God's attributes of faithfulness, truthfulness, and beauty are reflected in logic.
5. Explain how God's attributes are revealed in a sample syllogism.

---

[5] On the biblical view of transcendence and immanence, see John M. Frame, *The Doctrine of the Knowledge of God* (Phillipsburg, NJ: Presbyterian & Reformed, 1987), especially pp. 13–15; and *Doctrine of God*, especially pp. 107–115.

Chapter 8

Logic as Personal

Many agnostics and atheists may by this time feel uncomfortable with the character of logical laws. It seems that the laws of logic are beginning to look suspiciously like the biblical idea of God. The most obvious escape is to deny that logic is personal. It is just "there" as an impersonal something.

Logic and Rationality

In fact, a close look at logic shows that this escape route is not really plausible. In practice all human beings believe that logic expresses rationality. This rationality in logic is accessible to human understanding. Rationality is a *sine qua non* for logic. But, as we know, rationality belongs to persons, not to rocks, trees, and subpersonal creatures.[1] If the logic is rational, which we assume it is, then it is also personal.

When we reflect on logic, we also assume that laws of logic can be articulated, expressed, communicated, and understood through human language. In practice logical reasoning includes not only rational thought but also capability for symbolic communication. Now, the original, the laws of logic "out there," are not known to be written or uttered in any particular human language. But they must be expressible in language in our secondary description. They must be translatable into not only one but many human languages. We may express definitions and contexts for a law of logic through clauses, phrases, explanatory paragraphs, and contextual explanations in human language.

Laws of logic are clearly like human utterance in their ability to be grammatically articulated, paraphrased, translated, and illustrated. Logic is utterance-like, language-like. And the complexity of utterances that we find among logicians, as well as among human beings in general, is not duplicated in the animal world.[2] Language is one of the defining characteristics

---

[1] The truths about rocks and the laws governing rocks are rational and personal, because truth and law originate in God. But a rock or a plant does not have a personal *subjectivity*.

[2] Animal calls and signals do mimic certain limited aspects of human language. And chimpanzees can be taught to respond to symbols with meaning. But this is still a long way from the complex grammar and mean-

that separates man from animals. Language, like rationality, belongs to persons. It follows that logic is in essence personal.

Are We Divinizing Nature?

But now we must consider an objection. By claiming that the laws of logic have divine attributes, are we divinizing nature? That is, are we taking something out of the created world, and falsely claiming that it is divine? Is logic a part of the created world? Should we not classify it as creature rather than Creator?[3]

But we already observed that logic seems to be independent of the world. We cannot imagine a world in which logic does not hold. This fact shows that we are confronted with a transcendent reality.

In addition, let us remember that we are speaking of logic as it really is, not merely our human guesses and approximations. Logic in this sense is an aspect of the mind of God. All God's attributes will therefore be manifested in the real laws of logic, in distinction from our human approximations to them.[4]

Logic and the Trinity

The key idea that logic is divine is not only older than the rise of modern science; it is older than the rise of Christianity. Even before the coming of Christ people noticed profound regularity in the government of the world, and wrestled with the meaning of this regularity. Both the Greeks (especially the Stoics) and the Jews (especially Philo) developed speculations about the *logos*, the divine "word" or "reason" behind what is observed.[5] In addition the Jews had the Old Testament, which reveals the role of the word of God in creation and providence. Jewish Targums, the Aramaic renderings of the Old Testament, sometimes use "Word" to render the Tetragrammaton, the proper name of God.[6] Against this background John 1:1 proclaims, "In the

---

ing of human language. See, e.g., Stephen R. Anderson, *Doctor Dolittle's Delusion: Animals and the Uniqueness of Human Language* (New Haven, CT: Yale University Press, 2004).

[3] In conformity with the Bible (especially Genesis 1), we maintain that God and the created world are distinct. God is not to be identified with the creation or any part of it, nor is the creation a "part" of God. The Bible repudiates all forms of pantheism and panentheism.

[4] Something similar to this argument can be found in James N. Anderson and Greg Welty, "The Lord of Non-Contradiction: An Argument for God from Logic," *Philosophia Christi* 13:2 (2011): 321–338. But it appears to me that this article does not take into account the presence of analogy and the Creator-creature distinction in logical reasoning about God (see chapter 24 below).

[5] See "Word" in *The International Standard Bible Encyclopedia*, ed. Geoffrey W. Bromiley et al., rev. ed. (Grand Rapids, MI: Eerdmans, 1988), 4:1103–1107, and the associated literature.

[6] See John Ronning, *The Jewish Targums and John's Logos Theology* (Peabody, MA: Hendrickson, 2010). The Targums were committed to written form later than when the Gospel of John was written, but they represent oral tradition going back to the first century AD and before.

beginning was the Word, and the Word was with God, and the Word was God." John responds to the speculations of his time with a striking revelation: that the Word (*logos*) that created and sustains the universe is not only a divine person "with God," but the very One who became incarnate: "the Word became flesh" (John 1:14).

The English word *logic* comes from Greek *logikē*, which is closely related to the Greek word *logos*. *Logos* in Greek has a range of meaning, including *reason, law, word, speaking, declaration*. The meaning "reason" explains why the study of reasoning came to be called *logic*. The meanings related to communication and discourse are most pertinent to understanding the word *logos* in John 1:1. In John 1:1 the phrase "In the beginning" alludes to Genesis 1:1. And John 1:3 explicitly says that "all things were made through him," alluding to God's works of creation in Genesis 1. Notably, in Genesis 1 God creates by speaking:

And God said, "Let there be light," and there was light. (Gen. 1:3)

And God said, "Let there be an expanse in the midst of the waters, and let it separate the waters from the waters." And God made the expanse and separated the waters . . . (Gen. 1:6–7)

And God said, "Let the waters under the heavens be gathered together into one place, and let the dry land appear." And it was so. (Gen. 1:9)

John 1:1–3, by reflecting back on Genesis 1, indicates that the particular speeches of God in Genesis 1 have an organic relation to a deeper reality in God himself. The particular speeches derive from the One who is uniquely the Word, who is the eternal speech of God. God has an eternal speaking, namely, the Word who was with God and who was God. Then he has also a particular speaking in acts of creation in Genesis 1. This particular speaking harmonizes with and expresses his eternal speaking.

God not only created the world by speaking; he also sustains the world by speaking. Whatever happens takes place because God specifies it in his powerful speech:

Who has *spoken* and it came to pass,
    unless the Lord has *commanded* it?
Is it not from the *mouth* of the Most High
    that good and bad come? (Lam. 3:37–38)

Though John 1:1–3 focuses on speech rather than reason, the two ideas are closely related. John was undoubtedly aware of Greek speculations, such as those from the Stoics and from Philo, about a transcendent "reason" that explained the regularities of the world. John is providing a divinely inspired reply to these speculations.

Moreover, in Genesis 1 God's speech is rational speech. By speaking he brings order out of an earlier disorder (Gen. 1:2). He names and distinguishes particular things, offering a basis for our human reasoning that uses names and distinctions. We can also see a kind of logical order in the days of creation, according to which the later acts of creation build on earlier ones. For example, when God makes the heavenly lights "in the expanse" on the fourth day (Gen. 1:14), he builds on the fact that the expanse itself was made on the second day (Gen. 1:6, 8), and that he made the light itself on the first day (Gen. 1:3–5). The living creatures in the waters on the fifth day depend on the waters that were separated on the third day (Gen. 1:10). The land creatures on the sixth day depend on the dry land and the vegetation made on the third day.

So logic or reason is an aspect of God's speaking. We can see this is true when God created the world in Genesis 1. His speech includes logical self-consistency and rationality. The same truth holds supremely for the eternal Word of God who is God. This eternal Word is the eternal speech of God. He is therefore also the eternal logic or reason of God, as an aspect of God's speech.

Logic, we said, is personal. Now it becomes more evident why it is personal. It is not only personal, but a person, namely, the Word of God. But we should be careful to underline the fact that this person, the second person of the Trinity, is much richer than our human conceptions, either of logic or of reason or of language as a whole. He is infinite, an infinite person, with all the richness of God himself: "for in him [Christ] the whole fullness of deity dwells bodily" (Col. 2:9). Thus logic in a narrow sense focuses on only one aspect of who God is.

Moreover, God the Father, God the Son, and God the Holy Spirit are all *logical* in the sense of being consistent with who they are. The mutual indwelling of the persons of the Trinity guarantees coherence among the persons. The Father and the Spirit glorify the Word.

For Further Reflection

1. What is the role of God's speech in creation and providential rule over the world?
2. What is the relation between God's speech recorded in Genesis 1 and what is said about the Word of God in John 1:1–3?
3. Study the relation between Christ and the wisdom of God in Colossians 2:2–3 and 1 Corinthians 1:30. Study the role of Christ in creation according to Colossians 1:15–17; 1 Corinthians 8:6; John 1:1–3; and compare with Proverbs 8:22–31. How do these passages supplement what we have said about God and creation?
4. In the light of Genesis 1 and John 1:1–3, what can we say about the relation of logic to God?
5. How could the idea that Christ is the Logos of God be abused by people who might try to bring God down to the level of their limited understanding of God?

Chapter 9

Logic within Language

We can confirm the close relation of logic to language by observing that logic has to be explained and communicated to other human beings by means of language. We started off this book with examples of informal arguments. These informal arguments used language. We also provided an example of a piece of formal syllogistic reasoning: "All men are mortal. Socrates is a man. Therefore Socrates is mortal." We used language—sentences in English.

Previous Knowledge of Reasoning

Textbooks on logic work as well as they do because we have some tacit familiarity with reasoning in everyday life. Suppose a person has no previous formal training in logic. He can still follow the explicit logic about Socrates, because he can think and reason. Comprehension of logic textbooks depends not only on the language within the textbooks but also on the accessibility of the subject matter—the subject of logic—to human beings.

Human beings can grasp discussions of logical arguments because they have thinking capability. And their capability is somehow in tune with the logic that is written down on paper. In this sense, logic as personal, that is, logic belonging naturally to the thinking capabilities of persons, is inherently *prior* to logic as worked out explicitly in a theory on paper. Neither Aristotle nor his readers would have been able even to begin to discuss logic if they had no previous ability to think and to reason.

This priority belonging to persons suggests that the formalization of logic is a kind of *reduction*. It selects out *one* aspect from the whole of human thought. It focuses on that aspect, in the hope of understanding it more deeply and more precisely through careful concentration. But such a focus, valuable and insightful though it may be in drawing attention to some details, never really dispenses with the environment of persons. *We* as persons must be there to do the thinking and to recognize the relationship between special logical forms and the actual characteristics of our thinking, which are already there. If all of us persons were to die, God would still be there.

Language Delineating Logic

Logic is often focused on the study of the "formal" or general principles of argument, principles independent of content. Consider again the general syllogism that we already discussed:

> All Bs are As.
> All Cs are Bs.
> Therefore, all Cs are As.

The form is a *general* form because we can substitute many particular cases for A, B, and C. The symbols *A*, *B*, and *C* are logical placeholders rather than ordinary pieces of natural language. But they are still symbols, which function within a larger symbol system. When we first introduced them, we explained and illustrated them using natural language. We illustrated logical principles using particular examples, such as Socrates, men, and mortality, and we described the examples using ordinary language.

The general syllogistic form has the symbols *A*, *B*, and *C* instead of particular classifications like "being mortal." But it still contains some pieces of the English language, such as the words *all*, *are*, and *therefore*. In more formal logic even the words *all*, *are*, and *therefore* can be replaced—but not without first explaining the replacements using plenty of ordinary language (see parts II and III).

The teaching of logic uses ordinary language to start out. Then it can introduce special symbols like *A*, *B*, and *C*. These special symbols function as a kind of extension of language. So we still have logic functioning within the context of a creatively extended language.

How does special symbolism like *A, B, C* arise? The capability for introducing new words or new symbols into an exposition depends on powerful complexities within natural language and within our minds. Ordinary language has resources belonging to three distinct subsystems, namely, a referential subsystem, a grammatical subsystem, and a subsystem for sound (a "phonological" subsystem).[1] For example, the word *dog* has meaning (referring to canines). This meaning belongs to the referential subsystem. The word *dog* has grammatical form (singular or plural *dogs*); it has a sound (pronounced d-ŏ-g). For written language, a *graphological* subsystem substitutes for the sound subsystem.

---

[1] Vern S. Poythress, *In the Beginning Was the Word: Language—A God-Centered Approach* (Wheaton, IL: Crossway, 2009), chapter 32.

Now consider the symbol *A* used to stand for a general term within a syllogism. Like the word *dogs*, it enjoys coherence with all three subsystems of language. First, it has a meaning: roughly speaking, it means "you may substitute in here any general classifying term, and you then should substitute the same term for other occurrences of *A*." Second, it has a grammar. It is supposed to function in a way similar to a noun. It has a singular form *A* and a plural form *As* when we say that "All Bs are As." Third, it has a graphology. In this case, its graphical form is identical with the graphological form for the capital letter *A*. Technically speaking, there are two distinct linguistic elements *A*, with the same graphological form. The one is the ordinary letter capital *A*, while the other is the special symbol *A*, used in the context of syllogisms to stand for a classifying term. Having two distinct linguistic elements with the same graphological form is potentially confusing, but no more so than the existence of two words with the same graphological form *spring*. *Spring* is a season of the year. A *spring* is a mechanical device that exerts force when compressed or stretched. Human beings using language easily distinguish the two distinct words, because they occur in distinct contexts.

In sum, the symbol *A* belongs to all three subsystems, referential, grammatical, and graphological, and does so in an interlocking way. It can be written, read, and interpreted only by relying simultaneously on all three subsystems. We also have to rely on context, in order to disambiguate it; we distinguish the special symbol *A* from an ordinary capital letter *A* used as part of a longer word (or as the indefinite article: "*A* book").

The three subsystems interlock, and it turns out that they derive from the Trinitarian character of God. Let us see how.[2] According to John 1:1, God speaks his Word—his Word is the second person of the Trinity. Human beings who are made in the image of God speak their words. In doing so, they are imitating God, but they do so as creatures, on a subordinate level. The Spirit of God also is present with God. The Holy Spirit, like the breath in human communication, carries the word to its destination and works the effects. Psalm 33:6 says, "By the word of the LORD the heavens were made, and by the breath of his mouth all their host." The Hebrew word here for breath is *ruach*, the same word that is regularly used for the Holy Spirit. Indeed, the designation of the third person of the Trinity as "Spirit" (Hebrew *ruach*) already suggests the association that becomes more explicit

---

[2] See also ibid., chapter 32.

in Psalm 33:6. Similarly, Ezekiel 37 uses three different meanings of the Hebrew word *ruach*, namely, "breath" (37:5, 10), "winds" (v. 9), and "Spirit" (v. 14). The vision in Ezekiel 37 clearly represents the Holy Spirit as like the breath of God coming into human beings to give them life ("I will put my Spirit within you"; 37:14). Thus all three persons of the Trinity are present in distinct ways when God speaks his Word. The three persons are therefore all present in logic, which is an aspect of God's word.

Within God's original divine speaking, the meaning of his speech has a correlation with the plan of God the Father; the "grammar" has a correlation with the Word; and the speech has specific form through the Holy Spirit as the divine breath. The interlocking of subsystems within human language reflects the original divine coherence of the three persons of the Trinity. All language, including the specialized language within formal logic, depends on God as the original speaker. All language should be a motive for praising God and admiring his wisdom and infinity.

In our use of language we can be creative, as a reflection of the creativity of God.[3] We can add to language a written notation system. We may proceed to invent new graphical symbols like the symbol *A* to represent a classifying term. The new graphical symbol is an addition to the graphological subsystem. We also have to explain what this new symbol is going to *mean*. The meaning adds to the referential subsystem. We have to tell students, "This symbol stands for some classifying term like *dog*." This new symbol *A* then begins to function within the graphological, grammatical, and referential subsystems of the newly extended language.

All this work depends not only on the complexity of existing language but on its flexibility and extendability. Logic in this way depends on language for its intelligibility and its coherent functioning.[4] It also depends on our capability as human beings with minds. Our minds give us the ability to work flexibly with language and its meanings, and to grasp new meanings as well as new graphological symbols when someone else introduces them.

Mentioning Symbols

In introducing a new symbol we may often use the capability of language to talk about itself. Note that we can distinguish between *using* a word and

---

[3] Ibid., p. 30, and chapter 6.
[4] Later we will consider so-called formal languages that are deliberately "drained" of meaning, at least temporarily. It turns out that though they are unusual, they are not a real exception to the dependence of new symbols on natural language.

mentioning or talking about it. If I say, "I saw a stray cat on the street," I am *using* the word *cat*. If I say, "The word *cat* in the plural is *cats*," I am *mentioning* the word *cat* (and *cats* as well). If a scholar introduces a new technical word or technical symbol, he typically mentions the symbol in order to define it. The chemist may say, "C stands for the chemical element carbon." The chemist is *mentioning* the symbol C. Later, when he draws a diagram or writes an equation for a chemical reaction, he *uses* the symbol C already defined.

We can also meet a new word without an accompanying definition, in which case we may be expected to "catch on" from observing the word being used repeatedly in various contexts. We try to zero in on what it must mean by making sense of it from the contexts. This ability to discern new meanings, often by intuition, is mysterious. It doubtless depends on very complex abilities and complex interactions of human beings with their environment, including the language environment. But if the new contexts for a symbol are strange or technical in nature, it may be difficult for us to catch on. We may have to ask the expert, "What does the word *neutrino* mean?" in which case we are *mentioning* or talking about the word *neutrino*.

The mention of a word, in distinction from its use, involves a kind of stepping back. We step back from merely using the word *cat* in order to examine the word itself. We ask what the word means. Or we explain its meaning to someone else. We are, as it were, doing dictionary work or linguistic analysis rather than merely proceeding to use language unreflectively. We think and speak *about* our thinking and speaking, rather than about cats.

But then can we take another step back? If linguistics is the study of language, we can also practice "meta-linguistics," which studies linguistics. If epistemology is the study of knowledge, "meta-epistemology" will be the study of epistemology. And meta-meta-linguistics will be the study of meta-linguistics.

We can always consider the option of stepping back from what we were doing a moment earlier. We can reflect on what we were doing, and then reflect on our act of reflection, and then reflect on that. We can go on until we become confused!

Human Transcendence in Mentioning a Word

This standing back already exists when we *mention* a word rather than merely using it. We are, as it were, standing back to look at the word rather than unself-consciously using the word to look at something else. This standing back is a kind of human form of transcendence. We can transcend our immediate situation by reflecting on it. And we can transcend our reflections by reflecting on them. We can take a kind of God's-eye view, viewing ourselves from above, as another human being might see us or as God might see us.

This transcendence is then one way in which we think God's thoughts after him. God is *transcendent* in an absolute sense. He is infinite. We are creatures. But we do have a kind of imitative, creaturely ability to transcend our immediate environment or our immediate thoughts or our immediate speeches.[5] And we use this transcendence when we investigate logic. Every time we think, we imitate God's thinking. Every time we think about logic, we also imitate God's transcendence over the immediate.

We can put it another way. General rules of logic, in their generality, can find a home in our minds because we can transcend the particular instance of reasoning (e.g., about Socrates). We can see the generality belonging to many particular cases of reasoning. And we can employ language and thought to speak about and think about this general pattern. In doing so, we depend on the harmony between ourselves, our world, and our language. All three obey the same logic. We are depending on God, who has made us and our world and who has given us language. God in his wisdom holds together the various aspects of our thinking. And because we are made in his image, we are able in a creaturely way to imitate his transcendence.

Perspectives on Logic

Let us look more closely at the relation among three sides: (1) persons, (2) the world, and (3) language. God is the source for all three. All three function together, and by God's design they interlock. These three are closely related to John Frame's three perspectives on ethics.[6] People are the focus of Frame's existential (or "personal") perspective; the world is the focus of the situational perspective; and norms for language are the focus of the normative perspective. All three perspectives are tacitly involved in any practical analysis of language or logic.

John Frame first developed the three perspectives in the context of eth-

---

[5] See Poythress, *In the Beginning Was the Word*, chapter 12.
[6] John M. Frame, *Perspectives on the Word of God: An Introduction to Christian Ethics* (Phillipsburg, NJ: Presbyterian & Reformed, 1990); John M. Frame, *The Doctrine of the Christian Life* (Phillipsburg, NJ: Presbyterian & Reformed, 2008).

ics. The existential perspective focuses on persons and their motives. Our primary motive must be love. The situational perspective focuses on the situation, that is, the world, and asks what actions will promote the glory of God in our situation. The normative perspective focuses on norms, the commandments of God given in Scripture. The norms from God command us to love and to pay attention to our neighbor's need, which means paying attention to the situation. The most important person in the situation is God, and so the situational perspective implies attention to God's norms. The perspectives interlock. Rightly understood, each perspective implies the others. They are in harmony with one another.

Logic, as an aspect of language, is closely related to God's norms. Love is closely related to the persons and their motives. The full picture of God's plan includes both in harmony. In particular, in the wisdom of God's plan the normativity of logic is in harmony with the personal dynamic of love, and with the emotions that it draws in its train. Spock and McCoy actually belong together.

If we like, we can add to the picture a third character that *Star Trek* provides: Data. Data, a character from *Star Trek: The Next Generation*, is a sentient computer. Data, as his name suggests, stands for data. He is filled with facts about the world. He represents focus on the world of facts, that is, the situation. In God's plan, logic and emotion and data harmonize.

For Further Reflection

1. What is the relation of logic to language?
2. How does language depend on God?
3. How does human thinking about logic show imitative transcendence? How does it reflect abilities that image God's character?
4. What might be the advantages and disadvantages of introducing new special symbolism?
5. What benefits do we receive from our ability in imitative transcendence? How might this ability be misused in rebellion against God?

Chapter 10

Suppressing the Truth

Let us return to the main point in our argument. Logic, we have said, is personal. But logic does not depend on any one human person, since it would still hold if we had never existed. Logic transcends the world, including the world of human persons. That is another way of saying that it is divine. It belongs to God, as a feature of his speech. It displays his attributes because it is an aspect of his character. Hence, we rely on God every time we think and every time we engage in logical reasoning. We can praise God for what he has given us in our logic and our ability to reason.

Why do people not notice this relationship to God? The Bible has an answer. We suppress what we know about God:

> [18] For the wrath of God is revealed from heaven against all ungodliness and unrighteousness of men, who by their unrighteousness *suppress the truth*. [19] For what can be known about God is plain to them, because God has shown it to them. [20] For his invisible attributes, namely, his eternal power and divine nature, have been clearly perceived, ever since the creation of the world, in the things that have been made. So they are without excuse. [21] For although they knew God, they did not honor him as God or give thanks to him, but they became futile in their thinking, and their foolish hearts were darkened. [22] Claiming to be wise, they became fools, [23] and exchanged the glory of the immortal God for images resembling mortal man and birds and animals and reptiles.
>
> [24] Therefore God gave them up in the lusts of their hearts to impurity, to the dishonoring of their bodies among themselves, [25] because they exchanged the truth about God for a lie and worshiped and served the creature rather than the Creator, who is blessed forever! Amen. (Rom. 1:18–25)

At the time when the book of Romans was written, Greeks and Romans made statues of gods and bowed down to them. But in modern cultures we have another kind of substitute, namely, the idea of an impersonal something that governs the world. This impersonal something is a substitute for God.

This process of substitution takes place in the case of logic as well as in other areas.[1] We engage in substituting an *impersonal* conception of logic for the reality of its *personal* character. This substitution is a form of idolatry.

Modern conceptions of logic recapitulate the description in Romans 1:18–25. According to Romans 1:20 God's "invisible attributes, namely, his eternal power and divine nature, have been clearly perceived." They are perceived "in the things that [he has] made." The things God has made testify to the logical ordering of the world. And logic itself, as an aspect of the mind of God, is reflected in human minds. Our own minds and their reasoning reflect the logic of God, which is eternal and all-powerful. We cannot escape this testimony because it is there indelibly whenever we think or reason. Whenever we use language we exhibit logic in our speech. Here, as well as elsewhere, God's attributes "have been clearly perceived." As a result, "they [ultimately all human beings everywhere] are without excuse" (Rom. 1:20). Everywhere we are confronted with the reality of God—and everywhere we flee from this reality.

We are in rebellion against God, and we do not like to submit to him. We do not like the obligation of being thankful to him, because we have failed to be thankful. We are in flight from this God because it is too morally painful to contemplate our guilt and our failure. We make substitute gods in order to soothe our conscience. An impersonal something, or an impersonal logic, can safely be ignored, and lets us off the hook morally and religiously. We thereby fool ourselves.

Even in their rebellion, people continue to depend on God being there. They show *in action* that they continue to believe in God. Cornelius Van Til compares it to an incident he saw on a train, where a small girl sitting on her father's lap slapped him in the face.[2] The rebel must depend on God, and must be "sitting on his lap," even to be able to rebel against him.

Logic and History

We can see human rebellion work itself out in history. In the history of Western philosophy, many philosophers have sought to master logic as a

---

[1]See Vern S. Poythress, *Redeeming Science: A God-Centered Approach* (Wheaton, IL: Crossway, 2006), chapter 1, for a similar substitution in the case of scientific law; and Poythress, *In the Beginning Was the Word: Language—A God-Centered Approach* (Wheaton, IL: Crossway, 2009), chapter 9, for substitution in the theory of language.
[2]Cornelius Van Til, "Transcendent Critique of Theoretical Thought" (Response by C. Van Til), in *Jerusalem and Athens: Critical Discussions on the Theology and Apologetics of Cornelius Van Til*, ed. E. R. Geehan (n.l.: Presbyterian & Reformed, 1971), 98. For rebels' dependence on God, see Cornelius Van Til, *The Defense of the Faith*, 2nd ed. (Philadelphia: Presbyterian & Reformed, 1963); and the exposition by John M. Frame, *Apologetics to the Glory of God: An Introduction* (Phillipsburg, NJ: Presbyterian & Reformed, 1994).

means of mastering truth, mastering wisdom, and mastering the world. There is an innate desire within mankind for mastery, a desire and a drive put there by God himself when he created mankind and gave him a task:

> Then God said, "Let us make man in our image, after our likeness. And let them have *dominion* over the fish of the sea and over the birds of the heavens and over the livestock and over all the earth and over every creeping thing that creeps on the earth." . . .
>
> And God blessed them. And God said to them, "Be fruitful and multiply and fill the earth and *subdue* it, and have *dominion* over the fish of the sea and over the birds of the heavens and over every living thing that moves on the earth." (Gen. 1:26, 28)

But beginning with Adam and Eve human beings have been in rebellion against God's ultimate dominion. They seek to establish their own dominion independent of God—they seek *autonomy*, to be a god to themselves. "You will be like God," the serpent says (Gen. 3:5).[3] So they have pursued the mastery of logic *autonomously*. Pursuing autonomy means pursuing mastery independent of God; as human beings we want to be our own law, our own god. In fact this pursuit is an impossibility, because logic is an aspect of God's mind. But human beings suppress the truth and tell themselves that logic is impersonal.

This distortion of the truth has had its effect ever since Adam. And I suggest that it continues through the course of Western philosophy. Philosophy in most of its forms, from the time of Aristotle, clings to the foundational conception that logic is impersonal, and that certain modes of valid reasoning can be construed as mechanistic forms independent of the language of God. (For further discussion of logic and philosophy, see appendices F1–F5.)

The widespread idea that logic is impersonal and mechanistic explains the difficulty that we find with Spock. If logic is ultimately impersonal, and if Spock is purely logical, the impersonality of logic bleeds into Spock's entire character, and he becomes no better than a caricature of a robust human person. We may still admire his logic. After all, it is still a distorted reflection of God. But we feel its limitations. We feel unsatisfied. Or, conversely, we may feel that Spock's character is an ideal to emulate. But by our emulation we show our own one-sidedness, and we distort our own personhood.

---

[3] See the discussion of the fall in Poythress, *In the Beginning Was the Word*, chapter 14.

Do We Christians Believe?

The fault, I suspect, is not entirely on the side of unbelievers. The fault also occurs among Christians. Christians have sometimes adopted an unbiblical concept of God that moves him one step out of the way of our ordinary affairs. We ourselves may think of logic as a kind of cosmic mechanism or impersonal clockwork that holds the world in its grip, while God is on vacation. God becomes aloof and uninvolved. But this is not biblical. The Bible says, "You cause the grass to grow for the livestock" (Ps. 104:14). "He gives snow like wool" (Ps. 147:16).[4] His involvement includes involvement with every human mind:

> But it is the spirit in man,
>> the breath of the Almighty, that *makes him understand.*
> It is not the old who are wise,
>> nor the aged who understand what is right. (Job 32:8–9)

> O Lord, you have searched me and known me!
> You know when I sit down and when I rise up;
>> *you discern my thoughts* from afar.
> You search out my path and my lying down
>> and are acquainted with all my ways.
> Even before a word is on my tongue,
>> behold, O Lord, you know it altogether. . . .
> Where shall I go from your Spirit?
>> Or where shall I flee from your presence? (Ps. 139:1–4, 7)

Let us not forget it. If we ourselves recovered a robust doctrine of God's involvement in daily caring for us and our minds *in detail*, we would find ourselves in a much better position to dialogue with fellow human beings who rely on that same care.

Principles for Witness

In order to use this situation as a starting point for witness, we need to bear in mind several principles.

First, the observation that God underlies logic does not have the same shape as the traditional theistic proofs—at least as they are often understood. We are not trying to lead people to come to know a God who is completely

---

[4] See also the discussion in Vern S. Poythress, "Science as Allegory," *Journal of the American Scientific Affiliation* 35/2 (1983): 65–71.

new to them. Rather, we show that they *already know* God as an aspect of their human experience in thinking. This places the focus not on intellectual debate, but on being a full human being.

Second, people deny God within the very same context in which they depend on him. The denial of God springs ultimately not from intellectual flaws or from failure to see all the way to the conclusion of a chain of syllogistic reasoning, but from spiritual failure. We are rebels against God, and we will not serve him. Consequently, we suffer under his wrath (Rom. 1:18), which has intellectual as well as spiritual and moral effects. Those who rebel against God are "fools," according to Romans 1:22.

Third, it is humiliating to be exposed as fools, and it is further humiliating, even psychologically unbearable, to be exposed as guilty of rebellion against the goodness of God. We can expect our hearers to fight with a tremendous outpouring of intellectual and spiritual energy against so unbearable an outcome.

Fourth, the gospel itself, with its message of forgiveness and reconciliation through Christ, offers the only remedy that can truly end this fight against God. But it brings with it the ultimate humiliation: that my restoration comes entirely from God, from outside me—in spite of, rather than because of, my vaunted abilities. To climax it all, so wicked was I that it took the price of the death of the Son of God to accomplish my rescue.

Fifth, approaching people in this way constitutes spiritual warfare. Unbelievers and idolaters are captives to Satanic deceit (1 Cor. 10:20; 2 Thess. 2:9–12; 2 Tim. 2:25–26; Eph. 4:17–24; Rev. 12:9). They do not get free from Satan's captivity unless God gives them release (2 Tim. 2:25–26). We must pray to God and rely on God's power rather than the ingenuity of human argument and eloquence of persuasion (1 Cor. 2:1–5; 2 Cor. 10:3–5).

Sixth, we come into this encounter as fellow sinners. Christians too have become massively guilty by being captive to the idolatry in which logic is regarded as impersonal. Within this captivity we take for granted the benefits and beauties of rationality for which we should be filled with gratitude and praise to God.

Does an approach to witnessing based on these principles work itself out differently from many of the approaches that attempt to address non-Christians? To me it appears so.

For Further Reflection

1. In what way does the display of God's character in logic "prove" or not "prove" God's existence?
2. Can you explain how non-Christians rely on God at the same time that they deny him?
3. What distinction needs to be made between evidence and reception of evidence when it comes to believing in God?
4. What does 2 Corinthians 4:4–6 say about human resistance to God?

Chapter 11

Logic and the Trinity

Logic as we human beings experience it has roots in eternal logic, namely, the eternal Word, the second person of the Trinity, in fellowship with the Father and the Spirit. We can see more of the roots of logic by reflecting further on what the Bible says about God speaking.

God Speaking His Word

First, as we indicated earlier, logic is an aspect of God's speech. And his speech is Trinitarian.

Second, we can see an analogy between God as an author and a human author. Dorothy Sayers acutely observes that the experience of a human author writing a book contains profound analogies to the Trinitarian character of God.[1] An author's act of creation in writing imitates the action of God in creating the world. God creates according to his Trinitarian nature. A human author creates with an Idea, Energy, and Power, corresponding mysteriously to the involvement of the three persons in creation. Without tracing Sayers's reflections in detail, we may observe that the act of God in creation does involve all three persons. God the Father is the originator. God the Son, as the eternal Word (John 1:1–3), is involved in the words of command that issue from God ("Let there be light"; Gen. 1:3). God the Spirit hovers over the waters (Gen. 1:2). Psalm 104:30 says that "when you send forth your Spirit, they [animals] are created." Moreover, the creation of Adam involves an in-breathing by God that alludes to the presence of the Spirit (Gen. 2:7). All three persons of the Trinity are involved in God's work of creation. Though the relation among the persons of the Trinity is deeply mysterious, and though all persons are involved in all the actions of God toward the world, we can distinguish different aspects of action belonging preeminently to the different persons.

Logic in its divine origin belongs to the eternal self-consistency of God.

---

[1] Dorothy Sayers, *The Mind of the Maker* (New York: Harcourt, Brace, 1941), especially pp. 33–46.

God created the world in harmony with his own internal self-consistency. Logic within God corresponds most aptly to the plan of the divine Author. Logic is then one aspect of the "Idea," representing the plan of God the Father. Second, the creation of the world involves an articulation, a specification, an expression of the plan, with respect to all the particulars of a world. God specifies that logic will apply to the particulars of the world that he is going to create. For example, in God's plan he specifies that Socrates will be a man. This particularity corresponds to Sayers's term "Energy" or "Activity," representing the Word who is the expression of the Father. Third, God's activity in creation and providence involves holding things responsible to logic, a concrete application to creatures. At a particular time God actually brings Socrates into the world, and the Holy Spirit is present in his formation (Ps. 139:13–16). The Holy Spirit forms Socrates in harmony with the logic of God. As a result, Socrates is mortal. This action of God corresponds to Sayers's term "Power," representing the Spirit.[2]

We may see a reflection of the Trinity in still another way by using the categories that have already been developed in Trinitarian theological meditations on the character of God and his Word.[3] According to Trinitarian thinking, the unity and diversity in the world reflect the original unity and diversity in God. First, God is one God. He has a unified plan for the world. The universality of logic reflects this unity. God is also three persons, the Father, the Son, and the Holy Spirit. This diversity in the being of God is then reflected in the diversity in the created world.[4] The many instances to which logic applies express this diversity. For example, the general pattern "all Bs are As" expresses a unity common to many particular premises. Each instance, such as "all men are mortal," is a particular case, and the instances together show diversity.

Moreover, unity and diversity are expressed in another way. The unity of God's plan has a close relation to the Father, the first person of the Trinity, who is the origin of this plan. The Son, in becoming incarnate, expresses the particularity of manifestation in time and space. He is, as it were, an instantiation of God.[5] Thus he is analogous in his incarnation to the fact that one universal logic expresses itself in particular instances.

[2] See also John Milbank, *The Word Made Strange: Theology, Language, Culture* (Oxford: Blackwell, 1997), on the Trinitarian roots of communication.
[3] Vern S. Poythress, *God-Centered Biblical Interpretation* (Phillipsburg, NJ: Presbyterian & Reformed, 1999), especially pp. 69–94, where all meaning exhibits Triune character.
[4] See Cornelius Van Til, *The Defense of the Faith*, 2nd ed. (Philadelphia: Presbyterian & Reformed, 1963), 25–26.
[5] An *instantiation* is an individual expression of some reality (in the case of Christ, the reality is the reality of God). Christ's incarnation is unique, and yet we can still see analogies to other cases where an instance expresses a principle. See Appendix F5.

Love in the Family

God also uses an analogy between himself and a human family. The Bible indicates that God the Father is Father to the Son, in communion with the Holy Spirit. The designations "Father" and "Son" indicate that there is an analogy between the divine and the human. The roles and relationships between God the Father and God the Son have analogies to the roles and relationships between a human father and a human son.

Modern reasoning may be tempted to say that the use of words like "father" and "son" for God is "merely" metaphorical, an extension of their human use. But it is actually the reverse. God is the original. God made man to be like God, not vice versa. So it is appropriate to point out that God is the *original* Father. In comparison to this original, human fathers are derivative, "metaphorical" extensions of meaning from the original Fatherhood.[6]

We can say more about the divine original in God. The Holy Spirit, as the third person of the Trinity, has a role in the relationship of the Father to the Son:

[34] For he whom God has sent utters the words of God, for he gives the Spirit without measure. [35] The Father loves the Son and has given all things into his hand. (John 3:34–35)

The giving of the Spirit in verse 34 is one gift, while in verse 35 the Father gives the gift of "all things" to the Son. The gift of all things expresses the Father's love for the Son. And verse 34 indicates that the principal gift is the Holy Spirit. So the Holy Spirit expresses the Father's love.

Later in the Gospel of John, we learn that the Son in turn loves the Father: ". . . but I do as the Father has commanded me, so that the world may know that *I love the Father*" (John 14:31). The Son's love for the Father is made manifest in his obedience to the Father's commands: "I do as the Father has commanded me." The Son shows himself to be in harmony with the commands of the Father, and therefore with the will of the Father. This harmony implies consistency in the thinking and actions of the Father and the Son.

The Spirit also is in harmony with the Father and the Son, as we see by the fact that he speaks what he hears:

[6] On metaphor, see Vern S. Poythress, *In the Beginning Was the Word: Language—A God-Centered Approach* (Wheaton, IL: Crossway, 2009), chapters 34 and 35. See also J. I. Packer, "The Adequacy of Human Language," in *Inerrancy*, ed. Norman L. Geisler (Grand Rapids, MI: Zondervan, 1980), 195–226. Some of the language of this chapter is taken from Vern Sheridan Poythress, *Redeeming Sociology: A God-Centered Approach* (Wheaton, IL: Crossway, 2011), 28–29.

... for he [the Spirit] will not speak on his own authority, but whatever he hears he will speak, and he will declare to you the things that are to come. He will glorify me, for he will take what is mine and declare it to you. All that the Father has is mine; therefore I said that he will take what is mine and declare it to you. (John 16:13–15)

The Spirit speaks in harmony with what belongs to both the Father and the Son. Harmony includes consistency in mutual action. Consistency among the persons of the Trinity reflects itself in consistency in what they do toward human beings and the world. This consistency in God is the origin of logic as we experience it. The Father and the Son and the Spirit act in harmony with their love for one another. Logic, in this respect, is an implication of love.

This inner loyalty and love of God also explains why logic expresses *necessary* truth. The Father *necessarily* loves the Son through the Spirit. God is love (1 John 4:8). Each of the persons of the Trinity is a perfectly lovely object of love. It is inconceivable that God would not have this love. God necessarily acts in accord with his character and with the love among the persons of the Trinity, and this necessity means that the consistency of God with himself is a necessity. Therefore the consistency of logic in God's acts toward the world is also a necessity.

Logic and Love

The nature of God's love shows that love and logic are closely related. God the Father loves the Son through the Holy Spirit. Mutual love implies harmony among the persons of the Trinity. Harmony in turn implies consistency. Logic, we have said, is God's self-consistency. Thus, love implies logic. Conversely, logic implies love. Because God is consistent with himself, he is consistent also with his loving character. God the Father therefore loves the Son, who is the worthy object of love.

Within God's character, logic and love are perspectives on each other. Each implies the other. Each is characterized by the other, because God's logic is a loving logic and his love is a logical love. Both are expressed in God's Trinitarian nature, in which the persons of the Trinity love one another and are in harmony with one another.

We can put it another way. God is logical, and each of the persons of the Trinity is logical. But the second person, who is the Word and Logos of God, is the most prominent expression of the logical aspect of God's character. Likewise, God is loving, and each of the persons of the Trinity is full of love. But the third person, the Holy Spirit, is a prominent expression of love, because the Father loves the Son through giving the Spirit. The Spirit also brings the love of God to our hearts: "God's love has been poured into our hearts through the Holy Spirit who has been given to us" (Rom. 5:5). The Holy Spirit who indwells us empowers us to love: ". . . the fruit of the Spirit is love, . . ." (Gal. 5:22).

Thus, if we want to simplify, we can say that the Son represents logic and the Spirit represents love. The doctrine of coinherence says that the persons of the Trinity indwell one another. So each person expresses in himself characteristics that belong to the others. Love in the Holy Spirit expresses itself in the logic of the Son, and vice versa. This harmony in God through coinherence is utterly unique to God. But it is also the foundation for all harmonies among creatures. Harmonies in creatures reflect the original, uncreated harmony of the God who says, "I AM WHO I AM" (Ex. 3:14).

We are made in the image of God. So when we are right with God, logic and love will be in harmony in us, by analogy with their harmony in God, who is their original. Love includes an "emotional" side (though Christian love is not sentimentality). In love we are fervently committed to doing good to the other person. So the rationality of logic and the fervency of love go together. We love because it is logically right to do so, by the logicality of the Logos himself. Conversely, we are truly logical only when we love Christ the Logos of God. True logic can only operate in our lives through love of logic, that is, love of the true logic of God.

If we come to know Christ, who is the true Logos, we experience his beauty and we grow in love. If we love Christ, we want to know him better, and knowing him includes knowing the purity of his self-consistency. We want to imitate him, and in imitating him we follow the true source of all rationality. We follow the rationality and the logic of God.

In a word, logic and love, Spock and McCoy, come together in harmony. However, this key harmony does not come into our lives because we decide to follow a "moderate" middle ground, in which we settle for a noncommittal, in-between compromise. Nor do we get harmony because we affirm a little of Spock and a little of McCoy at just the right points. Nor do we just let them fight it out until they have each knocked off the unhealthy side of their counterpart.

No. Spock and McCoy are both distorted images, distorted by the corruptions of non-Christian thinking and non-Christian desire. Logic and emotion both need reconfiguration, yes, transfiguration, through renewal into the image of Christ (2 Cor. 3:18). Knowing Christ is the way to know God. And knowing God deeply leads to transforming our logic and our love, until they harmonize according to the inner harmony of God.

Understanding Omnipotence

Now let us consider God's omnipotence. Some people have imagined that God's omnipotence makes it possible for him to do anything at all, including the production of inconsistencies. But this is not true. The Bible clearly indicates that God acts in harmony with his character. He cannot act in a way that violates his character:

> . . . he *cannot deny himself.* (2 Tim. 2:13)

> God is not man, that *he should lie,*
>   or a son of man, that he should change his mind. (Num. 23:19)

> . . . God, *who never lies,* promised before the ages began. (Titus 1:2)

The Bible also indicates the close relationship and harmony between God's character and the expressions of his character:

> *Righteous* are you, O Lord,
>   and *right* are your rules. (Ps. 119:137)

God's rules are necessarily right because his character is righteous. The verse in Psalm 119:137 has two distinct words, "righteous," and "right," rather than one, but they are closely related in meaning. The next verse goes on to use the cognate noun "righteousness":

> You have appointed your testimonies in *righteousness*
>   and in all faithfulness. (Ps. 119:138)

The relation between God's character as righteous and the righteousness of his speech is further elaborated in following verses:

> Your *righteousness* is *righteous* forever,
>   and your law is true. (Ps. 119:142)

> Your testimonies are *righteous* forever;
>   give me understanding that I may live. (Ps. 119:144)

Thus, God is always consistent with his character. If we follow the Bible, we should use a definition of omnipotence that accords with God's character. That God is omnipotent means that God can do anything he pleases (Ps. 115:3; 135:6). What he "pleases," that is, what he wants, is always in accord with his character. We can therefore trust him and we can have confidence that he is perfectly consistent with himself and with the logic of his character. God's omnipotence is never in tension with his logic.

For Further Reflection

1. What main analogies does God use in the Bible to help us understand his Trinitarian nature? What practical benefits might follow from what he says about himself?
2. Can we comprehend completely the relation among persons of the Trinity? Are there mysteries in logic?
3. What implications does the nature of God have for the relation between logic and love?
4. How do we move toward having a harmony in our own lives between logic and love?
5. Does God have the power to destroy himself? Can God make a rock so heavy that he cannot lift it? Can God change the past? If we find that we answer "no" to one of these questions, does it imply that God is not omnipotent? Why or why not?

Chapter 12

The Absoluteness of God

We have traced the foundations of logic back to God. But this may seem strange to some people. Let us reflect on what we have done.

Clear and Unclear

First, why should we seek to find a foundation for the clarity of logic in the mystery of God? People might ask, "Why trace the clear to the unclear?"

Particular cases of logical reasoning can sometimes seem to be very clear. But why such reasoning works at all is not so clear, if we leave God out of our reckoning. Is logical reasoning just a path of approximations and guesswork and steady improvement on a pragmatic level? Is our whole reasoning process just the mindless and purposeless product of an allegedly undirected evolution? Or is there something deep about logic? And if there is, what is it?

When we study logic, are we grasping some ultimate structure of the world? Or is it just the ultimate structure of our own minds looking back at us as if in a mirror? After more than two thousand years of Western philosophy, philosophers still do not have a clear and coherent answer on which they can agree.

In addition, we can ask, What is the relation of logic to love? What has Spock to do with McCoy? Philosophy has no satisfying answer.

Reality of Analogies

In reflecting on logic, we have relied on analogies. We have said that there is a kind of analogy between the human mind and the mind of God, so that we can think God's thoughts after him. There is a kind of analogy between God speaking and human speech, so that the logic in human reasoning imitates the logic in divine speech. There is an analogy between God the Father and human fathers. There is analogy between the loving faithfulness of the persons of the Trinity and the consistency of logic.

Or is there? Are some or all of these analogies overdrawn or fanciful? And even if they are not, what good do they do us?

The heritage of intellectual life in the Western world owes a good deal to the Greeks. Greek philosophers wanted to make the nature of things transparent to the human mind. And we can sometimes achieve a good deal by seeking to understand more deeply.

But the quest for understanding gets corrupted by sin. We want to be God. We want to have God-like understanding. But absolute, transparent understanding belongs to God alone. What we understand, we understand by analogy to God's own understanding. The presence of analogy implies that we always confront remaining mysteries, not merely at the edge but at the heart of understanding, because we are finite and God is infinite. Every growth in understanding generates a new "why?" question: "Why are things this way?" For us there is mystery at every point in our experience, because at every point we experience the presence of God, and the truths that we know reflect the mind of God, who is infinite.

It is wise to acknowledge our dependence on God and to go to God for answers. For one thing, we should acknowledge that all our knowledge comes from God:

> But it is the spirit in man,
>   the breath of the Almighty, that *makes him understand*. (Job 32:8)

> He who *teaches man knowledge*—
>   the LORD—knows the thoughts of man,
>   that they are but a breath. (Ps. 94:10–11)

Our thoughts imitate God's thoughts. So when we think about logic, we should realize that our thinking has its foundation in God's thinking. The mystery of who God is should fire our love for God, right in the midst of our reflections on logic.

Foundations of Existence

Next, we should acknowledge that God is also the ultimate foundation for the *existence* of things, their very being and their characteristics. God exists eternally. He is his own foundation for existence. Everything else has been created by God. Its existence depends on God. "In him [God] we live and move and have our being" (Acts 17:28). Created existence comes about and receives its structure from God's word, which he uttered in acts of creation: "And God said, 'Let there be light,' and there was light" (Gen. 1:3).

God is not dependent on any outside source. So he does not need any ideas from outside himself in order to produce a plan to create the world:

> Whom did he consult,
>   and who made him understand?
> Who taught him the path of justice,
>   and taught him knowledge,
>   and showed him the way of understanding? (Isa. 40:14)

Who is a source for God's knowledge? The implied answer from Isaiah 40 is "no one." Or we could also say that God has his own wisdom and his own Spirit to consult (Prov. 8:22–31; Isa. 40:13). The mention in the Old Testament of the wisdom of God and the Spirit of God foreshadows the full revelation of the Trinitarian character of God in the New Testament. The New Testament identifies Christ as the wisdom of God (Col. 2:3; 1 Cor. 1:30). God consults himself. His plans and his speech issue from himself.

So it should not be surprising that two things are true about what God creates. First, the creature is not the Creator. God makes a world distinct from himself. Second, the creature reflects the Creator. It reveals God's "invisible attributes, namely, his eternal power and divine nature" (Rom. 1:20). In addition to this general display of God's attributes, God creates specific creatures that reflect him in specific ways. Created light reflects the fact that God *is light* in an uncreated sense (1 John 1:5). We can say that this kind of statement about light is a metaphor. But God is the original. Created light is derivative. So there is a sense in which created light is a metaphor for God. Similarly, earthly fathers and sons reflect the uncreated relationship between God the Father and God the Son within the Trinity. Consistency in logic in our reasoning reflects the consistency of the Father's love.

Imaging

All these reflections in created things are not identical with their original. Human fathers are not God the Father. They reflect him in the midst of being different from him. This reality of created reflection is itself analogous to an aspect of God. The eternal Son is the eternal *image* of the invisible God (Col. 1:15). He is the one and only original uncreated reflection. Human beings made in the image of God are made in the Son's image.

They are, so to speak, a reflection of a reflection. The Son is divine, but is not the Father. We as human beings are not divine and are not the Father. The Bible underlines the distinctions. But it also invites us to see the relationships and the analogies between God the Creator and the creation that reflects his glory.

We can say also that God is the foundation for the *meaning* of created things. God not only created them but gave them particular characteristics and gave them meaning within his comprehensive plan for the world. That meaning includes their function in displaying his glory. Each created thing displays God's goodness and his wisdom in its own distinctive way (Psalm 104). The worm displays God's glory by its amazing worminess. It does not need to be anything other than a worm in order to do so. It is fulfilling God's plan and showing his wisdom precisely by being a worm and living out its life as a worm. Likewise, logic displays the wisdom and self-consistency of God.

Following Lines back to God

The Bible invites us to see the world in relation to God who made it and sustains it. There is no other source for the world than in God himself. He is the *sole* creator. So *every* aspect, not just some, finds its origin and explanation ultimately in him. This reality should embolden us to notice analogies to what we know of God, even when the analogies are partial. For example, God is not a human father. He does not die, and he did not have a father who fathered him. He does not have a body. The analogy between God as Father and a human father is therefore *partial*. But it is real. God got his idea for human fatherhood from himself.

We should see in God the source and foundation for the world for several reasons.

First, God is ultimate. The ultimate Fatherhood belongs to God. So we are invited to reason downward, from God's Fatherhood to the meaning of human fatherhood. This downward reasoning can be helpful in a very practical way when people have had the experience of a bad human father. The proper response is to say not that fatherhood in itself is bad, but that the bad human father has corrupted the real and true fatherhood, which is ultimately rooted in God. And redemptively, we say that God offers himself as true Father, through Christ, to those who have suffered the effects of sin in bad human fathers.

Second, God is absolute. This absoluteness means that there is nothing behind or above God, to which he is subject. We have already used this reasoning with respect to logic. Laws of logic are not impersonal rules above God, because then they would play the role of being the true absolute.

If God is absolute, logic must be traced back to him. Logic is personal, not an impersonal something, a disconnected abstraction.

Worship

Third, God's uniquely glorious character demands our exclusive worship. Exclusive worship is the implication of the first commandment, "You shall have no other gods before me" (Ex. 20:3). Exclusive worship is also implied by the great commandment, "You shall love the LORD your God with all your heart and with all your soul and with all your might" (Deut. 6:5). All our being and all our action and all our thought must be devoted to him. Exclusive and radical loyalty to God implies giving him the praise for all our benefits. No benefit ought to be regarded as merely "there" and then taken for granted. The beauty of clouds or of trees or of a sunset, or the affection of a dog, or the humorous behavior of monkeys, should lead us to praise God, rather than merely to enjoy the effect but unconsciously to shrug our shoulders as to its source. The same principle then extends to logic. Logic is not just "there" impersonally. If it were, it would diminish our worship. We should *love* God because of what we learn in logic.

We know that we are supposed to praise God for the beauty of a rose, because a rose is special. God made roses as one kind of flower in distinction from many other kinds of flowers. And he made a choice to create plants with flowers, when he could have made many other alternative kinds of things. So we praise God for what is unique and for what did not have to be.

We should also praise God for what is *necessary*. God is necessarily righteous, because righteousness is part of his character. He is necessarily truthful. He is necessarily loving. He is necessarily all-powerful. Is he less great because these characteristics are necessary? Of course not. The Psalms praise God both for his acts of righteousness and power and for who he is, namely, righteous and powerful:

> They shall speak of the glory of your kingdom
> and tell of your power,
> to make known to the children of man your mighty deeds,
> and the glorious splendor of your kingdom. (Ps. 145:11–12)

The LORD is righteous in all his ways
   and kind in all his works. (Ps. 145:17)

The contingent acts in their particularity lead the psalmists to notice the glory and praiseworthiness of characteristics that reach beyond the particularities. So we should praise God for his character, for what is necessary about him, as well as for the particular events in this world that display his character. We should praise God for his self-consistency, which we see reflected in logic.

The apostle Paul touches on a similar point when he says concerning his ministry that, "We destroy arguments and every lofty opinion raised against the knowledge of God, and take *every thought* captive to obey Christ" (2 Cor. 10:5).[1] We cannot leave any thought outside the circle of our obedience to Christ and our praise to God offered through Christ. And if that is so, we are religiously constrained to praise God for logic. We are invited to discern his wisdom and his beauty, as they are reflected in the power of logical reasoning.

The Sovereignty of God

Fourth, God is absolutely sovereign. He rules everything:

  . . . he does according to his will among the host of heaven
    and among the inhabitants of the earth;
  and none can stay his hand
    or say to him, "What have you done?" (Dan. 4:35)

Absolute sovereignty implies that God specifies several kinds of realities in the world.

(1) First, he specifies what happens contingently—"by chance" we sometimes say. ". . . a certain man drew his bow *at random* and struck the king of Israel between the scale armor and the breastplate" (1 Kings 22:34). The flight of the arrow happened "by chance" in the sense that the bowman did not intend a particular target. But God had prophesied it earlier (v. 20). It took place in accord with God's control over the world as a whole, his control over human action,[2] and his control over the flight of arrows.

---

[1] Second Corinthians 10:5 has become an important "theme verse" in presuppositional apologetics. See Richard L. Pratt, *Every Thought Captive: A Study Manual for the Defense of Christian Truth* (Phillipsburg, NJ: Presbyterian & Reformed, 1979).

[2] For the compatibility of God's sovereignty with human free agency, see the discussions in Reformed theology, e.g., John M. Frame, *The Doctrine of God* (Phillipsburg, NJ: Presbyterian & Reformed, 2002), 119–159.

"The lot is cast into the lap, but its every decision is from the LORD" (Prov. 16:33). The casting of a lot, or the rolling of dice, is a classic instance of a so-called "chance" event. Human beings cannot predict the outcome. The Lord not only is able to predict, but controls the outcome—it is "from the LORD."

(2) Second, God specifies the regularities in this world. God spoke the universe into existence, according to Genesis 1. His speech governs the growth of plants (Gen. 1:11–12) and the existence and movements of the heavenly bodies (Gen. 1:14–18). *Within* the world that God has established, the growth of plants and the movements of the sun represent regular events rather than completely unpredictable events.

(3) Third, God specifies the *necessities* of which we become aware. God is necessarily righteous. Why? Because that is his character. Nothing above him constrains him. His own character is the only source for this stability and this necessity.

Sometimes we may confuse genuine necessity with regularity. People might say that the sun must rise tomorrow. The word *must* indicates necessity. But strictly speaking, the rising of the sun is not among those things that are rooted in ultimate necessity. The sun will continue to rise each morning because God has committed himself to the regularity of its rising, as long as the world lasts:[3]

> While the earth remains, seedtime and harvest, cold and heat, summer and winter, *day and night*, shall not cease. (Gen. 8:22)

The promise of God about day and night contains an explicit qualification, "While the earth remains." There is no specification here as to what will happen when Christ returns. Once we make this qualification, and say "While the earth remains," we can also say that it is completely certain that the sun will rise. That is, we can be certain that "While the earth remains, the sun will rise." That certainty is not grounded in some mechanical necessity, as if the world were ultimately a machine, with invisible wheels working in the background. The certainty is grounded in God's word. And in addition it is grounded in God's faithfulness. His character commits him to being true to his word and carrying out his promises and commitments. Hence, we go back to the necessity of God's character.

---

[3] On the nature of scientific laws, see Vern S. Poythress, *Redeeming Science: A God-Centered Approach* (Wheaton, IL: Crossway, 2006), chapter 1.

Though God's character is necessary, it was not necessary for him to produce a creation outside of himself. Given that he decided to create a world, it was still up to him to determine just what kind of a world he would create. We can imagine a world that had no sun, if God had decided to create it that way. So the "necessity" for the sun, if we want to call it "necessity," is limited and qualified.

By contrast, the righteousness of God and the infinity of God are necessities of another kind. If God had created a very different world, he would still be the same righteous and infinite God. He would be so even if he had created no world at all, but simply remained himself. The necessities of God's character condition any world that might be.

We may conclude that God sovereignly ordains logic and the laws of logic. Even if logic is a necessity, we should praise God for it and see its source in God.

For Further Reflection

1. Why is it legitimate to see analogies between God and things that he has made?
2. How does the Creator-creature distinction influence our understanding of analogies between God and created things?
3. How is logic related to worship? to God's sovereignty?
4. Which of the following are "necessary," and in what respect?
   a. God is loving.
   b. God created the world.
   c. God is omniscient.
   d. God created a world with lions.
   e. God knows all about lions.
   f. The apostles appointed Matthias after casting lots (Acts 1:26).
5. What danger is there in the idea of placing logical necessity "above" God?

Chapter 13

Logic and Necessity

What about the necessity of logic? Is it in fact necessary? Or is it merely a contingent product of mindless evolution? Our discussions in previous chapters have led to the conclusion that logic is an expression of God's mind and his self-consistency. Since God is always faithful, the principles of logic are necessary. Since human beings are made in the image of God, they can reason in imitation of God's rationality. So they have an inward sense of logic. In fact, we have an inward sense of the *necessity* of logic as well as its reality.

Logic in the Human Race

We can confirm the universality of logic within the human race by looking at the Bible's teaching on redemption. We have observed that human beings were created in the image of God. They were created with rationality imitating God's rationality. But more must be said.

Human beings have strayed from their original relation to God through their sins. Sin has an effect on the mind as well as having other consequences. The Bible describes pagans as "darkened in their understanding, alienated from the life of God because of the ignorance that is in them, due to their hardness of heart" (Eph. 4:18). Has human sin corrupted logic? Sin has brought not only darkness to the mind, but indirect effects as well. Brain injuries, developmental defects, and insanity can undermine people's normal ability to reason.

But God's goal in history includes restoration from the damage due to the fall. Since the first century, the gospel has been going out to the nations and languages of the world. The arguments and reasoning found in the Bible can be translated into other languages, and have been translated into many languages, more languages than any other book. God's purpose in sending the gospel to the nations guarantees that people within those nations can experience the enlivening action of the Holy Spirit and respond to the gospel. So the logic within the arguments in the Bible, as well as the many other dimensions of its message, belongs to every nation.

Logic and Materialistic Evolution

We should look at this question of the universality of logic in more depth. Let us consider what people might propose as alternatives. One alternative is to say that the principles of logic are simply principles for the operation of the human mind, and that our minds are the contingent product of mindless evolution.

What about the question of evolution? Did the human mind evolve gradually from apes, who evolved gradually from other mammals, and so on back? We cannot here enter into every aspect of the debates on evolution.[1] The word *evolution* is slippery and has many meanings. In some contexts, it can mean merely change over time.[2] We can speak of the "evolution" of the automobile or the "evolution" of communist ideology or the "evolution" of the solar system.

We must be more focused. Near the center of modern debates lies *evolutionary naturalism*, a worldview that eliminates God. Evolutionary naturalism does not merely say that we can breed dogs and see the development of a new breed. It does not merely say that God may have used processes like breeding. By "evolutionary naturalism" we mean a worldview that systematically eliminates the involvement of God. It is mainly within this worldview that people might propose that logic is merely the functioning of the human mind, and that the human mind is a product of undirected, purposeless evolution. They may then conclude that logic is an evolutionary product.

Do they think that logic is *merely* an evolutionary product and a pragmatic tool for survival? Or has the human mind—even if by accident—succeeded in touching something transcendent?

Evolutionary naturalism is in something of a dilemma at this point. One way or another we as human beings have become aware of logic. If this logic is transcendent, it threatens naturalism, because it suggests by its transcendence that it comes from God who is the source of transcendence. Logic reveals the attributes of God, and God comes flooding in.

So suppose naturalism says that logic is merely a pragmatic tool for survival. Let us think about what might help survival. Members of a primi-

---

[1] For an introduction, see Vern S. Poythress, *Redeeming Science: A God-Centered Approach* (Wheaton, IL: Crossway, 2006), chapters 18 and 19; C. John Collins, *Science and Faith: Friends or Foes?* (Wheaton, IL: Crossway, 2003).
[2] *Webster's Ninth New Collegiate Dictionary* (1987) offers as the first meaning "a process of change in a certain direction."

tive tribe might perhaps survive more effectively if they cooperate with one another. And they may be more willing to cooperate if they believe that their tribal god requires them to cooperate. Belief in their god promotes survival, but it may have nothing to do with real truth. Similarly, if people believe that logic is merely a pragmatic tool, they imply that logic promotes survival but has no transcendence, no necessary contact with truth. Then evolutionary naturalism, which uses logic for its erection, is merely a convenient means of survival, and has no guarantee of truth. The whole worldview collapses. In fact, any worldview that maintains that logic is merely accidental or unstable loses all rational support.

Postmodern Multiculturalism and Logic

We may also consider briefly a multicultural approach to logic. People may claim that each culture has its own logic. In making this claim, people may be stretching the word *logic* to cover the genius of the culture and all its particular patterns for working through difficulties. If that is what people mean, then, yes, we might admit that the cultural differences include differences in how communities confront difficulties, conflicts, and apparent paradoxes. But we achieve this conclusion only by radically stretching the more usual, technical meaning of the word *logic*.

If we focus on more formal study of logic, the situation shows complexities. Reflections on logic developed independently in at least three ancient cultures, namely Greece (especially Aristotle), India,[3] and China (especially Mo Zi).[4] These reflections on logic show a coloring from the cultures and philosophies and religious contexts in which they arose; but they also have considerable overlap. The differences do not result in an insuperable barrier to one understanding the other or enriching the other. In short, the various studies in logic do show cultural influence, but not in the radical, dramatic manner that pure cultural relativism might postulate.

If we go beyond acknowledging cultural influence, and instead postulate that logic is purely relative to culture, we get ourselves into difficulties.

---

[3] Brendan S. Gillon, "Logic and Inference in Indian Philosophy," in *Encyclopedia of Philosophy*, 2nd ed., ed. Donald M. Borchert, 10 vols. (Detroit/New York/San Francisco/ . . . : Thomson Gale, 2006), 5:410–414; Satis C. Vidyabhusana, *A History of Indian Logic: Ancient, Mediaeval, and Modern Schools* (Delhi: Motilal Banarsidass, 1971).

[4] A. C. Graham, "Chinese Logic," in *Encyclopedia of Philosophy*, 2nd ed., ed. Donald M. Borchert, 10 vols. (Detroit/New York/San Francisco/ . . . : Thomson Gale, 2006), 5:414–417; Chad Hansen, *Language and Logic in Ancient China* (Ann Arbor: University of Michigan Press, 1983). There are also developments in the Islamic world, but these are influenced by Aristotelianism (Nicholas Rescher, "Logic in the Islamic World," in *Encyclopedia of Philosophy*, 5:417–420).

Consider, for example, our reasoning about Socrates's mortality. Do we really want to claim that other cultures reason about Socrates in a radically different way? Do we want to claim that other cultures cannot follow syllogistic reasoning about Socrates? Such a claim sounds more like a cultural insult than a demonstration of enlightened tolerance. If nevertheless someone wants to make such a claim, he runs into serious difficulties.

The first difficulty is like the difficulty with the naturalistic account for the nature of logic. It self-destructs. Why do people come to embrace multiculturalism? Is it because they just "feel" like it? Perhaps so, but then other people who "feel" differently have just as much right to their feelings. If multiculturalism is just due to feeling, it has no claim to being stronger than ethnocentrism, which can also coexist with strong feelings. On the other hand, many have presented arguments for multiculturalism. In these cases, logic underlies the process by which people come to their convictions. If logic is not universal, multiculturalism falls to the ground, and with it the claim that other cultures follow different logics or none at all.

Second, as we have observed in our syllogism about the speeding bus, human survival depends on everyday use of logic. If a whole culture ceases to use logic or undertakes to adopt a radically different logic, that culture is not long for this world. The cultures that now exist testify by their existence to their sanity and therefore to their continued use of logic, at least in many of the spheres that touch on bodily survival.

To be sure, there are within some cultures pockets of superstition and magical practices and failure to pay attention to hygienic practices recommended in modern medicine. These failures are partly a matter of ignorance rather than logic. But when they do involve failures of logic (which some kinds of religion may endorse when they move toward fuzzy antirational mysticism), they are failures that confirm the main point, namely, that logic is important for survival.

Third, modern computer technology provides a fascinating confirmation of the universality of logic. The heart of a computer is the "CPU," the central processing unit. Within current technology, this unit typically consists in microscopically small electronic circuits etched on silicon wafers. The circuits are so constructed that they embody binary logic, so-called Boolean logic. In the nineteenth century George Boole originally developed this logic on the basis of reflection on earlier work on logic going all the way back to Aristotle.[5] It is the logic of truth and falsehood, and represents within itself the way in which reasoning can proceed from one truth to another.

Electronic circuits can embody this logic, because electronic switches and memory elements are either on or off, representing the possibilities of "true" or "false" within logical reasoning. Computer programmers use this logic when they write computer programs, which string together a large number of these small logical operations to perform all the operations that users later ask the computer to perform. Programs called compilers then translate the programs into "machine language," a sequence of binary signals that the central processing unit uses as directions. The translation and the central processing unit both use binary logic.

What relevance does the computer have to multicultural relativism? Computers work wherever you take them, all over the world. The logic embodied in computer circuits works within any cultural environment you may choose. Logic is universal.

For computers, the alternative to logic is to retreat not into some admirable form of multicultural "tolerance" but into gross superstition. The animist may postulate that the computers function because tiny little silicon "spirits" detect the will of the computer user. These spirits band together with thousands of other spirits, and together produce an outcome more rapidly than could any human user.

A truly relativistic multiculturalist has to say that the animist is just as right as the Western programmer. If he really believes such nonsense, let him set the animist to work to induce his "spirits" to perform a new computer task, and set the Western programmer to work on the same task, and let us see who will succeed.

In practice, multiculturalists are usually not consistent relativists. The ones who achieve prominence in the West do not believe in practice either in the relativity of computer programming or in the relativity of logic. They confine their relativity to some special spheres—perhaps religion, perhaps ethics. A few of them may talk boldly about science being a social construct. And indeed science is socially *influenced*. It cannot take place unless scientists act as human beings with social relationships to fellow scientists. But is science *merely* a social construct? Whenever the radical multiculturalists

---

[5] We will touch on Boolean logic in chapter 35. Boole may also have been acquainted with work in logic from India or China.

take out a laptop or a cell phone (whose innards contain a CPU and its logic), they show that they do not really believe their own pronouncements.

Human Understanding of Logic as Limited

Might there still be a grain of truth in multicultural ideas? Science, we observed, is socially *influenced*. Likewise, human reasoning is socially and culturally influenced. Let us think again about the way in which we know God.

We know God, but we do not know him exhaustively. We know him according to our finite human capacity. So we can speculate that angels or personal creatures radically different from us might know God in a way that would radically exceed our capacity. We can speculate that God could have created a whole universe quite different from our own. The particular syllogism about Socrates might not make sense to a personal being in another universe in which there was no Socrates, no human beings, and no mortality.

The particular examples of reasoning that we use clearly have to do with this world, or with hypothetical situations quite like this world. We can imagine a world with green horses, but such a world would still have "horses," somewhat like the horses of this world. Or would it have unicorns, still somewhat like horses but with horns? Or would it have bug-eyed science-fiction monsters, but still like bugs in this world? We show our anchorage in this world by the kind of examples that we use.

So our conception of logic is in a sense tied in with our experience of this world. God's knowledge, by contrast, is infinite, and is not limited by experience within creation. That is an all-important distinction.

Is Logic Merely a *Creation* of God?

So let us consider another alternative. We believe that God created man. Can we say that logic is limited to *this creation* or to the mind of man? Perhaps it does not manifest the mind of *God*, but only the mind of *man*.

The difficulty here is that, if logic belongs only to man and not to God, God is unknowable. And indeed a number of religious practitioners and philosophers have maintained that God is unknowable. But the Bible does not. It says bluntly that even unbelievers and rebels know God: "For although they *knew* God, . . ." (Rom. 1:21). They know God's "invisible attributes" (Rom. 1:20). When God gives us the Bible, we know even more, because he speaks to us in human language. In fact, the Bible is designed by

God to provide not merely a minimal knowledge such as a nonbeliever has, but *saving* knowledge (see, e.g., John 17:3). God's communication in human language includes the logical aspect involved in language and in what he says. Because God is faithful, we can trust what he says, and so we trust also the logical aspect.

It is important to see that God makes himself known in the Bible, and that the Bible provides true knowledge of God. When we read the Bible, and when the Spirit works in us to open our hearts to what it says, we know God. We do not merely know the best substitute that could be cooked up within the confines of logic and language. Any such substitute for God, even the best substitute, if it is not the real thing, would constitute idolatry. Idolatry destroys the purpose that God himself has in giving us the Bible.

It can sound humble when people say that God lies "beyond" all language and logic. But it is a false humility. In fact, they are claiming to know more than (and other than) what God himself has undertaken to tell us in the Bible. That is arrogance. If they think that God is unknowable, they are producing for themselves a substitute for God.

For Further Reflection

1. How does the spread of the gospel testify to the universality of logic in the human race?
2. What is the difficulty with claiming that logic is merely a pragmatic tool cast up by purposeless evolution?
3. What is the difficulty with postulating radically different "logics" among different cultures, and claiming that logic is purely relative to culture?
4. Can culture or religious background influence evaluation of reasoning? How?
5. What is the difficulty with saying that God is unknowable?
6. If God is knowable, can our minds comprehend everything about him? What is the difference between mystery and unknowability?

Chapter 14

Transcendence and Immanence

As we have seen, the relation of logic to God presents us initially with a dilemma. If logic is merely a creation of God and is subject to him, it would seem to follow that God is beyond logic and we cannot know him. If, on the other hand, logic characterizes God and not merely man, it might seem that we can use our understanding of logic to subject God to our own standards. In that case, has God ceased to be God? Has he ceased to be absolute? And would we also be able to say that angels or creatures unknown to earth must necessarily think in exactly the same way that we do? For practical purposes, we end up making ourselves the real lords over reality.

This dilemma is not unique to logic. A similar dilemma arises with respect to language. If language belongs merely to the created world, do we conclude that God is beyond language and we cannot know him through language? On the other hand, if language *does* characterize God, does it subject God to its own standards?

In the case of language, the answer provided by the Bible is that language exists first of all with God, and then is provided as a gift to mankind, to be used in divine-human as well as human-human communication.[1] Language use takes place on two distinct levels, the divine level and the human level. The Bible indicates that the distinction between Creator and creature is fundamental. At the same time, precisely because God is the all-powerful Creator, he can reveal himself truly to human beings through the medium of language that he has himself ordained for that purpose.[2]

Exactly the same reasoning holds in the case of logic, which is an aspect of language on both the divine and the human level.

---

[1] Vern S. Poythress, *In the Beginning Was the Word: Language—A God-Centered Approach* (Wheaton, IL: Crossway, 2009).
[2] J. I. Packer, "The Adequacy of Human Language," in *Inerrancy*, ed. Norman L. Geisler (Grand Rapids, MI: Zondervan, 1980), 195–226.

John Frame's Square on Transcendence and Immanence

We can re-express these truths in terms of the ideas of the transcendence and immanence of God. John Frame has conveniently summarized biblical teaching about God's lordship in a diagram, which is reproduced in figure 14.1:[3]

Fig. 14.1: Frame's Square on Transcendence and Immanence

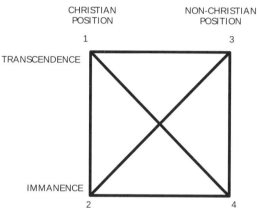

Frame explains that there are two distinct understandings of God's transcendence and immanence, namely, the Christian understanding, articulated in the Bible, and the non-Christian understanding. The left-hand side of Frame's square has two corners, labeled 1 and 2, representing the Christian understanding of transcendence (corner #1) and immanence (corner #2). The Christian view of transcendence says that God is the final and absolute authority and that he has complete control in his rule. In all his interactions with human beings, God is fully in control and he has the moral right to control. He is the standard for human understanding and evaluating.

The Christian view of immanence says that God is present to human beings, and that through Christ he makes it possible for them to draw near to him in fellowship.

This Christian view does not come out of nowhere. It comes up over and over again in the Bible, and John Frame's book provides abundant texts that support it.[4]

---

[3] The original diagram is in John M. Frame, *The Doctrine of the Knowledge of God* (Phillipsburg, NJ: Presbyterian & Reformed, 1987), 14.

[4] Transcendence and immanence are aspects of the biblical doctrine of God's *lordship*, which is a fundamental thread in the Bible. See especially Frame, *Doctrine of the Knowledge of God*, 9–61.

The non-Christian view is represented by the right-hand side of the square, which has two corners, labeled 3 and 4. These represent the non-Christian view of transcendence (#3) and immanence (#4). The non-Christian view of transcendence says that God is remote and uninvolved, perhaps also unknowable. The non-Christian view of immanence says that God is virtually identical with the world or indistinguishable from the world.

The non-Christian view gains plausibility by describing transcendence and immanence with expressions similar or even identical to what a Christian view might use. The terms "transcendence" and "immanence" are used on both sides. The non-Christian side may also say that God is "exalted" (transcendence) and that he is "near" and "present" (immanence). Frame's square represents these similarities in expression by the two horizontal sides of the square. The similarity is also called "formal" similarity, because the "form" of the expressions seems to be the same. But the two sides *mean* different things.

Careful listening to the non-Christian view reveals that the non-Christian view of transcendence in corner #3 contradicts the Christian view of immanence in corner #2. The non-Christian claim that God is uninvolved contradicts the Bible's claim that God is intimately involved and present in the world. Similarly, the non-Christian view of immanence in corner #4 contradicts the Christian view of transcendence in corner #1. If God is indistinguishable from the world (#4), he no longer serves as standard or authority—contradicting the Christian view of transcendence in corner #1. God no longer controls a world from which he is distinct. Rather, we ourselves are free to be our own immanent authority, because God is no longer distinguishable from us. The contradictions between the Christian view of the left and the non-Christian view on the right are represented within the square by the diagonal lines. The diagonal from corner #1 to corner #4 indicates that the non-Christian view of immanence in corner #4 contradicts the Christian view of transcendence in corner #1.

Transcendence and Immanence in Epistemology and Ethics

Frame's square applies not only to the topic of the basic status of God but also in the areas of epistemology (what we know) and ethics. Christian transcendence says that God knows all things and is the final standard for knowledge. Christian immanence says that God draws near to human beings and makes himself clearly known to them. Non-Christian transcendence says that God is unknowable and inaccessible. Non-Christian immanence says that what we feel that we know about God conforms to our own minds, so that our own minds can for practical purposes serve as the foundation for what we say about God.

Similar observations can be made about ethics. Christian transcendence in ethics says that God in his goodness and holiness is the standard for ethical goodness, and that he has the capability and authority to specify what is good. Christian immanence says that God makes his standards clearly known, both in the human conscience and in written form, in the Ten Commandments and other biblical commandments.

Transcendence and Immanence Applied to Logic

Frame's square can now be applied to our questions about logic. Christian transcendence says that God is ultimate, and there is no other. He is the source of all norms, including norms in logic. God's self-consistency is the source and foundation for all logical consistency that we as human beings experience. Logic is not an impersonal, abstract principle or set of principles *above* God. Rather, logic is personal. Ultimately, it *is* a person, namely, the second person of the Trinity, the Logos. God comprehends himself perfectly, and he is the standard for logic.

But we as creatures do not know God exhaustively; we do not know him with the depth with which he knows himself (1 Cor. 2:10). God's logic, which is preeminently the second person of the Trinity, is *incomprehensible*, in the technical sense of the word. "Incomprehensibility," in theological discourse, means that we do not know God exhaustively. We experience mystery in our knowledge. But we do know God truly, and that falls under the Christian view of immanence.

Christian immanence, applied to logic, says that God makes himself known both in the human mind and in the external world that he created. He is *present* ("immanent") in the world in general and in human minds in particular. He is present in his full character, and that implies that he is present in his logical self-consistency. We see logical consistency both in the world at large and in our own thinking processes. This logical consistency genuinely reveals God in his self-consistency. It is not merely a shadow of something totally inaccessible or totally unknowable. We do know God. We know his self-consistency in the Logos. But we do not *comprehend* his self-consistency.

We can rely on the world being in conformity with logic, and on our own minds being in conformity with logic. The trains of reasoning within our minds can include fallacious reasoning. But even in this case God is present as the standard by which fallacious reasoning can be judged fallacious. A stubborn person may sometimes refuse to budge out of a piece of fallacious reasoning. But we can also find cases in which a person comes to his senses and sees through a fallacy to which he formerly held. In such a case, he shows that he in some way has access to a standard that is not merely a description of how he always reasons, but a norm specifying how he ought to reason—for example, by avoiding fallacies.

Non-Christian Transcendence and Immanence in Logic

Non-Christian views can corrupt the understanding of transcendence and immanence in a variety of ways. But at a deeper level these views boil down to pretty much the same thing. They are all variations on attempts to retain "formal" similarity to the truth of the Christian view, and through formal similarity to retain plausibility. At the same time, they corrupt or distort the Christian view, in order to escape the clear revelation of God and our human responsibility to give him thanks and to obey his moral will. They are not merely innocent intellectual games or cases of innocent ignorance. Frame observes, "Those false concepts of transcendence and immanence fit together in a peculiar way: both satisfy sinful man's desire to escape God's revelation, to avoid our responsibilities, to excuse our disobedience."[5]

A typical non-Christian view of transcendence in logic (corner #3) might say that God is beyond logic. That is similar to the claim that God is unknowable, and contradicts the accessibility of God in logic, according to the Christian view of immanence (corner #2). Non-Christian immanence in logic (corner #4) might say that we cannot jump out of our skin. We must use our own immanent standards for what is logical and consistent. This view contradicts the Christian view that says that God is the standard for logic. People espousing a non-Christian view may then say, for example, that the doctrine of the Trinity is "illogical" or that divine sovereignty and human responsibility are logically incompatible. Any supposed revelation, they might say, must conform to reason—meaning human reason, not divine reason. Hence, special revelation can really be dispensed with, and

---

[5] Ibid., 14.

virtually replaced by reason (which is more or less what the deists did). A summary of Christian and non-Christian views of logic can be found in figure 14.2:

Fig. 14.2: Frame's Square: Summary of Christian and Non-Christian Views of Logic

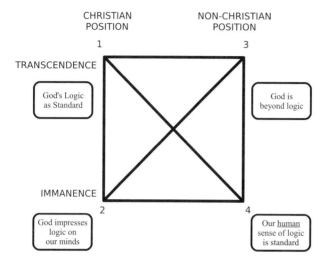

CHRISTIAN POSITION

NON-CHRISTIAN POSITION

1

3

TRANSCENDENCE

God's Logic as Standard

God is beyond logic

IMMANENCE

2

4

God impresses logic on our minds

Our human sense of logic is standard

Frame observes that despite the appeal of non-Christian views to our sinful desires, non-Christian views generate unresolvable tensions:

> How can God be infinitely far removed from us [non-Christian transcendence] and wholly identical to us [non-Christian immanence] at the same time? . . . If God is "wholly other," then how can we know or say that He is "wholly other"?[6]

The same fundamental tensions arise with respect to logic. If God is beyond logic, how can we use language—which includes a logical aspect—to say that he is beyond logic? If non-Christian immanence (#4) says that we are right to use our own human logic as if it were ultimate, does that not imply that we can simply dispense with God? But if we dispense with God, what makes logic binding or normative? We can describe empirically specific cases of human reasoning that follow logical norms and others that do not. What makes one superior to the other? We are in danger of losing all norms, because the fallibility of human reasoning destroys its value as a norm.

---

[6] Ibid.

Knowability of Logic

We can make similar points if we think about the *knowledge* of logic rather than logic itself. The Christian view of transcendence says that God knows himself perfectly and exhaustively. In knowing himself, he knows the Logos, and he knows all logic in perfection. He is the standard for logic, so that all human beings everywhere have a uniform standard for the workings of their reasoning.

Second, the Christian view of immanence says that God makes himself known. In making himself known, he makes known his self-consistency, which is the foundation of logic. In addition, since human beings are made in the image of God, they can reflect God's thinking at a creaturely level. When they reason logically, they reflect God's self-consistency.

Logical reasoning is natural to unfallen mankind. When human beings rebel against God, they corrupt their reasoning, but they cannot escape the logicality of God either in the world or in their minds.

So we now have an explanation for two sides to logic. First, logic in basic instances is accessible to human beings. Someone who has never had a course in logic can recognize the validity of a syllogism like the one about Socrates:

> All men are mortal.
> Socrates is a man.
> Therefore Socrates is mortal.

The validity of this syllogism is present to our mind because God is present to our mind in his logicality.

Second, logic is deep. We can always ask *why* syllogistic reasoning works. Why is there a distinction between the way our minds *actually* work (sometimes succumbing to fallacies) and the way they *ought to* work to produce valid reasoning? The standards for reasoning are transcendent. And that transcendence leads ultimately to the divine Logos, who is incomprehensible.

The Creator-creature Distinction

We can re-express the issue in a different way. God instructs us in the Bible that there is a distinction between the Creator and his creatures. Logic as God knows it can be distinguished from logic as we know it. God's mind is infinite; we are finite. God's logic is the Logos, the second person of the Trinity, who exists in communion with the self-consistency of the Father and the Holy Spirit. He is infinitely rich. God's knowledge is also his self-consistency, which expresses the love between the Father and the Son through the Spirit. All these matters are rich beyond measure. God comprehends them perfectly by knowing himself. We do not comprehend them; they are mysterious to us.

The Bible clearly teaches a radical distinction between Creator and creature. God is the Lord; we are his subjects. But this radical distinction must be interpreted in accord with Christian rather than non-Christian conceptions of transcendence and immanence. We interpret the distinction in accord with what the Bible teaches.

It would be easy to smuggle in a non-Christian view of transcendence and to conclude that, because we can distinguish logic in God from logic in our own minds and in our own understanding, the two are *unrelated*. Once again we are in danger of falling into the non-Christian view that God is unknowable. The Bible answers this danger by telling us that we are made in the image of God, so that we can think God's thoughts after him. And the Bible repeatedly shows that God can speak to human beings. God's speech conveys his thoughts and his self-consistency, that is, his logic. God makes himself known.

Even before the fall of Adam into sin, God made himself known through speech, through the divine Logos. After the fall, God overcomes the barrier of sin through the Logos who becomes incarnate in Christ and who offers sacrifice to take away our sin and cleanse us from it. In communion with the Father and the Spirit, the Logos is both the source of the human mind as created, and the source of redemption through which our minds and hearts are restored into the image of God (Col. 3:10). Praise be to God—Father, Son, and Holy Spirit!

Attitudes

The characteristics of logic encourage us to have a redeemed attitude when we engage in logic. Christ came to the earth and overcame the alienation between God and man. He overcame it *objectively* by his sacrificial death and his resurrection life. He overcomes it subjectively by sending his Holy Spirit to renew our minds (Rom. 12:1–2). Our rebellious hearts are changed by his work. So we are supposed to have new attitudes. We should humble ourselves before God in every area of life.

With respect to logic, we should acknowledge that God, not man, is the standard for logic and logical reasoning. At the same time, we should have confidence that he is faithful, and that we can know him. Our own minds have been restored so that they can begin to function in conformity with the mind of Christ, which is the mind of the Logos (see 1 Cor. 2:16). We have not been perfected, but we have been made *sane* in our basic mental orientation. We are not supposed to give up thinking (as some mystics have advocated) but should think more and more deeply and robustly as we are instructed by God's speech. "You shall love the Lord your God with all your heart and with all your soul and with all your *mind*" (Matt. 22:37). Loving God includes learning how to love him with our *mind*. It includes loving the Logos, the eternal Word of God. It therefore includes growing in our ability to reason soundly, and growing in appreciation and praise for the gift of a sound mind. We praise God for his logic.

For Further Reflection

1. What is the difference between a Christian and a non-Christian view of God's transcendence and immanence?
2. What is the difference between a Christian and a non-Christian view of logic?
3. What is the difference between a Christian and a non-Christian view of the pursuit of clarity in reasoning?
4. What is the difference between a Christian and a non-Christian view of the role of the human mind in relation to logic?
5. What is the difference in *attitude* between a Christian and a non-Christian approach to logic?

Chapter 15

Reflections on the Mediation of Human Knowledge of Logic

We may deepen our view of logic by reflecting on what it means to know logic when logic originates in God. A key reality in the nature of human knowledge is that knowledge brings us into relation to God through *mediation*. The teaching of the Bible about mediation deserves our attention.

We have said that logic reveals God. It reveals the true God. If so, it reveals God in his personal character, in his infinity, and in his holiness. We ought to give him thanks, but we have failed to do so and are therefore guilty. There is a difficulty, because we are sinful.

The Difficulty with Sin

How can we survive an encounter with God and his holiness? The same difficulty that we have with logic confronts us with all of general revelation, as described in Romans 1:18–25. How can human beings escape death?

Romans 1:18 underlines the difficulty by mentioning the "wrath of God," which "is revealed from heaven against all ungodliness and unrighteousness of men, who by their unrighteousness suppress the truth." People who are still alive in this world have not yet died physically because of God's wrath. But they experience God's wrath. They do not know God as they should.

Christ as Mediator

The Bible indicates that we can be reconciled to God through the death of his Son (Rom. 5:10). He is the "one mediator between God and men" (1 Tim. 2:5). His work has resulted in the forgiveness of sins (Col. 1:14). Through being united to Christ in a personal relationship, empowered by the Holy Spirit, we become progressively transformed into his image (2 Cor. 3:18). We are renewed in our knowledge (Col. 3:10). Since knowing logic truly involves knowing God, Christ must be our mediator in knowing logic.

We do not mean to imply that non-Christians know nothing about logic. They still receive benefits from God. Blessings that come to unbelievers are sometimes called "common grace."[1] "For he [God] makes his sun rise on the evil and on the good, and sends rain on the just and on the unjust" (Matt. 5:45). "Yet he [God] did not leave himself without witness, for he did good by giving you rains from heaven and fruitful seasons, satisfying your hearts with food and gladness" (Acts 14:17). Even these benefits are not deserved, and so we may infer that they are a benefit of Christ's work. Such benefits fall short of providing eternal salvation, however, unless the people who receive the benefits also turn to God in repentance and faith in Christ.

Christ's Knowledge and Ours

How does Christ's mediation take place? We know from the Bible that Christ is fully God (John 1:1) and fully man (John 1:14; Heb. 2:14–17). As God, he knows all things in infinitude. He is the Logos of God and his knowledge encompasses all of the rationality and self-consistency of God. His knowledge continues to be what it has been from all eternity. As man, he knows finitely, in accord with human capacity. Finally, he knows as one person who unites the two natures, the divine nature and the human nature. We cannot say how this is so; it is a deep mystery.

Our knowledge of logic is mediated through Christ, who is God and man in one person. He has reconciled us to God through his death, in which he bore the penalty for our sins, and through which we receive forgiveness and a clean standing before God (1 Pet. 2:24; Rom. 3:23–26; 5:1). Through his flesh (Heb. 10:20) we have communion with the full person of Christ and with the fullness of God. This communion includes forgiveness of sin and being clothed with Christ's righteousness, so that we are fit to be in God's presence. We ought not to think that we merely have communion with Christ's human nature as if it were in isolation from his person and his divine nature. We access *divine* power in order to be saved. Divine power goes together with divine meaning. We access divine meaning through Christ, but in the process we receive it according to our capacity as human beings renewed by the Spirit of Christ dwelling in us.

---

[1] Cornelius Van Til, *Common Grace and the Gospel* (n.l.: Presbyterian & Reformed, 1973).

Knowledge of Logic

Our knowledge of logic must conform to these realities. Our knowledge is finite but is surrounded by infinities: the infinite knowledge of God the Father, the infinite mediation of God the Son, and the infinite presence of God the Holy Spirit. Finite knowledge of logic is possible only through access to infinite presence. So finite knowledge cannot be disentangled from mystery—the mystery of God's infinite knowledge, the mystery of Christ's sacrifice, the mystery of the union of divine and human natures in one person, and the mystery of the indwelling of the Holy Spirit.

We may make more explicit application to logic. We know logic as a whole, and we know any part of logic, such as the validity of the syllogism about Socrates, only through communion with infinity. We know in analogy with the infinite self-consistency of God, who is the standard for logic. We know through knowing the Logos who is the logic of God. We know through the mystery of Christ's sacrifice, which has opened the way to communion. We know by communing with the Logos through the flesh and humanity of Christ, which is united to his deity in one person; we know through the presence of and instruction from the infinite rationality of the Holy Spirit, who comes to indwell us and gives us communion with the Son and the Father.

I believe, then, that there is mystery in *all* our knowledge, including our knowledge of logic and each of its parts. God displays himself and is present in all parts of logic and all its operations.

The same principle holds with respect to attempts to clarify knowledge. We can deepen our knowledge, and we can become clearer about what we know and how we know it. But the goal of *perfect* clarity usually amounts to a goal of dispensing with mystery, at least within a limited sphere. That goal innately belongs to non-Christian immanence, corner #4 in Frame's square of transcendence and immanence.

Dispensing with the Divine?

I do not believe that we can dispense with divine presence. Suppose we try to purify or clarify logic by saying that we will examine only the human level of logic, not the divine level. We will take logic as God has given it to us in finite form, rather than presumptuously pry into God's divine logic. The project may sound reasonable. But what do we mean by "the human level of logic"? Can we isolate it from God's presence and his self-consistency, which he reveals to us in the very character of our minds? The idea of a "human level of logic" is not clear.

To "pry into God's divine logic" is indeed inappropriate, if it means that we try to master God. That is non-Christian immanence. But to leave God's logic alone is non-Christian transcendence, where we claim that God is unknowable—at least with respect to logic. And if we claim that God is inaccessible, it will leave us free *in practice* to use a supposed "finite form" of logic as if it were everything—because, we reason, we have nothing better to use. But we do have something better, namely, communion with the Logos through the flesh of Christ, and through the Scripture which is his word. Our minds are not closed vessels that have a certain stock of logical pieces that are just "there." That would be to fall back into impersonalist thinking. Rather, we exercise reason at every moment in *communion* with the infinitude of God in Christ. We cannot isolate a purely human level, nor can we eliminate mystery, because the sacrifice of Christ and the union of two natures in Christ are mysteries.

Covenantal Knowledge

The structure of biblical covenants confirms this reality rather than offering another route. There is only one mediator between God and men, Christ Jesus (1 Tim. 2:5). The covenants in the Old Testament are shadowy anticipations of this one mediation. Isaiah 42:6 and 49:8 identify the prophesied servant as "a covenant": "I will keep you and give you as a *covenant* to the people . . ." (Isa. 49:8). The Messiah *is* the covenant, in its heart. As a consequence, knowledge by the people of God within a covenant with God is always mediated knowledge in communion with the infinitude of God. In particular, knowledge of logic is Christ-mediated knowledge of the Logos of God. There is no other knowledge of logic to be had.

Before the fall into sin, there was no need for substitutionary mediation in the presence of God in order to remove sin. But we see even within the pre-fall situation an analog to later mediation. We see the operation of the Word of God, coming from the Logos, and the role of the Spirit of God, giving life (Job 33:4; Ps. 104:30).

As a result, I believe no finite knowledge can be isolated from the infinite knowledge that God has, and no finite knowledge is isolatable from communion with infinitude. I also believe that all finite knowledge has mystery for us, but is without mystery for God, who has infinite understanding.

Imitative Transcendence

As human beings in the image of God, we can think about the relation of God who is infinite to man who is finite. We can talk about both the finite and the infinite. We can do so not only because we are created imitators of God's transcendence, but because God has instructed us about himself in Scripture, and his instruction is true.

But we cannot become infinite. We cannot specify the exact distinctions and parallels between the infinite and the finite without being infinite ourselves. We can describe the distinctions and parallels in part, as the Lord gives us ability through his word and through communion with Christ. But we do so *in part*. The attempt to "solve" the problem of infinitude by specifying a precise boundary, below which we can have finite logic, is itself a non-Christian move in which we temporarily make ourselves to be a god.

The idea of a "boundary" must be used with care. God is Creator and we are not. So there is a distinction. There is a "boundary," if that is what we want to call it. But the "boundary" is not a barrier. Christ gives us knowledge of God. Scripture as the word of Christ gives us knowledge. All God's covenantal dealings with us give us communion with God, because in them God gives us wise and true guidance without our having to become infinite. Scripture affirms the reality of mediation by which we have *real* communion with the infinitude of God himself. The alternative is to say that we have communion only with a finite replica of God, and that would be idolatry.

Jesus says, "Whoever has seen me has seen the Father" (John 14:9). He does not say that we have seen merely a finite model of the Father. He says, "And this is eternal life, that they know you the only true God, and Jesus Christ whom you have sent" (John 17:3). He does not say that we know only a finite model of the true God. He says, "I have given them the words that you gave me, and they have received them" (John 17:8). He does not say that the disciples have heard only a finite model of the words that the Father spoke.

These positive statements about human knowledge of God are theologically important, because they affirm the Christian concept of God's immanence in the sphere of knowledge, and they repudiate a non-Christian concept of transcendence, according to which we have knowledge only of what is finite (i.e., it postulates that God is unknowable).

These truths need to be applied to the arena of logic. We know the Logos of God, not merely a finite model. Yet we know him as creatures, dependent on mediation from God himself. Scripture is given to us as the word of God and the word of Christ who is the mediator of the knowledge of God. We do well to listen to Scripture, and not to listen to autonomously conceived philosophy, when we desire knowledge of logic.

Mediation through Christ is mysterious to us, because Christ is fully God and fully man. Such access to knowledge of logic does not "solve" anything in a manner that would be satisfying to a non-Christian.

For Further Reflection

1. What difficulty confronts us if we say that we have communion merely with a finite version of the logic of God?
2. What difficulty confronts us if we say that our logic is identical with God's?
3. Why is reflection on mediation important in evaluating human knowledge and philosophical claims in particular?
4. How does mediation of knowledge take place?
5. What mysteries belong to human knowledge? To knowledge of logic?

Chapter 16

Fallacies and God

Human reasoning includes not only good reasoning but bad. For instance, we may hear Bill say, "My doctor misdiagnosed my illness, and I ended up wasting a lot of money on him. All doctors are quacks." His conclusion, that all doctors are quacks, is not sound. This fault in reasoning is common enough that it has been given a name, *the fallacy of hasty generalization.*

Most fallacies crop up in the context of informal reasoning. So let us temporarily step back from our focus on formal deductive logic, in order to consider the topic of fallacies more broadly. We include fallacies in both informal and formal reasoning.

Does bad reasoning reveal God? Clearly God does not *endorse* bad reasoning. Bad reasoning by definition is reasoning out of accord with the rationality and self-consistency of God. But bad reasoning testifies to God indirectly, precisely by being bad. We judge reasoning to be flawed or bad because it is out of accord with what is sound. We show thereby that we have a normative knowledge of good reasoning. The difference between good and bad is based on a standard. And the standard goes back to God. Ultimately, God's self-consistency is the standard.

Bad reasoning sometimes does occur in a world in which God sovereignly controls the events, including human reasoning. Bad reasoning still lies within the range of God's plan, his decrees for the course of history. In a broad sense, then, even fallacious reasoning reveals God as the Lord of all history, including events that are human failures in history.

But is that all we can say? What makes fallacious reasoning so attractive at times? Fallacious reasoning is identifiable partly by its contrasts with sound reasoning. But typically, fallacious reasoning is not mere gibberish. It appears to make sense, at least superficially. It attracts people, and maybe it fools them, precisely because it still *sounds* logical.

Fallacies as Counterfeits

Many fallacies take people in because they are closely related to something true. They are *counterfeit* arguments. A counterfeit $20 bill can more often succeed if it looks and feels like the real thing. Similarly, a counterfeit argument may be attractive because it superficially looks like a sound argument.

Bill's argument about all doctors being quacks is pretty easy to see through, and may not convince anyone. But more subtle cases of hasty generalization may sway us. These cases are subtle counterfeits for something true. What is the underlying truth that they counterfeit?

Let us consider again Bill's argument that all doctors are quacks. Is it a counterfeit of a good argument? If so, what is the corresponding form of good argument? In many circumstances it is legitimate for us tentatively to draw a general conclusion when we have examined enough cases. One case of one doctor's failure is surely not enough. But if 100 doctors taken at random failed to diagnose 100 cases of fairly routine diseases, we would suspect that there is something the matter with the institutions that gave them medical training. The fallacy of hasty generalization is a counterfeit for the process of inductive generalization from a sufficient number of examples.

So counterfeits rely on truth. And truth comes from God. The principle is a general one. In the book of Revelation, Satan counterfeits the activity of God.[1] The apostle Paul says that Satan "disguises himself as an angel of light. So it is no surprise if his servants, also, disguise themselves as servants of righteousness" (2 Cor. 11:14–15). The book of Revelation and the apostle Paul are talking about major attacks on the Christian faith. But the principle can be applied to minor cases as well.

A fallacy works by "disguising itself": it sounds somewhat like a sound argument. The disguised mode still ends up testifying, in a kind of backhanded way, to truth, righteousness, and sound reasoning. It still partially relies on truth and reason in order to achieve its deceitful effect. So God is revealed, even though it is by way of a counterfeit that is out of conformity with his rationality.

Types of Fallacy

Let us see how this counterfeiting works out with some examples.

There are a number of types of fallacies. Over the centuries people have

---

[1] Vern S. Poythress, *The Returning King: A Guide to the Book of Revelation* (Phillipsburg, NJ: Presbyterian & Reformed, 2000), 16–22.

identified common fallacies and have given them names. Some fallacies go by more than one name, and sometimes people disagree over how best to classify them. For convenience I have followed the names and classifications offered in S. Morris Engel, *With Good Reason: An Introduction to Informal Fallacies.*[2]

The Fallacy of Bifurcation

In an earlier chapter we mentioned the fallacy of *bifurcation.* "Either you get an A in the course or you show that you are an idiot." No third alternative is offered. "Either you give in to his demands or you fight him." Is there no possibility of negotiation or mediation? The difficulty lies in the assumption that there are only two possible alternatives, when in fact a third or a fourth might be possible.

If this is a fallacy, what truth does it counterfeit? It counterfeits the truth that in some cases there are actually only two alternatives. Either Christ is Lord or he is not. Either Israelites serve the Lord God, as Joshua proposed in Joshua 24:14–15, or they refuse (overtly or covertly). And if they refuse, realistically they will end up serving some other god or gods.

Fallacies of Presumption

The fallacy of bifurcation belongs to a larger cluster of fallacies called *fallacies of presumption*, where the argument presupposes questionable assumptions. The fallacy of bifurcation presumes there is no third alternative. The fallacy of *hasty generalization* falsely presumes that one case (or a small number of cases) is enough to establish a general conclusion. It goes too *hastily* from one or a few cases to a generality. The claim that "All doctors are quacks" falsely presumes that all doctors will show the same faults as Bill found in one case with one doctor.

Next, the *fallacy of sweeping generalization* unsoundly presumes that there are no exceptional cases. If we say, "All human beings must die," we ignore Enoch and Elijah, who were caught up to God's presence without going through death (Gen. 5:24; 2 Kings 2:11). But the fallacy of sweeping generalization is a counterfeit of something true. A generalization, if it has truth at all, will at least apply to the great majority of cases, and exceptions should be justified on a case-by-case basis. And of course some generalizations will have no exceptions.

---

[2] S. Morris Engel, *With Good Reason: An Introduction to Informal Fallacies* (New York: St. Martin's, 1982).

Next, the fallacy of *false cause* postulates a causal connection on the basis of merely temporal or accidental connections. Alan says to Beatrix, "You jinxed me. Every time you are in the class when I am taking a test, I foul up the test." Alan has noticed a pattern in which the presence of Beatrix is followed by his failure to test well. He concludes that the temporal relationship between Beatrix's presence and his failure is also a *causal* relationship. Beatrix's presence (or her "jinx") causes Alan's failure. This kind of reasoning is also called the fallacy of *post hoc, ergo propter hoc* (Latin for "after this, therefore on account of this").

This fallacy is a counterfeit of something true. It is true that many temporal connections are also causal connections. One billiard ball hits another, and the second one suddenly starts moving. There is a temporal connection between the hit and the motion. In this case we are actually justified in seeing a causal connection. Even in the case of Alan, there may be some psychological causes involved. Suppose that Alan *thinks* that Beatrix is jinxing him. Alan's belief may so fluster him that his mind is distracted and he does foul up the test. Or Alan may become nervous because he is afraid of what Beatrix will think if he does not do well on the test. This nervousness causes Alan to do poorly. In these cases there is actually a genuine causal relationship between Beatrix's presence and Alan's failure. But the connection is not what Alan thinks it is; it is not a "jinx," but something that Alan largely brings on himself.

Next, the *fallacy of complex question* sets up a question that includes a false assumption. One well-known instance is the question, "Have you stopped beating your wife?" If you say "yes," it implies that you did beat her earlier. If you say "no," that is even worse! The fallacy of complex question is a counterfeit of a frequent situation where we do want to ask a specific question, and its clear formulation has to include assumptions. "When did you last go to the grocery store?" assumes that you have gone to the grocery store at some time or other. "What is your favorite book that you have read?" assumes that you can read and that you have read at least one book.

The *fallacy of special pleading* involves using a double standard, one for yourself or your favorite group, and another for others. "I am open-minded; he is wishy-washy." The fallacy of special pleading is a counterfeit for many situations where context may rightly make a big difference in how we evaluate someone's action. If someone does not take a stand on some issue, is he being open-minded or is he being wishy-washy? A fair evaluation takes into account the situation. Someone who refuses to stand up for what is right because he wants to avoid trouble is at fault, while someone who takes time to evaluate a difficult issue and does not prematurely take sides is open-minded. The fallacy arises only when favorable or unfavorable judgments are based on prejudice, rather than on a careful analysis of the situation.

The *fallacy of false analogy* is an argument from analogy where the analogy does not result in appropriate parallels. Someone says, "In argument as in war, you have to destroy completely the opponent's capacity to fight." But might it be easier in argument than in war to win over an opponent, or at least to appropriate some of his good points even if his overall position is wrong? So is the analogy between war and argument appropriate? The fallacy of false analogy is a counterfeit for the positive use of analogy in many situations in which it is appropriate. And the line between appropriate and inappropriate use of analogy is not always easy to discern.

Fallacies of Relevance

We also encounter fallacies of *relevance*. Arguments can bring in irrelevant information and distract us from the main point, making us feel that a conclusion has been supported when it has not been.

In *Pilgrim's Regress*, C. S. Lewis provides a humorous case:

> ". . . What is argument?"
>
> "Argument," said Master Parrot, "is the attempted rationalization of the arguer's desires." . . .
>
> ". . . What is the answer to an argument turning on the belief that two and two make four?"
>
> "The answer is, 'You say that because you are a mathematician.'"[3]

Instead of pointing out some flaw in the substance of the arguments, the character called "Master Parrot" attacks the motives or the character of his opponent. But even if his claims about his opponent are true, and even if the opponent is guilty of all kinds of wickedness, the opponent's *arguments* could still hold weight. Master Parrot has deflected people's attention from the real issues, rather than settling them.

---

[3] C. S. Lewis, *The Pilgrim's Regress: An Allegorical Apology for Christianity, Reason, and Romanticism,* 3rd ed. (Grand Rapids, MI: Eerdmans, 1943), 62–63.

This kind of stratagem is called the *ad hominem* fallacy. (*Ad hominem* is Latin for "toward the person," describing an attack on the person presenting the argument rather than on the argument itself.) It is a counterfeit. What truth does it counterfeit? It counterfeits the truth that in some situations the character of a person is relevant to evaluating his arguments. If we know that Spencer is a charlatan and a perpetrator of scams, we will look with suspicion on an invitation from him for us to invest in a gold mine that he has allegedly discovered. Whether we believe an otherwise unsubstantiated claim about his gold mine clearly depends on his character. Even if his arguments contain no unsubstantiated claims, we would be wise to inspect the arguments very carefully, looking for a trick that he could use to capture us in some scam.

Another kind of irrelevancy crops up in the *appeal to pity*. A speaker appeals for sympathy in order to induce people to judge in favor of someone in a pitiable state. In many cases this appeal is a fallacy, because the person's pitiable state is irrelevant to the question of whether, let us say, he has committed a crime. However, this counterfeit appeal depends on a truth. God does counsel us to have compassion on the weak. If we learn about a person's pitiable state, we may rightly decide to help in some other way than by evading a sound argument or succumbing to an unsound argument.

The fallacy of *appeal to authority* makes its appeal based on the opinion of someone famous, even though the famous person is not an expert or especially qualified to offer help in judgment. This fallacy involves an irrelevancy. Just because a person is famous as an actor, for instance, it does not mean that he is especially qualified to judge the virtues of different auto insurance companies. This fallacy is again a counterfeit, because we might legitimately appeal to an expert in real estate fraud when someone is being tried for a charge of real estate fraud, or appeal to an expert in airplane crashes when assessing the causes leading to a particular crash.

Then there is the fallacy of *argument by consensus*. "Everybody is doing it." Advertising can use this route: "90 percent of the people use our brand." Once we think about it, we can see that the numbers do not actually imply that their brand is any better. So this is a fallacy. But it counterfeits a truth: we might expect that in quite a few cases the lion's share of customers know something. Their choices in an open market, plus word-of-mouth testimony about the satisfying or unsatisfying features of competing brands, may eventually lead a large number people to settle on the optimal brand.

Then there is the fallacy of *snob appeal*. "Only the elite use our brand." The use of one brand of skin lotion or perfume by a certain key portion of the population does not establish its superiority. But there is a grain of truth here. In some areas, the elite may be "fussier" or more well-informed than the masses, so their use may be evidence for a superior product. The advertisers may also be appealing to elitism not to establish the innate superiority of their product but only to hint that using their product will give the customer added social prestige. And in some cases this may be true. People sometimes watch what brands you use.

Formal Fallacies

Some fallacies have a closer relationship to formal syllogistic reasoning. We have mentioned earlier the fallacy of false conversion:

> All dogs are animals. [mentally converted to "All animals are dogs."]
> All cats are animals.
> Therefore, all cats are dogs.

The conclusion is invalid. But the form of the syllogism is close to the valid form that we have discussed:

> All Bs are As.
> All Cs are Bs.
> Therefore all Cs are As.

It has some of the linguistic "feel" of this latter form, and so some people may be fooled. In addition, the two premises "All dogs are animals" and "All cats are animals" draw into close association the three categories, "dogs," "animals," and "cats." If someone is sloppy and inattentive in his thinking, he may just collapse the three categories in his own mind, and conclude that A, B, and C are all virtually identical with one another. Of course, this is not likely to happen with dogs and animals and cats, because we know too much about them and the conclusion that all cats are dogs is absurd. But it may happen in other cases if we get logically "sleepy."

The example given above of false conversion is closely related to another fallacy, called "affirming the consequent." This fallacy has to do with reasoning with if-then statements. Suppose we convert the statement "All collies are dogs" into a statement with an if-then format:

If anything is a collie, then it is a dog.

Or we use a particular case:

If Fido is a collie, then Fido is a dog.

Now consider the reasoning:

If Fido is a collie, then Fido is a dog.
Fido is a dog.
Therefore, Fido is a collie.

This reasoning is invalid. If Fido is a greyhound rather than a collie, the two premises are true, but the conclusion is false. The initial premise, "If Fido is a collie, then Fido is a dog," has two pieces. The "if" part is called *the antecedent* and the "then" clause, "then Fido is a dog," is called *the consequent*. The fallacy is called *affirming the consequent* because the second premise, "Fido is a dog," affirms the consequent in the if-then premise.

Though this reasoning is fallacious, it is closely related to a valid form of reasoning, called *modus ponens*:[4]

If Fido is a collie, then Fido is a dog.
Fido is a collie.
Therefore, Fido is a dog.

Classifying Fallacies

Are there other kinds of fallacies? We have not attempted to be exhaustive. People find many ways to counterfeit the truth, and people may fall into traps in reasoning even when no one has deliberately set a trap. The possibilities are innumerable. And yet a certain amount of classification is possible. More common fallacies have been given names, and the fact that they receive standard names indicates that they are common. S. Morris Engel's book, *With Good Reason: An Introduction to Informal Fallacies*, helpfully classifies informal fallacies under three broad headings: fallacies of ambiguity, fallacies of presumption, and fallacies of relevance.[5]

Fallacies of ambiguity focus on meanings that prove slippery. Fallacies of presumption involve untrustworthy assumptions or "presumptions."

---

[4] *Modus ponens* is a Latin expression meaning "the way that affirms."
[5] Engel, *With Good Reason*, 75–206.

Fallacies of relevance hope to sway people through irrelevant appeals. These three types cannot be perfectly separated, but they involve different focal difficulties.

If we wish, any one of the three types can be viewed as a perspective on the other two. In a broad sense, presumptions and irrelevant appeals involve misuse of meanings. Ambiguity and irrelevant appeals both involve false assumptions (the assumption that meaning is unambiguous or that an appeal is relevant). Ambiguity and presumption both involve a kind of irrelevance (since a second meaning in an ambiguous formulation is not actually relevant, and a presumption is irrelevant to the actual facts).

In this chapter we have considered a sample of fallacies of presumption and fallacies of relevance. We have not yet considered fallacies of ambiguity, that is, fallacies of meaning. These will be treated indirectly in the next few chapters, as we discuss issues of meaning.

Since all three kinds of fallacies counterfeit truth, and truth comes from God, the three kinds are in fact loosely related to God's lordship over truth. We can fruitfully use John Frame's triad of perspectives on ethics: the *normative*, *situational*, and *existential* perspectives.[6] The normative perspective is related to fallacies of meaning, since God's meanings are normative for truth. The situational perspective is related to fallacies of presumption, because presumption makes mistakes in assumptions about the world. The existential or personal perspective is related to fallacies of relevance, since irrelevant appeals often work by using something about us as persons. They appeal to some of our motives in order to make themselves effective in spite of the irrelevance of their content. All three forms of counterfeiting derive from twisting the original truth coming from God.

The *formal* fallacies mentioned above, such as the fallacy of affirming the consequent, do not fall so clearly under any one of these three categories. In some sense they show aspects of all three kinds of fallacies. People make mistakes about the meaning of logical derivation by drawing a conclusion when the premises do not warrant it. They make a mistake of presumption by assuming that they have a valid syllogistic form when they do not. They make a mistake of relevance when they falsely suppose that the premises are relevant to one another in a way that leads to a valid deductive conclusion. Perhaps formal fallacies are most easily classified as fallacies of meaning,

---

[6] John M. Frame, *Perspectives on the Word of God: An Introduction to Christian Ethics* (Phillipsburg, NJ: Presbyterian & Reformed, 1990); Frame, *The Doctrine of the Christian Life* (Phillipsburg, NJ: Presbyterian & Reformed, 2008).

since people are getting confused about meaning at the general level where they assess which syllogistic forms represent valid reasoning.

The Revelation of God

All these fallacies, and more that we might inspect, reveal God. By counterfeiting or aping the truth, they testify in spite of themselves to the truth. They testify to the final standard of God's rationality, even in the very process of deviating from his rationality.

For Further Reflection

1. Identify the kind of fallacy in the following arguments:
   a. You will have to accept that my fits of anger come along with my help, just like the light and heat of the sun come together.
   b. American-style government is either good or bad.
   c. Sue had chocolate ice cream at the cafe. Chocolate must be her favorite.
   d. I should buy a BMW because that is what rich people buy.
   e. Either you love our team or you hate it.
   f. I should buy a Toyota because the ad said it is the most popular brand.
   g. We should elect Jim as class secretary because it would be emotionally devastating to him if he lost.
2. Explain how each of the fallacious arguments listed above are counterfeits of a form of sound argument.
3. Why do fallacious arguments frequently counterfeit sound arguments?
4. How do fallacious arguments testify to God?

Part I.C

The Problem of Classification

Chapter 17

Analogy

In part I.B we saw that God reveals his character throughout logic, because his own self-consistency is the very foundation for logic. Christian thinking about logic is radically different when we open our eyes to see the glory of God being displayed in the field of logic as well as everywhere else.

Now we turn to consider difficulties in reasoning that are related to the meaning of the terms that we use. We expect that here also God reveals his character, and that Christian thinking will be distinctive.

Difficulties with respect to the meaning of terms crop up not only in informal reasoning but also in the context of formal reasoning in syllogisms. Syllogisms use terms like *men, mortal, dogs,* and *animals*. In syllogisms, terms like these are used to classify things. When we say that "all dogs are animals," we make two classifications. We classify some things as "dogs," and some things as "animals."

Reasoning depends on classifications. The terms that we use to make classifications must function coherently. So we will now consider how classification functions within syllogisms.

Relationship to Language

Consider again our starting example of a syllogism:

All men are mortal.
Socrates is a man.
Therefore Socrates is mortal.

People regard this syllogism as valid within any language in which it is expressed. But it does take language to express it. The logic of this syllogism coheres with functions of language. And language, even for human beings, is complex, many-dimensional. The sentence that says "All men are mortal" needs to be considered in its written texture, in its grammar, in its meaning, and in its relations to many other sentences. God's speech is even more complex and many-dimensional than human speech. It is infinite. When we think of logic as it originates in God, logic cannot be strictly isolated from who God is and how he speaks.

So in this and the following chapters we look at some of the ways in which a syllogism about Socrates has multidimensional connections. We focus not on the whole syllogism, but only one key part: the terms like *mortal* and *men*. The use of these terms depends on a number of assumptions, whose meaning and validity depend on God.

Analogy

First, a term like "man" depends for meaning on a fundamental analogy between God and man. God is the first one to have provided labels or terms. In Genesis 1:5, he "called the light Day, and the darkness he called Night." In Genesis 2:19–20 Adam gave names to the animals, and these names were additional labels. Adam's naming imitated God's acts of naming in Genesis 1. From these examples we may draw the general conclusion that our labels within human language imitate God's language. Or, if we focus on thinking rather than on speaking, we say that our thinking about men or mortality imitates God's thinking about those things. Our thinking and our speaking are *analogous* to God's thinking and speaking. And this analogy extends to the specific case of terms or classifications.

In Genesis 1, the names that God gave were not merely empty counters, but said something about what was named. He called the light Day, and the word *Day* said something meaningful about the light. Our thinking about the world depends constantly on meanings that are originally in God's plan and God's mind, and that we then take up in our minds.

Our dependence on God is more obvious in the case of the label *men* in the syllogism about Socrates. The word *men* in this context means human beings, not male human beings. (As previously noted, the syllogism about Socrates was regularly used as an example in discussions of logic before the rise of social pressures toward gender-neutral expressions in English.) What is a human being? The Greeks might have said, "A rational animal." A modern biological taxonomist might say, "Homo sapiens," and he might go on to describe certain distinctives in the DNA of human cells. But in the Bible, human distinctiveness is related to the fact that God made man "in the image of God" (Gen. 1:26–27), in analogy with God. Our understanding of man is related to our understanding of God, by way of analogy.

The differences in definition do make a difference. A one-dimensional definition (in terms, say, of rationality or DNA) is not the same as a many-dimensional definition such as "man is made in the image of God." Suppose that a one-dimensional definition succeeds in capturing the right list of members, that is, all the people whom we would in ordinary terminology classify as human beings. It nevertheless does not capture the full meaning of what it is to be a human being. And we may always wonder whether the one-dimensional definition has quite the right fit. For example, according to the Bible, human beings who believe in Christ go to the presence of God when their bodies die (Phil. 1:21–23; Rev. 6:9). They are still in the image of God, and therefore they are still human beings. But the DNA that is contained within their earthly bodies in the grave is nonfunctional and disintegrating. A definition in terms of DNA is therefore inadequate.

We have a similar challenge when dealing with mortality. What is it? To be mortal is to be subject to death. But within a biblical worldview, life and death have an innate relationship to God. God is the living God. The living things that he created have life in a manner analogous to his life, but within the realm of creation. Life has built into it an analogical relationship to God. Perhaps a one-dimensional definition might do well for some limited purposes, but life in our actual experience is multidimensional.

The Fallacy of Equivocation

The presence of analogy can create difficulty for reasoning. Consider the following reasoning:

> All foxes are carnivores.
> Herod the king is a fox.
> Therefore Herod the king is a carnivore.

Is this reasoning valid? In Luke 13:32 Jesus says that Herod the king is a fox. But he spoke metaphorically. He meant that Herod was analogous in some ways to a fox. On the other hand, the premise that "all foxes are carnivores" uses the word *fox* literally. The syllogism as a whole (the three lines together) is not valid, because the word *fox* is used in two different ways in the first two lines.

Aristotle recognized that shifts in meaning resulted in invalid reasoning. A shift in meaning makes the meaning "equivocal," because two different meanings belong to the two different lines. The resulting reasoning exhibits what has been called the *fallacy of equivocation*. In order for the reasoning to be formally valid, Aristotle required the meaning in different lines to be *univocal*.[1] That is, there should be one meaning common to all occurrences of a particular term.

Here is another example of equivocation:

> All tails are parts of animals.
> The back end of an airplane is a tail.
> Therefore the back end of an airplane is a part of an animal.

The word *tail* has two different meanings in the first two lines.

Syllogistic reasoning gains some of its power and prestige from the fact that the argument is considered valid by virtue of the *form* alone. We might therefore be tempted to say that we can be sure about syllogistic reasoning, even without checking out the content. The content may be about mortality, about foxes, or about tails. The content is irrelevant to the validity, because the syllogistic *form* guarantees validity. But that is not completely true, because an equivocation in meaning can destroy validity.

A syllogism could be guaranteed beforehand to work only if the argument is *purely* formal, and it can be purely formal only if it is not "contaminated" with the possibilities of ambiguity that crop up in ordinary language. But in fact ordinary language goes back by analogy to divine language, so it always rests on analogies. The analogies include both the analogy between human language and divine language and the analogy between human thought and divine thought. In addition, specific words like *mankind* and *life* evoke specific analogies with the Creator.

In our discussions of syllogisms in previous chapters, we did not bring into focus the fact that syllogisms are not purely formal, because they depend on the meanings of the terms. It is now time to take up this difficulty, and so we must qualify what we said previously. The validity of a sample syllogism holds within a context in which we understand meanings, and these meanings ultimately have a foundation in God who is their source. Syllogisms can function only in the context of meanings known to persons, and persons can function only in the context of the personal character of God.

---

[1] Thus the terms *equivocal* and *univocal* are opposites. The Latin terms from which they derive mean "equal voice" and "one voice," and are used to describe situations in which more than one meaning is an "equal" possibility (*equivocal*) or there is only *one* available meaning (*univocal*).

The Creator-creature Distinction

The Bible teaches that God the Creator is distinct from the creatures he has made. This distinction is called the *Creator-creature distinction*. There are two levels of being, God and creature, rather than one.

This two-level situation has implications for the use of terms in logic. Can we have one term, *father*, that applies both to God and to human creatures who are biological fathers? Clearly we can. But God's fatherhood and human fatherhood are not on the same level. So the relation between the two is one of analogy rather than strict identity. The introduction of analogy means that syllogistic reasoning will not necessarily be valid when applied to "fatherhood" as a general category. Similar results follow even if we talk about God as "creator," because we also use the word *creator* in a looser sense for human creators. Henry Ford "created" the automobile assembly line. An artist "creates" a masterpiece. These acts of "creation" are "subcreations," in contrast to the original act of God in creating the world. Thus the word *creator* can be used in at least two different ways.

We might suppose that syllogistic logic would work with less difficulty if we used it only for a one-level situation. So logicians confront the temptation to pretend that reality has only one level. Or, to put it another way, a logician may imagine that he can subject all of reality to the requirement that we have terms without any built-in analogies. He attempts to view God and God's creatures "from above," from a superior point of view that can capture everything in one grand viewpoint. He hopes to make reasoning work in a uniform way over the whole field. He will have high-level labels that apply equally and uniformly to both Creator and creature.

To do so, he tacitly makes himself superior to God. He has to be superior, in principle, if he is to control precisely the expressions that he will employ in order to determine what can be the case both with the Creator and with the creature. He denies his creaturely status. He also denies the fundamental character of the Creator-creature distinction.

Deductive reasoning in syllogisms promises rigor, and with rigor a kind of intellectual power. Seduced by the desire for power, we can try to make ourselves gods. In our minds we may try to force reality into the one-level machinery of syllogisms. If reality does not actually fit, so much the worse for reality! We end up systematically neglecting and suppressing those truths that do not fit the requirements of a supposed logical system.

Patching Up the Operation of Syllogisms

If we see the problem here, we can try to patch it up. For example, could we just specify that syllogisms apply only to creatures and not to the Creator? We confine them to working on one level of reality. But a non-Christian idea of transcendence threatens us. If we say that the Creator is completely inaccessible to the logic of syllogisms, we suggest that he is unknowable and irrational. That is a form of non-Christian transcendence. The other side of the coin is the threat of a non-Christian immanence. For practical purposes, we use our human level of logic as if it were ultimate.

In fact, it is impossible in practice to isolate in our minds one level, the level of created things. If we could, it would show that God is essentially irrelevant to the logic of created things and is not present. God is present, and created things testify to his character (Rom. 1:18–25). It is rebellious to try to remove his presence and our awareness of him in the process of reasoning.

Consider a particular example. An artist who creates a masterpiece is using the creativity that God gave him. God is present, and God's creativity works alongside human creativity. This is more obviously so in the case of an artist who is a Christian, because the Christian is trying to cooperate with God. But it is so even in the case of a non-Christian artist, who would consciously deny that God is helping him. God gives blessings to people who do not deserve them, blessings of "common grace." In particular, God blesses artists and other people with creativity.

We can try to imagine what it would be like if God were not acting in creativity. But if he were not acting, there would be no creative product. So it is impossible rigorously to imagine a human act of creation in such a way that we do not tacitly "mix" it with divine creativity. We do not know what it would be like to have human creativity "pure," unmixed with the action of divine creativity, partly because we have no examples, and also because in principle we cannot have such examples. Artists depend on God.

Similarly, logicians depend on God. God's logic is always sustaining the human reasoning going on in human minds. We cannot have reasoning at all without the presence of God and his power to sustain creatures.

So if we try to confine reasoning to the one level, the level of the creature, we are pretending that creatures are essentially independent of their Creator. We are presupposing a false view of reality.

Similar difficulties confront any proposal to confine reasoning to the level of the divine. Do we have a special logic that applies only to God? One difficulty here is that a "special" logic threatens to have no relation to common experience. It threatens to make God unknowable in practice. (This is non-Christian transcendence, corner #3 of Frame's square.) And then, if nevertheless we could somehow master this special logic, we would have mastered God and would be making ourselves superior to him. (This is non-Christian immanence, corner #4 of Frame's square.)

So can we rescue syllogisms in another way? Could we affirm that there are two levels of reality, and that a single syllogism needs to function on both levels? Would the two levels run parallel, never touching, like the two rails on a railroad track? Consider the following syllogism:

> All persons have a sense of right and wrong.
> You are a person.
> Therefore you have a sense of right and wrong.

The word "you" could refer to a human person, an angelic person, or one of the persons of the Trinity. The syllogism seems to work both on the human level and on the divine level.

The Creator, however, is not identical to the creature. In this sense the two rails never touch. But they are not simply parallel to one another. The creature depends on the Creator, and the Creator is infinitely deep. We cannot master him in our thought. And that implies in particular that we cannot master him with our syllogistic thought. The apparent rigor of a syllogism does not make our mind temporarily superior to God, or even on the same level with God. We should not aspire to force him to conform to our ideas, even our ideas of logic. (This is the Christian view of transcendence.) On the other hand, God does conform to his own logic, and he gives us access to logic through our being made in his image. Knowledge is genuine (the Christian view of immanence). We can see how the danger of lapsing into a rebellious attitude confronts us at every point. We can fall away from a Christian view into a non-Christian view of transcendence and immanence.

So should we work on this problem of rebellion entering into logic? If we could isolate this problem, dominate it, and solve it transparently to our intellectual satisfaction, we would have saved ourselves—we would have eliminated the problem of rebellion. By saving ourselves, we would also have made ourselves gods, and so paradoxically we would be displaying in ourselves the heart of rebellion.

The Bible indicates that God must save us (Jonah 2:9); we do not save ourselves. Christ must remove our rebellion, in the area of logic as well as in every other area. And this removal is not easy, partly because sin can be subtle and deep. We can begin in our discussions here to touch on some aspects of the remedy. But the full work of God is necessary for the full remedy. And the remedy is not complete within this life, but only in the new heaven and the new earth (Rev. 21:1–4).

How Did We Get This Way?

Human beings have had rebellion against God in their hearts ever since the first man and woman instigated rebellion (Genesis 3). All human beings have the temptation to practice rebellion in the area of logic as well as in other areas. But in addition, the human study of logic has a history. The history can influence us for good or ill, because we follow others whose rebellion has had its influence on them.

Historically speaking, the study of logic in the West owes much to Aristotle, who inaugurated the systematic study of syllogisms. Aristotle along with his predecessors, Plato and Socrates, were not followers of the true God, the God of Israel, but sought to practice *autonomous* thought in their philosophical reflections. They practiced their thinking and reflection in a manner that strove not to depend on God. They relied on reason, not on God's revelation.

Religious Commitment

Did Aristotle's religious commitment affect his philosophy? Of course it did, because all human thought imitates divine thought.[2] According to Romans 1:18–25, rebellion against God takes the form of making substitutes for God, and an impersonalist conception of reason or truth can be one form of substitute. This substitution corrupts human thought. But how?

Does the corruption mean that human beings can no longer reason at all? Have they completely lost touch with logic? No. God in his kindness is still gracious to those in rebellion. Thus, we can understand that Aristotle

---

[2] We cannot here undertake a full analysis of what has been called the noetic effects of sin, the effects on the mind and on thought. I owe much to Cornelius Van Til and John Frame (see, e.g., Cornelius Van Til, *The Defense of the Faith*, 2nd ed. [Philadelphia: Presbyterian & Reformed, 1963]; Van Til, *A Survey of Christian Epistemology*, volume 2 of the series *In Defense of Biblical Christianity* (n.l.: den Dulk Christian Foundation, 1969); John M. Frame, *Apologetics to the Glory of God: An Introduction* (Phillipsburg, NJ: Presbyterian & Reformed, 1994); Frame, *The Doctrine of the Knowledge of God* (Phillipsburg, NJ: Presbyterian & Reformed, 1987).

and other Greek philosophers received genuine insights from God. We can find elements of truth in their work. Aristotle's study of syllogisms has proved wonderfully useful ever since his time. Yet truth is corrupted when a human being is out of harmony with God, who is the source and standard of all truth. All human beings in rebellion against God act to make themselves a god; rebellion is deep. But in detail it takes many forms.

So we need to consider both what insights and what corruptions might be present with Aristotle and those after him. We have already seen that the idea of purely formal reasoning in syllogisms tempts us to suppress the presence of analogy, and to think that logic can operate on one level. We ignore the distinction between Creator and creature. Do other difficulties crop up in using syllogisms? In the next few chapters we consider the difficulties.

For Further Reflection

1. What complexities enter syllogistic reasoning because of equivocation?
2. What complexities enter syllogistic reasoning because of the Creator-creature distinction?
3. Can we fix the problem of analogy by confining logic to one level? Why or why not?
4. How does the Creator-creature distinction affect our view of informal reasoning?

Chapter 18

Unity and Diversity

In syllogistic reasoning we confront the issue of unity and diversity, which is also called the issue of the one and the many. How do unity and diversity relate to each other?

The Issue of General Categories

Unity and diversity operate in syllogisms in at least two ways. First, the general pattern of a syllogism is a unity in relation to its diverse instantiations. One general pattern that we have been considering is the syllogism of the form

> All Bs are As.
> All Cs are Bs.
> Therefore all Cs are As.

Here is a particular instance:

> All dogs are animals.
> All collies are dogs.
> Therefore all collies are animals.

The one general pattern, "All Bs are As, etc." shows the *unity* in many instances. The many instances, including "All dogs are animals, etc." show the *diversity* of instances.

Second, we confront the issue of unity and diversity within any one category, such as the category of animals. Any one animal, whether a collie or a cat, is a particular instance; it is one among many. The general category "animal" shows the unity among the many instances of animals. For the syllogism to work, it has to presuppose that general categories like "animal" function in a coherent way. The general category has to be understood as potentially allowing many instances.

What is the relation between the one, namely, the general category of "animal," and the many, namely Fido the dog, Felix the cat, and many other animals? The relation of the one and the many is related to the status of "universals," that is, general categories like *animal* or *humanity*.[1]

Nominalism and Realism

Medieval philosophers split over the issue of the status of universals. "Realists" believed that universals existed in reality, in addition to their instantiations. For example, they believed that "the beautiful" as a universal exists in addition to beautiful things. The universal concept of "horse" (or perhaps "horseness") exists in addition to particular horses. According to the Platonic version of realism, the universal is always there, even before God created any individual horse. So it has a kind of priority to individual horses.

How do the individual horses come to be? Perhaps they come into being by participating in "horseness"? But if they all participate, what differentiates them? How does the diversity come about, if we start with only abstract unity?

In medieval thought, the nominalists started at the other end of the spectrum. They denied the existence of universals. The particulars, the individual horses, then have priority. We invent the name *horse* to label them. The word *horse* is only a name,[2] produced by us after we have experience with horses. But how then does the unity in the label *horse* come about, if all we start with is an absolute diversity? Is the unity an illusion or a convenient fiction? The realists and the nominalists were both addressing what has been called "the problem of universals."

Trinitarianism

If we affirm the Creator-creature distinction, we have to say that the issue of one and many must distinguish two levels. We have one and many in the Creator and one and many in creatures.[3] In the Creator, one and many are equally ultimate. God always exists both in his unity as one God and in his plurality, consisting in the three persons of the Trinity. We must avoid saying that the oneness in God is more ultimate, so that the three persons of

---

[1] To his credit, Aristotle's discussion of syllogisms shows that he was aware of one aspect of the problem. The discussion of syllogisms in his work *Prior Analytics* depends on two other works, *Categories* and *On Interpretation*. The first of these deals with the issue of "categories," which is closely related to the issue of the one and the many. The second deals with terms, predication, and the formation of assertions, which are essential in considering propositions. Unfortunately, both of these works are at odds with a Trinitarian view of the foundations of language and thought. This chapter and subsequent chapters in this section will explore some of the difficulties in Aristotle's approach.

[2] The term *nominalism* comes from *nominal*, which is cognate to *name*.

[3] Cornelius Van Til, *The Defense of the Faith*, 2nd ed. (Philadelphia: Presbyterian & Reformed, 1963), 25–28.

the Trinity somehow come about after one God exists, or that God is really one and that he merely appears to us as three when he interacts with us (the error of modalism). We must also avoid saying that the diversity in God is more ultimate, so that the three persons exist first and then somehow join together into a three-member society that agrees to act jointly (the error of tritheism). So we can see that God is both one and many, and neither can be reduced to the other.

Now what about the issue of one and many among creatures? God in speaking through his Word creates the universe with its own created unity and diversity. Both unity and diversity owe their reality to God's speech, which expresses his character. God himself is one and many. He then expresses his inner unity and diversity in his speech. God the Father functions as speaker, God the Son as the Word, and God the Spirit as the breath of God's speech.

Let us become more specific by considering what happens with horses. We have already observed that there are many horses, but they belong together because they are all horses. They belong to the same species. They share common characteristics. How does this one and many come about?

God has planned to create a universe with horses. The universe includes many horses in their diversity, and each particular horse in all its particularity comes into being according to God's plan. Likewise, God planned a universe in which the distinct horses are united in belonging to one species, the species of horse.[4] They have common characteristics because God planned their commonality. Their commonality or unity is no more ultimate than their diversity, because God's plan includes both unity and diversity. His speech articulating his plan includes unity and diversity.

Thus, Christian thinking in terms of the Creator-creature distinction leads to a distinct approach to the issue of universals. The Christian position is not merely a realist position, because "horseness" is not prior to the particularities of individual horses. God's plan is of course prior to the actualization of his plan in the creation of particular horses. It is also prior to the actualization of his plan in the creation of the *species* of horse within the world. God's plan includes unity and diversity for the race of horses and for the particular horses. The execution of his plan in time and space manifests unity and diver-

---

[4] Genesis 1 indicates specifically that God created plants and animals "according to their kinds" (1:11–12, 21, 24–25). The Hebrew word for "kind" is not a technical scientific classification like our modern terms *genus* and *species*. Nevertheless, it indicates in a less technical way that God ordained both unities and diversities in the character of the plant kingdom and the animal kingdom.

sity. We now have around us both a species, namely, the species of horse, and the particular horses. God's plan includes both the generality, that is, the unity, and the particularities that show the diversity among living things.

Using the Creator-creature distinction, we naturally have to distinguish God's knowledge of horses from our knowledge. God knows comprehensively and originally, while we know partially and derivatively. We do know about the existence and characteristics of particular horses, like Sally the palomino mare. We also recognize that, by God's design, all horses belong together and share some characteristics. But we do not know everything that God knows about the particular mare Sally, nor do we know everything about horses in general. We can point to some characteristics that make us think that it is appropriate to classify Sally under the general term *horse*. But we could perhaps be fooled by some clever ruse, and we do not know everything that goes into God's making Sally a horse.

It is worthwhile dwelling on the nature of God's unity and diversity for a bit longer, because it is important as a foundation for creation and for logic.

The class *God* applies to all three persons of the Trinity. It is the general category. The persons are distinct; each one is fully God; each is an *instantiation* of God. Thus, within the Trinity we find a unity in the class and a diversity in the instantiations.

We can see a divine manifestation of generality and particularity at another level. When God the Son becomes incarnate, he is the unique manifestation of God on earth. Jesus says to Philip, "Whoever has seen me has seen the Father" (John 14:9). Jesus is the unique *instantiation* of God on earth in his incarnation. Thus the idea of instantiation, though applicable to all three persons, is especially seen in the person of Christ. What about the idea of class, the generality? The category *God* covers all three persons. God the Father is more often the most prominent representative in the Godhead, as when Jesus says that he is ascending to "my God and your God" (John 20:17). Thus we have reason to associate class or *classification* with the Father. Finally, the Holy Spirit represents the presence of God in believers, and unites us to Christ. He acts as the bond of *association* or relationship. So we can link the Holy Spirit to relationships—including even the relationship between the generality or *classification* ("God") and the *instantiation* (Christ in his incarnation).[5]

---

[5] On classification, instantiation, and association, see also Vern S. Poythress, "Reforming Ontology and Logic in the Light of the Trinity: An Application of Van Til's Idea of Analogy," *Westminster Theological Journal* 57/1 (1995): 187–219; reprinted in appendix F5.

God is absolute and original. Hence classification, instantiation, and association have their origin in him. They also apply derivatively to created things. Each dog is an instantiation of the species of dogs, where the species is the classification. Each dog in its individuality has an *association* with the species to which it belongs, with the other instances of dogs, and with other kinds of creatures as well.

Implications for Syllogistic Logic

The relation of unity to diversity has implications for our use of syllogisms. In syllogisms we are always relying on a prior understanding of unity and diversity. It is easy to pretend that syllogisms operate only with unities, namely, purely general categories like *dogs, animals, collies*. The pure generality of the categories guarantees the success of the inferences.

But the categories are not in fact "pure" in the required sense. They are not pure in our own minds, since we learn about dogs or animals through a combination of particular examples and more general statements related to examples. We learn about horses by a complex combination of particulars and generalities—particular horses like Sally and general talk using the word *horse*. We also learn in the context of *associations*. We interact with horses in association with other people, whom we hear using the word *horse*, and in association with an environment in which we see horses or pictures of horses.

Our knowledge of the general category *horse* is entangled with our experience of particular horses and our associations with environments in which we learn about them. What difference does this entanglement make for syllogisms?

Here is a syllogism for horses:

All horses are mortal.
All Clydesdales are horses.
Therefore all Clydesdales are mortal.

The syllogism works, does it not? Yes, it does. But for many people the ideal for syllogistic logic has been that logic would work in a purely *formal* way. Formal validity is supposed to hold by virtue of the general form of reasoning. If the general form is "contaminated" by particulars, the reasoning is not purely formal, and we may have to check out in detail the ways in which our particular experience with horses has colored our conception of the concept of horse. What happens when someone grows up around only one breed of horses—let us say Arabian? Does the word *horse* function in exactly the same manner for him as it does for others with different experience?

God's Knowledge of General Categories

Someone might suggest that we can escape our limitations by rising from our own knowledge of horses to God's knowledge. As usual, we have to be careful about our conceptions of God's transcendence and immanence. God's knowledge has to be like our knowledge in some ways, if our knowledge is to be real (the principle of God's immanence). At the same time, God's knowledge is superior to ours, not only in extent but also in texture (the principle of transcendence). If we imagine that we can unproblematically picture every aspect of God's view of things, we deny his transcendence.

What about the category *horse*? What is it like for God? Divine knowledge includes knowledge of the particulars (Sally the horse) and the generalities (all Clydesdales; and all horses). It includes all the relations between the particulars and the generalities, all the environmental associations, and all knowledge about how these unities and diversities relate to the ultimate unity and diversity in the Creator, the unity and diversity in the Trinity.

Unity and diversity in the Trinity exist not in isolation but in relation to each other. That mystery is the ultimate foundation for creation. So could we postulate that God's thinking isolates a universal ("horseness") with no relation to particulars (Sally)? Would that universal be ultimately an impersonal category, unrelated to the persons of the Trinity or to any other category? That picture would seem to be at odds with the interrelatedness of persons in the Trinity, and the interrelatedness of the knowledge that the three persons have of one another.

Similar conclusions hold for possibilities that never become actualized. God's mind can of course include possibilities about which he knows but that he never brings to pass.[6] The mare Sally, let us say, could have given birth to a foal but never did. Because we are subordinate creators in the image of our Creator, we may even imagine animals like unicorns that have never existed. But even here our minds use both particular hypothetical

---

[6] For a particular example, consider 1 Samuel 23:10–12, where David learns from God what *would happen* were he to remain in the city of Keilah. On the basis of this information, David leaves Keilah, and the hypothesized situations never come to pass in actual history.

examples (one particular unicorn, white and four feet high at the withers) and an idea of a general pattern: body like a horse, horn in the middle of the forehead. This interrelatedness of generalities and particulars has an ultimate ontological foundation in the interrelatedness of God and the persons of the Trinity.

A Paradox of Generalization

We might try another escape route. We might ask whether the entanglement of unity and diversity makes any practical difference. Can we not act *as if* we had perfect knowledge of ideally "perfect" general categories? But pretending as if reality were different from what it is always runs the risk of resulting in error. One of the original goals of analyzing syllogistic reasoning was rigor and a freedom from error. It is odd to introduce risk of error for the sake of maintaining the purity of syllogisms.

In fact, the risk is not merely theoretical. It has been known for about a century that unrestricted formal reasoning about very general categories leads to antinomies (see appendix A1). So we must respect the entanglement of unity and diversity, and not pretend that we can somehow surpass it.

Knowledge of Logic Interlocked with Particulars

The interrelation between unity and diversity in knowledge applies to the knowledge of logic itself. We know logic in the form of universal principles. We illustrate these principles using particular instances of reasoning about collies, dogs, animals, mortality, and other kinds of things. The particulars are naturally particulars taken from this world. Or they are particulars from our imagination, such as unicorns and bug-eyed monsters, but still related to our capacity for imagination, which we use in connection with ideas suggested by this world. The universals—the principles of logic—are entangled with the particulars by which we illustrate them. The entanglement is one way in which our knowledge is limited but still true.

As we observed earlier, we can imagine the possibility of an angelic being or a creature belonging to another world. Suppose this other world has no dogs or horses or animals. Suppose that a creature in this other world is still personal and is in communion with God's logic. So he can think rationally, by God's standards, but not necessarily with the same detailed textures as we do. We do not know exactly how such a being might think, because our own thinking has textures related to *this* world.

C. S. Lewis produces an interesting example of major differences in thinking when he imagines three "races" of intelligent beings on Mars. The first race inclines toward science and scientific thinking. The second is poetical, and the third is mechanico-technical in inclination.[7] He achieves his fascinating result partly by blowing up and exaggerating different styles of thinking that exist even among human beings! So we should not forget human differences. In a sense we share a common "logic" because we are made in the image of God. But in another sense, each of us is unique, and our style of rationality does not duplicate exactly the style of anyone else. In a world without sin, the entanglement of unity and diversity allows for differences without threatening human fellowship.

The possibility of ways of thinking different from our own should not disturb us, as long as we remember the Christian principles of transcendence and immanence. The possibility of difference simply underlines the principle of transcendence. God is greater than we are, in his thoughts as well as in his other characteristics. And that greatness is not merely quantitative, as if we could achieve infinity just by multiplying the number of our thoughts or increasing their speed or accuracy. We may not be able to imagine some aspects of God's thinking. And some other created being, created in a different way, might be able to imagine some of these aspects. We do not know, and we do not need to know.

On the other side we have the principle of immanence. What we do come to know, about God and about the world in which he put us, can be fully true. The logic in our reasoning can be fully valid, because it imitates God's logic, even though it does not capture his infinity. We can reason safely, because God made us using infinite wisdom. That is, we are safe if we follow his ways. The difficulty is sin, not finiteness.

[7] C. S. Lewis, *Out of the Silent Planet* (New York: Macmillan, 1943).

For Further Reflection

1. Illustrate how unity and diversity interact in your learning what a bicycle is.
2. What are the philosophical views called *realism* and *nominalism*?
3. How does a Christian view based on the Trinity interact with realism and nominalism?
4. How do the entanglement of unity and diversity affect syllogistic reasoning?
5. What difficulties do people find if they try to give an impersonalistic explanation of unity and diversity, starting with unity as more ultimate? Starting with diversity as more ultimate?

Chapter 19

Stability of Meaning

The formalization that takes place in syllogistic reasoning involves an idealization. It picks out one dimension from the total texture of reasoning and attempts to isolate it. In the process of isolation, interesting patterns come to light. But careful analysis shows that the process involves simplifications and passes over difficulties. In this chapter we continue to discuss the difficulties, concentrating now on the issue of stable meaning.

The Necessity of Stability

If a syllogism is going to work by virtue of its form alone, the meanings that reoccur must be stable. For example, in the syllogism about Socrates, the reoccurring labels "Socrates," "men/man," and "mortal" have to have the same meaning in all their occurrences. Otherwise, as we have seen, the syllogism becomes an instance of the fallacy of equivocation. Remember the instance of equivocation with the word *tail*:

> All *tails* are parts of animals.
> The back end of an airplane is a *tail*.
> Therefore the back end of an airplane is a part of an animal.

The two occurrences of the same word *tail* exhibit a relation of unity and diversity. There is one word, exhibiting unity. There are two occurrences, exhibiting diversity. A syllogism depends on this kind of unity and diversity, as well as the unity and diversity that relates a general category like *horse* to particular horses. This unity and diversity depends on the Trinity.[1]

But the validity of the syllogism depends on the *kind* of unity and diversity that we encounter in a particular case. Do we have two occurrences of the same word, with two meanings (equivocation), or two occurrences of the same word with one and the same meaning? That latter situation is sup-

---

[1] See the further discussion in Vern S. Poythress, *In the Beginning Was the Word: Language—A God-Centered Approach* (Wheaton, IL: Crossway, 2009), chapter 19, on contrast and variation.

posed to occur with a valid syllogism. Now, since the reoccurrence of the same word does not guarantee, merely by its form, the reoccurrence of the same meaning, what do we mean by "same meaning"? Meanings have to be expressed by words, so how might we "independently" check sameness? The sameness depends ultimately on unity in the mind of God.

Relative Stability versus Perfect Stability

Can we fix the difficulty? Words in natural language are *relatively* stable in meaning.[2] Some words like *tail* have more than one sense. The word *tail* can designate either the rear part of the body of an animal or the rear part of an airplane (or still other things). But as long as we stick to a single sense, we might think we will be all right.

The single sense that we choose is stable. But is it *perfectly* stable? A closer analysis of word meanings reveals that they involve contrast, variation, and distribution.[3] The word *tail* contrasts in meaning with words designating other parts of the body: head, torso, legs. The word has *variation* in that it applies to tails of various animals, such as cats, dogs, horses, and monkeys. The word has *distribution* in that it occurs in contexts in which we make whole statements involving tails, or ask questions about tails.

The aspect of *contrast* is closely related to stable meaning. There are stable contrasts between tails and other parts of the body. A tail can be defined as "the rear end or prolongation of the rear end of the body of an animal."[4] The more precise description of contrast is "contrastive-identificational features." Various features serve not only to make contrasts between tails and other parts of the body, but positively to identify tails for what they are. The contrastive-identificational features mean that words do label classes or categories. And in the world itself, there are classes of creatures.

These classes are particularly visible in the world of plants and animals. In the system of biological classification, there are species and genuses and families and orders and "classes" in the technical sense. God created a world in which such classifications are appropriate. We can thank him for this kind of stability in the world. Stability makes possible the working of syllogisms. All people who use syllogisms depend on the stability of God and of his governance of the world. But such stability does not imply that

---

[2] Ibid., chapters 7, 20, 33.
[3] Ibid., chapters 19 and 33; Kenneth L. Pike, *Linguistic Concepts: An Introduction to Tagmemics* (Lincoln: University of Nebraska Press, 1982), 42–65.
[4] *Webster's Ninth New Collegiate Dictionary.*

all classes have equally sharp boundaries, or that all classes are defined with great precision.

For example, with the word *tail* there is still an ambiguity, since we can speak of the "tail end" of an animal like a worm or an insect or a spider, which, strictly speaking, has no "tail." What is the difference between "the rear end" and the "prolongation of the rear end" of an animal? How distinct and how narrow does the "prolongation" have to be to count as a tail? An ant has an abdomen which is a distinct part, positioned to the rear of its legs, while the legs themselves are attached to its thorax. So does the abdomen count as a "tail"? Probably not, but it depends on how flexible we want the word *tail* to be.

Boundaries to Meaning

What is the boundary between what is a tail and what is not? The stability of meaning and the presence of contrast imply that there is at least a rough boundary. But the edges are "fuzzy." We could also say that because of the interlocking contrast and variation, the contrast between tail and not-tail also possesses variation when we look at it more minutely. The variation may depend on a larger context, that is, a "distribution" of the word *tail* in a sentence, and the distribution of the sentence within a context of discourse. The discourse may be of a more technical scientific kind, or may function as a simple explanation to a child, or may encourage metaphorical or poetic stretches in meaning.

We might argue that it does not make any difference in the case of tails. Whatever the exact definition of the word *tail*, as long as we are dealing with animal tails the syllogism holds true:

> All *tails* are parts of animals.
> The back part of a cat is a *tail*.
> Therefore the back part of a cat is a part of an animal.

The syllogism does hold true. But we have had to assure ourselves first that the word *tail* was used with an appropriate kind of stability.

Consider another syllogism:

> All *tails* are controlled by muscles.
> All tentacles of jellyfish are *tails*.
> Therefore all tentacles of jellyfish are controlled by muscles.

It is not so clear how to evaluate this syllogism, because some of the key words have fuzzy boundaries. What counts as a tail? What counts as a muscle? And is the first premise true, that "all tails are controlled by muscles"?

One of the difficulties we experience is that many things we think we know about the world arise partly from induction. Mammals and other large animals are the most likely candidates to use as a starting point for generalizing about tails. The obvious mammals like cats, dogs, cows, horses, and monkeys all have tails whose motions can be controlled by muscles. But maybe somewhere there is a less well-known mammal with no muscular control. I do not know for sure.

We have other difficulties when we travel beyond mammals. Some jellyfish have tentacles. Do these tentacles jointly constitute a "tail"? It depends on whether we want to use the word *tail* more broadly or more narrowly. The word *muscle* also shows some potential difficulty with boundaries. By "muscle" do we mean a distinct macroscopic tissue whose function is mostly to produce motion by contraction? Some jellyfish can exert some control over the motion of their tentacles. But the tentacles do not have the complex musculature of vertebrates. So the tentacles have "muscles" if we use the word broadly to cover anything that can produce macroscopic motion. They do not if we look for a complex, specialized muscle tissue.

The joint effect of these various difficulties is that it is not so clear whether the syllogism about jellyfish works. And if it does not work, why does it not work? Is the difficulty that the first premise is untrue? Or that the second premise untrue? Or does the word *tail* or the word *muscle* involve an equivocation? Or is it just that language is not precise and "stable" in quite the way it would need to be in order to guarantee beforehand the correct working of the syllogism?

If we have difficulties with this one example, clearly we may have difficulties with many other similar examples. If someone promises to present us with a particular case of a syllogism, we cannot say beforehand whether it will involve difficulties.

Why do these difficulties exist? People fascinated with the power of logic or the potential promised in syllogisms might want to say that these difficulties arise from the imperfections of natural language. But how do they know that the fault is with language rather than with the syllogistic pattern? Or rather, does the fault lie in an unrealistic expectation that we could reduce reasoning to a purely *formal* process?

When we obtain our basic guidance from the Bible, we can begin to move toward answers. God created man morally upright (Eccles. 7:29). God communicated with mankind even before the fall into sin (Gen. 1:28–30; 2:16–17).[5] The fall disrupted human language along with other aspects of human life. But the disruption was a moral and spiritual disruption, not a metaphysical change in the very nature of language. Moreover, God continued to communicate to mankind after the fall, thereby tacitly endorsing language as a suitable vehicle for divine communication. This suitability implies that the difficulty in guaranteeing syllogisms is a difficulty with syllogisms and our expectations, not a difficulty with language as God has given it to us. Syllogisms are designed to focus single-mindedly on one aspect of how reasoning functions in language and in thought. The single-minded focus can be useful. But it leaves out much. Distorted human expectations lead to a desire to force the richness of language into a small box that has been created by this reduced focus.

Precision

The word *tail* is not infinitely precise in its contrasts. Even within a technical scientific context, there may remain difficult cases, and it may be partly just a matter of definition (shall we use the word to cover a wider or a narrower range of cases?), rather than a crucial functional distinction. This lack of complete precision frustrates the idea of making syllogisms completely formal.

We can try to produce an ideal case by *imagining* that the word *tail* is given a completely precise and completely invariant meaning. But we should have some concern about this ideal of complete precision. Does complete precision mean *infinite* precision? If not, the remaining area of imprecision may prove to ruin the purity of syllogistic process. If it does mean infinite precision, we need to ask whether finite human beings can achieve infinite precision. Does the ideal of infinite precision represent an element of inward rebellion, in which we aspire to be godlike—to be omniscient?

In addition, this step toward imagination is artificial. In practice, context always colors meaning. The tail of a cat is not the same as the tail of a horse or the tail of a fish or the tentacles of a jellyfish. Even if we could perfectly define the boundary between tail and not-tail, these variations would remain, and in practice our experience of cats "bleeds into" the associations

---

[5] Poythress, *In the Beginning Was the Word*, chapters 3, 4, and 14.

with the word *tail* when we hear of the tail of a cat. Syllogisms are idealizations that leave things out. To know whether syllogisms constitute valid reasoning in the real world, we have to reckon with whether, in any particular case, what is left out disrupts an initial impression of valid reasoning. We have to reckon with meaning in context.

For Further Reflection

1. Discuss the difference between relatively stable meaning and perfect precision.
2. Illustrate the phenomenon of relative stability with another word besides the word *tail*.
3. Illustrate the potential effect on syllogisms of the ambiguity of the word *cat*, which can refer to domestic cats or to the cat family. Illustrate using some other word of your own choosing.
4. Why might syllogisms work with fewer problems in scientific discourse than in ordinary discourse?

Chapter 20

Form and Meaning

In natural language, form and meaning come together. What are "form" and "meaning"? The "form" of the word *tail* includes the fact that it is a noun, with the plural form *tails*. The "form" also includes its spelling and pronunciation. The "meaning" of the word is what we would find in a dictionary: "the rear end or prolongation of the rear end of the body of an animal." We need to consider the issue of form and meaning, because the interlocking of form and meaning disturbs the attempt to make syllogisms a matter of pure form, which would operate on purely abstract meanings.

We have said that form and meaning interlock. Once a person has learned English, the meaning of the word *tail* is evoked from the form "t-a-i-l," and the form is produced in order to communicate the meaning to others. In practice, the two sides go together.[1] In naive use of language, people usually do not distinguish them. The word *tail* produces simultaneously awareness of the form "t-a-i-l" and the meaning "rear end."

The Importance of Form and Meaning in Syllogisms

The working of a syllogism depends on both form and meaning. General syllogisms exhibit a constant form:

All Bs are As.
All Cs are Bs.
Therefore all Cs are As.

The constant structure of the form is an essential part of the generalization

---

[1] Ferdinand de Saussure distinguished the two, labeling the form the "signifier" (French *signifier*) and the meaning the "signified" (French *signifié*). The distinction with respect to the language system (*langue*) opened the way for the development of structural linguistics (de Saussure, *Course in General Linguistics* [New York/Toronto/London: McGraw-Hill, 1959]). But it involved an idealization and a simplification. In practice, one side always comes with the other, in what Kenneth L. Pike dubbed a "form-meaning composite." See Kenneth L. Pike, *Language in Relation to a Unified Theory of the Structure of Human Behavior*, 2nd ed. (The Hague/Paris: Mouton, 1967), 62–63, 516–517; Pike, *Linguistic Concepts: An Introduction to Tagmemics* (Lincoln: University of Nebraska Press, 1982), 16; Vern S. Poythress, *In the Beginning Was the Word: Language—A God-Centered Approach* (Wheaton, IL: Crossway, 2009), 263–264, 375–376.

that makes a syllogism what it is. It is intended that this form will be essentially independent of the content or meaning that fills the As, Bs, and Cs. At the same time, in practice analysts are not interested in syllogisms merely because of their form. Syllogisms are important in practice because they have a bearing on meanings.

The point of the exercise of learning about syllogisms is that we would be able to identify which reasonings are valid, and would have a means of evaluating conclusions about Socrates or about cats' tails. The study of syllogisms has a point because it leads to evaluation of meanings. Thus, syllogisms depend on both form and meaning. Form and meaning operate in natural language, and they operate in syllogisms as a kind of extension or formalization or schematic representation of one aspect of language.

God as Sustainer of Form and Meaning

How do form and meaning relate to each other? A speaker communicates ideas, that is, content. So it is natural to associate the particular meanings of a particular discourse with the speaker. The meanings are expressed in discourse which has grammar. And they are carried through a medium such as breath and sound. The threefold distinction between content, grammar, and medium has its origin in God. God as Father gives content; the Son as the Word gives the "grammar" of divine speech; and the Spirit as breath provides the medium for delivery of the speech.

The three persons of the Trinity indwell one another. So it is impossible to isolate perfectly the action of one. All three persons act together in speech. And the speech has content, grammar, and breath.[2] Likewise human speech has content, grammar, and breath. Traditionally, content has also been called *meaning*, while grammar and breath (sound or written form) together constitute *form*. Form and meaning go together, in analogy with the joint action and mutual indwelling of the persons of the Trinity. Through hearing or seeing the form we discern the meaning. And we re-express the meaning, perhaps in more than one form (paraphrase).

Syllogisms, we have said, depend on form and meaning. So they depend on a structure that derives from God. And God is not a deistic God who puts these structures in place in the distant past and then disappears from the scene. According to the biblical doctrine of God's immanence, he is

---

[2] Content, grammar, and breath correspond respectively to the three subsystems of language mentioned in chapter 9, namely, the referential subsystem, the grammatical subsystem, and the phonological subsystem.

continually present in the world. He is therefore continually present in language, even in human language—though he does not necessarily morally endorse everything that we say. He is therefore also present in the operation of form and meaning in syllogisms. Syllogisms should therefore stimulate us to praise him.

God as Sustainer of Syllogisms

Syllogisms depend on the *distinction* between form and meaning. We have the same syllogistic form:

> All Bs are As.
> All Cs are Bs.
> Therefore all Cs are As.

This form must apply when a variety of meanings are plugged into A, B, and C as placeholders.

At the same time, syllogisms depend on a tight *correlation* between form and meaning. We have already seen the necessity for correlation in discussing the issue of the meaning of the word *tail*. The word *tail* occurred more than once in the syllogistic patterns that we discussed. It was demonstrably the *same* word, in terms of form, because the form is revealed through the spelling, t-a-i-l. For the syllogism to work correctly, the form t-a-i-l must correlate with the same meaning throughout. We must be talking about the same kind of tail.

The correlation between form and meaning is even more crucial when we come to the form of the syllogism as a whole. The form "All Bs are As, etc." is a form of valid argument. To speak of "validity" is to make a statement about content and about meaning. If the premises are true, the conclusion must be true. To speak of "truth" is also to be concerned with meaning. The very form of the argument is important only because it points to something about the nature of truth and validity. It correlates with meaning, namely, the meanings associated with "if-then" reasoning and with truth being deducible from prior truths.

A syllogism works because in fact this particular correlation between form and meaning is a tight and consistent one. "If-then" as a grammatical form correlates with hypothetical reasoning with particular content. Similarly, the statement "All Bs are As" as a linguistic form with grammar and graphical symbols is correlated tightly with content, namely that, if we fill B and A with material referring to the world, we simultaneously make the form "All Bs are As" correlate with a claim about reality, that is, about content: we claim that whatever has character B or belongs to category B also belongs to category A.

Form and meaning in a syllogism have to be distinct. This distinction relies on and testifies to the distinction between the persons of the Trinity, who are present in language. Form and meaning also correlate with each other tightly. This correlation relies on the mutual indwelling of the persons of the Trinity. The persons of the Trinity love one another and are in harmony with one another. Through their presence in language, they sustain form and meaning in harmony with each other.

Awareness

Most of the time we are not consciously aware of God's presence in a syllogism, or of his presence in language. Being finite, we cannot possibly be consciously aware of everything at once, or be aware of all aspects of a complex reality. Rather, we rely on the faithfulness of God even in areas of which we are not aware. Our situation becomes a problem not because we are unaware, but because we avoid awareness. In rebellion we want to be our own gods, and we resist the idea of dependence on God. So we systematically suppress the presence of God rather than seek him (Rom. 1:18–25). If we are made aware of God's presence, we should be encouraged and stimulated to give thanks and to stand in awe of him. Instead, through suppressing the truth (Rom. 1:18), we "did not honor him as God or give thanks to him" (Rom. 1:21). This dishonoring of God is sin. Sin affects logic.

Platonic Ideas

The interlocking of form and meaning becomes more important because there is a philosophical tradition, namely, the Platonic tradition, which desires to purify concepts by separating the idea (the meaning, the content) from its embodiment in language. Plato counseled aspiring philosophers to seek to know the *idea* of the good, the beautiful, and the just. The idea was thought to be in its essence a transcendent idea, independent of any particular language—also independent of God. It was an impersonal idea. And so Plato's vision tacitly assumed an impersonalist universe.

Plato toyed with the concept of a demiurge, a god-like being who made individual things by following the pattern of the idea. For example, the demiurge may have made individual horses by copying the general pattern, the idea of a horse. But the pattern itself was superior to the demiurge. Plato's demiurge is not the God of the Bible, but an inferior substitute. If we are to speak plainly, the demiurge is a counterfeit. Plato tacitly rejected the absoluteness that the Bible ascribes to the true God when he made the ideas impersonal and superior to his demiurge.

Plato produced other difficulties. Plato thought that, to grasp pure ideas with the greater purity, the philosopher has to be free from the body, which drags the soul down into ignorance of the true nature of things. Plato despised the body; he despised matter. Thereby, he also tacitly despised the particular. Without having heard the New Testament gospel, he rejected in principle the incarnation. Though Plato along with many other brilliant people had insights into the truth by virtue of common grace, his ideas cannot safely be combined or synthesized with Christian teaching—despite repeated attempts to do so over the centuries.[3]

In particular, I suggest that we do well to be suspicious of Plato's ideal of pure ideas, disembodied ideas, that is, general concepts that do not need particulars and have no intrinsic entanglement with particulars. Plato's idea of the good is the principal example. In Plato's idealization, the ideas have meaning but no form—no specific realization in grammar, in sound, and in writing in any language. If we think about the ideas, the ideas are still supposed to be independent of the particular representations that we have of them in our minds and our brains. This striving for pure generality without particularity is in tension both with the intertwining of unity and diversity that we examined in chapter 18 and with the intertwining of form and meaning in language. It is analogous to a denial of the incarnation.[4]

Aristotle differed from Plato in that he thought of Plato's ideas not as ideas merely "in the sky" (the world of "Forms" or ideas) but as ideas embodied in the particular instances: the idea of horse is embodied in particular horses, the idea of the good is embodied in particular examples of goodness, and so on. In a way, this association with the particulars is an

---

[3] John Frame says, "Combining the Christian perspective with the Greek is not advisable. We can learn today from the questions the Greeks asked, from their failures, from the insights they express in matters of detail. But we should rigorously avoid the notion of rational autonomy and the form-matter scheme as a comprehensive worldview" (John M. Frame, "Greeks Bearing Gifts," in *Understanding the Flow of Western Thought*, ed. W. Andrew Hoffecker [Phillipsburg, NJ: Presbyterian & Reformed, 2007], 33).

   Plato, see ibid., 18–23. See also Cornelius Van Til, *A Survey of Christian Epistemology*, volume 2 of the series *In Defense of Biblical Christianity* (n.l.: den Dulk Christian Foundation, 1969), 24–43.

[4] See also Poythress, *In the Beginning Was the Word*, appendix D; and Poythress, "Reforming Ontology and Logic in the Light of the Trinity: An Application of Van Til's Idea of Analogy," *Westminster Theological Journal* 57/1 (1995), reprinted in appendix F5.

improvement. But within logic, the ideal is still to work with the general ideas. Their embodiment is only a means, a starting point from which we travel in order to grasp the idea in its purity. So the goal of a pure idea, independent of language, remains in place.

This ideal of having a pure, precise concept, as we have indicated, is at odds with the character of God as Creator and God as the Trinitarian origin for unity and diversity. This ideal has corrupted the history of Western thought, including thinking about logic.

For Further Reflection

1. Illustrate the involvement of the Father, the Son, and the Holy Spirit in God's providential government in Psalm 104:30 and 147:15.
2. What are the difficulties with the ideal of a pure idea, pure meaning without form?
3. In Plato's thought, how was the ideal of a pure idea entangled with non-Christian assumptions about the nature of reality?

Chapter 21

Context for Meaning

We should also notice the influence of context on verbal meaning. In natural language, meaning is influenced by context. Syllogistic reasoning, by contrast, invites us to confine our attention to idealized propositions that are seemingly independent of context. In fact, in the context of discussions in logic, the word *proposition* is often used to describe the content of a declaration, with the assumption that the content has been made independent of a larger context of verbal discourse, and with the additional assumption that we are focusing on a content independent of the particular human language in which it is expressed.

Let us first consider ordinary language. The context for communication in language includes a context of other things being said, and the context of a human situation. Sometimes a whole utterance consists of only one word ("What?") or one sentence. But people can also produce paragraphs, essays, and whole books. Any one sentence in a book is qualified by what comes before and after. The significance of a speech depends on who says it and why.

Examples of Contextual Influence

For example, consider one sentence taken out of the Bible: "And when he saw their faith, he said, 'Man, your sins are forgiven you'" (Luke 5:20). We have to derive from the context of the passage and the whole book of Luke extra information about what is going on. Who is "he"? Who is being referred to in the expression "their faith"? Who is the man whose sins are forgiven? When we look at the context, we also see that the pronouncement of forgiveness is linked with the miraculous healing of a paralyzed man, so that the healing confirms Jesus's authority to forgive sins. In the whole Gospel of Luke, in which this verse appears, the act of healing and the act of forgiveness are both linked to the theme of fulfillment. The Old Testament had promised a coming day of climactic salvation that would accomplish both healing and forgiveness. Thus, the one sentence in Luke needs interpretation by a rich interaction with the context of the rest of the Bible.

In addition, meaning can be qualified by the *situation* in which an utterance is produced. A smile may be an indication that a particular statement is meant humorously or ironically. A "tail" in the context of a discussion of vertebrates means the tail of an animal, while a "tail" in the context of aeronautics means the tail of an airplane.

Even within a single narrower area we can see differences due to context. The tail of a cat is different from the tail of a horse. When we watch the behavior of a domestic cat, the tail of a cat sometimes seems to have a mind of its own. The cat chases its tail, or plays with it, as if not knowing that the tail is part of its own body. The tail can have complex behavior because it has its own bones and musculature. Or consider monkeys. Some monkeys have prehensile tails, which they use to grab things. The tail becomes like a fifth limb.

A horse's tail, by contrast, is made of hair—no bones. It is a different *kind* of tail from a cat, which in turn is a different kind of tail from a monkey. We can even ask whether it is very helpful to group together a horse's tail and a cat's tail under a single word *tail*, because the resemblances are superficial and the differences are notable. Some other language might have two different words for these two different kinds of tail. So the meaning of the word *tail* is colored by whether the context indicates that it is a horse's tail, a cat's tail, or a monkey's tail. Or consider the tail of a boxer (a variety of dog), which is not much of a tail at all, but little more than a stub. Context influences meaning.

Context and Syllogisms

Syllogisms function best if context can be ignored. The idea of a "proposition" often connotes a statement that needs no context for its interpretation. Typically, it contains words like *Socrates* with a definite referent, rather than words like *he* and *their* whose referent has to be determined from context. It contains a timeless statement, like "Socrates is a man" (not "was a man," that is, when he was alive), rather than tensed statements like "Socrates went to the forum yesterday." A "proposition," ideally, contains all its meaning.

But such a conception is an idealization in comparison with natural language. To come close to the idealization, we would have to pack extra meaning into a sentence that we would afterwards place in isolation from contexts. The extra meaning has to be added in order to include information that normally comes from context. We would replace any pronouns with unambiguous descriptions. We would also have to give up the opportunity to introduce nuances in meaning through the multitude of interactions in paragraphs and in human situations. Even in the process of packing in extra meaning and giving up nuances, we would be exercising human intentions. And these intentions, to be effective, would have to be understood by other human beings who examine what we are saying. Thus *some* context of meaning is always there, even if it is the rather special context of trying to eliminate direct contextual influence on meaning.

When we have gone this far, we still have to deal with other aspects of context, like the difference between the tail of a cat and the tail of a horse. If we form a syllogism in which we talk about "tails" in general, we have to inspect whether the working of the syllogism might be interfered with by the difference between the two kinds of tails.

The attempt to eliminate context can be motivated by the desire to have specialized language that is more precise in one dimension. There are benefits to precision.[1] But the desire also has *religious* motivations, behind which may lie once again the desire for autonomy. To be dependent on context is one aspect of our finiteness.

Suppose we focus on one item, let us say a single sentence within a syllogism. We simultaneously leave in the background a whole host of other items, which lie as it were in the periphery of consciousness. We do not attend simultaneously to everything. Only God is capable of exhaustive knowledge. But the desire for autonomy can push us to wish to be like God. And since we cannot directly be God by knowing everything, we can at least try to know one thing in a way that is uninfluenced by what we do not know, and uninfluenced by context.

God himself has a context in himself. The three persons of the Trinity act in the context of the actions and the knowledge of the other persons. So context is built into divine knowledge and divine action. By God's design, it is also reflected in what God has made. The desire to eliminate context is therefore suspect. And the necessity of eliminating context for the sake of "pure" form in a syllogism is also suspect.

---

[1] Shawn Hedman is matter-of-fact: "This demonstrates the fundamental tradeoff in using logics [formal logical systems] as opposed to natural languages: to gain precision we necessarily sacrifice expressive power" (Hedman, *A First Course in Logic: An Introduction to Model Theory, Proof Theory, Computability, and Complexity* [Oxford: Oxford University Press, 2004], xiii).

For Further Reflection

1. Discuss the influence of context on the interpretation of Luke 4:10–11 and 4:22.
2. What advantages or disadvantages may there be in trying to pack meaning directly into a single sentence rather than relying on context?
3. In what way are "propositions" within the context of a syllogism purified from contexts?

Chapter 22

Persons and Logic

We now look at another dimension in syllogistic reasoning, namely, the involvement of persons. Persons and their intentions are one aspect of the context in which logic operates.

For logic to be purely *formal*, it should be independent of persons. And indeed there is a *kind* of independence. As we observed earlier, different people and different cultures can recognize valid reasoning when they see it. Validity holds no matter which person is inspecting a syllogism or thinking it through. Any one human person can be eliminated without affecting the validity.

But God as divine personal absolute cannot be eliminated. The harmony between the judgments of two different human persons rests ultimately on the fact that both are created in the image of God, and both reflect the divine harmony among the persons of the Trinity. It is important to maintain this personal character of logic in order to have a basis for harmonizing logic and love.

Persons in Syllogisms

We can return to our old example of reasoning about Socrates and his mortality. In practice, such reasoning is significant to us as human beings because from time to time some human person is thinking through this reasoning. And for this example with Socrates to be effective, it has to be communicated. The discussion of logic and the communication of logical principles to the next generation involves communication between persons. A speaker speaks a discourse to an audience. The speaker is a person; the audience is composed of persons. The discourse is not itself a person, but it is personal. It makes sense and has meaning because persons are involved in its production and reception.

If we think about it, the involvement of persons provides another instance of unity and diversity or one and many. There is commonality in the reasoning about Socrates, as is represented by the fact that we can use a fixed sequence of words in English to express it. This sequence of words can be shared in principle among all those who know English. This commonality is an instance of *unity*. The unity is shared among a *diversity* of speakers of English. Each brings his own coloring to the language—some people know more about the historical Socrates than others.

If we are right in maintaining that unity and diversity interlock (chapter 18), they also interlock in the unity of a principle and the diversity of people thinking about the principle. Thus the unity is not in fact totally independent of the diversity. It is not isolatable. People cannot be cut out of our thinking about logic.

Interlocking Meaning

We can arrive at the same result from a different starting point. Suppose that Abigail is talking to Carol about the syllogism concerning Socrates. Abigail as a speaker has intentions. Her intentions are expressed in the discourse, at whose heart is a syllogism. Carol as listener receives an impression of the point of the discourse. Here we have three foci for meaning, namely, a focus on the speaker, on the discourse, and on the listener. The meaning of Abigail as speaker is the speaker-meaning or intention. The meaning of the discourse is what it expresses within the constraints of English. The meaning for Carol is the impression that she receives.

If the communication is successful, the three meanings harmonize. But they do not completely collapse into one; each is colored by the persons involved. (In the case of the meaning of the discourse, the persons would be all native speakers of English.) We can of course *stipulate* a special meaning for the word *meaning*, and say that it stands for only what is *common* to all three points of view. But when we do this, we rely on the interlocking of unity (the commonality) and diversity (the distinct viewpoints of different persons). The commonality does not dissolve the diversity.[1]

Thus the persons, the persons of speakers and listeners, cannot be dissolved out of meanings. And that principle includes the meanings involved in logic. It is people like Abigail and Carol who engage in syllogistic reasoning. If we rebel against God, we will be tempted to try to become a god, and to strive for exhaustive understanding of a syllogism. We want utterly to dominate the reasoning. To do so, we have to eliminate the "messiness"

---

[1] For further discussion of this point in the context of language, see Vern S. Poythress, *In the Beginning Was the Word: Language—A God-Centered Approach* (Wheaton, IL: Crossway, 2009), chapters 2, 20.

and multidimensional complexities of human persons with their desires and fears and bodily weaknesses. We postulate an ideal meaning of the discourse. In our mind we try to make the discourse—let us say the syllogism about Socrates—completely independent of any speaker or listener. We picture it as just "there," perhaps in Plato's abstract world of pure ideas. But Plato's world becomes in practice inaccessible to real human beings. Without words and connections with ordinary life, a pure abstraction is also a pure emptiness.[2] Logic cannot be separated from persons, including preeminently the personality of God.

Time and Logic

We can see another aspect of the personal involvement with logic by focusing on time. Logical principles are supposed to hold independent of time. And there is truth in that perception, because logic is grounded in God, who is independent of time and exists eternally. But it is also true that God acts in time. And he created human people who act in time. God has purposes that he works out in time. And human actors have their own purposes. When we think or communicate about logic, we think and act and communicate as *purposeful* actors. Logic in our lives is bound up with purposes.

Even the reasoning in a syllogism has temporal aspects to it. We move from the claim that "All men are mortal" to the claim that "Socrates is a man." And then we may say, "Therefore, Socrates is mortal." The word *therefore* implies a movement, not in space, but in thought. We travel from the premises to the conclusion. And the premises are put forward in the way that they are *on purpose*. We bring them together because we have plans—we have a purpose. Our plan is to draw a conclusion. And then, acting in time, we *do* draw the conclusion. And the word *therefore*, by connecting premises and conclusion, indicates at least tacitly that there are purposes and there is a movement in time from premise to conclusion.

God, we say, is above time. But his logic is reflected in the temporal sphere when we as temporal creatures move from premises, which we grasp at an earlier time, to a conclusion, which we contemplate at a later time. God, who is above time, knows all about time. In his infinity he knows not only the foundations of logic, which are found in his own self-consistency and inner harmony, but he also knows all the ways in which those founda-

---

[2] See John Frame, "Greeks Bearing Gifts," in *Revolutions in Worldview: Understanding the Flow of Western Thought*, ed. W. Andrew Hoffecker (Phillipsburg, NJ: Presbyterian & Reformed, 2007), 21, 32.

tions can be worked out in time by personal creatures who reason in time. God knows every point of view, including the point of view and experience in time that we have as creatures.

> You [God] know when I *sit down* and when I *rise up*;
>   you discern *my thoughts* from afar. (Ps. 139:2)

God discerns "my thoughts." He is able to discern them in their temporal order. He is not himself *subject* to the limitations of temporal order that a creature possesses in his creatureliness. But he knows these limitations and he knows this temporal order completely. In that knowledge, he knows also all the temporal successions in logical reasoning that take place among human persons. Their validation, including the validation of their temporal aspects, comes from him.

The basic principles of logic remain the same over time. But those principles also interact with and interlock with time, because we as temporal persons work them out in thought and in language in time and in the rich phenomena of temporal succession. Once again the one and the many belong together. The "one" is the general principle, let us say the principle of the validity of the syllogism about Socrates. The "many" consists in the many concrete experiences of people walking through this syllogism in their temporal experience. The one summarizes the many and is expressed in the many, rather than being alien from the many. Thus time cannot be cut out of logic.

We might qualify that idea. Time cannot be cut out of human use of logic. But if logic is founded in God, can we say that time can still be cut out of divine logic? God is above time, but as Creator he is also the foundation for time. His logic contains within it the basis for temporal reasoning.

We cannot comprehend how this is so. But we may perhaps see at least a sliver of the infinite truth if we contemplate an eternal act of God, such as God's act in the fact that God the Father begets God the Son. The Father was active when the Son became incarnate through the virgin Mary: "the power of the Most High will overshadow you" (Luke 1:35). This act of God in time is consistent with who God always is. It is consistent with the eternal relations between the Father and the Son. So we speak of eternal begetting to express the fact that the eternal relations are expressed in time when the incarnation comes about.

Similarly, the Father always loves the Son. Love is an eternal act. The

Father acts in time when he loves the Son day by day through the time when the Son lives on earth in his incarnate state. The eternal love is the foundation for the love expressed in time. The eternal begetting is the foundation for the conception of Jesus in Mary's womb. The eternal imaging relation between the Father and the Son (Col. 1:15; Heb. 1:3) is the foundation for the fact that now, in time, we can see the Father in the Son (John 14:9). The eternal speaking of the Father in the Word is the foundation for his speaking in time, when he creates light, and when he speaks to us in the Bible.

Likewise, God's eternal self-consistency, which is expressed in the Father's love for the Son, is manifested in time in the consistency of logic as we experience it temporally. God ordains that this logical reasoning of ours goes forward in time, and that its going forward matches the eternal logic within God. We can say this also in terms of speech. God speaks the Word eternally, and this Word is his eternal logic. God speaks to create the universe and sustain it. His speaking carries with it its logical consistencies in conformity with his original consistency in his eternal Word. His speaking governs the world not only in its particular events but in its logical structures. His speaking therefore specifies each act of human reasoning that proceeds from premises to conclusion.[3] His speech produces the temporal order in human reasoning, in conformity with the eternal order in divine reasoning in his self-knowledge. God controls through his speech the human process leading to conclusions that we reach at a point in time later than our consideration of the premises. This too is logical. Logic in this way is *in time*.

For Further Reflection

1. In what way can we see a temporal succession in human reasoning? In a syllogism?
2. In what way does this temporal succession have its foundation in God?
3. How does sleep and health affect human reasoning?
4. How do human attitudes toward rationality influence receptivity to argument?
5. Use an example of informal reasoning and communication, such as Acts 13:16–49, to illustrate the work of logic in time.

---

[3] Here I presuppose a strong view of God's sovereign control over details as well as general principles with respect to the world; and I presuppose the compatibility between his control and human ethical responsibility. For a defense of these views, see, e.g., Poythress, *In the Beginning Was the Word*, chapters 3–6; John M. Frame, *The Doctrine of God* (Phillipsburg, NJ: Presbyterian & Reformed, 2002), 21–182.

Chapter 23

Logic and Religious Antithesis

What effects does religious commitment have on logic?

The Religious Commitments of Persons

People act according to their own motivations when they study logic as well as when they use it. And people are not religiously neutral. God made us for communion with himself. If we rebel against him, we erect substitute gods. And truth is corrupted by the distortions of the substitute.

We see the corruption most directly when we consider the question of whether the rules of logic are personal or impersonal. They are in fact personal; they are the expression of the language of God and the self-consistency of God, which is in harmony with the personal love of the Father for the Son and the Son for the Father, through the Holy Spirit. When we convert this personal texture of consistency into an impersonal abstraction, we corrupt the truth.

The Ideal of Pure Oneness, without Diversity

Another area of corruption lies in the ideal of achieving pure unity without diversity in the categories that we use in logic. We should return for a moment to the point made earlier about the relation between one and many. Consider a particular case, namely, the relation between the generality of being "human" and the particular cases of particular human beings. The one is "humanness." The many are particular humans, Socrates and Plato and Aristotle—as well as you and me. In practice, our knowledge of the one, of what it means to be human, is bound up with the knowledge of particular human beings, including self-knowledge. And all this knowledge is also bound up with knowledge of God, in whose image we are made.

We have said, "in practice." Within finite human experience, and within human use of ordinary language, the one and the many belong together. But if Christian theology is right about the Trinitarian character of God, and the dependence of human thought on divine thought, the expression "in practice" can be extended to "in theory" as well. God's knowledge is also "contextualized" knowledge, that is, his knowledge exists in the *context* of the interaction and mutual indwelling of the persons of the Trinity.

In natural language, then, the descriptive term *human* has meaning in interaction with particular human beings like Socrates and ourselves. We may say, "Socrates is human" and "Plato is human." And in each sentence, the word *human* is subtly colored by its association with a particular example or instantiation of the classification *human*. When we consider the assertion "Socrates is human," Socrates is our prime example of humanity. We are invited to think of what it means to be human with Socrates as our prime example. What might come to mind? To be human means to think, to exercise reason. To be human means entering into dialogs and discussions. To be human includes not knowing everything, and includes the opportunity, if one is inclined as Socrates was inclined, to admit one's ignorance on certain subjects.

Instantiation and classification interpenetrate, rather than being purely isolated. The ultimate basis for this interpretation lies in the plan of God to create human persons in analogy with divine persons. So we also take into account the persons of the Trinity—the Father, the Son, and the Holy Spirit—who exist not only as distinct persons but as persons in relationship. Likewise, the word "human" has contrast, variation, and distribution.

In contrast to this complexity, logical analysis often wants to have an ideal, context-free symbol, the word *human*, which is often regarded as having purely identical meaning no matter to which item it applies. This ideal wants unity without any diversity in the label *human*. If we relate this ideal to the question of God, an ideal of unity without diversity is *unitarian*. Unitarianism is the belief that there is one God (unity), but *not* a Trinitarian God. God is one, but not three persons. This ideal is innately untrue to reality, but true to the desires for human autonomy. In other words, there is an underlying religious motivation.

Christian Evaluation

How should a Christian react? With concern, certainly. But should we conclude that human reflections on logic are wholly the work of the devil? Of course not. Human logic, as we have said, reflects divine logic. And this reflection remains, at least in some ways, even when the religious motivations of human beings and their corrupt concept of God lead to distortions. In addition, we know that God is good to those who do not deserve it. He gives "common grace." Unbelievers as well as believers receive insights about the world, including the world of logic.

We must simply recognize that an ideal based on pure unity captures only one dimension from natural language, and reflects only one dimension from God's language. The ideal has a context, namely, the context of simplification. Within this context, we can enjoy regularities, and we know that these regularities reflect the regularities of God's self-consistency and his plan for the world.

At the same time, we must be circumspect. People who are overattracted by the insights of the unbelieving world may swallow bits of unbelieving presuppositions and distortions along with the attractive bits of truth. Conversely, people who are keenly aware of the dangers of sin may reject all insights out of the non-Christian world, for fear of swallowing sinful poison. Both sides have something to say for themselves, but both sides are incomplete and miss something. I am writing this book so that we may think carefully about human achievements in the area of logic. And in so thinking, we may begin to sort through the difference between good and bad, truth and distortion, common grace and effects of sinful desires for autonomy.

Readers may refer to appendices F1–5 for further reflections on the relation of logic to philosophy and its history.

For Further Reflection

1. Why do we need a specifically Christian evaluation of human motives in logic?
2. How can human knowledge of logic include sinful corruption?
3. What sinful motivations can influence human attitudes toward logic?
4. In what ways do these motives make a difference in the actual working out of arguments?

Chapter 24

Theistic Proofs

We now have traveled far enough in our exploration of logic that we may begin to analyze theistic proofs. The traditional theistic proofs are a handful of arguments for the existence of God that have been discussed for centuries. There are several, the most prominent being the *ontological argument*, which takes its start from the nature of perfect being; the *cosmological argument*, which is based on causes; and the *teleological argument*, which is based on evidence for design.

Each of these arguments has appeared in various forms. Much has been said about them, pro and con. We cannot cover all the history or all the approaches without going outside the scope of the present book. But we have come to understand something about logic. And so we may venture, at least tentatively, to explore what may be the implications of our approach when dealing with theistic proofs.

Presupposing God

Logic, we have claimed, depends on God and manifests God. It is one aspect of the display of the glory of God and the character of God. As Romans 1:18–25 indicates, the display of God's character leaves human beings "without excuse" (v. 20). Not only God's existence but his character is "plain to them" (v. 19), and "they knew God" (v. 21). This knowledge is available from the whole of creation. Logic is one source. The obstacle is that human beings in rebellion suppress this clear knowledge (v. 18).

We can use arguments to present to human beings both the testimony to God in creation and the testimony about the way of salvation opened by God through Christ. As we have seen, the apostles present such arguments. The arguments take place against the background of the knowledge of God that people already have, and which they suppress in their guilt.

Theistic proofs can be added to all these other kinds of argument. They may be used to try to awaken people to the reality of the God that they already know, even in their unbelief. But there is something peculiar about the proofs, because they do not come in a vacuum. They come against a background of who human beings are—created in the image of God and yet rebellious against their Creator. And they come against the background of what logic itself is—the revelation of the Logos of God.

So it should not be supposed that the unbelievers who listen to the proofs are innocent or entirely ignorant of God to begin with. And it should not be supposed that anyone will be convinced as he ought to be unless he experiences a supernatural work of the Holy Spirit, which comes in connection with the application of the work of Christ. So theistic proofs ideally go together with the message of the gospel of Christ, which calls people out of darkness into forgiveness and reconciliation with God. Through the gospel rebellious resistance to the clear reality of God is healed, and the guilt is cleansed by the blood of Christ. Mere argument, as such, does not heal sinners.

Misunderstanding of Argument

Second, people in rebellion will regularly misunderstand theistic proofs for various reasons. One reason is that there is a non-Christian as well as a Christian view of logic. Non-Christians like to think that logic is just there, as an impersonal something, rather than being a manifestation of the personal presence of God. They may suppress the reality of logic itself even as they are engaged in reasoning about God. How might this happen? There are many forms of unbelief. But we will focus on difficulties associated with people's conception of logic.

The Argument from Design

For the sake of concreteness, let us consider a simple summary form of the teleological argument, that is, the argument from design. Here it is in the form of a syllogism:

> Everything designed has a designer.
> The universe is designed.
> Therefore, the universe has a designer.

How do we evaluate this syllogism?

We consider the syllogism against the background of what we have said about the limitations of syllogistic reasoning. For one thing, arguments are used among persons. And the persons have already taken an attitude toward God. The effect of an argument may be that a resistant person denies one of the premises rather than accepts the conclusion. The agnostic or atheist may simply deny that the universe is designed. So arguments, even good arguments, do not always persuade people.

Second, we can see a difficulty because the words "designed" and "designer" may be used in more than one way. Is there equivocation in the words? The word "designer" can apply to human designers who design watches, automobiles, and buildings. It can also apply to God as the divine designer. Are God and man "designers" in the same sense?

As noted in chapter 11, Dorothy Sayers vigorously uses the analogy between God and a human creator when discussing how creative artistry shows analogies to the Trinitarian character of God. But she is well aware that God is unique in his Trinitarian character. Human creators are subcreators, and they reflect the Trinity without being identical to God.

We can arrive at the same conclusion if we reflect on what we have said about logic operating on two levels, the level of the Creator and the level of the creature. If we insist, erroneously, that there is only one level, we will arrive at a kind of attitude where we want to insist on bringing the Creator down to the level of the creature. In a non-Christian view of immanence, God is indistinguishable from his creation. A syllogism operating with this kind of logic concludes at best that God is a finite designer, on the same level as a human designer.

Non-Christian Assumptions Creeping In

Syllogisms within an Aristotelian conception have other difficulties that show up their underlying non-Christian assumptions. To operate impersonally and in a purely formal manner, syllogisms have to have (1) no use of analogical structure, and so be independent from God to whom our thoughts are analogous (chapter 17); (2) universals independent of particulars (unity without diversity, chapter 18); (3) perfectly precise categories (chapter 19); (4) meaning independent of all form (chapter 20); (5) decontextualized propositions, whose meaning is wholly self-contained (chapter 21); (6) impersonal and nontemporal propositions, independent of all persons who invoke them and of the constraints of time (chapter 22).

A non-Christian is tempted to start the whole process of syllogistic reasoning with a cluster of assumptions about logic. And these assumptions already tacitly deny the existence of the God of the Bible. Any so-called "designer" who can fit *within* the confines of these assumptions must be a "designer" tailored to the requirements of non-Christian assumptions about the "right" of human beings to reason as if they were completely *autonomous*. Reasoning itself must be independent from God. In particular, logic itself cannot be allowed to depend on God and to testify to God, because it would make the non-Christian give up his desire for autonomy *at the beginning* of the argument. Or better, he would have to give up before the actual beginning, at the point when he is negotiating the ground rules for argumentation.

The ground rules for argument are the rules ordained by God, which testify unambiguously to his eternal power and deity. They already demonstrate not only the existence of God but his character, and they do so before any particular argument can be mounted.[1]

The Value of Arguing for Design

If non-Christian assumptions can creep into logical reasoning, does that make worthless all arguments from design? Human beings still live in God's world. The things that God has made testify to his "eternal power and divine nature" according to Romans 1:20. If they testify to his "divine nature," we may conclude that they also testify to his wisdom. Proverbs 8:22–31 shows awareness that the mountains, the skies, the fountains, and the sea show God's marvelous wisdom:

> The LORD possessed me [wisdom (here personified)] at the beginning
>   of his work,
>   the first of his acts of old.
> Ages ago I was set up,
>   at the first, before the beginning of the earth.
> When there were no depths I was brought forth,
>   when there were no springs abounding with water.
> Before the mountains had been shaped,
>   before the hills, I was brought forth,
> before he had made the earth with its fields,
>   or the first of the dust of the world.
> When he established the heavens, I was there;
>   when he drew a circle on the face of the deep,
> when he made firm the skies above,

[1] "Arguing about God's existence, I hold, is like arguing about air. You may affirm that air exists, and I that it does not. But as we debate the point, we are both breathing air all the time. Or to use another illustration, God is like the emplacement on which must stand the very guns that are supposed to shoot Him out of existence" (Cornelius Van Til, *Why I Believe in God* [Philadelphia: Commission on Christian Education, Orthodox Presbyterian Church, n.d.], 3).

when he established the fountains of the deep,
when he assigned to the sea its limit,
    so that the waters might not transgress his command,
when he marked out the foundations of the earth,
    then I was beside him, like a master workman,
and I was daily his delight,
    rejoicing before him always,
rejoicing in his inhabited world
    and delighting in the children of man.

What God has created shows design. The argument from design can be viewed as a way of drawing explicit attention to this testimony. The universe is designed, and testifies to its designer. The argument from design is sound when we understand it as a summary of the character of the world as explained in the Bible. But it is not valid *merely* by virtue of "form." It is sound by virtue of pointing to content, the content of what is called "general revelation," which is the revelation of the character of God through what he has made. The argument might better be called "the argument *for* design" rather than "the argument *from* design," because accepting the reality of God leads human beings to acknowledge design, but as long as human beings are in rebellion they suppress the character of the designs.

It should also be clear, from what we have said in previous chapters, that God's design is visible in the very character of logic and the workings of logic. Every human being who uses logic is like the daughter who sits on her father's lap in order to slap his face. There is something guilty about a person starting into an argument about God, and therefore depending on him and knowing him, and yet hoping that in the argument he will be able to continue not to repent and not to ask mercy, but rather to slap God in the face. Perhaps one person's way of slapping God in the face is by tacitly or overtly claiming to use logic as a "thing" independent of God and his existence.

The Cosmological Argument

We may now briefly consider the cosmological argument. The cosmological argument is an argument that proceeds from causes back to the first cause. Here is one form of the argument:

Everything that has a beginning has a cause.
The universe has a beginning.

Therefore, the universe has a cause.

We are supposed to see that the "cause" of the universe is God, because the cause must precede the universe, and must be adequate to bring about the entire universe.

We may see in this syllogism difficulties similar to the difficulties we found in the argument from design. What about the word *cause*? Does it have the same sense throughout the syllogism? In the first premise, the word *cause* seems to have a focus on immanent causes within the world, that is, secondary causes. Water vapor in the air is a cause for water condensed into droplets in clouds, and the droplets in clouds are a cause of rain, and rain is a cause for rivers. These are causes within the world. If the universe as a whole has a "cause" on the same level, it is a finite, secondary cause. We arrive at a finite god, rather than the true God.

In contrast to this attempt to reason with a one-level logic, we can acknowledge that the word *cause* has analogy built into it. God is *not* one more cause like a secondary cause, but he does bring things into being and he does act to produce results. He is a cause by analogy with the forms of secondary causation within the world. Better, he is the archetype, and secondary causes are ordained by him to display his glory through analogy.

Syllogisms, to be purely formal, cannot allow analogy. If we hold rigorously to this requirement, we end up either with a finite first cause or with a syllogism that is invalid because of equivocation. As with the argument from design, so here: a non-Christian conception of logic wants purely formal syllogisms with purely univocal (nonanalogical) meanings. This opening conception already excludes God at the outset, by disallowing the analogical structure inherent in the Creator-creature distinction. Any such argument will obviously fail completely to establish, in a genuinely sound fashion, the existence of God.

The Value of Arguing for God as a Cause

But the cosmological argument can also be viewed from a Christian point of view, according to which logic is a reflection of the Logos of God. In this understanding of logic, analogy has a substantive, positive role. The argument for the first cause is sound, not as a purely *formal* argument but as a substantive argument that summarizes the way in which creatures testify to God as their Creator, their first cause. He is the cause of each particular creature, and the cause of the world as a whole. "In the beginning, God created the heavens and the earth" (Gen. 1:1). He is the cause who by his decrees ordains each causal relation between one billiard ball and another, or the causal relation between a human person's plans and his execution of the plans. We must only add that we use the word *cause* analogically. God is not "a cause" on the same level as secondary causes.

In fact, the cosmological argument can be viewed as a special instance of the argument from design. God's design of the world is comprehensive. He designed everything. One aspect of his design is the system of secondary causes:

> And God said, "Let the earth sprout vegetation, plants yielding seed, and fruit trees . . . (Gen. 1:11)

God specified that the earth would sprout vegetation (the earth being one cause), and that plants would yield seed (the plants being a cause for the seed). Causes are designed. They point to God the Designer who designed them, that is, who caused them.

The Ontological Argument

The ontological argument is an argument based on the conception of a perfect being or a greatest being.[2] It was first set forth by Anselm of Canterbury, but not in precise syllogistic form. In one simple form, it runs as follows:

> Anything that can be conceived not to exist is not the greatest being.
> Therefore the greatest being cannot be conceived not to exist.
> Therefore the greatest being necessarily exists.

How do we evaluate this argument?

To work, the argument has to have an additional assumption, namely, that we can conceive of something that is the greatest being. Otherwise, we might confront a situation where several beings are equally great, or where there is a whole sequence of beings, each of which is greater than the last, but with no one being greater than them all.

If we can solve these issues, we still confront issues similar to those with the other theistic proofs. Do we have here an analogy and an equivocation,

---

[2]See Graham Oppy, "Ontological Arguments," *Stanford Encyclopedia of Philosophy (Fall 2011 Edition)*, ed. Edward N. Zalta, http://plato.stanford.edu/archives/fall2011/entries/ontological-arguments/, accessed August 24, 2012.

with the word *being*? The word *being* can refer either to created beings or to the Creator. Apples and horses are created beings, and we can conceive that they might not exist. On the other hand, the expression *the greatest being* is intended to refer to God the Creator. A relationship between the two levels of being is implicit in the first line of the argument, where it talks about "anything that can be conceived not to exist" and brings this kind of "being" into relation to "the greatest being."

If formal argument requires univocal terms, the word *being* is in danger of requiring us to bring God down to the level of creatures. If there is only one level of being, God is the greatest being among "beings," but he remains restricted by our conception of uniform "being." He is not truly infinite.

On the other hand, if we work with a Christian conception of logic, we allow for two levels of being, the Creator and the creature. And we acknowledge analogies between them. So then the argument can be an argument that draws attention to ways in which God manifests his glory in the things that he has made, while remaining distinct from and superior to them.

Human Thought and Standards

We can see a second difficulty in the transition between the second and third lines in the argument. The second line is about what we can conceive. The third line is about what exists—about reality. In a non-Christian conception of logic, human reasoning can *legislate* for reality. Reality must conform to the basic structures of human thought. The result is that human conceptions of logic function as an ultimate standard. This ultimate standard represents a non-Christian concept of immanence (corner #4 in Frame's square). God must exist because our minds postulate him to exist. God becomes dependent on man.

On the other hand, we can reinterpret the same argument on the basis of Christian assumptions about logic. On Christian assumptions, God is the standard for logic, but his wisdom and self-consistency are still reflected in human minds. We are unable to think away the *concept* of the greatest being—though atheists would say that they do not think that this concept refers to anything that actually exists. The presence of this particular concept is one way in which God continues to be present and to reveal himself to us, even within the structure of our minds. Rightly understood, the presence of the concept testifies to the presence of the reality—namely, God himself. Atheists do not agree with the conclusion that God exists because they have suppressed the revelation of God that is present in their minds. So the argument is sound, if it operates on Christian assumptions.

Non-Christians might quarrel with the argument in another way. They might dispute the truthfulness of the assumption that "anything that can be conceived not to exist is not the greatest being." Romans 1:18–25 indicates that, in fact, non-Christians cannot completely think God away. They cannot completely get him out of their minds. They know God (Rom. 1:21). But they suppress that knowledge (v. 18). So they may indeed *claim* that they can think away the existence of the greatest being.

They may also quarrel about the nature of "the greatest being." When a Christian uses that expression, he refers to God, the true God who is described in the Bible and whose character is displayed in the creation. But according to Romans 1, unbelievers distort the knowledge of "the greatest being." So what they mean by the expression may have confusions, or they may partly attach the expression to false gods of their own making. We must say clearly that such false gods do not exist, even though an unbeliever may think that they are "the greatest."

If we wish, we can treat the ontological argument as a special form of the argument for design. God designed the human mind in such a way that it cannot successfully think God out of existence. This design reflects the character of God the Designer.

General Evaluation of Theistic Proofs

The theistic proofs have an interest for us because they use logic. But what kind of logic? Because context cannot be completely eliminated (chapter 21), and because persons are always present who participate in the arguments (chapter 22), the proofs operate in a context of assumptions. The assumptions color the nature of the arguments. The arguments are not purely formal, because context cannot be eliminated. Non-Christians and Christians bring different assumptions about the role of context and the character of logic itself. These differences generate subtle and yet sometimes weighty differences in the meaning of the arguments themselves.

Each of the arguments that we have considered ends with a finite god if we start with human autonomy in logic. On the other hand, each of the arguments is sound if we consider it as contextually qualified by the meaning of God's inescapable presence, a presence that he manifests in the created world, in the mind of human beings, and in logic itself.

In addition to the traditional theistic proofs, many other kinds of argument may be of help. The Bible as a whole can be considered as an argument, designed by God to persuade unbelievers and to confirm and strengthen believers (chapter 2). Within the pages of the Bible are further, subordinate arguments. We ourselves may produce arguments based on the life, death, and resurrection of Christ, or based on the fulfillment of prophecies or the evidence of miracles. But all of these arguments occur within the context of assumptions that people make about logic. Argument can be corrupted by the assumption of autonomy.

Responsibility and Guilt

We can see still another difficulty with the theistic proofs if we focus on human responsibility in the reception of these proofs. If we insist on treating the proofs as merely formal in nature, unbelievers can claim that the formalism does not work properly, and use the deficiency as an excuse. Or they can deny the truth of one of the premises and escape in a similar manner. They might then say, "I am excused from believing in God because the arguments are not cogent." In this response they would be evading their guilt. Though one argument may have deficiencies, God's own revelation does not. God has shown himself, according to Romans 1:18–25. Guilt is the result, independent of our judgments as to whether a particular proof "works."

One of the points of Romans 1:18–25 is that human beings are "without excuse" (Rom. 1:20). They are without excuse because the universe shows the hand of its Designer, because the universe points to its Cause, and because the very mind of man cannot evade the reality of God's existence. When unbelievers complain about the deficiencies of theistic proofs, they may easily use these complaints to conceal their lack of excuse.

In addition, theistic proofs presented to a non-Christian may reinforce his desire to evaluate the arguments on the basis of human standards of cogency, and to act as if his standards were ultimate. Non-Christians already have a non-Christian view of logic.

Particularly in modern times, the theistic proofs are often viewed as if they promise to listeners a route for knowing God independent of the Bible. And there is a grain of truth in this idea. The Bible itself, in Romans 1:18–23, indicates that people know God even when they have never read the Bible. But God's way for fallen human beings to recover and to be reconciled to him involves submission to the teaching of Scripture, not another independent effort to establish knowledge by deliberately setting Scripture aside. The setting aside of Scripture as a key resource for knowledge is itself an act of autonomy, in which we want to reason things through for ourselves rather than merely submit to God's voice.[3] So theistic proofs, when viewed apart from God's instruction in Scripture, easily become part of a human context that has already committed itself to the principle of autonomy.

Finally, theistic proofs operate in a human context. Unless we are careful, it may prove to be a context in which people want to assume that logic is a neutral something, not dependent on God and not clearly revealing God. If, as I have argued, logic itself displays the character of God, we hardly "need" theistic proofs, except as a reminder and further pointer to what we already know and rely on before we even start our arguments.

Our analysis of theistic proofs has confirmed what we found in earlier chapters, that the Christian conception of logic differs from a non-Christian conception, and that this difference affects the understanding of and evaluation of cases of syllogistic reasoning as well as arguments of an informal sort. The difference has effects throughout our reasoning, not just for theistic proofs. Western thought needs to be redone.

For Further Reflection

1. What are the strengths and weaknesses of theistic proofs?
2. In what ways do Christians and non-Christians differ in their understanding of theistic proofs?
3. In what respect do the theistic proofs represent valid or invalid argumentation?
4. In what way can theistic proofs actually end up being interpreted in line with a prior presupposition of autonomy?
5. Are the theistic proofs needed? Explain your answer.

---

[3] Of course, we also have to face the issue of whether Scripture is the voice of God or merely human voices. That issue leads to arguments pro and con about the nature of Scripture. See John Murray, "The Attestation of Scripture," in *The Infallible Word: A Symposium by the Members of the Faculty of Westminster Theological Seminary*, 3rd rev. printing (Philadelphia: Presbyterian & Reformed, 1967), 1–54.

Chapter 25

Rethinking Western Thought

Logic, we have said, is a foundation for Western thought. If we transform logic, we should also ask what transformation should ensue for Western thought as a whole.

By common grace, much that is good has arisen in the intellectual life of the West. Common grace has operated in non-Western cultures as well. But sin contaminates human thought, both in the West and elsewhere. The contamination is obvious when a human being uses a brilliant mind to plot a brilliant murder. Or a tyrant may use clever rhetoric and technologically advanced weapons to support his tyranny.

But the contamination may also be subtle, through deeply concealed desires for rebellion against God. Contamination can enter even within the positive contexts of scientific achievements or the exquisite beauties of paintings and poems. Sin cannot easily be uprooted. It takes the redemption of Christ, not autonomously motivated critical rethinking. Christ's redemption touches every aspect of life, not merely intellectual endeavors and not merely logic. We need purification in the heart and in our deeds, not merely in our thoughts. The three interact. But purity in thought remains one of the needs.

The Foundational Corruption

The deepest corruption is the corruption of the heart. We are rebels against God. And rebellion gets expressed in all kinds of ways. It gets expressed unknowingly even in theological expositions, even expositions by sincere Christians. We are not going to get free from such a Western heritage without taking seriously the need for spiritual purification and the full resources for purification that we find only in fellowship with Christ the purifier.

The corruption of the heart takes the form of desire for autonomy. Autonomy expresses itself in many ways. But one way is in an autonomous conception of logic. Logic becomes an impersonal something, which we think we can access independently of God. An impersonalist conception of logic is one of the direct corruptions.

Other Expressions of the Corrupting Effects of Corrupt Logic

But we can also see more indirect effects. For example, consider again the polarity between the *Star Trek* characters Spock and McCoy. In a way, Spock is an embodiment of an impersonalist conception of logic. McCoy is an embodiment of passion. His passion may in some ways be driven by love for humanity, and such love is admirable in a way. But in the *Star Trek* series McCoy's love for humanity remains disconnected from love of God, and from the love that God has shown to us through sending his Son.

Logic in Spock and passion in McCoy produce tension. But the tension is not necessary. Both logic and love originate in God, and in him they are in harmony. If we come to him and have our logic and love purified by fellowship with him through the Spirit of Christ, we begin to move beyond the tension. The tension, in the end, is a fruit of sin, whether directly or indirectly. So one key area for purification lies in the impersonalist conceptions of logic that have been with the Western world since the time of Aristotle.

We can also see a need for purification when we consider the difficulties concerning classification (part I.C). Embedded in Western thought we can see longings for perfectly "pure" categories. Or, to put it differently, we see longings for univocal meanings without any analogies (chapter 17), universals without particulars, unity without diversity (chapter 18), stabilities in categories without flexibilities (chapter 19), meanings without forms (chapter 20), meanings without contexts (chapter 21), propositions without persons (chapter 22), and truth without religious commitment (chapter 23). Plato set before us an ideal for knowledge in which human knowing penetrates to the "bottom" of the world, and that bottom consists in pure "forms" like goodness or justice. Aristotle gave more weight to particulars, and not just universals, but the same tendency remains in Aristotle's logic, because the proper functioning of syllogisms in a purely formal way depends on categories that have an essentially Platonic character. This Platonic ideal poisons not only the ideal for human knowledge, but the ideal for what the world is.

Aristotle thought of the world as composed of substances with essences (for example, being a cat), to which there attach additional qualities in the form of accidents (for example, color).[1] Immanuel Kant undertook to shift the focus from things to what we *think* about things. And in the twentieth century we have seen further shifts in philosophy and in the sciences, from focus on things to focus on relationships and on the dynamics of change. But study of relationships and change can still be captive to the same old ideal of perfectly precise categories. If I am right, this ideal is, at root, a non-Christian ideal, which implicitly rejects the Trinity and pursues human autonomy. We need to root it out.

It is not easy, because rooting out the effects of sin is never easy. The task is difficult because sin gets entangled with what is good. People live in God's world, in God's presence. Even when desire for autonomy is strong, people do not escape God, either in logic or in any other field of endeavor. We ought to admire and appreciate people's work even when we engage in critical sifting.

Immanuel Kant and Effects of the Critique of Theistic Proofs

An additional effect of logic on Western thought has come through Immanuel Kant's philosophy. Kant reflected on the classic theistic proofs and endeavored to show that they did not work. Why not? Kant thought that pure human reason could operate safely only when reflecting on the sphere of sensory phenomena such as science studied (see appendix F1). By contrast, when reason was used for reflecting on the existence of God and the nature of God, it led to antinomies, because it was being used in a sphere beyond its competence and its reach. Kant thought that belief in God could still be motivated on a practical level by concerns for moral standards, but God could not be rationally proved.

In fact, as we have seen from the preceding chapter, reasoning about God relies on the analogical relation between God and man, between Creator and creature. If indeed reason is treated as univocal and purely human, if reason can deal only with univocal terms and not with analogy, it is not adequate for God. Neither is it adequate for anything else, because it is a distortion of the truth (chapter 17). Kant did not see that he was using a corrupted conception of reason, but he was at least partly right: an autonomous conception of reason does not work for reflections about God.

But the legacy of Kant has not led to the repudiation of autonomous reason. It has led instead to the repudiation of knowledge of God. The Kantian

---

[1] See S. Marc Cohen, "Aristotle's Metaphysics," *Stanford Encyclopedia of Philosophy (Spring 2009* Edition*)*, ed. Edward N. Zalta, http://plato.stanford.edu/archives/spr2009/entries/aristotle-metaphysics/, accessed October 11, 2011.

approach, if affirmed, leads to the conclusion that God is inaccessible to purely rational knowledge. Thus, Kantianism offers a form of non-Christian transcendence. And something similar to Kantian thinking has had a widespread influence on Western culture. Nowadays most of the Western intelligentsia think that science is reliable in its own sphere of phenomena, but that religious thoughts are merely subjective. Everyone can have his own ideas, and those ideas may have some moral effects, but no one really knows God. This effective repudiation of knowledge of God includes skepticism about the classic theistic proofs. They become merely pointers to something transcendent, but they are not hard, stable sources for genuine knowledge.

Our own analysis of logic is quite different from a Kantian analysis. God is not only knowable but is clearly known (Rom. 1:19–21). He reveals himself not only in the things that he has made (v. 20) but in the very structure of logic and rationality. The Kantian heritage needs to be replaced.

For Further Reflection

1. What main distorted conceptions about logic need to be transformed?
2. How do distorted conceptions within logic have a broader effect on thought?
3. How should knowledge of common grace affect our attitude toward work produced by non-Christians?
4. What is Kant's critique of the classical theistic proofs? How does Kant's critique have a wider effect?

Part I.D

Aristotelian Syllogisms

Chapter 26

Theistic Foundations
for a Syllogism

Aristotle classified several forms of valid syllogistic reasoning. By common grace, he identified some valid forms of reasoning. But he left undone reflection on how syllogistic reasoning reveals God and reflects the glory of God. So let us consider some of Aristotle's syllogisms in the light of the full revelation of God in the glory of Christ.

Limitations in Syllogistic Form

First, we should recall our discussion in part I.C about the difficulties in trying to make syllogisms purely formal. God's logic is infinite. Human reflection of that logic takes place in the rich context of language and thinking that imitates the language and thinking of God. That which is "formal" cannot be purely separated from content, that is, meaning. Yet it is still useful to consider the syllogisms that Aristotle studied. Even though we must pay attention to content as we consider validity, we may acknowledge that syllogisms express patterns of reasoning that prove to be valid in many cases, and this validity reflects the ultimate soundness of the self-consistency of God, which is also the soundness and faithfulness of God the Father loving the Son.

So our treatment of syllogisms takes place within the context of our understanding of logic and language. We acknowledge our finiteness, our dependence on God, and we commit ourselves to give thanks to him as he deserves. Within that context, we may rejoice in particular jewels of God's glory on which Aristotle focused.

The First Type of Syllogism: Barbara

The first form of syllogism considered by Aristotle, which is was named *Barbara* in later times,[1] has the form that we have already seen several times:

---

[1] See chapter 28 for an explanation of the naming system.

All Bs are As.
All Cs are Bs.
Therefore all Cs are As.

We may illustrate it with a particular case:

All dogs are animals.
All collies are dogs.
Therefore all collies are animals.

Foundations in God

The conclusion of the syllogism follows from the premises. And this in itself is striking. We sense the necessity. Necessity derives from God. We are experiencing an effect of God's character and his commitment to his character. Moreover, there is power in necessity. The world is constrained in such a way that all collies are animals. We ourselves are constrained by the obligation to follow reasoning of this kind. Power as well as necessity comes from God, who has ordained the nature of the world according to his will. We are invited to be in awe of God as we contemplate with awe the power of a syllogism.

We can also reflect on the relation of one to many. The form of syllogism called "Barbara" has many instances. As usual, the instances cohere with the general pattern. The one, that is, the general pattern, and the many, that is, the instances, belong together. The logic of all instances and the logic of the general pattern derive from God. God is self-consistent. And his self-consistency is manifested in many instances in the world. The primacy belongs to God. From him come the instances, because he is pleased to manifest his glory in the world that he has made. And the manifestation of his glory includes the manifestation of the glory of his self-consistency, as it is reflected in the consistency of human reasoning and the consistency in the world that he has made. So it is fitting to ask whether we can see in God an origin for this particular kind of syllogism, named Barbara.

Roots in the Trinity

In fact, when the Gospel of John describes the relations of speech to the persons of the Trinity, we can see some similarities to the Barbara pattern. Consider John 12:49:

> For I [the Son] have not spoken on my own authority, but the Father who sent me has himself given me a commandment—what to say and what to speak. (John 12:49)

John 12:49 implies that whatever the Son says, the Father says.

John 17:7–8 has a similar implication:

> Now they know that everything that you [the Father] have given me [the Son] is from you. For I have given them the words that you gave me, and they have received them . . .

To show the relation of these verses to syllogisms, we pick out only one dimension from their meaning. We simplify by putting the truth into the standard form for a syllogistic premise. "All words that the Son says are words that the Father says."

We may notice also that the Holy Spirit speaks what he hears:

> When the Spirit of truth comes, he will guide you into all the truth, for he will not speak on his own authority, but whatever he hears he will speak, and he will declare to you the things that are to come. He will glorify me, for he will take what is mine and declare it to you. (John 16:13–14)

Again, these verses are rich. We may single out one dimension to use in a syllogism: "All words that the Spirit says are words that the Son says." Now we have the two premises for the syllogistic form Barbara:

> All words that the Son says are words that the Father says.
> All words that the Spirit says are words that the Son says.
> Therefore, all words that the Spirit says are words that the Father says.

This syllogistic form is a simplification. But it is a simplification of a rich reality in the way in which God speaks to the disciples in accord with his Trinitarian character.

In John 16:15 Jesus makes a connection in another way: "All that the Father has is mine; therefore I said that he [the Spirit] will take what is mine and declare it to you." The statement "All that the Father has is mine" applies in context especially to the words and truth of the Father. So we can simplify it and say, "All words that the Father says are words that the Son says." The conclusion of the verse, introduced with "therefore," says that "he [the Spirit] will take what is mine and declare it to you." We may simplify that statement to say that all words that the Spirit says are words that the Son says. This latter statement can be treated as if it were the conclusion of a syllogism. If we fill in a second premise, we can obtain a syllogism as follows:

> All words that the Father says are words that the Son says.
> All words that the Spirit says are words that the Father says.
> Therefore, all words that the Spirit says are words that the Son says.

The second premise, "all words that the Spirit says are words that the Father says," is not made explicit in John 16, but is presupposed on the basis of the Old Testament testimony that the Spirit of God represents God himself in action.[2]

The passages in John focus on the giving of redemptive truth to the disciples. They talk about God's speech as it took place while Christ was on earth, and subsequently when the Holy Spirit comes in fullness to guide and teach the disciples (John 16:13). This speaking is thus divine speaking in time that becomes accessible to the disciples as human beings. But since God reveals himself in harmony with who he is, this speaking in time and space is in accord with the eternal speaking of God among the persons in the Trinity. This speaking within the Trinity has an inner harmony, as illustrated by the syllogism. As the word "therefore" in John 16:15 illustrates, this harmony expresses the logical self-harmony of God's self-consistency, which, as we earlier observed, comes from the Father's love for the Son through the Spirit.

May we then say it? The syllogistic form Barbara exists first of all in the self-harmony of Trinitarian love and Trinitarian speaking. The use of the syllogism "on earth" imitates the original logic of the Trinity.

For Further Reflection

1. How might syllogisms display the glory of God?
2. What information do we find in the Gospel of John that shows a Trinitarian analogy to the Barbara syllogism?
3. Discuss the temptation to use a non-Christian view of immanence in logic to force Trinitarian speech into a nonmysterious syllogism.
4. Discuss the temptation to use a non-Christian view of transcendence in logic to discount the foundational character of Trinitarian speech. (Hint: non-Christian transcendence might object that God's speech is mysterious and so cannot be a foundation.)

---

[2] See also 1 Corinthians 2:10–11: "For the Spirit searches everything, even the depths of God. For who knows a person's thoughts except the spirit of that person, which is in him? So also no one comprehends the thoughts of God except the Spirit of God."

Chapter 27

Venn Diagrams

Now let us consider how we might represent the reasoning in the Barbara syllogism by a diagram. Consider a particular case of reasoning:

> All dogs are animals.
> All collies are dogs.
> Therefore, all collies are animals.

We begin with the first premise, "All dogs are animals." We can begin to represent it in a spatial diagram if we draw two circles, one circle including all dogs and the other circle including all animals (see figure 27.1):

Fig. 27.1: Dogs and Animals

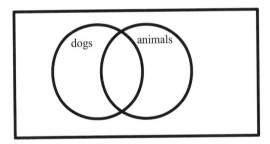

When we say that all dogs are animals, we imply that the circle representing dogs is entirely inside the circle representing animals (see figure 27.2):

Fig. 27.2: All Dogs Are Animals

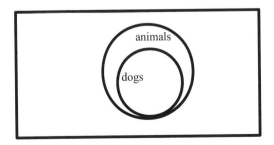

The second premise, that all collies are dogs, can similarly be represented. We draw a circle to represent collies. Then we put the circle for collies completely inside the circle for dogs (figure 27.3):

Fig. 27.3: All Collies Are Dogs

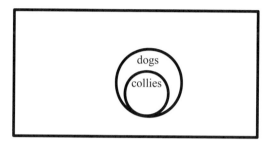

When we combine these two spatial relations, we see that being inside the circle for dogs makes collies inside the circle for animals as well. That is, all collies are animals (figure 27.4):

Fig. 27.4: Therefore, All Collies Are Animals

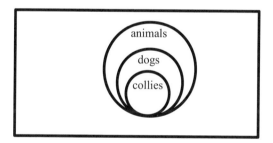

The Idea of Venn Diagrams

In about 1880, John Venn invented a visual way of representing logical relations using spatial regions. We have been using a variation of his method, which was employed even earlier by Leonhard Euler. Euler put one circle entirely inside another when one category, such as collies, was included within another category, such as dogs.[1] The diagrams that we

---

[1] Technically, when using Euler's circles, several cases have to be considered. The premise "all dogs are animals" does not indicate whether "dogs" represents the same set as "animals" or represents a smaller subset within "animals." So unless we bring in extra information about the nature of the world, we have to have two diagrams, one diagram in which one circle is inside the other, and a second in which the two circles are identical. The extra complexity can be remedied either by going to Venn diagrams, or by stipulating that some distinct spatial subregions within a Euler diagram need not have any members.

have just introduced above are examples of Euler diagrams. Instead of using Euler's approach, Venn made all the circles intersecting circles. He did not allow any one circle to be put entirely inside another. The advantage is that we can see all the potential combinations for any possible categories like A, B, and C.

Let us illustrate using the same categories that we had before, namely collies, dogs, and animals. Let us begin with only two circles, one for dogs and one for animals. We draw them so that they intersect each other (figure 27.5):

Fig. 27.5: Venn Diagram for Dogs and Animals

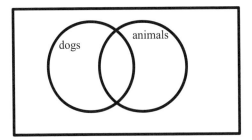

Next, we represent the truth "all dogs are animals" by X-ing out the subregion representing dogs that are *not* animals. We put an X in the region inside the circle for "dog" and outside the circle for "animals" (figure 27.6):

Fig. 27.6: Venn Diagram for Dogs and Animals

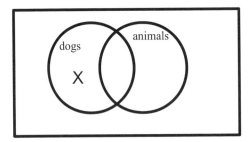

To make more vivid the fact that we are canceling out a whole region, we can, if we like, add shade to the region, as in figure 27.7:

Fig. 27.7: Venn Diagram for Dogs and Animals, with Shading

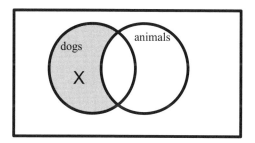

Either of these diagrams, with one region X-ed out or shaded, represents the same truth that we represented earlier by putting the circle for dogs completely inside the circle for animals. The overlap between the two circles, one for dogs and one for animals, represents the things that are *both* dogs *and* animals. Since in this case all the dogs are both dogs and animals, the rest of the circle for dogs, that is, the part *outside* the circle for animals, is X-ed out. We can even picture it by imagining that, once we know that the X-ed out region is empty, we erase it (figure 27.8):

Fig. 27.8: Dogs and Animals Diagram with Empty Region Erased

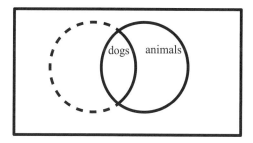

What is left of the circle for dogs is then entirely inside the circle for animals. We are now essentially back to an Euler diagram, where one region is entirely inside another.

Now go back to the Venn diagram, with two intersecting circles, one for dogs and one for animals. We can go to another stage by adding a third circle for collies (figure 27.9):

Fig. 27.9: Venn Diagram for Collies, Dogs, and Animals

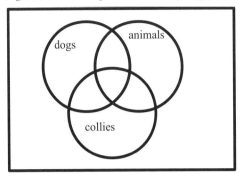

Since all dogs are animals, we cross out the part of "dogs" outside of "animals." See figure 27.10 ("X$_1$" indicates the regions crossed out at this stage):

Fig. 27.10: Collies, Dogs, Animals Diagram, with Cross-outs for Dogs

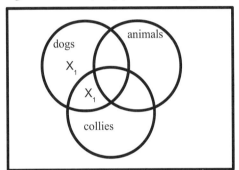

Then, to represent the fact that all collies are dogs, we have to cross out the regions within the circle for "collies" that are outside of the circle for "dogs." The result is shown in figure 27.11 ("X$_2$" indicates the crossed-out regions):

Fig. 27.11: Collies, Dogs, Animals Diagram, with Cross-outs for Collies and Dogs

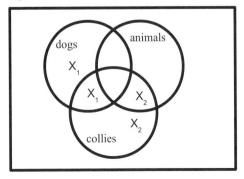

All that is left of "collies" is inside the circle for "animals." That is, all collies are animals. If we shade out the empty regions, we obtain figure 27.12:

Fig. 27.12: Venn Diagram for Collies, Dogs, and Animals, with Shading

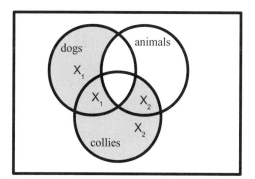

The only part of the circle for collies that is still unshaded is entirely inside the circle for animals. So we can see that all collies are animals.

When we use these diagrams, the circles represent classes: the class of all animals, the class of all dogs, and the class of all collies. The region formed by the intersection of two circles represents the things that are both dogs and animals, or both dogs and collies, or both collies and animals. The diagrams also allow us to visualize the *complement* of each such class. The *complement* of the class of animals is the class of all things that are *not* animals. It is represented by the entire space outside the circle that represents animals (figure 27.13). Likewise, the complement of the class of all dogs is the region outside the circle representing dogs:

Fig. 27.13: Venn Diagram for Nonanimals

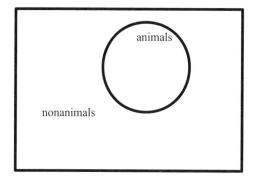

To say that all dogs are animals is equivalent to saying that if anything is a dog, it is *not* in the region outside the circle for animals; that is, if anything is a dog, it is not nonanimal.[2] Or we can say that no dogs are nonanimals. Or we can say that all nonanimals are nondogs (see figure 27.14):

Fig. 27.14: Nondogs and Nonanimals

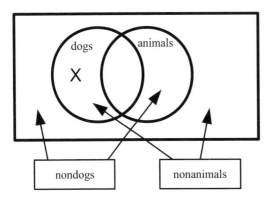

We have now seen two kinds of diagrammatic representation of logical relationships, namely, Euler diagrams and Venn diagrams. In Euler diagrams, one spatial region can fit entirely inside another (a circle for "dogs" fits inside a circle for "animals"). In Venn diagrams, the regions remain distinct and overlapping, but some regions are X-ed out to show that they have no instances.

Either type of diagram represents the same logical relationships. In the end, it makes no difference which kind of diagram we use, as long as we are consistent. From now on we will use Venn diagrams, both because they are more common and because Euler diagrams can become more complicated if we have to consider more than one possibility for which area is included within which.

Venn diagrams leave some areas blank. A blank area symbolizes a combination that may or may not have instances. For example, figure 27.14 for nondogs and nonanimals shows a blank area for the right-hand part of the circle for animals. The right-hand part is the part representing animals that are nondogs. The fact that it is blank means that there may or may not be animals that are nondogs. The information given in the premises has not

---

[2] In ordinary English.

yet specified whether there are such creatures. We know from looking at the world that there are animals that are not dogs. But in formal reasoning we are supposed to use only the premises that we are actually given; we are not permitted to use extra information that we derive from our knowledge of the world.

A blank area clearly is different from an area that is X-ed out. Any X-ed-out area is an area that we know is empty. For example, there is nothing that is a dog and also a nonanimal. So the left-hand part of the circle for dogs is X-ed out in figure 27.14.

Indwelling of Persons

The representation of logical relationships by spatial relationships has an analogue in God. The persons of the Trinity *indwell* one another. The Father is in the Son and the Son in the Father (John 17:21) and the Spirit indwells them. God is not spatially confined, nor are the distinct persons of the Trinity. So the expressions about "indwelling" are understood *analogically*. The Trinitarian relations are the uncreated foundation for spatial relations within the created order.

In particular, the mutual indwelling among the persons of the Trinity is the foundation for God indwelling believers (John 14:23; 17:21). The biblical expressions about indwelling use an analogy with spatial relations, in which one thing is inside another. The picture of the human body as analogous to a temple is relevant: "your body is a temple of the Holy Spirit within you" (1 Cor. 6:19). In a temple, God uses physical space to picture spatial inclusion, which is analogous to the inclusion of the presence of the Holy Spirit *within* a believer. And the dwelling of the Holy Spirit within a believer is analogous to the original indwelling of the persons of the Trinity, as is pointed out in John 17:21:

> . . . just as you, Father, are *in* me, and I *in* you, that they *also* may be *in* us, . . .

In close connection with these expressions we also find expressions about the Father, the Son, and the Holy Spirit dwelling in believers: "I *in* them" (John 17:26); ". . . make *our home with* him" (14:23); ". . . will be *in* you" (v. 17).

Once we see the roots for spatiality in God, we can correlate spatiality to logic. Venn diagrams express logical relations and truth relations spatially. We conclude that the logic of Venn diagrams has coherence with the logic expressed in truth and falsehood, because God is consistent. God's truth-fulness and self-consistency form the foundation for logic. The indwelling of the persons in one another forms the foundation for spatial realities. Logic and space cohere because God coheres with himself. His truthfulness coheres with the indwelling of persons.

The indwelling of the persons implies that what belongs to one belongs to the other. That is, all that belongs to the Father belongs to the Son, and all that belongs to the Son belongs to the Father. These relationships are the original, uncreated fullness of belonging. All Bs are As, where B is what belongs to the Father and A is what belongs to the Son. So indwelling is a suitable starting point for showing that God is the foundation for the logical relations in the Barbara syllogism.

The indwelling of the persons of the Trinity also indicates the limita-tions of the attempt to make the Barbara syllogism merely formal. God himself in his Trinitarian nature is the opposite of merely "formal." He is infinitely rich in complex meaning. Now consider John 16:15, "All that the Father has is mine." This statement is close to what we have already said, that all that belongs to the Father belongs to the Son. The comprehensive-ness of belonging includes words, as we have seen. All words that the Father says are words that the Son says. But we also know that the Son is not the Father and the Father is not the Son. So the personal distinctives of each person are *not* shared. The Father begets and the Son is begotten, while the reverse is not true. So the word "all" is contextually colored. It does not include the features that distinguish one person of the Trinity from another. The original "syllogism" concerning the indwelling of the persons is not abstract and impersonal, with no context, but is personal and contextual. Likewise, the reflected syllogisms that we apply to the created world are colored by the personal character of God. There is no such thing as valid impersonal reasoning.

Imaging in the Trinity as Foundational

We may also consider the theme of *imaging*. The presence of *imaging* in the Trinity can be viewed as the background for the Barbara syllogism. The Son is eternally the "image of the invisible God" (Col. 1:15). In his relation to God the Father he is the divine original for the imaging present in theophany, that is, special appearances of God to human beings. In some of the theophanies God appears as a human figure (for example, Gen. 18:1–2; Ezek. 1:26–28).

The human form foreshadows the final appearance of God when Christ becomes incarnate. Since theophanies anticipate the coming of God the Son, who manifests God the Father, we can say that theophanies involve both God the Father and God the Son. In these special temporary appearances in the Old Testament, as well as in the permanent appearance when the Son became incarnate (John 1:14), the Holy Spirit is present in power.[3] Hence, theophany is Trinitarian in character. In addition, man is made in the image of God (Gen. 1:26–27). He is an image of the original image that is the Son.

Now we can reconsider the Barbara syllogism from the standpoint of imaging. Because the Son is the exact image of the Father (Heb. 1:3), all that the Son says reflects what the Father says. All that belongs to the Son belongs to the Father. So we see in the relation between the Father and the Son the prime or original instance of premise 1, that all Bs are As. We can represent it as shown in table 27.1a:

TABLE 27.1a: Imaging the Father-Son Relationship

Original Imaging	Original Premise	Derivative Instances
The Son (B) images the Father (A).	All that belongs to the Son (B) belongs to the Father (A).	All Bs are As.

The original instance is then reflected or imaged in other instances, such as the principle that all that the Spirit says the Son says. That relation of the Spirit to the Son is the prime instance of the principle that all Cs are Bs. To say that all Bs are As, in the instance of the persons of the Trinity, is a manifestation of imaging, namely, that Bs image As. Likewise, all Cs are Bs because Cs image Bs. We can add to the table (table 27.1b):

TABLE 27.1b: An Image of the Holy Spirit

Original Imaging	Original Premise	Derivative Instances
The Son (B) images the Father (A).	All that belongs to the Son (B) belongs to the Father (A).	All Bs are As.
The Spirit (C) manifests the Son (B).	All that belongs to the Spirit (C) belongs to the Son (B).	All Cs are Bs.

C images B, which images A. An image C of an image B of an archetype

---

[3] See Meredith G. Kline, *Images of the Spirit* (Grand Rapids, MI: Baker, 1980).

A is still an image, because of the fellowship in the harmony of persons in imaging. So all Cs are As. See the complete table (table 27.1c):

TABLE 27.1c: Imaging Trinitarian Relationships

Original Imaging	Original Premise	Derivative Instances
The Son (B) images the Father (A).	All that belongs to the Son (B) belongs to the Father (A).	All Bs are As.
The Spirit (C) manifests the Son (B).	All that belongs to the Spirit (C) belongs to the Son (B).	All Cs are Bs.
The Spirit (C) manifests the Father (A).	All that belongs to the Spirit (C) belongs to the Father (A).	All Cs are As.

The Barbara syllogism exists in the Trinity in the form of imaging in its self-consistency. Barbara is reflected in the created world because God loves the Son as his image, and therefore is pleased to make images of his eternal relations within the world that he has created.

Perspectives on the Barbara Syllogism

We have now presented three different analyses of the divine foundation for the Barbara syllogism. The first uses the example of the speech of the persons of the Trinity. The second represents Barbara in spatial relationships, using a Euler diagram or a Venn diagram. It then proceeds to reflect on the spatial expressions used to describe the mutual indwelling of the persons of the Trinity. The third starts from imaging, and notes that an image of an image is itself an image, thereby providing a foundation for the Barbara syllogism.

These three analyses are three perspectives on Barbara. They are obviously in harmony, because all three express God's self-consistency. But they are also distinct. One is not reducible to the other, since God is rich, and the glory of his nature includes speaking and indwelling and imaging relations. All three persons are involved in all three activities, speaking and indwelling and imaging. We may nevertheless note a certain correlation. Speaking can be associated preeminently with God the Father, who is the original speaker. Indwelling can be associated preeminently with God the Spirit, who brings to us the presence of God, who indwells us (1 Cor. 6:19), and whose indwelling is the means for the indwelling of the Father and the

Son in us. Imaging can be associated preeminently with God the Son, who is the eternal image of God.

All three of these perspectives are related in turn to God's love, so that love can be another perspective on the same syllogistic logic. Love implies sharing, according to John 3:35. Sharing includes sharing in speaking and sharing in what belongs to each person in intimacy. This intimacy in the case of the Trinity is particularly intimate, and thus it constitutes a kind of indwelling. Finally, those whom we love we imitate. The Son is the image of the Father in imitation of the Father. Barbara is valid because the Father loves the Son through the Spirit.

For Further Reflection

1. How does the Barbara syllogism have its roots in God?
2. Explain how imaging can be viewed as the background for the Barbara syllogism.
3. On what basis are analogies from speaking, from indwelling, and from imaging coherent with one another?
4. How could the Barbara syllogism be misunderstood if one started from a non-Christian view of transcendence and immanence?

Chapter 28

Syllogisms of the First Figure

We may now proceed to consider some of the other kinds of syllogistic forms that Aristotle explored. Aristotle had a detailed system of classification, which we need not explore in all its details.[1] Traditionally, the major subdivisions of kinds of syllogisms are determined by the position of the so-called "middle term," that is, the term that occurs in both premises. In the Barbara syllogism, the middle term is B, which occurs in both the first and second premises. Consider again the particular example,

> Premise 1: All dogs are animals.
> Premise 2: All collies are dogs.
> Conclusion: Therefore all collies are animals.

In this example the middle term is *dogs*, because it occurs in both premises.

In a number of kinds of valid syllogism, the middle term (*dogs* above) appears in the subject in the first premise ("All dogs are . . .") and in the predicate in the second premise (". . . are dogs"). These syllogisms are classified as belonging to the "first figure" in the traditional classification. We now consider valid syllogistic forms belonging to the first figure. The first form, called *Barbara*, was already considered in the previous chapters. Now we need to consider the rest.

Kinds of Premises and Conclusions

Each form of syllogism consists of two premises and a conclusion. We can further distinguish different forms of syllogism by looking at what are the different possibilities for each premise or for the conclusion. Each premise and each conclusion can be classified as one of four kinds of statement, as follows:

---

[1] See A. N. Prior, "Logic, Traditional," in *Encyclopedia of Philosophy*, 2nd ed., ed. Donald M. Borchert, 10 vols. (Detroit/New York/San Francisco/ . . . : Thomson Gale, 2006), 5:495–498.

1. Universal affirmative: "All Bs are As." Example: "All dogs are animals." Such an assertion is called *universal* because it is speaking about *all* dogs or all entities belonging to some classification B.

2. Particular affirmative: "Some B is A." Example: "Some sea creature is a mammal." This premise is called *particular* because the word *some* refers to some particular entity, not to all. In the example with a sea creature, the word *some* indicates that there is some particular sea creature that is a mammal. That is, there is at least one; there may or may not be more.

3. Universal negative: "No Bs are As." Example: "No dogs are cats." The word *no* indicates that the assertion denies rather than affirms. At the same time, the assertion is still universal, because it makes a claim about *all* the members of the class of dogs. "No dogs are cats" is equivalent to "All dogs are not cats."[2]

4. Particular negative: "Some B is not A." "Some sea creature is not a fish." The presence of the word *not* indicates that the assertion is a denial, a *negative*. The presence of the word *some* indicates that it is a particular rather than a universal statement about all sea creatures.

In Aristotle's syllogisms, each premise and each conclusion has one of these four forms. In the Barbara syllogism, the two premises and the conclusion are each universal affirmatives.

Foundation for Distinctive Types of Proposition

These distinctions between universal and particular, and between affirmative and negative, are possible because of the richness of language and the richness of human thought. We can see ways in which both distinctions have their ultimate foundation in God.

Let us begin with the distinction between universal and particular statements. This distinction is closely related to the distinction between unity and diversity. A property that is true for every case within a certain category is a unity with respect to that category. For example, "All dogs are animals" is an expression of unity with respect to everything that is a dog. On the other hand, each dog is distinctive. Some dogs are black, some are brown, some are male, some are female, and so on. Particular statements, that is,

---

[2] There is a potential ambiguity in the expression "all dogs are not cats." In ordinary English it is possible to interpret it as meaning either "if anything is a dog, it is not a cat," or "it is not the case that all dogs are cats." The meaning we want is the first. The same must be said for other cases involving universal negative assertions.

statements with the word *some*, come into play because there are many situations in which a property belonging to a particular individual member of a class (e.g., a particular dog) does not necessarily belong to every member of the larger class (all dogs). Particular statements become important because of diversity within classes (like the class of dogs).

Next, let us consider the distinction between affirmative and negative statements. Does this distinction have its foundation in God? God is a God of truth. And truth contrasts with falsehood, because of the self-consistency of God. So negative statements contrast with affirmative statements. The contrast ultimately depends on God being a God of truth whose nature forbids falsehood.

We have to be careful, because affirmative and negative statements go together with universal and particular statements in a complex way. Suppose we start with a particular individual dog, Fido. An affirmative statement would say that Fido is an animal (which would be true), while a negative statement would say that Fido is not an animal (which would be false). If we try to generalize, and make a universal statement, the universal affirmative would be "Fido and Rover and Rex and all the other dogs are animals," that is, "All dogs are animals." The generalization for the negative, "Fido is not an animal," would be "Fido and Rover and Rex and all the other dogs are not animals." That is, "All dogs are not animals," which is understood as equivalent to "If anything is a dog, it is not an animal."

But suppose we ask what is the negation or contradictory of "All dogs are animals"? We can formulate the contradictory by adding the expression "It is not the case that . . ." The contradictory of "all dogs are animals" is "It is not the case that all dogs are animals." This latter statement is equivalent to "Some dogs are not animals." That is, the contradictory of a universal affirmative is a particular negative. Similarly, the contradictory of "No dogs are cats" is "It is not the case that no dogs are cats," which is equivalent to "Some dogs are cats." The contradictory of a universal negative is a particular affirmative. To put it another way, the opposite (contradictory) of saying that all instances have property A (universal affirmative) is to say that at least one instance does not (particular negative). The opposite of saying that no instances have property A (universal negative) is to say that at least one does (particular affirmative).[3]

---

[3] More will be said about the relation of universal to particular in chapters 48–50.

The Second Type of Syllogism: Celarent

Each form of Aristotelian syllogism has been given a traditional shorthand name, which we will supply for the sake of historical reference. The name of the second form of syllogism is *Celarent*. It has the following form:

> No Bs are As.
> All Cs are Bs.
> Therefore, no Cs are As.

Here is an example:

> No dogs are cats.
> All collies are dogs.
> Therefore, no collies are cats.

Unlike the Barbara syllogism, which uses three universal affirmatives, the first premise of Celarent is a universal negative, "*No* dogs are cats." The conclusion is also a universal negative ("*No* collies are cats"). The second premise, "All collies are dogs," is a universal affirmative. The Celarent syllogism is the name given to all syllogisms with precisely this sequence of premises and conclusion.

The name "Celarent" and the other traditional names for the various syllogisms use a memory aid probably based on Latin. In Latin, *affirmo* means "I affirm." The first two vowels of *affirmo*, namely, the vowels A and I, are used when describing premises or conclusions that have an affirmative form. A universal affirmative proposition such as "All collies are dogs" is type A. A particular affirmative such as "some dog is a collie" is type I. For negative premises or conclusions, people use the first two vowels E and O of the Latin word *nego*, "I deny." A universal negative such as "No dogs are cats" is type E. A particular negative such as "Some dog is not a collie" is type O.

Now in the Celarent syllogism, the first premise, "No Bs are As," is a universal negative, that is, type E. The second premise, "All Cs are Bs," is universal affirmative, type A. The conclusion, "No Cs are As," is universal negative, type E. The three letters for the two premises and the conclusion are in the following order: (1) E, (2) A, and (3) E. These three are then used as the three vowels of the name CElArEnt, retaining the proper order. Given the three vowels, one can reconstruct the pattern for the Celarent syllogism.

Consider now the name "Barbara" for the earlier form of syllogism. The three vowels of the name "Barbara" in order are A, A, and A. The vowel *A* indicates a universal affirmative. The three As in order indicate that the first premise, the second premise, and the conclusion are all universal affirmative.[4]

Trinitarian Basis for Celarent

We can, if we wish, see connections between Celarent and Trinitarian speech, when we note that in one case in the Gospel of John, the speaking of the Son is described through a denial as well as an affirmation. "For I [the Son] have not spoken on my own authority" (John 12:49). As we have observed in the previous chapter, this context of Trinitarian speech is rich. We may single out one dimension in order to bring it into relation to the syllogistic form. No words that the Son says are words on his own authority. We then have the possibility of a syllogism:

> No words that the Son says are words on the Son's own authority.
> All words that the Father says are words that the Son says.
> Therefore, no words that the Father says are on the Son's own authority.

This syllogism holds because of the harmony among the persons of the Trinity, which can be seen as an expression of their love, their speech, their imaging, or their mutual indwelling. The negative, "no words," rejects the possibility of disharmony or independence, rather than directly affirming the harmony. These modes of expression have unity and diversity. The diversity is expressed in the distinction between negative and positive expressions of truth. The unity belongs to the character of the harmony that is affirmed in both expressions.

We can again proceed to show the relationships among different perspectives on the harmony within the Trinity. The persons of the Trinity indwell one another. This indwelling can be expressed positively by saying that the Father is in the Spirit. It can be expressed negatively by denying that the Father is apart from or independent of the Spirit in some activity:

---

[4] In addition, traditional logic distinguishes four different "figures," based on the relative arrangements of subjects and predicates in the two premises and the conclusion. The term in the predicate position of the conclusion (the term that we have labeled A in Barbara) is called the *major* term. The term in the subject position of the conclusion is called the *minor* term (the term C in Barbara). The *middle* term is the term that occurs in both premises but not in the conclusion (the term B in Barbara). The *major premise* is the premise that contains the major term, while the *minor premise* is the premise that contains the minor term. By convention the major premise is written first. Syllogisms of the *first figure* all have the pattern: major premise B − A, minor premise C − B, conclusion C − A. The *second figure* has the pattern: major premise A − B, minor premise C − B, conclusion C − A. The *third figure* has B − A, B − C, conclusion C − A. The *fourth figure* (not separately discussed by Aristotle) has A − B, B − C, conclusion C - A.

Some of the consonants used in the names also have significance. Syllogisms closely related to one another share the same initial consonant, and later consonants may also indicate relationships.

No activity of the Father is apart from the presence of the Spirit.
All the activities of the Son are activities of the Father. [See John 14:10,
    "The Father who *dwells* in me does his works."]
Therefore, no activity of the Son is apart from the presence of the Spirit.

The Syllogism Celarent in a Diagram

We can represent the syllogism of the form Celarent in a diagram, with
three circles, one each for A, B, and C. No Bs are As implies that we must
X-out the overlap between circle B and circle A (see figure 28.1):

Fig. 28.1: Venn Diagram for "No Bs are As"

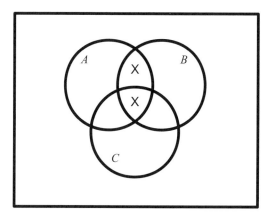

All Cs are Bs implies that we must X-out the overlap between C and not-B.
So add more X's, and we get figure 28.2:

Fig. 28.2: Venn Diagram of the Celarent Syllogism

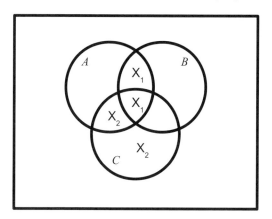

We can see from the diagram that the overlap between circle A and circle C is completely X-ed out. That is, no Cs are As.

The Relation between Celarent and Barbara

We may also discern a relation between syllogisms of the form Celarent and those of the form Barbara. As we observed with relationships in Trinitarian speech, the relationships can be expressed either positively or negatively. Positively, Jesus says, "What I say, therefore, I say as the Father has told me" (John 12:50). Negatively, he says, "For I have not spoken on my own authority" (v. 49). Speaking on his own authority is the opposite of speaking "as the Father has told me." What God *is* always contrasts with what he is not, and what he does do contrasts with what he does not do.

The close relationships among these contrasts gives us the opportunity to deduce the syllogistic form Celarent from the form Barbara, by substituting a negative property for A in Celarent. The argument is easy to see if we use an example. Suppose that we want to establish the validity of the following instance of a Celarent syllogism:

> No dogs are cats.
> All collies are dogs.
> Therefore, no collies are cats.

We have to substitute a negative formulation for "cats."

> All dogs are not-cats.
> All collies are dogs.
> Therefore, all collies are not-cats.

If the expression "not-cats" is too awkward, we may find something better:

> All dogs are nonfeline.
> All collies are dogs.
> Therefore, all collies are nonfeline.

This form of argumentation is an instance of the Barbara syllogism. Thus, if we know that Barbara is valid, we know that this instance is valid. (Validity, of course, always takes into account a larger context; but granted that we have normal contexts, we can see the legitimacy of moving from Barbara to Celarent.) Hence we know that Celarent is valid.

We can also argue in the reverse direction. Given the validity of the Celarent syllogism, we can derive from it the validity of Barbara. Again, we use an example. Suppose that we want to establish the validity of the following example of Barbara:

> All dogs are animals.
> All collies are dogs.
> Therefore, all collies are animals.

If we substitute a negative property, we obtain:

> All dogs are not nonanimal.
> All collies are dogs.
> Therefore, all collies are not nonanimal.

We then have to observe that "All dogs are not nonanimal" is equivalent to "No dogs are nonanimal." And "All collies are not nonanimal" is equivalent to "No collies are nonanimal." So we have:

> No dogs are nonanimal.
> All collies are dogs.
> Therefore, no collies are nonanimal.

This syllogism now has the form of Celarent. Thus, if Celarent is valid, Barbara is valid.

The conversion of one form to the other is a matter of perspective. We can view Celarent as a form of Barbara, if we view the negation "no" in Celarent (premise 1) as implying a universal affirmation that all Bs are not-As. We can view Barbara as a form of Celarent, if we notice that "All Bs are As" can be translated into the equivalent, "No Bs are not-As." Multiple perspectives, as usual, reflect the richness of the self-consistency of God.

The Third Type of Syllogism: Darii

A third type of syllogism, named *Darii*, has the following form:

> All Bs are As.
> Some C is B.
> Therefore, some C is A.[5]

---

[5] The first premise is universal affirmative, type A. The second premise is particular affirmative, type I. The conclusion is particular affirmative, type I. The three vowels A, I, and I are the three vowels of "Darii" in order.

The word "some" in this context means at least one. It does not indicate one way or the other whether there is more than one such C. Nor does it indicate one way or the other whether *all* Cs are Bs. It makes a more modest assertion that "some" C is B, but does not imply by that modesty that it is not true that all Cs are Bs.

We can provide an example:

All mammals breathe air.
Some sea creature is a mammal.
Therefore, some sea creature breathes air.

Does this form of syllogism have roots in God? We may think back to what we observed concerning the Barbara syllogism, which we illustrated using words coming from the persons of the Trinity. Shall we say that "some" of the words are shared? The harmony among the persons of the Trinity is exhaustive, so that not only some but all of the words are shared. But we can easily illustrate the Darii syllogism if we focus first on the words that the disciples of Jesus receive and that they are supposed to pass on.

In John 17, in the context of expressions about indwelling, Jesus indicates that he will be "in them," that is, he will indwell the disciples (John 17:23). In verse 23 he also says that "you" (the Father) will be "in me." He also sends the disciples, which implies that they will speak the words that he has given them: "As you [the Father] sent me [the Son] into the world, so I have sent them [the disciples] into the world" (v. 18). This commissioning does not imply that the disciples become God themselves. In their commission they bear the words that Jesus has given them (v. 14), but they remain human, and when they are acting as ordinary people rather than under the commission, they remain fallible, as Peter illustrated by his behavior at Antioch (Gal. 2:11–14). Thus we may say that *some* of the disciples' words are words given by the Son, namely, the words that are part of their commission. But not all their words have this status. Therefore, we have syllogisms like the following:

All the words of the Son are words of the Father.
Some of the words of Peter are words of the Son.
Therefore, some of the words of Peter are words of the Father.

This and other similar syllogisms concerning the disciples show that the communication of God through the disciples illustrates the logic of the

Darii syllogism. Darii is in this sense rooted in God's plan for the spread of the divine word, and therefore expresses his self-consistency. But would Darii have any role if we did not bring in the humanity of the disciples?

We know that God is Lord over possibilities as well as what actually takes place in the world according to his plan. God by nature contrasts with anything creaturely, including a creature that he *might* create but did not. The contrasts are rooted in the unity and diversity in divine truth, truth that includes truths about what God might create.

In addition, we can observe that the syllogism Barbara that we considered earlier is actually a "stronger" case of the syllogism Darii. The word *some* in Darii does not imply one way or the other whether all Cs are Bs. It is more "modest," we said. So the premises in Darii are actually still true in the case when all Cs are Bs.[6] When all Cs are Bs, surely it is true that some are. And when all Cs are As, surely it is true that some are. In the previous chapter we saw that the Barbara syllogism holds in God himself as the Trinitarian archetype, where all words of one person in the Trinity are also words of another. These relationships are therefore also expressions of the Darii syllogism. Hence, Darii has its foundation in the Trinity.

We can represent Darii in a Venn diagram if we use a check mark to indicate that at least one member belongs to a particular spatial area. Darii then is expressed by figure 28.3:

Fig. 28.3: Venn Diagram of the Darii Syllogism

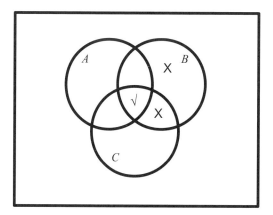

---

[6] That is, the premise "some C is a B" follows from "all Cs are Bs" provided we make the additional assumption that the category C is not empty. We will encounter the need for such an additional assumption at a few other points.

As usual, the blank areas are areas that we have not further specified. For example, in figure 28.3 (above) consider the part of the circle C that is outside both circles A and B. It is blank, which represents the fact that our information does not specify whether or not there is any C that is both non-A and non-B. By contrast, the check mark in the central area indicates that we do know that there is some C that is both A and B.

The Fourth Type of Syllogism: Ferio

A fourth type of syllogism, named *Ferio*, has the following form:

No Bs are As.
Some C is B.
Therefore, some C is not A.

We may provide an example:

No reptiles are fish.
Some vertebrate is a reptile.
Therefore some vertebrate is not a fish.

Ferio can be represented in a Venn diagram as in figure 28.4:

Fig. 28.4: Venn Diagram of the Ferio Syllogism

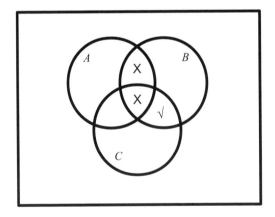

We can show that Ferio can be derived from Darii. We start with the example we just gave, and alter the wording:

All reptiles are nonfish.
Some vertebrate is a reptile.
Therefore, some vertebrate is nonfish.

The resulting form is the form of Darii. Darii and Ferio serve as perspectives on each other. We can convert Ferio to Darii by changing from a negative "no" to a positive "all" in premise 1, and adjusting the category A ("fish" changes to "nonfish") accordingly.

Similarly, we can convert Darii to Ferio by changing our descriptive term A from positive to negative. Start with an example of Darii:

All mammals breathe air.
Some sea creature is a mammal.
Therefore, some sea creature breathes air.

We convert to equivalent expressions with "non-air-breathing":

No mammals are non-air-breathing.
Some sea creature is a mammal.
Therefore, some sea creature is not non-air-breathing.

The result is the form of Ferio.

The four different kinds of syllogism, Barbara, Celarent, Darii, and Ferio, have other relations to one another. Some can be derived from others using the principle of *reductio ad absurdum* ("reduction to absurdity"). That is, we show that a conclusion is true by showing that the assumption that it is not true leads to a contradiction. The derivations are found in appendix A2.

Conclusion

All the distinct forms of syllogism, as well as other aspects of logic, have their ultimate foundation in the self-consistency of God and the character of God. They are naturally related to one another because they express in distinct ways the harmony in God's character. We can praise him that his harmony is reflected in all of the world, including the operations of our own minds when we use logical reasoning. Logic reveals God. Logic is a manifestation of his self-consistency and the harmony in God among the persons of the Trinity. We can be grateful for his faithfulness and the beauty of his character.

For Further Reflection

1. Write other examples of the syllogistic forms Celarent, Darii, and Ferio.
2. What is the relation between a universal affirmative (all dogs are animals) and a particular negative (some dogs are not animals)? What other two kinds of statements are related to one another in a similar way?
3. How do universal affirmatives, particular affirmatives, and the contrast between them have a foundation in God?
4. How do the syllogisms Celarent, Darii, and Ferio display the glory of God?

Chapter 29

Checking Validity by Venn Diagrams

The syllogistic forms Barbara, Celarent, Darii, and Ferio are all valid forms of argumentation. We have seen how their validity can be checked using Venn diagrams. Venn diagrams can also check the validity of other forms, and detect those forms that represent *invalid* reasoning. That is, a Venn diagram can detect when the conclusion does not logically follow from the premises.

An Invalid Form

Consider the following reasoning:

> All dogs are mammals.
> No fish are dogs.
> Therefore, no fish are mammals.

The two premises are true, and the conclusion is true. But the conclusion does not *follow* from the premises. So the reasoning is invalid. We can see the invalidity by using another example with the same form:

> All dogs are mammals.
> No cats are dogs.
> Therefore, no cats are mammals.

The two premises are both true, but the conclusion is false, showing that the reasoning is invalid.

The general pattern in both cases runs like this:

> All Bs are As.
> No Cs are Bs.
> Therefore, no Cs are As.

We start with a Venn diagram for A, B, and C. The premise "All Bs are As" is recorded by crossing out that part of circle B that is outside circle A (see figure 29.1):

Fig. 29.1: All Bs Are As

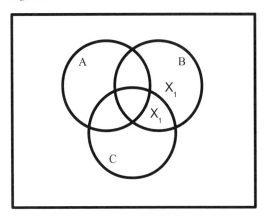

Now we add to the diagram the information that no Cs are Bs. We cross out the region where C and B overlap (see figure 29.2):

Fig. 29.2: All Bs Are As, No Cs Are Bs

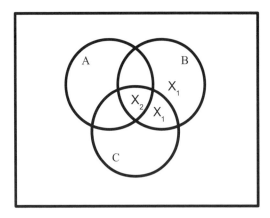

Is it now the case that no Cs are As? No. There is still a region where C and A overlap, as indicated by the arrow in figure 29.3:

Fig. 29.3: Some C May Still Be A

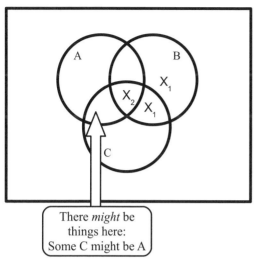

Another Case of Invalidity

Consider now the following reasoning:

All geniuses are talented.
Some doctor is talented.
Therefore, some doctor is a genius.

Is the reasoning valid?

To check validity, construct a Venn diagram with three circles for geniuses, the talented, and doctors (figure 29.4):

Fig. 29.4: Genius, Talent, and Doctors

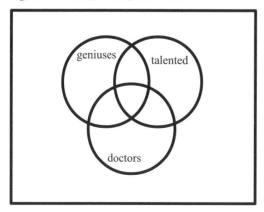

Then enter the information represented by "All geniuses are talented." This premise implies that the part of the circle for geniuses that is outside of the circle for talented should be X-ed out (figure 29.5):

Fig. 29.5: "All Geniuses Are Talented"

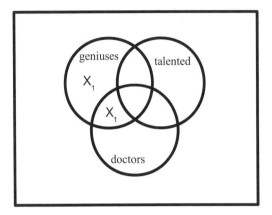

The second premise, that some doctor is talented, can be represented by a check mark in the intersection of the circle for doctors and the circle for talented. But there are two subregions in the intersection, one inside the circle for geniuses and one outside. Should we check both (figure 29.6)?

Fig. 29.6: "Some Doctor Is Talented" (Both Subsections Checked)

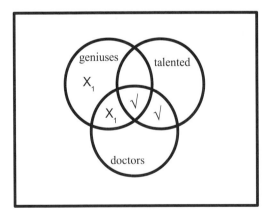

But if we use two check marks, we are implying that we know there is at least one thing in each of the subregions. The second premise says only that there is at least one thing in one *or* the other of the two subregions. This situation can be represented by placing the check mark on the boundary between the two subregions (figure 29.7).

Fig. 29.7: "Some Doctor Is Talented" (Check Mark on Boundary)

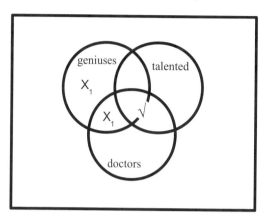

The conclusion that is claimed to follow is that some doctor is a genius. This conclusion would hold if we knew that the region in the intersection of "geniuses" and "doctors" was not empty. The check mark is halfway into that region. If the check mark were in that region, it would say that we have at least one doctor who is a genius. As it is, the check mark is on the boundary. It means that we know only that some doctor is talented. But it could still be the case that such a doctor is talented but is not a genius. The check mark would end up in the region outside of "geniuses." The reasoning is therefore invalid. The conclusion does not follow from the premises.

If the conclusion does not follow, we ought to be able to produce a case with the same form, but whose conclusion is obviously false.

All dogs are mammals.
Some sea creature is a mammal.
Therefore, some sea creature is a dog.

This reasoning has the same *form* as the earlier one. The two premises are true, while the conclusion is false, showing that the overall pattern of reasoning is invalid.

For Further Reflection

1. Use Venn diagrams to check the validity of the following:

    a.
    No collies are cats.
    All collies are dogs.
    Therefore, no dogs are cats.

    b.
    All mammals breathe air.
    Some sea creature is not a mammal.
    Therefore, some sea creature does not breathe air.

    c.
    Some mammal is a sea creature.
    All mammals are vertebrates.
    Therefore, some vertebrate is a sea creature.

    d.
    No cats are dogs.
    No bears are cats.
    Therefore, no bears are dogs.

2. For each invalid argument from question #1 above, write an argument with the same form but using different categories (e.g., not "collies," "cats," and "dogs" as in 1a). Pick the categories so that the two premises are true but the conclusion is false.

Part II
Aspects of Propositional Logic

Propositional logic studies whole propositions and their combinations. Propositions are either true or false. Special notation is introduced to represent propositions and to represent the logical relations between them.

Part II.A

Truth in Logic

Chapter 30

Truth in Logic: Truth Functions

We now consider developments within modern symbolic logic.

The Nature of Modern Symbolic Logic

What is symbolic logic, and why does it matter? Symbolic logic is a subdivision of *formal logic*. Traditional formal logic, based on Aristotle, focused on syllogisms. But in the nineteenth and twentieth centuries logicians developed additional tools, which included special logical symbols with specific technical meanings. Because of the use of special symbols, this kind of logic is called *symbolic logic*.[1]

As an example, we may take one of the axioms of Whitehead and Russell's *Principia Mathematica*:

$$\vdash : p \lor p \, . \supset . \, p[2]$$

This axiom is written in a specialized formal language, with special symbols: $\vdash \lor . \supset$. These symbols have to be defined to have specialized, precise meanings. If we translate this special symbolism back into ordinary language, it says roughly the following:

---

[1] Sometimes the choice of tools has been correlated with deeper philosophical assumptions. Aristotle thought that the world consisted of things (e.g., Socrates) and natural classes of things (e.g., mortal things), and that things had properties (being mortal, being snub-nosed). The simplest truths were therefore truths that ascribed properties to things. It was natural for him to study propositions like "All Bs are As." By contrast, some twentieth-century philosophers have thought that the world consisted in *facts*. The simplest truths were statements of fact, that is, whole propositions. So it seemed natural to study whole propositions. However, the situation is more complicated, because the fully developed apparatus for twentieth-century symbolic logic includes resources rich enough to express Aristotelian syllogisms, and includes notation for individuals (which are thing-like) and predicates (which are like properties of things). See part III.A, part III.B, and appendix C2. Aristotelian syllogisms can be treated as *one part* of twentieth-century symbolic logic. So the two kinds of logic need not be seen as in tension with each other. Moreover, since we can distinguish a system of formal logic from the richness of natural language describing the world, and from the infinite knowledge of God, we need not maintain that a particular logical system has direct implications about the ultimate structural organization of the world.

[2] Alfred North Whitehead and Bertrand Russell, *Principia Mathematica*, 2nd ed., 3 vols. (Cambridge: Cambridge University Press, 1927), 1:96, proposition 1.2.

The symbol *p* stands for any proposition we like, such as "Snow is white." The axiom as a whole says: It is the case (⊢) that if snow is white (*p*) or (∨) snow is white (*p*), then (. ⊃ .) snow is white (*p*). (The extra dots in the notation indicate how the material is grouped together.[3])

The specialized formal language serves to condense some aspects of what happens in reasoning in ordinary language.

The Challenge

When we use logical argumentation *informally*, our informal reasoning has close connections with the operations of language and the ways in which we use language in persuading others. It is easy to remind ourselves that the whole process is personal and many-dimensional. The validity of the reasoning is one aspect of larger personal purposes in reasoning and in communication.

On the other hand, formal logic is not so obviously personal. It deliberately generalizes. We may say that it "abstracts" away from any particular person and any particular argument, in order to put all the focus on the general forms of reasoning.

Aristotelian syllogisms represent one kind of generalization. Modern symbolic logic continues this pattern and intensifies it. Formalized reasoning of this kind represents a greater challenge, if we believe that logic has its foundations in God, who is personal. It might seem that formal logic is designed precisely to sit out there with no relation at all either to human persons or to God. The same impression may become even stronger with symbolic logic, because it introduces formal symbols and moves farther away from the familiarity of ordinary language.[4]

Simple and Compound Propositions

Symbolic logic includes within its scope the study of the relationships between simple propositions like "Snow is white" and compound propositions like "Either snow is white or the moon is made of green cheese." To

---

[3] The dot immediately before the implication sign ⊃ indicates that the antecedent for the implication is the composite proposition p ∨ p. In addition, two dots represent a more "powerful" grouping than does one dot. The two dots that immediately follow the assertion sign ⊢ indicate that the assertion sign governs the whole remaining part of the line.

[4] We focus on "classical logic," which is closer to Aristotle. Other special logics are considered in part III.E.

study the general pattern of such relationships, symbolic logic often symbolically represents a whole proposition such as "Snow is white" by a single letter. For example, we can specify that the symbol S will stand for the proposition "Snow is white." In addition, we can specify that the symbol M will stand for the proposition "The moon is made of green cheese." The compound proposition, "Either snow is white or the moon is made of green cheese," can then be represented as "Either S or M."

In a sense it makes little difference whether we use a whole sentence "Snow is white" or a single symbol S. But using a symbol S rather than a whole sentence can have an advantage. It makes it easier to focus on the general relationship between S, M, and the compound proposition "Either S or M." We are not distracted by the demand to pay attention to the specific content of S. We are not as likely to ask ourselves about the nature of snow, and whether it is always white. In addition, using the symbol S makes it easy to generalize. What if, instead of standing for "Snow is white," we had chosen to have S stand for "Sheep produce wool"? We could still make the same basic observations about the compound structure "Either S or M." The use of the single symbol S also helps to move reasoning in the direction of isolating propositions from a larger context of knowledge that helps to define their meaning. S is understood to stand for a proposition that has been isolated. It is not part of a larger paragraph that helps to understand its meaning and implications, and in which the sentence S in turn helps us to understand the thrust of the paragraph. In addition, the meaning of S is isolated in relation to the compound structure "Either S or M." We are not supposed to let the specific content of the proposition S, and the nature of snow and whiteness, affect the interpretation of the truth or falsehood of the larger structure "Either S or M." This isolation and lack of interference on larger meanings differs from the behavior of natural language. In natural languages the meaning of a smaller piece of text can influence the interpretation of a larger construction. For example, a potential ambiguity between two meanings of the word *tail* can be cleared up by a neighboring sentence talking about animals (making us infer that the word *tail* refers to an animal tail) or about airplanes. This kind of influence is now forbidden. The symbol S is supposed to stand for a self-contained sentence. It is an idealization in comparison with natural language.

Logical "Or"

Symbolic logic takes a further step by replacing the either-or structure with a special symbol for "or." The word "or" in English has a range of functions, and its exact function in any one occurrence is influenced by the context. Sometimes it is used in persuasive contexts where the speaker is setting up two alternatives, one of which is supposed to be rejected as abhorrent:

> Do you not know that . . . you are slaves of the one whom you obey, either of sin, which leads to death, *or* of obedience, which leads to righteousness? (Rom. 6:16)

Sometimes the word "or" stands between two alternatives that are mutually exclusive, without any indication that one alternative is preferred:

> No one can serve two masters, for either he will hate the one and love the other, *or* he will be devoted to the one and despise the other. (Matt. 6:24)

Sometimes "or" separates two overlapping alternatives:

> . . . do not be anxious how you are to speak *or* what you are to say, . . . (Matt. 10:19)

Logicians construct a special symbol for "or," for which they typically use the symbol $\vee$.[5] Logicians want to "drain out" all the extra associations and leave only one precise function. They specify that the new logical "or" symbol $\vee$ deals exclusively with truth value. Its meaning is closer to the "overlapping" meaning of "or."

Given this special understanding of the new symbol $\vee$, the compound sentence "either snow is white or the moon is made of green cheese" can be written symbolically. It is represented as $S \vee M$. The proposition S, that snow is white, is true, so that the compound proposition $S \vee M$ is true. The same notation can be used with any other propositions. Suppose we have two propositions that we label D and E. The combination D *or* E, or more precisely $D \vee E$, is true if either D is true or E is true or both D and E are true. Here are some further examples:

> $(1 + 1 = 2) \vee (2 + 2 = 4)$ is true because both entries are true.
> $(1 + 1 = 2) \vee (2 + 2 = 5)$ is true because the first entry ("$1 + 1 = 2$") is true.

---

[5] Logical "or" ($\vee$) is unicode symbol U2228.

(1 + 1 = 1) ∨ (2 + 2 = 4) is true because the second entry is true.
(1 + 1 = 1) ∨ (2 + 2 = 5) is false because both entries are false.

We can indicate how the logical "or" symbol operates by drawing up a summary that shows each of the four possibilities given above. Within this summary, we will let T stand for *true* and F stand for *false*. The symbol T is actually not completely equivalent to the English word *true*, because the word *true* in natural English, like the word "or" in natural English, has a range of meaning; that is, it has "variation." For example, Jesus in John 6:32 speaks about "the true bread from heaven," meaning the real or genuine bread. The special symbol T "drains out" all the extra associations of this kind, and is supposed to be used only to label true propositions within a purely "formal" setting.

Since we want to discuss the general character of truth, we need to distinguish between particular propositions, like "1 + 1 = 2," and the general pattern. The symbols D and E, as well as the symbols S and M, are supposed to stand for particular propositions. But we can also use symbols to stand for any proposition whatsoever, when the proposition has not yet been specified. For this purpose, we use symbols p, q, r, s, etc. Now we consider the combination $p \lor q$. Within this combination, the proposition p can be either T or F, and the proposition q can be either T or F. Altogether there are four possible combinations: p is T and q is T; p is T and q is F; p is F and q is T; p is F and q is F. For each of these combinations, we can tell whether $p \lor q$ is T or F (because $p \lor q$ depends only on the truth values of p and q, not on the detailed content within each proposition). We summarize all the possibilities for truth values in figure 30.1:

Fig. 30.1: Truth Values for (p or q)

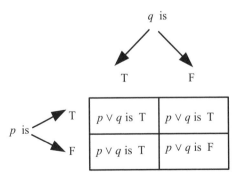

Or we may present it in a tabular arrangement (table 30.1):

TABLE 30.1: Truth Table for Logical "Or" ($\vee$)

p	q	$p \vee q$
T	T	T
T	F	T
F	T	T
F	F	F

This kind of tabular arrangement is called a *truth table*, because it is a table that specifies the truth or falsity of a compound proposition ($p \vee q$) for every possible combination of truth and falsehood of its component parts (the parts p and q).

We can also describe the information in the truth table in this way: $p \vee q$ is false (F) only if[6] both p and q are false; otherwise $p \vee q$ is true (T). The "or" symbol is intended to be purely "formal." So the propositions p and q do not need to have any relation to one another in their content. For example, in the sentence, "Either snow is white or the moon is made of green cheese," the two simple propositions do not have closely related meanings. This sentence is a suitable example of the use of English "or" in a manner similar to the one-dimensional, "drained-out" function of $\vee$. If we need to distinguish the special function of $\vee$ from the ordinary, richer use of "or" in English, we can call the symbol $\vee$ *logical "or."* It is also called *logical disjunction* or simply *disjunction* for short.

Symbols

How does a special symbol like *S*, *M*, or the symbol $\vee$ for logical disjunction originate? The special symbols are like extensions to the alphabet. Human beings have designed and crafted the symbols. In the nineteenth and twentieth centuries, the process of introducing special symbols took place over a period of some decades and received input from a number of notable figures. Considerable knowledge went into the process. And this knowledge involves persons, who use language and symbols, and who think through what it might mean for a precise system of symbols to

---

[6] It is customary within formal logic to use the expression "if and only if," abbreviated as "iff," to describe a situation where one expression is the case if and only if the other is the case. In more informal discussion, I have preferred to use "only if" in many of these cases, because in ordinary English the context indicates well enough that "if and only if" is implied. There is a trade-off between the rigor and explicitness of "if and only if" on the one hand, and the naturalness of "only if" on the other.

express processes of reasoning. So symbolic logic involves persons in its origin. The human persons share an understanding of reasoning in general and of the special symbols that they use. This shared understanding has as its foundation the creation of man in the image of God. Our capacity to reason, and our capacity to represent reasoning in special new symbols, derived from God's reasoning and God's original capacity for producing languages and symbols.

Second, the particular symbols in symbolic logic, like the symbol p for a proposition and the symbol ∨ for "or," have to be explained. Textbooks in symbolic logic begin with ordinary English (or some other natural language). They rely on readers' understanding of natural language. And readers must already have some intuitive experience with informal reasoning and with the logical meaning of words such as "or."

Third, in introducing symbolic logic, teachers rely on students' ability to adjust and to gain new understandings beginning with old meanings. The special symbols in symbolic logic are not completely identical in meaning to words in ordinary language; rather, they are specialized. Students have to "catch on" to the way in which they are specialized.

Logical "Not"

The relationship of logical disjunction is only one example of a simple logical relationship between simple propositions like S and M and a compound proposition like $S ∨ M$. There are other logical relationships. Symbolic logic represents each of these relationships symbolically, using special technical symbols that have greater precision than natural language. For example, there is the "not" symbol, usually represented as a tilde ∼ or a bent line ¬.[7] The expression ∼p stands for the negation of the truth value of the proposition p to which the tilde is attached. "Not-p" (∼p) is true if p is false, and vice versa. The truth value of ∼p depends only on the truth value of p, not on the specific content of p. The truth table for logical "not" (∼) is presented in table 30.2:

TABLE 30.2: Truth Table for Logical "Not" (∼)

p	∼p
T	F
F	T

---

[7] The bent line is unicode symbol U00AC.

If *p* stands for the proposition that snow is white, ~p stands for the proposition that it is not true that snow is white. The symbol ~ is called the operation of logical negation. It is a simplification from the use of "not" in ordinary language.

Logical "And"

Starting with the English word "and," we can produce another special logical symbol that focuses on the truth values T and F. The proposition "*p* and *q*" is to be taken as true only if *both p* and *q* are true. Several notations for the logical symbol "and" have been used: the ampersand &, a simple period '.', or the special symbol ∧. We will use the symbol ∧. The truth table for logical "and" (∧) is presented in table 30.3:

TABLE 30.3: Truth Table for Logical "And" (∧)

p	*q*	*p* ∧ *q*
T	T	T
T	F	F
F	T	F
F	F	F

The logical function ∧ is called *logical conjunction*.[8] As an example, consider the compound proposition "(Snow is white) and (The moon is made of green cheese)." It is represented as *S* ∧ *M*. The first component proposition, "Snow is white" (*S*), is true, while the second component proposition, "The moon is made of green cheese" (*M*), is false. So the compound proposition *S* ∧ *M* that links the two together with logical "and" is false (F).

Logical Implication

We can produce another special logical symbol starting from the if-then relationship in English. Consider the following if-then statement:

> For if the dead are not raised, not even Christ has been raised.
> (1 Cor. 15:16)

There are two pieces, the hypothetical part introduced by "if" ("if the dead are not raised") and the conclusion, "not even Christ has been raised."

---

[8] The unicode for the symbol ∧ is U2227.

These two parts are conventionally called the *antecedent* and the *consequent*, respectively. The word *if* indicates a logical connection. Logicians "drain out" extra associations from natural language and produce a concept of *logical* implication, usually called *material implication*. It is often symbolized using the symbol ⊃ or the right arrow → or a right arrow with two parallel shafts ⇒.[9] "$p \supset q$" says that p "materially implies" q.

The essential property of this kind of implication—"material implication"—is obtained by draining out everything except the most essential relation between the truth of the parts. If the first part, the antecedent, is true, the second part, the consequent, will also be true—it cannot be false. That is to say, $p \supset q$ is true if p is true and q is true. But $p \supset q$ is false if p is true and q is false. (Remember that $p \supset q$ designates the relation of material implication, not the truth of either p or q separately.) But what happens if the antecedent p is false? Nothing follows in terms of an implication relation. The consequent can be either true or false. So logicians specify that, if p is false, $p \supset q$ is automatically taken to be true. The truth table for logical ("material") implication is presented in table 30.4:

TABLE 30.4: Truth Table for Logical ("Material") Implication (⊃)

p	q	$p \supset q$
T	T	T
T	F	F
F	T	T
F	F	T

The formal symbol ⊃ does not exactly match our everyday use of an "if-then" grammatical structure in English. The formal symbol is built by design to be purely "formal," to ignore everything except truth values. So when we consider a formal implication from p to q ($p \supset q$), the propositions p and q do not need to have any relationship in their content. Here is a valid implication:

(Snow is white) ⊃ (2 + 2 = 4).

The implication is true because both of the embedded propositions are true—even though they have no direct relationship to each other in their content. Here is another instance:

---

[9] ⊃, →, and ⇒ are represented in unicode as U2283, U2192, and U21D2, respectively. The double-shafted arrow ⇒ is also sometimes used to denote a stronger kind of implication, such as necessary implication.

(The moon is made of green cheese) ⊃ (2 + 2 = 4).

The implication as a whole is defined as true because the second part is true. The first part is not true, but that does not negate the truth of the whole.

The special symbols ∨, ~, ∧, and ⊃ are sometimes called *truth functions*, because they operate on propositions that are either true (T) or false (F), and the result is either true or false depending only on the truth or falsity of the pieces.

The introduction of special symbols allows us to focus carefully on one dimension of logical relationships. We "strip out" from the meaning of English sentences everything except the truth value, and then we define simple relationships between the truth values of the simple pieces ("Snow is white") and compound sentences. At every point we are implicitly relying on the richness of language, which God has given us, and the richness of our minds, which God has made in his image. Our language and our minds allow us to grasp the meaning not only of sentences in natural language but of special notational systems that extend and condense language, starting with pieces of natural language.

For Further Reflection

1. Let *W* stand for the proposition "Water is wet," and *D* stand for "Dogs are friendly." Write in symbolic notation the following:
   a. Water is not wet.
   b. Water is wet and dogs are friendly.
   c. Dogs are friendly or water is wet.
   d. If dogs are friendly, water is wet.
   e. Dogs are not friendly.
2. In computer science there is what is called a "nand" gate, whose output is the negation of "and." The output is true except in the case that the two inputs (say *p* and *q*) are both true. Represent this logical truth function in a truth table.
3. In computer science a "nor" gate represents the negation of logical "or." Take two inputs (*p* and *q*), combine them with "or," and then take the negation. Represent the "nor" function in a truth table.
4. What human capabilities underlie our ability to create these specialized logical truth functions?

Chapter 31

Divine Origin of
Logical Functions

Since logic as a whole originates in God and in God's rationality (the Logos), the same holds for parts of logic, including truth functions.

Theistic Meaning of Truth Functions

What shall we say about truth functions and their tables? The concentration on truth values T and F results in a very precise system that reduces logic to a formal notation. The result is "formal" or mechanical. We can proceed to check out results through a mechanical sequence, filling out the tables for truth functions. It might seem to be the case that we have now arrived at something that is independent of God. But is it?

As we observed earlier in discussing the role of persons in logic, it is always we as persons who do the thinking, whether we conduct that thinking informally with thoughts and ordinary language, or whether we do it with special symbols. The symbols have a meaning because we as persons have put meaning into them. It is we who have agreed that the symbols will behave in the way specified in their truth tables. It is we who know that these symbols are intended to represent in a simplified way something like the operations of "or" and "and" and "not" in English. It is we who know that T and F are intended to translate back into *true* and *false* in English.

Symbolism within Language

We observed earlier that logic functions within language (chapter 9). The introduction of new symbols depends on language. The same is true with the new symbols for truth functions: ∨, ~, ∧, and ⊃. As extensions of language, these symbols depend on the theistic foundations for language.

As an example, consider the symbol ~ for logical negation. Like the word *dogs*, it enjoys coherence with all three subsystems of language (introduced in chapter 9). First, it has a meaning: roughly speaking, it means "it is not the case that . . ." Second, it has a grammar. It is supposed to occur preceding a proposition, and at no other place. Third, it has a graphology. The tilde symbol ~ has a form consisting of a horizontally oriented line with two curves, the left-hand curve facing downward and the right-hand curve facing upward. The symbol ~ belongs to all three subsystems—referential, grammatical, and graphological—and does so in an interlocking way. It can be written, read, and interpreted only by relying simultaneously on all three subsystems. The three subsystems derive their meaning and their interlocking function from God, who is the archetypal speaker (see chapter 9). Thus the symbol ~ reveals the glory of God in language and symbolism.

Form-meaning Composites

We can proceed to operate on complex expressions in symbolic logic without always keeping meaning in mind. The symbolic expressions are meant to behave well whether we are thinking of the meaning or not. But when we perform operations on symbolic expressions, we are relying on the coherence of form with meaning. The individual symbols ∨, ~, ∧, and ⊃ are form-meaning composites (see chapter 20). The graphic forms ∨, ~, ∧, and ⊃ have the *same* meaning in each occurrence. This coherence between form and meaning has its foundation in the ultimate coherence of God and his specifications for truth and for language.

Coherence among Fields

The use of special symbols relies on further coherences in the world that God has ordained. (1) We rely on coherences between ordinary language and special logical symbols; (2) we have coherences between our *minds* and language and the special symbols; (3) we have coherences between formal operations on the symbols and logical relationships between truths and falsehoods in the real world. All these coherences hold because God is coherent with himself. His speech offers the basis for (1) ordinary language, (2) specialized symbolic notation, (3) human rationality in the mind, (4) truth and falsehood in ordinary life, and (5) the specialized, reduced form of truth and falsehood in truth tables.

The Origin of Truth

We can also consider the origin of the ideas of truth and falsehood. A logical symbol focusing wholly on the truth values T and F is a simplification.

From what does it simplify? The distinction between truth and falsehood in ordinary language is one starting point. And this distinction has its roots in the truthfulness of God, who is truth (John 14:6).[1] God knows all truths, in all their richness. So the simplification involved in a truth table has its roots in him.

We have already explained how the truth functions have a close relation to corresponding functions in ordinary language, namely "or" and "and" and "not." Somewhat more loosely (because the correspondence is not as close), the idea for material implication ⊃ goes back to the structures in ordinary language related to the word *implies*, as well as to clausal structures with "if-then" (called *conditionals*). It is also similar to instances of reasoning with the word *therefore*. Language—not only English but all human language—is a gift from God. In addition, God speaks and uses human language. We can see uses of "or," "and," and "not" (or their analogues in the original languages, Hebrew, Aramaic, and Greek) in the Bible. In this prosaic sense, logical truth functions have their origin in God.

Divine Origin of Logical Negation ("Not")

Now consider the different truth functions, one by one. We begin with logical "not" (~). God's speech in the Bible distinguishes truth and falsehood. "The fool says in his heart, 'There is no God'" (Ps. 14:1). By ascribing the saying to "the fool," as well as through other passages of the Bible affirming the existence of God, the Bible indicates that Psalm 14:1 presents us with a falsehood. It is false that "there is no God." God's speech to us indicates that he knows about falsehoods that people entertain, as well as about truth. The two are not confused in his mind. He knows falsehoods to be false, and truths to be true. His consistency with himself involves opposition to what is not consistent with himself. He has expressed to us in time, in a verse like Psalm 14:1, one aspect of what he has always known. Thus the opposition between truth and its negation is eternal.

We can see further roots for the relation of negation by considering unity and diversity. Diversity implies negations. If A differs from B, A is not the same as B. Or, to put it more explicitly, it is *not true* that A is the same as B. These relations have their ultimate roots in Trinitarian diversity. The Father is not the Son.[2]

---

[1] See Vern S. Poythress, *In the Beginning Was the Word: Language—A God-Centered Approach* (Wheaton, IL: Crossway, 2009), chapter 35.

[2] "So there is one Father, *not* three Fathers" (Athanasian Creed).

We can also see a relation between God's holiness and negation. God in his holiness is distinct from all that is unholy. Before the world was created, there did not exist anything unholy. But according to the consistency of his character as holy, God would be distinct from any unholy thing that arose within creation. And this distinction is known by God before he created the world, as part of his foreknowledge. Negation, therefore, exists first of all in God. Negation taking place in our minds is derived from God. Finally, negation as a logical symbol is a piece of meaningful specialized language representing one aspect of the logic of God's original character. It depends on his self-consistency, his holiness, and his moral opposition to what is opposed to him.

Divine Origin of Logical "Or"

Now consider the function of logical "or" (symbolized as $\vee$). We can see the divine origin of this logical relation by starting with the creation of the world. God created a particular world by speaking. "And God said, 'Let there be light,' and there was light" (Gen. 1:3). The particularity of his speech implies choices.

God is absolute. He did not have to create. And having chosen to create, he was free to create whatever he wished. He might have done otherwise. That word *otherwise* represents alternatives in his choices. We as human beings make choices in imitation of God's divine choice-making. We consider alternatives, including ethically reprehensible alternatives:

> And if it is evil in your eyes to serve the Lord, *choose* this day whom you will serve, whether the gods your fathers served in the region beyond the River, *or* the gods of the Amorites in whose land you dwell. (Josh. 24:15)

The original power of choice-making is in God, as Creator. Even before the creation of the world, God has the choice in his plan of whether to create and what kind of world to create. The plurality of options is a diversity in the mind of God. And the plurality of God's speech when he speaks the creation into existence has its foundation in God the Son, who is the Word of God, distinct from God the Father. The "or's" within this world, that is, the different options of which we become aware, rest on the diversity in God's thought.

Divine Origin of Implication

Next consider the true function of *material implication*, that is, $\supset$. Implication in symbolic logic has ties with reasoning. If we think that p is true, and we also think that *p* implies *q*, we reason from the truth of *p* to the truth of *q*. This kind of reasoning is common enough that it has received its own name, *modus ponens*. The Bible contains examples of this kind of reasoning in an informal context. Consider Colossians 3:1:

> If then you have been raised with Christ, seek the things that are above, where Christ is, seated at the right hand of God.

The context in Colossians 3:1 tacitly implies that you have been raised with Christ. So the apostle Paul expects his readers to draw a conclusion from his if-then sentence in Colossians 3:1. You have been raised with Christ. Therefore seek the things that are above, . . .

It is a simplification or reduction of the riches of this passage if we convert it into formal logic, but it is possible to represent one aspect of the reasoning in a more formal structure:

> If you have been raised with Christ, seek the things that are above.
> You have been raised with Christ.
> Therefore, seek the things that are above.

We can represent the structure of this argument by letting *R* represent "you have been raised with Christ" and *S* represent "seek the things that are above."

> $R \supset S$
> R
> Therefore *S*.

We may give another example of informal reasoning from 1 Corinthians 15:16–22:

> For if the dead are not raised, not even Christ has been raised.

The apostle Paul then turns this reasoning around in order to convince the Corinthians that they need to believe in a future bodily resurrection:

> But in fact Christ has been raised from the dead, . . . (1 Cor. 15:20)
> So also in Christ shall all be made alive. (1 Cor. 15:22)

It is possible to represent one aspect of the reasoning through using formal logic:

For if the dead are not raised, not even Christ has been raised.
But in fact Christ has been raised from the dead.
Therefore, the dead are raised.

If D stands for "the dead are raised," and C stands for "Christ has been raised," the simplification goes

$\sim D \supset \sim C$
C
Hence D.

This is a recognized valid form of argumentation, called *modus tollens*.[3]

Consider another piece of informal movement in thought:

For as the Father raises the dead and gives them life, so also the Son gives life to whom he will. (John 5:21)

The expression "so also" indicates the movement of thought. The statement in John 5:21 is preceded by a general statement that expounds the relation of the Father's actions to the Son's:

For whatever the Father does, that the Son does likewise. (John 5:19)

The word *whatever* invites us to apply the general principle to particular examples such as raising the dead. If the Father raises the dead, the Son raises the dead. If the Father gives life, the Son gives life. John 5:21 then reasons on the basis of the fact that the Father does raise the dead and does give them life. It invites us to the conclusion that the Son "gives life to whom he will." We can see here the operation of informal implication. Formal implication within symbolic logic is a simplification and reduction that starts from one aspect of informal implications.

The particular kind of implication that we have in John 5:19–21 is significant because it shows how implication is rooted in the Trinity. The relation between the Father and the Son, the Son's love for the Father, and the Son's imitation of the Father, are all a foundation for drawing implications from the Father's acts to the Son's acts.

The acts of which John 5 speaks are redemptive acts within history.

---

[3] Alfred North Whitehead and Bertrand Russell, *Principia Mathematica*, 2nd ed., 3 vols. (Cambridge: Cambridge University Press, 1927), 1:103, proposition 2.17; Irving M. Copi, *Symbolic Logic*, 5th ed. (New York: Macmillan, 1979), 22–23. *Modus tollens* is a Latin expression meaning "the way that denies."

But God's acts within history are always consistent with who he always is. It is always the case, even before the foundation of the world, that the Son is "the radiance of the glory of God and the *exact imprint* of his nature" (Heb. 1:3). The eternal harmony between the Father and the Son is the basis for their harmony when they act within creation. That eternal harmony includes implications. We might say that the Father's character *implies* the Son's character. Divine implication in this sense is the ultimate foundation for logical relations of implication among truths about the world and truths that we think through in our minds—minds made in the image of God.

Divine Origin of Logical Conjunction ("And")

We can also see roots for the relationship of logical conjunction, that is, logical "and." The Father raises the dead and gives them life. The Son also gives life. Both are true. Joint truth belongs to God's acts within history. Many things are true concerning God's character even before the foundation of the world. The Father is holy and the Son is holy and the Holy Spirit is holy. The Father is almighty and the Son is almighty and the Holy Spirit is almighty.[4] Joint truth expresses the harmony among the persons of the Trinity. We can also see unity and diversity. Each truth is a distinct truth, and the persons of the Trinity are distinct from one another. Each truth belongs to a complex of truths: God is holy; God is almighty. The particularity of truths about the persons goes together with the generality of the same truth for God. Logical relations of conjunction among truths about this world have their foundation in the unity and the diversity of the Trinity.

For Further Reflection

1. How do each of the main logical truth functions, ~, ∨, ⊃, ∧, have a foundation in God?
2. Show a relation between material implication and 1 Thessalonians 4:14.
3. Discuss the relation of Colossians 3:2 to logical negation and logical disjunction.
4. Discuss how Christian and non-Christian views of transcendence and immanence affect our view of the truth functions ~ and ⊃.

---

[4] The formulation about the persons being "almighty" is found in the Athanasian Creed.

Chapter 32

Complex Expressions

Using the truth functions ~, ∨, ∧, and ⊃, we can construct more complicated combinations. For example, ~(~p) is the result of applying the function of logical negation (~) twice to p. If p is the proposition "Snow is white," ~p is the proposition "It is not true that snow is white," or equivalently, "Snow is not white." ~(~p) is the proposition "It is not true that snow is not white." Or consider another example. (p ∨ q) ∧ r is the result of first applying logical disjunction ∨ to p and q, and then taking the result, namely p ∨ q, as one of the starting points to which we then apply the operation of logical conjunction ∧. All expressions that use truth functions in addition to propositional symbols like p and q are called *compound propositions*. By contrast, p and q are simple propositions.

The Use of Parentheses

We have to be careful about the grouping of operations, which we have indicated by using parentheses. (p ∨ q) ∧ r is not the same as p ∨ (q ∧ r). Consider a particular example, where p stands for "It is raining," q stands for "It is dark," and r stands for "It is cold":

> (p ∨ q) ∧ r is exemplified by: (It is raining or it is dark) and it is cold.
> p ∨ (q ∧ r) is exemplified by: It is raining or (it is dark and it is cold).

Suppose that in fact it is raining (p is T), it is dark (q is T), but it is not cold (r is F). Then (p ∨ q) ∧ r, which means "(It is raining or it is dark) and it is cold," is false, because it is not cold. p ∨ (q ∧ r), which means "It is raining or (it is dark and it is cold)," is true, because it is raining.

In the case of p ∨ (q ∧ r) we first apply the operation of logical conjunction to q and r, and obtain q ∧ r. Then the result gets used as an input for logical disjunction ∨. Suppose p is true, q is true, and r is false. Then what is the truth value of p ∨ (q ∧ r)? Using the truth table for ∧, we see that q ∧ r is F. We can substitute F for q ∧ r in p ∨ (q ∧ r) and get p ∨ F.

p is T. Substituting into $p \lor F$, we get $T \lor F$. Using the truth table for $\lor$, we can see that, since the first entry of $T \lor F$ is T, the value of $T \lor F$ is T. Thus, $p \lor (q \land r)$ is T, even though $q \land r$ is F. Now ask what is the truth value of $(p \lor q) \land r$? Note the different grouping of the parentheses. p is T. So, using the truth table for $\lor$, $p \lor q$ is T. Substituting T for $p \lor q$, we get the expression $T \land r$. r is F. So $T \land r$ is F. $(p \lor q) \land r$ is F. Thus in this case $(p \lor q) \land r$ and $p \lor (q \land r)$ have different truth values. (See table 32.1 for the calculation.)

TABLE 32.1: Calculating Truth Values

(p is T, q is T, and r is F.)

Start:	$(p \lor q) \land r$	$p \lor (q \land r)$
	$(T \lor T) \land r$	$p \lor (T \land F)$
	$(T) \land r$	$p \lor (F)$
	$T \land F$	$T \lor F$
	F	T

We can consider all possible truth values by drawing up a table in which we have rows for every possible combination of truth values for p, q, and r (see table 32.2a):

TABLE 32.2a: All Possible Combinations of Truth Values for p, q, and r

p	q	r
T	T	T
T	T	F
T	F	T
T	F	F
F	T	T
F	T	F
F	F	T
F	F	F

To make sure that we have not omitted any possible combination, it is best to have a systematic way of arranging the rows. On the first row after the headings p, q, r, we make p, q, and r all have the value T. Then on the next row we vary *r* alone, leaving *p* and *q* with the same value (T). When we have finished dealing with both possibilities for *r*, we change the value of *q*. We let *q* be F. All this time *p* constantly has the value T. With *p* as T and *q* as F, we must once again let *r* take on both its values. We first make *r* have the value T, and then in the next row we give *r* the value F.

We have now gone systematically through all the possible combinations for *q* as T or F and *r* as T or F. But for all these combinations, *p* is always T. To cover all the possible combinations involving all *three* propositions, *p*, *q*, and *r*, we must now change *p* to its other value, namely F. We then produce a new series of rows. We repeat all the possible combinations for *q* and *r*, starting, as usual, with the value T for both *q* and *r*. With *q* as T, we let *r* take each of its two possible values, and then we vary *q*, all the time retaining *p* with the value F.

Once we have the table for all possible combinations for *p*, *q*, and *r*, we can add columns to the right of it. The extra columns will be used to calculate compound propositions like $p \vee q$ (see table 32.2b):

TABLE 32.2b: All Possible Combinations for *p*, *q*, and *r* Plus Compounds

p	*q*	*r*	*p* ∨ *q*	(*p* ∨ *q*) ∧ *r*	*q* ∧ *r*	*p* ∨ (*q* ∧ *r*)
T	T	T				
T	T	F				
T	F	T				
T	F	F				
F	T	T				
F	T	F				
F	F	T				
F	F	F				

Now we can calculate the truth values of $(p \vee q) \wedge r$ and $p \vee (q \wedge r)$ (table 32.2c):

TABLE 32.2c: All Possible Combinations for
p, q, and r Plus Compounds, with Calculations

p	q	r	$p \lor q$	$(p \lor q) \land r$	$q \land r$	$p \lor (q \land r)$
T	T	T	T	T	T	T
T	T	F	T	F	F	T
T	F	T	T	T	F	T
T	F	F	T	F	F	T
F	T	T	T	T	T	T
F	T	F	T	F	F	F
F	F	T	F	F	F	F
F	F	F	F	F	F	F

Column 4, for $p \lor q$, is calculated by paying attention to the information about p and q that is provided in the first two columns. When p is T and q is T, in the top two rows, $p \lor q$ is T. Likewise we get $p \lor q$ as T in the other rows until we come to the last two rows. In these last two rows, p is F and q is F, so $p \lor q$ is F. In the same way we can fill out the entries in the other columns to the right.

When we compare the columns for $(p \lor q) \land r$ and $p \lor (q \land r)$, we can see that they are not always the same.

Similarly, $(\sim p) \lor q$ is not the same as $\sim(p \lor q)$. The expression $(\sim p) \lor q$, when translated into English, says that either not-p is true or q is true. The second expression, $\sim(p \lor q)$, says that it is not true that p or q is true. That is, $(p$ or $q)$ is false, and it follows that both p and q must be false.

To avoid using too many parentheses, logicians have agreed to have a common understanding: logical negation $\sim$ has highest "precedence." Unless parentheses indicate the contrary, the operation of negation is applied only to the immediately following symbol. Thus $\sim p \lor q$, without any parentheses, means the same as $(\sim p) \lor q$. If we want to talk about $\sim(p \lor q)$ we have to leave in the parentheses.

Potential Ambiguities

The use of a precise notation can eliminate certain ambiguities that crop up in natural language. Consider the sentence,

It is not true that snow is white and the moon is made of green cheese.

Theoretically, this sentence could have two distinct meanings, which we can indicate by adding parentheses:

It is not true that (snow is white and the moon is made of green cheese).
(It is not true that snow is white) and the moon is made of green cheese.

The first of the two sentences negates the compound proposition, "Snow is white and the moon is made of green cheese." Since the moon is not in fact made of green cheese, the compound proposition combining it with "Snow is white" is false. Accordingly, the sentence as a whole is true. Now, consider the second sentence, "(It is not true that snow is white) and the moon is made of green cheese." Since snow is white, the negation "It is not true that snow is white" is false. It is also false that the moon is made of green cheese. Accordingly, the proposition represented by the whole sentence is false.

Let S stand for the proposition that snow is white, and M stand for the proposition that the moon is made of green cheese. Then in symbolic notation the first sentence is

$$\sim(S \wedge M)$$

Logical negation $\sim$ is applied to the compound proposition $S \wedge M$. The second sentence, "(It is not true that snow is white) and the moon is made of green cheese," is represented as:

$$\sim S \wedge M$$

We can verify that if S is T and M is F, the two expressions have different truth values.

Logical Relations between Truth Functions

Because the truth functions $\vee$, $\sim$, $\wedge$, and $\supset$ are precisely defined to operate rigidly on truth values, they have precise relations to one another. For example:

$p \wedge q$ is equivalent to $\sim(\sim p \vee \sim q)$.

Again consider an example. If p stands for "It is raining," and q stands for "It is dark," we obtain the following expressions:

$p \wedge q$ means: (It is raining) and (It is dark).
$\sim(\sim p \vee \sim q)$ means: It is not true that [(It is not raining) or (It is not dark)].

When we say that two expressions are equivalent, we mean that they always have the same truth value.

[(It is raining) and (It is dark)] is T if and only if
It is not true that [(It is not raining) or (It is not dark)]

For a general statement that "$p \wedge q$ is equivalent to $\sim(\sim p \vee \sim q)$," we can check an equivalence by testing that the two sides have the same truth value for all possible combinations of true or false p and true or false q.

Let us actually carry out the calculation. We aim to show that $p \wedge q$ is equivalent to $\sim(\sim p \vee \sim q)$. To show that they are equivalent, we have to check that both sides produce the same truth value for any of the possible starting combinations, with p as T or F and with q as T or F. There are four combinations: p is T and q is T; p is T and q is F; p is F and q is T; p is F and q is F. Take these one at a time. Suppose p is T and q is T. $\sim p$ is F (using the truth table for $\sim$). Likewise $\sim q$ is F. $\sim p \vee \sim q$ is F (using the truth table for $\vee$). Finally, $\sim(\sim p \vee \sim q)$ is T (using the truth table for $\sim$). Once again, we can draw up a table, whose columns show the steps in reasoning. Table 32.3a shows the necessary columns, and then fills in the first row, which deals with the case where p is true (T) and q is true (T).

TABLE 32.3a: Calculating the Truth Value of $\sim(\sim p \vee \sim q)$

p	q	$\sim p$	$\sim q$	$\sim p \vee \sim q$	$\sim(\sim p \vee \sim q)$
T	T	F	F	F	T

Now we can fill out the rest of the table (see table 32.3b):

TABLE 32.3b: Calculating the Truth Value of $\sim(\sim p \vee \sim q)$ for All Possibilities

p	q	$\sim p$	$\sim q$	$\sim p \vee \sim q$	$\sim(\sim p \vee \sim q)$
T	T	F	F	F	T
T	F	F	T	T	F
F	T	T	F	T	F
F	F	T	T	T	F

The last column of the table agrees exactly with the table for logical "and" ($p \wedge q$). So we have checked that $p \wedge q$ is equivalent to $\sim(\sim p \vee \sim q)$.

Because of the equivalence between $p \wedge q$ and $\sim(\sim p \vee \sim q)$, the logical symbol $\wedge$ (logical "and") can actually be *defined* using the expression $\sim(\sim p \vee \sim q)$. Rather than explaining logical "and" separately, we can simply specify that it is a shorthand expression for $\sim(\sim p \vee \sim q)$. More precisely, we say that any expression of the form $A \wedge B$ is shorthand for the corresponding expression $\sim(\sim A \vee \sim B)$. It is up to us whether we want to introduce logical "and" by a separate explanation or whether we want to define it as a shorthand expression for something else. We just need to make sure first that the expression $\sim(\sim A \vee \sim B)$ really is equivalent to the function of logical "and."

We know, then, that logical "and" can be *defined* using two other logical symbols, namely, logical negation $\sim$ and logical disjunction $\vee$. Is the same true for other logical symbols? If we like, any one of the symbols $\vee$, $\wedge$, and $\supset$ can be *defined* using the symbol $\sim$ for logical negation and one other symbol. Here are the equivalences that enable us to do it:

> $p \wedge q$ is equivalent to $\sim(\sim p \vee \sim q)$ (already checked).
> $p \wedge q$ is equivalent to $\sim(p \supset \sim q)$.
> $p \supset q$ is equivalent to $\sim p \vee q$.
> $p \supset q$ is equivalent to $\sim(p \wedge \sim q)$.
> $p \vee q$ is equivalent to $\sim(\sim p \wedge \sim q)$.
> $p \vee q$ is equivalent to $\sim p \supset q$.[1]

The equivalences mean that there is more than one perspective available in dealing with truth functions. We can start with $\sim$ and $\vee$ alone, and use them to define $\wedge$ and $\supset$. We thereby use $\sim$ and $\vee$ as a perspective on $\wedge$ and $\supset$. Or we can start with $\sim$ and $\wedge$, and use them as a perspective on the rest. Each perspective involves a difference in detail about the meaning of the symbols. In addition, the English renderings of the meanings of the expressions depend on which perspective we use. But the truth values are the same, no matter which perspective we choose.

---

[1] In fact, all four of the logical symbols can be defined using only one symbol to start with, namely, the Sheffer stroke $|$. $p \mid q$ is interpreted as meaning "p is incompatible with q." $p \mid q$ is equivalent to $\sim(p \wedge q)$. See Alfred North Whitehead and Bertrand Russell, *Principia Mathematica*, 2nd ed., 3 vols. (Cambridge: Cambridge University Press, 1927), 1:xvi. We could also use as the starting symbol $\downarrow$ ("nor"). $p \downarrow q$ is equivalent to $\sim p \wedge \sim q$.

For Further Reflection

1. Why can logical disjunction ∨ be defined using logical negation ~ and material implication ⊃?

2. Let A, B, be true propositions and G, H be false propositions. Determine the truth value of the following:
   a. $\sim A \vee B$
   b. $\sim(H \supset G)$
   c. $A \supset (H \supset \sim G)$.
   d. $(A \supset H) \supset (A \wedge \sim B)$

3. Let B stand for the proposition "Bob is intelligent," let C stand for the proposition "Charlotte is tall," and let D stand for the proposition "Donna is happy." Convert into symbolic notation the following:
   a. Either Bob is intelligent or Charlotte is not tall.
   b. If Donna is not happy, Charlotte is not tall.
   c. Bob is not intelligent, and either Charlotte is tall or Donna is not happy.
   d. If Charlotte is tall, then Bob is not intelligent and Donna is happy.

4. Use truth tables to verify that
   a. $p \vee q$ is equivalent to $\sim(\sim p \wedge \sim q)$.
   b. $p \supset q$ is equivalent to $\sim(p \wedge \sim q)$.
   c. $p \vee q$ is equivalent to $\sim p \supset q$.
   d. $p \wedge q$ is equivalent to $\sim(p \supset \sim q)$.

5. a. Suppose we define $p \mid q$ as meaning "p is incompatible with q." $p \mid q$ is equivalent to $\sim(p \wedge q)$. Write out the truth table for $p \mid q$. (When so defined, the symbol | is called the Sheffer stroke [see chapter 41].)
   b. Verify the following equivalences using truth tables.
      a. $\sim p$ is equivalent to $p \mid p$.
      b. $p \vee q$ is equivalent to $(p \mid p) \mid (q \mid q)$.
      c. $p \supset q$ is equivalent to $p \mid (q \mid q)$.
      d. $p \wedge q$ is equivalent to $(p \mid q) \mid (p \mid q)$.

6. Is there any limit to the complexity of compound formulas using the logical truth functions? Write out a formula using at least seven instances of truth function symbols (i.e., ∨, ~, ∧, ⊃, or |), and all four propositional symbols p, q, r, s.

Part II.B

Perspectives on Truth in Logic

.

Chapter 33

Venn Diagrams for Truth Functions

We have represented the meaning of logical connectives like "or" and "and" using truth tables. But there are other ways of explaining these connectives. Let us look at some of these ways, beginning with Venn diagrams.

Venn Diagrams for Propositions

Suppose p and q are two general statements that may or may not be true in particular cases.[1] We picture the cases where p is true as a circle with the label p. We picture the cases where q is true as a second circle with the label q. The region where the two circles overlap (intersect) then represents the area where *both* p and q are true. (See figure 33.1.)

Fig. 33.1: Venn Diagram of Conjunction ("And")

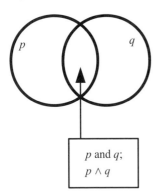

p and q;
$p \land q$

In addition, the total region enclosed by both circles represents the area where either p or q is true. (See figure 33.2.)

---

[1] In our examples at this point we are simplifying by ignoring the issue of "quantification," that is, the treatment of propositions that may be true in all or some or no cases. See chapter 48.

Fig. 33.2: Venn Diagram of Conjunction ("Or")

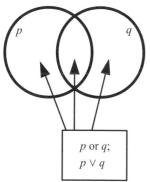

The region outside the circle of p represents the area where p is not true ($\sim p$). (See figure 33.3.)

Fig. 33.3: Venn Diagram of Negation ("Not")

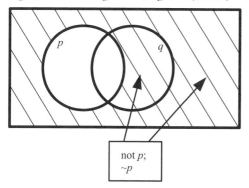

What is the region that represents the area where q is not true (where q is false)? See figure 33.4:

Fig. 33.4: Venn Diagram of $\sim q$

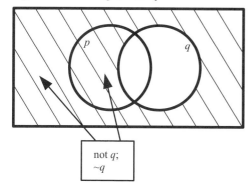

Finally, how do we represent the proposition $p \supset q$? Remember that $p \supset q$ is true except when p is true and q is false. So, in a Venn diagram, we must cross out only one region, namely, the region where p is true and q is false. The region to be crossed out is the region inside the circle p and outside the circle q. (See figure 33.5.)

Fig. 33.5: Venn Diagram of Implication ('$\supset$')

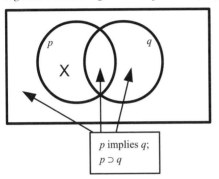

Most of the time when we are reasoning using a proposition like $p \supset q$, we are in a situation where we know that $p \supset q$ is true. We can represent that situation in a diagram by simply eliminating the region where p is true and q is false, that is, the region inside the circle p and outside the circle q. If we collapse that region down to nothing, we obtain a diagram in which the region representing p is completely inside the circle q. (When we eliminate the empty regions, we have a Euler diagram instead of a Venn diagram.) This situation of inclusion of one region within the other represents the reality where we know that $p \supset q$. (See figure 33.6.)

Fig. 33.6: Alternate Diagram when $(p \supset q)$

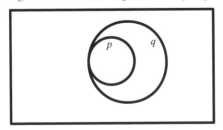

Venn diagrams and Euler diagrams are convenient for representing logical relations, because more complex logical relations can often be "read off"

from the diagrams. We have already illustrated the process, when we considered how to represent the Barbara syllogism and other syllogisms using Venn diagrams (chapter 27).

Why do Venn diagrams and Euler diagrams work? They are spatial representations of logical relations. They work because there is a harmony between logic and space. Or we might say that the facts concerning what belongs to spatial regions obey the laws of logic. If we occupy an impersonalist worldview, we may be tempted to claim that the spatial relations "reduce" to logic. But God rules the world personally. His speech governs space; his speech governs human reasoning and human logic. The coherence between space and logic goes back to the coherence of God's speech.

Once again we see unity and diversity. There is unity in the general coherent principles that operate both in spatial regions and in reasoning about "or" and "and." There is diversity in the expressions of the general principles. The truths can be illustrated either in spatial relationships or in reasoning in language, and these two demonstrations are distinct in texture.

We can see here one of the benefits of formalization. In moving toward formalized versions of "or" and "and," we necessarily simplify the richness of natural language. We reduce the function of "or" and "and" to one dimension. In previous chapters we have sometimes stressed what is lost in this kind of reduction. But we can also ask what is gained. By stripping truth and falsehood down to "bare bones," we can show that these bare bones, in their simplicity, have several parallels in various fields of study.

Venn diagrams can also represent the logical relations among three distinct propositions *p*, *q*, and *r*. We represent each proposition by a different circle, and make sure that the circles overlap, so that there is a spatial region for each combination of truth and falsehood (see figure 33.7):

Fig. 33.7: Venn Diagram of *p*, *q*, *r*

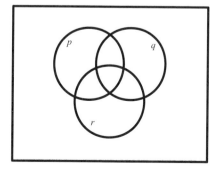

For Further Reflection

1. Represent in a Venn diagram
   a. $\sim p \vee \sim q$
   b. $p \mid q$, which is defined as being false only if p and q are both true.
   c. $\sim p \wedge q$
   d. $\sim(p \wedge q)$

2. Use Venn diagrams to check the logical equivalences mentioned in the exercises of chapter 32:
   a. $p \vee q$ is equivalent to $\sim(\sim p \wedge \sim q)$.
   b. $p \supset q$ is equivalent to $\sim(p \wedge \sim q)$.
   c. $p \vee q$ is equivalent to $\sim p \supset q$.
   d. $p \wedge q$ is equivalent to $\sim(p \supset \sim q)$.

3. With the definition that $p \mid q$ is false only if p and q are both true, use Venn diagrams to check the following equivalences:
   a. $p \mid q$ is equivalent to $\sim(p \wedge q)$.
   b. $\sim p$ is equivalent to $p \mid p$.
   c. $p \vee q$ is equivalent to $(p \mid p) \mid (q \mid q)$.
   d. $p \supset q$ is equivalent to $p \mid (q \mid q)$.
   e. $p \wedge q$ is equivalent to $(p \mid q) \mid (p \mid q)$.

4. Check the following equivalences by using Venn diagrams:
   a. $p \wedge (q \vee r)$ is equivalent to $(p \wedge q) \vee (p \wedge r)$.
   b. $p \vee (q \wedge r)$ is equivalent to $(p \vee q) \wedge (p \vee r)$.
   c. $p \wedge (p \vee q)$ is equivalent to p.
   d. $p \vee (p \wedge q)$ is equivalent to p.

Chapter 34

Other Representations
of Logical Truth
and Falsehood

We now consider some other ways of representing logical truth and falsehood and logical truth functions.

Sets

Let us first consider sets. Mathematicians and logicians have a special technical concept of "set." Roughly speaking, a set is a collection, and its members are whatever individuals belong to the collection. A collection with one small apple, one medium-sized apple, and one large apple is a set with three members. In parallel with the development of technical concepts in logic, the technical concept of a *set* puts to one side the many-dimensional complexity of our experience of the world and concentrates on only one dimension: it concentrates on the idea of a member belonging to a whole. In addition, a set is assumed to be well-defined, so that what does and does not belong to a particular set is precisely specified. Sets are often designated by listing their members, enclosed in braces. {1,2,3} is a set consisting of the members 1, 2, and 3.

It turns out that we can define certain operations that can be performed on sets. For example, we can define the *union* of two sets A and B as the set whose members are exactly the members of A or B. Suppose A is the set {1,2} and B is the set {2,3}. Their union is the set that contains all the members of set A, namely, 1 and 2, and *in addition* all the members of set B, namely, 2 and 3. The union is {1,2,3}. It so happens that 2 is in both sets A and B, but it does not get listed twice when we form the union. It is enough to list it once, because even a single listing already indicates that 2 is a member of the union. That is, {1, 2, 2, 3} is the same set as {1, 2, 3}. The order in which the elements are listed is irrelevant. {1,2,3} is the same set as {2,3,1}.

In mathematical notation, the union of sets A and B is denoted $A \cup B$.

$A \cup B = \{$members x such that x is a member of A or x is a member of $B\}$

This idea of union has a close connection with Venn diagrams. In the Venn diagram with the circles p and q, the interior of the circle labeled p can represent all the points belonging to the *set P*. The interior of the circle q can represent all the points belonging to the *set Q*. The union, namely $P \cup Q$, is then the set of all points that belong either to the set P or to the set Q. This set corresponds to the points that are inside one or both of the circles. (See figure 34.1.)

Fig. 34.1: Union of Two Sets ($P \cup Q$)

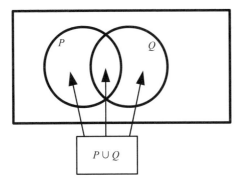

The property of "being a member of" is denoted by a special symbol $\in$. The expression $x \in A$ means "x is a member of A." Using this new notation, we can write:

$x \in A \cup B$ if and only if $x \in A$ or $x \in B$.

Note that set union $\cup$ has a close relation to the logical connective "or." An element x is in the union if it is *either* in A or in B.

We can also define the *intersection* of two sets. The intersection of sets A and B is the set whose members are exactly the members that belong *both* to A *and* to B. The intersection is denoted $A \cap B$.

$x \in A \cap B$ if and only if $x \in A$ and $x \in B$.

The intersection of two sets has a close relation to the logical connective "and."

It also has a connection to Venn diagrams. The area within the intersection of the two circles p and q represents the intersection of two sets. (See figure 34.2.)

Fig. 34.2: Intersection of Two Sets ($P \cap Q$)

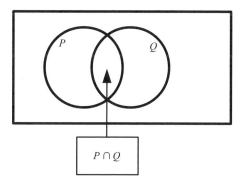

Finally, we can define a *complement* relation. The complement of the set A consists in everything that does not belong to A. The complement is sometimes denoted A'. (See figure 34.3.)

Fig. 34.3: Complement (') of Set A

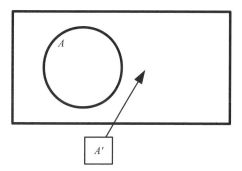

We can summarize the idea of a complement set using our usual notation:

$x \in A'$ for all x such that it is not true that $x \in A$.[1]

The complement of a set has a close relation to the logical connective "not." The three operations, union ($\cup$), intersection ($\cap$), and complement ('), together

---

[1] Care must be exercised with this definition of complement. We have to make sure that we have a reasonable idea about the total range for the members x. The definition of complement tacitly assumes that there is a large set U that is the total range for x. Within this "universe" U we are considering all the smaller sets like A and B. Otherwise, we can run into the paradox discussed in appendix A1, concerning the "set of all sets."

act like the operations of disjunction (∨), conjunction (∧), and negation (~). Thus there is a correlation between sets, Venn diagrams, and the logic of truth functions ("or," "and," and "not").

If we like, we can also add in the logical operation of implication (⊃). The analog for sets is the relationship of set inclusion. We say that a set A is *included* in B if every member of A is also a member of B. More compactly,

If $x \in A$ then $x \in B$.

Or we can write the same condition in a way that actually uses the implication symbol ⊃:

x ∈ A ⊃ x ∈ B.

The usual symbolic notation for saying that A is included in B is $A \subseteq B$. If we want to represent this relationship in a spatial diagram, we can do it just by putting a circle representing A completely inside the circle representing B. (See figure 34.4.)

Fig. 34.4: Set Inclusion: $A \subseteq B$

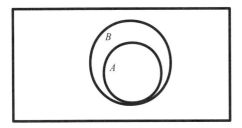

If $A \subseteq B$ and $B \subseteq C$, it follows that $A \subseteq C$ (figure 34.5):

Fig. 34.5: Set Inclusion: $A \subseteq B \subseteq C$

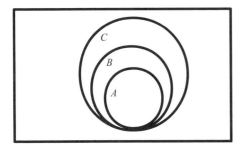

We can see that relationships between sets can model logical relationships such as "or," "and," "not," and "implies."

Lattices

Mathematics has another subfield, called *lattice theory*. This field is related to the patterns that we have explored for truth functions. So we need to dip into this theory.

Lattice theory is a theory that studies partial orderings of certain kinds. First we have to understand what a partial ordering is.[2] A partial ordering, roughly speaking, is an ordering of "greater" and "lesser," where some items are greater than others but where other items may be unordered relative to one another. For example, the natural numbers 1, 2, 3, 4, … have a natural ordering of greater and lesser. The natural numbers are one example of a partially ordered set. In fact the natural numbers are not merely *partially* ordered but *totally* ordered, since for any two distinct numbers one is greater than the other.

But there are other examples where partial orderings are *not* total orderings. Think of a ladder. The higher rungs of the ladder can be regarded as "greater than" the lower rungs. But two points on the same rung do not have any definite order. Neither one is greater than the other. To make it more complicated, we can consider several ladders side by side. Or we can consider a trellis or latticework consisting in a pattern of crisscrosses or X's (see figure 34.6):

Fig. 34.6: A Trellis

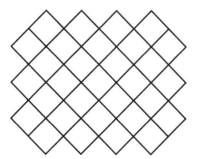

Each intersection point on a trellis can be considered to be "greater than"

---

[2] For an exact definition and technical discussion, see Garrett Birkhoff, *Lattice Theory*, 2nd ed. (New York: American Mathematical Society, 1948), 1; George Grätzer, *Lattice Theory: First Concepts and Distributive Lattices* (reprint; Mineola, NY: Dover, 2009), 1–2.

the points immediately below it, at a 45 degree angle to the right or to the left. Thus in figure 34.7 point *A* is "greater than" point *B*. Point *A* is also "greater than" any points further down the 45-degree downward paths: points *C*, *D*, and *E*. But points on the same level are not ordered relative to one another. Point *A* has no order relative to *G*.

Fig. 34.7: Trellis Plus Letters

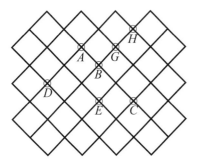

In addition, point *A* has no ordering with respect to point *H*, because *H* is not above or below *A by means of* 45-degree paths.

Another example of a partial ordering occurs with sets. Suppose that we consider the ordering in which one set is defined as "less than" another if it is included within the other, but is not exactly the same set as the other.[3] For example, the set {2} is included in {1,2,3}. So {1,2,3} is greater than {2}. On the other hand, {1,2} and {2,3} do not have an order, because neither is completely included within the other. The set of dogs is included in the set of animals. So the set of animals is "greater" in the specified sense. The set of collies is included in the set of dogs, and so the set of dogs is greater than the set of collies. However, the set of horses is unordered in relation to the set of dogs, because neither set includes the other.[4]

It turns out that sets form a lattice when we use the relationship of inclusion to order them. The term *lattice* has a special technical definition within mathematics. It is not just any arrangement of latticework with a

---

[3] In mathematical terminology, such an inclusion is a "proper inclusion." {1} is properly included in {1,2,3}. By contrast, the inclusion of {1,2} in {1,2} is "improper," because the two sets are identical.
[4] We can generalize from these examples. Any *partially ordered set* has an ordering relation, which can be denoted by the "less-than" symbol <. But we must understand that this ordering relation can apply to other items besides numbers. For any elements *a*, *b*, and *c*, $a < b$ and $b < c$ implies that $a < c$. Also, it is never true that $a < a$. These properties clearly hold for the natural numbers and for the set of positions on a ladder or trellis. If, in addition, for all distinct elements *a* and *b*, either $a < b$ or $b < a$, the set composed of these elements is *totally ordered*. See Birkhoff, *Lattice Theory*, 1.

relation of "greater" and "lesser." In addition to having a partial ordering, a lattice has an operation called *join*. The join of two elements *x* and *y* is the unique element that is greater than or equal to *x*, greater than or equal to *y*, and less than any *other* element greater than or equal to both *x* and *y*. For example, if sets are ordered by the relationship of set inclusion, the join of the set of dogs and the set of horses is the set of animals that are either dogs or horses. The join operation has some of the same properties that we have already seen with logical "or." Because of the similarity, the same symbol is often used. The join of *x* and *y* is written as *x* ∨ *y*. There is also an operation called *meet*. It is similar to logical "and."[5] The meet of *x* and *y* is the unique element that is less than or equal to *x*, less than or equal to *y*, but greater than any other element less than or equal to *x* and *y*. The meet of the set of dogs and the set of female animals is the set of animals that are both dogs and female. The meet of *x* and *y* is written as *x* ∧ *y* (see figure 34.8):

Fig. 34.8: The Join (∨) and Meet (∧) of x and y

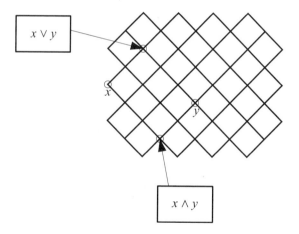

Thus logic correlates with lattices and partial orderings, as well as with sets and Venn diagrams. In accordance with the personalist worldview where God speaks, all these correlations derive from the speech of God.

Computer Technology

Next, consider computer technology. Computer technology embodies logic. The central processing unit in an electronic computer operates using elec-

---

[5] For an exact definition, see Birkhoff, *Lattice Theory*, 16; Grätzer, *Lattice Theory*, 3.

tronic circuits in which, within a particular wire or transistor, the current is either on or off. These two conditions, on and off, symbolize two states, yes and no (or T and F). Data gets recorded on hard drives or permanent media like CDs in microscopic areas. The magnetic polarity within a particular area, or the presence or absence of a pit, symbolizes yes or no. These two states can also represent the truth values T and F.

Within a central processing unit the connections between the transistors enable simple logical operations: logical "or," logical "and," logical "not," and logical implication. By combining simple logical operations into longer programs, the central processing unit mimics longer pieces of reasoning. The combinations of logical operations also include numerical operations such as addition, multiplication, and complementation performed on numbers represented in a binary base (base 2 instead of the usual base 10). The elementary logical operations are strung together by programs that have their own logic, using logical "and," "or," "not," and "implies."

In short, computer technology is heavily dependent on logic. Logic is used in the minds of the programmers in their planning. It is also used in the process of writing the programs, in recording the programs in computer memory, and in the central processing unit. Logic is pervasive.

So we have another correlation. God governs the whole world, including the human beings who over a period of years invented the various pieces that go into the heart of contemporary computer technology. The human beings had to think God's thoughts after him. Their logic had to conform to his logic. God by his speech specified both the development of computer technology and its current state. His speech governing computers coheres with his speech specifying logic, Venn diagrams, and the use of "or" and "and" in ordinary language. It all works because God is self-consistent, and because he expresses his consistency in every aspect of the world that he has made and over which he rules. Praise the Lord!

For Further Reflection

1. Draw a spatial diagram representing simultaneously the following relations of set inclusion: $D \subseteq C$, $C \subseteq B$, $B \subseteq A$.

2. Draw a spatial diagram representing the situation where $A \cap B$ has no elements (the intersection is "empty").

3. Draw a spatial diagram to check that the following two sets are equal:

    $A' \cap B' = (A \cup B)'$

4. What are the members of $A \cap A'$?

5. Draw a diagram of a partial ordering where $x < y$, $y < z$, $u < z$, and u is *not* ordered with respect to x and y. (Hint, place "greater" elements above the elements that are lesser, and draw a line between any two elements that are ordered relative to each other.)

6. a. In the trellis below, find the meet and the join of A and B.

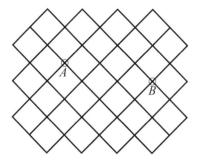

   b. Do every two elements in the trellis above have a meet and a join? Find two that do not have a meet. Find two that do not have a join.

   c. Indicate how you could extend the trellis by drawing more lines, until every two elements have a meet and a join.

7. How do computer central processing units depend on God?

Chapter 35

Boolean Algebra

The logical relations that we have seen in truth functions, in sets, and in computer programming have a correlation with one more field of study, namely, *Boolean algebra*. George Boole in the nineteenth century explored symbolic representations of logical relationships, and the field called Boolean algebra is named in honor of his pioneering study.[1] Boolean algebra is still another way of representing logical relationships.

Some of the ideas are fairly abstract. For the benefit of people without previous knowledge of Boolean algebra, we will approach the ideas by stages. If the material proves difficult for some readers, they may simply pass on to the next chapter.

Elementary Algebra

We start with arithmetic. Here is one example:

$2 + 3 = 5$

Now compare this example with a question posed in elementary algebra:

If u represents an unknown number, and we know that $u + 3 = 5$, what is u?

Since we know that $2 + 3 = 5$, the answer is that u is 2. If we do not already recognize that the number 2 fits the bill, we can follow a standard procedure for determining u. We undertake to isolate u on one side of the equation.

Begin with the original equation:

$u + 3 = 5.$

Now subtract 3 from both sides of the equation:

$u + 3 - 3 = 5 - 3.$

---

[1] Garrett Birkhoff, *Lattice Theory*, 2nd ed. (New York: American Mathematical Society, 1948), 152.

Now simplify. Since $3 - 3 = 0$ and $5 - 3 = 2$,

$u + 0 = 2$.
$u = 2$.

Here is another arithmetic truth: $2 \times 4 + 3 = 11$. And here is a question from elementary algebra: if $2 \times y + 3 = 11$, what is y?

Now let us ask ourselves what is the difference between arithmetic (like $2 + 3 = 5$) and elementary algebra (like $u + 3 = 5$). Arithmetic works with numbers like 2 and 3 and 5. By contrast, in elementary algebra we introduce letters (u, x, y) in addition to numbers. The letters are like placeholders for numbers. Frequently, they represent unknown numbers. We can perform operations of addition, subtraction, multiplication, and division on them, just as if they were specific numbers. At the end of our work we find out what specific number—a previously unknown number—was being represented by u or x or y.

We can also use the same notation with u or y or a or b not to represent one specific unknown number, but any number we wish. Consider:

$a + b = b + a$

No matter which number a may represent, and which number b may represent, the result is true. Addition produces the same result whichever number we put first. We say that addition (+) is *commutative*, because we can "commute" (interchange) the positions of a and b and still obtain the same result for the sum of the two numbers. Now consider the operation of multiplication ($\times$). For any two numbers a and b,

$a \times b = b \times a$

Multiplication is commutative.

Operations

Abstract algebra starts with these kinds of observations about numbers and makes another step of generalization. Rather than generalizing from a specific number 2 to a general number a, we generalize the idea of an *operation*, such as addition or multiplication. Instead of addition or multiplication, we talk about a generalized operation that has two numbers as its inputs. It produces a single number as an output. We can represent this situation as a box with two wires to feed information into the box from the left, and one wire to feed information outward to the right (see figure 35.1):

Fig. 35.1: Binary Operation of Addition

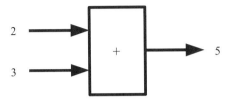

What do we use as a symbol to represent such an operation? We can use any symbol we want, provided we know what it means. We can use an old symbol like the plus sign + provided we understand that it no longer stands *just* for the operation of addition, but for a *general* operation that we may not want to specify further. For the moment, let us use a new symbol *. If we put in the numbers 2 and 3 as inputs into the box representing the operation *, the result, the output, can be written as 2*3. Likewise, the result of putting in numbers a and b is $a*b$. The operation * is commutative if $a*b = b*a$ for all choices of a and b. In this way we can express the commutativity of addition and multiplication with a single expression.

Addition and multiplication have some other properties. For example,

$$a + (b + c) = (a + b) + c$$

This rule says that a decision about the grouping of several different operations of addition does not make any difference in the final result. We can first add b and c and obtain $b + c$. Then we can take the result of this operation, and add it to a, obtaining $a + (b + c)$. Or we can start by adding a to b to obtain $(a + b)$, and then continue by adding c to obtain $(a + b) + c$. An operation + with this general property is called *associative*. Addition is associative. So is multiplication, because

$$a \times (b \times c) = (a \times b) \times c$$

The general operation * is called associative if

$$a * (b * c) = (a * b) * c \text{ (for all values of } a, b, \text{ and } c)$$

Operations like addition and multiplication are called *binary* operations because they need two inputs. The operation of adding three numbers is a *ternary* or 3-ary operation, because it takes three inputs (see figure 35.2):

Fig. 35.2: Ternary Operation of Addition

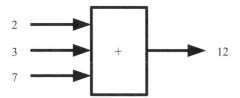

Normally we do not worry about an operation like this, because it is enough to consider the *binary operation* of addition, which we can use to define how to add three or four or more numbers.

We have assumed that the individual elements like *a* and *b* are numbers. But they may be other types of things. They may be rotations in space. They may be propositions like *p* or *q*. For propositions *p* and *q*, we could define a binary operation * that results in another proposition, namely, *p*q* .

Suppose we have a collection of elements *k*, *l*, *m*, ... They may or may not be numbers. And suppose we have a binary operation * that yields new elements. We can ask whether this binary operation is commutative or associative.

We can now begin to see a possible connection between binary operations and logical truth functions. Suppose the propositions like *p* and *q* are regarded as "elements" that we can use as inputs into a "box" which represents a logical operation. Suppose that the operation is logical "or" ($\lor$). Then $p \lor q$ ("*p* or *q*") is another proposition, that is, another element. The operation $\lor$ is a binary operation because it yields a single output $p \lor q$ when it starts with two inputs, *p* and *q*. If we are concerned only for truth value, the binary operation $\lor$ is commutative, because $p \lor q$ and $q \lor p$ are equivalent in truth value. Similarly, logical "and" ($\land$) is a binary operation. It is commutative, because $p \land q$ and $q \land p$ are equivalent in truth value.

What about the operation represented by logical "not" ($\sim$)? It is a *unary operation*: it needs only one input. If *p* is the input, not-*p* ($\sim p$) is the output.

Fig. 35.3: The Unary Operation of Negation

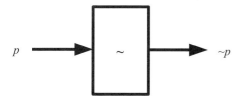

Boolean Algebra

Now we are ready for Boolean algebra. Boolean algebra studies the properties that are common to logical truth functions and some other kinds of systems with similar behavior. We can start again with a collection of elements $k, l, m, \ldots$. (These are akin to the starting propositional symbols $p, q, r, \ldots$.) We consider a binary operation $\oplus$ that takes these elements as inputs. The symbol $\oplus$ consists of a plus symbol (+) with a circle around it. What symbol we choose does not really matter. But by using a symbol that is similar to the symbol for ordinary addition (+), we can produce a reminder that in some ways the new operation will act in a manner similar to the ordinary operation of addition (+). We specify that this binary operation must obey the rule:

$$a \oplus b = b \oplus a$$

In other words, the operation $\oplus$ is commutative. This commutative rule represents a *common pattern* that has several different appearances in different contexts. If a and b are numbers and the operation $\oplus$ stands for addition, we are claiming that addition is commutative. If the operation $\oplus$ is numerical multiplication, we are claiming that multiplication is commutative. If the operation $\oplus$ stands for logical "or" and the symbols a and b stand for propositions (or rather their truth values), we are claiming that logical "or" is commutative. If the symbols a and b stand for sets and the operation $\oplus$ stands for the operation of set union ($\cup$), we are claiming that set union is a commutative operation (which it is).

We should recognize that when we talk about a general operation $\oplus$ we are relying on the interlocking of unity and diversity. In this case, the unity is the unity of a common pattern. The pattern is the pattern for a binary operation. If we specify that the rule of commutativity must hold, commutativity is part of the general pattern. If the common pattern represents unity, where is the diversity? The diversity is the diversity of various instances that illustrate the pattern. The operation of addition on numbers is one instance of the pattern. The operation of multiplication is another instance. The logical operator "or" is another instance. The operation of the union of two sets is an instance.

If there were no significant instances of a pattern, we could not talk about it or conceive of it, since a conception in the mind or a sentence discussing a pattern shows at least one instance of it. Moreover, there would be little point in singling out a general pattern if it had no instances that were significant in some way for human purposes. The operation of addition is significant because we use it in calculations about distances, money, and quantities of goods, to name a few.

So what is a Boolean algebra? It is anything that has a collection of elements $k, l, m, \ldots$ plus some operations with specific properties. We have not yet specified all the properties, but we will now proceed to do so.[2]

1. A Boolean algebra has a binary operation $\oplus$. The newness of the symbol may help to remind us that this symbol can stand for any of several operations with which we are already familiar in other contexts. At the same time, since it looks a little like the operation of addition (+), it reminds us that the operation of addition on numbers is one of the instances that helped to inspire the generalization.

2. The operation $\oplus$ is commutative:

$$a \oplus b = b \oplus a$$

3. The operation $\oplus$ is associative:

$$a \oplus (b \oplus c) = (a \oplus b) \oplus c$$

As we have observed, the operation of numerical addition (+) is associative. So is the logical operator "or."

4. A Boolean algebra has a second binary operation $\otimes$. Note that this symbol is a multiplication symbol (×) with a circle around it. The idea for this symbol is partly inspired by the ordinary operation of multiplying numbers. At the same time, it need not have exactly the same properties as ordinary multiplication. This binary operation can stand for logical "and" ($\wedge$) or for the operation of taking the intersection of two sets ($\cap$).)

5. The operation $\otimes$ is commutative:

$$a \otimes b = b \otimes a$$

6. The operation $\otimes$ is associative:

$$a \otimes (b \otimes c) = (a \otimes b) \otimes c$$

---

[2] Ibid.

7. The operations $\oplus$ and $\otimes$ are "distributive" with respect to each other:

7a: $a \otimes (b \oplus c) = (a \otimes b) \oplus (a \otimes c)$
7b: $a \oplus (b \otimes c) = (a \oplus b) \otimes (a \oplus c)$

The first of these last two properties (7a) holds for ordinary addition and multiplication. The second (7b) does not. (It may hold for arithmetic for a few special choices of values of a, b, and c. The point is that it does not hold *in general* for ordinary arithmetic.) The second distributive law (7b) shows an important difference that distinguishes Boolean algebra from ordinary arithmetic. Even though arithmetic was one of the inspirations behind Boolean algebra, we must now ignore the intuitions that we have about arithmetic and deal with Boolean algebra as a distinct kind of object.

8. Some specific combinations return to the starting point (called the *law of absorption*):

8a: $a = a \otimes (a \oplus b)$
8b: $a = a \oplus (a \otimes b)$

These rules do not hold for ordinary arithmetic (except that they may hold for a few special choices for the values of a and b).

9. A Boolean algebra has a unary operation $\ominus$. A *unary operation* takes only *one* input. For each input it produces a determinate output. For numbers, the numerical operation of negation '-' is an example of a unary operation. If we put in 4 as an input, we get -4 as an output. If we put in -7 as an input, we get -(-7) = 7 as an output. Likewise, the operation of logical negation ~ is a unary operation. We have chosen the symbol $\ominus$ for our unary operation, because it is the symbol '-' for numerical negation, with a circle placed around it. The new symbol $\ominus$ is meant to remind us that in some ways it is similar to the operation of numerical negation '-'.

10. There are two special elements, normally denoted 1 and 0, which have the following properties:

10a: $(\ominus a) \oplus a = 1$ (for any a)
10b: $(\ominus a) \otimes a = 0$ (for any a)

The symbols 1 and 0 are potentially confusing. 1 and 0 in the context of Boolean algebra are not the same as 1 and 0 in the context of arithmetic. In Boolean algebra, $(\ominus a) \oplus a = 1$. In ordinary arithmetic, $(-a) + a = 0$. We must just accept that Boolean algebra does not match the properties of ordinary arithmetic at this point. As usual, we must not let our previous experience with arithmetic interfere with Boolean algebra. Boolean algebra has its own kind of behavior, which is defined by the properties that we have just listed. In some ways it is similar to arithmetic, and in some ways not.

Implications from Boolean Algebra

Using these starting rules for Boolean algebra, we can deduce additional properties. For example, let us try to deduce

11. $a \oplus (\ominus a) = 1$

The only properties we can use are the properties just listed, the properties 1–10 above. Using these properties alone, can we deduce property 11?

Property 11 is closely related to 10a. The one difference is in the order of elements. We can prove it using the commutative rule 2. The commutative rule says that

$a \oplus b = b \oplus a$

for all a and b. So it holds in particular when b is $\ominus a$.

$a \oplus (\ominus a) = (\ominus a) \oplus a$

Rule 10a says that $(\ominus a) \oplus a = 1$. So $a \oplus (\ominus a) = 1$, which is what we wanted to prove. Since we have proved rule 11, it is now a *theorem* (a result established by a proof). It can be used in later proofs.

Here is the way we would write up the proof:

$a \oplus (\ominus a) = (\ominus a) \oplus a$ (by rule 2, commutativity of $\oplus$)
$= 1$ (by rule 10a).
So $a \oplus (\ominus a) = 1$.

Here is another rule that can be deduced:

12. $a \otimes (\ominus a) = 0$

This rule is just like rule 10b, except for the order on the left-hand side. The proof of it is just like the proof for rule 11. Here is the write-up:

$a \otimes (\ominus a) = (\ominus a) \otimes a$ (by rule 5, commutativity of $\otimes$)
$= 0$ (by rule 10b).
So $a \otimes (\ominus a) = 0$.

In fact, there is a general principle of *duality* in Boolean algebra. A careful inspection of the starting rules 1–10 shows that they are exactly the same when we exchange the two symbols $\oplus$ and $\otimes$ for one another and also exchange 1 and 0. So for every theorem with respect to $\oplus$ there is a matching theorem with respect to $\otimes$. We know there will be a matching theorem, and that it can be proved, because we can go through exactly the same steps of proof, each time exchanging the appropriate symbols for one another.

Now let us try something a little more difficult:

13. $a \oplus 0 = a$

From rule 8b, we know that $a = a \oplus (a \otimes b)$.
Substitute $\ominus a$ for b in rule 8b.
We get $a = a \oplus (a \otimes (\ominus a))$.
By rule 12, $a \otimes (\ominus a) = 0$.
Substituting into the line $a = a \oplus (a \otimes (\ominus a))$, we get $a = a \oplus 0$, which is what we wanted to prove. Here is a condensed write-up:

$a = a \oplus (a \otimes (\ominus a))$ (by rule 8b)
$= a \oplus 0$ (by rule 12).
So $a = a \oplus 0$.

Using commutativity, it follows also that

14. $0 \oplus a = a$

$0 \oplus a = a \oplus 0$ (by commutativity, rule 2)
$= a$ (rule 13).

Any reasoning within the proofs must appeal to specific rules, either the initial rules that define Boolean algebra (rules 1–10), or additional rules like 11–13 that have already been proved using the initial rules. The initial rules are usually called *axioms*, while any proved results are called *theorems*. Once a theorem has been established, it can function in additional proofs just as if it were one of the initial axioms.

In a similar way, we can prove:

15. $a \otimes 1 = a = 1 \otimes a$
16. $a \oplus a = a$
17. $a \otimes a = a$
18. $a \oplus 1 = 1 = 1 \oplus a$.
19. $a \otimes 0 = 0 = 0 \otimes a$.
20. $\ominus\ominus a = a$
21. $\ominus(a \oplus b) = (\ominus a) \otimes (\ominus b)$
22. $\ominus(a \otimes b) = (\ominus a) \oplus (\ominus b)$

For the proofs, see appendix B1.

The last two rules, 21 and 22, are called *De Morgan's theorems*. In addition, only one of the two forms of the distributive law (7) is necessary. The other can be derived from it (see appendix B1 for the proof).

The advantage of working with Boolean algebra is that any results we obtain apply to everything that has the same starting properties as a Boolean algebra.

Sets act like a Boolean algebra once we make the proper connections. We can begin with a set U. A *subset* of U is any set whose elements are all in U. For example, {1,3} is a subset of {1,2,3}. The subsets of U will make up the elements k, l, m, ... within a Boolean algebra. Set union $\cup$ acts like the operation $\oplus$. Set intersection $\cap$ acts like the operation $\otimes$. Taking the complement of a set (A') acts like $\ominus$. The special element 1 corresponds to the starting set U. The special element 0 corresponds to the empty set, the set with no elements at all {} (also written as $\varnothing$). We then have to check that the subsets of U form a Boolean algebra, that is, that they satisfy all the starting rules that define a Boolean algebra. Once we have checked that the subsets form a Boolean algebra, we know immediately that all the results obtained for Boolean algebras also hold for relations between sets.[3]

We can also make a correlation between the rules for Boolean algebra and the rules for truth functions. All the starting rules for Boolean algebra hold for logical truth functions, once we adopt the understanding that two propositions are treated as "equal" within the setting of Boolean algebra whenever they are logically equivalent, that is, whenever each implies the other.[4] For example, in logic $p \vee q$ is equivalent to $q \vee p$, because each implies

---

[3] George Grätzer, *Lattice Theory: First Concepts and Distributive Lattices* (reprint; Mineola, NY: Dover, 2009), 76.
[4] See Birkhof, *Lattice Theory*, 4.

the other and because one is true if and only if the other is true. The logical operation ∨ is therefore commutative. The correspondence between logic and Boolean algebra is actually complete. Logical "or" (∨) corresponds to ⊕. Logical "and" (∧) corresponds to ⊗. Logical "not" (~) corresponds to ⊖. All the results that can be derived in Boolean algebra correspond to results in logic. The correspondence is so important that it has become conventional to use the symbols ∨ and ∧ within the context of Boolean algebra to denote the two operations that we have symbolized as ⊕ and ⊗. The unary operation that we have called ⊖ is usually denoted ¬, which is also one of the symbols often used for logical negation. All the theorems of truth functions can then be derived within Boolean algebra.[5]

Boolean algebra also has a close relation to mathematical lattices. Every Boolean algebra can be viewed as a lattice (once we do appropriate changes in notation). But not every lattice has all the properties of a Boolean algebra. All lattices share *some* properties with Boolean algebras, and this sharing accounts for the commonalities.[6]

For Further Reflection

1. How is Boolean algebra related to ordinary elementary algebra?
2. How do the properties for the Boolean operation ⊗ differ from the properties for ordinary multiplication of natural numbers?
3. Prove #15 above, namely, that $a \otimes 1 = a = 1 \otimes a$. (Hint: it is the "dual" of the results #13 and 14 above. So the proof can imitate the steps for proving 13 and 14.)
4. Why is it useful to have a series of properties for the operations ⊕ and ⊗ that do *not* match exactly the properties of ordinary addition and multiplication?
5. What is the relation of Boolean algebra to sets?

---

[5] A theorem within propositional logic, such as $p \supset p$ (Alfred North Whitehead and Bertrand Russell, *Principia Mathematica*, 2nd ed., 3 vols. [Cambridge: Cambridge University Press, 1927], 1:99, proposition 2.08), must first be "translated" by using $\sim p \vee q$ as the definition of $p \supset q$ (ibid., 1:94, proposition 1.01). Translating $p \supset p$ results in $\sim p \vee p$, or, in the earlier symbolism for Boolean algebra, $(\ominus p) \oplus p$. In the context of Boolean algebra, a concatenation of operations on elements $p, q, r, \ldots$ is a "theorem" of logic if the result is equal to the special element 1. In this case, the verification is easy: $\sim p \vee p$ is equal to 1 according to rule 10a.
[6] Birkhoff, *Lattice Theory*, 152.

Chapter 36

Truth-functional Equivalence

We have introduced four main special symbols for truth functions, namely, logical disjunction (∨), logical negation (~), logical conjunction (∧), and material implication (⊃). Logicians often use one other symbol, namely, *truth-functional equivalence*, symbolized by ≡ (other people use a doubled-headed arrow ↔). We write $p \equiv q$ for "p is equivalent to q." Or we can reexpress it as "p is true if and only if q is true." This kind of equivalence is called truth-functional equivalence because the truth value of $p \equiv q$ depends wholly on the truth values of the constituents p and q. It is also called *material equivalence*. Like material implication, it does not depend on the meanings of the components p and q but only on their truth values.

Definition of Truth-functional Equivalence

Two propositions are truth-functionally equivalent if they have the same truth value. So "Snow is white" is equivalent to "The moon is not made of green cheese." Likewise any two false statements are equivalent. "1 + 1 = 3" is equivalent to "The moon is made of green cheese." The truth table for truth-functional equivalence is shown in table 36.1:

TABLE 36.1: Truth Table for Truth-functional Equivalence

p	q	$p \equiv q$
T	T	T
T	F	F
F	T	F
F	F	T

We can also represent the equivalence $p \equiv q$ in a Venn diagram (see figure 36.1):

Fig. 36.1: Venn Diagram of Equivalence

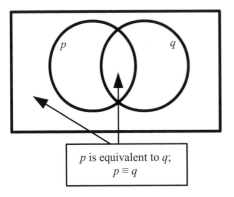

p is equivalent to q;
$p \equiv q$

With propositional variables like p and q, the equivalence relation $p \equiv q$ can be either true or false, depending on the truth or falsehood of p and q. If two complicated expressions are always equivalent, no matter what the truth or falsehood of the starting components like p and q, they are said to be *logically equivalent*. Two expressions are logically equivalent if they are materially equivalent for all possible assignments of T and F to their constituents p and q.

We have already observed that a number of expressions are logically equivalent. For example, $\sim p \lor q$ is logically equivalent to $p \supset q$. In fact, in Whitehead and Russell's system for logic, $p \supset q$ is actually defined as shorthand for $\sim p \lor q$. But some other system may choose to define $\lor$ using $\sim$ and $\supset$ (for example, by saying that $p \lor q$ is shorthand for $\sim p \supset q$). Or a system may treat the symbols as independent of one another, and then prove on the basis of suitable starting axioms that two expressions are equivalent.

Defining Material Equivalence

If we wish to use the symbol $\equiv$ for equivalence within a particular logical system of deduction, we must first define it in terms of other symbols, or else introduce rules that specify its properties. Most logical systems choose to define material equivalence using two of the other logical truth functions. One definition would be that

$p \equiv q$ is shorthand for $(p \supset q) \land (q \supset p)$.

Some Equivalent Expressions

With this definition, we can check using truth tables that the following expressions are equivalents:

$(p \supset q) \equiv (\sim p \lor q)$
$(p \lor q) \equiv (\sim p \supset q)$
$(p \land q) \equiv (\sim(p \supset \sim q))$
$\sim(p \land q) \equiv (\sim p \lor \sim q)$
$\sim(p \lor q) \equiv (\sim p \land \sim q)$

The last two equivalences are sometimes called De Morgan's theorems. They exactly match De Morgan's theorems for Boolean algebra (chapter 35 and appendix B1).

Here are some more equivalences:

$\sim\sim p \equiv p$
$(p \lor q) \equiv (q \lor p)$ (commutativity of $\lor$)
$(p \land q) \equiv (q \land p)$ (commutativity of $\land$)
$((p \lor q) \lor r) \equiv (p \lor (q \lor r))$ (associativity of $\lor$)
$((p \land q) \land r) \equiv (p \land (q \land r))$ (associativity of $\land$)
$(p \land (q \lor r)) \equiv ((p \land q) \lor (p \land r))$ (distributivity)
$(p \lor (q \land r)) \equiv ((p \lor q) \land (p \lor r))$ (distributivity)
$p \equiv (p \land (p \lor q))$ (absorption)
$p \equiv (p \lor (p \land q))$ (absorption)
$(p \supset q) \equiv (\sim q \supset \sim p)$
$(p \equiv q) \equiv (q \equiv p)$ (commutativity of equivalence)
$(p \equiv q) \equiv ((p \supset q) \land (q \supset p))$
$(p \equiv q) \equiv ((p \land q) \lor (\sim p \land \sim q))$
$p \equiv (p \land p)$
$p \equiv (p \lor p)$

Some of these equivalences correspond to properties in Boolean algebras. This correspondence is not an accident. If, using generic symbols p, q, r, s, t, ... for propositions, we can find two propositional formulas that are logically equivalent, the corresponding expressions in Boolean algebra are equal. We simply make the substitutions:

$\ominus$ for $\sim$
$\oplus$ for $\lor$
$\otimes$ for $\land$
$\ominus x \oplus y$ for $x \supset y$.

Logically Equivalent Expressions as Replacements

One convenient principle about equivalence is that logically equivalent expressions can replace one another inside a single compound proposition, without changing the truth value of the total proposition. For example, consider expression A:

$$\sim(p \wedge q) \supset (\sim\sim r \vee (q \supset \sim\sim\sim r))$$

We know that

$$\sim(p \wedge q) \equiv (\sim p \vee \sim q)$$

So $(\sim p \vee \sim q)$ can replace $\sim(p \wedge q)$ in expression A. We obtain an expression B:

$$(\sim p \vee \sim q) \supset (\sim\sim r \vee (q \supset \sim\sim\sim r))$$

We know right away that $A \equiv B$, because replacing an included expression $\sim(p \wedge q)$ with its logical equivalent cannot change the truth value of the larger expression in which it is included. Let us write out the result that $A \equiv B$:

$$\{\sim(p \wedge q) \supset (\sim\sim r \vee (q \supset \sim\sim\sim r))\} \equiv \{(\sim p \vee \sim q) \supset (\sim\sim r \vee (q \supset \sim\sim\sim r))\}$$

Since $r \equiv \sim\sim r$, we can also replace one or both occurrences of $\sim\sim r$:

$$\{\sim(p \wedge q) \supset (\sim\sim r \vee (q \supset \sim\sim\sim r))\} \equiv \{\sim(p \wedge q) \supset (r \vee (q \supset \sim\sim\sim r))\}$$

$$\{\sim(p \wedge q) \supset (\sim\sim r \vee (q \supset \sim\sim\sim r))\} \equiv \{\sim(p \wedge q) \supset (r \vee (q \supset \sim r))\}$$

Divine Origin of Material Equivalence

Finally, can we see a foundation in God for the truth function of material equivalence? Two propositions are materially equivalent if each implies the other. This kind of relationship is exemplified in many cases within God's creation. For instance, consider the equivalence $\sim\sim p \equiv p$. It says that a double negation ($\sim\sim$) is equivalent to an affirmation.

We can illustrate it with a simple proposition S, "Snow is white." $\sim\sim S \equiv S$. In ordinary English, "It is not true that snow is not white" is equivalent to "Snow is white." We can also find examples in the Bible where a double negative re-expresses a positive affirmation. Consider the last part of John 3:16:

. . . whoever believes in him [the Son] should not perish but have eternal life.

"Whoever believes in him should not perish" contains implicitly a double negative, since "perish" is a negative idea, meaning "not live, not have life." Since the context is talking about "eternal life" rather than merely ordinary physical life, "perish" means "not have eternal life." So the whole expression can be rewritten, "Whoever believes in him should *not* (*not* have eternal life), but have eternal life." The first *not* corresponds to the original *not* occurring in John 3:16; the second *not* has been teased out of the meaning of "perish." The total effect is to have a double negation, which is then expressed positively in the next clause, "have eternal life." The two ways of saying it are equivalent.

Or at least they are roughly equivalent. As usual, natural language has nuances and complexities. When we try to make it correspond to simple structures in formal logic, we have to treat it "one-dimensionally," so to speak, and ignore complexities.

Truth is in harmony with itself when we are dealing with creation. But as usual, harmony in creation derives from the original, archetypal harmony in God.

To see one form of logical harmony in God, consider the verses in the Gospel of John that talk about the relation of the words of the Father to the words of the Son:

> For I [the Son] have not spoken on my own authority, but the Father who sent me has himself given me a commandment—what to say and what to speak. (John 12:49)

> Now they know that everything that you [the Father] have given me [the Son] is from you. For I have given them the words that you gave me, and they have received them . . . (John 17:7–8)

Both of these passages have meanings within a rich context of the Gospel of John. They enjoy a relationship to themes expressed at many points in the Gospel of John, such as that the Father and the Son are in harmony in their work, that the Father loves the Son (John 3:35), that the Son loves the Father, as expressed by keeping his commands (14:31), that the Son does what the Father does (5:19–26), and that the Son shows us the Father (14:9–10). In addition, John 12:49 has relations to other verses in John that speak about authority. John 12:49 has as its background rich personal relations between the Father and the Son. But we can single out one dimension in order to show a relation to the simplified idea of material equivalence.

John 12:49 indicates that the words of the Son are not his own, but the words of the Father. We can represent it as:

(w is a word of the Son) $\supset$ (w is a word given by the Father)

John 17:7–8 indicates that the words of the Father have been passed on to the disciples by the Son:

(w is a word given by the Father) $\supset$ (w is a word of the Son)

Together, these two truths imply an equivalence, which we may write:

(w is a word given by the Father) $\equiv$ (w is a word of the Son)

The context is discussing the Father's speech to human beings. But as usual, his speech to human beings has as its deeper foundation his speech to himself. The logical equivalence between words of the Father and words of the Son reflects the harmony in the purposes of the Father and the Son. Whatever attributes the Father has, the Son has: righteousness, omnipotence, holiness, and so on. And the same may be said concerning the Spirit. The harmony among the persons of the Trinity is thus the deepest *equivalence*. It is a personal relation, infinitely rich. Material equivalence (truthfunctional equivalence) is a one-dimensional reflection of this archetypal equivalence. It is still important, because it reflects God and testifies to God. God is present in each relation of truth-functional equivalence.

For Further Reflection

1. Check out the equivalences mentioned in this chapter using truth tables.
2. Use truth tables to show that
   a. $(p \equiv q) \supset (\sim p \equiv \sim q)$
   b. $(p \equiv q) \supset ((p \lor r) \equiv (q \lor r))$
   c. $(p \equiv q) \supset ((p \land r) \equiv (q \land r))$
   d. $(p \equiv q) \supset ((p \supset r) \equiv (q \supset r))$
   e. $(p \equiv q) \supset ((p \equiv r) \equiv (q \equiv r))$

Chapter 37

Harmony in Truth

God has created a world with fascinating complexity and diversity. In previous chapters we have shown that the logical pattern that we see in truth and falsehood for truth functions like "or" and "and" has analogies in several different fields of study. We find analogies in space in the form of Venn Diagrams, and in the form of latticework drawn in space. We find analogies in realms of distinct collections (sets), natural language, human minds, computers, and formal algebra (Boolean algebra). The coherence among these realms goes back to the inner coherence in God himself. In addition, in some cases at least we can see analogies that show the roots of these created manifestations in the Creator and his character.

Deducibility

But first, let us deal with an objection. We have already encountered the idea that logic is just "there" as an impersonal something (chapters 7 and 9). The same idea crops up again when we admire the coherence between logic and other fields. An objector may say that the coherence between the patterns in all these areas is just there as an impersonal something. This idea is more plausible when the coherence is exact. We can have an exact match between (1) logical truth functions; (2) regions of space in Venn diagrams; (3) specialized use of "or," "and," and "not"; (4) sets; (5) thoughts in human minds; (6) logic in printed circuits and in computer programs; and (7) Boolean algebras. The match between the specialized logical meaning of "or" and "and" and what happens with sets is a suitable example. Here the analogy between the two is especially close, because we can define relationships between sets using the logical meaning of "or" and "and." The union $A \cup B$ is defined by

$x \in A \cup B$ if and only if $x \in A$ or $x \in B$.

We can see the logical truth function "or" used in the definition of $A \cup B$. The exact match between logical functions on the one hand and sets on the other hand is guaranteed by the properties of "or," "and," and "not." We can *deduce* properties of sets from properties of logical "or" and the other logical functions.[1] We can *deduce* properties of spatial regions using set theory. We can *deduce* logical results using Boolean algebra. So, an objector may reason, it really boils down to the same thing several times over.

But it is still true that on an elementary level we are dealing with several different kinds of entities. We have propositions with their logical connectives, spatial regions with their spatial relations, sets with their relationships of membership, and Boolean algebra with its abstract operations. These several things are distinct within the world that God made. God is Lord over them all.

God has created the world with diversity. He has created our minds with ability to grasp diversity. The diversity can never be completely explained merely from unity. (Remember the problem of medieval realism: how do you get diversity out of pure unity?) In the case before us, the unity is the unity of a common pattern belonging to truth functions, spatial regions, and so on. Each realization of the pattern in a particular sphere, like the sphere of sets or collections, is a manifestation of the goodness of God. And the relation of the particular to the general, that is, the relation of diversity to unity, derives ultimately from the diversity and unity in God himself, in the persons of the Trinity. God's logic is a unity because there is one God, and the three persons are in harmony. God's logic is manifested in truth functions, spatial regions, latticework, and sets because God ordains diversity. This diversity is in harmony with unity but not reducible to it.

It is wonderful to find that sets in their relationships show a pattern analogous to the logic of "or" and "and." Logic applies to sets, and it is wonderful that it does. It is a source for praise, not something to be taken for granted.

Boolean Algebra as a Possible Unifying Solution?

People who desire a purely impersonal explanation for unity and diversity might appeal to Boolean algebra. Is Boolean algebra the unifying factor in all the domains? Boolean algebra is attractive in a context where we are looking for unification. It seizes on a common pattern belonging to several different fields.

---

[1] Whitehead and Russell's *Principia Mathematica* undertakes such a deduction in an extensive way. Volume 1, section 1a, handles "The Theory of Deduction," which deals with propositions. Section 1c, "Classes and Relations," includes "Calculus of Classes" (1c:§22) (Alfred North Whitehead and Bertrand Russell, *Principia Mathematica*, 2nd ed., 3 vols. [Cambridge: Cambridge University Press, 1927]).

Logic itself is a kind of unifying procedure, because in studying logic we are looking at *general* patterns of reasoning, rather than merely looking at a single particular syllogism about, for example, Socrates. Boolean algebra can be viewed as a further generalization. Why should we go through the same observations and the same processes of reasoning several times over, when we are dealing with a common pattern (the unity)? Boolean algebra offers us a notational system and a way of thinking that says, in effect, "Let's do it only once." Then it can apply to all the fields where the axioms of Boolean algebra hold true.

The whole idea of a generalized operation like ⊕ has this effect. A generalized operation, together with the notation that goes along with it, seizes on a common pattern. The common pattern belongs to logical connectives ("or," "and"), Venn diagrams, union and intersection of sets, computer circuits, and so on. So the reasoning can take place once for all within the generalized setting of Boolean algebra. Then, we may say, it "automatically" applies to all the relevant domains. The application is "automatic" because the correspondence among domains is exact. But the correspondences have to be there in the first place, before we even starting thinking about them. Boolean algebra is possible only *because* of prior correspondences and analogies. An appeal to Boolean algebra as an ultimate *explanation* for the correspondences seems to have things backward. The correspondences, ordained by God, explain how we arrive at Boolean algebra as a unified description.[2]

Boolean algebra does "explain" the correspondences at one level, by offering a unified general treatment. But then we still have the problem of unity and diversity. The treatment in Boolean algebra is *unified* and *general*—it is a unity. It is a unity in relation to the diversity of applications to the diverse fields. How do we explain the diversity?

It looks as though we can escape into an impersonalist explanation of this world of ours only by virtually ignoring the diversity. Someone starts with unity, which he conceives as a pure abstraction, an impersonalist something. And then he "explains" language, Venn diagrams, and sets by saying that these are merely the *same* thing all over again. If later on he has to concede that Venn diagrams are neither sets nor language, at the level of ordinary experience, he backs away from pure unity and says that his original

---

[2] Here again, the unified description offered in Boolean algebra is a way of thinking God's thoughts after him. We human beings have not invented Boolean algebra out of nothing, but out of minds in tune with truth—ultimately the truth in God's mind.

pure unity, which is a high-level abstraction, *applies* to diverse realms. Why does it apply? Why is the world so wonderfully coherent?

Boolean algebra in the end does not serve to provide an ultimate philosophical explanation any better than if we had started with logic as the final unifying factor. In fact, Boolean algebra is worse off as an ultimate explanation, because we end up asking ourselves why a seemingly arbitrary list of starting rules (two binary operations, commutativity, associativity, and so on) has relevance. Why *these* rules rather than others that we could dream up? At least if we start with logic, we have an arena that intuitively seems more basic. We say to ourselves, "It is the way we reason." "Things *must* be this way," we say. But that kind of start leads us back to our earlier discussion about how logic reveals God. Things *must* be that way because God is Lord over all, not because our own minds are little gods that can legislate for reality.

God as the Original of Spatial Structure

Once we recognize the absoluteness of God, it is natural to look at the character of God as the original, in comparison to any structure in creation that reflects God's character. The same holds in particular for the principle of spatiality. As we indicated earlier (chapter 27), according to the Bible the persons of the Trinity indwell one another (John 17:21; Luke 4:18). This Trinitarian interrelationship is the ultimate foundation for spatial relations in creation. Likewise, God in his Trinitarian self-consistency is the ultimate foundation for logic. Truth-functional logic and Venn diagrams cohere because God coheres with himself.

God as the Original, Who Is Reflected in Language

Next, consider the relation of logic to language. What is the original reality behind human languages? We have already seen that the Word of God, the second person of the Trinity, is the original or archetype for language. Formal logic invents special symbols like logical "or" (∨) and logical "and" (∧). The ability to invent and define special symbols is itself part of the capability of human beings to use language. The special symbols belong to a special logical symbolism that is language-like, and their origins in human language make them a specialized part within ordinary language. Human language has its origin in the divine language of the Word. Therefore the special capabilities in logical symbols also have their origin in the same place. Truth and falsehood cohere with logical symbols because truth has its roots in the truthfulness of God, and logical symbols have their roots in the language of God. The language of God coheres with his truthfulness.

God as the Original for Minds

Next, consider how God is at the root of human thinking and mental reasoning. As human beings, we can think about logic. Our mental activity is another dimension to the character of logic. And again our minds have their roots in God's mind. We are made in his image, and our thoughts imitate his thoughts. We think his thoughts after him. The coherence of logic with our minds rests on divine coherence. God's logical consistency and his truthfulness cohere with his ability to think, and his thoughts are consistent.

God as the Original behind Computers

It is more challenging to try to understand the roots of modern computers. Computers carry out reasoning and computations *automatically.* Despite the fruitful analogies between electronic computers and the human mind, our present-day computers do not actually think. Rather, they imitate human thinking. They can accomplish the imitation very impressively because of previous cleverness and insight from human beings. Computer programmers have thought hard and long, and have written programs that make explicit every single step in a long process of reasoning, as well as the exact connections between the steps. Everything is made explicit so that electronic circuits can exactly duplicate the steps automatically. "Automatically" is the key word. "Automatically" is the opposite of something taking place "by thinking." On a literal level, there is no real thinking or understanding exercised by the circuits themselves.

So where does the genius of computers reside? Partly we are dealing with the minds of computer programmers, and therefore with the coherence between their minds and the mind of God. Partly we are dealing with programming language, as a kind of artificial language with roots in ordinary language—and ordinary language has roots in divine language. Programmers also rely on "compilers," which are programs that automatically make a translation between a programming language and the machine script that is actually read by a central processing unit. Such translation has roots. Where? God is capable of speaking in all languages, and human translators reflect his capability, because they are made in his image. Compilers, written by human beings, express the translation capabilities of the pro-grammers who write them.

In actual computer computations, we deal with other pieces as well, especially computer hardware. A computer is a complex machine whose hardware parts are so constructed that the machine as a whole can carry out the purposes of those who construct it. And the main purpose in the case of a general-purpose computer is for the machine to duplicate exactly the logical steps contained in any number of computer programs, whose logic is supposed to duplicate exactly the logic in the minds of the programmers.

Human beings have the capability of constructing machines because of a large number of abilities and skills that they can bring together in a coherent way. Among these abilities is the ability to exercise thoughtful, purpose-directed control over silicon, plastic, and other materials, such as iron, copper, aluminum, or gold. These materials go into the material construction of a typical computer. Moreover, human beings use machines and multiple steps of processing in order to transform the silicon into com-plex final forms. It takes extensive planning and extensive construction of machines to do manufacturing steps with precision and consistency.

In their control, human beings imitate God's control. They are subor-dinate kings over the world, imitating God who is the great king. He is also the greater maker who made the world itself. Human beings are subordinate makers, "subcreators." Their kingship is a purposeful kingship, the control of a designer. The designer leaves his stamp of purpose on the product.

We can extend a bit further the principle of imaging. God made human beings in his image. Human beings make computers. Are computers in the image of human beings? They are not an exact image. They reflect only certain limited aspects of humanity. But we have here a kind of reflection of some aspects of human reasoning and human computation. So, yes, they are a limited image. They owe their existence to the creativity of human beings, who owe their creativity to God.

Moreover, God's power has to sustain the human beings in the process of manufacturing. Human abilities in manufacturing reflect God's power and wisdom. By wise manufacturing, human beings are able to create a limited image of their reasoning. Computers in their operations coherently correspond to human reasoning, because God ordains that his creative operations of making things cohere with human operations. God's creativ-ity also coheres with his truthfulness and with his logic. Human beings reflect this coherence. So, when they do well, their creativity coheres with truth and logic. Computers exist only because of this coherence.

God as the Original behind Sets

In the preceding chapter we also noticed a correlation been truth-functional logic and sets. The union and intersection of sets exactly imitate Boolean algebra, which also holds for sets.

Sets exist because God through his language has made distinctions in the world. We can distinguish human beings from horses, and horses from cats. A set is an abstract object, crafted by mathematicians to capture only one dimension from the richness of God's creation. That one dimension is the dimension of making distinctions, which implies the inclusion of some items within a collection and the exclusion of other items that do not belong to the collection. The collection of cats includes all cats and excludes dogs and horses. The collection {1,2,3} includes 1, 2, and 3 and excludes all other numbers.

God ordained all the distinctions that we ever think of. Remember, our thinking imitates God's thinking. God's making of distinctions is the root for sets. God's truthfulness and his consistency are the root for logic. Sets follow logic because God's distinctions cohere with his consistency and his truthfulness.

God as the Original behind Boolean Algebra

Next, consider how God is at the root of Boolean algebra. Boolean algebra is like a specialized language. It has specialized terms like a and b that function in imitation of ordinary language. The terms a and b may be compared to clauses. The operations $\oplus$ and $\otimes$, which in the more common notation are denoted $\vee$ and $\wedge$, are like the conjunctions "or" and "and" that link clauses together into sentences. Boolean algebra has a kind of "syntax," in the form of rules for forming more complex structures out of simpler ones. For example, the structure $p \vee q$ is a complex structure formed out of the three simpler units p, q, and $\vee$. There are rules for how to make "well-formed" structures. Putting two "clauses" p and q before and after the central symbol $\vee$ results in a more complex "clause." But putting several truth functions together with no other symbols results in something like $\vee\vee\sim\wedge$. The result is not a well-formed structure, and does not have a well-defined "meaning" or "grammar" within the specialized "language." We can see here imitations of features of ordinary language. These features have their root in God and his divine speech.[3]

Boolean algebras are described by certain axioms, such as the commutative laws:

$$p \vee q = q \vee p$$
$$p \wedge q = q \wedge p$$

These laws imitate similar laws concerning meaning in natural language. For example, the words "or" and "and" can link two clauses in either order, and many times the meaning is about the same. (But because of the complexities of natural language, a larger context of a paragraph may sometimes influence the meaning, and then one or the other order of the parts may be important for the meaning of the whole.) The laws of language go back to God's specifications for language. God speaks to specify the character of each and every human language.[4]

For Further Reflection

1. Spell out the kind of correspondences that exist between sets, logical truth functions, and Boolean algebra.
2. How do sets have their foundation in God?
3. How may the *exactness* of the correspondences tempt people to oversimplify the issue of unity and diversity?
4. How do computers reflect the glory of God?

---

[3] Vern S. Poythress, *In the Beginning Was the Word: Language—A God-Centered Approach* (Wheaton, IL: Crossway, 2009), especially chapter 32. For an illustration from elementary algebra, see Vern S. Poythress, "Tagmemic Analysis of Elementary Algebra," *Semiotica* 17/2 (1976): 131–151.
[4] Poythress, *In the Beginning Was the Word*, chapters 8 and 9.

Chapter 38

Perspectives on Truth Functions

The multiple relationships of logic with various fields, like Venn diagrams, sets, lattices, computers, and Boolean algebras, lead naturally to the topic of multiple perspectives. Venn diagrams and each of the other fields of study can be treated as a perspective on logic.

Venn Diagrams as a Perspective on Logic

Venn diagrams offer one perspective on logic. It is an attractive perspective because we can visualize what is going on. For example, does $p \wedge q$ imply $p \vee q$? Within the standard Venn diagram for p and q, we locate the regions representing $p \wedge q$ and $p \vee q$. We can see that the region for $p \wedge q$ is completely inside the region for $p \vee q$. (see figure 38.1):

Fig. 38.1: Venn Diagram for $(p \wedge q) \supset (p \vee q)$

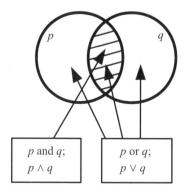

p q

p and q;
$p \wedge q$

p or q;
$p \vee q$

So yes, $(p \wedge q) \supset (p \vee q)$. By contrast, if we try to reason out the result starting with the axioms of Whitehead and Russell, it is not obvious how to proceed. And the process of deduction involves several steps.[1] Or let us try to verify that $p \wedge q$ is equivalent to $\sim(\sim p \vee \sim q)$. Begin with the standard Venn diagram representing p and q by overlapping circles. $\sim p$ is the region outside the circle p. $\sim q$ is the region outside the circle q. We can represent the relationships in a diagram, where $\sim p$ is the region that is hatched with lines going from upper left to lower right. $\sim q$ is the region with hatching that goes from the upper right to the lower left (see figure 38.2):

Fig. 38.2: Venn Diagram for $\sim p$ and $\sim q$

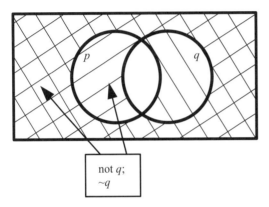

Now $\sim p \vee \sim q$ consists in all of the region that belongs either to $\sim p$ or to $\sim q$, that is, all the hatched region. $\sim(\sim p \vee \sim q)$ is the negation of the hatched region, which is $p \wedge q$.

Sets as a Perspective on Logic

Next, we can consider sets as a perspective on logic. For a proposition p, we can consider a set whose members are all the possible situations in which p turns out to be true.[2] Call this set P. Similarly, for a proposition q, let Q be the set whose members are all the possible situations in which q turns out to be true. The set $P \cup Q$, the union of P and Q, then corresponds to the proposition $p \vee q$. The intersection $P \cap Q$ corresponds to the proposition

---

[1] Whitehead and Russell, *Principia Mathematica* (2nd ed., 3 vols. [Cambridge: Cambridge University Press, 1927], 1:100 proposition 2.06) says that $(p \supset q) \supset ((q \supset r) \supset (p \supset r))$. In this proposition, substitute $(p \wedge q)$ for p and $(p \vee q)$ for r. We get $((p \wedge q) \supset q) \supset ((q \supset (p \vee q)) \supset ((p \wedge q) \supset (p \vee q)))$. By proposition 3.27 (p. 1:110), $(p \wedge q) \supset q$. By *modus ponens*, $(q \supset (p \vee q)) \supset ((p \wedge q) \supset (p \vee q))$. By axiom 1.3 (p. 1:96), $q \supset (p \vee q)$. By *modus ponens*, $(p \wedge q) \supset (p \vee q)$. Most people would find this kind of deduction harder to follow than the inspection of a Venn diagram.

[2] As usual, to be sure of avoiding paradoxes we have to presuppose that the total scope for the "situations" is limited to some specified domain, let us say a universal set U. The logical negation of the proposition p is then represented by exactly those situations within U where p is false.

$p \wedge q$. In this way we can establish a correspondence between any composite proposition and a set representing the situations in which this proposition turns out to be true. Logical relations between propositions are represented by relationships among sets.

This representation of logical relations does not necessarily help us to see logical consequences more quickly. But it offers a concrete embodiment of logic in possible situations. We see a correlation between logic and the "world" of situations.

Boolean Algebra as a Perspective on Logic

Next, consider Boolean algebra as a perspective on logic. In Boolean algebra propositions are correlated with elements a within a set. But instead of operations of set union and set interaction, we have general operations $\oplus$, $\otimes$, and $\ominus$. Or, if we use the same notation as we have in logic, the general operations are $\vee$, $\wedge$, and $\sim$. The operations conform to rules (such as commutativity and associativity). We calculate according to the rules rather than making deductions. The calculations are simply manipulations of letters and symbols on paper, following specified rules. We can also describe the process as manipulating a specific formal "language" according to specific formal rules. A person need not know the meaning of the symbols or the rules in order to do this. But of course he needs to know the meaning if he is to see "the point" and make a practical application at the end. This perspective shows that there is more than one way of looking at rule-governed inference.

The Mind as a Perspective on Logic

We can also use the human mind as a perspective on logic. From this perspective, logical arguments and logical inferences, as well as the logical connectives "or," "and," and "not," take place primarily in our minds. We reason. We see that one truth follows from another. We group truths together in considering whether two propositions both hold, which is an expression of logical conjunction, that is, logical "and." We consider whether we know that at least one of two propositions holds, and in so doing we express in our minds the operations of logical disjunction, that is logical "or." And so on.

The expressions on paper, whether in the form of written propositions, Venn diagrams, or algebraic symbols from Boolean algebra, all express in some form what goes on in our minds. Once they are on paper, they can be understood by human minds, either our own or someone else's with whom we are communicating. Logic on paper is a kind of shorthand and a communicative aid for something else, which we treat as the main starting point. That something else is the operation of the mind. We treat what is *common* to many human minds, rather than what is idiosyncratic (e.g., a stomach ache as perceived in the mind).

When we talk about minds, we can see another instance of the interlocking of the one and the many. There are many human beings. Each of our minds is unique. But there are also commonalities, among which are commonalities in reasoning. The common pattern represents a unity. The many minds represent diversity. Because we are all made in the image of God, we can all think alike. Because God made each of us in his individuality, we all think differently when we inspect the details in texture. We rely on unity and diversity when we look at logic through the perspective of human thinking.

Perspectives in General

We may recall John Frame's three perspectives on ethics: the normative, the situational, and the personal/existential perspectives.[3] In looking at the human mind as a perspective, we have adopted a perspective similar to Frame's existential perspective. The existential perspective works as a perspective because we can always observe that, whatever it is that we know, it is *we* who know it. The whole world can be viewed from the *perspective* of the involvement of the human observer. This kind of viewpoint is valid and harmless as long as we do not claim that it is the origin of everything else. God made the world and he made us. Apart from sin and its effects, we and the world would be fundamentally in harmony, and both we and the world would be in harmony with God's purposes and his standards (norms). Starting with the human mind naturally leads to acknowledging both God and the world. In particular, we acknowledge logic as something inside us, in our minds, and also something outside us, as ordained by God in harmony with the consistency of his character and in harmony with the world that God made.

The flexibility of our minds includes our ability to begin to appreciate other people. If we love them, we listen to them and begin to appreciate their *perspectives*. The diversity of people leads naturally to acknowledging

---

[3] See chapter 16 and John M. Frame, *Perspectives on the Word of God: An Introduction to Christian Ethics* (Phillipsburg, NJ: Presbyterian & Reformed, 1990).

a diversity of perspectives. In addition, we begin to incorporate a second or a third perspective into *our* mind. Then one mind has several perspectives. This kind of diversity of perspectives includes the perspectives on logic that we have just surveyed. We look at logic through the perspective of Venn diagrams or sets or Boolean algebra or mental logic.

Multiple human perspectives exist because multiple human beings exist. This multiplicity is due to the plan of God. He created the race of human beings as a single race (unified in Adam) and as a diversity of individuals. Unity and diversity go together. It is not too hard to see that this unity and diversity echoes the original unity and diversity in God. God is one God in three persons. Each person of the Trinity knows from his own personal perspective.[4] The persons know one another (Matt. 11:27; 1 Cor. 2:10), so that there is an interlocking in the knowledge of each. This divine knowledge is incomprehensible. But it is reflected at the creaturely level in us, because in our experience of knowledge different perspectives can interlock. John Frame demonstrates how the normative, situational, and existential perspectives interlock; each leads naturally to acknowledging the other and even in a sense incorporates the other.[5]

Likewise, the different perspectives on logic, when properly understood, interlock and affirm one another. Venn diagrams, for example, can be viewed from the perspective of sets. Each spatial region can be seen as corresponding to the set consisting of the points in the interior of that region. Sets can be viewed as a particular case of Boolean algebra. Conversely, Boolean algebra can be viewed as a set, namely, the set of elements a, b, c, ... on which the operations $\vee$, $\wedge$, $\sim$ operate. It is a set with certain extra features defined by the operators and their rules.

Thus the diversity of perspectives on logic has its ultimate root or original in the diversity of perspectives in the persons of the Trinity. Unity is displayed in the fact that there is one consistent pattern of logic, as represented by any one of the perspectives. This unity has its root in the unity of one God. The fact that the perspectives interlock has its root in the mutual indwelling of the persons of the Trinity, which is called *coinherence.*

---

[4] Vern S. Poythress, *Symphonic Theology: The Validity of Multiple Perspectives in Theology* (reprint; Phillipsburg, NJ: Presbyterian & Reformed, 2001), especially chapter 5, pp. 50–51.
[5] Frame, *Perspectives on the Word of God.*

For Further Reflection

1. In what ways does the adoption of one perspective aid human beings in understanding? Illustrate using Venn diagrams as a perspective.
2. How does the diversity of perspectives among human beings reflect a Trinitarian origin?
3. Explain how the human mind can be used as a perspective on truth and logic.
4. How does a Christian explanation of diversity of perspectives differ from a non-Christian approach to logic?

Part II.C

Propositional Logic

Chapter 39

Introducing Propositional Logic

We have seen that modern symbolic logic simplifies and formalizes the process of reasoning. Formal propositions serve as a kind of refinement or one-dimensional simplification of ordinary sentences. In this refinement, the sentences are supposed to be exactly defined, independent of a larger discourse context. They are supposed to be either true (T) or false (F). Smaller sentences are put together using the logical connectives "or," "and," "not," and "implies." Given these simplifications, logicians can study which composite sentences are always true. For example, for any proposition p, either not-p is true (i.e., p is false) or p is true.[1] We get a particular example if p stands for the proposition "It is raining." Either it is not raining or it is raining. In the modern notation of symbolic logic, we can write:

$\sim p \vee p$

The notation is interpreted to mean, "Either not [$\sim$] p or [$\vee$] p."

We can check that $\sim p \vee p$ is always true by constructing a truth table for it. There are only two alternatives, namely, p is T or p is F. Either way, $\sim p \vee p$ is T (see table 39.1):

TABLE 39.1: Truth Table for $\sim p \vee p$

p	$\sim p$	$\sim p \vee p$
T	F	T
F	T	T

Logicians have studied which formulas of this kind are always true.

---

[1] Alfred North Whitehead and Bertrand Russell, *Principia Mathematica*, 2nd ed., 3 vols. (Cambridge: Cambridge University Press, 1927), 1:101, proposition 2.11. We ignore for the moment alternatives to classical logic, in which a proposition may have unknown truth value, or may be probably true, or may be undefined (chapters 63 and 64). The assumption that propositions are clearly defined and are either true or false dispenses with these complexities.

This study is called *propositional logic*. The formulas that come out true for all possible truth values of their constituents p, q, r, ... are called *tautologies*. It turns out that an indefinite number of true formulas can be deduced from a small number of starting formulas, which can be regarded as *axioms*. Assuming that the axioms are true, logicians deduce other truths using a small number of formal rules for valid deduction. There is more than one possible choice of starting axioms, and more than one collection of formal rules with which to start. If the axioms and formal rules are properly chosen, they all lead to the same result. They all allow us to deduce from the axioms all possible tautologies.

The most common formal rules are two rules: substitution and *modus ponens*. Let us look at them.

Rule of Substitution

The rule of substitution says that if any formula is always true, it remains true when we substitute more complicated propositional expressions for a symbol p or q or another symbol standing for a proposition. For example, consider

$\vdash \sim p \lor p$

Substitute for p the expression $(q \land \sim(r \supset s))$. We obtain:

$\vdash \sim(q \land \sim(r \supset s)) \lor (q \land \sim(r \supset s))$

The result is always true. By substituting other expressions for p, we can obtain any number of additional tautologies.

If we *start* with an expression with several propositional symbols, let us say p and q and r, then we must take care that we substitute the *same* expression for each occurrence of p. We may substitute a second expression for each occurrence of q, but this second expression must be the same expression substituting for *each* occurrence of q. The same must hold for r or any other symbol for a proposition.

Logicians have often preferred not to treat the rule of substitution as a separate rule, but to include more axioms instead.[2] Instead of starting with

---

[2] For example, see Irving M. Copi, *Symbolic Logic*, 5th ed. (New York: Macmillan, 1979), 227. Whitehead and Russell (*Principia Mathematica*, 2nd ed., 3 vols. [Cambridge: Cambridge University Press, 1927], 1:98), take a slightly different path. In their exposition, each axiom is understood as asserting all its cases. For example, in the axiom $(p \lor p) \supset p$ the letter p stands for any proposition that one wishes to plug in. When we plug in a specific composite proposition, such as $(q \land \sim(r \supset s))$, it is still the *same* axiom, only in the form of a particular case. We find it convenient in our exposition to call substitution a "rule" rather than to treat

one axiom, such as ~p ∨ p, they include as axioms all propositions that have the form ~p ∨ p. So, for example, ~$(q$ ∧ ~$(r ⊃ s))$ ∨ $(q$ ∧ ~$(r ⊃ s))$ would be an axiom because it has the same general form as ~p ∨ p. There are many other axioms with the same form. Each choice for a substitute for p results in another axiom. Since there are an infinite number of axioms with this form, they cannot be written out one by one. But they can be summarized in an *axiom schema*. An axiom schema is a single pattern, or "schema," that shows in one line the common form of all the axioms of one kind. In this case the schema is

~p ∨ p

where p stands for any proposition, including compound propositions like $(q$ ∧ ~$(r ⊃ s))$.

The advantage of this kind of treatment is that we do not have to worry about having "substitution" as a separate rule. Nor do we have to worry about qualifying our rule of substitution later on, in more complex situations.[3] The disadvantage is that we need more axioms. If we have more axioms, the force of the rule of substitution is being built into the axioms themselves. So one way or another it is present.

The Rule of *modus ponens*

The second general rule for deducing truths is the rule called *modus ponens*.[4] This rule says that if q is true and if $q ⊃ r$ is true, that is, if q implies r, we can deduce that r is true. Of course for many cases of q we cannot establish that q is true. *Modus ponens* does us no good. But suppose that for q we substitute the expression ~p ∨ p. The rule says in the case of this particular q, that is, for ~p ∨ p, if ~p ∨ p is true and if $($~p ∨ $p) ⊃ r$ is true, we can deduce that r is true. Depending on what r is, there is hope that we might be able to use *modus ponens*, because there is hope that we can establish that ~p ∨ p is true for all possible truth values of p.

The rule called *modus ponens* follows from the nature of the meaning of implication. It can be represented schematically as a series of steps, as follows:

---

it as a notational convention or to multiply the number of axioms. The results are the same (we are using different perspectives).
[3] Later we discuss qualifications needed in the context of conditional proof (chapter 42) and in the context of quantification (chapter 50).
[4] Whitehead and Russell, *Principia Mathematica*, 1:94, proposition 1.1; Copi, *Symbolic Logic*, 228.

Premise 1: q is true.
Premise 2: $q \supset r$ is true.
Conclusion: r is true.

The premises must have already been established in order to reach the point where we deduce that r is true. The premises may be axioms, or theorems already deduced from axioms, or theorems obtained by using the rule of substitution.

God as the Original for the Rule of Substitution

Both the rule of substitution and the rule of *modus ponens* have their roots in God.[5] The rule of substitution uses the relationship of unity to diversity. The unity here is the unity of the general proposition with which we start. Let us say that we start with the proposition $\sim p \vee p$. This proposition is a generality because p stands for any of a number of particular propositions. One particular example would be obtained if for p we substitute "snow is white." We obtain,

$\sim$(Snow is white) $\vee$ (Snow is white)

In more ordinary English, "Either snow is not white or snow is white." This particular application of the general proposition $\sim p \vee p$ is one of *many*. We have a diversity of many possible particular ways of substituting various propositions for the symbol p. The unity is the unity of a common form or structure, a unity that belongs to all such instantiations. Among these instantiations is the one in which we substitute for p the expression $(q \wedge \sim(r \supset s))$. This latter expression still retains some generality, since we can make an additional substitution in which we substitute some particular expression for q or r or s. If we substitute for q another general expression, such as $\sim u$, then we can perform still another substitution by substituting something else for u, and so on indefinitely. All of these substitutions use relationships of unity and diversity.

We have already seen that unity and diversity go back to God and have God as their ultimate root (chapter 18). God is the original. But his character is reflected in our thinking as creatures. Classification, instantiation, and association are therefore also at work with the process of deduction

---

[5] See Vern S. Poythress, "Reforming Ontology and Logic in the Light of the Trinity: An Application of Van Til's Idea of Analogy," *Westminster Theological Journal* 57/1 (1995), reprinted in appendix F5.

by substitution. The original *p* is the classification. It is a general symbol, representing any proposition. The substitute, let us say $(q \land \sim(r \supset s))$, is the instantiation. The two are related by association. The result of applying the substitution to a particular proposition such as $\sim p \lor p$ is to produce a new proposition. This new proposition is an instantiation, and it has a relationship (an association) with the original proposition.

Classification (generality): $\sim p \lor p$
Instantiation (particularity): $\sim(q \land \sim(r \supset s)) \lor (q \land \sim(r \supset s))$
Association: relation between the general pattern and its
particularization.

God as the Original for *modus ponens*

Already in chapter 31 we introduced the idea that God is the original root for *modus ponens*. We looked at John 5:19–21 and saw how implication is rooted in the Trinity. We can begin to formalize the reasoning in John 5:19–21 if we like. The Father gives life. If the Father gives life, the Son gives life. Therefore, the Son gives life. This reasoning is an instance of *modus ponens*. Because God is the original for logic, God's inner coherence is a basic instance on which the general use of *modus ponens* rests.

A Sample Deduction

We are now ready to show the way in which deduction operates in practice. We consider two examples from the early part of Whitehead and Russell's book *Principia Mathematica*.

First, let us try to show that $(p \supset \sim p) \supset \sim p$. One of Whitehead and Russell's axioms (which we will discuss in the next chapter) says that $(p \lor p) \supset p$. Using the rule of substitution, substitute $\sim p$ for p in this axiom. We obtain

$$(\sim p \lor \sim p) \supset \sim p$$

Now in Whitehead and Russell's system, the only starting logical connectives are $\lor$ and $\sim$. The implication symbol $\supset$ is then defined by saying that $p \supset q$ is short for $\sim p \lor q$. So we can replace one notation by the other. We get

$$(p \supset \sim p) \supset \sim p$$

which is what we wanted to demonstrate.

We can write out the course of our reasoning in a series of lines. With each line we include a reason justifying how we obtained the line. Here is the reasoning that we just did:

(1) $(p \lor p) \supset p$ (an axiom; [any axiom can be used in a deduction])
(2) $(\sim p \lor \sim p) \supset \sim p$ (by substituting $\sim p$ for p in (1))
(3) $(p \supset \sim p) \supset \sim p$ (from (2) by the definition of $\supset$)

Each of the lines (1)-(3) is justified either by an axiom or by results from previous lines. A series of lines of this type, each justified by axioms or previous lines, is called a *proof*.

The result on line (3) is actually significant. It is a form of the principle of *reductio ad absurdum*. The general principle of *reductio ad absurdum* says that if an assumption leads to a contradiction, that assumption must be false. To see how line (3) is related to *reductio ad absurdum*, we can translate it into ordinary English. Suppose we were to start by assuming a proposition p, and then from p we were able to deduce its opposite, that is, not-p. In symbolic notation, we would have shown that $p \supset \sim p$. In that case, assuming p has led to a contradiction (both p and $\sim p$ are true). The principle of *reductio ad absurdum* then says that p itself must be false. The deduction as a whole, that is, the fact that $p \supset \sim p$, shows that our initial proposition p was not in fact true. That is, it shows that $\sim p$ is true. If $p \supset \sim p$, then $\sim p$. So $(p \supset \sim p) \supset \sim p$. With line (3) above, we have just proved one form of the principle of *reductio ad absurdum*.

We now try to demonstrate that $(p \supset \sim q) \supset (q \supset \sim p)$.[6] We start with another axiom of Whitehead and Russell, namely, that $(p \lor q) \supset (q \lor p)$. In this axiom, substitute $\sim p$ for p and $\sim q$ for q. We obtain

$(\sim p \lor \sim q) \supset (\sim q \lor \sim p)$

Using the definition that $p \supset q$ is shorthand for $\sim p \lor q$, we obtain

$(p \supset \sim q) \supset (q \supset \sim p)$

which is the result we wanted. Here is the same deduction or proof, done as a series of lines:

(1) $(p \lor q) \supset (q \lor p)$ (an axiom)

---

[6] Whitehead and Russell, *Principia Mathematica*, 1:100, proposition 2.03.

(2) $(\sim p \lor \sim q) \supset (\sim q \lor \sim p)$ (by substituting $\sim p$ for p and $\sim q$ for q in (1))

(3) $(p \supset \sim q) \supset (q \supset \sim p)$ (from (2) by definition of $\supset$)

Deductions can of course involve more steps than these. They may use as starting premises results that have already been previously deduced as well as the starting axioms. But the patterns of deduction are always the same. Deductions use axioms, previous results, the rule of substitution, and the rule *modus ponens*, that is, that "anything implied by a true . . . proposition is true."[7] Each line in a proof must be justified in one of these ways. The rules for deduction must be completely explicit, so that the validity of the deduction can be checked by a merely mechanical inspection of the relation of one line to the preceding lines from which it is deduced.

For Further Reflection

1. Describe the role of axioms in a deductive system. What is a proof?
2. What are the significant differences between establishing the truth of a tautology by a proof and establishing it by checking using truth tables?
3. How does the rule of substitution have its root in God? What about the rule of *modus ponens*?
4. Given the results already established in this chapter, prove that

   $(\sim p \supset \sim q) \supset (q \supset \sim\sim p)$

   Also prove that

   $(r \supset \sim p) \supset (p \supset \sim r)$

---

[7] Ibid., 1:94, principle 1.1.

Chapter 40

Axioms of Propositional Logic

We now consider some of the axioms that have been used for propositional logic. Do these axioms have roots in God?

More than one choice of axioms is possible. In fact, we can use any collection of tautologies, as long as we have enough tautologies to deduce all the rest. We will focus on the axioms given in Whitehead and Russell's *Principia Mathematica*, because it was a landmark book in the attempt to put not only deductive logic but all of mathematics on a rigorous basis. Whitehead and Russell offer five starting axioms.[1] Using these axioms alone, plus the rules of deduction, it is possible to deduce all tautologies, that is, all the logical formulas that are always true for any truth values chosen for the propositional symbols p, q, r, etc. There are an infinite number of such tautologies, but given any one of them, it is always possible to find a proof that leads from Whitehead and Russell's axioms to the tautology that we have picked. The axiom system of Whitehead and Russell is an impressive achievement, when one thinks about it. It displays the wonderful coherence in the logic of tautologies.

Whitehead and Russell's book does not fully explain why they chose the five axioms that they offer. But we can guess that it is partly because when we understand their meaning we can intuitively confirm that they are true. Let us consider them one by one.

The Principle of Tautology

The first axiom says that if p or p, then p. In symbolic notation,

$$(p \lor p) \supset p^2$$

---

[1] Alfred North Whitehead and Bertrand Russell, *Principia Mathematica*, 2nd ed., 3 vols. (Cambridge: Cambridge University Press, 1927), 1:96–97. Later a few other axioms are added, to deal with "quantification" and other needs.

[2] Whitehead and Russell, *Principia Mathematica*, 1:96, proposition 1.2. We call it "the first axiom," but it is not the first principle in Whitehead and Russell's book: it follows the statements that express the principles

Illustration: If (it is raining or it is raining), then it is raining.

Whitehead and Russell call this principle the *principle of tautology*. But, as we have indicated, the word *tautology* is also used in the broader sense to label any compound proposition in symbolic logic that is always true.

Whitehead and Russell's principle is indeed obvious. Like all the axioms, it does presuppose a larger context. In the background, we presuppose that we as human beings are thinking and communicating; we have invented and explained special technical symbols; we have agreed to idealize reasoning and reduce one aspect of reasoning to its bare bones; we agree that the "propositions" we treat are idealized versions that reduce the richness of ordinary language. We ignore all the complexities belonging to the problem of classification (part I.C).

God as Origin for the Axiom of Tautology

God in his self-consistency is the origin for all human reasoning. So he is the origin for the principle of tautology. Can we say anything more?

In an elementary way, this axiom uses unity in diversity. The three occurrences of the symbol p are all occurrences of *one* identifiable symbol. There is unity is all three occurrences. On the other hand, there are *three* occurrences, not one. Each occurrence is distinguishable from the other two. Each has a different position in the compound proposition $(p \lor p) \supset p$. Each is an *instantiation* of the proposition p. We have seen that such unity and diversity has its root in the Trinity.

We can even see in our knowledge of the Trinity ways in which such unity in diversity operates. For example, consider the proposition that God is righteous. We can describe how we know that God is righteous by saying that he reveals himself as righteous through the work of Jesus the Son. We can also say that we know that God is righteous because the Holy Spirit teaches in the Bible that God is righteous. In the Bible we also come to know about the work of Jesus the Son. In addition, the Holy Spirit by dwelling in us confirms in our hearts the conviction that God is righteous. If the symbol p stands for the proposition that God is righteous, we experience the occurrence of p in at least two different contexts, the context of the revelation of p

---

of deduction (*modus ponens*), which are articulated in propositions 1.1 and 1.11 (1:94–95). Note that in presenting the axioms we use parentheses rather than Whitehead and Russell's convention of grouping material together with dots. The dots are convenient for dealing with situations that would otherwise require several layers of nested parentheses. But as a specialized notation they represent one more thing that would have to be learned by a beginner.

through the Son and the context of the revelation of p through the Spirit. For the sake of clarity, we should also say that because of the mutual indwelling of the persons of the Trinity, these two revelations come in the final analysis from all three persons. The Holy Spirit indwelt the Son during his life on earth, and so the Spirit was at work in the Son's works of righteousness. In addition, the Son pours out the Spirit on the church (Acts 2:33) and the Spirit is the Spirit of the Son (Rom. 8:9; 2 Cor. 3:17). The Spirit comes to the apostles and writers of the New Testament, so that what they write is the word of the Spirit and the word of the Son. The witness of the Spirit in our hearts is also the work of the Son, because the Son has sent his Spirit.

We can choose to describe the source of our knowledge in these two ways. That choice is an either-or. But it is basically the *same* content for knowledge. This situation is like the composite proposition $p \vee p$. Whichever source we choose, we arrive at the general conclusion that God is righteous. p holds. Thus in our knowledge of God we have an illustration of the principle of tautology: $(p \vee p) \supset p$.

God's own knowledge of himself is the original knowledge (what may be called the *archetype*). Our knowledge is derivative (what may be called the *ectype*). But our knowledge imitates God's knowledge, because we are made in his image. This imitation suggests that God's knowledge of himself also illustrates the principle of tautology. God the Father knows his own righteousness both through knowing the character of the Son, who is righteous, and through knowing the character of the Spirit, who is righteous. Hence, at this level, the principle of tautology belongs to God himself, not merely to creatures. Since God is the original, this principle in God is not only one instance of the principle, but the *prime* instance. God is the origin for the principle.

The Principle of Addition

The second axiom in *Principia Mathematica*, called the *principle of addition*, says that if q, either p or q. In symbolic notation,

$$q \supset (p \vee q)$$

Illustration: If it is dark, then (either it is raining or it is dark).

This principle is obvious. We may say that it is built into the meaning of logical "or" ($\vee$). Because God is the origin for all of logic, he is the origin for this principle. Can we see any more specific way in which he is the origin?

It is convenient to begin with our knowledge of God. We know that God made choices in his acts of creation. He decided to create horses and *not* unicorns. This choice-making is one illustration of the operation of "or." God creates this creature *or* that creature. When we find that he created horses, we can also infer that he created horses instead of any number of other alternatives. And he created horses in addition to other creatures, such as donkeys and cats. Among these other alternatives, some are realized (donkeys) and others are not (unicorns).

This kind of knowledge is akin to what is summarized in the principle of addition. The symbol p could stand for "horses exist." q could stand for "donkeys exist" or "unicorns exist." When we know that horses exist, we can add other pieces of knowledge about donkeys and unicorns. These other facts color our view of the universe as a whole, but it does remain true that horses exist. We can rely on the faithfulness of God, and therefore subordinately on our finite reasoning processes in the imitation of God. When we know that horses exist and that unicorns do not exist, the transition from earlier knowledge ("horses exist") to later knowledge ("horses exist or unicorns exist") is akin to the formal rule of the principle of addition.

Once again, we can suggest that our knowledge concerning horses imitates God's original knowledge. God knows many things. His knowledge of one truth, namely, that he has created horses, is not disrupted by his knowledge of other truths. The unity of God's mind goes together with the diversity of distinct truths in his mind.

The Principle of Permutation

The third axiom, called the *principle of permutation*, says that if p or q, then q or p. The order can be reversed without affecting the truth of the compound propositions. In symbolic notation,

$$(p \lor q) \supset (q \lor p)$$

Illustration: If (either it is raining or it is dark) then (either it is dark or it is raining).

The relation between $p \lor q$ and $q \lor p$ expresses a symmetry. The result is the same in its truth no matter which order we choose. Symmetries of many kinds exist in the world that God has created. Many kinds of trees have roughly symmetric shape; they grow symmetrically around a central trunk. Many flowers unfold symmetrically around the center of the blossom. The tabernacle that God instructed Moses and Bezalel to make in the wilderness has symmetries in its rooms and furnishing. These symmetries all reflect the beauty of God.[3] The most basic symmetry of all is the symmetry among the persons of the Trinity. The Son is "the radiance of the glory of God and the *exact imprint* of his nature" (Heb. 1:3). Whether we consider the knowledge of God coming by means of the Son or by means of the Spirit, and with whichever order we start, we come to the same knowledge of God. To put it another way, logic has symmetries because God is beautiful and has symmetries within himself. He delights in his own beauty, and out of this delight he reflects his beauty not only in the Son but in the works that he creates through the Son and the Spirit. He reflects his beauty in human language, and in the human use of logic.

The Associative Principle

The fourth axiom, called the *associative principle*, says that if p or (q or r), then q or (p or r). In symbolic notation,

$$(p \lor (q \lor r)) \supset (q \lor (p \lor r))$$

Illustration: If (either it is raining or (it is dark or it is cold)), then (either it is dark or (it is raining or it is cold)).

The difference between the left side and the right side in the formula is a difference in the order of the two propositions p and q. More commonly, associative laws are expressed in a notation in which the order of elements remains the same, but the parentheses are grouped differently. The difference in grouping of parentheses is then the difference in "association." If we keep the order p, then q, then r the same for the left-hand side and the right-hand side of the formula, a difference only in grouping of parentheses would look like this:

$$(p \lor (q \lor r)) \supset (p \lor q) \lor r))$$

Illustration: If (either it is raining or (it is dark or it is cold)), then (either (it is raining or it is dark) or it is cold).

In *Principia Mathematica* Whitehead and Russell explain that they chose a less common form of the associative principle because "the natural

---

[3] Vern S. Poythress, *Redeeming Science: A God-Centered Approach* (Wheaton, IL: Crossway, 2006), chapters 17, 20, and 22.

form of the associative law . . . has less deductive power, and is therefore not taken as a primitive proposition [an axiom]."[4] In other words, the unusual form is chosen because, when taken together with the rest of the axioms, it more easily enables a number of key deductions, in order to obtain the full spectrum of tautologies.

God is the original for all of logic. But we can also see a more particular expression of a principle of associativity. First, we have to consider again the Trinitarian character of God. We have earlier indicated that the Holy Spirit as the Spirit who indwells us functions as a bond or "association." This kind of associative function represents one way in which God is a source for association.

The three persons of the Trinity are in fellowship with one another. They indwell one another. When they act in the accomplishment of creation, redemption, and consummation, they act together, though in distinct ways that correspond to the nature of each person in relation to the other two. For example, God the Father, God the Son, and God the Spirit are all active in creation. The Father speaks, such as in the command, "Let there be light" (Gen. 1:3). The Son, who is the eternal Word, is the original for the words spoken. The Spirit is like the breath of God (Ps. 33:6; see also Ps. 104:30).

The actions of the persons of the Trinity have natural groupings. For example, the Father and the Son both send the Holy Spirit in his redemptive presence: ". . . the Holy Spirit, whom *the Father* will send in my name" (John 14:26); "I [the Son] will send him to you" (16:7). Similarly in Acts 2 the Holy Spirit is "poured out" from the Father and the Son: "Being therefore exalted at the right hand of God, and having received from *the Father* the promise of the Holy Spirit, *he* [Jesus] has poured out this that you yourselves are seeing and hearing" (Acts 2:33). The Father and the Son are grouped together, because together they are the agents in sending the Spirit. The Spirit is the recipient and the one who executes their commission. In Romans 8 the Spirit is called the "Spirit of God" (especially God the Father) and the "Spirit of Christ" (Rom. 8:9).

We also see the Father and the Spirit grouped together. In the incarnation of the Son, the Father and the Spirit act together: "The *Holy Spirit* will come upon you [Mary, the mother of Jesus], and the power of *the Most High* will overshadow you; therefore the child to be born will be called holy—the

---

[4] Whitehead and Russell, *Principia Mathematica*, 1:96.

Son of God" (Luke 1:35). The Father and the Spirit together are agents. The Son is the recipient of their action. In addition, the Father and the Spirit are active together in raising Christ from the dead (Rom. 8:11).

Finally, the Son and the Spirit are grouped together in bringing about the plan of God the Father on earth. In Luke 3:22, at Jesus's baptism, the Holy Spirit "descended on him in bodily form, like a dove; and a voice came from heaven [the voice of God the Father], 'You are my beloved Son; with you I am well pleased.'" The Holy Spirit is sent as the Spirit anointing Jesus for ministry. And the voice of the Father, by alluding to Psalm 2:7 and Isaiah 42:1, implies a commission to Christ to carry out the work of the Messiah as prophesied in Psalms, Isaiah, and other parts of the Old Testament. Note also Luke 4:18: "The *Spirit* of the Lord is upon *me*, because he has anointed me . . ."

When Jesus begins his public ministry, Luke says, "And *Jesus* returned in the power of the *Spirit* to Galilee, and a report about him went out through all the surrounding country. And he taught in their synagogues, being glorified by all" (Luke 4:14–15). Jesus is preaching and working miracles as the Son, sent by the Father. He has the power of the Spirit in so doing. Both the Spirit and the Son are at work.

We may conclude, then, that in the works of redemption there are natural groupings of the persons of the Trinity. Two of the persons are described as active together in relation to the third. And all three possible groupings of two occur in the Bible.

There is only one God. All his works are works of the one God. But the "associative" grouping of two persons in relation to the third still makes sense. Whatever grouping we use, the implications for the work of God as one God are the same. This kind of grouping is then the original, while groupings with respect to mundane truths, such as we see in the associative principle, are a reflection of the divine original.

The Principle of Summation

The fifth axiom, called the *principle of summation*, says that if *q* implies *r*, then (*p* or *q*) implies (*p* or *r*). In symbolic notation,

$$(q \supset r) \supset ((p \vee q) \supset (p \vee r))$$

Illustration: If (it is dark implies it is cold), then (the assumption that (it is raining or it is dark) implies the conclusion that (it is raining or it is cold)).

This principle is a little more complex. It is not as obvious.[5] But further reflection may help to make it intuitively plausible. If we know that q implies r (for example, if we know that (it is dark implies that it is cold)), we are supposed to verify that $(p \lor q) \supset (p \lor r)$. Suppose we know that p is true. It is clear that p implies p. Adding the q and the r does not affect the implication. So indeed $(p \lor q) \supset (p \lor r)$. Next, suppose that q is true. We have assumed that q implies r. So r also must be true. Then the full implication $(p \lor q) \supset (p \lor r)$ is also true. The final case is when p and q are both false. Then $p \lor q$ is false. Then there is nothing to prove, since the implication symbol $\supset$ has been previously defined so that the whole implication is true whenever the antecedent (in this case $p \lor q$) is false.

We can express the idea in another way. We start with $q \supset r$. If we know that q implies r, will the implication still be valid when we add "or p" to both sides? It will, because the valid implication "p implies p" can be "added to" the existing implication "q implies r." In fact, we can state more generally, if q implies r and s implies t, then $(q$ or $s)$ implies $(r$ or $t)$. In symbolic notation,

$$((q \supset r) \land (s \supset t)) \supset ((q \lor s) \supset (r \lor t))^6$$

Illustration: If (it is raining implies it is wet) and if (it is cold implies I am shivering), then (it is raining or it is cold) implies (it is wet or I am shivering).

Once again, we can obtain a helpful illustration by reflecting on God's action in creating the world. He made choices with respect to what kind of world he would create, and what kinds of creatures he would create within the world. Let us imagine two possible choices for worlds, represented by q and s. Because God is self-consistent, whichever choices he makes, he will make a world that expresses his inner self-consistency. So q will have certain implications, according to God's consistency. Let us say that r is among those implications. And likewise s will have some implications. Let us say that t is among those implications. The diversity of choices q and s is consistent with the unity of God and the unity of his self-consistency. So it would seem reasonable to contemplate what might be true assuming either one of the opening choices, q or s. And so we arrive at a process of implication similar to the principle of summation.

---

[5] In fact, it is violated in so-called quantum logic. One way of explaining this difficulty is to say that, according to quantum theory, finding out whether a quantum state q is actually realized requires a measurement, and the measurement disturbs the system (e.g., p). It can be disputed whether this difficulty is a difficulty in logic or in physics. For simplicity we are considering *classical* logic, which ignores these complexities (see further discussion in chapter 63).

[6] Whitehead and Russell, *Principia Mathematica*, 1:114, proposition 3.48.

But we should exercise caution. Our minds imitate God's mind. But God's mind is infinite and incomprehensible. We are creatures within the world that God created. He could have created worlds of other kinds. Because we are made in the image of God, we can imagine how he might have created worlds different from this one. But some of the possibilities beyond this world may be beyond our minds. We cannot simply identify our minds with God's mind, because then we abolish the distinction between Creator and creature. The fifth axiom, along with the other axioms, should be viewed as a human attempt to express one dimension in the logic of ordinary language, and this language reflects the original logic of God, which is incomprehensible.

For Further Reflection

1. Which of Whitehead and Russell's axioms are most "obvious"?
2. How does the principle of permutation have its foundation in God?
3. How does the associative principle have its foundation in God?
4. Verify each of the axioms using truth tables.

Chapter 41

Alternative Axioms

The axioms used by Whitehead and Russell's book are reasonable, but they are not the only ones possible. It is a matter of choice, because it is possible to deduce Whitehead and Russell's axioms from an alternative collection, and this collection can in turn be deduced from Whitehead and Russell's axioms. Some people have explored whether the number of starting axioms can be reduced. They have also asked whether the number of starting *logical symbols* can be reduced. As we observed in chapter 32, logical implication ($\supset$) can be defined in terms of logical "or" and "not." Whitehead and Russell's system actually begins with only two logical symbols, namely, "or" and "not" ($\vee, \sim$). It then defines implication ($\supset$) and logical conjunction ($\wedge$) as shorthand notations for certain specific combinations of "or" and "not." But there are other ways of proceeding. Logical "or" can be defined in terms of implication and "not":

$p \vee q$ is equivalent to $\sim p \supset q$

Jan Łukasiewicz showed that it was sufficient to start with two logical operations, namely, $\sim$ ("not") and $\supset$ ("implies"), plus three axioms:[1]

$(p \supset q) \supset ((q \supset r) \supset (p \supset r))$[2]
$(\sim p \supset p) \supset p$[3]
$p \supset (\sim p \supset q)$[4]

We may consider these axioms one at a time.

The Principle of the Syllogism

The first of Łukasiewicz's axioms, called the principle of the syllogism,[5] says that if p implies q, then if q implies r, p implies r. In symbolic notation,

---

[1] *Encyclopaedia Britannica* (1963), 14:296.
[2] Alfred North Whitehead and Bertrand Russell, *Principia Mathematica*, 2nd ed., 3 vols. (Cambridge: Cambridge University Press, 1927), 1:99, proposition 2.06.
[3] A form of the principle of the *reductio ad absurdum* (ibid., 1:103, proposition 2.18).
[4] Ibid., 1:104, proposition 2.24.
[5] Whitehead and Russell, *Principia Mathematica*, 1:100–101, proposition 2.06.

$(p \supset q) \supset ((q \supset r) \supset (p \supset r))$

Illustration: If (it is raining implies it is wet), then [the assumption that (it is wet implies the grass is wet) implies the conclusion that (it is raining implies the grass is wet)].

It is called the principle of the syllogism because it is related to the earlier syllogism with Socrates. We can see a relationship if we reformulate the syllogism with Socrates as follows:

Being Socrates (p) implies being a man (q).
Being a man (q) implies being mortal (r).
Then: being Socrates (p) implies being mortal (r).[6]

Intuitively, the chain of inferences makes sense. If we can reason from Socrates to man, and from man to mortality, then we can do both steps together and reason from Socrates to mortality. In general terms, if we can reason validly from p to q, and also from q to r, we can do both steps together and validly reason from p to r.

Chains of reasoning of this kind occur in ordinary life, though often in shorthand form. Some of the steps in the reasoning may have to be inferred rather than being spelled out explicitly. For example, we have reasoning in John 5:26, 28–29:

For as the Father has life in himself, so he has granted the Son also to have life in himself. . . .

Do not marvel at this, for an hour is coming when all who are in the tombs will hear his [the Son's] voice and come out, those who have done good to the resurrection of life, and those who have done evil to the resurrection of judgment.

With some reflection, we can simplify and extract a syllogistic chain:

If the Father has life in himself (p), the Son has life in himself (q).
If the Son has life in himself (q), the Son gives life in resurrection (r).
If the Father has life in himself (p), the Son gives life in resurrection (r).

We can thus suggest that syllogistic reasoning among human beings reflects

---

[6] For simplicity I have suppressed the universal quantifier, "*All* men are mortal." Quantifiers are treated symbolically in predicate logic, which is more complex than propositional logic and presupposes it. See chapters 48–50.

the consistency of God, and the consistency of life between the Father and the Son, through the Spirit. The so-called principle of the syllogism is one reflection of God's consistency.

The Principle of *reductio ad absurdum*

The second of Łukasiewicz's axioms is a form of the principle of *reductio ad absurdum*. It says that if assuming p is not true leads to the conclusion that p is after all true (a contradiction), then p is true. In symbolic notation,

$(\sim p \supset p) \supset p$

Illustration: If (it is not raining implies that it is raining), then it is raining.

God is not only the God who knows all truth and who is truth itself (John 14:6), but a God who knows all the trails of reasoning in the human mind, including false trails (Ps. 139:2, 4, 16). When a false assumption leads to contradiction, we know from the self-consistency of God that the assumption must be false.

The apostle Paul uses a form of the argument of *reductio ad absurdum* in 1 Corinthians 15:12–20:

> But if there is no resurrection of the dead, then not even Christ has
>   been raised. (1 Cor. 15:13)
> . . .
> But in fact Christ has been raised from the dead, . . . (v. 20)
> . . .
> . . . then, at his coming those who belong to Christ [will be raised]. (v. 23)

We can simplify it as follows:

> If there is no resurrection of the dead, Christ has not been raised.
> Christ has been raised.
> Therefore, there is a resurrection of the dead.

Let p stand for the proposition that Christ has been raised. Let q stand for the proposition that there is a resurrection of the dead. Then the argument runs as follows:

$\sim q \supset \sim p$
p
Therefore q.

This form of argument can be viewed as a form of *reductio ad absurdum*. If the assumption that q is false ($\sim q$) leads to affirming both $\sim p$ and p, we have a contradiction. Hence the assumption that q is false is incorrect. Hence q is true.

The Principle of Falsehood

Łukasiewicz's third axiom says that if p is true, the assumption that p is false can lead to any conclusion whatsoever. In symbolic notation,

$$p \supset (\sim p \supset q)$$

Illustration: If it is raining, then (the assumption that it is not raining implies that the moon is made of green cheese).

It is not so easy to see intuitively how this is so. It is indeed so that trying to hold to two contradictory ideas at the same time is destructive to sound reasoning. Falsehood leads to more falsehood. Formal logic simplifies by reducing reasoning to one dimension, namely, simple truth or falsehood, independent of content. And that reduction leads to the simplified formal statement that falsehood leads to all propositions.

We can find an intuitively more appealing equivalent by making a replacement. Remember that

$r \supset s$ is equivalent to $\sim r \vee s$.

Substituting $\sim p$ for r and q for s,

$\sim p \supset q$ is equivalent to $\sim(\sim p) \vee q$.

Also, $\sim\sim p$ is equivalent to p, so

$\sim p \supset q$ is equivalent to $p \vee q$.

If we substitute $p \vee q$ for $\sim p \supset q$ in Łukasiewicz's third axiom, we obtain

$$p \supset p \vee q$$

This result is similar to Whitehead and Russell's principle of addition. It makes intuitive sense. Surely if p is true, we can also say that p or q is true. Illustration: If it is raining, then either it is raining or it is dark.

The Sheffer Stroke

It is not so surprising that logicians should explore whether the number of starting symbols and starting axioms can be reduced in number still further. The answer offered by Jean Nicod is that we need only one starting logical symbol, one axiom, and one rule of deduction in addition to the rule of sub-stitution.[7] The starting logical symbol is |, which is called the *Sheffer stroke*. It denotes logical incompatibility. $p \mid q$ means that p is incompatible with q. Or we could say, "not both p and q." The composite proposition $p \mid q$ is true if at least one of p or q is false. The truth table for the Sheffer stroke | is given in table 41.1:

TABLE 41.1: Truth Table for the Sheffer Stroke (|)

p	q	$p \mid q$
T	T	F
T	F	T
F	T	T
F	F	T

The one rule of inference (in addition to the principle of substitution) is that if p is true and $p \mid (q \mid r)$ is true, one may deduce that r is true. The one axiom is the following:

$$\{p \mid (q \mid r)\} \mid [\{t \mid (t \mid t)\} \mid \{(s \mid q) \mid ((p \mid s) \mid (p \mid s))\}]^8$$

This axiom is pretty opaque, in contrast to most of the axioms we have already discussed.[9] The opacity is part of the price we pay if we want to pack all the axioms into one.

---

[7] Jean Nicod, "A Reduction in the Number of Primitive Propositions of Logic," *Proceedings of the Cambridge Philosophical Society* 19 (1917): 32–41; cited in Whitehead and Russell, *Principia* Mathematica, 1:xvi.

[8] Whitehead and Russell, *Principia Mathematica*, 1:xix.

[9] Pieces within this axiom are nevertheless related to the axioms we have already seen. The left-hand side, $p \mid (q \mid r)$, is equivalent to saying that p implies both q and r. The right-hand side contains two pieces. The first piece, $t \mid (t \mid t)$, is similar to the tautology $t \supset t$. The second piece, $(s \mid q) \mid ((p \mid s) \mid (p \mid s))$, when related to the left-hand side, is an expression of one form of the principle of the syllogism. For those interested in still more details, here is a brief explanation. Begin with the expression on the left-hand side, namely, $p \mid (q \mid r)$. If p is true, $q \mid r$ must be false for $p \mid (q \mid r)$ as a whole to be true. $q \mid r$ is false only if both q and r are true. Thus $p \mid (q \mid r)$ as a whole is equivalent to "p implies q and r." If p does indeed imply both q and r, the left-hand side is true. For the whole axiom to be true (which it must be, if it is going to serve as an axiom), $\{t \mid (t \mid t)\} \mid \{(s \mid q) \mid ((p \mid s) \mid (p \mid s))\}$ must be false. The only way for the right-hand side to be false is for both of the two major "pieces" within it to be true. That is, $t \mid (t \mid t)$ is true and $(s \mid q) \mid ((p \mid s) \mid (p \mid s))$ is true. $t \mid (t \mid t)$ is automatically true (check it out by plugging in the two alternative values for t, T or F; or notice that, by the earlier reasoning about the meaning of $p \mid (q \mid r)$, $t \mid (t \mid t)$ is equivalent to saying that t implies (t and t), which is surely true). Now what about $(s \mid q) \mid ((p \mid s) \mid (p \mid s))$? $(s \mid q)$ is equivalent to q implies not-s. If q does indeed imply not-s, and (as we have deduced) $(s \mid q) \mid ((p \mid s) \mid (p \mid s))$ is true, then the half of the expression which follows $(s \mid q)$, namely, $((p \mid s) \mid (p \mid s))$, must be false, which implies that $(p \mid s)$ is true, that

Perspectives on Axioms

All lists of starting axioms, and all the variations on the rules of deduction, are like so many perspectives on the truths of logic and how we arrive at them. Multiple perspectives are possible because of the diversity in the Trinity, which is reflected in the diversity of the human mind.

For Further Reflection

1. How does Łukasiewicz's first axiom, the principle of the syllogism, have its foundation in God?
2. How is Łukasiewicz's logical system as a whole related to Whitehead and Russell's system? How do both systems display the glory of God? What should be our response?
3. In what ways is Nicod's system a special achievement?
4. Use Frame's square for transcendence and immanence to discuss the difference between a Christian and a non-Christian view of the relation of one axiom of propositional logic to the origin of the axiom in God.

---

is, that p implies not-s. Thus, taking everything together, if p implies q, which is part of the meaning of the left-hand side, and q implies not-s, then p implies not-s. This chain of reasoning is one form of the principle of the syllogism. The principle of syllogism together with the principle of tautology and the rule of deduction suffice to deduce all the other tautologies.

Nicod has found an impressively compact starting point. It is to be admired. But its importance is decreased by the fact that there are many other possible starting lists of axioms, all of which lead to the same results in the long run. Nicod's system offers one perspective (see chapter 38).

Chapter 42

Dispensing with Axioms

Whitehead and Russell's system for propositional logic has five axioms (see chapter 40) and two rules of deduction, namely, the rule of substitution and *modus ponens*. If we like, we can add further rules of deduction, provided we make sure that these additional rules always lead from truth to more truth. Having more rules of deduction may make it easier to figure out how to deduce new theorems. So there is potential practical value in adding some more rules of deduction. It turns out that, if we add enough rules, we can dispense with having any axioms at all! A system of this kind can be constructed so that the rules for inferences mimic more "natural" ways in which human beings reason. For this reason it is called a *natural deduction system*. It is useful because it is usually easier within this kind of system to figure out a way to deduce a theorem that we have decided we want to prove.

So let us look at some additional rules, which together enable us to deduce all five axioms of Whitehead and Russell. Under this new way of organizing the system, the five axioms of Whitehead and Russell become theorems instead of axioms. But whether they are axioms or theorems, they can be used as a starting point for all further deductions. So the new system, with no axioms, is equivalent in its results to the system of Whitehead and Russell.

Rule of Addition

Our first rule, which we call the rule of *addition*, is similar to axiom 2 of Whitehead and Russell (the principle of addition, $q \supset (p \lor q)$).

Rule of addition: If q is a theorem, $p \lor q$ is a theorem.

Illustration: If we have established that it is dark, we can legitimately deduce that (either it is raining or it is dark).

To put it in different words, if we know that q is true we can infer that $p \lor q$ is true. The rule of addition says that if we have a number of lines in a proof, and *q* represents one of the lines, then on a later line we may deduce *p* ∨ *q* from the earlier line. We can add a second version of the rule:

Second rule of addition: If *p* is a theorem, *p* ∨ *q* is a theorem.

Illustration: If we have established that it is raining, we can legitimately deduce that (either it is raining or it is dark).

In practice, the rule would operate by moving from one line of a proof to the next:

p (Premise)
p ∨ *q* (Conclusion from the preceding premise, using the rule of addition)

Here is an example that starts from a proposition *q* that is one of the theorems in Whitehead and Russell:

p ⊃ *p*[1]
Therefore *r* ∨ (*p* ⊃ *p*)

Here we have used *p* ⊃ *p* instead of *q* and *r* instead of *p* in the first form for the rule of addition. The rule of addition is understood as including all possible substitutions of this kind for the starting symbols *p* and *q*.

Having this new rule of inference does not alter the capabilities of Whitehead and Russell's system in any substantive way, since even without the extra rule we can deduce the same result by a different route:

(1) *p* ⊃ *p* (theorem already proved in Whitehead and Russell)
(2) *q* ⊃ (*p* ∨ *q*) (axiom 2 in Whitehead and Russell)[2]
(3) (*p* ⊃ *p*) ⊃ (*r* ∨ (*p* ⊃ *p*)) (by substituting *r* for *p* and *p* ⊃ *p* for *q* in (2))
(4) *r* ∨ (*p* ⊃ *p*) (by *modus ponens* from (1) and (3))

Thus Whitehead and Russell's axiom 2, namely, *q* ⊃ (*p* ∨ *q*), together with the deduction rules already in place in Whitehead and Russell's system, enables us to achieve the same results as could be achieved using the *extra* rule for deduction. But the converse is also true. If we add enough extra rules of deduction, we can produce a situation in which we no longer need axiom 2.

---

[1] Alfred North Whitehead and Bertrand Russell, *Principia Mathematica*, 2nd ed., 3 vols. (Cambridge: Cambridge University Press, 1927), 1:99, proposition 2.08.
[2] Ibid., 1:96, proposition 1.3.

Rule of Conditional Proof

Our next rule is more complicated and more significant. Suppose we can deduce the conclusion q by assuming, earlier in the lines of a proof, that p is true. Then we can infer that $p \supset q$ is true. We call this the rule of *conditional proof*. Intuitively, this principle makes sense, because it is close to the real meaning that we want the symbol ($\supset$) for implication to have. Here is how it works on a particular example:

(1) Assume that q is true.
   (2) $p \lor q$ (by the rule of addition applied to (1))
(3) $q \supset (p \lor q)$ (by the rule of conditional proof applied to the sequence (1)-(2))

Here is an illustration where p and q are replaced by specific propositions:

(1) Assume that it is dark (q).
   (2) either it is raining (p) or it is dark (q) (by the rule of addition applied to (1))
(3) If it is dark (q), then either it is raining (p) or it is dark (q) (by the rule of conditional proof applied to the sequence (1)-(2))

We have indented line (2) to make it easier to remember that line (2) is written *within* a schema where we have added an extra assumption (namely, line (1)). We then back out of that extra assumption in line (3), using the rule of conditional proof. So line (3) itself is no longer "conditional"; it is valid in general. It does not receive an extra indent. We have now proved that $q \supset (p \lor q)$ using our two new rules of deduction. $q \supset (p \lor q)$ was an axiom for Whitehead and Russell's system. We no longer need it as an axiom in our new system, because the additional rules of deduction allow us to prove it.

We can also produce another version of the principle of addition.

(1) Assume p.
   (2) $p \lor q$ (by the rule of addition applied to (1))
(3) $p \supset (p \lor q)$ (by the rule of conditional proof applied to the sequence (1)-(2))

So we have proved that $p \supset (p \lor q)$.

We have to introduce two provisos, however, when we use our new rule, the rule of conditional proof. First, when we are in the middle of the lines leading from an assumption (line (1) above) to a conclusion (line (3) above), we are not allowed to apply the rule of substitution to these middle lines. The rule of substitution applies only to axioms and to theorems already established on the basis of axioms. It does *not* apply in the middle of a conditional proof. Why not? We have to "keep track" of the earlier assumption, in this case the assumption that p holds true. If we substitute some other expression for p, we destroy validity in the process. Watch:

(1) Assume p.
  (2) p (from (1))
  (3) q (by substituting q for p in (2)) [but this is not an allowed kind of substitution]
(4) $p \supset q$ (by the rule of conditional proof applied to the sequence (1)-(3))

The final line, $p \supset q$, expresses the principle that any proposition p implies any other q. That is clearly unsound. An illegal kind of substitution, which is what took place in step (3), ruins the validity of the deduction. An illustration may help. If p stands for the proposition "it is raining," we cannot just substitute "it is dark" for it in the middle of a conditional proof that depends on the assumption that it is raining.

A second proviso says that once we have "backed out" of the extra assumption involved in a conditional proof by the final step, we cannot appeal to any of the intermediate steps later on. Consider the following reasoning, which becomes invalid at step (4):

(1) Assume p.
  (2) p (from (1))
(3) $p \supset p$ (conditional proof applied to (1)-(3))
(4) p (from (2))—illegal, because we are appealing to the line (2) inside the conditional proof.

Rule of Reiteration

The rule of *reiteration* says that we may repeat a result obtained from a preceding line, or repeat an axiom or a theorem already proved elsewhere. Whitehead and Russell's system allows for this procedure but does not explicitly name it. For convenience and clarity, we give it a name.

Rule of Disjunction Elimination

Next, the rule of *disjunction elimination* allows us to make a deduction from a disjunction $p \lor q$ without necessarily knowing which of the two propositions p or q holds. Suppose we have already established (by lines of proof) that for some particular value of p, q, and r, (a) $p \lor q$; (b) $p \supset r$; and (c) $q \supset r$. Then we may infer r. Schematically, the lines of proof look like this:

(1) $p \lor q$
(2) $p \supset r$
(3) $q \supset r$
(4) r (by disjunction elimination applied to (1), (2), and (3))

Illustration: suppose we know three different pieces of information:

(1) Either it is raining or it is dark.
(2) It is raining implies it is cold.
(3) It is dark implies it is cold.

Then we can legitimately deduce that it is cold.

This rule makes intuitive sense. Suppose we know that $p \lor q$. We may not know *which one* of p and q is true, but at least one is. If p is, then we deduce r using the additional proposition $p \supset r$ (we use *modus ponens* for this deduction). If q is true, then we deduce r using the proposition $q \supset r$. Either way, we deduce r. So, yes, we may legitimately infer r once we have in place the propositions (1), (2), and (3) above.

Deducing the Axioms of Whitehead and Russell

Using these rules, we may now deduce the axioms of Whitehead and Russell. We have already deduced above Whitehead and Russell's second axiom, the principle of addition, namely, that $q \supset (p \lor q)$. We now need proofs for the remaining axioms.

The principle of tautology. Whitehead and Russell's principle of tautology says that $(p \lor p) \supset p$. Can we prove it? Let us start by proving something simpler, namely, that $p \supset p$. It is easy using the rule of conditional proof.

(1) Assume p.
(2) p (by the rule of reiteration from (1))
(3) $p \supset p$ (by the rule of conditional proof, applied to lines (1)-(2))

Illustration:

(1) Assume that it is raining.
(2) It is raining (from (1)).
(3) If it is raining it is raining (conditional proof, from (1)-(2)).

Now we are ready to show that $(p \lor p) \supset p$.

(1) $p \supset p$ (previous theorem)
(2) Assume $p \lor p$.
   (3) p (by the rule of disjunction elimination, applied to (2), (1), and (1))
(4) $(p \lor p) \supset p$ (by the rule of conditional proof, applied to lines (2)-(3))

The principle of permutation, the associative principle, and the principle of summation. The remaining axioms of Whitehead and Russell take more work in deduction, but the principles remain the same. (See appendix B2 for the explicit deductions.)

Something Out of Nothing?

All of the original axioms in Whitehead and Russell's system have become theorems in our new system. Once these axioms are established as theorems, we can use these theorems in further deductions, and thereby prove any conclusion that can be proved in Whitehead and Russell. In our new system, we need no starting axioms. We start from zero.

But how can deduction start from zero? Many discussions of the process of deduction point out that deduction must always have some starting premises to work on. The truth or falsehood of these premises has to be established from *outside* the deduction. For example, think of our syllogism about Socrates:

Premise 1: All men are mortal.
Premise 2: Socrates is a man.
Conclusion: Therefore Socrates is mortal.

The conclusion follows inexorably from the premises. The argument is *valid* in the technical sense of validity. But does the argument get us anywhere? Does it do us any good? We gain something only if we can first establish the truth of the two premises. We might try to supply other syllogisms to argue for Premise 1 or for Premise 2. But these other syllogisms would have their own premises. We never come to an absolute bottom. We never start from zero. Likewise, the deductive system of Whitehead and Russell includes axioms. So does the alternative system offered by Łukasiewicz. These axioms are not themselves deduced. Their truth must be established from outside the system.

In our new system, we start with no axioms but only with rules for deduction. The rules for deduction contain information within them, and this information means that in reality we do not start from absolutely nothing. So where did the rules for deduction come from? We codified them, but we did not invent them arbitrarily. We selected them to express explicitly some of the ways in which people already know unself-consciously how to reason. So the rules came from our minds. And our minds came from the mind of God, because he created us in his image.

When we start from Whitehead and Russell's axioms, we have a certain perspective on deduction and propositional truth. When we start with Łukasiewicz's axioms, we have a different perspective. When we start with an expanded number of rules of deduction, we have still a different perspective. These perspectives all have their own flavor. But at a deep level, they imply one another, which is what we should expect from God, who is in harmony with himself.

Nevertheless, the perspective in which we start with no axioms at all still has a striking character. Let us ask more carefully how it is possible. We added to Whitehead and Russell's rules of deduction (substitution and *modus ponens*) three more rules: the rule of addition (which has two forms), the rule of conditional proof, and the rule of disjunction elimination. The rule of addition allows us to deduce $p \lor q$ if we know that q. But we still have to have a starting premise, namely q. The rule of disjunction elimination also requires starting premises—not one, but three. So neither of these rules allows us to start with no premises at all.

What about the rule of conditional proof? It is the key rule. Why? It does not need any starting premises. It can begin with an *assumption*. For example, the derivation of the principle of addition $q \supset (p \lor q)$ begins with an assumption:

(1) Assume q.

The rule of conditional proof allows us to start with any assumption we want. We need no external justification—we need no premises.

The whole process starts as if by magic. We seem to produce an assumption out of nothing. Then, some lines later, when we arrive at a result, we "close out" the initial assumption using the rule of conditional proof, and we obtain a proof that is actually valid.

We do not literally start with nothing. First, as we already indicated, the rule of deduction contains information. The theorems that result already have their principles mysteriously concealed, albeit in a different form, in the rules of deduction. We can even see to some extent how this "conceal-ment" takes place. The rule of addition, whereby we deduce $p \vee q$ from q, already expresses in principial form some of the force of Whitehead and Russell's principle of addition, $q \supset (p \vee q)$. The rule for disjunction elimina-tion already has within it some of the force of Whitehead and Russell's prin-ciple of permutation and their associative principle. The rule of conditional proof is the most powerful, but within Whitehead and Russell's system it corresponds to some extent to what they call the "principle of the syllo-gism," which takes the form of two theorems each of which are deduced using the starting axiom of the principle of summation. The theorems are:

$$(q \supset r) \supset ((p \supset q) \supset (p \supset r))$$
$$(p \supset q) \supset ((q \supset r) \supset (p \supset r))^3$$

These theorems, along with a few others, can be used repeatedly in order to reproduce within Whitehead and Russell's system the power of the rule of conditional proof.

The Power of Making Assumptions

But we should not minimize the significance of the rule of conditional proof or the principle of the syllogism that corresponds to it. Both of these prin-ciples touch on the question, "What if?" They deal in hypotheticals. The rule of conditional proof invites us to think about a possibility that we may not yet know to be true. We begin to construct a picture imaginatively. "Imagine that p is true. What would follow?" In some cases, much follows, and what follows is interesting.

The principle of the syllogism, as expressed in Whitehead and Russell's notation, contains within it a similar kind of meaning, if we reflect on it carefully. Consider the first form of the principle of the syllogism:

$$(q \supset r) \supset ((p \supset q) \supset (p \supset r))$$

This principle tells us a conclusion $(p \supset q) \supset (p \supset r)$ that follows once we know that $q \supset r$. But in particular cases we may not know for sure whether $q \supset r$. Even if we do, we may not know whether $p \supset q$. And if we know that also, we know that $p \supset r$, but we *still* have no assurance that p or r is true when taken by itself. The formulation, when translated back into ordinary

---

3 Ibid., 1:100, propositions 2.05 and 2.06.

English, is full of hypotheticals. It takes the form: if *A* is true, then *B* is true, where we may not know whether in fact *A* is true. We are only told what we should imagine within a world *if A were* true.

An appreciation for the practical import of this principle depends on our understanding the meaning of hypotheses or suppositions or conditionals. It depends on our being able to imagine what might be but which we do not know to be and which indeed might *not* be.

Two aspects of human thinking come to the surface when we put things this way. One aspect is the limitation of our knowledge. There are things we do not know. We use hypothetical constructions partly because we are finite. Even within the limitations of our finiteness, we do know *some* things. And among these are conditionals: if we *did* know some additional truth *A*, we would, according to the nature of the connection between *A* and *B*, also be able to know that *B*. Knowledge is connected in this way. It is connected in us because we are imitating an archetype, namely God, in whom all knowledge is connected by the unity of his person and the self-consistency of his character.

The second aspect about hypotheticals and imagination is its aspect of creativity. We can picture imaginary situations in our minds, not only when we do not know what the facts are, but even when we do. We can imagine situations or even whole worlds that do not actually exist. Does this creativity operate in a vacuum? No, it is an imitation of God's creativity.

God showed his creativity by creating an actual world, the world around us. But he need not have exercised his creativity in exactly the way he did. He made choices. As we have observed, he created horses and not unicorns. In his infinity, he also knows about the choices that he did not make but could have made (1 Sam. 23:10–13). He knows about unicorns. We did not invent the idea; he had it first.

We said at one point that the rule of conditional proof enabled us to start "from zero." We meant that we started with no axioms at all. But it also may give us the feeling that we start literally from nothing. We "create" a proof "out of nothing." The Bible indicates that God created the universe out of nothing (Col. 1:16). God alone, in his infinity and self-sufficiency, is able to be the absolute creator in this way. But we imitate him, do we not?

We do not literally create out of nothing. We must first exist ourselves. We must first have minds. We must first have some practical experience in reasoning. If we have practical experience with this world, we gain ideas that enable us to create fantasy worlds. We become in this way "subcreators," though we still owe our creativity itself as well as our individual creative ideas to God, who thought them first.

We can create not only fantasy worlds, but fantasy proofs. Assume that p is true. (Illustration: assume that it is raining.) That assumption is a kind of fantasy. It creates a "world," albeit a world with very minimal structure. We have become subcreators. We are imitating God's creativity—not apart from him, but by his power and in his presence. Precisely through God's creativity being exercised in us, we become creative. Now we use the rule of addition, which imitates the mind of God. We reason that this new world, in accordance with the mind of God, must also have the structure p or q if it has the structure p. Moreover, there is a relation between the two structures, p on the one hand and p or q on the other hand. The one implies the other, according to the rationality of God. Our creativity is bounded by the creativity of God and the rationality of God. But that is not a threat or a straitjacket. Having no bounds at all leads to meaninglessness. God's bounds give meaning to creativity.

In chapter 9 we noted that we have ability to *mention* a word like *cat* as well as to *use* it in a sentence, "The *cat* is on the mat." When we *mention* a word, we engage in a kind of "standing back" or transcendence, in which we stand above a particular sentence or linguistic unit and discuss how it operates. Linguistics itself is possible because we can stand back from everyday unreflective language *use*, and make observations about that use.[4] Likewise, in this case, when we create a fantasy world, we are standing back from the world as it is. We exercise a kind of miniature transcendence.

Strikingly, our fantasy proofs have value in the real world. It is in fact the case that p implies (p or q), that is, $p \supset (p \lor q)$. We must always bear in mind the qualifications that we investigated earlier. Formal logic is a one-dimensional simplification. It singles out one dimension only from the full power of language and reason, as God gave them. Yet it is wonderful. We reflect on our level as creatures God's transcendence by being subcreators who imagine fantasy worlds or fantasy proofs.

We also exercise transcendence by standing back from particular cases of reasoning and making a very generalized statement, namely, $p \supset (p \lor q)$. That statement holds not only for the particular cases of reasoning that we

---

[4] See Vern S. Poythress, *In the Beginning Was the Word: Language—A God-Centered Approach* (Wheaton, IL: Crossway, 2009), chapter 11.

have examined one by one. It holds in general. It holds for future cases. It holds for fantasy cases in hypothetical situations. It holds for fantasy cases in fantasy worlds. When we say that, we stand, as it were, "above" the particular cases. Or we stand "above" all the fantasy worlds that we survey in our minds. We transcend them. We transcend whole worlds.

Have we become gods? Maybe we think we have, in the recesses of our hearts. We want to be God. We lust insatiably for the satisfaction of absolute transcendence and absolute autonomy. But if so, we lust for something that is not true and that we can never have. We are not God. Even in the process of standing above particular cases of reasoning, we rely on the inner relationship or association between the general rule for reasoning and its particular manifestations. We rely on unity and diversity. And that means that we rely on God.

Likewise, when we imagine whole worlds, we imagine a variety of possible worlds, each world with its own diversity. The imagination is interesting not only because of the diversity but because of the unity. All the worlds are worlds. They are unified by sharing common features of rationality, and maybe additional features that we have added by analogy with the world that we experience. The unity of common features goes together with and coheres with the diversity of worlds. We rely on unity in diversity. We rely on God. We also rely on God who sustains our neurons, our brains, our breathing, and our heartbeat.

We are made in God's image. That character of being in his image means that we do have miniature transcendence of a sort in us. But God's image in us takes two forms. The original form with Adam was a form in which we thought God's thoughts after him in an analogical way because we loved him. We enjoyed him, desired him, and rejoiced unspeakably in the glory that he revealed in our minds through his infinity and his transcendence.

The other form is the fallen form. Instead of desiring fellowship with God, and instead of rejoicing in the wonder of his presence and the presence of his ideas, we pervert our desire into its opposite: we want to be away from God, independent of him, so that we may praise the glory of ourselves as if we were God.

The two forms of the image are irreconcilable. We are either one or the other. Either we are fulfilled in fellowship with God or we are frustrating the very character of our minds by seeking a phantom, the phantom of being God rather than enjoying him.

For Further Reflection

1. Which of the rules for natural deduction is the most powerful?
2. How are rules of natural deduction related to Whitehead and Russell's axioms?
3. In what ways does the rule of conditional proof manifest the glory of God?
4. Discuss whether a natural deduction system starts "from zero."
5. How do hypotheses reflect in our minds the glory of God?

Chapter 43

Perspectives on Propositional Logic

We observed earlier that we can use several different perspectives on logic (chapter 38). These perspectives can be used not only in looking at simple truth functions ($\lor$, $\sim$, $\land$, $\supset$) but also in looking at the larger system consisting of composite propositions, deductions, and tautologies. Whitehead and Russell, Łukasiewicz, and Nicod all chose to work within the bounds of the notations of a formalized language. But the framework of tables for truth functions offers a creative alternative. We will use truth tables as a perspective on the logical systems of Whitehead and Russell, Łukasiewicz, and Nicod.

(Note that this use of perspectives is *not relativistic*. The same tautologies occur in each of the systems. But the route by which we deduce them is different.)

Truth Tables as a Perspective on Propositional Logic

Can we *deduce* the axioms for propositional logic from the truth tables for the logical connectives? For example, let us consider Whitehead and Russell's first axiom,

$(p \lor p) \supset p$[1]

We can use truth tables to show that this axiom is always true. There are only two possibilities to consider. p is T or p is F. Suppose p is T. Then $p \lor p$ is T (using the truth table for $\lor$). So then $(p \lor p) \supset p$ is T (using the truth table for $\supset$). A true proposition ($p \lor p$) does imply ($\supset$) a true proposition (p). Suppose on the other hand that p is F. Then $p \lor p$ is F (using the truth table for $\lor$). So then $(p \lor p) \supset p$ is T (using the truth table for $\supset$). A false proposi-

---

[1] Alfred North Whitehead and Bertrand Russell, *Principia Mathematica*, 2nd ed., 3 vols. (Cambridge: Cambridge University Press, 1927), 1:96, proposition 1.2.

tion $(p \lor p)$ does imply $(\supset)$ another false proposition (p). The whole course of reasoning is summarized in table 43.1:

TABLE 43.1: Truth Values of $(p \lor p) \supset p$

p	$p \lor p$	$(p \lor p) \supset p$
T	T	T
F	F	T

Since $(p \lor p) \supset p$ is always true, it is legitimate as an axiom—or, as we have done it here, as a deduction from truth tables. Similarly we can verify the truth of the other axioms. For the fourth and fifth axioms, namely

$$(p \lor (q \lor r)) \supset (q \lor (p \lor r))$$
$$(q \supset r) \supset ((p \lor q) \supset (p \lor r))$$

the verification is the most tedious, because we have to consider eight possible cases for all the combinations of T and F for three distinct propositions, p, q, and r (see table 43.2):

TABLE 43.2: Truth Values for $(p \lor (q \lor r)) \supset (q \lor (p \lor r))$

p	q	r	$(p \lor (q \lor r)) \supset (q \lor (p \lor r))$
T	T	T	T
T	T	F	T
T	F	T	T
T	F	F	T
F	T	T	T
F	T	F	T
F	F	T	T
F	F	F	T

The process of verification takes time, but it is completely mechanical.

In the same way we can verify or disconfirm the truth of any composite proposition made up by combining elementary propositions p, q, r, ... together with logical connectives $\lor$, $\land$, $\supset$, and $\sim$.

Thus truth tables and the procedures generated by them represent an alternative perspective. They are not only an alternative perspective on the logical connectives, but on the entirety of propositional logic. Propositional logic as a whole studies the general conditions under which composite propositions like $(p \lor q) \supset p$ are true. We can deduce which such composite propositions are true, given the truth values of the elementary propositions p, q, r, ... out of which they are composed. Propositional logic also studies which composite propositions are tautologies, that is, which are *always* true, for any starting truth values of p, q, r, ... The axioms provided in Whitehead and Russell and the axioms of Łukasiewicz are examples of such propositions. We can tell whether a given proposition is a tautology by testing all the possible truth values of p, q, r, and seeing whether in every case the resulting composite proposition comes out with the value T.

Curious people might well ask why we bother with axioms at all, if we can test the truth value in this way. But in more complex cases, which involve more than unanalyzed elementary propositions like p and q, it is not always so easy. Moreover, propositional logic also is interested in the *relations* between propositions, especially in inferential relations. When can we validly infer that p implies q? Or, to put it another way, given that we know that a certain complex proposition p is true, can we infer that another proposition q is also true? For simple propositional logic, truth tables are adequate to this task as well. We simply test when the composite proposition $(p \supset q)$ is true. By contrast it is not so easy to see which propositions can be deduced by the purely formal rules of deduction when we start only with Whitehead and Russell's five axioms, or Łukasiewicz's three axioms, or Nicod's one axiom. It takes work. All the approaches are *perspectives* on propositional logic. They are different perspectives, and it takes work to assure ourselves that they are actually equivalent.

Venn Diagrams as a Perspective on Propositional Logic

We can also use Venn diagrams as a perspective on the whole of propositional logic. To begin with, Venn diagrams can be used to check that the truth tables for the logical connectives are indeed correct. How would we proceed? For two propositions p and q, let us check the truth table for $p \lor q$. If we have a circle for p and a second circle for q, the circle for p will represent the circumstances in which p is true. Likewise the circle for q represents the circumstances in which q is true. The area that represents where $p \lor q$ is true is the area enclosed by one circle, added to the area enclosed by the other. (The hatched area in figure 43.1 represents where $p \lor q$ is true.)

Fig. 43.1: Venn Diagram of Conjunction ("Or")

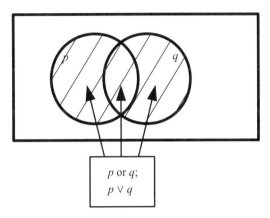

Now test all the alternatives, *p* as T or F and *q* as T or F. If *p* is T and *q* is T, we are in the region where the circles intersect. This is included in the hatched area that represents where $p \lor q$ is true. So $p \lor q$ is T in this case. If *p* is T and *q* is F, we are in the region inside circle *p* and outside circle *q*. This region also is within the hatched area. So again $p \lor q$ is T. If *p* is F and *q* is T, we are in the region inside circle *q* and outside circle *p*. This region is within the hatched area. So $p \lor q$ is T. Finally, if *p* is F and *q* is F, we are in the region outside both circles. That is, we are outside the hatched area. So $p \lor q$ is F. In every case, the truth value of $p \lor q$ is the same as what is indicated in the truth table that we drew up earlier.

Why is this kind of confirmation important? We already knew what the truth table was. The confirmation shows that there is more than one way of looking at the issue of truth. There is more than one perspective. And the perspectives confirm one another. They are in harmony.

We can also use Venn diagrams to confirm the axioms of propositional logic, such as the axioms of Whitehead and Russell or of Łukasiewicz. Let us try to confirm the axiom $q \supset (p \lor q)$ (Whitehead and Russell's second axiom). We need only to inspect the Venn diagram for *p* and *q*. The circle for *q* is entirely inside the hatched area that represents $p \lor q$. The fact that it is entirely inside means that $q \supset (p \lor q)$.

The process gets complicated when we have three distinct propositions *p*, *q*, and *r*. We have to have a more complicated Venn diagram. (See figure 43.2.)

Fig. 43.2: Venn Diagram of *p, q, r*

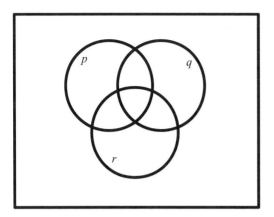

For more than three propositions, it becomes difficult (but still possible) to represent all the possible overlapping regions in one plane.[2]

Sets as a Perspective on Propositional Logic

Next, we can use sets as a perspective on propositional logic. We associate a set P with proposition p, a set Q with proposition q, and so on. A composite proposition such as

$(p \lor p) \supset p$

can be tested by asking whether the corresponding relationship holds among sets. Is it true that $P \cup P \subseteq P$? (We have to note first that set inclusion $\subseteq$ corresponds within the realm of sets to logical implication $\supset$; see chapter 34.) Yes, it is true that $P \cup P \subseteq P$. It follows from the definitions of set union ($\cup$) and inclusion ($\subseteq$). The main deductions that we can draw about sets we can also draw within the context of Boolean algebra, because sets form a Boolean algebra with union and intersection of sets taking the role of the two complementary algebraic operations ($\oplus$, $\otimes$).[3] So Boolean algebra can also be used as a perspective, from which we can deduce the axioms of propositional logic.

---

[2] Vern S. Poythress and Hugo Sun, "A Method to Construct Convex, Connected Venn Diagrams for Any Finite Number of Sets," *The Pentagon* 31/2 (1972): 80–82.
[3] Garrett Birkhoff, *Lattice Theory*, 2nd ed. (New York: American Mathematical Society, 1948), 153. Taking the complement of a set is the analogue of the unary operation $\ominus$.

Logic as a Perspective on Truth Functions

We can also move in the opposite direction, and use logic as a perspective on truth functions. If we inspect carefully what we did with truth functions, we can see that we were using logic informally in the process of reasoning about them. Consider again our truth-functional demonstration that $(p \lor p)$ $\supset p$. We began with the choice of p as T or p as F. We knew that there were no other alternatives, because p as F means the same as p not being T. This dichotomy of alternatives is a logical dichotomy, which we can express formally as p or $\sim p$, that is, $p \lor \sim p$. $p \lor \sim p$ is a tautology. It is always true. If we wish, we could take it as a logical axiom. Instead, Whitehead and Russell chose to derive it by using their five axioms. Whatever starting point we use, we are using this piece of logic informally.

Once we have assumed that p is T, we calculate from the truth table for logical disjunction $\lor$ the truth value of $p \lor p$. In this calculation, we use the relationship of one to many. The truth table as a whole, which is a truth table for all values of p and q, presents the function of $\lor$ as a whole. The application to $p \lor p$ is a particular instance, where we substitute the symbol p for the symbol q. It is an informal instance of the principle of substitution. We also have a kind of substitution to an even more particular case or instantiation, namely, the case where p has the value T. This move also is like a kind of informal substitution. Then we are in a situation where both "inputs" to the operator $\lor$ are T. Therefore the output (using the table, namely, the first line beneath the headings p, q, and $p \lor q$) is T. We have made an informal inference. If we make it more formal and explicit, it goes like this:

> (1) If p is T and q is T, then $p \lor q$ is T. (This truth is part of the meaning of $p \lor q$ or the meaning of the truth table for $\lor$.)
> Substitute p for q in (1):
> (2) If p is T and p is T, then $p \lor p$ is T.
> (3) Premise: p is T.
> (4) p is T and p is T. (From (3))
> (5) Conclusion (by *modus ponens* applied to (2) and (4)): $p \lor p$ is T.

We must then go through another substitution and another use of *modus ponens* to draw a conclusion with respect to the entire proposition $(p \lor p)$ $\supset p$. Here is the reasoning, made explicit:

> (1) If p is T and q is T, then $p \supset q$ is T. (This truth is part of the meaning of $p \supset q$ or the meaning of the truth table for $\supset$.)

Substitute $p \lor p$ for p and p for q in the truth (1):

(2) If $p \lor p$ is T and p is T, then $(p \lor p) \supset p$ is T.

(3) Premise: $p \lor p$ is T. (As derived from the preceding series of inferences.)

(4) Premise: p is T (by assumption).

(5) $p \lor p$ is T and p is T. (From (3) and (4). This result can be obtained more formally using still more rules.)

(6) Conclusion (by *modus ponens* applied to (2) and (5)): $(p \lor p) \supset p$ is T.

Logic as a Perspective on Venn Diagrams

In like manner we may use logic as a perspective on Venn diagrams. We used Venn diagrams earlier to confirm Whitehead and Russell's second axiom, $q \supset (p \lor q)$. We return to the same argument and inspect it carefully. It uses informal inference. It is a general principle in Venn diagrams that if the area representing proposition A is completely included in the area representing proposition B, it indicates for the corresponding logical relations that $A \supset B$.[4] Take this principle as the starting point.

(1) If the area for A is completely included in the area for B, then $A \supset B$. In (1), substitute q for A and $p \lor q$ for B by the principle of substitution:

(2) If the area for q is completely included in the area for $p \lor q$, then $q \supset (p \lor q)$.

(3) The area for q is completely included in the area for $p \lor q$. (By visual inspection.)

(4) Conclusion: $q \supset (p \lor q)$ (by *modus ponens* from (2) and (3)).

We can also confirm that we use informal logic when we reason about sets or Boolean algebra. This logic can be written out in formal lines with premises and conclusions if we wish. Logic is indispensable to close reasoning.

Logic as a Foundation?

This indispensability of logic may be one reason why Whitehead and Russell undertook to treat their subject matter as they did. It is much easier for an untrained person to learn Venn diagrams than to wade into the highly abstract symbolism in formal propositional logic. Why then use such symbolism? But we have just seen that the use of Venn diagrams covertly

---

[4]Remember that the area representing B represents all the circumstances where the proposition B is true. If the area representing A is inside the area representing B, then every case where A is true implies that B is true. There may still be other cases (outside the area representing A) where B is true.

depends on logic. With Venn diagrams we have not reached a real foundation—we have not touched the bottom, as it were. We have to go to logic itself to build the real foundations for the reasoning processes. These logical processes are behind or underneath Venn diagrams and truth tables and other areas of study.

Whitehead and Russell's achievement is impressive, and people may think that it shows that logic is a foundation for other things in a one-way sense. That is, they may think that logic is a foundation for reasoning in various spheres of life, but it has no further foundation itself. It is simply "there," independently. But we have already tried to show that that impression is an illusion.

The indispensability of logic is actually a two-way street. Logic is indeed indispensable for truth tables. But there are dependencies in the other direction. We cannot understand the meaning of the logical symbols for "or," "and," and "not" without tacitly understanding and using in some form or other the information contained in truth tables. We cannot understand these meanings in truth tables or in formal logic without first having some experience in ordinary life, in which we experience the ordinary linguistic meanings and functions of words like "or," "and" and "not" (or their analogues in other languages).

Moreover, ordinary language is indispensable for the communication of the meaning of both truth tables and the special symbols introduced in formal logic. Ordinary reasoning by ordinary people, using ordinary human minds, is indispensable as a background for understanding the specialization and reduction that takes place in formal logic. Above all, God is indispensable for logic, as well as for Venn diagrams, truth functions, sets, and whatever else we may think of. He thought it all first. We are thinking his thoughts after him. His rationality—his logic—is the foundation for the use of logic in both formal and informal ways. If we try to build a foundation without acknowledging God, what we build is an idol, a substitute for God who is the foundation.

Religious issues will not disappear. We have heart motivations, even if we often conceal these motivations from ourselves. We build for ourselves structures of meaning. And when we are in rebellion against God, we want to be autonomous. We want our structures of meaning to be autonomous.

We do not know all the motivations that Alfred North Whitehead and Bertrand Russell had in producing their work *Principia Mathematica*. We do not know all the motivations that Aristotle had in working out his principles for syllogisms. These men did not know all their motivations themselves, because deeper motivations, particularly religiously rooted motivations, often conceal themselves. We do know from the Bible that religious motivations are unavoidable in all of life. You are either for God or against him. In whatever you do, you strive to do all for the glory of God (1 Cor. 10:31) or you have some other motivation. Perhaps you do all for the glory of *you*. In the case of Whitehead and Russell and Aristotle, we do know something more about their views in philosophy. All three make it clear in their writings that they reject the God of the Bible.[5] That rejection has subtle consequences outside of the sphere of explicit religious reflection.

Whatever Whitehead and Russell intended by way of personal motivation, their work *Principia Mathematica* has an ambivalent status. It is brilliant and monumental and has many particular truths. But the work as a whole can also tempt people into thinking that they can treat logic as a foundation that is not itself more deeply founded. Logic then becomes a god substitute. The result is a form of idolatry. Logic takes some of the role that is reserved for God alone.

Perspectival Dependence

We can use logic as a *perspective* on truth functions and Venn diagrams and ordinary language and the reasoning operations in our minds. We can also use these other spheres as a perspective on logic. The relationship and dependence is mutual. These perspectival relations, as we have already noted, have their original in God. God the Father knows all things by knowing the Son. The Son knows all things by knowing the Father (Matt. 11:27). We see this foundational, archetypal divine perspectivalism reflected in the world that God has made and in the truths about the world. We see it reflected also in our own minds. We use our minds as an existential perspective on truth. Through one perspective we view the whole. Likewise, through the perspective of logic we may view everything as logical. And indeed it is, because it has its foundation in the speech of God, which is simultaneously the Logos of God. God's attributes are like perspectives on God.[6] God's

---

[5] Aristotle lived before the time of the New Testament, and it is not clear whether he ever encountered the Old Testament. In any case, what he has to say about the unmoved mover is incompatible with the Bible. Aristotle's unmoved mover is a kind of godlike figure but is wholly uninvolved. That picture invokes a false view of transcendence.

[6] Vern S. Poythress, *Symphonic Theology: The Validity of Multiple Perspectives in Theology* (reprint; Phillipsburg, NJ: Presbyterian & Reformed, 2001), 37–38.

rationality and God's self-consistency are among his attributes. They offer one perspective on God. But it is only one of many. It feels "ultimate" in a sense because God is ultimate. But it is not more ultimate than a perspective through speech or through righteousness or through love. God the Father loves the Son through the Spirit. Out of love he displays the logicality of the Son through all of reality. The Spirit who loves the Son impresses the logicality of the Son on our minds, both when he forms them and as he maintains them (Ps. 139:13–16; compare Luke 1:35).

For Further Reflection

1. In what way can we use truth tables as a perspective on propositional logic?
2. How is logic a perspective on truth tables and sets?
3. In what way does logic appear to some people to be the deeper foundation for reasoning about truth functions and sets?
4. In what way is the relationship between logic and other fields a two-way relation?
5. What does it mean to try to make logic autonomous?

Chapter 44

Soundness and Completeness of Propositional Logic

Within propositional logic, let us consider again the choice of axioms and the description of rules for deducing further results. Several choices of axioms are possible. Each of these choices is meant to represent within formal symbolism some of the properties of statements about the real world. Do the different choices of axioms lead to exactly the same results in deductions? How can we tell? And even if they do lead to the same results, how can we be sure that all these results correspond well with the real world?

We have seen that symbolic logic is a simplification in comparison with the real world. But we at least want it to be a consistent simplification. For instance, we have the formalized symbol T, standing for truth. It is a simplification in comparison with what we mean by truth in the real world. But can we at least be sure that the formalized deductions from the chosen axioms always result in propositions that come out T? Can we be sure that the axioms are sufficient for deducing *all* the propositions that are always T (all tautologies)?

These are fascinating questions, which have interested logicians. Some are easier to answer than others. Logicians distinguish two big questions, the question of *soundness* and the question of *completeness*. We can consider a particular logical system like the system of Whitehead and Russell, with its axioms and rule(s) of deduction. Such a system is *sound* only if all the axioms are tautologies (they always come out T, no matter what are the truth values of the smallest constituents p, q, r, etc.) and all the deductions result in tautologies.

The other question is the question of completeness. A system is *complete* only if all the tautologies can be deduced.

If there are not enough axioms, the system may be incomplete. It may turn out to be too weak to deduce everything that we might desire. In such a case, deductions from the axioms lead only to further always-true propositions (tautologies), but some always-true propositions can never be obtained in this way.

The opposite problem is the problem of unsoundness. The system may be too strong, in that it allows the deduction of some propositions that may be false (F) as well as tautologies.

We can picture the various possibilities in a diagram. Let us represent the set of all deducible propositions with a circle *D*, and the set of always-true propositions (tautologies) with a circle *T*. See figure 44.1.

Fig. 44.1: Soundness and Completeness

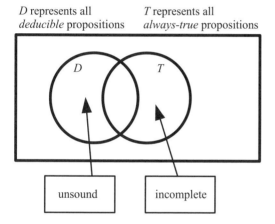

If *D* has no untrue propositions, the system is *sound*. This situation would be represented either by crossing out the part of *D* outside *T*, or by placing *D* wholly inside *T*. On the other hand, if part of *D* is outside *T*, the system is *unsound*.

If part of *T* is outside *D*, there are some always-true propositions that are not deducible, and the system is incomplete. If *T* is wholly inside *D*, the system is complete. If *D* and *T* are identical, the system is both sound and complete. This result is usually what logicians desire. It is the ideal situation, the "Goldilocks" solution. The system is not so weak that it leaves some always-true propositions undeducible, nor so strong that it leads to erroneously deducing some untrue propositions.

Soundness: Truthfulness of Conclusions

Now let us ask ourselves whether Whitehead and Russell's system for propositional logic is *sound*. It is sound only if all the deducible propositions are true, whatever may be the truth value assigned to the propositional symbols $p, q, r, \ldots$.

Whitehead and Russell's axioms were chosen in such a way that most if not all of them seem intuitively obvious. Once we understand their meaning, we can see that they are true. If they are true, and if the rules for deduction always lead from truth to more truth, we can conclude that everything derivable from the axioms is indeed true.

We can choose another route to establish soundness. We can verify the truth of the axioms by deducing them from another set of axioms. For instance, we can deduce Whitehead and Russell's axioms from Łukasiewicz's or Nicod's, or from the system of "natural deduction" with no axioms (chapter 42). But of course such deductions give us confidence only if we *already* have confidence in the axioms and rules that we use instead of Whitehead and Russell's.

Still another route exists, which is the use of truth tables. The verification contains several steps.

First, we ask ourselves whether an assignment of truth values T and F to simple propositions p and q unambiguously determines the truth values of compound propositions like $\sim p \vee q$ that are constructed out of them. The answer to this first question is "yes," because the truth tables for the logical connectives $\sim$ and $\vee$ produce unambiguous results, once the truth values of p and q and other proposition symbols are assigned.

Second, we ask whether the starting *axioms* are always true, when we substitute into them all the possible assignments of truth value to the atomic propositions $p, q, r, \ldots$. In the previous chapter we checked that Whitehead and Russell's first axiom, namely, $(p \vee p) \supset p$, is true for each of the two possibilities, namely, when p is T and when p is F. We could proceed to do the same for each of the other axioms, and in each case they check out.

Third, do the rules of deduction always lead from truth to more truth? There are two rules of deduction, namely, substitution and *modus ponens*. Does substitution always lead from truth to truth? Consider a typical case of substitution, such as when we substitute $\sim p$ for p and $\sim q$ for q in Whitehead and Russell's third axiom,

$$(p \vee q) \supset (q \vee p).$$

We know that the third axiom is always true, no matter what assignments of truth values are given to p and q. If we substitute a more complex proposition such as ~*p* for *p*, this more complex proposition will itself have an unambiguous truth value in all its occurrences. Suppose the truth value is T. This truth value will behave within the third axiom in the same way as would the simple step of assigning the truth value T to the original symbol *p*. The same reasoning holds if the truth value is F. Hence the third axiom will always be true even after we have made the substitution.

We also have to consider the rule of *modus ponens*. This rule says that if we know that *p* is true, and if we also know that *p* ⊃ *q* is true, we can deduce that *q* is true. Again we can translate this procedure into observations about truth values. For an arbitrary proposition *p*, *p* can have either truth value, T or F. When we say that we know that *p* is true, we are saying that it is a composite proposition such that for any assignment of truth values to its component parts, it comes out true. We are saying the same for the proposition *p* ⊃ *q*. If *p* ⊃ *q* is true, it disallows the case where *p* is true and *q* is false. Since we know that *p* is true, *q* cannot be false. Therefore it must be true. Hence, when *modus ponens* acts on true propositions, we arrive at another proposition, namely *q*, which must also be true.

With a logical system such as Whitehead and Russell's, we may go through a large number of deductions. We may arrive at conclusions that become the starting point for still further deductions. And this process may go on indefinitely. However long it goes on, as long as we stick to the rules we never arrive at anything except always-true propositions.

Verification through Boolean Algebra

If we like, we could also do a similar kind of verification using Boolean algebra. First, check that each of the axioms of Whitehead and Russell hold true when we translate them into Boolean algebra. For example, consider Whitehead and Russell's second axiom, *q* ⊃ (*p* ∨ *q*). We have to translate the meaning of ⊃. *r* ⊃ *s* is shorthand for ~*r* ∨ *s*. The second axiom means ~*q* ∨ (*p* ∨ *q*). Now treat this expression as an expression in Boolean algebra. Logical disjunction ∨ corresponds to the operator ⊕ in Boolean algebra, while logical negation ~ corresponds to ⊖. Rather than converting all the symbols, we will just treat ~ and ∨ as if they were the names of operators in Boolean algebra (remember, our notation does not really matter; what matters is the substance).

By the commutative law within Boolean algebra,

~*q* ∨ (*p* ∨ *q*) = ~*q* ∨ (*q* ∨ *p*).

By the associative law,

$$\sim q \vee (q \vee p) = (\sim q \vee q) \vee p.$$

By the definition of 1,

$$\sim q \vee q = 1.$$

So we can reduce $(\sim q \vee q) \vee p$ to

$$1 \vee p.$$

By a property of 1 (see appendix B1, rule 18),

$$1 \vee p = 1.$$

Anything that Boolean algebra equates to 1 is a tautology. As result of the total process of reasoning, we can conclude that $q \supset (p \vee q)$ is a tautology, that is, that it is always true no matter what the truth values of p and q.

Next, we may check within Boolean algebra that the rules of deduction always lead from tautologies to more tautologies. This is indeed so.[1]

Finally, we may check that Boolean algebra is nontrivial, that is, that there exist Boolean algebras with more than one element. For this purpose, consider a set consisting of two distinct elements, T and F: {T,F}. We may define the operations $\vee$, $\wedge$, and $\sim$ in the normal way. We then check that these operations, so defined, satisfy all the rules for a Boolean algebra.

Actually, these checks have already been done in a more general context. It is a standard result within the theory of Boolean algebra that the set of all subsets of a single nonempty starting set U forms a Boolean algebra.[2] If we start with the set with one element {c}, there are only two subsets, namely, {c} and {} (the empty set). These can be renamed T and F or 1 and 0. We then have a ready-made Boolean algebra that we can use to verify the axioms of Whitehead and Russell or another logical system.

Completeness

Our next question is about *completeness*. A system of logic is called *complete* if, by using it, we may succeed in deducing every proposition that is

---

[1] See the verification of the rule of *modus ponens* in appendix B1.
[2] Garrett Birkhoff, *Lattice Theory*, 2nd ed. (New York: American Mathematical Society, 1948), 153.

always true, within the specialized language that the system provides. In the context of propositional logic, the propositions that are always true are the *tautologies.*

It is not so easy to see whether Whitehead and Russell's system or Łukasiewicz's system is complete.

Deducibility of One System from Another

Would it help to use a second system of deduction to establish the capabilities of the first?

Using the normal rules of deduction, we can deduce Whitehead and Russell's five axioms from Łukasiewicz's three axioms. Conversely, we can deduce Łukasiewicz's three axioms from Whitehead and Russell's five. The rules for deducing further conclusions are the same in both systems. So, having once deduced Łukasiewicz's axioms from Whitehead and Russell's, we can exactly reproduce any proofs that use Łukasiewicz's axioms, and produce any conclusion that Łukasiewicz's system can derive. If we are told that Łukasiewicz's system is complete, it means that his system is capable of deducing every tautology. For each tautology, we take its proof within Łukasiewicz's system and simply reproduce the same proof in Whitehead and Russell's system. So we know that Whitehead and Russell's system is complete.

The same is true if we start with Łukasiewicz's axioms and deduce the axioms of Whitehead and Russell. If Whitehead and Russell's system is complete, so is Łukasiewicz's. The same is true if we start with Nicod's one axiom.

We have to be a little careful, because the systems offered by Whitehead and Russell, by Łukasiewicz, and by Nicod have different starting symbols. Whitehead and Russell start with the symbols for "or" (∨) and "not" (~), and then use them to define the symbols for "implies" (⊃) and for "and" (∧). Łukasiewicz starts with the symbols for "implies" (⊃) and "not" (~), and uses them to define "or" and "and." Nicod starts with only one symbol, the Sheffer stroke (|), and uses it to define all the rest. The meaning of the rule for *modus ponens* is not the same in these three systems, since logical implication ⊃ has a different status in the systems. Nor is the meaning of the individual propositions the same, since a starting symbol like ∨ in Whitehead and Russell's system is a defined symbol in Łukasiewicz's and Nicod's systems, and we must "translate" compound propositions accordingly when moving between two systems.

So we have to assure ourselves that we can appropriately "translate" propositions from one system to the other, and that the proofs within one system can also be translated. Once we have done this, we can see that each system establishes the axioms of the others, and when the axioms are established, each system can exactly imitate the proofs that derive from the axioms.[3]

Of course, none of the systems can be established except by using assumptions. If we assume that one is capable, then we can establish the others *based on the initial assumption*. Behind all three systems lies God, who is the ultimate foundation and guarantee for each of them.

By processes such as we have described, we can show that all three systems lead to the same deductions and the same list of provable "theorems." We can also go through the same kind of reasoning with the system of natural deduction that we introduced in chapter 42. It too leads to the same deductions and the same list of provable theorems. But do these theorems include *all* tautologies or only some? How do we tell?

The more theorems that we prove from Whitehead and Russell's system or from our system of natural deduction, the more satisfied we may feel. But might there be some obscure, horrendously complex proposition that is a tautology but is *not* provable? How do we tell without surveying every possible proposition? Starting with our propositional symbols p, q, r, s, ... (indefinitely extendable) and our logical connectives $\vee$, $\wedge$, $\supset$, $\sim$, we may produce an unending number of increasingly complex propositions. So the task of proving all tautologies will never come to an end.

Logicians have discovered some ways to avoid this interminable task. One route is to show that we can reproduce within the notation and rules of Whitehead and Russell's system all the steps that go into the process of verifying a tautology using truth tables (see appendix B5 for a sketch of the process). Or, in a second route, we can use enough theorems from Whitehead and Russell to show that any tautology can be converted into a standard form, and we can shape this standard form in such a way that any proposition that has this form turns out to be easy to prove.[4] Or we can break the task up into three stages: (1) show that the results of truth-table reasoning

---

[3] Dealing with Nicod's system is slightly more complex, since within his system the rule of deduction that expresses the principle of *modus ponens* has a different form. But once we have established that Nicod's rule is implied by the rule of *modus ponens* in the other systems and vice versa, the systems can be shown to produce equivalent results.

[4] See Irving M. Copi, *Symbolic Logic*, 5th ed. (New York: Macmillan, 1979), 260–276, for a completeness proof for the "Hilbert-Ackerman system," which is very similar to Whitehead and Russell's system.

can be mimicked using their analogues in Boolean algebra; (2) show that the axioms of Boolean algebra are, when suitably translated, theorems of Whitehead and Russell; and (3) show that deductions within Boolean algebra correspond to deductions within Whitehead and Russell.

These routes show that it can help us to use perspectives. We succeed in the task by showing that one task can be "translated" into the conceptions of another field. The logic of truth tables gets translated into Whitehead and Russell's notation. Or it gets translated into reasoning in Boolean algebra.

Dependence

In the process of providing answers to key questions about the capabilities of systems of propositional logic, we have used processes of reasoning. For example, we have reasoned our way toward the conclusion that Whitehead and Russell's system is *sound*. The processes of reasoning, under close inspection, show signs of presupposing logic. We are using logic to verify logic. Does such verification make sense?

As one part of the answer, we may observe that there is no other way to produce support for a logical system or increase our confidence in it. Would it do any good to produce an *illogical* argument in favor of logic?

As another part of the answer, we may observe that the use of multiple perspectives, from truth tables or Boolean algebra or sets or alternate axioms, helps to assure us that we have not overlooked something crucial in the process of narrowly studying from one perspective only.

For Further Reflection

1. What does it mean for a system of propositional logic like Whitehead and Russell's to be *sound*? to be *complete*?
2. Why do logicians typically want their systems to be sound? to be complete?
3. What advantage may we obtain by looking at systems that start with a different set of axioms than Whitehead and Russell's system?
4. To show that a system like Whitehead and Russell's is sound, what do we have to verify about each of the axioms?

Chapter 45

Imitations of Transcendence

Finally, we may note the way in which examination of a whole logical system uses human mental ability to transcend the immediate circumstances.

Human "Transcendence"

This ability to transcend the immediate, or to think about what we are thinking, shows itself when we examine a whole logical system like Whitehead and Russell's. While we are immersing ourselves in Whitehead and Russell's system, the symbols p, q, r, ... and the logical connectives have meanings. We know that p stands for a proposition (usually it is supposed to represent the general case, not merely a particular proposition like "snow is white"). We associate logical meanings with the logical symbols $\vee$, $\wedge$. But then we can stand back and look at what is going on in Whitehead and Russell as a rule-based game played with symbols. We can discuss as a general question what sequences of symbols, out of all possible sequences, can be deduced using these rules. We can make correlations between this system and other systems of rules, like the rules for calculating from truth tables. And we can endeavor to show, using ordinary informal logic, that the two sets of rules lead to the same results.

God is transcendent in a unique sense. He transcends the whole world. We are finite and we do not. But we have capabilities as human beings that imitate or reflect divine transcendence on our own human level. We can picture for ourselves what it is like to stand back from the immediacy of our situation.

Patterns of Inference

We can see a particular special instance of a small transcendence or imitative transcendence when we reconsider our discussion in the previous chapter. When we gave evidence that Whitehead and Russell's system is sound, we used some complex reasoning. Consider the point at which we observed that the rule of substitution and the rule of *modus ponens* always lead from truth to more truth. This connection of truth leading to truth holds for any one step, when we consider it by itself. But then we can stand back in order to consider a whole series of steps. This standing back is a kind of miniature imitation of transcendence.

Suppose we picture a whole series of deductions leading to new theorems:

(1) Axiom 1.
(2) Axiom 2.
(3) Axiom 3.
(4) Theorem 1 (obtained by substitution from (1)).
(5) Theorem 2 (obtained by *modus ponens* from (3) and (4)).
(6) Theorem 3 (obtained by substitution from theorem (2)).
(7) Theorem 4 (obtained by substitution from axiom (2)).
(8) Theorem 5 (obtained by *modus ponens* from (7) and (1)).

The details are not important. The axioms could be the axioms belonging to any particular deductive system. The theorems would then be theorems obtained within the system. When we call the deductions "theorems," we make them sound important. But some of them could be small steps that are not very significant in themselves, but that lead somewhere further on to a significant result. From the standpoint of whether the individual lines follow from the rules, all of the lines (except the axioms) are theorems that follow from previous lines.

Now, let us ask ourselves whether the first three lines are true. They are, because they are axioms, and we are assuming that we have checked that the axioms are true. How do we know that line (4) is true? We have obtained line (4) by using the rule of substitution on line (1), which we already know is true. What about line (5)? It is obtained from lines (3) and (4), which we have already assured ourselves are true. Clearly we can reason in the same way to line (6), and line (7) and line (8). Can we go on? How do we know?

We know because, after working through a few lines, we can understand that there is a regular pattern. The truth of each line is guaranteed by the truth of one or more of the previous lines. And this pattern holds for *any number of lines* through which we may proceed. That phrase "any number of lines" represents a point of miniature transcendence. When we speak in that way, we are standing back from the particulars of the reasoning that establishes how we know that line (6) is true. We are generalizing. This step of generalization relies on and presupposes the relationship between unity and diversity. We have the unity that belongs to the general pattern. In this case, the unity is the general fact that any one line has an assurance of its truth from the preceding lines and from the truth-preserving character of the rules of deduction. The diversity is the diversity of what we do with each new line. Each new line may refer back to earlier lines in a different manner than the way the previous line did. Each new line may use the rule of substitution or the rule of *modus ponens* in a somewhat different way, when it comes to the details.

As usual, the interlocking of unity and diversity goes back to God's Trinitarian character. We are relying on the faithfulness of God.

But there is a further element in this reasoning that we should notice. It is the idea of number. We used the phrase "any *number* of lines," and that is no accident. Whether or not we use actual numbers as labels for the lines, the lines form a sequence from top to bottom. The sequence is important, because the earlier lines have to be deduced first. Otherwise we produce a deductive circle:

(1) p (by substituting p for p in line (2))
(2) p (by substituting p for p in line (1))

Both lines are deduced by using the rule of substitution. But the argument is circular, viciously circular. The difficulty comes from line (1). On this line, we ought first to establish that p is true from *previous* lines. It is not legitimate for us to appeal to a later line, namely line (2). If p is an arbitrary proposition, it could be either true or false. We cannot possibly succeed in proving its truth by a linear chain of reasoning, that is, noncircular reasoning.

We can now see that we must have within our heads and use within our reasoning an idea of order. Order of all kinds has God as its origin, but we need not explore that issue further at this point. This particular order is used in another way when we ask ourselves whether we can go on from line (8)? Can we add more lines? Clearly we can. How many? As many as we want. We just have to make sure that we keep using the rules of deduction, and that we keep appealing only to previous lines (not subsequent lines) as the basis for the deduction on the current line.

When we say that Whitehead and Russell's logical system is *sound*, we mean that no matter how far we go down the list of theorems, we always produce more truths. Deduction leads from truth to more truth. But have we traveled all the way down every list of lines in order to check out that conviction? We have not. We cannot, because the lists can be made indefinitely long.

In fact, then, we have *not* checked out each individual stage. We have made an inference from the general pattern. How does this inference get off the ground? This kind of inference has a name: *mathematical induction.*

Mathematical Induction

Just like the principle of *modus ponens*, the principle of mathematical induction uses two premises and one conclusion. *Modus ponens* says that the following reasoning is valid:

> Premise 1: p.
> Premise 2: $p \supset q$.
> Conclusion: q.

If you have confirmed both premises, you can draw the conclusion.

Mathematical induction says that the following sequence of reasoning is valid:

> Premise 1: A property M is true for the number 1.
> Premise 2: If M is true for the positive integer k, M is also true for the number $k + 1$.
> Conclusion: M is true for all positive integers n.

(Depending on what property M we are talking about, Premise 1 or Premise 2 may fail to be true. The principle of mathematical induction says only that *if* Premise 1 and Premise 2 both hold true, we can legitimately draw the conclusion: M is true for all positive integers n.)

For example, using the principle of mathematical induction, we can establish, for all positive integers n, the property M that says that the sum of the first n positive integers is $n(n + 1)/2$. That is, $1 + 2 + 3 + \dots + n = n(n + 1)/2$.[1]

Let us check out the first few cases for the sum of n positive integers. If n is 1, the sum of the first n positive integers is the sum of one integer, which is simply 1. For $n = 1$, $n(n + 1)/2 = 1(1+1)/2 = 1$. So the formula is valid for $n = 1$. If n is 2, the sum of the first n positive integers is $1 + 2$. $1 + 2 = 3$. And for $n = 2$, $n(n + 1)/2 = 2(2+1)/2 = 3$. The formula is valid for $n = 2$. If n is 3,

---

[1] For proofs, see Vern S. Poythress, *Redeeming Science: A God-Centered Approach* (Wheaton, IL: Crossway, 2006), 331–334.

the sum is $1 + 2 + 3 = 6$. $6 = 3(3+1)/2$. If n is 4, the sum is $1 + 2 + 3 + 4 = 10$. $10 = 4(4+1)/2$. We have now checked that the property M holds for $n = 1$ through 4. We can continue to check out more cases. But we would soon tire ourselves out. We cannot check an infinitude of cases one by one. So we need some other type of reasoning if we are going to establish a general truth about the sum of the first n integers. This new type of reasoning is presented to us in the principle of mathematical induction.

If we know that premises 1 and 2 above hold true, does the conclusion follow that the property M holds for all positive integers?

The conclusion does make sense. See how the reasoning goes:

Line (1): M is true for 1. (From Premise 1.)

Line (2): If M is true for 1, M is true for 2. (Substituting 1 for k in Premise 2.)

Line (3): M is true for 2. (*Modus ponens* from (1) and (2).)

Line (4): If M is true for 2, M is true for 3. (Substituting 2 for k in Premise 2.)

Line (5): M is true for 3. (*Modus ponens* from (3) and (4).)

Line (6): If M is true for 3, M is true for 4. (Substituting 3 for k in Premise 2.)

Line (7): M is true for 4. (*Modus ponens* from (5) and (6).)

Using this kind of step-wise reasoning, we can, in a finite number of lines, establish the truth of M for any single number n. How do we know we can do it? Only by standing back and transcending the reasoning involved in any one line. We see a general pattern. We extrapolate.

But we are not yet done. What we want is not merely to establish the truth of M for the number 256 (let us say). We want to know that M is true for *all* numbers n. How do we do that? We cannot do it by *modus ponens* and substitution *alone*. We have to think and see a pattern.

We may put it more pictorially. We imagine ourselves traveling along the line of numbers, 1, 2, 3, 4, 5, and going on and on, never stopping. We have to imagine ourselves as achieving an infinite result, namely, checking out the truth of M for every single integer. But we do not need actually to do the checking on each number individually! That is the power of the principle of mathematical induction. We just do it once. We go from k to $k + 1$. We treat that one move as sufficient because we can *see* how things might go if we had infinite patience and infinite time and infinite resources.

That idea of going to infinity is actually built into us in our capacity for miniature transcendence. It is a gift from God who is infinite. It reflects our capacity as people made in the image of God to have a taste of infinity, a sense of the infinite, even though we are not infinite. It is wonderful. And it is useful! It saves us the trouble of checking out truth for each number individually.

Using Mathematical Induction

Now we are ready to use the principle of mathematical induction to assure ourselves that, no matter how long a list of deductions we produce, we always get theorems that are true. We chose as our property M the following: all theorems obtained by proofs consisting of n lines or less are always true (they are tautologies).

First, is the property M true for $n = 1$? A proof one line long is an axiom. We assume that we have checked by some other means that the axioms are true. So M is true for $n = 1$.

Second, assume that M is true for $n = k$. Then all theorems obtained from proofs k lines or less are true. Suppose we have a proof of $k + 1$ lines. The first k lines are all true, by assumption. Since the $(k + 1)$-th line is derived by valid principles from previous lines, it also is true. So all theorems derived from proofs of $(k + 1)$ lines are true. We have now established both premises for mathematical induction. Therefore, all theorems obtained from proofs of n lines are true. But all theorems that can be derived at all are derived by proofs with a finite number of lines. So all theorems that can be proved (within the system) are true.

For Further Reflection

1. What is the principle of mathematical induction?
2. Why is mathematical induction useful?
3. Why do we need mathematical induction to establish that all provable propositions in Whitehead and Russell's system are true?
4. How does mathematical induction display human imitative transcendence?

Part III
Enriching Logic

Propositional logic as discussed in part II can undergo enrichment in several respects. We consider predicates, quantification, equality, functions, formal systems, proofs, models, and special logics.

Part III.A

Predicate Logic

Chapter 46

Introducing Predicate Logic

In part II we looked at the way we can represent whole propositions like "Snow is white" or "The moon is made of green cheese" with simple symbols like *S* and *M*—or *p*, *q*, and *r* to stand for any proposition at all. We represent logical relations like "and" and "or" with technically precise symbols ∧ and ∨. The study of these matters has been called *propositional logic*, because it treats propositions as wholes that are not further analyzed. Now we take a further step by going "inside" propositions and analyzing their pieces. We study *predicate logic*.

Understanding Logical Predicates

What is a "predicate"? When the word is used in the context of modern logic, it is a kind of refinement and simplification in comparison to ordinary language. In ordinary language the "predicate" in a simple clause is the part of the clause that is not the subject. In the clause "snow is white," the expression "is white" is the predicate. We have already met predicates in the context of Aristotelian syllogisms. Within the proposition "All men are mortal," the expression "are mortal" is the predicate, grammatically speaking. Ignoring the verb "are," which is a simple linking verb, we can say in the context of logical analysis of the proposition that "mortal" functions as a predicate. "All men" is the grammatical subject. Logical analysis splits this expression in two. "Men" is the logical subject and "all" is called a "quantifier."

Symbolic logic has undertaken to treat subjects like "men" as if they were "predicates" in the logical sense. Take the proposition "All men are mortal." We can rephrase it as "Everything that is human is mortal." The expression "is human" is the predicate within the relative clause, "That is human." Once again if we ignore the linking verb "is," we can consider "human" as the logical predicate.

Logicians have developed specialized notation to represent what is going on. We will introduce this notation bit by bit, so that it is more digestible. First, how do we represent predicates? The predicate *mortal* is not a proposition by itself. But it is a piece that can serve as one part of a proposition. "Socrates is mortal" is a proposition. So are "Plato is mortal" and "Aristotle is mortal." The predicate can be represented as a symbol with an empty place to hold the subject, thus: Mortal(...). It may seem counterintuitive to put the empty place *following* the predicate symbol *Mortal*, because in English the subject typically precedes the predicate. But there are historical reasons why the notation has been chosen in this way. So here are some propositions:

> Mortal(Socrates)
> Mortal(Plato)
> Mortal(Aristotle)

For convenience, writers in logic often represent the predicates by single letters rather than whole words. So we have

> M(Socrates)
> M(Plato)
> M(Aristotle)

where *M* represents the predicate *mortal* or "is mortal." The use of a single symbol *M* rather than a full English word reminds us that the logical notation is trying to refine and simplify English or some other natural language. The notation is not merely a re-expression with identical meaning but is intended as a more rigorous, more precise, less ambiguous expression.

Now how do we represent "men"? It too becomes a predicate, if we rephrase "Socrates is a man" as "Socrates is human." The predicate is *human*. We then have notation as follows:

> Human(Socrates)
> Human(Plato)
> Human(Aristotle)

So we can represent the proposition "If Socrates is human, Socrates is mortal" as follows:

> If Human(Socrates), then Mortal(Socrates).

Using the normal symbol ⊃ to represent implication (the if-then relation), we get

> Human(Socrates) ⊃ Mortal(Socrates).

Likewise,

Human(Plato) ⊃ Mortal(Plato).

Variables

Next, we should differentiate between particular cases like Socrates and Plato and a general case, when we want to consider the predicate *human* in general. We can represent the predicate in general by writing "Human( )," leaving an empty space. Or we can fill in the space with a kind of "place-holder," which will represent *any* particular individual that we might after-wards want to put in as the subject of "Human( )." Thus

Human(x)

is our shorthand for "x is human."

In this context, x is called a *variable*. It stands not for any particular individual, like Socrates, but for anything that we might put in. We could of course represent Socrates by a single letter, say s. Plato will be p. (Here s and p do not stand for propositions, as they sometimes did earlier in the book, but for individuals, namely, Socrates and Plato, respectively.) When used in this way, s and p are not variables. They stand for individuals. They are called *constants*. "Human(s)" says that Socrates is human. "Human(p)" says that Plato is human. By contrast, "Human(x)" says that x is human, where x has yet to be specified.

Expressions like "Human(x)" are not propositions, because they have no determinate truth value. They are called *propositional functions*. Once the variable x is assigned a particular value, such as s for Socrates, then we obtain a proposition, Human(s), and it has a truth value. The elements like s, p, and x are called *individual symbols*. An individual variable x ranges over all individuals. Individual *constants* like s and p have a fixed referent (like Socrates). The individuals may include not only persons, but animals, plants, or any individual entities whatsoever. The context around the logical systems must specify what kind of individuals and what kind of application we are contemplating.

For Further Reflection

1. What is a "predicate" in formal logic? Explain using "is white" and "is canine" as examples.
2. How does a predicate in formal logic differ from a predicate in the context of grammar?
3. What is a variable?
4. If we use the letter W to symbolize the predicate *wise* and the letter *s* to symbolize Socrates, what is the meaning of W(*s*)? Represent in symbols the proposition that Felix is a cat.

Chapter 47

Theistic Foundations for Predicates

What is the relation of logical predicates to God? We should remember that, according to a Christian point of view, logic in God is an aspect of divine language. Logic among human beings is a reflection of logic in God. It is an aspect of language.

Relationships to Natural Language

Both modern symbolic logic and traditional syllogistic logic have developed as attempts to capture some of the processes of reasoning that have been exhibited for centuries in natural language and users of natural language. Sometimes in the process, logicians have judged that natural language is *defective*. For example, in symbolic language sentences are typically treated wholly in terms of their truth value—true or false—while other dimensions of meaning are placed in the background. This focus on truth value represents a gain in precision of a certain kind. But it also results in a reduction of the total meaning to one dimension. A logician can pronounce natural language "defective" because it does not have technical precision about truth values.

But in another way, the shoe is on the other foot. Formal language is highly simplified and stereotyped language. From a certain point of view, it is "defective" in comparison with the richness of natural language. And, as we have seen, formal language depends on natural language for its starting point. We have to explain new symbols like $M(\ldots)$ using a good deal of natural language before people are able to grasp the symbols' meaning and use them in the way in which they are intended.

In fact, natural language and the specialized, derivative language of symbolic logic serve complementary purposes. Neither is innately "defective," provided we appreciate their positive purposes.

Theistic Foundations for Predicates

So now consider the foundations for logical predicates like Human(…). Without using the term *predicates*, we have already discussed some of the key ideas about predicates in part I.C, where we considered the problem of classification. Aristotelian syllogisms work only if the terms like *human*, *mortal*, *dog*, *animal*, *reptile*, and so on, have a stable meaning. Natural language shows stability in meaning, but also has complexities that are put to one side in the process of adapting language to a syllogistic form.

What happens when we make for ourselves predicates like Human(…)? What happens when we make a further condensation of a predicate into one letter H: $H(x)$ for x is human? Do we intend that the predicate H is perfectly precise, and that the reasoning processes concerning it are purely formal and purely context-free? It is easy to fall into a false confidence, or to wish for reality to conform to an autonomous ideal and to pronounce language "defective" because it does not conform to this ideal.

We should remember what we have earlier observed (chapters 18–22) about the problem of classification and the problem with the ideal of achieving perfect unity and perfect clarity in a concept. In natural language, the word *human* is subtly colored by its association with particular examples, such as "Socrates is human" and "Plato is human." Instantiation and classification interpenetrate, because both are ultimately rooted in God's Trinitarian character.

Now the technical symbol H can stand for the predicate *human*. But in contrast to the complexity in natural language, the symbol H is an ideal, context-free symbol, which is often regarded as having purely identical meaning no matter which item fits into its empty space. "H is H," it may be said. H(Socrates) and H(Plato), or better, $H(s)$ and $H(p)$, must according to this ideal use a purely identical H. This ideal is in effect a *unitarian* ideal, an ideal that wants unity without any diversity in the symbol H. And the symbols s and p standing for Socrates and Plato must have pure diversity, without any unity. This ideal is innately untrue to reality, but true to the desires for human autonomy. In other words, there is an underlying religious motivation.

As usual, we can appreciate the insight from symbolic logic into the regularities of language and the regularities of God's harmony with himself. But we should beware of adopting the ideal that is often an underlying presupposition.

Complex Predicates ("Relations")

In natural language we have terms like *human*. But natural language is richer. It is about sentences and complex communication in discourses. It is about thinking and communicating with other persons. And it is well for us repeatedly to recognize the simplifications. If we compare Aristotle's syllogisms with natural language, we can see that syllogisms deal mainly with one kind of clause structure, namely, a clause of the kind "The boy is human," where the predicate has a linking verb "is" and an attributive adjective "human." Or else the clause has a noun in the predicate, such as "is a reptile," "is an animal." But there are other basic clause types, such as clauses with transitive verbs and objects: "The boy fed the dog." Or we can have a verb such as "give" that usually functions together with two objects, a direct object designating the gift and an indirect object designating the recipient: "The boy gave the food to the dog."

We can represent a proposition like "The boy gave the food to the dog" in a simple way if we keep strictly to the pattern where we separate the predicate from the subject. "The boy" is the subject. The rest of the clause is the predicate. So let us symbolize the predicate "... gave the food to the dog" by the symbol G. Symbolize the subject "the boy" by the letter b. The whole proposition then becomes $G(b)$. The difficulty is that this symbolic representation does not recognize a distinct role for the food or for the dog. It is rather impoverished. Thus, clauses of these kinds do not mesh as well with Aristotle's syllogistic forms.

Modern symbolic logic has developed a way of incorporating another dimension of this kind of language by using multi-place predicates, which are usually called *relations*. We need some explanation.

The logical predicate Human(...) is a one-place predicate, because there is one empty place in which to put a particular entity such as Socrates. The predicate Human(...) by itself is not a complete proposition. Once we put in *Socrates*, it becomes a proposition: "Human(Socrates)," which translates as "Socrates is human." In English, the expression "... is human" has a single "slot" or empty space. Now in the sentence, "The boy fed the dog," if we take "fed" as central, there are two empty spaces, one for the grammatical subject, and another for the grammatical object: "_____ [space 1] fed _____ [space 2]." How do we represent this situation symbolically? We represent it with a two-place predicate, which can be written: Fed(x, y), where x and y are placeholders. x will indicate the subject and agent in feeding, while *y* will indicate the object of feeding. We need two distinct symbols, *x* and *y*, because we need to distinguish the agent from the recipient. Thus:

Fed(the boy, the dog)

symbolically represents the English sentence, "The boy fed the dog." The order matters. "Fed(the dog, the boy)" represents the proposition that the dog fed the boy.

The word *give* requires three entries, for the subject (agent), object (gift), and indirect object (recipient). Thus:

Gave(the boy, the food, the dog)

If we want, we can also incorporate the time as an extra element, and specify that a predicate like *Fed* takes three values, namely, the agent ("the boy"), the recipient ("the dog"), and the time ("yesterday"). So

Fed(the boy, the dog, yesterday)

represents the English sentence, "The boy fed the dog yesterday." Similar treatment can aid us in representing complicated clauses.[1]

The Divine Original for Clauses

Language itself has its foundation in divine language. Various types of clauses have their archetype in truths about God. God is righteous (Ps. 119:137). The expression "is righteous" shows the kind of attributive structure that we can represent with a one-place predicate: "Righteous(God)." We can see here the importance of underlining the fact that the unity of one universal category, namely righteousness, is associated with the diversity of things to which righteousness is attributed. Righteousness belongs not only to God but to the distinct persons of the Trinity. And the meaning of righteousness is colored by the one to whom we ascribe it. The righteousness of God is original, while the righteousness of his laws is derivative, and the righteousness of human beings is derivative.

Consider another example. "The Father loves the Son" (John 3:35). The

---

[1] On the complexities, see, e.g., Robert E. Longacre, *An Anatomy of Speech Notions* (Lisse, Netherlands: De Ridder, 1976), 40–97; Robert E. Longacre, *The Grammar of Discourse* (New York/London: Plenum, 1983), 151–241.

full clause is a transitive clause, which shows the kind of transitivity that we can represent in a two-place predicate: Love(the Father, the Son). The meaning of "love" is qualified by context. "Love" among the persons of the Trinity is the original, archetypal love. Love among human beings is derivative.[2] Hence, an attempt to make the predicate Love(x, y) purely a "formal" notation reduces a rich reality to one dimension.

We may also emphasize the presence of context. Every truth about God exists within the context of all that God is. No truth is really context-free. And this presence of context has implications for our thinking about predicates. Predicates exist within a context, which can further qualify their meaning. Think again, for example, of our example with the boy feeding the dog. We represented it symbolically as a two-place predicate:

Fed(the boy, the dog)

But it can also be represented by a three-place predicate if we make explicit the role of time:

Fed(the boy, the dog, yesterday)

We can make it a four-place predicate if we make explicit the role of motive:

Fed(the boy, the dog, yesterday, love)

We can make it a five-place predicate if we make explicit the location:

Fed(the boy, the dog, yesterday, love, in the kitchen)

Just how much context do we want to pack into one proposition? It depends on us. The idea that predicates are uniquely defined as having so many slots or placeholders is an idealization, in which we put into the background the role of context.

The variability concerning the number of placeholders is one illustration of the more general principle that meaning interlocks with context (chapter 21). The context supplies a rich texture of meaning. It depends on us how much of this texture we want to make explicit by including it in a single sentence. And we must decide how much to make explicit by

---

[2] On the roots of clauses in God, see Vern S. Poythress, *In the Beginning Was the Word: Language—A God-Centered Approach* (Wheaton, IL: Crossway, 2009), chapter 31.

including separate slots when we write a simplified notation for predicate logic, "Fed(… , … , …)."

The Range for Individuals

As we indicated in the previous chapter, the context must also indicate what kind of individuals we have in mind. Do we intend that an individual variable x should range over all human beings, or all animals, or what category? Here we are confronted again with the limitations of formal logic, because of the challenges in classifying (part I.C).

We also find another assumption in the formal notation, namely, a strict distinction between individuals a, b, c, … and predicates F, G, H, … . The notation insists that we must not confuse the two. But natural language allows us to talk not only about creatures such as human beings and animals but also about abstracts, such as *human*. We can say, for example, "'Human' is a category," or "'Abstract' is an abstract category." So predicates like "abstract category" can be applied to predicates such as *abstract*.

For Further Reflection

1. Give an example of a clause in natural language that can be represented formally by a two-place predicate. What is gained and lost by such a formalized representation?
2. What is the ultimate foundation for predicates?
3. Explain how the idea of a fixed number of empty slots for a predicate is an idealization in comparison to natural language.
4. What simplifications take place in making the transition from natural language to a formal symbolic system for predicates?
5. Represent in the notation of symbolic logic the following propositions:
   "Mary loves John."
   "Mary is happy."
   "Mary put her coat on the chair."

Part III.B

Quantification

Chapter 48

Quantification

Now we consider the functions of words like "all," "some," and "no."

Quantifiers: "All"

Consider the proposition "All men are mortal." If we are to represent this proposition in a completely formalized notation, we must have a way of representing the word *all*. "All," "some," and "no" are called *quantifiers*. The field of logic that studies these ideas is called *quantification theory*.[1]

We begin with the word *all*. More than one formal notation has been used to represent it. One common notation is an upside-down A: ∀.[2] If we want to say, "All things are mortal," we need a variable x to represent the various possibilities for things that might be mortal. The propositional function "x is mortal" is our starting point. We can paraphrase "All things are mortal" by saying "for all x, x is mortal." We write it as follows:

($\forall x$) (x is mortal)

Or, in the notation we have developed,

($\forall x$) (Mortal(x))

The notation ($\forall x$) means, "For any entity x …" or "For all x." It is called a *universal quantifier*. Logicians sometimes also use a convention in which they dispense with the symbol ∀. Instead of ($\forall x$) they write simply (x). Or they write ∀x without parentheses. We will use the more explicit notation ($\forall x$). The proposition "All men are mortal" can be paraphrased as "For anything x, if x is human then x is mortal. Symbolically, such a proposition is represented as follows:

($\forall x$) (If x is human, then x is mortal)

---

[1] Technical discussion nowadays distinguishes different levels of complexity (see chapter 62). In this and the next few chapters, we discuss for simplicity only "first order quantification."
[2] The symbol ∀ is unicode character U 2200.

In our new notation for predicates, this proposition is written,

$(\forall x)$ (Human(x) $\supset$ Mortal(x))

If we use a single letter to represent each predicate, we have

$(\forall x)$ $(H(x) \supset M(x))$

$(H(x) \supset M(x))$ is not a *proposition*, but a *propositional function*, with no determinate truth value, because x is not determined. Once we add the notation $(\forall x)$ to the front, the entire expression $(\forall x)$ $(H(x) \supset M(x))$ becomes a proposition, which is true only if $H(x) \supset M(x)$ is true for all possible choices of x. That is, the proposition $(\forall x)$ $(H(x) \supset M(x))$ implies that $H(s) \supset M(s)$ is true (for s representing Socrates) and in addition $H(p) \supset M(p)$ is true (for p representing Plato) and in addition $H(a) \supset M(a)$ is true (for a representing Aristotle), and so on for every individual that we substitute for the place-holder x. Since x is a variable, it does not matter what letter we use to represent it. We can use y instead:

$(\forall y)$ $(H(y) \supset M(y))$

The meaning is the same.

Now consider a whole syllogism:

All dogs are animals.
All collies are dogs.
Therefore, all collies are animals.

Let $D(\ )$ represent the predicate for "dog"; let $A(\ )$ represent the predicate for "animal"; let $C(\ )$ represent the predicate for "collie." In modern notation, the first premise, "All dogs are animals," becomes:

$(\forall x)$ $(D(x) \supset A(x))$

When translated back into ordinary English, this symbolic line says, "For any entity x, if x is a dog $[D(x)]$, then x is an animal $[A(x)]$."

In a similar manner, we may represent the second premise and the conclusion in symbolic notation. The syllogism as a whole then comes out as follows:

$(\forall x)\ (D(x) \supset A(x))$
$(\forall x)\ (C(x) \supset D(x))$
Therefore, $(\forall x)\ (C(x) \supset A(x))$

We can, if we wish, combine the whole syllogism into a single long prop-osition, which says that if the two premises hold, they imply the conclusion.

$$[(\forall x)\ (D(x) \supset A(x)) \land (\forall x)\ (C(x) \supset D(x))] \supset (\forall x)\ (C(x) \supset A(x))$$

Quantifiers: "Some" and "No"

In Darii and other syllogisms from Aristotle the word *some* is used. Consider again our usual example for Darii:

All mammals breathe air.
Some sea creature is a mammal.
Therefore, some sea creature breathes air.

The first premise, "All mammals breathe air," would be represented in the new notation as:

$(\forall x)\ (\text{Mammal}(x) \supset \text{Air-breathing}(x))$

Now what is the meaning of "Some sea creature is a mammal"? It is not talking about all entities x, but about "some." At least one, we have said. We re-express it as "There exists an x such that x is a sea creature and x is a mammal." The idea of existence ("there exists …") is usually symbolized in modern symbolic logic by a reversed E: $\exists$.[3] How do we say that "there exists a mammal"? We mean that at least one mammal exists, but we do not name any particular one. We represent this situation with a variable, such as x. We reinterpret "There exists a mammal" as "There exists an x such that x is a mammal. We write it:

$(\exists x)\ (\text{Mammal}(x))$

Once again, we can use y or some other variable (say z) to say the same thing:

$(\exists z)\ (\text{Mammal}(z))$

The notation $(\exists z)$ is called an *existential quantifier*.

---

[3] The unicode symbol is U 2203.

So how do we represent the complete proposition, "Some sea creature is a mammal"? We mean that there exists an x such that x is a sea creature *and* x is a mammal. Expressed in symbolic notation, the meaning comes out:

$(\exists x)$ (Sea-creature$(x) \land$ Mammal(x))

The complete Darii syllogism comes out as follows:

$(\forall x)$ (Mammal$(x) \supset$ Air-breathing(x))
$(\exists x)$ (Sea-creature$(x) \land$ Mammal(x))
Therefore, $(\exists x)$ (Sea-creature$(x) \land$ Air-breathing(x))

Consider next the Celarent syllogism. Here is an example:

No dogs are cats.
All collies are dogs.
Therefore, no collies are cats.

How do we symbolize that "no dogs are cats"? We can paraphrase it as, "For any x, if x is a dog, x is not a cat." In symbolic notation, this comes out as

$(\forall x)$ (Dog$(x) \supset {\sim}$Cat(x))

The syllogism as a whole then comes out as follows:

$(\forall x)$ (Dog$(x) \supset {\sim}$Cat(x))
$(\forall x)$ (Collie$(x) \supset$ Dog(x))
Therefore $(\forall x)$ (Collie$(x) \supset {\sim}$Cat(x))

Consider one final example (an example of the Ferio syllogism):

No reptiles are fish.
Some vertebrate is a reptile.
Therefore some vertebrate is not a fish.

How do we represent the notion that "No reptiles are fish"? It is equivalent to saying that if anything is a reptile, it is not a fish:

$(\forall x)$ (Reptile$(x) \supset {\sim}$Fish(x))

The complete syllogism then looks as follows:

($\forall x$) (Reptile(x) $\supset$ ~Fish(x))
($\exists x$) (Vertebrate(x) $\land$ Reptile(x))
Therefore ($\exists x$) (Vertebrate(x) $\land$ ~Fish(x))

Or, alternatively, the first premise could be paraphrased as saying that there does not exist an x such that x is a reptile and x is a fish. So:

~($\exists x$) (Reptile(x) $\land$ Fish(x))

Representation of Four Kinds of Aristotelian Propositions
    In Aristotle's syllogisms there are altogether four kinds of propositions:

All Bs are As. (universal affirmative)
No Bs are As (universal negative)
Some B is an A (particular affirmative)
Some B is not an A (particular negative)

These four types, as we have seen, each have their own symbolic representations, as follows:

All Bs are As: ($\forall x$) ($B(x) \supset A(x)$)
No Bs are As: ($\forall x$) ($B(x) \supset$ ~$A(x)$)
Some B is an A: ($\exists x$) ($B(x) \land A(x)$)
Some B is not an A: ($\exists x$) ($B(x) \land$ ~$A(x)$)

Using these representations, we may express the pattern of any of the Aristotelian categorical syllogisms.
    We now need to consider the relation of these new concepts to their theistic foundations.

For Further Reflection

1. Convert the following syllogisms into symbolic notation:
   a. All fish are vertebrates.
      Some sea creature is not a vertebrate.
      Therefore, some sea creature is not a fish.
   b. All artists are creative.
      All artists are human.
      Therefore, some human is creative.

Chapter 49

The Theistic Foundation for Quantification

We now consider the theistic foundations for quantification: "all," "some, "no."

The words "all," "some," and "no," and similar words in other natural languages, exist prior to the introduction of special explanations of the technical meanings in symbolic logic. Once again, language with its foundations in God is the ultimate background for the conceptions found in formal logic.

The idea of quantification is closely related to the idea of one and many. The "many" are the particular things. The "one" is the general group. If we want to say something about every member of the group at once, we may use "all" or "every." The general truth, applicable to all, is the one. The particular truths with respect to each particular member of the group are the many. The one and the many are coherently related, because they image the one and the many in the Trinity. The archetype is found in the Trinity.

The Universal Quantifier, "All"

How may we see roots for the word *all*? All the persons of the Trinity are God. Each person is a particular person. The three persons in their distinctiveness are the many. God is one. The universal truth, applied to each person, is also one. The word *all* in the context of the Trinity functions to relate the one and the many in a particular way, namely, by exhibiting one truth holding for the three persons.

According to our reasoning in chapter 18 about the roots of unity and diversity, unity and diversity in the created world have their root in the unity and diversity in the Trinity. Analogously, the unity and diversity expressed in the function of the word *all*, as applied to the world, have their root in the unity and diversity in the function of the word *all* within the Trinity. Universal quantification, as expressed by *all*, functions reliably because of the self-consistency of God. The word *all*, through its root in God, reflects the "eternal power and divine nature" of God (Rom. 1:20).

We could proceed, as we did earlier, to remind readers that the regularities with respect to the functions of the word *all* are regularities of divine specification. God speaks. His speech, including his speaking these regularities, shows omnipresence, eternality, immutability, omnipotence, truthfulness, immateriality, transcendence, immanence, and rationality. As a result, we should give thanks. But we often fail. Here, as everywhere in human thought, sin corrupts the knowledge of God and the praise of God.

The Existential Quantifier, "Some"

What do we say about the word *some*, an *existential quantifier*? The word *some* invites us to pick one from among the many. Again, we see an interplay between one and many. But the meaning is not the same as with the word *all*. The truth to be expressed is a truth that may hold for one out of the many, without holding for all. These relations hold within the Trinity. The Son is a person, begotten by the Father. In symbolic notation,

x is the Son $\wedge$ x is a person $\wedge$ x is begotten by the Father.

The proposition that is expressed in this way does not hold when x is the Holy Spirit or the Father. It holds only when x is the Son. So we cannot say that it is true for "all x," but only for "some x":

$(\exists x)$ (x is the Son $\wedge$ x is a person $\wedge$ x is begotten by the Father).

This example, and others like it with respect to the Trinity, represent the *archetype*, the original or root for the use of existential quantification. Other uses are *ectypes*, or derivative. They reflect the glory of God, and should lead us to the worship of God who is their origin.

The Negative, "No"

How do we think about the negative quantifier, "no"? It is the negation of the existential qualifier *some* ($\exists$). If we say, "no dogs are cats," it is equivalent to saying that it is not the case that some dog is a cat.

$\sim(\exists x)$ $(\text{Dog}(x) \wedge \text{Cat}(x))$

Consider now an archetypal case: The Son is not the Father. Or, to put it another way, there is no one who is the Son and who is also the Father:

$\sim(\exists x)$ (x is the Son $\wedge$ x is a person $\wedge$ x is the Father).

This and other similar truths about the Trinity are the archetypes of the derivative truths with the quantifier "no."

The Creator-creature Distinction with Quantification

As we indicated earlier, the Creator-creature distinction is important for logic (chapter 17). Formal logic can present us with the temptation to treat logic as one-level logic applying to both Creator and creature in the same way. We attempt either to bring the Creator down to the level of the creature, or to leave the Creator "beyond" logic and unknowable. Quantification presents us with the same issues all over again.

What is the range of the variable x or other variables governed by the quantifiers $\forall$ and $\exists$? In a typical case, people hope to apply logic to human beings like Socrates and Plato, and to animals, plants, and other entities. In these cases, x ranges over *creatures*. If we exclude God, he may become irrelevant—we might claim that he is not in our "universe of discourse," and he is "beyond logic." On the other hand, if we include God or the persons of the Trinity within the range of x, we may wrongly suggest that God is on the same level as the creatures.

The discussion in chapter 17 already indicated that either route, followed thoughtlessly or purely "formally," results in a non-Christian concept of transcendence and immanence of God. If, on the other hand, we allow analogical relations between Creator and creature, and analogical expressions in our language that discusses our Creator, analogy ruins the formal "purity" of the logic.

In particular, the question arises as to whether x should stand for God or for one of the distinct persons of the Trinity. Either alternative is not completely adequate in itself, because God is both one God and three persons. We can legitimately use the word *all*: "all the persons of the Trinity are one God." But this use of *all* must be classified as *analogous* rather than identical with the use with respect to "all dogs," because the dogs do not indwell one another and do not constitute one individual.

In addition, the other difficulties discussed in part I.C under the problem of classification also touch on quantification. The problem of the one and the many is central in quantification, and it is not "formalizable," since it is founded on the Trinitarian character of God.

Stability in meaning is at issue, since for purely formal reasoning we must have perfect stability for the range of the variables x. The typical explanation in expositions of logic is to say that x ranges over *all individuals*. But what counts as "an individual" is not defined with infinite precision. Logic texts tend to give us open-ended lists of the "kind of things" that can be viewed as individuals.

In many cases the scope of what is an "individual" varies with the context in which the formal apparatus is used. Maybe in one context it is human beings, animals, plants, and nonliving things that actually exist on earth at one particular time. Maybe in another context it ranges over (say) all human beings existing on earth at any time whatsoever, so that Socrates even today counts as an individual about whom we may inquire as to whether "Socrates is human." Maybe in another context an "individual" may be a social institution like a government, a city, a corporation, or a club. Maybe an individual may also be a part of a creature, such as my right arm or my left leg. Surely my right arm is something to which we may ascribe certain properties, so that, for example, it is or is not muscular or tanned. But if we start including parts, there is no obvious stopping point. We have not really specified what counts as an individual in a context-independent way.

The interlocking between form and meaning and the contextual influences on meaning afflict us, because they enter into the understanding of the words *all*, *some*, and *no* in natural language. If we are going to use formal logic in an application to the actual world in which we live, rather than in a very "pared-down, bare-bones" world consisting of (say) six entities $\{a, b, c, d, e, f\}$, we should recognize that we have imprecision about the range of x over "individuals."

In these ways, then, the formal representation of quantification, like the formal representation of propositions in simple propositional logic, is a simplification and a reduction. It does not capture every dimension of reality, but chooses to single out one dimension. It seeks to represent one dimension within a context where we as persons still have to understand the meanings of the symbols and to make judgments as to how they align with real-world issues. The alignment always contains mystery, and mystery is especially noticeable when we are dealing with truths about God.

Disambiguation

Natural language contains ambiguities that symbolism is designed to eliminate. We can use an example having to do with quantification. Consider the sentence in English,

Every doctor likes some lawyer.

How would we convert this sentence into a proposition in modern logical notation? It has two quantifiers, *every* and *some*. It has three predicates, *doctor*, *likes*, and *lawyer*. (As in the case with Aristotelian syllogisms, nouns like *doctor* and *lawyer* have to be converted into predicates.) The central propositional meaning has the form

Likes(x, y)

"Likes(d,l)" says that individual d likes individual l.

To say that "every doctor likes l" means that, if x is a doctor, x likes l:

$(\forall x)\ (\text{Doctor}(x) \supset \text{Likes}(x, l))$

The expression "some lawyer" corresponds to the expression $(\exists y)\ \text{Lawyer}(y)$ … . So, putting everything together,

$(\forall x)\{\text{Doctor}(x) \supset (\exists y)\ [\text{Lawyer}(y) \wedge \text{Likes}(x, y)]\}$

In English, "for every individual x, if x is a doctor, we can infer that there is some individual y such that y is a lawyer and x likes y."

We can also pull forward the symbol $(\exists y)$ without changing the substance of the meaning:

$(\forall x)\ (\exists y)\ \{(\text{Doctor}(x) \supset (\text{Lawyer}(y) \wedge \text{Likes}(x, y))\}$

The meaning in English is that every doctor can find at least one lawyer whom he likes, but the lawyer in question may not be the same one as the next doctor likes. This interpretation is one possible meaning of the English sentence, "Every doctor likes some lawyer."

But there is another possible meaning that would be more appropriate in some contexts (note that context can often disambiguate a sentence in English). The meaning may be that there is some one lawyer, let us say Mr. Likable, who is liked by all the doctors. In symbolic notation, this second meaning gets written as follows:

$(\exists y)\ (\forall x)\ \{(\text{Doctor}(x) \supset (\text{Lawyer}(y) \wedge \text{Likes}(x, y))\}$

The order in which $(\forall x)$ and $(\exists y)$ occur is crucial. If $(\forall x)$ comes first, we first pick x, then y. That is easier. For each doctor x, all we have to do is find at least one lawyer y whom that particular doctor likes. It need not be the same y every time. On the other hand, if the order of quantifications is reversed, if we write

$$(\exists y)\ (\forall x)\ \{(Doctor(x) \dots \}$$

the situation is different. The proposition says that we must pick y first, then x. Pick one y before any decision is made about x, which is going to represent the doctors. One y—the same y—must work for every x. We must find Mr. Likable, whom every single doctor likes. Every doctor must agree with every other doctor in his liking for Mr. Likable. Here is how we might express the two meanings in English:

Every doctor can find at least one lawyer whom he likes.

There exists a lawyer [we have called him Mr. Likable], at least one particular person, whom every doctor likes.

Here are the same two meanings, with the English structure more adapted to the nature of technical quantification:

For every doctor, there exists an individual [y] such that he is a lawyer and the doctor likes him.

Some individual y exists such that, for every doctor, the doctor likes y and y is a lawyer.

Thus the symbolic notation does have an advantage in clearing up a potential ambiguity. And such ambiguity may on occasion lead to fallacious reasoning.

As we might expect, this potential for two different meanings has an archetype in the Trinity. Every person within the Trinity is distinct from another person within the Trinity. But it is not true that every person is distinct from every person, which would mean that each person would be distinct from himself. Nor is it true that there is some person within the Trinity who is distinct from every person in the Trinity.[1]

---

[1] For those who want a technical representation, here it is. Each person in the Trinity is distinct from another person in the Trinity:

$$(\forall x)\ (\exists y)\ \{Person\text{-}of\text{-}the\text{-}Trinity(y) \wedge (Person\text{-}of\text{-}the\text{-}Trinity(x) \supset \sim(x = y))\}$$

Derivation

Logicians have recognized that one quantifier can be used to define the other. The universal quantifier ($\forall x$) can be defined as $\sim(\exists x)\sim$. Thus:

($\forall x$) $H(x)$ is defined as $\sim (\exists x) \sim H(x)$.

Intuitively, this equivalence makes sense. For example, suppose that the variable x ranges over human beings. To say that all individuals are human, that is, ($\forall x$) Human(x), is equivalent to saying that there does not exist any individual who is not human ($\sim (\exists x) \sim$ Human(x)). In general, saying that for all x, $H(x)$ is true is equivalent to saying that there does not exist x such that $H(x)$ is not true.

Here is another equivalence:

($\exists x$) $H(x)$ can be defined as $\sim (\forall x) \sim H(x)$.

To say that there exists an individual who is human (($\exists x$) Human(x)) is equivalent to saying that it is not true that all individuals are nonhuman ($\sim (\forall x) \sim$ Human(x)). In general, to say there is some individual for which the predicate H is true is equivalent to saying that it is not true that for all individuals H is false.

In this sense, the two quantifiers are perspectives on one another. Either one can be used as the starting point.

Similarly,

$\sim(\forall x)$ $H(x)$ is equivalent to ($\exists x$) $\sim H(x)$.

"It is not true that all individuals are human" is equivalent to "it is true that some individual is nonhuman." In general, "It is not true that for all x, $H(x)$" is equivalent to "For some x, it is not true that $H(x)$."

$\sim(\exists x)$ $H(x)$ is equivalent to ($\forall x$) $\sim H(x)$.

"It is not true that there exists an individual who is human" is equivalent to "All individuals are nonhuman."

The perspectival relation between ($\forall x$) and ($\exists x$) has its root in the

---

No person in the Trinity is distinct from all persons in the Trinity simultaneously. It is not true that:

($\exists y$) ($\forall x$) {Person-of-the-Trinity(y) $\land$ (Person-of-the-Trinity(x) $\supset \sim(x = y$))}

Trinity. We already observed that one and many are interrelated, and that the three persons of the Trinity can be loosely associated with the three perspectives, classification, instantiation, and association. Classification focuses on the generality, and is thus closely related to the universal quantifier ($\forall x$). Instantiation focuses on the particular manifestation, and is thus closely related to the existential quantifier ($\exists x$). Association invites us to remember the association between classification and instantiation. The particularity represented in the word *some* is a particular out of a group, that is, the class, and conversely the class is made up of particulars, instantiations. The formal symbolism focuses on one dimension from a rich reality.

For Further Reflection

1. How can the existential quantifier ($\exists x$) be defined in terms of the universal quantifier ($\forall x$)?
2. Eliminate all the existential quantifiers from the following, by substituting equivalent expressions that involve universal quantifiers.

$$(\exists y)(\forall x)(\exists z)\{S(x, y) \supset (\exists w)\ T(\ w, x, z)\}$$

3. What are the roots for quantification in the Trinity?
4. Illustrate the use of the words "all," "some," and "no," using statements about the persons of the Trinity.

Chapter 50

Axioms and Deductions for Quantification

If the logic of quantification is to become part of a formal deductive system, the system must include axioms and rules that include quantification. The same rules that we have discussed in dealing with truth-function logic or propositional logic can serve as a starting point. We only have to understand that instead of proposition symbols like p and q we can also have "propositional functions." A propositional function is an incomplete proposition like $H(x)$ that may include variables. For example, if F, G, and H are predicates, and s is an individual (Socrates), the following are propositional functions:

$H(y)$
$G(x) \lor \sim H(x)$
$G(x) \lor (\sim H(x) \lor p)$ (where p is a simple proposition, with no variable)
$F(x) \supset [(\sim H(y) \lor \sim G(x)) \lor G(s)]$
$(\forall x)\{F(x) \supset [(\sim H(y) \lor \sim G(x)) \lor G(s)]\}$

If we add extra quantifiers, we can obtain complete propositions. The following are complete propositions:

p
$H(s)$
$(\forall x)(G(x) \lor (\sim H(x) \lor p))$
$(\forall x)\{F(x) \supset [(\sim H(s) \lor \sim G(x)) \lor G(s)]\}$
$(\forall x)(\exists y)\{F(x) \supset [(\sim H(y) \lor \sim G(x)) \lor G(s)]\}$

The axioms that we discussed for propositional logic can now be extended, so that each symbol p, q, r, etc., for a proposition is now understood to stand for both propositions and propositional functions. The propositional functions may include individual variables (x), individual constants (s), and quantifiers $(\forall x)$. Consider, for example, the first axiom in Whitehead and Russell's system:

$(p \lor p) \supset p$

We can now substitute for p any propositional function and obtain an instance of the axiom:

$(H(y) \lor H(y)) \supset H(y)$
$(H(s) \lor H(s)) \supset H(s)$
$[(\forall x)(F(x) \supset \sim H(y)) \lor (\forall x)(F(x) \supset \sim H(y))] \supset (\forall x)(F(x) \supset \sim H(y))$

and so on.

Free and Bound Variables

The different examples illustrate a difference between two different uses of variables like x and y. In one use, the variable is governed by a quantification symbol, such as $(\forall x)$, $(\forall y)$, $(\exists x)$, $(\exists y)$. In all the complete propositions, the variables x and y are governed by corresponding quantifiers. Such variables are called *bound* variables. (An individual constant like s is simply a constant, and so a quantifier is not relevant for it.) In the other type of use, a variable is not governed by a quantification symbol, but is *free*. In the example

$F(x) \supset [(\sim H(y) \lor \sim G(x)) \lor G(s)]$

both x and y are free. In the example

$(\forall x)\{G(x) \supset [(\sim H(y) \lor \sim G(x)) \lor G(s)]\}$

y is free and x is bound. Whether a variable is bound or free may depend on the *scope* of quantifiers around it. Consider

$F(x) \supset [(\sim H(y) \lor (\exists x) \sim G(x)) \lor G(s)].$

In this expression, the quantifier $(\exists x)$ governs only what is within its scope, a scope defined by the use of parentheses. $(\exists x)$ governs only $\sim G(x)$. So the x in $\sim G(x)$ is *bound*. On the other hand, the x in the opening expression $F(x)$ is free. It is independent of the x's occurring later on. This kind of situation is potentially confusing, so it is in general better to use a distinct variable for each quantifier. We can use z instead of x in the existential quantification without changing the meaning:

$F(x) \supset [(\sim H(y) \vee (\exists z) \sim G(z)) \vee G(s)]$.

With this notational change, it becomes clearer that x is free and z is bound.

By definition, the *scope* of a quantifier $(\forall x)$ or $(\exists z)$ is the subformula that it governs. By convention, the scope is the smallest possible subformula that a quantifier can govern, consistent with the use of parentheses. For example,

$(\exists z) F(z) \vee G(z, x)$

means the same as

$((\exists z) F(z)) \vee G(z, x)$

The scope of $(\exists z)$ is only $F(z)$, not $F(z) \vee G(z, x)$. If we want it to have the larger scope, we must explicitly include parentheses:

$(\exists z) (F(z) \vee G(z, x))$

Ways to Build Quantificational Logic

As in the case of propositional logic, we can go about building a logical system either by adding axioms or by adding rules of deduction. Whitehead and Russell's system chooses to add axioms. Some of the extra material that Whitehead and Russell add to deal with quantification has to do with specifying what counts as a meaningful ("well-formed") proposition or propositional function. In addition, Whitehead and Russell offer two ways to build the system for quantification. In one way, both universal quantification $(\forall x)$ and existential quantification $(\exists x)$ are new kinds of symbols. In the second way, only universal quantification is a genuinely new kind of symbol. Existential quantification is defined in terms of universal quantification as the more basic concept: $(\exists x)$ is treated as shorthand for $\sim (\forall x) \sim$. These two approaches are perspectives on one another. The second of these two methods has the simpler set of axioms, since only the behavior of universal quantification has to be specified by axioms. The behavior of $(\exists x)$ can be deduced from its definition.

Axioms of Whitehead and Russell for Quantification

Let us look at the axioms added to deal with quantification, in order to understand their significance. The first axiom says that we can go from a general truth to any particular instance:

$((\forall x)\, F(x)) \supset F(y)^1$

It is called the principle of *universal instantiation*. The truth of this axiom follows from the meaning of the word *all*. If something is true for all cases, it is true for any particular case, as symbolized by y. (It does not matter whether we use y or some other symbol, such as z. The principle also holds if instead of y we write a constant symbol s: $((\forall x)\, F(x)) \supset F(s)$.) Here we can see again the interplay between the one, namely, the general truth that $F(x)$ is always true, and the many, namely, the particular truths for particular y's: $y_1, y_2, y_3, \dots$.

The principle holds because God is faithful to himself. We can see an archetypal form of the principle in God. In fact, we can see particular examples of this archetype. God is righteous. Every person in the Trinity is righteous. Therefore, the Father is righteous, the Son is righteous, and the Holy Spirit is righteous. The general principle, namely, that every person in the Trinity is righteous, leads to the application to each person of the Trinity, the Father, the Son, and the Spirit. We can see similar logic at work with respect not only to God's righteousness, but also his love, his holiness, his omnipotence, and his immutability.

Actually, we want not one axiom alone, but a general *schema* or pattern of axioms, which would apply to any propositional function, not simply to a simple predicate F. For example, we want to be able to say,

$[(\forall x)\, (G(x) \vee {\sim}H(x))] \supset (G(y) \vee {\sim}H(y))$
$[(\forall x)\, (G(x) \vee {\sim}H(x))] \supset (G(z) \vee {\sim}H(z))$ [it does not matter what new
     variable z we use]
$[(\forall x)\, (G(x) \vee {\sim}H(y))] \supset (G(y) \vee {\sim}H(y))$
$[(\forall x)\, (G(x) \vee {\sim}H(y))] \supset (G(z) \vee {\sim}H(y))$
$[(\forall x)\, ((G(x) \vee {\sim}H(y)) \supset p)] \supset [(G(y) \vee {\sim}H(y)) \supset p]$

And so on. We can sum up all these cases in one compact formula:

$((\forall x)\, \varphi(x)) \supset \varphi(k)$

The formula says that if a propositional function $\varphi(x)$ is true for all values of x, it is true for any particular value k. For example, if all individuals are human, then individual y is human. Here φ stands for any propositional

---

[1] Alfred North Whitehead and Bertrand Russell, *Principia Mathematica*, 2nd ed., 3 vols. (Cambridge: Cambridge University Press, 1927), 1:140, proposition 10.1. See also 1:133, proposition 9.2. My notation differs from theirs, but the substance is the same.

function whatsoever that has x as a variable. It does not matter *which* symbol we use for an individual variable: $((\forall y)\ \varphi(y)) \supset \varphi(k)$, $((\forall z)\ \varphi(z)) \supset \varphi(k)$, and so on. We use the Greek letter φ instead of a normal letter, to remind ourselves that it need not consist of a single predicate like F, but can stand for a complex expression like $(G(x) \lor {\sim}H(y)) \supset p$. The placeholder k, in this case, can be either a new variable (y, z, etc.), or a variable already occurring elsewhere in φ, or a constant (e.g., s or c). We should also note that the propositional function $\varphi(x)$ may include other free variables such as y and z as well as the variable x. These free variables are not affected.

It should be noted that in this formulation, *all* the occurrences of x within the original complex expression $\varphi(x)$ must be replaced by the same k, whether k is a variable like y or a constant like c. For example, suppose that we start with

$(\forall x)\ ((G(x) \lor {\sim}H(x)) \supset p)$

We may infer $(G(z) \lor {\sim}H(z)) \supset p$ or $(G(c) \lor {\sim}H(c)) \supset p$. We may *not*, however, infer

$(G(z) \lor {\sim}H(y)) \supset p$ or
$(G(z) \lor {\sim}H(c)) \supset p$

We need one more restriction. When we replace the bound variable x, governed by the universal quantification $(\forall x)$, and we introduce a variable y to replace x, y must be *free* in the places where it is introduced. Suppose we know that

$(\forall x)\ (\exists y)\ (H(x) \equiv {\sim}H(y))$

(As an example of the meaning here, consider the proposition "for all individuals x there exists some individual y such that x is human if and only if y is nonhuman." This proposition is true if the universe of individuals includes both humans and animals. For each x that is human, we pick a y that is an animal, and for each x that is nonhuman, we pick a y that is human.)

Starting with this formula, can we substitute y for x:

$(\exists y)\ (H(y) \equiv {\sim}H(y))$???[2]

---

[2] As an example of the meaning, consider the proposition: "There exists a y such that y is human if and only if y is nonhuman." The proposition is false, because no y can be both human and nonhuman.

No, because the new occurrence of y is within the scope of the quantifier $(\exists y)$. All such problems can be solved by first rewriting the original statement with a new choice of quantifiers.

$$(\forall x)\ (\exists z)\ (H(x) \equiv \sim H(z))$$

Now substitute y for x:

$$(\exists z)\ (H(y) \equiv \sim H(z))$$

This inference is legitimate, because y is free in its new occurrence.

The Axiom of Generalization

The second axiom of Whitehead and Russell is an axiom that allows us to move from the particular to the general: If $F(y)$ is true for whatever y we may choose, then $(\forall x)\ F(x)$ is true. Or, using our previous generalized notation, if $\varphi(y)$ is true for whatever y we may choose, then $(\forall x)\ \varphi(x)$ is true. This principle applies for any variable symbols y and x. This principle is the converse of the principle of universal instantiation.

Once again, this principle has its archetype in the Trinity. What is true of each person of the Trinity is true of all. We may call this axiom the principle of *universal generalization*.

Restrictions on Substitution

It is to be understood that in making the transition from $\varphi(y)$ to $(\forall x)\ \varphi(x)$, *all* instances of the free variable y in $\varphi(y)$ must be replaced by x, and that the variable x must not already occur in $\varphi(y)$. Let us illustrate. From

$$(\exists z)\ (H(y) \equiv \sim H(z))$$

we infer

$$(\forall x)\ (\exists z)\ (H(x) \equiv \sim H(z))$$

But from

$$(\exists x)\ (H(y) \equiv \sim H(x))$$

we may not infer

$(\forall x) (\exists x) (H(x) \equiv \sim H(x))$

because x already occurs in the expression $(\exists x) (H(y) \equiv \sim H(x))$.

Likewise, from

$H(y) \equiv \sim H(x)$

we may not infer

$(\forall x) (H(x) \equiv \sim H(x))$

In addition, within a system of natural deduction, we need to deal with the situation of conditional proofs. Conditional proofs introduce extra assumptions. In theory, *any* assumption is allowed at the beginning of a conditional proof. If an assumption includes a free variable y, it creates a potential difficulty, because the assumption does not specify for which y it is true.

Consider :

> (1) Assume $G(y)$.
>   (2) $(\forall x) G(x)$ (from (1) by universal generalization???)

(As an example, consider the following sequence: (1) Assume y is human. May we deduce: (2) For all x, x is human?) Step (2) is not allowed because in the assumption (1) it is not clear that one is assuming truth for all y. If we were allowed to continue, we could falsely deduce:

> (3) $G(y) \supset (\forall x) G(x)$ (conditional proof from (1) and (2))

But this says that if $G(y)$ is true for a particular y, it is true for all.

The natural interpretation of the step "Assume $G(y)$" is that it is saying, "Assume $G(y)$ for some particular y, which is yet to be specified." Then see what happens. So we must specify a restriction: we are not allowed to use the principle of universal generalization on a variable y when the variable occurs as a free variable in an assumption within whose scope we are currently operating. If, on the other hand, we close out the extra assumption by the method of conditional proof, we are *then* free again to use the principle of universal generalization.

Hence, we may work forward in a conditional proof, without universal-izing y, and then close off the conditional. The following is legitimate:

(1) Assume $G(y)$
   (2) Assume p.
      (3) $G(y)$ (reiteration from (1))
      (4) $p \supset G(y)$ (conditional proof from (2) and (3))
   (5) $G(y) \supset (p \supset G(y))$ (conditional proof from (1) and (4))
   (6) $(\forall y)[G(y) \supset (p \supset G(y))]$ (universal generalization from (5))

In (6) the universal generalization on y takes place after exiting the conditional introduced in step (1).

The Axiom of Quantification Movement

The third axiom in Whitehead and Russell is an axiom allowing us to move the position of the quantification:

$$[(\forall x)(q \lor \varphi(x))] \supset [q \lor (\forall x)\, \varphi(x)]$$

In English, this axiom says that if for all x either q is true or $\varphi(x)$ is true, then either q is true or for all x $\varphi(x)$ is true. It is understood that q does not itself contain the variable x. It may, however, contain other variables, either bound or free. If q is true, both of the sides separated by $\supset$ are true. That is, the antecedent $[(\forall x)(q \lor \varphi(x))]$ is true and the consequent $[q \lor (\forall x)\, \varphi(x)]$ is true. The antecedent is true because $q \lor \varphi(x)$ is true—for any x whatsoever. The principle of generalization allows us to conclude that $[(\forall x)(q \lor \varphi(x))]$. If q is *not* true, then the antecedent is equivalent to $(\forall x)\varphi(x)$. If it is not true, there is nothing to prove. If it is true, the consequent is true by the principle of addition, $p \supset (q \lor p)$, with $(\forall x)\, \varphi(x)$ substituted for p.

Possible Rules of Natural Deduction

As in the case of propositional logic (part II), we may choose to add rules of deduction instead of adding axioms. This alternative again illustrates that we may choose one of several perspectives on how we construct a logical system. In a system of natural deduction, what do the rules look like? In this case, the rules are very much like the axioms. The rule of universal instan-tiation says that if we know that $(\forall x)\, \varphi(x)$, we may deduce $\varphi(y)$. The rule of universal generalization says that if we know that $\varphi(y)$ for any arbitrarily chosen y, we may deduce $(\forall x)\,\varphi(x)$. The axiom for quantification movement can be added as an additional deduction rule:

If we know that $(\forall x)(q \lor \varphi(x))$, we may deduce that $(q \lor (\forall x)\,\varphi(x))$

This rule is not actually necessary, because it can be deduced within a natural deduction system using the rules for universal instantiation and universal generalization. (See appendix C1.)

Existential Generalization

It is convenient if we also add rules for natural deduction for the existential quantifier $\exists$. These extra rules are not necessary, because they can be deduced from the rest. But they are convenient.

The rule for *existential generalization* says that, if $F(x)$ holds for a particular case c, there exists at least one x for which it holds:

$F(c) \supset (\exists x)\, F(x)$

The same is true if we know that $F(y)$ is true for some case of a variable y:

$F(y) \supset (\exists x)\, F(x)$

To cover both of these cases, we write

$F(k) \supset (\exists x)\, F(x)$

where k stands for either a constant or a free variable.

In keeping with our general approach, we may generalize this principle to include any propositional function φ.

$\varphi(k) \supset (\exists x)\, \varphi(x)$

It is understood that the variable x does not already occur in φ. (If it does occur as a bound variable, replace x by some new variable z: $\varphi(k) \supset (\exists z)\, \varphi(z)$.)

We can establish this result using the rule of universal instantiation (see appendix C1.)

Existential Instantiation

Finally, we may add a rule allowing us to move from an existential quantification to a particular case. (Once again, this rule is not strictly necessary, but may be convenient in shortening and simplifying some proofs.)

Rule of existential instantiation: if we have shown that $(\exists x)\ \varphi(x)$, we may infer $\varphi(k)$, where k is either an individual constant (for example, c) or an individual variable (such as y). But there are restrictions:

(1) k must not occur in any earlier line of the proof.
(2) The principle of universal generalization cannot be applied to k.
(3) The closing line of the proof must not include k.[3]

Other Deductions

The syllogistic forms from Aristotle can be deduced using this system of rules. In appendix C2 we present a few cases. In more traditional logic the syllogistic forms were regarded as virtually "axiomatic." But we have some choice as to what we are to treat as more fundamental. Logic "hangs together" because of the self-consistency of God. God produces a derivative self-consistency and a kind of "hanging together" among various manifestations of his consistency. Any way we proceed, we are using our own rational powers, the powers of our mental reasoning, and the powers of language. In addition to these, we are using one part of formalized logic to confirm another part.

The axioms and the system of deduction, taken together, are nowadays called *first order quantification theory*, which can be distinguished from theories that have still more layers of complexity (see chapter 62).

---

[3] The restriction (1) is necessary because the proposition $(\exists x)\ \varphi(x)$ says only that there is *some* x such that $\varphi(x)$. It does not specify *which* instance might work. If k already occurs in an earlier line of the proof, we cannot guarantee that *for this same* k it would be true that $\varphi(k)$. We have to protect ourselves by picking arbitrarily some new symbol k, which we will use to stand for some individual for which $\varphi(k)$.

The restriction (2) is necessary because we know only that $\varphi(k)$ for some k, not for all. We cannot generalize to $(\forall k)\ \varphi(k)$.

The restriction (3) is necessary because the particular choice of k is pertinent only within the temporary bounds of a proof where, in effect, it is defined by a preceding proposition $(\exists x)\ \varphi(x)$. We cannot carry it outside the proof.

For Further Reflection

1. Convert the following argument to formal symbols, and then derive the
   conclusion, using the rules of natural deduction and specifying what
   rule justifies each step.
   a. All dogs are animals.
      Fido is a dog.
      Therefore, Fido is an animal.
   b. Sally-the-whale is a mammal.
      Sally-the-whale is a sea creature.
      Therefore, some mammal is a sea creature.

Chapter 51

Soundness of Quantification

Just as we asked about the soundness and completeness of propositional logic in chapter 44, we may ask about the soundness and completeness of the theory of quantification presented in the previous chapter.

Soundness

The theory of quantification is sound if all its theorems are always true. We can show that all the theorems are always true if we show (1) that the axioms are always true and (2) that the principles for making deductions always lead from true premises to true conclusions. We will take these two steps one at a time.

Soundness of the Axioms

The axioms for our theory of quantification include the axioms for propositional logic. These axioms are, however, interpreted in a more "generous" fashion. The propositional symbols p, q, etc., may stand not only for elementary propositions but for propositional functions. This expansion leaves intact the truth-functional properties belonging to the axioms. So all the axioms are still tautologies.

In addition, the theory of quantification provides for two new axioms, or rather axiom schemas. For any propositional function $\varphi(x)$,

$$((\forall x)\, \varphi(x)) \supset \varphi(k)$$

This is the principle of universal instantiation. Is this principle always true?

Assume $(\forall x)\, \varphi(x)$. The proposition says that for all x, $\varphi(x)$ is true. So for any particular chosen value, let us say k, $\varphi(x)$ is true. That is, $\varphi(k)$. $(\forall x)$ $\varphi(x)$ says that $\varphi(x)$ is true for all instances: $\{[(\varphi(a) \wedge \varphi(b)) \wedge \varphi(c)] \wedge \varphi(d)\} \wedge$ $\varphi(e)$ … for all the individuals a, b, c, d, e, … . The conjunction is true only if each element is true. So we may legitimately deduce any particular case, let us say $\varphi(b)$.[1] Since the principle is general, it is true not only for any *fixed* individual b, but for a variable y representing any individual. It follows that the axioms of universal instantiation always lead to more propositions that are always true.

Next, consider the axiom of universal generalization. It says that if $\varphi(y)$ is true for whatever y we may choose, then $(\forall x)\,\varphi(x)$ is true. It is clear that if $\varphi(y)$ is true for each particular case, it is true for all. Suppose that we know that

$\varphi(a)$
$\varphi(b)$
$\varphi(c)$
$\varphi(d)$
$\varphi(e)$
...

Then $\{[(\,\varphi(a) \wedge \varphi(b)) \wedge \varphi(c)] \wedge \varphi(d)\} \wedge \varphi(e) \ldots .$[2]

The latter is equivalent to $(\forall x)\,\varphi(x)$. In sum, the principle of universal generalization always leads from true propositions to more true propositions.

Finally, consider the axiom of quantification movement,

$$[(\forall x)(q \vee \varphi(x))] \supset [q \vee (\forall x)\,\varphi(x)]$$

It can be deduced from the other axioms within our system of natural deduction (see appendix C1).

Or we can simply interpret it in terms of truth. $(\forall x)(q \vee \varphi(x))$ says that $q \vee \varphi(y)$ for each y. If $\varphi(y)$ is true for every y, $(\forall x)\,\varphi(x)$ is true and so $q \vee (\forall x)\,\varphi(x)$ is true. If $\varphi(y)$ is *not* true for some y, q must be true, and so $q \vee (\forall x)\,\varphi(x)$ is true. So the new axiom always leads from true propositions to more true propositions.

The Soundness of Deductions Using Quantification

Now we are ready to consider the second issue: do the deductions permitted within quantification theory always lead from true propositions to conclusions that are true propositions? Within quantification theory, the rules for deduction include all the rules for deduction in propositional logic. These

---

[1] This result can be viewed as a kind of generalized form of the rule of conjunction elimination, as discussed in appendix B3.
[2] This result can be viewed as a kind of generalization from the rule of conjunction introduction, as discussed in appendix B3.

rules always lead from truth to truth. Quantification theory has two additional rules, namely, universal generalization and existential instantiation. The principle of universal generalization says that if we know that $\varphi(y)$ for an arbitrarily chosen individual y, we may deduce that $\varphi(x)$ is true for all x: $(\forall x)\varphi(x)$. Intuitively, we can see that this deduction moves from truth to truth. Second, consider the rule for existential instantiation. Suppose that in a proof we have arrived at the result $(\exists x)\varphi(x)$. Can we deduce that $\varphi(c)$ for some constant c? The proposition $(\exists x)\varphi(x)$ implies that there is some individual x for which $\varphi(x)$. But we do not know which one. So we just let a new constant c (or a new variable y) stand for this individual. The rule for existential instantiation specifies that the symbol c or y must be a *new* symbol, not one occurring earlier in the proof. That restriction ensures that we do not illegitimately claim to know exactly *which* individual satisfies $\varphi(x)$. In the deductions that follow, we just need to make sure that we do not use the symbol c or y in a way that assumes that we know more about it than we in fact do.

(An additional check on the soundness of quantification theory will be given in chapter 54, by relying on the soundness of propositional logic.)

Completeness of Quantification Theory

Our quantification theory is also *complete*. That is to say, any proposition within the system that is always true is also deducible from the axioms. But it is more difficult to show that this is so. Demonstrations can be found in a number of logic textbooks.[3]

For Further Reflection

1. Why is it important for logicians to know that the axioms for quantification are sound and complete?
2. Discuss how to use mathematical induction to fill in the steps needed to show the soundness of quantification theory. (Hint: do induction on the number of lines in the proof; see chapter 45.)
3. Check that the rule of existential generalization always leads from truth to truth.
4. Explain how there is a relation between universal quantification ($\forall x$) and the repeated use of logical conjunction to link propositional functions $\varphi(x)$ that hold for each particular individual: $\varphi(a), \varphi(b), \varphi(c), \varphi(d), \ldots$.

---

[3] For one such demonstration, see Irving M. Copi, *Symbolic Logic*, 5th ed. (New York: Macmillan, 1979), chapter 10.

Part III.C

Including Equality and Functions

Chapter 52

Equality

The resources for quantification theory can be further expanded by adding a symbol for equality. Why should we bother and why should we care?

Quantification theory is a kind of formalized language that represents parts of the logical reasoning that takes place in ordinary language. Expanding quantification theory to include equality is an expansion of the language. It enables us to represent more aspects of the reasoning that takes place in ordinary language. The more aspects we represent, the more complex our language.

This expansion has both advantages and disadvantages. The main advantage is that we have richer resources in the expanded formal language. The disadvantage is that we have more complexity. It is easier to become confused or to get lost in the complexity. And there is also the danger, as the resources expand, that we may find it easier to ignore the difference between the reduced system of formal language and the full resources of natural language.

We will now introduce symbolism for equality, so that we have some experience with this kind of expansion and so that we can reflect on its relationship to its foundations in God.

A symbol for equality can be added to the other notations that we already have for quantification theory. The symbol = is used. We need to explain just how it is used.

The Function of the Symbol for Equality

In the context of arithmetic, the symbol = for "equals" indicates that two numbers are equal: $3 + 5 = 8$; $3 \times 5 = 15$. The meaning of the symbol is extended when we use it in the context of quantification theory. The symbol now indicates that two symbolic notations designate the same *individual*. If s stands for Socrates and t is a second symbol standing for Socrates, $s = t$. Usually it is not necessary to have two constant symbols for the same individual, but it is permitted. Sometimes formal logic is used in describing parts of mathematics, and the realm of individuals, that is, the "universe of discourse" over which an individual variable x ranges, is the realm of numbers—the individuals x, let us say, are all positive integers. Or, in another context, x may range over all integers (positive, negative, or 0), or all rational numbers, or all real numbers. The equality symbol then has its normal arithmetical meaning.

In the context of ordinary life, we encounter a use for equality whenever we offer two descriptions for the same entity. If we say that "Paris is the capital of France," we can write it as "Paris = the capital of France." We can represent this claim in formal symbols by letting p stand for Paris, and c stand for "the capital of France." Then $p = c$. Or we can choose to analyze the conception "the capital of France" and break it down into smaller constituents. Let $C(x, y)$ stand for the binary (two-place) relation "is capital of." $C(x, y)$ if and only if x is capital of y. Then $C(p, f)$, where f stands for France. Normally, there is only *one* capital of any particular nation or state. We can express this extra condition by saying:

If x is capital of France, $x = p$.

Or, in formal notation,

$$(\forall x)(C(x, f) \supset (x = p))$$

If we also want to include the information that $C(p, f)$, we may write

$$(\forall x)(C(x, f) \equiv (x = p))$$

Note that we must keep straight the difference between the symbol $\equiv$ for material equivalence and the symbol $=$ for the equality of two individuals. Material equivalence $\equiv$, which uses three parallel lines, is a relation between two complete propositions or propositional functions. ($C(x, f)$ and $(x = p)$ are both propositional functions.) Equality $=$, which uses two parallel lines, is a relation between individuals (that is, are they the same individual?).

Technically, equality $=$ is a two-place predicate, since it has two blank spots that we fill with individual symbols. If we write it like any other two-place predicate, we would have to write $E(x, p)$, where the symbol E stands for the predicate "equality." If we use the normal symbol $=$ for "equals" instead of using the symbol E, we get the expression:

$$=(x, p)$$

That way of writing it is strange. So it is customary with the equality symbol = to write it in the normal way with which we are familiar from arithmetic:

$$x = p$$

We have to have extra axioms to specify how the new symbol = will function. For one thing, for any individual x,

$$x = x$$

We need to say that if $x = y$, they can replace one another in any context.

$$(x = y) \supset (G(x) \equiv G(y))$$

for any predicate symbol G. In fact, the same holds for any propositional function φ with one free variable x:

$$(x = y) \supset (\varphi(x) \equiv \varphi(y))$$

This formulation is an *axiom schema*. It represents a separate axiom for each propositional function φ and for each choice of individual variable symbols x and y. Some or all of the free occurrences of x in $\varphi(x)$ are replaced by free occurrences of y in $\varphi(y)$. (We must be careful if there are quantifiers with x or y somewhere in φ.)

Theistic Foundations for Equality

As usual, special notation represents a gain in precision but a loss in the multidimensional characteristics of natural language. The special notation assumes that the referent for a particular symbol is uniquely identified. Paris is the capital of France. But we have to know which Paris: Paris, France; not Paris, Illinois.

Individuals can be identified with more than one description, and this multiplicity of description involves the relation of unity to diversity. We have the unity of one individual, namely Paris, France, and a diversity in ways of describing it, namely as "Paris" or as "the capital of France." The unity of a single individual depends on God. It is God who has established stable wholes. Paris remains Paris. It does so because God remains God.

The unity of one God is the ultimate foundation for the unity of individuals in the world. Moreover, God can be described in more than one way: he is "God," "Creator," "the Holy One," "the Almighty." Each person of the Trinity has unity and diversity of descriptions. God the Son is also "the Word" and "the Son of God." The Holy Spirit is also "the Spirit of God" and "the Spirit of Christ." The ultimate, foundational cases of equality are the cases with God. God is God, and each person of the Trinity is himself.

For Further Reflection

1. In what ways may the equality symbol = in logic be a *reduction* from the fuller meanings in natural language?
2. What is the foundation for the stability of identity in the created world?
3. Assign a meaning to new special symbols, if necessary, and then write in your symbolic notation "Madrid is the capital of Spain." Use symbolic notation to assert that Madrid is the *only* capital of Spain.
4. Using the axiom schema $(x = y) \supset (\varphi(x) \equiv \varphi(y))$, prove
   a. $(x = y) \supset (y = x)$ [Hint: use the expression $x = y$ itself as φ and do two partial replacements.]
   b. $((x = y) \wedge (y = z)) \supset (x = z)$
   c. $\sim(x = y) \supset \sim(y = x)$ [Hint: use the truth functional tautology $(p \supset q) \supset (\sim p \supset \sim q)$.]
   d. $(\sim(x = y) \wedge (y = z)) \supset \sim(x = z)$

Chapter 53

Functions

Next, we can expand the notation of quantification theory by adding *functions*. What are functions? And why should we care?

Adding functions to our theory is like adding equality. It is a further expansion in the resources of the formalized language for logic. What we have already said about the advantages and disadvantages of adding resources holds true for this kind of addition. We introduce functions so that we have some experience with this kind of expansion and so that we can reflect on the relationship of functions to their foundations in God.

Functions in Algebra

Algebra forms the most useful background for building up an understanding of what a function is. Let us begin with an example. We can add 3 to each positive integer in the sequence 1, 2, 3, 4, … . We obtain the sequence 4, 5, 6, 7, … . We can indicate the relationship between the numbers in the two sequences by using arrows to correlate the numbers, one by one, as follows:

$$1 \rightarrow 1 + 3 = 4$$
$$2 \rightarrow 2 + 3 = 5$$
$$3 \rightarrow 3 + 3 = 6$$
$$4 \rightarrow 4 + 3 = 7$$
…

If we omit the middle part, we have two columns:

$$1 \rightarrow 4$$
$$2 \rightarrow 5$$
$$3 \rightarrow 6$$
$$4 \rightarrow 7$$
$$5 \rightarrow 8$$
…

The relationship between the two columns is a *function*. A function is like a box, inside which calculations may take place (see figure 53.1):

Fig. 53.1: Illustration of a Function

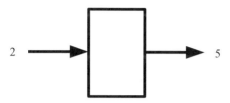

For each appropriate input (such as the number 2) it produces an output (the number 5) according to some rule (the internal workings of the box).

We can summarize the entire process by letting *n* stand for any positive integer. The process of adding 3 to *n* moves us from *n* to *n* + 3, *for any n.*

Because there are many instances where we want to discuss such operations, we need a general notation. We let the letter *f* stand for the function itself, that is, the correlation between each number *n* and the output *n* + 3. *f* is like the box itself. The number *n* is the input to the box, and *n* + 3 is the output. When the input to the function *f* is the number 2, the notation *f*(2) is the standard way of denoting the output of *f*. We write *f*(2) = 5, *f*(1) = 4, *f*(3) = 6, and so on. If we want to describe *f* all in one line, we write

$f(n) = n + 3$ (for any positive integer *n*).

Here is another function: $g(n) = 2 \times n$. The letter *g* stands for the function itself, that is, the box into which we feed numbers. The function *g* is a correlation between the input to the box *g* and its output. In this case, the function *g* doubles whatever number is fed into it. It does not matter whether we use the letter *n* or some other letter to describe the numbers that are fed into the box. The function *g* can also be described by writing $g(x) = 2 \times x$.

The most common occurrence of functions is in manipulating numbers. But we can generalize the idea of function so that it applies to other realms. For example, for any person *x*, let *f*(*x*) be defined as the father of *x*. Then this *f* is a function. To distinguish it from other functions, we can write it out more fully: *father*(*x*) is the individual who is the father of individual *x*.

There is one key requirement for a function f. Whenever $f(x)$ is defined for a particular individual x, it must produce a *unique* value. "Child of x" is not a function, because a parent may have more than one child.

Functions and Relations

The example with father-child relations illustrates an important relationship between functions on the one hand and relations on the other. Any function can be construed (or redefined) as a relation between inputs and outputs. Let $R(x, y)$ be a binary predicate or binary relation, that is, a relation with two inputs x and y. Let us say that R represents the relation of child to father. $R(x, y)$ means "person y is father of x." $R(x, y)$ has the value T (true) when y is the father of x; otherwise it has the value F. Then the binary relation R contains all the information that is contained in the earlier function f. We can summarize the situation by noting

$R(x, y)$ if and only if *father*$(x) = y$.

This situation is true in general. For the function $f(n) = n + 3$, we have a corresponding relation $A(x, y)$ such that $A(x, y)$ is true if and only if $x + 3 = y$. For A to represent a *function* (and not just a binary relation) from x to y, we must have

$(A(x, y) \land A(x, z)) \supset (y = z)$ for all x, y, and z.

Such a condition guarantees that there will not be more than one y that could be the output for any particular x. If we want to guarantee that a function is actually defined for all individuals x, we have to specify it: $(\forall x)(\exists y)A(x, y)$.

Functions on Multiple Variables

So far we have considered functions that have only one input x (or n). We can generalize this situation to consider functions that operate on more than one input. We may define a function

$h(a, b) = a + b$, for all whole numbers a and b.

h requires two inputs, a and b. When it receives these inputs, it performs a calculation and produces a single output, namely, $a + b$. Just as a function with one input can be correlated with a relation with two inputs, a function with two inputs can be correlated with a three-place predicate, that is, a relation taking three inputs. We define

$H(x, y, z)$ if and only if $x + y = z$.

As usual, for $H(x, y, z)$ actually to correspond to a function, we require

$(H(x, y, z) \wedge H(x, y, w)) \supset (z = w)$ for all x, y, z, and w.

This condition states that there can be at most *one* element z that has the relation $H(x, y, z)$ for any starting choices of x and y.

In a similar fashion a function $f(x_1, x_2, x_3, ..., x_k)$ with k variables x_1, ..., x_k can be correlated with $(k + 1)$-place predicate, a relation on $k + 1$ variables:

We define F so that $f(x_1, x_2, ..., x_k) = y$ if and only if $F(x_1, x_2, ..., x_k, y)$.

If we include functions and equality in a logical language, we must distinguish between two kinds of formal expression, namely, *propositions* and *terms*. A *term* is either (1) a symbol for an individual constant (a, b, c, ...) or (2) a symbol for an individual variable (x, y, z, ...) or (3) the value $f(t_1, t_2, ... , t_n)$ of a function f (which takes n variables) where $t_1, t_2, ... , t_n$ are terms. (Note that the word *term* is used here with a special technical meaning. It should not be confused with the word *term* used to describe the word *dog* or *animal*.)

Because of the close relationship between functions and multi-place predicates, predicates *alone* could theoretically do all the work that we normally accomplish with predicates and functions *together*. For this reason, quantification theory is often introduced in its simpler form, with predicates but no explicit functions. This simpler form allows a simpler analysis. But it has a practical disadvantage. If we use predicates to represent functions, we must for each such predicate carry along a specification that says that only one element y can make the predicate true for any one x. $(\forall x)(\forall y)(\forall z)\{(P(x, y) \wedge P(x, z)) \supset (y = z)\}$. We must also use a roundabout way to represent the value $f(x)$ of a function with input x. It is much less cluttered if we allow ourselves to use functions like addition and multiplication using a normal notation.

Functions as a Perspective on Predicates

We have just seen that functions can be regarded as a special kind of predicate. We can also go in the opposite direction. Predicates can be regarded as a special kind of function. How?

So far we have considered functions f only in a few limited contexts. The function $f(x) = x + 3$ takes as its input a whole number x, and results in an output $f(x)$ that is another whole number, namely, $x + 3$. We have also considered the function *father*(...) ("father of") that has an individual human being as input, and whose output is an individual human being. As a more general case, we may consider functions f that take an input from a set A and have as output a member of the set B. A and B need not be the same set. The set of all $x \in A$ such that $f(x)$ is defined is called the *domain* of f. The set $R = \{f(x) \mid x \in A\}$ (the set of all values $f(x)$ such that $x \in A$) is called the *range* of f. If D is the domain of f, we write $f: D \to B$ to indicate that f is defined for all the elements x in D and that the values $f(x)$ are in B (but the range of f could be a subset R of B that does not include all of B). We say that f maps D into B.

Now return to the context of formal logic and quantification theory. Suppose that U is the "universe" of individuals x over which individual variables range, and that $H(x)$ is a predicate in our logic. If we know all the values x for which $H(x)$ is true, we have fully described the behavior of H. Suppose we specify a function h such that, for all x in the universe U, $h(x) =$ T if and only if $H(x)$ is true. If $H(x)$ is false, we make $h(x) =$ F.

For example, suppose that the universe U has only three individuals, a, b, and c. Suppose further that $H(a)$ is true, $H(b)$ is false, and $H(c)$ is false. The corresponding function h is then to be defined so that $h(a) =$ T, $h(b) =$ F, and $h(c) =$ F. The function h has all the information that we need about the predicate H. It is simply that we have represented the information in a different form. While H is a one-place predicate, h is a function with U as its domain. It maps U into the special set $S = \{T, F\}$. We write $h: U \to S$.

Given such a function h, we can exactly reconstruct the corresponding predicate H. Similarly, corresponding to each predicate of the form $G(x)$ we have a function $g: U \to S$ that completely specifies the truth values of $G(x)$ for all x. Thus, each predicate can be represented as a function.

What about multi-place predicates? For a k-place predicate symbol $G(x_1, \ldots, x_k)$ we can specify a function $g(x_1, \ldots, x_k)$ with k variables, whose values are in $S = \{T, F\}$:

$G(x_1, \dots, x_k)$ is true if and only if $g(x_1, \dots, x_k) = \text{T}$.

In sum, predicates can be represented as functions, and functions can be represented as predicates. The two serve as perspectives on each other. One or the other kind of representation may be more convenient depending on context. As usual, these perspectives have their ultimate foundation in the unity and diversity of the Trinity. Their unity is expressed in the fact that they represent the *same* information. Their diversity is expressed in the choice of two different notations and two distinct clusters of extra information that must be supplied to interpret properly the meaning.

Theistic Foundations for Functions

We introduce functions into logical systems because functions, or their less-formalized analogues, exist in other contexts. We have already observed that ordinary addition (+) and multiplication (×) on numbers are functions. The expression "the capital of" can be regarded as being something like a function that takes a country of the world as an input and produces the capital of that country as output. Similarly, "the father of" or "the mother of" is like a function. God created not only things in the world but also structure. There are relationships of a multitude of kinds, and these relationships are planned and ordained and controlled by God. The multidimensional relationships in the world are reduced to one-dimensional relationships in formal logic. And multidimensional functions are reduced to one-dimensional functions in formal logic. God also has provided us with the ability to think, and he has ordained the relationships between the multidimensional world and its one-dimensional analogues within the realm of formal logic. All the riches of the intellectual world, as well as the creatures in the world, come from God and his plan.

We also know, in the area of functions as well as in all other areas, that we must reckon with the Creator-creature distinction. Relationships and functions exist among creatures in the created world. Do relationships and functions exist in God as well? Clearly relationships exist. We have had many occasions to reflect on the relationships among the persons in the Trinity. The Father is Father to the Son. The Father loves the Son and the Spirit. The Spirit is sent by the Father in an eternal sending. These relationships are *uncreated*. They are eternal. They are also archetypal. They are the original relationships, and so they are the ultimate foundation for relationships among creatures.

We can be even more specific: relationships among creatures are specified by God. He does so by speaking his word. And when he speaks, he speaks in accord with his eternal Word. So we can see that relationships among creatures have a specific foundation in divine speech, and that divine speech involves eternal relationships among the persons of the Trinity. Each person of the Trinity participates distinctively in divine speech, and the persons enjoy distinctive *relationships* with one another in the act of speaking. These relationships are thus an archetypal foundation for relations among creatures, and also for relations between God and creatures (especially, the relation between God and human beings).

The correlation between functions and relations, which we have seen earlier, has a theistic foundation, as we would expect. God the Father is Father to the Son. The Father is the Father-of the Son. "Father-of" is an archetypal function. Starting with the Son, and looking for his Father, we arrive at the Father. Because there is only one eternal Son, "Son-of" is also a function. Starting with the Father, and looking for his Son, we arrive at the Son.

It is easier to see an archetypal foundation for functions by considering the fact that the Son is "the image of the invisible God" (Col. 1:15), "the exact imprint of his nature" (Heb. 1:3). The expressions "image" and "exact imprint" imply a panoply of correlations between God the Father and God the Son. What God is, is revealed in the Son. So we have correlations: God the Father is righteous, holy, loving, all-knowing, eternal, and all-powerful. The Son likewise, as his image, is righteous, holy, loving, all-knowing, eternal, and all-powerful. We have here relations between attributes of the Father and attributes of the Son. We can say, with an archetypal use of the word *function*, that one is a function of the other. All functional relations that we see in our minds, whether they belong directly to God's revelation of himself, or to aspects of created things, derive from this original (archetype).

God reveals his eternal power and divine nature (Rom. 1:20). His power is revealed in his specifying of all relationships by his word. All functions, whether functional relationships among creatures or formal functions within mathematics or logic, reveal God's eternal power and divine nature. Let us give thanks, and praise his glory!

For Further Reflection

1. Define some extra symbols, if necessary, and then, using a function, represent in symbolic notation the proposition "Monica is the mother of Augustine."
2. With the universe of individuals {2,3,4}, (a) represent the predicate "is even" as a one-place predicate; (b) represent "is even" as a function; (c) represent the two-place predicate "is less than" (<) as a function; (c) represent the function $f(2) = 3$, $f(3) = 4$, $f(4) = 2$ as a predicate.
3. What are the advantages and disadvantages of including functions in a formal system with quantification?
4. What is left out when we move from relationships in the world to formalized functions?
5. In what way do functions have an archetype in God?
6. Prove that $2 + 1 = 3$ and $2 + 3 = 5$ together imply $2 + (2 + 1) = 5$. (What axiom do you appeal to?)

Part III.D

Introducing Formal Systems

Chapter 54

Troubles in Mathematics

So far we have examined two different systems of symbolic logic: first the system of propositional logic, and then a more complicated system of quantificational logic, which includes predicate logic. In both of these cases, simple axioms and deduction rules make it possible to derive all the "right" propositions, that is, the propositions that are always true. (The systems are complete.) At the same time, the systems avoid deriving any "bad" propositions that are not always true, or deriving a contradiction. (The systems are sound.) All seems to be well in the "house" of logic built by these systems.

We have seen in part I.C how we have to qualify the way in which these artificially simplified and reduced systems relate to the world that God has made and to God himself in his self-consistency. Yet, still, when we take into account these qualifications, the systems of propositional logic and first-order quantificational logic are impressive and beautiful. Their impressiveness and beauty reflects the majesty and beauty of God.

Non-Euclidean Geometry

But the course of history has shown that there are problems in the wings. These have come to light primarily in connection with work in mathematics. Mathematics is a broader area of study that uses logic. Mathematics, like formal logic, has traditionally aspired to have complete certainty and necessity in its results.

For centuries, Euclidean geometry was regarded as a model of logic and certainty. The Greek mathematician Euclid in about 300 BC summarized the results of previous generations of mathematicians in his book *Elements*.[1] His book showed how to derive theorems in geometry by deducing them from a few starting postulates. His postulates play a role like the axioms in a formal logical system. The theorems followed by necessity from the postulates.[2]

[1] The work exists in many modern editions: e.g., Euclid, *Euclid's Elements*, ed. Dana Densmore, trans. T. L. Heath (Santa Fe, NM: Green Lion, 2002).
[2] In the nineteenth century mathematicians found that Euclid's postulates needed to be supplemented by some additional postulates that he used without realizing it. See, e.g., Roberto Torretti, "Nineteenth Cen-

But one of the postulates raised questions. It was Euclid's "parallel postulate." The parallel postulate says that given any line L and any point P not on the line, one and only one line M can be drawn through P such that M is parallel to L, that is, such that M does not intersect L[3] (see figure 54.1):

Fig. 54.1: Nonparallels versus One Parallel

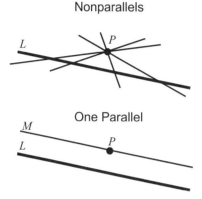

It seemed to the ancient Greeks, from just looking at the possibilities, that the parallel postulate must be true. But it was less obvious than Euclid's other postulates. So attempts were made to derive it from the remaining postulates. Those attempts were unsuccessful.

Finally, in the nineteenth century, the mathematicians Johann C. F. Gauss, János Bolyai, and Nikolai Lobachevsky independently showed that alternatives to the parallel postulate could lead to consistent results.[4] In one form of geometry, which can be represented with "lines" that are great circles on a sphere, there are no parallel lines at all. All lines intersect. In another form of geometry there are an infinite number of lines M that do not intersect L.

This result was disturbing enough. But things got worse for those who

---

tury Geometry," *Stanford Encyclopedia of Philosophy (Summer 2010 Edition)*, ed. Edward N. Zalta, http://plato.stanford.edu/archives/sum2010/entries/geometry-19th/, accessed August 26, 2011, §4; David Hilbert, *The Foundations of Geometry*, trans. E. J. Townsend (reprint; La Salle, IL: Open Court, 1950), online at http://www.gutenberg.org/files/17384/17384-pdf.pdf, accessed August 25, 2011).

[3] The parallel postulate comes in several forms, not all of which are completely equivalent. We have chosen one, which is not precisely the formulation that Euclid himself used.

[4] Roberto Torretti, "Geometry," in *Encyclopedia of Philosophy*, ed. Donald M. Borchert, 2nd. ed., 10 vols. (Detroit/New York/San Francisco/ . . . : Thomson Gale, 2006), 4:58–59; Torretti, "Nineteenth Century Geometry," §1. Earlier, Gerolamo Saccheri (1667–1733) attempted to derive the parallel postulate by assuming the contrary and trying to deduce a contradiction (using the principle of *reductio ad absurdum*). He discovered many results in non-Euclidean geometry, but found them so counterintuitive that it is disputed whether he saw them as *positive* results in a new kind of geometry rather than merely results whose counterintuitive character seemingly confirmed Euclidean geometry.

longed for traditional security. In 1915 Albert Einstein proposed his general theory of relativity. It theorized that physical space and time in our actual universe could be "curved" and show properties belonging to these alternate "geometries." In 1919 the general theory of relativity was first confirmed experimentally by observing the bending of starlight as it traveled close to the sun during a total solar eclipse. When applied to the physical world, the parallel postulate turned out to be not only unprovable but also false.

These developments raised questions about the security of conventional mathematics. If the parallel postulate could fall to the ground, how do we know that other postulates or axioms are secure?

Calculus

At least in the area of arithmetic, all seemed to go well. But there were difficulties that gradually dawned. Calculus, as originally formulated by Sir Isaac Newton and Gottfried Leibniz, dealt with infinities. And in the early days, before it was put on a more rigorous basis, these infinities could lead to erroneous results.[5] Calculus was obviously useful, and no mathematician wanted to give it up. But how were we supposed to protect ourselves from the erroneous results?

Mathematicians and logicians began to be concerned to place the practice of mathematics on a more secure basis. One important work was by Gottlob Frege, who attempted to derive all the laws of arithmetic starting with axioms from logic. But Bertrand Russell discovered that Frege's axioms led to contradiction. (For details, see appendix A1, under "Russell's Paradox.")

Hilbert's Program

The German mathematician David Hilbert wanted to see mathematics established on a certain foundation. He proposed to achieve this result by reducing mathematics to axioms and rules of deduction, and then showing that the axioms and rules could never lead to a contradiction. In 1900 he proposed to achieve this result by watching the way that the axioms and

---

[5] A simple example comes from considering the infinite series $1 - 1 + 1 - 1 + 1 - 1 + \ldots$. What is its sum $s = 1 - 1 + 1 - 1 + \ldots$? If we group numbers together, we can get $s = (1 - 1) + (1 - 1) + (1 - 1) + \ldots = 0 + 0 + 0 + \ldots = 0$. But we can also group them in a second way: $s = 1 - (1 - 1) - (1 - 1) - (1 - 1) - \ldots = 1 - 0 - 0 - 0 - \ldots = 1$. We can also write $s = 1 - (1 - 1 + 1 - 1 + 1 - 1 + \ldots)$. The expression within the parentheses is the same as s. So $s = 1 - s$. Solving for s, $s + s = 1 - s + s$. $2s = 1$. $s = 1/2$. With the order $1 - 1 + 1 - 1 + \ldots$ with which we started, the sum of any odd number of terms is 1, and the sum of any even number of terms is 0. The sums oscillate between 1 and 0; they never *converge* to any particular value. So the infinite sum s simply is not defined.

rules functioned in proofs, rather than by merely looking at the *meaning* of the axioms.

We can use as an example our discussion of the soundness of propositional logic (chapter 44). We can establish, using truth tables, that each of the axioms is a tautology. Then we test whether the rules of deduction always lead to more tautologies. These two steps both inspect characteristics of the axioms and the rules of deduction, rather than focusing on the *meaning* of the axioms when they are applied to situations in the real world. Together, the steps reassure us that propositional logic proves only tautologies and never leads to a contradiction. A logical system that never deduces a proposition p and its opposite $\sim p$ is called *consistent*.

We can never establish consistency without using some assumptions. In this case, we have to assume that we know what we are talking about when we use the tables for truth functions. And we actually use mathematical induction as well (chapter 45). But Hilbert hoped that the consistency of large parts of mathematics might be established using only a minimal starting point, such as arithmetic.

Establishing the Consistency of First-order Quantification Theory

We can give another example of establishing consistency that helps to illustrate what Hilbert desired. We may attempt to confirm the consistency of our quantification theory (part III.B), assuming the consistency of propositional logic. By so doing, we reassure ourselves about the soundness of a more complex theory on the basis of a simpler one.

We can be assured of the consistency of our quantification theory by reducing everything back to "bare bones," as it were.[6] Suppose a is an individual constant. For any predicate $F(x)$ with one variable, we look at a transition in which we replace the variable x by a. We obtain $F(a)$. For multi-place predicates $K(x, y, z)$, replace all the variables by a, obtaining $K(a, a, a)$. For a quantifier $(\forall x)G(x, y)$ erase the quantifier $(\forall x)$ itself and replace all instances of the variable x (and other variables) by a. So $(\forall x)G(x, y)$ becomes $G(a, a)$. Because the expression $(\exists x)$ is defined as $\sim(\forall x)\sim$, $(\exists x) G(x, y)$ becomes $\sim(\forall x)\sim G(x, y)$, which reduces to $\sim\sim G(a, a)$.

In this way, we can reduce any propositional function $\varphi(x)$, of whatever complexity, to a proposition $\varphi_r(a)$ with no quantifiers and no variables. The

---

[6] Our method is similar to that in Irving M. Copi, *Symbolic Logic*, 5th ed. (New York: Macmillan, 1979), 295.

expression φ_r (with the special subscript r) denotes the propositional function φ with all the quantifiers stripped out. Each predicate $G(x, y, z)$ within φ reduces within φ_r to a proposition $G(a, a, a)$ which is true in all of its occurrences, or else false in all its occurrences. $G(a, a, a)$ functions for all essential purposes as if it were a simple, atomic proposition p. We essentially reduce quantification theory to simple predicate logic by "smashing out" all the variables. Or we can go a further stage, and reduce the predicates $G(a, a, a)$ to simple propositions $p, q, \ldots$, by substituting a distinct propositional symbol p for each distinct predicate G (more precisely, we substitute p for $G(a, a, a)$). We get a further reduction of φ_r to φ_{r2}.

Now we are ready to derive the consistency of quantification theory from the consistency of simple propositional logic. We do it by *reductio ad absurdum*. Suppose quantification theory is inconsistent. By definition, inconsistency means that there is a proof within quantification theory of some proposition φ and also its negation $\sim\varphi$. We repeat the exact same proof, line by line, smashing out all the quantifiers and replacing all the predicates with propositional symbols. The proof still conforms to the required rules of deduction. The resulting proof is a proof that uses only the axioms of propositional logic and that results in theorems in propositional logic. So now we have a proof that φ_{r2} and that $\sim \varphi_{r2}$. That is, we have deduced a contradiction *within* propositional logic. Since we already know from chapter 44 that propositional logic is consistent, this is impossible. Hence, by *reductio ad absurdum*, the initial assumption is incorrect. We cannot have a proof within quantification theory of both φ and $\sim\varphi$. So quantification theory is consistent.

For Further Reflection

1. What was troubling about non-Euclidean geometry?
2. What difficulties arose when calculus was first developed?
3. How did David Hilbert propose to go about establishing a secure foundation for mathematics?
4. What do we have to assume to deduce the consistency of quantification theory? What does the presence of assumptions have to say about the prospect of finding an ultimate secure foundation?

Chapter 55

Axiomatizing Mathematics

Hilbert, we said, wanted to see mathematics converted to an axiomatic system, and then to show that the resulting system was first of all consistent, but then also complete. Just as we have established the consistency of our quantification theory on the basis of the consistency of propositional logic, maybe the consistency of mathematics as a whole could be established using some smaller piece, such as quantification theory.

The Role of Mathematical Induction

But quantification theory alone will not actually suffice. Without making it completely explicit, we have actually used the principle of mathematical induction a number of times in our arguments. The idea of converting from one kind of proof to another contains within itself the idea of a proof consisting of any number n of steps. To make explicit all the steps in our reasoning, we would have to use mathematical induction on the number of steps. We first establish that a principle holds for a proof that is one step long. And then, assuming that a principle holds for a proof n steps long or less, we show it must hold for a proof $n + 1$ steps long. We have to use numbers in keeping track of proofs. So the number system has a key role.

Could we then establish consistency of mathematics using arithmetic, but nothing more complicated? Hilbert thought it was an achievable goal, because the characteristics of proofs could be described using numbers.

Kurt Gödel and Incompleteness

It came as a shock when mathematicians found out that proving consistency or completeness by such means is impossible. The shock was produced by the mathematician Kurt Gödel in 1931.[1] Gödel presented a proof that

---

[1] Kurt Gödel, "Über formal unentscheidbare Sätze der *Principia Mathematica* und verwandter Systeme, I," *Monatshefte für Mathematik und Physik* 38 (1931): 173–198; translated into English in a number of places. See, e.g., Kurt Gödel, *On Formally Undecidable Propositions of* Principia Mathematica *and Related Systems*, trans. B. Meltzer (New York: Dover, 1992); see also Martin Hirzel, translator, "On Formally Undecidable Propositions of *Principia Mathematica* and Related Systems," online at http://www.research.ibm.com/

showed that if we had a system with axioms for arithmetic, and if the axioms could themselves be enumerated, it was possible to produce a formula G in arithmetic that was true but not provable.[2] That is, it would not be provable if the axioms themselves were consistent. (If they were inconsistent, any formula whatsoever could be proved.) As a result, we know that it is not possible to enumerate a set of axioms that would be complete. Any ordinary set of axioms for arithmetic is *incomplete* in the logical sense.

The naive response to this claim might be to try to add a new axiom to remove the incompleteness. The new axiom will be the formula G that Gödel showed to be unprovable but true. If the formula G is treated as an axiom, in addition to the axioms already in use in the system, G is automatically a theorem (after all, any axiom is automatically a theorem, because we can "prove" it in one line). So then, in the new, altered system, the formula G would be provable as well as true. Would this take care of the problem of incompleteness?

But Gödel's proof is more subtle. He has a recipe that starts with the list of axioms for a given system. Given those axioms, his recipe builds up the formula G. If we add a new axiom, namely, G, the overall situation has changed. The recipe must include this new axiom in its reckoning. The recipe then produces a new formula, say G_2. So do we add G_2 as an axiom? If we do, the recipe produces still another formula, G_3. And so on. Each formula is unprovable in the system comprised by the axioms of the preceding system. We never achieve completeness.

By a second step Gödel showed that if the system for arithmetic contains axioms powerful enough to include a reasonable part of arithmetic and theory of numbers, it can prove its own consistency only if it is inconsistent.

Other mathematicians have since offered proofs of the consistency of arithmetic.[3] But the proofs take place within mathematical systems that not only include arithmetic but are more powerful than arithmetic. So the hope of building up mathematics from a simple, stable foundation is frustrated.

people/h/hirzel/papers/canon00-goedel.pdf, accessed January 18, 2011. But Gödel's original work is hard for the uninitiated to digest. It is better to approach it by way of the simpler, "stripped-down" explanations that are offered both online and in print.

[2] Gödel actually achieved his result for one specific system, namely, Whitehead and Russell's axiomatic system for arithmetic. But he commented that the same procedure would work for any system that included a sufficient amount of arithmetic. Barkley Rosser in 1936 showed that Gödel's assumption of a stronger form of consistency for the axioms could be reduced to normal consistency (no proof of both p and $\sim p$). For the sake of simplicity we leave aside these details.

[3] Jan von Plato, "The Development of Proof Theory," *Stanford Encyclopedia of Philosophy (Summer 2010 Edition)*, ed. Edward N. Zalta, http://plato.stanford.edu/archives/sum2010/entries/proof-theory-development/, accessed August 26, 2011, §5; Wolfram Pohlers, *Proof Theory: An Introduction* (New York: Springer, 1989), 7–76.

Studying Proofs

Gödel's results give people extra motivation for studying logical systems and the proofs that these systems produce. What is provable cannot necessarily be equated with what is true. So it is not enough to study what is provable from the axioms. *As a separate task*, we have to ask what is true. We know that, whatever list of axioms we start with, there will always be some always-true propositions that are beyond the scope of what is provable.

The methods that Gödel used to achieve his results also give us an extra motivation. His methods involve a process of looking at how proofs are constructed. So his methods themselves indicate one of the benefits of studying proofs.

Gödel's approach is subtle and complex. We will not get into all the details. But some of the key turning points are worth noting. (For more details, see appendix D1.)

First, Gödel specified a way to represent any propositional function by a natural number. He produced his specification by treating each propositional function as if it were merely a sequence of meaningless elementary symbols. These elementary symbols would include the symbols ∨, ~, ∀, of course. Gödel also included parentheses symbols, (), in order to specify the groupings of elements. The symbols also include individual variables x, y, z, etc. The logical system being examined can include still other symbols, as long as we specify exactly what they are. (We do not need to include symbols for logical conjunction ∧ and material implication ⊃, because we can agree that these extra symbols are "shorthand" for propositional functions constructed from the symbols ∨, ~, and ∀.)

The process of "encoding" any propositional function starts with the elementary symbols that are used to write out the propositional function. Each elementary symbol is encoded by a number. Then the whole series of symbols, taken as a whole, is encoded in a second number, which specifies which symbols occur in which order. Given a propositional function and Gödel's recipe, anyone can calculate the number that encodes the propositional function. Conversely, given the number, anyone can, with the help of a certain amount of numerical processing, read back out from the number all the information needed to reconstruct the series of symbols that the number encodes. The number in question is called the Gödel number of the propositional function, in honor of Gödel's achievement.

In a similar manner, one can construct a way of encoding a whole proof in a single number in such a way that the proof can be reconstructed from the number. The number in question is called the Gödel number of the proof. (See appendix D1.)

Given this representation of proofs using numbers, one can formulate *using numbers* what it means for a proposition to be provable. And then, if the logical system that one is studying contains enough resources to deal with arithmetic, one can express this very property of provability *inside* the system being studied. As a final stage, Gödel exhibited a particular formula G within the logical system whose real meaning outside the system is "I am unprovable (within the system)."

This state of affairs sounds paradoxical. But it is protected from being nonsense by the careful distinction between the logical system being studied and the numerical representation in Gödel numbers that one uses in doing the studying.

Nevertheless, consequences do follow. Suppose that, inside the logical system, we could succeed in finding a proof for G. Then from that proof we could construct the Gödel number of the proof. And the Gödel number would provide a counterexample to the numerical property "I am unprovable." Thus, from outside the system, we can see that G is indeed unprovable (if the logical system is consistent). Since it is unprovable, and its meaning (from outside the system) is to say that it is unprovable, it says what is true. The proposition G is thus both unprovable and true. So we have found a true proposition that is unprovable within the logical system. The system is incomplete.

Formal Systems

This whole process works only if, at the start, we have a clear distinction between the logical system being studied and the way in which we talk about it, using numbers to represent the propositional functions. The logical system we are studying is called a *formal system* or *logical calculus*. When we study such a system we use ordinary language. But we can also, in our study, use pieces of formal logic or arithmetic. Gödel did so by constructing numerical functions representing numerical properties. These numerical functions use numbers and their properties to represent the behavior of the formulas inside the formal system. Gödel then engaged in logical reasoning concerning these numerical properties, and produced theorems about the numerical properties. Such pieces of formal logic or arithmetic or set theory, if they are complex, can be regarded as constituting a *metalanguage*, that is, a language for talking about the language under investigation.

The formal language and the metalanguage in which we discuss it must be kept distinct in our minds. At the same time, there are two tight correspondences between the formal language and the metalanguage. One correspondence is expressed by Gödel numbers. Each formula in the formal system corresponds to a specific Gödel number, namely, the Gödel number of the formula. When we are studying the formal properties of the formal system, we may convert formulas into numbers and back, and we may map properties of formulas and proofs into properties of numbers.

The other correspondence is a correspondence in meaning. It consists in direct translation of the *meaning* of the symbols and formulas in the formal language, when we treat those symbols and formulas as corresponding to the meaning of the corresponding symbolic expressions in the metalanguage.

The presence of two distinct correspondences, plus the ability within number theory to represent the basic properties of proofs, allows us to construct a formula within the system whose meaning (outside the system) is to assert its own unprovability (unprovable within the system).

Larger Implications

Gödel's results were frustrating to people who had hoped to have a complete set of axioms that could lead to all mathematical truth. It *permanently* closed the door to the hope of completely reducing mathematics to logic, by providing a logically airtight proof that such a reduction could not be achieved. It also implied that human beings could never achieve exhaustive mastery of numbers. Finally, it showed that formal representations of the reasoning in mathematics always fell short of the imitative transcendence of human beings. In other words, it indirectly showed something about transcendence—that mathematics "transcends" logical axioms, in some sense. It also implies that human beings transcend formal representations of mathematical truth, and that God transcends human beings (because he knows the truths of mathematics that we do not access).

For Further Reflection

1. What is meant by a Gödel number of a formula?
2. Why did David Hilbert and others want to prove the consistency of mathematics? How did they hope to achieve this goal? Why is the goal not attainable except by using systems more powerful than the ones that one hopes to prove consistent?
3. What is a metalanguage?
4. On what two systems of correspondence between a formal language and a metalanguage did Gödel rely?
5. What may be the theological significance of Gödel's incompleteness theorems?

Chapter 56

Studying Proofs

We can now take a few steps in exploring the study of proofs. This study has developed into a complex field, called *proof theory*, in which we will take only a few preliminary steps. But these steps may help us to see how God shows his glory in this field of study.

Formal Language

In the previous chapter we have already considered the idea of a formal language and a formal system. But we have not yet given precise definitions. Precise definitions are needed if we are going to make a clear distinction between formal language and metalanguage, including ordinary language.

A *formal language* consists of two pieces: (a) a list of elementary symbols or characters a, b, c, etc.; and (b) rules for putting these characters into strings in specific ways. Let us begin with the idea of a string of characters. A string is simply an ordered list of one or more of the characters. The characters are simply written one after the other. If 0, S, (,), ~, and = are the characters or elementary symbols, the following are possible strings:

```
000
0((S
)=~=
=0~
```

However, *A* and *SA* and *(0A0000)* are not permissible strings, because *A* is not one of the characters.

(These symbols and others are used in appendix D1 in discussing Gödel's incompleteness theorem. When meaning is later given to them, *0* stands for the number zero and *S* stands for the successor function $S(n) = n + 1$ for any number n.)

The list of characters can be finite or infinite. Only a finite number of characters can occur in any one string. But strings can be as long as we like. So for some purposes it may be useful to have an infinite number of elementary symbols, in order to make sure that we never run out. Any particular formal language specifies exactly which elementary symbols belong to its list.

Well-formed Formulas

Not all strings are of equal interest. Any formal language has rules for putting its characters together in precise ways to produce those strings that are going to be the focus of attention. The strings that are singled out for interest are called *well-formed formulas*. The formal language must include rules specifying which strings are well-formed formulas. And these rules must be precise. It is usually required that a suitably written computer program could decide whether any particular string is a well-formed formula. Because the concept of a well-formed formula is so important, the literature in logic often uses a standard abbreviation: *wff* is short for "well-formed formula."

Now let us illustrate with a particular case of a simple formal language. Let x and y represent strings made up wholly of these characters: $\lor \sim ( ) p \ q \ r \ s \ t$. Some but not all of the strings x and y will be well-formed formulas. Which ones? First, we specify that the string consisting of a single character p, q, r, s, or t is a well-formed formula (wff). We also have to specify how, given a simpler well-formed formula x, we may construct a more complex one. One of our rules will be to say that if x is a well-formed formula, so is $\sim x$. That is, if we start with a well-formed formula x, we can produce a second, new well-formed formula by prefixing the character tilde $\sim$ to the string x. For example, since p is a well-formed formula, so is $\sim p$. So also is $\sim q$. So are $\sim\sim q$ and $\sim\sim\sim\sim q$.

Here now is the complete set of rules for producing well-formed formulas:

(1) p, q, r, s, and t are well-formed formulas (wffs).
(2) If x is a well-formed formula, $\sim x$ is a well-formed formula.
(3) If x and y are well-formed formulas, $(x \lor y)$ is a well-formed formula.

Using these rules, we can construct complex formulas that are well-formed.

$\sim p$
$\sim\sim p$
$\sim\sim\sim\sim\sim p$
$\sim(p \lor \sim q)$
$((p \lor r) \lor \sim\sim p)$
$(((p \lor r) \lor t) \lor \sim(s \lor \sim(\sim(p \lor r) \lor \sim\sim\sim p)))$

We can also tell when something is not a well-formed formula:

$a=$
$\lor\ p()$
$p \lor r$

The last item in the list, $p \lor r$, is not a well-formed formula because it does not include the necessary open and closed parentheses. By contrast, $(p \lor r)$ is a well-formed formula.

We can already see the relevance of formal languages to symbolic logic. We have been working with semi-formalized languages when we discussed propositional logic and quantificational logic. But the symbol system that we used was not completely formalized. We used substitutes like brackets [] for parentheses () when it seemed convenient. On occasion, we omitted parentheses when they were unnecessary. We did not exactly specify which symbols p, q, r, etc. could be used to represent propositions. A formal language, technically, allows no such imprecision. Everything must be "strictly by the book"—strictly formal.

Formal Systems

In proof theory, we are interested not in all formal languages, but in *formal systems*. A *formal system* is a formal language with some extra structure added to it. The extra structure consists in two pieces: (1) a list of axioms and (2) a list of rules for producing proofs (rules for deduction).

Let us consider the first piece, the list of axioms. Each axiom must be a well-formed formula. But normally the list of axioms includes only a few kinds of well-formed formulas, not all wffs. The list of axioms can be either finite or infinite. If the list is infinite, it is usually required that they must be specifiable according to some pattern.[1] For example, for one particular formal system, we might specify that $(\sim(x \lor x) \lor x)$ is an axiom whenever x is a well-formed formula. This specification generates an infinite number of axioms, since there are infinitely many well-formed formulas that could be plugged into the place of x. The specification makes it clear which formulas are axioms.

It is most common in formal systems to have an infinite number of

---

[1] Again, the appeal to computer programs is useful. A suitably written computer program must be able to determine whether or not any particular well-formed formula is an axiom. Such a collection of axioms is called "decidable" because the computer program can decide for certain whether a particular well-formed formula is an axiom.

axioms, described by an axiom schema of the type $(\sim(x \vee x) \vee x)$. In this way we avoid having to add a rule of substitution as an extra rule within the formal system.

In a formal system the second piece of added structure is the list of rules for deduction. Typically, for the sake of study, there is only one main rule, namely, *modus ponens*. But others may be added when we deal with more complex systems. The rule of universal generalization and the rule for mathematical induction are such rules.

A *proof* within a formal system is a series of well-formed formulas p_1, p_2, p_3, ..., p_n, such that each p_i is either (1) an axiom or (2) deducible (using the rules for deduction) from one or more of the preceding formulas in the series.

The well-formed formulas that can be proved using the axioms and the rules of deduction are said to be *provable* within the formal system. A well-formed formula that has been proved is called a *theorem*.

A Simple Formal System

As a start, we will define a simple formal system L. We are going to specify exactly what the formal system L is by specifying both the formal language and the added structure. The formal language for L has to be specified by providing two pieces, (a) the list of elementary symbols and (b) the rules for well-formed formulas. The first step (a) is to specify the elementary symbols. The elementary symbols or characters are as follows: $\vee \sim (\ ) P_1 P_2 P_3 P_4 \ldots$. The characters P_1, P_2, etc. are intended to stand for propositions. But what they "stand for" is not specified when we introduce the formal system L. The formal system has these characters, independent of any interpretation that we later give to them. As the next step (b), we must specify the rules for forming well-formed formulas. The first rule is

Each P_i is a well-formed formula (wff).

The other rules for well-formed formulas are like those already given in the previous example.

If p is a wff, so is $\sim p$.
If p and q are wffs, so is $(p \vee q)$.

Note that p and q are *not* characters within the formal system. They are symbols within our metalanguage, in which we describe the system. p and q

stand for any wff made up of characters within the system. The only minimal well-formed formulas within the system are P_1, P_2, P_3, ... The symbol p itself is not a well-formed formula (wff). It *stands for* something that is a well-formed formula. The starting well-formed formulas P_i are called *atomic formulas* because, within the formal language, they have no "inner structure." They cannot be pulled apart or further analyzed.

Here are some well-formed formulas in the formal system L:

P_3
P_7
$\sim P_1$
$(P_3 \vee P_2)$
$\sim\sim(P_4 \vee \sim P_9)$
$\sim(((\sim(P_3 \vee P_2) \vee P_3) \vee \sim P_1) \vee (\sim\sim P_4 \vee P_5))$

The only deduction rule is *modus ponens*. The rule runs as follows:

For any well-formed formulas p and q, if p and $(\sim p \vee q)$ are lines in a proof, you may deduce q.

This rule is the same form of *modus ponens* used in Whitehead and Russell's system. The symbol $\supset$ is not an elementary symbol in this formal system L. Neither is it an elementary symbol in Whitehead and Russell's system. So it cannot be used in describing *modus ponens* within the formal system. But it can be defined as a kind of shorthand:

For any well-formed formulas x and y, $(x \supset y)$ is shorthand for $(\sim x \vee y)$.

This "shorthand" is *not* part of the formal system. But it is convenient for us when we talk about the system from outside. It is convenient, in other words, in our metalanguage.

What are the axioms in this formal system? Anything we like. If we view the formal system L as purely formal, it is just a game with rules. It is up to us what rules we choose. The system does not have to correspond to anything in the real world. It does not have to be consistent, and its axioms do not have to be true when interpreted according to standard meanings for the formal symbols. As long as the system is purely formal, it does not "mean" anything.

But of course most of the interest lies not merely in the game-like character of the formal system, but in the possibility that later on we may attach meaning to the symbols and the axioms. So it is natural to think first of all of the possibility of using as axioms all the axioms of Whitehead and Russell's system of propositional logic. Let us begin with their first axiom:

A1: For all well-formed formulas p, $((p \lor p) \supset p)$ is an axiom.

Remember that $\supset$ is shorthand. With the shorthand removed, A1 "really says":

A1: For all well-formed formulas p, $(\sim(p \lor p) \lor p)$ is an axiom.

Since we are describing the axioms in our metalanguage, it is okay to use $\supset$ as shorthand. A1 is called an *axiom schema* rather than an axiom, because it specifies an infinite number of axioms, one for each well-formed formula p. Since we understand that we are dealing with all well-formed formulas p, we can write simply:

A1: $((p \lor p) \supset p)$ is an axiom.

Here are the rest of the axioms for Whitehead and Russell's propositional logic:

A2: $(q \supset (p \lor q))$ is an axiom.
A3: $((p \lor q) \supset (q \lor p))$ is an axiom.
A4: $((p \lor (q \lor r)) \supset (q \lor (p \lor r)))$ is an axiom.
A5: $((q \supset r) \supset ((p \lor q) \supset (p \lor r)))$ is an axiom.

If we like, we can add more axioms in addition to A1, A2, A3, A4, and A5. Adding axioms would make it easier to prove theorems. But we would have to be careful. If we add an axiom that is the negation of a tautology, say $\sim q$, then we would find that we could prove both q and $\sim q$, which is a contradiction. We can give a general definition:

A formal system L is *inconsistent* if there is some well-formed formula q such that q and $\sim q$ can be proved within L.

In any formal system that we intend eventually to apply to the real world, inconsistency is unacceptable. It means the complete failure of the system to represent logical truth. But in theory we can contemplate the possibility of a formal system in which, either by accident or deliberately, we introduce axioms that make the system inconsistent. When we "play the game" of examining a formal system, we can study either a consistent system or an inconsistent one. The choice is ours. When later we come to give meaning to the symbols in some application to the world, the inconsistent systems turn out to be uninteresting, because they do not succeed in distinguishing between true and false propositions.

We can also weaken the system if we stipulate that only *some* of the well-formed formulas A1, A2, A3, A4, and A5 are axioms. It is up to us what we choose as axioms (as long as the system is treated as purely formal).

We illustrate the development of this formal system and the study of its proofs in appendix D2. There are some specific payoffs. We can show that the rules for natural deduction that we developed in chapter 42 can be derived if we assume A1, A2, A3, and A5. From these rules or directly from A1, A2, A3, and A5 we may prove A4. Thus A4 itself is not needed as an axiom schema within the formal system.

For Further Reflection

1. What is a formal language?
2. What is a formal system?
3. Which of the following are well-formed formulas of the formal language *L* described above?
   a. $((P_2$
   b. (P_2)
   c. $\sim P_3$
   d. $(\sim P_1 \vee P_8)$
   e. $(\sim P_1 \vee P_8) \vee P_2$
4. What does it mean to say that a formal system is inconsistent?
5. Why would people want to study formal systems?

Chapter 57

Theistic Foundations for Proof Theory

What does this study of formal systems and proofs have to do with God? In a sense, a formal system like the example *L* in the previous chapter simply repeats what we have already done *informally* when we discussed Whitehead and Russell's system for propositional logic. We can repeat what we said earlier about the revelation of God's glory in truth functions, axioms, and propositional logic. We can also repeat what we said about the *limitations* that formal logic has in comparison with natural language. We need to be aware of sinful temptations to autonomy that crop up when people use formal logic in an overreaching manner or in a context where they deny the Creator-creature distinction.

Evaporating Meaning

In a sense, then, nothing is different. But in another sense there is a subtle but significant difference. In a formal system, we are taking another step in "evaporating" meaning out of the symbols. We can treat the characters or elementary symbols *as if* they were just markers that have to be manipulated according to specific rules. The formalizing of the rules means that we do not have to know what is the meaning of the character ~ or ∨ or left-parenthesis '(' in order to manipulate them. We could write a computer program to manipulate them according to the rules. A program could be written that would test whether a string fed in as input was a well-formed formula. A second program could test whether any series of well-formed formulas was a proof. The programs would not have to know the meaning of the characters.

We can illustrate by considering a change of notation. Suppose that we use *N* (for "not") instead of ~, and *O* (for "or") instead of ∨. We use *B* ("begin") instead of left parenthesis '(' and *E* ("end") instead of right parenthesis ')'. Then we specify:

If *p* is a wff, N *p* is a wff.

If *p* and *q* are wffs, B *p* O *q* E is a wff.

This new notation accomplishes the same thing as before. The formal system will be essentially the same whether or not we are told in the metalanguage what meaning will eventually be assigned to the characters.

Once we have evaporated meaning, or forgotten meaning, a formal system is simply a kind of game. We play the game by following the rules. And the goal of the game is to see what kind of strings we can produce as a result of following the rules. The game is a kind of mental puzzle. We can pretend that we do not care whether the results have any bearing on the outside world. We are just playing. It is a mental exercise that excites our mental curiosity. We are taking on the challenge of describing and analyzing what results follow from the rules.

So it may seem that a formal system consists in pure form without meaning. By arriving at pure form, have we finally arrived at a realm where God is absent or where he makes no difference?

The Presence of God in Imitative Transcendence

Actually, God displays his glory right in the midst of the process of constructing a formal system. A formal system has to be either constructed or *created*. We are using our creativity, which reflects God's original, archetypal creativity.

In doing the construction, we have to stand back from our immersion in language and reasoning and try to look down on language and reasoning as if from outside or above it. Gödel's results depended on his being able to distinguish between the formal system he was studying and the metalanguage that he used to study it. He was looking down on the formal system "from above," from a kind of *transcendent* position. In his personal thinking and in his metalanguage, he transcended the limitations of the formal system. In particular, he was able to *see* from his transcendent position that a certain formula in the formal system was true even though it could not be proved.

In a situation like this, the human investigator is showing an imitative form of transcendence (see chapter 45). He is not God, but he imitates God by his ability to transcend the immediate. He stands back and analyzes the thinking or writing or use of language in which he engaged a moment before.

This transcendence is itself reflected when we carefully distinguish between metalanguage and formal language about which we talk in metalanguage.

This imitative transcendence must have a role even in defining a single character such as tilde ~ that will be used in the formal language. When we put the character into the list, we and any readers must be able to distinguish between formal language and metalanguage. We must understand that the character as a graphic symbol is supposed to be a character in the formal language, and that we are stipulating in the metalanguage that such will be the case from now on. At the same time, we must understand that we will use the same symbol ~ within our metalanguage as a label to *refer to* the tilde character ~ in the formal language. To make clear the distinction, people have sometimes used a graphical sign ~ as the character in the formal language and the sign enclosed in single quotes '~' to refer to the formal character using the metalanguage. (In this book we have tried to avoid the extra clutter involved when we use single quote marks.) The distinction between metalanguage and the formal character tilde ~ within the formal language illustrates and displays the operation of imitative transcendence even in the case of a single character such as tilde ~.

Some people may like formal systems because they are seeking an impersonal realm of pure form. For them, formal systems get adopted as one further step in the attempt to flee God and to obtain a space where he is absent, namely, the "space of formal systems." But the goal is illusory.

When we try to escape God, we are trying to be our own god. So we are still imitating God, but in a perverse way. Our imitation *still* reveals the presence of God. When we stand above a system of reasoning and try to reduce it to pure form, we show imitative transcendence in the very process of standing above. We show imitative creativity in the creation of formal tools, and imitative sovereignty in our mastery over the forms that we have created. God is being displayed in his glory, transcendence, creativity, and sovereignty through the abilities that he has given us, through the power that he exerts in us, and through the meaning that he reflects in us as we study a formal system.

The Presence of God in Language

It is not an accident that formal languages are called "languages." Of course they are not ordinary human languages. But neither are they purely random. Logicians talk about the rules of formal language as rules of "syntax." The rules imitate or reflect at least one dimension of the syntactical rules that govern natural languages. In a formalized version of Whitehead and Russell's system, the well-formed formulas are like clauses or sentences. Within English, two clauses can be connected together using "or" to make a single larger clause. And this larger clause can be connected to still another clause using "or." The formal syntax of the formal symbols ~ and ∨ obviously imitates the more relaxed, multidimensional syntax of clauses in natural languages. Natural languages are what they are because they imitate or reflect divine language. And divine language is divine, reflecting the one original language, the Word of God who is God. So the syntax of formal languages reflects God.

The process of *reflection* or imitation or imaging that we see when we think about language has a source in God. The original or archetypal image is the Son, "the image of the invisible God" (Col. 1:15). All other imaging relations image this original.

We can also see a reflection of the character of God in the capability within natural languages for building more and more complex structures. We build up whole discourses from paragraphs, paragraphs from sentences, sentences from clauses, clauses from words. And within this complex discourse we are capable of standing back and referring to what we have been saying, or summarizing what we are saying in a single sentence or a single word. We exercise imitative transcendence in this process of standing back.

The complexities of language are reflected in a one-dimensional way in the typical character of rules for well-formed formulas. From one or two earlier well-formed formulas, like p and q, we are allowed to form a longer string $(p \lor q)$ that will incorporate the earlier strings and form a new, more complex well-formed formula. The process can then be repeated any number of times. This process of using earlier results and feeding them back again into the process is called *recursion*. Recursion is a form of imitative transcendence. After we have been dwelling in our thoughts inside p and q in order to construct them according to the rules, we *stand back* and let ourselves consider p and q as completed wholes. Once we recognize them as a whole belonging to the appropriate category of well-formed formulas, we produce still another well-formed formula. Then we can stand back and treat the new formula as a whole. We repeatedly transcend our earlier steps in analysis and synthesis.

We can see a particular case of imitative transcendence with Gödel's proof of incompleteness. Gödel exercised imitative transcendence first of all by distinguishing his formal system from the metalanguage in which he was analyzing the system. Then he obtained a well-formed formula G that was unprovable in the system. (This unprovability could be seen only by standing back in imitative transcendence.) G can be added as an axiom. But then, standing back another time, we can construct a second formula G_2 that is unprovable. By standing back a third time, we can construct a third formula G_3. We are displaying imitative transcendence that reflects the glory of God and his ability to transcend the entire world.

The Presence of God in Rules

Paul says, "In him [God] we live and move and have our being" (Acts 17:28) and ". . . in him [Christ] all things hold together" (Col. 1:17). God is present and sustains and holds together formal systems.

God is present not only in the persons who exercise transcendence over formal systems; he is also present in the rules. We invent formal rules in our creativity. Our creativity reflects God's creativity, because we are made in his image. Rules that we make to "rule over" a formal system are an image of the rules that God specifies to rule over the world that he has created. And the rules that we "create," we create in the presence of God, who gives life and breath and "teaches man knowledge" (Ps. 94:10). God has inspired our creativity and our thoughts, and he controls all the outcomes.

The rules we make, even *formal* rules for games, are God's before they are ours. God knew them first, from all eternity. He knew about formal systems—every possible formal system. He knew all rules for all systems. God's omnipotence, omnipresence, eternality, truthfulness, immateriality, and rationality are displayed in the rules that he speaks to govern the world. These attributes are also displayed in the rules that he contemplates for formal systems.

These rules that God has in his mind *govern* the formal systems to which they apply. They govern the formal systems in a manner independent of space and time, thus showing God's omnipresence and eternality. They do not change in time, thus displaying God's immutability. They are ideational rather than material, thus displaying God's immateriality. They govern, displaying God's omnipotence. They are rational, displaying God's rationality and personality.

In turn, the rules that we ourselves create display these characteristics because they are not rules that are just "there" independent of God. They come from him. We ourselves are not omnipresent or omnipotent, but our ideas about rules and our very ability to think about rules reflects God's eternal power and divine nature.

We are "without excuse" (Rom. 1:20) because we *know* God through his display of his glory in the rules. But we suppress that knowledge.

The Presence of God in Personal Purposes

God is also present in our purposes. In sin, our purposes can be perverse. But we still cannot avoid imitating God. We twist good purposes, and still reflect in our perversion the good purposes of God.

The purpose of playing a game is one example. We can play a game in order to escape from weighty matters of life. Is this escape a sinful flight from responsibility? Many times, it is. But could it also be an escape in order to rest, and to be refreshed? Could it be a kind of mini-sabbath rest, to be refreshed and then return to serious living with more godly zeal? Could we enjoy and praise God in a game? Again, yes.

So it is with the "game" of logic or the "game" of playing with formal systems. Even in playing a game, we have motives. We serve God, or we rebel against him, or we try to ignore him (which is a form of rebellion).

The Presence of God in Unity and Diversity

God is present in the unity and diversity of formal systems. Each character, such as the tilde symbol $\sim$, has both unity and diversity, and the two are intertwined. Each character is a unity, distinct from other characters. And each character has diversity, since it has *multiple* occurrences in the strings and well-formed formulas of the formal system. We must be able to understand and use this unity and diversity. And the unity and diversity are related to one another. The unity cannot be grasped except through instantiations, particular cases where we display the tilde symbol $\sim$. The diversity cannot be grasped unless, when we see particular instances of the tilde $\sim$, we are able to identify them as instances of tilde ($\sim$) rather than O or B. Everything we have said in part I about the revelation of God is still relevant.

Revelation of God in Form and Meaning

What about form and meaning? In God's speech, form and meaning go together, indwelling one another. His speech reflects his Trinitarian character. Our ordinary human speech reflects his speech, and possesses both form and meaning in an interlocking manner. But what about formal systems? Are they not pure form with no meaning?

One of the ironies about the process of trying to evaporate meaning is that the person doing the evaporating must supply meaning continually in the process. He must know and understand what he is attempting to do. And if another person is going to appreciate the meaning of the attempt, he too must understand that the task at hand is "evaporating meaning and moving toward pure form."

The result of the process is that we arrive at a list of characters, such as ~, ∨, etc. We may be told that "the characters have no meaning." But the person who has completed this process must tell us (directly or indirectly). When he tells us, he is still giving us meaning. And if we analyze the characters from a linguistic point of view, they still display form and meaning in the usual interlocking way. If they did not, they could not function as part of English, which has of course now been creatively extended to include them.

In the case of characters in formal languages, their *form* is a geometrical shape and size. Tilde ~ is a wavy line that curves first one way and then the other. It is to be sized so that it fits appropriately with the characters on either side of it. The wedge symbol ∨ is composed of two line segments of equal length, attached to each other at one end and forming an acute angle facing upward. So much for *form*. What about *meaning*?

The meaning of tilde ~ is, at the very least, something like the following:

> Tilde ~ functions as a special character used in a special context, defined as "formalized systems." In this context we are temporarily supposed to refrain from interpreting it as having any other special reference or function within natural language.

Moreover, this character tilde ~ functions in the context of syntactical rules that suggest greater similarity to some elements in natural language than to others. In addition to all this, we must be aware of another aspect of its meaning: tilde ~ is one counter or playing-piece within a game with rules. The game is a puzzle-like game that may involve challenges in problem solving. So there is lots of meaning here already.

Additional meaning remains in the background. In the larger context, we are interested in playing this "game" of formal systems not merely for its own sake, but because it does have interesting implications once we make ties between the formal system and informal logic. In the long run, those ties are essential for seeing the significance of what is going on, and for motivating us to study formal systems.

Translation

The ties between formal systems and the rest of the world represent a kind of *translation*. We translate between the formal system, which supposedly "has no meaning," and the metalanguage, in which we know that tilde ~ is eventually going to stand for logical negation. Logical negation within semi-formalized forms of logic is in turn a step toward formalization, in comparison with informal reasoning within natural language. We must translate between logical negation within the metalanguage and reasoning within natural language. And in a sense, because we acknowledge the Creator-creature distinction, we must translate between the meaning of reasoning and negation for human beings and the meaning for God.

Like translations between two natural languages, these metaphorical translations can take place only if we understand both languages between which we are translating. And understanding depends on context. The context of natural language includes both the world and God who made it. The context of formal systems is a context defined by us and by our metalanguage (against the background of God's sovereign control). The definition and explanation takes place *outside* the formal system. Context is a necessity. As usual, we cannot evaporate it or dispense with it. The contexts that we use reflect the final context, the context that God himself has—the original, ultimate context of the persons of the Trinity in fellowship with one another.

Consider another aspect of ordinary translation between natural languages. Ordinary translation takes into account the context of two different cultures. It translates between two different points of view enmeshed within these cultures. The two different points of view offer two perspectives. Perspectives belong to persons, and imitate the relation of persons in the Trinity. Translation is based on God. The diversity of two languages reflects the diversity of distinct persons of the Trinity. The unity of meaning inherent in translation reflects the unity of one God, who is in harmony with himself.

Likewise, translation between a formal system and its intended meaning within the metalanguage requires two perspectives. The investigator must be able to assume first one perspective, then the other. And he must keep straight in his mind which is which. To do so, he has context. The distinction of perspectives is a diversity. The unity of meaning is a unity. Unity and diversity coinhere, reflecting the coinherence of persons of the Trinity.

Recursively Ascending Languages

We study a formal system using metalanguage and metareasoning. In doing so, we transcend the formal system. In a second step of imitative transcendence, we can stand back and transcend our metalanguage and metareasoning. We then attempt, perhaps, to reduce this metalanguage and metareasoning to a formal system. We do so, then, using a meta-metalanguage. And then we stand back and examine our meta-metalanguage. We apply the process indefinitely. We ascend to heaven, as it were.[1]

But we never really get there. We remain creatures. The longing for exhaustive mastery is a twisting of the created longing to know God in full personal depth, and to have the satisfaction of knowing and loving him. People in rebellion turn to other paths, and the study of logic for the sake of mastery may be one of them.

Analogy and Stability of Meaning

Finally, consider the issue of analogy and the issue of stability in meaning, raised earlier in chapters 17 and 19. When we translate between two languages, we use analogy. The full meaning of a piece depends on the larger context. The transfer must use analogy. The meaning of tilde ~ within a formal system is analogous to the meaning of logical negation in semi-formalized logic, and that meaning in turn is analogous to the meaning of "not" within natural English. Without analogy, and a previous understanding of "not," we could not begin. We must also have difference. Tilde ~ cannot merely mean "not," but must be "purified" and one-dimensional in its meaning.

Within a formal system, does each element have stable meaning? Tilde ~ has a stable meaning. It can be re-identified in each of its occurrences, and it is always a part of the same logic "game" with the same rules of syntax. It is in a sense *very* stable, because we as persons have taken care to introduce formal systems with a lot of English prose, and by so doing we have

---

[1] See Vern S. Poythress, "The Quest for Wisdom," in *Resurrection and Eschatology: Theology in Service of the Church: Essays in Honor of Richard B. Gaffin, Jr.*, ed. Lane G. Tipton and Jeffrey C. Waddington (Phillipsburg, NJ: Presbyterian & Reformed, 2008), 86–114.

set up an elaborate context in the midst of which we can have extra stability through a kind of one-dimensionality of meaning.

On the other hand, the larger contexts and their influence will not go away. The point of setting up the "game" of formal systems includes understanding more, using the analogy between logical negation and "not" in ordinary language. We know this. And we know that the study of tilde ~ within the formal system is useless if we do not eventually relate it to meanings outside of it. At one point, within a very tightly controlled context, we may find ourselves saying that tilde ~ "has no meaning." But then later we will say things in the metalanguage, and we will impart meaning to the tilde through the metalanguage. At the point of impartation, we have in a sense *changed* the meaning. It is *not* perfectly stable. And we cannot allow perfect stability, because that would also imply perfect irrelevance. And perfect irrelevance would, taken seriously, result in no meaning. Stable meaning is always meaning in relation to God. And so it always interlocks with mystery.

Gratitude to God

Working with formal logical systems can be fun. It is like a game or a puzzle. We can enjoy it just for the fascination of the game. Or we can use it to practice creativity and insight, exercising our mental and logical capacities to enhance our skills for the future. When we solve a puzzle, we can have a sense of achievement and can thank God for giving us insight and enabling us to arrive. We can enjoy the beauty God displays in the coherence of a small, carefully constructed system. God's beauty has many reflections. And one of them is in logic, for those who have a taste or insight for it. All our blessings come from God. When unbelievers enjoy the challenge or insights of logic, they too are receiving a benefit and a joy from God. But they do not enjoy it to the full, because they do not give him thanks and enjoy him in the process of enjoying the gift. The Giver is always bigger than the gift. And the joy from fellowship with the Giver is richer than joy from interaction with the gift alone.

For Further Reflection

1. What are the benefits of formal systems?
2. How would we respond to the claim that within a formal system the characters and the strings "have no meaning"?
3. How do formal systems still have a relationship to personal purposes?
4. How do formal systems depend on a larger context of meanings?

Chapter 58

A Computational Perspective

Now we sketch a computational perspective on formal systems and Gödel's incompleteness theorem that we saw in chapter 55. We have seen that we can develop multiple perspectives on logic (chapter 43). One of these is the perspective of computers and computation. Computers use logic. So logic becomes a perspective on computers. But computers are sufficiently complex that they can embody in their programming considerable amounts of logic. We will develop this second route to use computers as a perspective on logic. We reflect on what a computational perspective can show us about formal systems, provability, and the study of formal systems using metalanguage.

Representing Formal Systems by Computation

The rules that describe the characters and the well-formed formulas of a formal language are almost always specific enough and simple enough so that a computer can capture the idea. A computer can be programmed so that, given any string of characters as input, it can determine whether the string is a well-formed formula. Given a series of lines, each of which is a string of characters, a computer can also determine whether the series of lines constitutes a valid proof within a specific formal system.

This conversion of formal languages and formal systems into computer programs is parallel to what Kurt Gödel accomplished by converting questions about formal systems into questions in number theory. Gödel made each character within a formal system correspond to a distinct number. Then the correspondence was extended, so that a specific number—later called the Gödel number—corresponded to each well-formed formula, and still another number corresponded to each proof. Gödel thereby translated questions about formulas and proofs into questions about numbers.

In a parallel manner, the questions about formal systems can be translated into questions about calculations and computer reasoning. In fact, computer programs can reason about numbers, so Gödel's correspondences between formal systems and arithmetical properties could be one way in which a computer program chooses to express the questions in programming language. Thus, through looking at the challenges concerning computation, we can develop insight into logic and proofs.

Representing Computers Logically: Turing Machines

Already before the dawn of the era of electronic computing in the 1940s, Alan Turing began to develop a theory of computing. He was aware of Kurt Gödel's 1931 result about the incompleteness of axioms for arithmetic (chapter 55). Turing explored what it meant to "translate" some of the key ideas of Gödel's proof into the context of computation. In 1936 he published his first paper that set forth some of the main connections.[1]

In this paper, Turing proposed an idea for a general purpose computer. He simplified by imagining a general, abstract representation for the kind of mechanical calculator that could follow a series of fixed rules in order to accomplish a calculation. He represented each such calculator as a programmed core plus a memory. The core for the calculator was what is now called a "finite state machine." It has a fixed number of internal "states." It also has fixed rules for making transitions from one state to another. If a memory is added (which Turing wanted), the machine also needs rules for reading and writing to a memory area. Turing pictured the memory area as a tape along which a reading-and-writing "head" could travel.

The transitions between the internal states were specified by rules that could say, "If you are in state A, go to state B if there is a symbol S recorded in the present location of the read head on the tape"; "If you are in state A, go to state C if there is a symbol T recorded in the present location"; "go from state A to state D if there is no symbol." The rules could also specify the recording or erasing of a symbol at the current spot on the tape. Finally, the rules specified movement along the tape: move to the right one space, or to the left one space. The computation started from a special "start" state, and might or might not include a situation in which there were already some symbols on the tape. The machine also had provision for stopping. It stopped whenever there was no rule telling it how to proceed onward from

---

[1] Alan M. Turing, "On Computable Numbers, with an Application to the *Entscheidungsproblem* [decision problem]," *Proceedings of the London Mathematical Society*, series 2, 42 (1936): 230–265; online at http://www.thocp.net/biographies/papers/turing_oncomputablenumbers_1936.pdf, accessed January 26, 2011.

its present state. If the machine stopped, the stopping signified that its computation was complete.[2] Such a machine was later called a *Turing machine.*

This conception of computation seems on the surface to be very elementary, but Turing showed that with sufficiently complex rules for the transitions (in effect, programming rules) and enough distinct internal states, a machine of this kind could in principle make any calculation that could be accomplished by any means whatsoever. The sole proviso was that the calculation must be purely "mechanical" or "algorithmic": it must be capable of being specified by precise rules that prescribe one step after another. Ordinary numerical addition and multiplication are algorithmic, because students can perform the calculations by following the rules that they learn in grade school. Electronic calculators can make the same calculations, because their internal programs spell out the logical equivalent of the same rules (though internally these calculators used binary-based rather than decimal-based arithmetic in their representations of numbers). Modern computers can carry out very complex calculations, but there must always be rules specifying the steps.

There could be many different arrangements of rules, and so there are many different machines. Because each machine has only a finite number of states and a finite number of rules, an exact description of the machine can be encoded in a single number. This encoding should remind us of Gödel's encoding of well-formed formulas using numbers.

Turing also devised the idea of a *universal machine*, since called a *universal Turing machine*. A machine is called *universal* if its program allows it to mimic exactly the behavior of any other Turing machine. The universal machine is assumed to start with a tape (the memory) which specifies the number that encodes the exact description of some particular Turing machine *T*. The tape also includes the marks (if any) that the machine *T* will be given as its input. The universal machine then calculates all the steps that the machine *T* has to go through, and produces the same result as the machine *T* would produce.

The total process may sound complicated. And there is indeed some complication in executing the idea in practice. But the core idea is fairly straight-forward. Producing a universal Turing machine is essentially equiv-

---

[2] Turing's original paper in 1936 focused on a situation where the calculator was programmed to print an indefinitely long sequence of 0s and 1s, which were supposed to represent the binary-based expansion for a particular real number. In this situation, a calculator that halted would be judged to have failed. But for other purposes such a calculator could be interpreted as having stopped because it had finished producing its result.

alent to programming a general purpose computer so that it digests the program of a second computer, and then carries out the calculations that this second program would supervise. Anyone who has explored computer programming realizes that this kind of process can be done in principle, though it is tedious to work it out in practice.

The Halting Problem

Turing then considered a particular question in computation, which is now called the *halting problem*. The problem arises because some computer programs never produce a result. They just go into an endless loop. State A, let us say, has a rule that says to go to state B, and state B has a rule that says to go to state A. If such a machine ever enters the state A, it will then go to state B, then back to state A, then to state B, and so on indefinitely. It will never reach its "stop" state. It will never "halt." By inspecting its rules or watching it go through its "calculation," we can quickly see that it will never halt. So far, so good.

Now let us ask, "Can we devise a general procedure so that we can always calculate, for each Turing machine, whether that particular machine will eventually halt? Will it at some point end up in the "stop" state? Or will it continue working forever and never reach a conclusion?"

Why does it matter? It matters in practice because we do not want to stand around forever if the machine is never going to produce an answer. But it also matters at the level of principle because, it turns out, the halting problem is akin to Gödel's incompleteness result. It just takes some work to see how.

If we know what characterizes a proof, we can program a computer so that it produces proofs automatically. Turing discussed only one kind of "computer," which subsequent history has labeled "Turing machines." But the basic idea can be explained in more familiar terms by talking in the language of modern computers. To produce proofs, a computer program just starts with one of the axioms. That is itself a one-line proof. It prints out several of these. Then it takes one of the axioms, puts a second axiom as the second line, and checks whether a deduction can be made by *modus ponens* (if p and $p \supset q$, then q). Then it tries another combination of axioms. And it begins trying proofs longer in length, with four or five lines instead of one or two. If we do our program right, we can make the computer produce mostly simpler proofs at first, but gradually expand in a systematic way. If it is systematic, it will gradually cover more and more territory, and no possible proof will be permanently overlooked.

So such a program will eventually be able to print out any proof that is valid in the formal system. If we give it a well-formed formula as input, and if the formula has a proof, eventually the computer will tell us that it has a proof, and will supply one. If, on the other hand, the formula has no proof, the computer will go on and never halt.

So now, if we have a general procedure for determining whether a computer will halt, we program a second computer to calculate whether the first will halt. If it says yes, we know that the formula being tested is provable. If it says no, we know that the formula in question is not provable. Such information would be potentially very valuable. It would give us a mechanical procedure for testing provability.

But Turing showed that it is impossible to solve the halting program, that is, to have a general procedure—an "algorithm"—that will calculate an answer. The reason why it is impossible is similar to the reason why normal axioms for arithmetic are incomplete.

Producing the Key Program

The basic idea goes like this.[3] Assume that we *do* have a program to solve the halting problem. Then, using the program as a starting point, we can construct a second computer program which goes through exactly the same calculations up until the endpoint, but then does not halt by putting out a "yes" or "no" (or symbolic equivalent). Rather, it is programmed to do one more step at the end. It halts if the program about which it was calculating does not halt. But if the program about which it was calculating does halt, it sends itself into an endless loop. In other words, it halts if and only if the program that it is inspecting does not halt.

After all this preparation, we proceed to calculate the coding number of the program that we have just constructed. We use that coding number as input to the program itself. If the program halts, in effect it puts out the message, "I do not halt." If it does not halt, it must be because it has gone into its endless loop, and this can happen only if it *does* halt. The result is that it halts if and only if it does not. We arrive at a contradiction. So the initial assumption that the halting problem was solvable is shown to be false.

It is actually not quite that simple, because a program that calculates the results of other programs needs two inputs, not one. A method similar to what Gödel employed (appendix D1) gets over the final obstacle (see appendix E1).

---

[3] Turing's original paper went about the issue differently, but the results were the same.

Pertinence to Proof Theory

The unsolvability of the halting problem is pertinent to proof theory and Gödel's incompleteness theorem (chapter 55). Remember that Gödel found a way to express the nature of a formal proof using numbers. He constructed a numerical correspondence, and then was able to write a property about numbers that corresponded to the fact that a series of formulas within a formal system constituted a proof. In a similar way, we may translate into numbers the property of halting. A program P with an encoding number e halts if there exists a number h such that, when the program executes the h-th step in its process of calculation, it halts—it enters the "stop" state. A program does not halt if there does not exist such a number h. We can write up these properties as properties of numbers. The properties of numbers encode the process of calculations by a Turing machine. The resulting formulas are formulas in number theory.

For any particular program P and input n that is fed into it, either the program halts or it does not. Corresponding to this situation, we know that one of two formulas in number theory is true: either h exists or it does not.

Now comes the important connection. Suppose we can find a system of axioms for number theory that are *complete*. That is, all true formulas in number theory can be derived from them. If we can describe the axioms so that a computer program can digest them, we can program a computer systematically to track through longer and longer proofs, until it finds either a proof that h exists or a proof that it does not. The computer would in this way have determined whether the program P halts. Thus, the completeness of axioms for number theory would result in a solution to the halting problem. Since the halting problem is unsolvable, any set of axioms digestible by a computer[4] is incomplete.

Computation and Functions

The theory of computation and the theory of formal systems are related in still another way, through functions. Each computer program can be regarded as a *function* that takes an input x and produces an output $f(x)$. (If the program does not halt, $f(x)$ is undefined.) By supplying complex

---

[4] Why the extra qualification, "digestible by a computer"? Suppose we specify that all true formulas of number theory are axioms. Then it follows (trivially) that we have a complete set of axioms. Every true formula is proved by a one-line proof, because it is an axiom. But if we use this definition of axioms, we have no way of calculating whether a formula is an axiom. Such a set of axioms is useless for proof theory, because we do not have it under our control. It is not calculable.

programming instructions, we can construct a great variety of functions, some very complex. These functions can also be represented in a formal system that is sufficiently rich. So the character of computations can be expressed in formal systems.

Because modern computers conduct their operations at rates over a billion times per second, they can accomplish calculations that would take human beings a lifetime. But they still have limitations. Any calculation must follow a specific set of rules. The functions on nonnegative integers calculable by computer are called *computable* functions. Because "computers" might conceivably include unusual arrangements as well as typical modern computers, there is still some vagueness about what is a computer. Alonzo Church first formulated what has come to be known as *Church's thesis*, namely, that the functions that are computable in some intuitive sense are precisely the same class as *recursive functions*.[5] Gödel originally introduced *recursive functions* for his incompleteness proof. They can be rigorously defined within a formal system that includes arithmetic. Thus there are perspectival relations between formal systems on the one hand and computation theory on the other.

For Further Reflection

1. What is a Turing machine?
2. Why is the concept of a Turing machine significant for modern computers?
3. What is the "halting problem"?
4. What similarities are there between the halting problem and Gödel's incompleteness theorem?
5. What does the halting problem say about the limitations of our knowledge? What is the relation of our knowledge to God's knowledge in these matters?

---

[5] Church's thesis is also called the "Church-Turing thesis" because of an analogous formulation of the same idea in Alan Turing's 1936 paper on computability (B. Jack Copeland, "The Church-Turing Thesis," *Stanford Encyclopedia of Philosophy [Summer 2010 Edition]*, ed. Edward N. Zalta, http://plato.stanford.edu/archives/sum2010/entries/church-turing/, accessed August 26, 2011). Church's original paper is Alonzo Church, "An Unsolvable Problem of Elementary Number Theory," *American Journal of Mathematics* 58 (1936): 345–363.

Chapter 59

Theistic Foundations
of Computation

What does God have to do with computation? Many of the observations that we made about the theistic foundations for proof theory (chapter 57) have analogues for the theory of computation.

Transcendence

The analysis of the halting problem, like the analysis of Gödel's incompleteness result, depends in an essential way on the ability to stand back from any particular calculation going on, and to analyze the meaning of the calculation as a whole. In fact, we have to be able to analyze the meaning of many possible calculations. We have to be able to think about the concept of any calculation that can be carried out by any computer (or Turing machine equivalent). We have to "transcend" any particular calculation.

As human beings, we exercise an imitative transcendence. We are still finite, but we imitate God's transcendence by our ability to stand back. The halting problem must distinguish carefully between a calculation by a specific Turing machine, a calculation that is mimicking this machine, and a reasoning that we ourselves are doing in a metalanguage in order to convince ourselves that the halting problem is unsolvable. (For further illustrations of imitative transcendence, see appendix E2.)

Translations

The halting problem also involves two distinct translations between formal machines—Turing machines—and metalanguage. In a manner analogous to formal systems, Turing machines are formal machines. The programs for the machines are just mechanical rules that can be followed even without knowing what the overall calculation is about. Likewise, modern computers are mindless. They understand nothing about the meaning of the programs that they are executing. They just go blindly on. But they also go with blinding speed, so that, when a computer programmer devises a program with a clear-cut goal, the computer can attain the goal with startling rapidity.

We translate between these "mindless" rules and our metalanguage in two ways. One is itself a kind of "formal" translation that expresses only the "syntax" of the machine. That is the encoding number e for a program. The number e uniquely represents the program, but does so not by spelling out its meaning or its purpose but by enabling us to reconstruct its rules with precision.

The other translation is the translation in meaning. For example, we know, because we have programmed it, that a particular program P calculates the double $2 \times n$ for any number n that it is given as input. We know that a certain program M mimics the behavior of other programs.

By using both of these translations, and by translating one back into the other, we produce the desired conclusion about the unsolvability of the halting problem. We are able to appreciate that such is the meaning of our metalanguage argument, because we transcend the specific programs.

As in the case of Gödel's incompleteness result, so here, the translations imitate the multiple perspectives among human languages, languages that can be translated into one another. And these multiple perspectives imitate the mystery of the Trinity, with the distinct perspectives belonging to each person of the Trinity.

The One and the Many

We depend on God, as always, for our understanding of the one and the many in relation to one another. We use the one and the many when we think about the general idea of algorithmic computation on the one hand, and a specific program with its specific computation on the other hand. We meet the one and the many again when we consider the unity of one program on the one hand, and the diversity of the different steps that it goes through in calculation on the other. We also meet the one and the many when we think of the unity belonging to one program, and the diversity of results that the one program calculates when given different numbers as inputs.

Computers as Reflecting Human Creativity

As we observed earlier in our reflections on computers as a perspective, computers reflect the glory of God by reflecting the ingenuity and insight of the programmers who write their instructions and of the manufacturers who make the computers. We have derivative creativity, which reflects on the level of our creatureliness the original creativity of the one Creator. And we have been given by our Creator a wonderful power to create images of ourselves, at least in a one-dimensional way, by embodying our creativity in computer programs.

Rules

Computer programs are structured collections of rules,[1] individual rules arranged into groups and connected by other rules. The rules for Turing's finite state machines are also rules, and together these rules allow Turing machines to perform the same calculations as modern computers. Rules, rules.

These rules are manmade rules. But they do not come from nowhere. They come from human purposes and human creativity and human wisdom. Human beings have to understand how to get from a purpose to a procedure that will accomplish the purpose. The planning and wisdom and understanding and rule-making capabilities of human beings all go back to God. We are made in his image. We make rules because he made rules first. His rules govern our very being, but his rules also specify what we know and what we learn and what we succeed in producing in the form of a computerized image of our thinking. We succeed only because God is empowering us and working with us and in us, giving both ideas and plans and powers to embody the ideas either in print or in silicon.

God's rules display his character. They are omnipresent, eternal, immutable, omnipotent, truthful. And they are rational and personal and purposeful. Our manmade rules do not have God's infinity, but they reflect his infinity. Our rules have efficacy only because they are sustained and empowered by his infinity.

The Halting Problem

The limitations of computation, as expressed in the halting problem, reflect God's transcendence, our finiteness, and the finiteness of any machine that we make. By transcending our immediate circumstances, and by reflecting on our own thoughts, our machines, and our computations, we may see the limitations of a "world" of computation that we have constructed. But as

---

[1] Some computer programming languages are designed to be "object-oriented" rather than rule-oriented. But these languages still presuppose an underlying level where rules specify the behavior of objects.

finite creatures we have no way of transcending our limitations all the way to infinity, and then knowing exactly which programs halt in every case. The capacities and limitations of our own minds, as well as the capacities of computational worlds that we construct in our creativity, reveal the glory of God and should evoke our praise.

For Further Reflection

1. In what ways do modern computers reveal the glory of God?
2. Indicate some specific ways in which human thinking about computing transcends computing.
3. In what way do rules for computation reflect the glory of God?
4. In what ways do the limits of modern computer reveal the glory of God?

Chapter 60

Models

Now we consider formal *models* in relation to logical systems, especially formal systems. Their study is called *model theory*. But what is a *model*? Let us set the stage for this new concept.

What Is a Model?

In constructing a formal system, we "evaporate" meaning out of the truth-functional symbols ~, ∨, the parentheses (), the propositional symbols P_1, P_2, P_3, ..., and whatever other symbols belong to a formal language. We operate in a sense as if we were just playing a game using the elementary symbols as counters and following certain arbitrarily invented rules. But of course we know in the back of our minds, when we transcend the formal system, that we have constructed the whole thing for a purpose. Eventually, we want it to correspond to something outside.

In the long run, people are interested in logic because eventually it impinges on or gets applied to the world. Logic may find application in the rather special "world" of mathematics. But logic could also be applied to the syllogisms of Aristotle: "All men are mortal. Socrates is a man. ..." This application to the world is closely related to the conception of a model. A model is a kind of application of a formal system to an example.

But in modern symbolic logic, the examples of application are typically not examples directly from the world of human beings and mortality. Rather, they are carefully defined abstract objects. A *model* is a set of objects, together with some extra structure, so that each well-formed formula within a logical system can be "translated" into the model and tested as to whether it comes out true or false in the model. The model is a kind of miniature world. But it is a very stripped-down world, whose "objects" have only a few abstract properties.

An Example of a Stripped-down World

Before considering completely abstract models, let us begin with a more concrete example. Suppose p and q are proposition symbols in some formal language. To construct a model for the language, we have to connect these two symbols to items outside the language, items belonging to the model. Let p be assigned to the proposition "Snow is white," which we designate S. And let q be assigned to the proposition "The moon is made of green cheese," which we designate M. Let us construct a "model" (but it will not be fully abstract). The model X begins with the set $\{S,M\}$. It has only two members, namely, the two propositions S and M. The model X also assigns a truth value to each of these propositions.[1] S is T and M is F. Finally, the model X includes a specification as to how to assign the symbols p and q. p is assigned to S, and q to M.

With this model X, some of the formulas in the formal language come out true, and some come out false. p, clearly, is true in the model, while q is false. $\sim p$ is false and $(\sim p \vee q)$ is false. And so on.

Logicians also have special terms to talk about the relations between models and formulas. A formula that comes out true in a model is said to be *satisfied* by the model, and the model *satisfies* the formula. Thus the model X satisfies p and $\sim q$, but does not satisfy $(\sim p \vee q)$. There is also a special notation:

$$X \models p$$

It is to be read as "X satisfies p." That is, p comes out true in the model X. (Note that the symbol $\models$ for satisfaction is not the same as the mathematical symbol $\neq$, which means "is not equal to.")

Every tautology is satisfied in every model. That is to say, it is true no matter what truth values are assigned to the atomic propositional characters within it. For example, $(\sim p \vee p)$ is satisfied in every model, because it is true whether the atomic propositional character p itself is T or F in the model X.

---

[1] The term *model* is sometimes used for the set X, *before* setting up correlations between the formal language and the set. The correlations are then added to indicate which propositional symbols are true in the model, which individual constants in the language correspond to which elements in the set of individuals in the model, and so on for the other elementary symbols in the formal language. These correlations are called *interpretations* of the formal language with respect to the model X. But the word *model* is also sometimes used to describe the set X together with all the correlations. This second kind of "model" includes the first kind of "model" *plus* the interpretation of the symbols with respect to the starting set. For simplicity, I am using *model* in the second sense. A model includes the interpretation of the symbols in the formal language. When such a model is fully formalized it is sometimes also called a *structure*.

Other well-formed formulas, however, may or may not be true, depending on the model chosen. For example, the well-formed formula (p ∨ q) is satisfied in the model X in which *p* is assigned to S and *q* is assigned to M. (*p* ∨ *q*) is not satisfied in the model X in which both *p* and *q* are assigned to M.

Models for Propositional Logic

What would it look like to have a model of propositional logic? To be concrete, we have to have a particular formal system first. Let us take the system L that we developed in chapter 56. It has as propositional symbols P_1, $P_2, P_3, \ldots$. Each of these propositional symbols must be correlated with a proposition in a model X, and the proposition in X must be either true or false. Or, to simplify matters, we can have X contain only two elements, T and F. The starting base for X is the set {T,F}. And the model X also specifies for P_1 whether we correlate it with T or F. We can say that P_1 is correlated with T. Then P_1 comes out true in X. P_2 is correlated with F. So P_2 comes out false in the model X. P_3 is correlated with F. P_4 is correlated with F. And so on.

Since there are an infinite number of propositional symbols P_i, we cannot physically write out all the correlations. Instead, we can represent the correlation as a mathematical function, say f. A function f specifies a correlation between two sets, let us say A and B. As an example, let the set A be composed of the three members $\{P_1, P_2, P_3\}$ and the set B be composed of {T,F}. We define the function f by specifying that $f(P_1) = T, f(P_2) = F, f(P_3) =$ F. Once we have specified the value of $f(P_i)$ for each P_i, X becomes a model for the formal system.

The function f provides a way of testing the truth value of any propositional character P_i. We can extend the function f so that it applies to compound expressions as well as to the starting characters P_i. For example, we say that for any well-formed formula p, $f(\sim p) = F$ if and only if $f(p) = T$, and $f(\sim p) = T$ if and only if $f(p) = F$. For well-formed formulas p and q, $f((p \vee q))$ = F if and only if $f(p) = F$ and $f(q) = F$, otherwise $f((p \vee q)) = T$. With this specification, all the tautologies come out true in X.

In general, suppose that we have a formal system L, which includes not only elementary symbols and well-formed formulas but also axioms and rules for constructing proofs. If all the provable formulas come out true in X, X is said to satisfy, not merely a particular formula, but the formal system as a whole.

Models for Quantification

What does a model for quantification theory look like? Quantification theory (part III.B) is more complicated, because we can have not only symbols p for propositions, but symbols $H(x)$ for predicates and symbols a, b, c, for individual constants. Each symbol p for a proposition has to be mapped into either T or F in the model X. Each symbol a, b, c, ... that is an individual constant has to be mapped into an individual element in a base set U for the model X. U is the "universe" of individuals. It contains as members all the elements in the model that are supposed to correspond to individual constants and individual variables within the formal system. Some of the individual symbols can be mapped into the same element in U.

So far we have a function f mapping proposition symbols p, q, ... into $\{T,F\}$, and a second function g mapping individual constants a, b, c, ... into U. Finally, we also have to have something correlated with each predicate symbol $H(x)$. We have to specify for which values of x $H(x)$ comes out true in the model. Let the symbol S stand for the set of all elements x such that $H(x)$ is true. If we already know for which x $H(x)$ is true, we can define the set S to include just these x's. In set notation, $S = \{x \in U \mid H(x)\}$ (S has as members those individuals x in U such that $H(x)$). On the other hand, if H is a new predicate symbol, and we want to specify for the first time when $H(x)$ is true, we can do it by picking a set S that is a subset of U. We then say that $H(x)$ will be interpreted as true in the model X if and only if x is a member of the subset S (that is, $x \in S$). Thus, once we know S, we have a complete specification for the truth value of $H(x)$ for every possible individual x in the "universe" U. Conversely, if we already know for which x's $H(x)$ is true, we also know what is the correlated subset S. We now have a correlation between the predicate symbol H and the subset S.

We have to establish a correlation of this kind for *each* single-place predicate symbol $H(\ )$ in the formal language. So let us now alter our notation a bit. We write the subset S as $S = m(H)$, where m is a function operating on H. With this new notation for m we are indicating that *which* subset S we have in mind depends on the predicate symbol H. m is a function mapping from predicate symbols H to subsets $m(H)$ of U. Thus, if H_1, H_2, H_3, H_4, etc., are predicates in the formal language, the function m specifies for each one of these predicates some subset of U. For example, $m(H_2)$ is a subset of U, and it precisely specifies for which individuals x in U the formula $H_2(x)$ comes out true in the model.

We also have to deal with multi-place predicates of the form $G(x, y)$. Let U^2 be the set of all ordered pairs (x, y) where x and y are individuals in U.[2] A subset J of U^2 will consist in some, but not necessarily all, ordered pairs of elements from U. We will consider $G(x,y)$ is true for particular values of x and y if and only if (x, y) is a member of the special subset J.

(As a particular example, consider a "universe" U with only two distinct elements, a and b, and with a binary predicate $G(x,y)$ which is true only if $x = y$. That is, $G(a,a)$ is T, $G(b,b)$ is T, $G(a,b)$ is F, and $G(b,a)$ is F. Together these represent all the possibilities. The corresponding set of ordered pairs J is $\{(a,a), (b,b)\}$, that is, precisely the ordered pairs (x,y) for which $G(x,y)$ is T.)

We must do the same for each binary (two-place) predicate of the form $G(x, y)$. So we have a function m_2, which maps each binary predicate symbol G into a subset $m_2(G)$ of U^2. Similarly, with each three-place predicate $G(x, y, z)$, we correlate a subset of U^3, the set of all ordered triples (x, y, z) of individual elements x, y, z in U. The full model X includes not only the set U of individuals, but all the mappings f, g, m, m_2, and so on, which specify the truth values associated with all the starting symbols in the formal language.

In a similar way, a model for a still more complicated logical system can be produced by adding more structure alongside the set U at the heart of the model.

Gödel's Completeness Theorem

A major result in model theory is Gödel's completeness theorem (not to be confused with his incompleteness theorem discussed in chapter 55). The completeness theorem says that a formal system for first-order quantification (part III.B) has a model that satisfies it if and only if it is consistent. This theorem is important because it assures us that there is a tight correlation between two distinct properties: consistency in the formal system (a purely internal property) is correlated to satisfaction (a property related to models). The correlation assures us that the formal system can actually mean something with respect to the possible models.

One half of this claim is easy. Let us show that, if a formal system has a model, it is consistent. We do it by assuming the contrary. Suppose that a formal system has a model but is inconsistent. By definition of consistency, this means that there is some formula p such that both p and $\sim p$ are

---

[2] The ordered pair (x, y) must not be confused with the *set* $\{x, y\}$ composed of the two elements x and y. Two ordered pairs are equal if and only if the first entries are equal and the second entries are equal: $(x, y) = (z, w)$ if and only if $x = z$ and $y = w$.

provable in the system. For the formal system to have a model X, both p and $\sim p$ would have to be satisfied by X, which of course is impossible. We have deduced a contradiction, so the initial assumption that the system is inconsistent must be false. Hence, if a formal system has a model, it is consistent.

The other half of the theorem says that if a formal system for first-order quantification is consistent, it has a model. This half is much harder, since we have to construct such a model. The model is built up gradually using information from the axioms, plus more axioms that can be added while still leaving the system consistent.

For Further Reflection

1. What is a model for a formal system?
2. Construct a simple model for a formal system with three propositional symbols p, q, and r, in which all three propositions are true. Construct a second model in which p is true but q and r are false.
3. Can we can construct a model in which p is both true and false?

Chapter 61

Theistic Foundations for Models

What does God have to do with models?

Logic got its start as a discipline in relation to reasoning about the world. "All men are mortal." The world, or at least a small part of it, can serve as a kind of informal "model" in which logic can be tested. This informal thinking about logic in relation to the world offers the starting point for the formal models that have been studied in the twentieth century.

God and World

The most obvious point about God is that God is the God who rules the world. He made it. He controls it. The truths that hold with respect to the world hold because he specifies them. He plans them in his eternal counsel. He brings them to pass by speaking. God's speech is thus not only the origin of logic but the origin of the world about which logic holds. His speech has syntax, a kind of inner organization and logic. And his speech has reference, in that he talks about things in the world that have been created or that he calls newly into existence: "Let there be light" (Gen. 1:3). These two dimensions, namely, syntax and reference, are represented in a simplified fashion in logical models. The world, and therefore the reference, is represented by a model. The speech in its inner articulation or syntax is represented by a formal logical language which specifies some truth in the model.

But we must recognize that models are *formal*. They are very exactly specified, and, as we have seen a number of times, extra meaning is "evaporated" out of the model in order that it may be "pure." This purity has an advantage in rigor and clarity. Its disadvantage is the normal one in such cases. The model is one-dimensional. We are no longer talking about Socrates as an individual but about individual a. Individual a is simply an abstract placeholder in the set U at the heart of a model. Likewise, we are no longer talking about being human or being mortal. We are talking about a general, abstract predicate $H(x)$. We represent the predicate by an equally abstract entity in the model, namely, a subset $m(H)$.

These representations are nevertheless interesting because they do represent one dimension of what is going on in more informal uses of logic. They interest us as *persons*. They are a kind of simplification of what is accomplished when God speaks to govern the world.

The Relation between Model and Logic

The operation of model theory depends on us. We have to use our ability to understand both the logical language of a formal system and a model as a kind of representation of a mini-world. We must, in addition, understand that the two have a relation to each other. The maps f, g, m, and so on are not constructed out of thin air, but with a view to establishing just the right kind of correlation to imitate the realities of relationships between logical language and the world. We have *prior* understanding of this relationship even before we begin formally to engage in logic. We understand the relation between language and the world. We have to, in order to use language.

Foundations for Language

As usual, our ability imitates God's ability. Because God speaks, and because he made us in his image, we can speak. Because God reasons, we can reason. His speech toward the world has its roots in his eternal nature and his eternal speech, namely, the Word. The Word represents the archetypal syntax of God, and the thoughts expressed are thoughts of the speaker, preeminently God the Father. The relation of Father to Son, through the Spirit, constitutes both the distinction between reference and syntax and the indissoluble relation between them. This relationship is imitated in model theory, at its foundation. God is pleased to display his glory in human thought, not least in the thoughts of model theory.

One and Many

Models involve the interaction of the one and the many. The one is the abstraction, for instance $H(x)$ or $m(H)$. The many are the many instances to which it might apply. Typically a single formal system has many models that satisfy it. Each model is one out of many. And the many models all illustrate the one system. Also, a formal system has within it many well-formed formulas. Each formula is illustrated in the model by being satisfied or not satisfied. Each formula is one among many, and its satisfaction in the model is one of many satisfactions of many formulas. This interplay of one and many, as always, has its foundation in the Trinity. God's one and many is the archetype for the instances of one and many in model theory.

For Further Reflection

1. How does natural language have analogies to formulas in a formal system and the models to which they relate?
2. What is the difference between syntax and reference in natural language? In model theory? How do the two have their foundation in God?
3. What familiarity with natural language must be presupposed in teaching model theory?

Part III.E

Special Logics and More Enriched Logics

Chapter 62

Higher-order Quantification

People have enriched logic in several ways. We will discuss some of these enrichments briefly, in order to appreciate how God's glory is displayed in them as well as in the forms of logic that we have already studied.

First, people have extended the concept of quantification. How?

Variable Predicates

When we introduced the concept of quantification, we introduced variables like x and y. These variables ranged over the realm of "individuals." We had in mind a picture where x could stand for Socrates, Plato, or another human being. If the universe of discourse were broader, x could stand for an animal, a plant, a rock—any individual thing. Or the individuals could be numbers. Predicates like "being human" or "being mortal" or "being a carnivore" apply to such individuals.

In addition to individuals, we had predicates such as $H(x)$. For simplicity, we began by treating these predicates $H(x)$ as if they represented some particular fixed predicates in the real world: $H(x)$, for example, might in a particular case represent the predicate "x is human." But we have an advantage when we use a notation like $H(x)$ rather than the fuller notation Human(x). We need not specify right away *which* predicate the letter H will denote. We could say that the letter H represents some predicate or other, which we will specify later. All the proofs involving H will work just as well. (Of course, the results from the proofs still depend on the starting axioms. If we apply a formal system to the real world, we still have to make sure that the axioms are true when interpreted according to the particular meaning that we give to the symbol H within the world.)

Since the meaning of the symbol H has not been specified, it is in fact possible to regard the notation $H(x)$ as representing a predicate H that is a *variable predicate*. It makes no real difference in the proofs. But we have *not* let ourselves use a *quantifier* like "some" or "all" that would *range over* predicates (like *H*) rather than over individuals (like *x* or *y*). We now consider how we might abandon this restriction.

How would we represent a proposition such as "Socrates has some of the same properties as Plato," or "Socrates has all of the same properties as Plato"? In these last two propositions, the words *some* and *all* apply to properties, or, as we are now relabeling them, to predicates. Suppose *s* stands for the individual Socrates, and *p* stands for the individual Plato. Suppose H(*x*) is the predicate for being human. Then we have propositions like H(*s*) to represent "Socrates is human," and H(*p*) to represent "Plato is human." But being human is just one particular predicate. What would it look like if we treat *H* as a variable predicate and then use quantification with *H*? We might try to write:

$$(\forall H)(H(s) \supset H(p))$$

Or, if we have already used *H* as a notation for a constant predicate "is human," we introduce a new letter to stand for a variable predicate over which we quantify:

$$(\forall P)(P(s) \supset P(p))$$

The above formula would mean, if any predicate *P* is true of Socrates (*s*), it also is true of Plato (*p*).

The quantification $(\forall P)$ differs from what we have seen before. The expression $(\forall x)$ quantifies over a variable *x*, where *x* ranges over all *individuals* in the universe of discourse: Socrates, Plato, all human beings, perhaps also all animals, plants, and other individual entities. But this variable *x* does not range over predicates like "is human" or "is mortal." We cannot reasonably allow it to do so, given the structures that we have set up in the formalized language of a formal logical system. In the formula H(*x*), standing for "*x* is human," *x* and *H* play different roles, and the roles are not reversible.

We have, however, seen at least two kinds of situations in which quantification over predicates might be useful. The first situation occurred when we discussed activities of God the Father and his Son. John 5:19 says, "For *whatever* the Father does, that the Son does likewise." The word *whatever* functions as a kind of quantification. What allowable range does the word *whatever* have? Its range is not a range over individuals, either the Father, the Son, or human individuals. Rather, it ranges over possible actions. And actions are more like predicates. Suppose we wanted to reduce John 5:19 to formal logic—and, as we have stressed before, it would indeed be a reduction, a kind of flattening of the passage to one dimension. We would have to have a quantification over the predicates representing the various actions that could be performed by persons.

We also met with a use of variable predicates in discussing mathematical induction. The principle of mathematical induction looks at the following situation:

> Premise 1: A property M is true for the number 1.
> Premise 2: If M is true for the positive integer k, M is also true for the number $k + 1$.
> Conclusion: M is true for all positive integers n.

It talks about a property M. The principle of mathematical induction holds for all properties M. To formulate the principle in its full generality, we have to have quantification over properties, which we can represent as follows:

> $(\forall M)$\{Premise 1: A property M is true for the number 1.
> Premise 2: If M is true for the number k, M is also true for the number $k + 1$.
> Conclusion: M is true for all positive integers n.\}

Or, if we use $M(n)$ to represent the property M being true for number n,

$$(\forall M)\{[M(1) \wedge (\forall k)(M(k) \supset M(k + 1))] \supset (\forall n)[M(n)]\}.$$

We can see in the formulation of mathematical induction two distinct kinds of quantification. One kind of quantification, represented by $(\forall k)$ and $(\forall n)$, is quantification over individuals. In this case the variables k and n range over all the natural numbers, each of which is treated as an individual. The second kind of quantifying expression $(\forall M)$ is quantification over predicates. The two kinds of quantification have to be kept distinct.

Higher-order Quantification Theory

In previous chapters on quantification (part III.B), we have allowed only quantification over individuals. (This kind of quantification is illustrated with $(\forall n)$ and by earlier notations like $(\forall x)$, $(\forall y)$, $(\exists x)$.) The resulting theory is called *first-order quantification theory*. It is called "first-order" because it is the simplest form of quantification, and there is only one kind of quantification, namely, over individuals x.

If we allow quantification over predicates ($\forall M$), the result is called *second-order quantification theory*.[1] The variables M for predicates are second-order variables.

We may also contemplate the possibility of examining properties of predicates. We may, for some purposes, want to have a variable predicate like M range not over all predicates whatsoever, but only over those with certain special properties. The properties would be properties, not of individuals x, but of predicates M. So how will we denote these properties? We will have type-two predicates to describe the properties of type-one predicates. Thus "is-a-numerical-property(M)" would denote that M is a numerical property, in distinction (say) from an ethical property or a physical property like hardness. As usual, shorthand symbolism would reduce a type-two predicate such as "is-a-numerical-property" to a single symbol, let us say J. $J(M)$ is true of the type-one predicate M if and only if M is a numerical property. In order to avoid confusing J with an ordinary type-one predicate, we could give it a superscript: $J_2(M_1)$. The letter M is given the superscript 1 to indicate that it is a type-one predicate.

We might want to deal not only with predicates that take only one variable, like $M(x)$, but with predicates (or "relations") that take two or more variables, like $R(x,y)$ or $S(x,y,z,w)$. These predicates would have their own variables and quantifiers like ($\forall R$) where the symbol R ranges over all type-one two-place predicates $R(x,y)$. But for simplicity we will ignore the treatment of such multi-place predicates.

As we might expect, it is possible to consider *third-order quantification theory*, which would allow quantification over type-two predicates of the form J_2. And then there would be type-three predicates J_3 describing properties of type-two predicates, and type-four predicates describing properties of type-three predicates, and so on. The distinction between different types is part of what is called the *theory of types*. The theory arose because it

[1] In most modern settings, what we have called *predicates* are usually represented by sets. Instead of the predicate "is human" we have the set of all individuals x who are human. The two ways of talking are obviously correlative. The properties of type-one predicates such as "is human" then become properties of sets. And these type-two properties are represented as sets of sets. For example, the property of "being a numerical property" is represented by the set that has as its members all sets that represent numerical properties. And so on. We are simplifying for the sake of introducing only the most basic constituents in what is called *the theory of types*.

turns out to be important in a formalized setting in order to avoid paradoxes that are generated by the idea that we can form the set of all sets or the set of all sets that do not contain themselves (appendix A1). The theory of types forces the formalization to proceed upwards in a hierarchy, rather than mixing levels and producing paradoxes.

Incompleteness of Second-order Quantification

We earlier indicated that Kurt Gödel had shown that first-order quantification theory is complete. With the axioms and rules of derivation that are usually given, it can prove any well-formed formula that is true in every model. But the same is not true for second-order quantification theory.[2] Why not? The basic elements of the theory of numbers can be embedded in the more expressive framework of second-order quantification theory. And that means that Gödel's proof of incompleteness for number theory carries over into the incompleteness of second-order quantification theory, as a larger theory in which number theory is embedded.

The decisive difference can be seen with the principle of mathematical induction. That principle can be expressed, as we have sketched above, within second-order quantification theory. The principle cannot be expressed within first-order quantification theory, where the symbolism $(\forall M)$ is not available. The principle can in part be set down in axioms by using an infinite number of axioms in an axiom schema. But then the first-order theory cannot itself have a formula that directly mentions this infinity. In addition, the language is not expressive enough to capture the full logical power that is available in the metalanguage or in second-order quantification. Its limitations protect it from being subject to Gödel's method of numerically encoding the logic of proof within the system.

All of these issues touch in one way or another on the power of imitative transcendence among human beings. We are able to transcend a particular formal system and analyze it. If the system itself can have encoded within it a complete analysis of provability, it can be used to generate a self-referencing formula like Gödel's.

---

[2] Leon Henkin did provide one kind of "completeness theorem," but it involved a notable alteration in the models to which second-order quantification theory applies. See Alonzo Church, *Introduction to Mathematical Logic* (Princeton, NJ: Princeton University Press, 1956), 307–315.

For Further Reflection

1. What does it mean to have second-order quantification? Why might it be useful?
2. Why is it important to avoid "mixing" types of quantification within a formal system?
3. Can there be such a thing as third-order quantification and higher? What does "and higher" reveal about human imitative transcendence?

Chapter 63

Multivalued Logic

We may discuss very briefly some alternative treatments of logic that have sprung up to supplement or replace classical logic. What are these other logics, and how do they differ from classical logic?

Truth

The fundamental difference among some of these alternative logics concerns the representation of truth. And the issue of truth makes us remember that in the Bible, truth has its source in God. God is the God of truth and is the origin of truth. Christ says that he is the truth (John 14:6). God knew all particular truths before mankind was created. Truth is personal. It is the truth of God, and truth is expressive of the Trinitarian relation among the persons, since Christ is the truth and is the manifestation of the Father, who is the God of truth. The Spirit is the Spirit of truth (John 14:17; 16:13). It follows that human thinking is always derivative. And formal logic *of any kind* will reflect the truth but will be one-dimensional in comparison to the fullness of who God is.

I suspect that alternative logics have come into being partly because people have felt inadequacies about the representation of truth in classical logic. Then they have looked for alternatives that capture some other dimension that is not as well represented in classical logic.

Multivalued Logic

First we consider *multivalued* logic. The multiple values of multivalued logic include truth values in addition to the alternatives true and false in classical logic. Now how can there be an additional alternative to true and false? It seems absurd, perhaps, to the person already immersed in the thinking encouraged by classical logic. Classical logic has a way of feeding back into our general thinking about the world, and then we can easily conceal from ourselves some of the complexities.

Many of the complexities have already been mentioned in part I.C.

Some assertions are vague and need to be further explained before we can decide whether they are true or false. In some cases we do not know whether they are true or false, even when they are explained. What about questions about the future? Are they true or false before the future arrives? Or are they indeterminate? What about questions about angels?

We are finite. We cannot confidently give answers to all yes or no questions. Moreover, some questions that seem to be definite may not be as definite as they seem. Can there be a set of all sets that do not contain themselves? Does a particular computer program ever halt (the halting problem, see chapter 58)? Multivalued logic represents an attempt, or rather several attempts (for there is more than one possibility), to represent the complexity involved in the fact that not every declarative sentence is clearly true or clearly false. We may have to say, "I don't know," or "We have to wait for the future to see," or "I am not sure we can ever answer that question," or "Maybe that question does not have a definite answer."

Multivalued logic is to be commended for the fact that it draws attention to such complexities. But there is a danger. In this as in other areas, we may end up ignoring or denying the Creator-creature distinction. Let us illustrate by considering the problem of questions about the future. We are ignorant of many future events. We cannot tell whether it will rain exactly one year from the present date. The assertion, "It will rain in Madrid on day X" has no truth value that we can hope to determine *from our limited, finite point of view*. But God knows. So from his point of view, the assertion can be evaluated as true or false, even though we are unable to evaluate it. We distinguish ourselves—the creature—from God, the Creator.

There are other kinds of indeterminateness besides the indeterminateness of the future. Does a jellyfish have a tail? It depends. It depends on how broadly or narrowly we want to use the word *tail*. Is the tail of an airplane a real tail or merely a metaphorical tail? How do we answer?

God knows all about the complexities of the English language, including the complexities about the word *tail*. The situation is richer than what can be captured by a simple true or false answer, which human beings sometimes give in an attempt to ignore or smash out the complexities. For example, they may assert bluntly that "It must be the case that a jellyfish has a tail or else it does not." But could we answer better by saying that it depends on what a person means and what are the circumstances (technical reports in biology versus a discussion with a three-year-old)? God knows the complexities in personal meanings and in circumstances, as well as the human tendency to want a simple, clear-cut answer that will settle all the issues at once.

So all the complexities are not going to dissolve magically if we say, "Well, what is true or false is what is true or false from God's point of view." It is true that God's point of view is ultimate. In all areas, God knows what is true. But his understanding of the word *tail* includes an understanding of the complexities of personal purposes and circumstances. It includes knowledge of multiple possible contexts. In this respect, God's point of view is richer than the T and F of classical logic.[1] The T and F of classical logic reflect one dimension of the richness of who God is. So we can rejoice in the insights that they give us. But they do not authorize us to forget the richness and majesty of the God we serve. One of the potential values of multivalued logic is to remind us of some of that richness.

Three-valued Logic

One kind of multivalued logic is three-valued logic, also called *trivalent logic*, with the values true, false, and unknown. Represented symbolically, we can have the three truth values T, F, and U. Table 63.1 shows the truth tables offered by Stephen Kleene for his three-valued logic.

TABLE 63.1: Truth Table for Kleene's Three-valued Logic

p	q	$p \lor q$	$p \land q$	$\sim p$
T	T	T	T	F
T	F	T	F	F
T	U	T	U	F
F	T	T	F	T
F	F	F	F	T
F	U	U	F	T
U	T	T	U	U
U	F	U	F	U
U	U	U	U	U

The assignments make intuitive sense. They are consistent with a temporal development in which we are eventually going to replace the unknown

---

[1] Remember that T and F represent a one-dimensional simplification that suppresses contexts and personal influences (chapters 21 and 22).

value with either T or F, and then the evaluations of logical truth-functions in two-valued, classical logic are consistent with the temporary values that we assign before we know some of the truth values. For example, if we know that p is T but the truth value of q is unknown (U), we can still confidently conclude that the truth value of $p \vee q$ is T, because of the definition of logical disjunction $\vee$. We cannot, however, say anything yet about $\sim q$ being either true or false. $\sim q$ has a truth value just as unknown as the truth value of q.

Unfortunately, the calculation of truth values for compound expressions does not work out quite in the same manner as for classical logic. Consider $\sim p \vee p$. Suppose p is unknown (U). The truth tables calculate out to show that $\sim p \vee p$ is U. p is U, and so $\sim p$ is U, and so finally $\sim p \vee p$ is U. By contrast, two-valued truth tables show that it is a tautology: it is true even if we ourselves do not know the truth value of p.

What is the difference between the two approaches? In three-valued logic, the calculation of the truth-table result carries along only the information that p has a truth value of unknown. By contrast, the two-valued approach tries out both combinations, when p is T and when p is F. By trying out the combinations separately, it is able to *correlate* between the truth value of p and the truth value of $\sim p$, rather than treating them both just as black boxes with unknown values concealed inside. The calculation using two values finds that one or the other of p and $\sim p$ is true, even if we do not know which. Hence $\sim p \vee p$ comes out true in either case. The two-valued approach ends up being more insightful, because it can correlate between truth values at two different places. The same thing happens if there are two or more propositions p, q, r, ... making up a single complex formula. Any one propositional symbol q is assigned the same truth value at every point where it occurs, and thus the calculation of the truth value of a large formula takes into account the correlation between truth values that crop up at two or more different points in the overall structure of the formula.

A three-valued logic with an extra value U has some use. The addition of the truth value *unknown* reflects the character of the world in which we live. We do not always know. But in the context of logic it could also represent a temptation, if we ignore the Creator-creature distinction. What is unknown to us is known to God. If we regard the category *unknown* as a one-level category operating in a one-level reality, we are ignoring God.

Infinite-valued Logic

Other multivalued logics exist besides Kleene's three-valued logic.[2] Jan
Łukasiewicz invented a form of logic with an infinite number of truth values, ranging from 0 to 1. 0 represents certain falsehood (F). 1 represents
certain truth (T). In between are uncertainties, represented by a real number between 0 and 1. If the truth value of a proposition p is c, the truth
value of $\sim p$ is $1 - c$. (For example, if the truth value of proposition p is 0.2,
the truth value of $\sim p$ is $1 - 0.2 = 0.8$.) If the truth value of q is d, the truth
value of $p \vee q$ is the maximum of c and d. (For example, if p has truth value
0.2 and q has truth value 0.4, the truth value of $p \vee q$ is the maximum of 0.2
and 0.4, that is, 0.4.) The truth value of $p \wedge q$ is the minimum of c and d.
This kind of assignment of truth value reduces to two-valued classical logic
if all the initial assignments of truth values are 0 (F) and 1 (T).

Łukasiewicz's infinite-valued logic, like Kleene's three-valued logic,
reminds us that a simple division into true and false is sometimes a simplification. Moreover, in addition to saying that we may not know for
certain the truth value of a proposition p, Łukasiewicz offers us a way of
quantifying our uncertainty. In some cases where we do not know, we
may still have our suspicions. We may estimate that it is highly likely that
p is true. So we can assign it a truth value of 0.9 or 0.95, let us say. Or
we think that it is unlikely. So we assign it a truth value of 0.2 or 0.03.
Łukasiewicz's logic is a reminder that things that are unknown may still
be estimable.

Much that we have said about Kleene's logic carries over to
Łukasiewicz's logic. Łukasiewicz's logic, like Kleene's, has trouble when
it comes to the *correlations* between truth values at different points in a
compound formula. Consider again the example of the formula $\sim p \vee p$.
Suppose we do not know the truth value of the proposition p. Suppose also
that we have no particular reason to think that it is likely to be true, or
likely to be untrue. We assign it a middle-of-the-road number, namely, 0.5.
Then, the proposition $\sim p$ has probability $1 - 0.5 = 0.5$. The proposition $\sim p$
$\vee p$, according to Łukasiewicz's recipe for calculating on $\vee$, has as its truth
value the maximum of 0.5 and 0.5, which is 0.5. This result suggests that
the truth value is completely uncertain, which of course is false. In two-
valued logic, the truth value is always T.

---

[2] Research has also explored possibilities with four or more discrete truth values.

Probabilistic Logic

The assignment of truth values between 0 and 1 in Łukasiewicz's infinite-valued logic is akin to what happens in probability theory. Probability theory deals with events whose outcome is uncertain. If we flip a coin, it comes up heads some of the time. It also comes up tails some of the time. We cannot predict it. If it is a fair coin, we can say that on the average it comes up heads 1/2 the time, and tails 1/2 the time. So we assign a probability of 1/2 to the event that it comes up heads (on one specific flip). An event that is certain has probability 1. An event that cannot occur has probability 0. In between 1 and 0 are all the probabilities for events that happen some of the time, but not always.

As with the previous example, we should distinguish between our knowledge and God's knowledge. We do not know beforehand the outcome of a flip of the coin. But God does. So the Creator-creature distinction is relevant to our understanding of probabilities.

Probabilities do not behave in quite the same way as do the numbers in Łukasiewicz's logic. In Łukasiewicz's logic, if p has truth value 1/2 and q has truth value 1/2, the truth value of $p \wedge q$ is the minimum of 1/2 and 1/2, that is, still 1/2. Now suppose that p stands for the proposition that coin A turns up heads, while q stands for the proposition that coin B turns up heads. p has probability 1/2, and q has probability 1/2. $p \wedge q$ stands for the proposition that *both* coin A and coin B turn up heads. Even if coin A turns up heads, which is 1/2 the time, we still have to have coin B turn up heads, which is only 1/2 of the time left. The probability of both events together is the product of the individual probabilities 1/2 × 1/2 = 1/4. Thus, probabilities behave differently from what is prescribed in Łukasiewicz's logic.

It is interesting to explore Łukasiewicz's logic as a kind of game, to see what happens in particular cases, and what proofs we can construct. But it is not likely to have many interesting applications in the real world. Probability theory is much more relevant, and is often used by mathematicians and statisticians in situations of uncertain outcomes. Probability theory can be viewed as a kind of infinite-valued logic. But our task is not over if we have assigned some probability to each simple individual event. The events have relationships to one another. In the case of flipping two coins A and B, the two events are described as *independent* because they do not influence each other. But events like burning wood and seeing smoke are correlated. The probability of seeing smoke in a forest on any one day is small. But if we know that someone has just started a fire, the probability is quite high.

Because of its importance and usefulness, probability theory deserves its own discussion. But we cannot undertake it here.

Quantum Logic

Quantum logic can be seen as another form of infinite-valued logic, closely related to probability theory. As the name suggests, quantum logic has arisen in connection with quantum mechanics, which describes the strange behavior of small particles and waves in the microscopic world.[3] Some of this behavior is counterintuitive in comparison to our normal experience in the macroscopic world. Many people have heard about the way in which microscopic particles such as electrons can behave either like waves or like particles, depending on the experimental setup.

Discussion of quantum theory is beyond the scope of our book. But we can alert readers to the fact that it has had some effect on thinking about logic. Some people have spoken about a distinctive "quantum logic" that differs from classical logic. What is "quantum logic" about?

Let us begin with something simpler. In the world of very small particles, research in physics has found that it is impossible to answer simultaneously all the questions we might want to ask about a particle's physical state. The impossibility is not merely a limitation in the technical precision of the apparatus used to make measurements. It seems to be inherent in the world. The inherent limitations show one way in which God's knowledge and control exceed ours.

For example, if we determine within narrow limits the position of an electron at a particular point in time, we cannot simultaneously determine how fast it is moving.[4] One of the effects of this foundational uncertainty is that quantum mechanics must continually deal with probabilities rather than certain predictions.

Of course we must also deal with probabilities in everyday life. Probabilities often crop up because of practical limitations, not because of the

---

[3] But microscopic quantum phenomena can show striking macroscopic effects, as in the case of superfluids and coherent laser light.

[4] The Heisenberg uncertainty principle says that the numerical product of the uncertainty in position (Δx) and the uncertainty in momentum (mass times velocity, Δp_x) can never be reduced below a certain minimum value, $h/4\pi$, where h is Planck's constant. $\Delta x \times \Delta p_x \geq h/4\pi$.

technical physical limitations uncovered in quantum mechanics. So why should there be any fuss when we come to quantum mechanics?

There is a fuss because probabilities in quantum mechanics do not behave in quite the same way as in ordinary life. In ordinary life, we assume that we can simultaneously obtain answers to several questions. Each of these answers provides us with a truth value. In quantum mechanics, we cannot get simultaneous answers, and that has an effect on how we would calculate truth values. Whenever we can get simultaneous answers, ordinary classical logic holds. When we cannot get such answers, we can still make some predictions, but the reasoning is more complicated.[5] However, the reasoning about the mathematical representation of quantum mechanics takes place within the ordinary world, and such reasoning can use classical logic when it analyzes the mathematical representation.

People debate the significance of the special phenomena in quantum mechanics. Is it really the case that we are changing logic? Or are we just meeting some special challenges in the way we represent quantum phenomena mathematically?

Quantum logic illustrates again that the adoption of classical logic involves simplifications. We take a kind of one-dimensional approach to reasoning, and leave aside analogy, personal involvement, and so on. It turns out, in the light of quantum research in the twentieth century, that we were also leaving aside some extra complexities that crop up in physics. We left aside such complexities without even knowing it.

Fuzzy Logic

Fuzzy logic is another kind of infinite-valued logic. In fuzzy logic, propositions have truth values anywhere from 0 to 1, just as in Łukasiewicz's infinite-valued logic. Fuzzy logic is closely related to *fuzzy set theory*. So we need to explain fuzzy set theory. In classical set theory, a set has certain

---

[5] In ordinary life, the distributive law for Boolean algebras can be applied to the probabilities of events. Suppose we have three events, A, B, and C. The probability that event A will occur and that in addition at least one of the events B or C will occur can be represented symbolically as $\text{Prob}(A \wedge (B \vee C))$. The distributive law for Boolean algebra says that $A \wedge (B \vee C) = (A \wedge B) \vee (A \wedge C)$. The probabilities are the same, no matter which way we look at it. That is, the probability that event A will occur, and that in addition B or C will occur $(A \wedge (B \vee C))$, is the same as the probability that at least one of two events will occur, namely, A and B together or A and C together $((A \wedge B) \vee (A \wedge C))$.

In quantum mechanics, it turns out, some of the fundamental structures are not Boolean algebras. The distributive law no longer holds. The structures in question are called complemented modular lattices. See George W. Mackey, *Mathematical Foundations of Quantum Mechanics* (New York/Amsterdam: Benjamin, 1963); Garrett Birkhoff and John von Neumann, "The Logic of Quantum Mechanics," *Annals of Mathematics* 37 (1936): 823–843.

definite members, and no more. For example, the set S = {horse1, horse2, horse3} has exactly three members, namely, the horses horse1, horse2, and horse3. But, as we have seen in chapter 19, classifications of objects in ordinary life often have fuzzy boundaries. A cat's tail is definitely a tail. But do a jellyfish's tentacles count as a "tail"? Does an airplane tail count as a "tail" when the context of our discussion is tails of animals? Unless we introduce a special technical definition, the word *tail* has a vagueness or indeterminateness at the edges. So do most words in English and other natural languages.

The route taken in classical logic is to ignore vagueness or indeterminacy, or else to claim to banish it: we imagine a world where the word *tail* has a perfectly precise boundary to its possible referents. But this is an idealization. The idealization limits the ability of classical logic to apply robustly to natural language. Fuzzy set theory presents itself as a partial answer.

How does fuzzy set theory work? The set S = {horse1, horse2, horse3} has a precisely defined list of members. But suppose we have another set-like object R, and we are not sure whether horse1 is a member of R. We can assign to its membership a real number between 0 and 1. If we assign the number 1 to horse1, horse1 is definitely a member of R. If we assign the number 0 to horse1, horse1 is definitely not a member. If we assign to horse1 a number in between, say 1/3, it says that horse1 has 1/3 of a membership in R. It is on the fuzzy line between being inside R and being outside. It is somewhat more toward the outside than the inside. If it has 0.04 membership in R, it is very much toward the outside, but still not quite definitely outside (not 0).

Suppose now that we are not sure whether horse2 or horse3 is a member of R. We assign a number to indicate a partial membership for each of them. But it need not be the same number. Maybe horse2 has 0.9 membership in R. It is near to the inside of the fuzzy boundary of R.

In general, we need to have a real number for each element horse1, horse2, and horse3 that may have partial membership in R. We can represent this information as a function. For any element x that could possibly be in R, there will be assigned to x a real number $m(x)$ between 0 and 1. $m(x)$ may also take the extreme values 0 and 1. We write $0 \le m(x) \le 1$, which reads: 0 is less than or equal to $m(x)$, and $m(x)$ is less than or equal to 1. So R can be represented as an ordinary set S plus a "membership function" $m(x)$.

Now let us consider a particular example. Let S = {a, b, c, d}. Construct the fuzzy set R by starting with the set S and adding a membership function m with the following values: m(a) = 1, m(b) = 0.3, m(c) = 0.6, m(d) = 0.

The element a is definitely in R, because $m(a) = 1$, and 1 represents certain membership. If $m(s) = 1$ for all s in S, R reduces for practical purposes to the original set S. Note also that in our case $m(d) = 0$. This means that d is definitely not in R, even though it is in S. It is convenient to allow this possibility, even though we could obtain the same result by leaving d out of the original set S. The interesting cases are the elements b and c, which are neither definitely in R nor definitely out.

Fuzzy set theory is a useful reminder that we may sometimes confront complexities in natural language and complexities in life. Boundaries for our categories or classifications may sometimes be fuzzy. Fuzzy set theory endeavors to model this practical fuzziness by sets with extra structure. It thereby moves beyond the simplification in which we pretend to have an allegedly "ideal" situation in which all boundaries are perfectly precise.

We have seen in examining this challenge earlier that the idea of a perfect boundary can easily tempt us to want perfect knowledge—exhaustive knowledge—and to make ourselves gods. Fuzzy sets can remind us of the complexities of language and the limitations in our knowledge.

But fuzzy sets do not do everything for us. In their own way they are still an idealization. For one thing, the definition of a fuzzy set R still starts with an ordinary classical set S. So the challenge of classification already appears with S. The concept of an "element" of a set strips out all the information from the world, leaving us with an "element" whose only properties are possible membership in sets. This kind of reduction from the full richness of the world still represents a collapse into a one-dimensional approach to classification.

Second, how do we know how to assign a real number like 0.3 or 0.6 to membership of b and c in R? Why 0.3 rather than 0.2 or 0.8? The lower numbers are supposedly to represent positions closer to the outside of the fuzzy boundary, while the higher numbers represent positions closer to the inside. But how do we measure this "position"? In practice, we may feel that a jellyfish "tail" is somewhere on the fuzzy boundary of the usual use of "tail." But where? Any number that we give, say 0.3, is a bit of a guess.

We could make the meaning more precise by saying that 0.3 is the *probability* that the word *tail* will be felt appropriate by an average native speaker of English. But the expression "felt appropriate" is itself fuzzy. A native speaker could react to a sample instance of "tail" by saying, "It is an appropriate use," or by saying, "It is inappropriate," or by saying, "Well, it is tolerable," or by saying, "It's a little awkward," and so on. There is a spectrum of possible responses. If we nevertheless decide to go toward a probability assignment, we are venturing into probability theory. Probability theory can then be allowed to take over the job that we thought we needed to assign to fuzzy sets.

Another difficulty with representing linguistic fuzziness using fuzzy sets is that linguistic fuzziness is colored by context. Suppose that I am a marine biologist, and that as a specialist I feel considerable awkwardness at the prospect of calling jellyfish tentacles a "tail." I certainly would not do it in a professional paper. Nor would I do it even in ordinary conversation. But suppose I have a picture book about marine animals that I am showing to my three-year-old daughter. I come down to her level, and for convenience I talk about the jellyfish's "tail." I know what I am doing, and my daughter understands too. I am not lying to her. A jellyfish's tentacles are 100 percent a "tail" *in this special context.* It is so convenient that in ordinary communication we can use context to save us from jargon and circumlocutions and vast, cumbersome explanations.

So we return to the question, "Is a jellyfish's set of tentacles a tail?" If we are thinking within the scheme offered by fuzzy set theory, we invite ourselves to assign a number, maybe 0.3. But that number is a pretty impoverished representation of what is going on. It does not represent *context.* It does not represent the distinction between writing for a professional journal of marine biology and talking to a three-year-old.

The issue of context is a serious one, because God is the ultimate context. Do a jellyfish's tentacles constitute a "tail" in God's sight? We have a Creator-creature distinction. God knows infinitely. So would God give us a clear yes-no answer, if only he consented to?

Because God knows infinitely, he also knows the complexities about jellyfish and about the fuzzy boundaries of the English word *tail,* and about the possibility of varying contexts that make the word more flexible or more precise. He knows it all. *Any* simple yes-no answer ignores detail about this situation. We can be glad that we cannot force God to give us a simple yes-no answer in a circumstance where such an answer is inappropriate and inadequate. The question itself is wrong if it has set up the situation *with the assumption* that all boundaries must be forced to be precise, regardless of complexities. The complexities exist in our human understanding. And we may infer that God's infinite understanding includes even more complexities. The question is in danger of forcing a reductionistic, one-dimensional answer for a many-dimensional world and a many-dimensional plan of God for the world.

Because the definition of fuzzy membership leaves behind context, fuzzy set theory has some of the same limitations that we encountered with Łukasiewicz's infinite-valued logic. In fuzzy set theory, set union, set intersection, and set complement are typically defined in a manner parallel to Łukasiewicz's logic.[6] The result is artificial in comparison to probability theory.

We have not yet explained *fuzzy logic*. Fuzzy logic is logic appropriate for fuzzy set membership. Suppose b has a 0.3 membership in the fuzzy set R. Then the proposition "b is in R" has a fuzzy logic value of 0.3. Fuzzy logic proposes to reason about propositions that make assertions about membership in fuzzy sets. That is the basic idea.

What we have already said about fuzzy sets carries over easily to fuzzy logic. It has a value for reminding us of something left out in classical logic. Classical logic assumes precise boundaries of the categories or classes with which it reasons. The categories are things like "being human," "being mortal," "being a dog," and so on. Classical logic builds patterns of formal reasoning that mimic reasoning in our minds and in our natural languages, but which ignore the complexities concerning boundaries. Fuzzy logic, like fuzzy set theory, says, in effect, "Look what you have left out." That is useful.

But the new approach is still one-dimensional and still has its own limitations. *We* as persons must still think about context, and must evaluate, before God and in the context of everything that we know about God's world, whether the analogue between the formal pattern and practical reasoning actually holds in a particular case. Is fuzzy logic an adequate representation of the reasoning about "All men are mortal"? And if so, is it an adequate representation of reasoning that undertakes a theistic proof? Our thoughts are analogically related to God's thoughts, so that the question of analogy in meanings always lurks in the background—in the context, we might say. Fuzzy set theory and fuzzy logic do not really have built into them, at their foundation, robust resources for dealing with analogy and metaphor.

---

[6] Let R and S be two fuzzy sets with membership functions m_r and m_s, respectively. $m_r(x)$ is the amount of membership of x in R, and likewise $m_s(x)$ gives the amount of membership in S. Then $R \cap S$, the intersection of R and S, has membership function $m(x) = \text{minimum}(m_r(x), m_s(x))$. $R \cup S$, the union of R and S, has membership function $m(x) = \text{maximum}(m_r(x), m_s(x))$. These definitions reduce to ordinary set intersection and union when R and S mimic ordinary sets, that is, when their membership functions always take the values 0 and 1. But the formal definition of intersection and union does not mimic probability theory, and is not influenced by possible correlations in the real world between membership in one of two imprecisely defined classes.

For Further Reflection

1. If $p \supset q$ is regarded as equivalent to $\sim p \lor q$, work out the truth table for $p \supset q$ in Kleene's three-valued logic.

2. What should be the truth-table definition of truth-functional equivalence in Kleene's three-valued logic? That is, what is the defining truth table for $p \equiv q$?

3. Using truth tables, check that $p \lor q$ is equivalent to $\sim(\sim p \land \sim q)$ in Kleene's system.

4. What are the strengths and weaknesses of Kleene's and Łukasiewicz's multivalued logics?

5. Calculate the union $(R \cup S)$ and intersection $(R \cap S)$ of the fuzzy sets R and S with membership functions $m_r(a) = 1$, $m_r(b) = 0.7$, $m_r(c) = 0.5$, $m_r(d) = 0.3$, $m_r(e) = 0$; $m_s(a) = 1$, $m_s(b) = 0$, $m_s(c) = 0.4$, $m_s(d) = 0$, $m_s(e) = 0.8$.

6. What features of natural language does fuzzy logic attempt to represent?

7. Why have some researchers thought that a special logic is needed for quantum mechanics?

Chapter 64

Intuitionistic Logic

Intuitionistic logic is a complicated alternative to classical logic. The outstanding feature of intuitionistic logic is that the law of excluded middle is not treated as a valid general rule. That is, $p \lor \sim p$ is not a theorem for arbitrary p. However, it is still the case that, if p is true for a particular chosen p, then $p \lor \sim p$ is true. Likewise, $p \lor \sim p$ is true in the case where $\sim p$ is true. The deduction rule of addition, which says that $p \lor q$ is deducible from p and is deducible from q, is still a valid rule of deduction.

Then what is the difficulty? There are mathematical conjectures for which no one knows the answer. For instance, the *Goldbach conjecture* says that every even integer greater than 2 can be expressed as the sum of two prime numbers. $4 = 2 + 2, 6 = 3 + 3, 8 = 3 + 5, 10 = 5 + 5$, and so on. (A prime number is a whole number greater than 1 that has no factors other than 1 and itself. 3, 5, and 7 are prime, but $9 = 3 \times 3$ and so 9 is not prime. $12 = 4 \times 3$, and so 12 is not prime.) As of 2011, it is not known whether the Goldbach conjecture is true. Let p stand for the Goldbach conjecture. Classical logic regards p as true or false. We just do not know which. Intuitionistic logic treats p as having an unknown status until (1) a counterexample is produced, in the form of a specific even number $2n$ that is not the sum of two primes, or (2) a proof of p is obtained based on normal axioms for arithmetic.

Origins

The approach called *intuitionism* first arose in mathematics, rather than merely within logic proper. It was primarily the product of the mathematician L. E. J. Brouwer (1881–1966), who adhered to a mentalist or intuitionistic philosophy. Influenced by the philosophies of Kant and Schopenhauer, Brouwer thought of mathematics as a creation of the human mind, based on the intuitive experience of time. The experience of time introduced the idea of oneness and twoness, and from there human thinking arrived at the concept of the natural numbers. In Brouwer's view, logic was a derivative aspect of mathematics, rather than the reverse. This philosophy of mathematics, which is now called *intuitionism*, opened to Brouwer the possibility of altering the conventional understanding of the laws of logic, based on his conception of mathematics.

The key element in intuitionist philosophy is the idea of mathematics as mental creation. A mathematical truth is not true eternally, but rather is found to be true when a mental construction shows that it is true.[1] As a result, the proposition $p \lor \sim p$ cannot be affirmed for a proposition p in mathematics for which we do not have a construction, either in the form of an explicitly constructed counterexample or in the form of a proof. And a proof must actively *construct* any particular numbers needed in its steps. In particular, in order to prove the existence of a number with certain properties, it is not enough to use *reductio ad absurdum* to show that assuming the contrary leads to a contradiction. One must actually produce the number in question by an explicit construction.

Evaluation

How shall we evaluate Brouwer's intuitionism? Brouwer paid attention to limitations in mathematical knowledge. We do not know the answer to certain conjectures like Goldbach's conjecture. Brouwer's concern for limitations was later supplemented by Gödel's incompleteness theorem. As a result of Gödel's theorem, mathematicians and logicians have grown to recognize that there are an indefinite number of arithmetic propositions whose truth or falsity cannot be established by routine proofs from well-known axioms.

This concern for human limitation is in fundamental harmony with the Christian distinction between Creator and creature. We do not know everything that God knows. And our limitations need to be reckoned with. We are in danger of subtly falsifying reality, and producing flawed results, if we

---

[1] Mark van Atten, "Luitzen Egbertus Jan Brouwer," *Stanford Encyclopedia of Philosophy (Summer 2010 Edition)*, ed. Edward N. Zalta, http://plato.stanford.edu/archives/sum2010/entries/brouwer/, accessed August 26, 2011, §3:

> As, on Brouwer's view, there is no determinant of mathematical truth outside the activity of thinking, a proposition only becomes true when the subject has experienced its truth (by having carried out an appropriate mental construction); similarly, a proposition only becomes false when the subject has experienced its falsehood (by realizing that an appropriate mental construction is not possible). Hence Brouwer can claim that 'there are no non-experienced truths.'

Brouwer's words come from L. E. J. Brouwer, *Collected Works 1. Philosophy and Foundations of Mathematics*, ed. Arend Heyting (Amsterdam: North-Holland, 1975), 488. See also Rosalie Iemhoff, "Intuitionism in the Philosophy of Mathematics," *Stanford Encyclopedia of Philosophy (Summer 2010 Edition)*, ed. Edward N. Zalta, http://plato.stanford.edu/archives/sum2010/entries/intuitionism/, accessed August 26, 2011. See also Dirk van Dalen, "Intuitionism and Intuitionistic Logic," *Encyclopedia of Philosophy*, 2nd ed., ed. Donald M. Borchert, 10 vols. (Detroit/New York/San Francisco/ . . . : Thomson Gale, 2006), 4:737–743.

think purely in terms of an ideal of absolute mathematical knowledge that we do not possess.

On the other hand, Brouwer's positive philosophy of mathematics cannot be endorsed.[2] A philosophy that conceives of mathematics as purely a matter of human mental operations makes man, not God, the real origin of mathematics. Moreover, it is reductionistic, in that it reduces mathematics to one dimension, namely, its presence in human mental intuition. It cannot explain the coherence between mental mathematics and other dimensions of the world (physical objects, space, physical laws, language, and the special symbolism of formal languages).[3]

Intuitionistic philosophy treats man as the measure of truth. It treats the Goldbach conjecture as neither true nor false—until we as human beings come up with a counterexample or a proof. But God's knowledge exceeds ours. God already knows whether the conjecture is true or false. It is true or false in God's mind, even before human beings find out which of the two alternatives is the case. It is possible, because of the limitations of the human mind and the limitations of axioms that we may devise, that we may never find out the answer while this world lasts.[4] Because of the knowledge that God has given us about himself, we as human beings can still know that the Goldbach conjecture is either true or false, measured by the final standard, namely, God's knowledge. We are, as it were, similar to intuitionists when we look at the limitations of human knowledge; but we adopt a stance similar to a classical logical viewpoint when we contemplate God's knowledge.

But we should also note that caution is appropriate when we think about God's knowledge. The Bible reveals a God who is beyond our comprehension. We must preserve a Christian view of God's transcendence and immanence. God's immanence implies that we can understand a good deal about his thinking. We can even talk about cases like the Goldbach conjecture where God knows more than we know. Quantitatively speaking, his

---

[2] See Vern S. Poythress, "A Biblical View of Mathematics," *Foundations of Christian Scholarship: Essays in the Van Til Perspective*, ed. Gary North (Vallecito, CA: Ross House, 1976), 158–188, especially 162.

[3] See also appendix F1 on Kantian subjectivism, which is related to Brouwer's approach.

[4] There are several possibilities. (1) It is possible that a counterexample to the Goldbach conjecture exists, in the form of a specific even number that is not the sum of two primes. If the smallest counterexample is a very large number, it may be beyond the calculating capabilities of even the most powerful computers of this and succeeding generations. Human beings may never discover a counterexample within the time that human beings live within this world. (2) It is possible that the Goldbach conjecture has a proof that uses only well-known axioms (such as Peano's axioms for arithmetic). But if the simplest proof is exceedingly long and intricate, it may never be discovered while human beings live within this world. (3) It is possible that the Goldbach conjecture is true but unprovable, in a manner parallel to what has been demonstrated by Gödel's incompleteness theorems. (4) It is possible that in our reasoning about God's knowledge we have omitted some additional possibility beyond (1)-(3) above.

knowledge is more extensive than ours. But his knowledge is also qualitatively different, because he knows as the absolute Creator (Christian transcendence). We cannot know with perfect clarity just *how* his knowledge transcends ours.

God's transcendence implies that we must be humble. We must recognize that it can be hazardous to claim to know too much about just what it means for God to know this or that fact. For a question like the Goldbach conjecture, it certainly looks to us as though the Goldbach conjecture is either true or false. That is why we can infer that God knows which is the case.

But there are other questions in modern mathematics where the situation is not clear. For example, consider one issue about infinite sets. The *continuum hypothesis* conjectures that there is no set of intermediate size between the set of positive integers and the set of real numbers (where "size" is suitably defined by the understanding that two sets in one-to-one correspondence with each other are the same size; see appendix E2). Both the continuum hypothesis and its negation have been shown to be consistent with standard axioms for set theory. So which is true? Do we just need more axioms? Or, when we deal with infinite sets, are we quite sure what we mean? Is it possible that the situation here is like the situation with the word *tail* in English? The word *set*, even in the technically precise context of mathematics, is not perfectly precise. Is it possible that the continuum hypothesis has no clear yes-no answer, because our words and mathematical constructions lack the necessary precision? What we thought was a clear-cut question turns out not to be clear-cut.

Developments

Intuitionistic logic has a history beyond Brouwer. Brouwer's philosophy led him to conceive of mathematics as foundational and not dependent on logic. Brouwer thought that mathematical intuition was not a form of logic, and so it would be inappropriate to try to *reduce* mathematics to formal axioms. In fact, Brouwer philosophically opposed the movement toward formalization that was championed by David Hilbert and others like him. But he allowed for a pragmatic value in formalization, and after him others developed formal axioms that gave expression to the ideas of intuitionism.[5]

As we have indicated, the axioms for intuitionistic logic do not allow

---

[5] Joan Moschovakis, "Intuitionistic Logic," *Stanford Encyclopedia of Philosophy (Summer 2010 Edition)*, ed. Edward N. Zalta, http://plato.stanford.edu/archive/sum2010/entries/logic-intuitionistic/, accessed August 26, 2011.

the deduction of the law of excluded middle, $p \vee \sim p$. How can the law of the excluded middle be itself excluded, and still preserve other parts of logic? In Whitehead and Russell's system for propositional logic, $\sim p \vee p$ is by definition the same as $p \supset p$, and the latter is still true in intuitionistic logic. The crucial difference is in the definitions of the logical operators. In intuitionistic logic, $\sim p \vee q$ is not equivalent to $p \supset q$, though the equivalence *does* hold in classical logic. In intuitionistic logic $\vee$ (logical disjunction) and $\supset$ (material implication) are defined separately and independently. Thus each formal system of logic must be treated on its own terms.

Relationships

Nevertheless, there are relationships between the two kinds of logic. Kurt Gödel and Gerhard Gentzen independently showed that any proposition p in classical logic can be "translated" in a formulaic way into an analogous proposition p' in intuitionistic logic, in such a way that p and p' are materially equivalent in classical logic, and such that if p is provable in classical logic then p' is provable in intuitionistic logic.[6] In this way, the essential power of classical logic can be embedded in intuitionistic logic.

But if intuitionistic logic has a weaker set of axioms than classical logic, how can it possibly "contain" classical logic?

In classical logic, p and $\sim\sim p$ are materially equivalent. But in intuitionistic logic, they are not always equivalent. If a particular proposition p can be proved by methods acceptable to intuitionism, intuitionism and classical logic are basically equivalent *for that proposition*. But in other cases the two forms of logic do not treat the relation between the propositions p and $\sim\sim p$ in the same way. The simple method of truth tables will not work in the context of intuitionistic logic, because of the problem with conjectures whose truth or falsehood has not been established. In intuitionistic logic, the operation of logical negation $\sim$ has slightly different properties. For a positive property p involving the existence of certain numbers, proving p means that you must construct the numbers. On the other hand, proving $\sim p$ means only that you show that the assumption of the existence of the numbers leads to a contradiction. Negative properties can be established by *reductio ad absurdum*. In intuitionistic logic, $p \supset \sim\sim p$. If p is provably true, it cannot be the case that you can find a counterexample. On the other hand, in general it cannot be proved that $\sim\sim p \supset p$. If you show that assuming $\sim p$ leads to a contradiction

---

[6] Ibid., §4.1.

(*reductio ad absurdum*), you establish ~~p. But until you construct suitable numbers that show that p is true, you have not yet proved p in a manner that is satisfactory within the intuitionistic context.

Granted this understanding, the fundamental element in the translation from classical logic into intuitionistic logic is to translate atomic propositions p into ~~p, and to translate compound propositions of the form $p \vee q$ using De Morgan's theorem, which expresses the equivalence in classical logic between $p \vee q$ and ~($\sim p \wedge \sim q$). In the process of making these translations, extra instances of logical negation (~) are introduced. These extra negations make no difference within classical logic, since $p \equiv$ ~~p. However, within the context of intuitionistic logic, the extra negations weaken the claim made by the formula as a whole. No longer is the new formula making a positive claim for having constructed certain numbers, but only a negative claim that a contradiction follows from assuming the contrary.

Conversely, intuitionistic logic finds a home within the classical world by way of the theory of computability. Constructible numbers are computable numbers. So Negri and von Plato observe,

> Intuitionistic logic, and intuitionism more generally, used to be philosophically motivated, but today the grounds for using intuitionistic logic can be completely neutral philosophically. Intuitionistic or constructive reasoning, which are the same thing, systematically supports computability: If the initial data in a problem or theorem are computable and if one reasons constructively, [intuitionistic] logic will never make one committed to an infinite computation. Classical logic, instead, does not make the distinction between the computable and the noncomputable.[7]

In these ways, intuitionistic logic and classical logic serve as perspectives on one another. We are richer for having both. We thank God for the perseverance of Brouwer and his followers in following a new idea, though we disagree with the philosophy that presided at its birth.

---

[7] Sara Negri and Jan von Plato, *Structural Proof Theory* (Cambridge: Cambridge University Press, 2001), 25. In addition, the meaning of intuitionistic logic can be interpreted in model theory (van Dalen, "Intuitionism," 739–742).

For Further Reflection

1. What philosophical ideas drove the original idea of intuitionism?
2. What is the conception of mathematics in philosophical intuitionism?
3. What positive insights belong to intuitionistic logic?
4. What are the potential liabilities of intuitionistic logic?
5. How does intuitionistic logic interpret logical negation differently from classical logic?
6. What issue does intuitionistic logic see in the law of excluded middle?
7. How can intuitionistic logic and classical logic be fitted together?

Chapter 65

Modal Logic

Modal logic means logic dealing with possibility and necessity. Classical logic considers what is the case. Snow is white. All cats are carnivores. The moon is not made of green cheese. Modal logic considers what *could* be the case. Is it possible that the moon could be made of green cheese? Is it necessary that the sun will rise tomorrow, or is it possible that it will not rise?

People have discussed issues of possibility and necessity for a long time. But possibility and necessity do not fit well into the core of Aristotelian logic, which was designed to deal only with simple truth and falsehood.[1] Nor do they fit directly into twentieth-century propositional logic (such as Whitehead and Russell's propositional logic) or quantificational logic.

Symbols in Modal Logic

Only in the twentieth century did the character of possibility and necessity begin to be included in formal logical systems. *Modal logic* is the name now given to symbolic logic that includes extra symbols to represent possibility and necessity. The usual symbol for possibility is a diamond ◊. The symbol for necessity is a square □.

> ◊*p* means "it is possible that *p*" or "*p* is possibly true" or "possibly *p*"
> (these three expressions are treated as equivalent).
> □*p* means "it is necessary that *p*" or "*p* is necessarily true" or
> "necessarily *p*."

As is usual in symbolic logic, the formal symbols are not designed to capture everything about the natural-language use of the words *possible* and *necessary*. They are a kind of specialization. They take one dimension from the richness of natural language, and endeavor to represent that one dimension in a rigorous, consistent, and well-defined way.

Just as the operations of universal and existential quantification can be

---

[1] Aristotle was aware of the issue of future contingent events, but his categorical syllogisms are not designed to include them.

defined in terms of one another, so the operations of possibility and necessity, when treated in this one-dimensional manner, can be defined in terms of one another. For example, the possibility symbol $\Diamond$ can be defined in terms of the necessity symbol $\Box$ by saying that the possibility symbol $\Diamond$ is shorthand for $\sim\Box\sim$. For any proposition p,

$\Diamond p$ means $\sim\Box\sim p$

Translated back into ordinary English, this formulation is saying,

> "It is possible that p is true" is shorthand for "It is not necessary that p is false (not true)."

This formulation makes reasonable sense in English. But we must remember that the symbolic notation with the symbols $\Diamond$ and $\Box$ is a "one-dimensional" simplification of the meanings of the words *possible* and *necessary* in English.

Instead of defining the possibility symbol $\Diamond$ using the necessity symbol $\Box$ as a starting point, we may do the reverse. We may define necessity in terms of possibility:

$\Box p$ is shorthand for $\sim\Diamond\sim p$

Translated into English, this formulation means roughly,

> "It is necessary that p is true" is shorthand for "It is not possible that p is false (not true)."

The more common approach is to take the necessity symbol $\Box$ as basic. It is added as an extra symbol in the formal language of the logical system of modal logic. Then the possibility symbol $\Diamond$ is defined in terms of it. Technically, the possibility symbol is not part of the formal language, but is shorthand for $\sim\Box\sim$. That is, the possibility symbol is part of the shorthand that exists in the metalanguage. In practice, logicians use both symbols freely. But they know in the back of their minds that they have defined one in terms of the other. And replacement of the possibility symbol $\Diamond$ by its definition $\sim\Box\sim$ takes place when they do their initial work to establish the fundamental logical properties of possibility.

Whichever approach we use, we can affirm several equivalences:

$\Diamond p$ is equivalent to $\sim\Box\sim p$
$\sim\Diamond p$ is equivalent to $\Box\sim p$
$\Box p$ in equivalent to $\sim\Diamond\sim p$
$\sim\Box p$ in equivalent to $\Diamond\sim p$

But in more ordinary, multidimensional contexts, we can find instances where the different wordings are not completely synonymous. Suppose that we have heard on tonight's news what we regard as a reliable weather report. We might say, "It is not possible that it will rain tomorrow." We are speaking loosely. We mean that it is extremely unlikely. Such a statement is not equivalent to saying that it is necessary for it not to rain. The latter wording suggests a continuation such as, "It is necessary for it not to rain if we are going to have a nice picnic." Necessity, in English, frequently addresses what is necessary for some purpose. Modal logic as a formal system is not intended to match English.

Axioms

In a system of symbolic logic, we also need some extra axioms to indicate how to manipulate formulas that include the extra symbols. The main extra axioms are of two kinds. The first kind adds extra axioms corresponding to the original axioms for classical logic.

1. If p is a theorem in modal logic, derivable using the minimal axioms of propositional logic and modal logic, you may infer $\Box p$.

This rule is called the *necessitation rule*.[2] This rule makes sense. The tautologies and other basic axioms in a system are meant to be chosen so that they are obviously true and we could not imagine them to be false. They are *necessarily* true. (We will, however, later add extra axioms for modal logic, and they are not included in this rule.)

The second kind is a rule more closely related to the deduction rule *modus ponens*:

2. If $\Box(p \supset q)$ then $(\Box p) \supset (\Box q)$.

This rule is called the *distribution axiom*. Usually we drop the extra parentheses around $(\Box p)$. We write $\Box p \supset \Box q$ when we mean $(\Box p) \supset (\Box q)$. The

---

[2] James Garson, "Modal Logic," *Stanford Encyclopedia of Philosophy (Winter 2009 Edition)*, ed. Edward N. Zalta, http://plato.stanford.edu/archives/win2009/entries/logic-modal/, accessed August 24, 2012, §2.

necessity symbol □, like the operator for logical negation ∼, has "higher precedence" and goes only with what is immediately after it, unless parentheses signal otherwise. Thus □$(p ⊃ q)$ means that it is necessarily so that p implies q. □$p ⊃ q$, by contrast, means the same as $(□p) ⊃ q$; it means that if p is necessarily true, we infer q. These are quite different meanings.

In classical logic, the deduction rule *modus ponens* allows us to deduce q once we have proved both p and $(p ⊃ q)$. The new rule, the "distribution axiom," allows us to deduce □q once we have proved both □p and □$(p ⊃ q)$. Thus, it extends the rule of *modus ponens* to cover situations that deal with necessity.

Some forms of modal logic add additional axioms to these basic ones. We will discuss some of these additional axioms when we discuss models for modal logic.

The Significance of Possibility and Necessity

What are the extra symbols ◊ and □ intended to represent? They represent possibility and necessity, we say. But what *kind* of possibility and necessity? We must be careful, because the words *possible* and *necessary* in English have a range of usages. As usual, natural language is flexible. A logical formalism will capture only one dimension of this richness.

We can talk of something being "necessary" in the context of moral obligation. "It is *necessary* for me to carry out the terms of the contract that I signed." Moral necessity has been studied by philosophers, and the term "deontic logic" has been used. Deontic logic has been treated as one kind of modal logic. But in this case the operation denoting necessity is customarily written with the symbol O ("It is *obligatory* that . . .") rather than the symbol □. We can also talk about possible or impossible events in the context of discussing the limitations of our knowledge. We might say, for example, that "It is possible that Don is guilty of the crime of which he is accused." In most situations of this type, the crime has already taken place. Either in fact Don is guilty or he is not (though we are ignoring the possibility that he is an accessory to some other person who directly did the deed). But we are in a situation where we do not *know* whether Don is guilty. This kind of possibility has been called *epistemic* possibility, that is, a kind of possibility having to do with capabilities in knowledge. It asks what follows from what we *know* or do not know. The operation denoting epistemic necessity is sometimes denoted K (for "known").

Epistemic possibility may also crop up in situations of future predictions. We might say, "It is possible that it will rain tomorrow." Or "It is not possible that it might rain tomorrow" (because we have received what we consider to be a definitive weather report on tonight's news). This situation might be regarded as essentially the same as the situation involving Don's guilt. But some philosophers have considered that future events are *innately* indeterminate rather than simply unknown to us. This kind of situation gives rise to what are known as *tense* logics (since truth value can vary with the *tense* of the verb, which indicates whether the proposition in question has to do with the past, the present, or the future).

As usual, ordinary conversation contains fuzzy boundaries. Just how unlikely or absurd does something have to be before we will say, at least loosely speaking, that it is "impossible"? What we say depends, as usual, on context, which enables hearers to discern whether we are speaking precisely, and whether we are including very unlikely "possibilities."

More often philosophers are concerned with what has been called *logical* or *alethic* possibility and necessity. They are not asking whether it is possible for it to rain tomorrow, given the weather report, but whether it is possible *in general*.

Are unicorns possible? Maybe not within this world. But are they possible in some world? Such very general possibility is to be distinguished both from moral possibility and from the kind of "possibility" deriving from limited knowledge.

So what is this kind of possibility? How do we think about it? We will evaluate these questions using the Bible as a resource, and by reflecting on the foundations for possibility and necessity in God.

For Further Reflection

1. What feature differentiates modal logic from propositional logic?
2. What standard equivalences hold that show the relations between possibility (◊) and necessity (□)?
3. Distinguish some different kinds of uses of the language of "possibility" and "necessity" in ordinary language.
4. What is the relation between possibility and necessity in the formal language of modal logic?

Chapter 66

Theistic Foundations for Modal Logic

Let us consider how the idea of possibility functions in relation to God.

Theological Reflection about Possibility

To begin with, theological discussion of human decision making sometimes distinguishes between moral and physical possibility. As an example, consider Jesus's prediction in the Gospels that Peter would deny him three times before the night was over (Matt. 26:34 and parallels). Physically speaking, it was *possible* for Peter to keep his mouth shut. He had voluntary control of his own body. No superscientist was manipulating his vocal apparatus and making it come out with sounds that Peter himself did not control. No physical force was applied to Peter from outside. But in another sense, we could argue that Peter did not have the moral fortitude to keep silent. We might claim that it was *morally* impossible for Peter to keep silent, because from a moral point of view he did not have what it takes.

Moral responsibility is a mysterious thing. Since the fall of Adam, every human being except Jesus has been infected with sin. We not only perform outward actions that are sinful, but have inward sinful desires that motivate the actions. We cannot stop sinning. Yes, people perform some good deeds, but even these are contaminated by mixed motives. Morally speaking, it is not *possible* for us to stop sinning completely. Yet we are still responsible for our sins. There is no physical compulsion. So it is clear that we have to make a distinction between moral and physical possibility.

Let us return to the case of Peter's denial. We can talk about still another sense of possibility, namely, possibility in the light of Jesus's prediction of the denial. If we knew nothing about Jesus's prediction, and we were bystanders observing Peter's situation, we might say, from the standpoint of our knowledge, that it was possible for Peter either to deny Jesus or not deny him. We would be saying that we did not know, and that both possibilities appeared to us to be open ("epistemic possibility"). On the other hand, if we knew Jesus's prediction, and believed it, we would have been able to say that it was "impossible" for Peter not to deny Jesus, because we know that divine predictions always come true.

The same holds in the case of any divinely inspired prophecy. In Micah 5:2 God prophesied through the prophet Micah that the Messiah (Jesus) would be born in Bethlehem. So, as soon as the prophecy was given, we could say that it was *impossible* for the Messiah to be born elsewhere. On the other hand, before the prophecy was given, we would have had to say that, as far as we knew, it was possible for the Messiah to be born anywhere.[1] We would still have the constraint that the Messiah had to be descended from David, as God promised in 2 Samuel 7:13 and in Isaiah 11:1.[2] This kind of possibility is one form of epistemic possibility.

Thus, in ordinary language we can talk about possibilities and necessities in a number of contexts. And these cannot be equated with one another. In fact, because of the general principle of contextual influence, *every* use of words like *possible* and *necessary* is colored in subtle ways by context. In particular, what we think is "possible" at an earlier point in time may become "impossible" or "necessary" when God speaks more words, indicating more details about his plans for the future. What God promises is necessary, and what contradicts his promises is impossible.

We also know that God is creative and free. He is not constrained from the outside to do anything he does. He is sovereign. So he did not have to create the world. When Adam fell, God did not have to undertake to redeem him. He nevertheless chose to do so. God did not have to choose Abraham, rather than someone else, to be the man beginning a special line of promise leading to Christ. But, since God did purpose to do these things, we can say that it was *necessary* for him to carry them out. He is a God of faithfulness, and his own character has implications. God cannot break his promises, because that is inconsistent with his character. So fulfilling his promises is *necessary*. We can count on it.

This kind of discussion of what is possible and necessary reckons with God. And so it must. Necessity originates with God. God does not betray

---

[1] Here as in other circumstances we can distinguish God's point of view from our limited knowledge. God knew from the beginning where the Messiah would be born. Given his plan, it was impossible that the Messiah would be born anywhere else.

[2] There are complexities here, because in 2 Samuel 7 there is an allusion also to Solomon, David's son, who functions as a type of Christ, the Messiah. Also, it is not clear whether the prophecy recorded in Micah 5:2 was originally given orally by Micah before or after the prophecy in Isaiah 11:1.

his character. The Bible says that God never lies (Titus 1:2). Why? It would be inconsistent with his character, which includes being truthful. The Bible also says that God "cannot deny himself" (2 Tim. 2:13). The word *cannot* represents an impossibility. It is *necessary* that God tell the truth. There is no outside constraint, but his character requires it. God is the original, and everything else derives from him. All necessity within this world, and within our thinking, has its ultimate roots in God.

Moreover, these roots are bound up with God's Trinitarian character. As we have seen in earlier chapters, God's faithfulness to his character coheres with his faithfulness to his Son, whom he loves through the Holy Spirit. God's character is expressed in his Son, and so loving the Son means faithfulness to the Son, which means faithfulness to God's character. Necessity coheres with love. Necessity is personal. Necessity is also moral. God's faithfulness is moral consistency as well as logical consistency. And necessity is epistemic: God is faithful to what he knows, and preeminently the Father knows the Son through the Spirit.

Thus, the distinctions between moral necessity, epistemic necessity, and alethic necessity are subtle. We cannot strictly separate them. They are aspects of God's character. Each kind of necessity implies the others. Each, we might even say, is a form or expression of the others. Each is a perspective on the others. Ultimately we have one God with whom we have to reckon.

Logical Necessity

Philosophers have sometimes focused on what they have called *logical* necessity. A logical necessity is a truth that follows directly from logic, and whose denial leads to logical inconsistency. For example, within a philosophical context, it may be claimed that Aristotle's syllogisms *necessarily* hold (that is, they are valid, and necessarily so, because they are part of logic). It may be claimed that $p \supset p$ is *necessarily* true.

But in this kind of reflection there looms up the temptation to regard "logic" as an impersonal something out there, independent of God. If so, a philosopher might even blasphemously say that it is logically possible for God to contradict himself. It is logically possible, he thinks, because he cannot derive a contradiction, within his own mind, from the premises. But then he is making his own mind the ultimate standard for logic. And that is illegitimate. It denies the Creator-creature distinction, and denies the *personal* character of logic as well.

In fact, possibility and necessity *make no sense* without God as their foundation. God's character is the limit of possibility. As people made in the image of God, we have the capability of thinking about possibilities because we imitate God, who knows all possibilities even before we were created.

Moreover, because we are finite, we do not comprehend exhaustively God's character. To put it differently, we do not comprehend the Logos. Living in *this* world, we do not have a God's-eye vision of all possibilities whatsoever, or of all possible worlds that God might have created to bring these possibilities to realization. So talk about "possibilities" beyond the edge of the universe is fraught with peril.

Nevertheless, such talk is not altogether useless. We can say, for instance, that God could have created a world very different from this one, because we know, from what he reveals to us about himself within this world, that he is free and creative. But we do not know the details of the possibilities and impossibilities. To know the limit of the possibilities, we would have to know the limits of his character. We would have to comprehend the Logos. And we do not know the Logos exhaustively.

The peril arises because it is tempting to fall back into the practice of making ourselves little gods. We try to imagine what is possible for God, and do not notice that in the process we allow the intrusion of a sinful desire to make our own judgments about possibility and necessity the ultimate standard to which we think God must conform. We will be a god, and we will tell God what we will and will not stand for. The Bible's own reply is pertinent:

> But who are you, O man, to answer back to God? Will what is molded say to its molder, "Why have you made me like this?" (Rom. 9:20)

Religious rebellion can easily lie beneath the surface, and even break out in our ideas about logic. And the temptation occurs in particular when we are dealing with the mystery of what is possible, that is, what is possible for God.

We are made in the image of God. Our thinking and talking about possibility and necessity imitates the mind of God and images God. But in rebellion we may pervert this ability into an attempt to be a god in matters of necessity and possibility.

Consider a particular example, going back to Peter and his denial. The philosopher who wants to be perfectly general might want to consider the possibility of another world in which Peter did not deny his Lord, and in which Jesus did not predict his denial. This possibility does make a certain amount of sense, because, as we observed, Peter was not under physical constraint. We can picture for ourselves an alternative scenario, and picture Peter boldly acknowledging that he was a disciple. We can picture it. And God is not surprised. We have imaginations and creativity and ability to make hypothetical pictures because God, as the original knower, knew all about such pictures and possibilities before we ever did.

But there are also difficulties and complexities, if we think about it. What kind of a world would this be, an alternative world with Peter in it? Peter is who he is. If we imagine a completely different world, while Peter as we know him belongs to *this* world, does it make clear sense to talk about Peter in that world? Are we going to say that Peter in the alternative world has exactly the same moral failings and fears as he does in this world? And if so, would he have the *moral* fortitude to withstand temptation?

Exactly what does it mean to have a different world and the *same* Peter? Are we "playing God" by assuming that we can work out a whole other world in a manner consistent with God's character? Or, more likely, are we assuming that we can work out a whole other world consistent with our own human conception of what is possible? We face the temptation to make our idea of possibility into an ultimate standard.

No, we are finite. I suspect that we do not thoroughly understand what we mean when we attempt to have another world with the *same* person Peter in it. We do understand somewhat: maybe we mean "a person just like Peter, but without all his moral failings," or something like that. But we do not know everything, and so we do not know all the limitations and the possibilities that would go into creating alternative worlds.

Affinities

Quantificational logic shows some concerns that are analogous to the issues of possibility. A quantifying term, the term *all* or the term *some*, is designed to range over a number of *possibilities*. Suppose we have a predicate $H(x)$. Let us say that it is intended to represent "x is human." x is a variable ranging over all humans and animals and plants. Each individual s (Socrates) or p (Plato) is like a possibility, for which $H(x)$ might be true. To say that it is "possible" that $H(x)$ (i.e., that "x is human") would be akin to saying that some x exists for which $H(x)$. That is:

$(\exists x)H(x)$

Likewise, to say that it is "necessary" that H(x) would be akin to saying that H(x) is true for all x:

$$(\forall x)H(x)$$

What we have earlier said about God as the foundation for quantification (chapter 49) applies by analogy to possibility and necessity in our new context.

Yet possibility and necessity in this new context do not simply reduce to using quantifiers in the usual way. What is the difference? With quantifiers, the variable x ranges over referents within this world: Socrates, Plato, and so on. Each individual is a possible instance of x. But the philosophical discussion of possibility wants to talk about possibilities that are not actualized within this world. We say, "it is possible that Peter could have refused to deny Christ, but in fact he did." We distinguish possibility from what actually happened. The Bible contains instances that discuss possibilities of this kind. Jesus says,

> For *if* the mighty works done in you [Chorazin and Bethsaida] had been done in Tyre and Sidon, they *would have* repented long ago in sackcloth and ashes. (Matt. 11:21)

> For if the mighty works done in you [Capernaum] had been done in Sodom, it would have remained until this day. (Matt. 11:23)

Tyre and Sidon "would have repented," he says. But the biblical record shows that they did not (Ezekiel 28). Jesus postulates a situation in which "the mighty works" were done in Sodom. But such mighty works did not happen in fact.[3] Such an illustration helps to illumine the depth of guilt in Chorazin and Bethsaida, in comparison with Tyre and Sidon. But Jesus's hypothetical situation for Tyre and Sidon does not change everything in the whole world into another whole world. Tyre and Sidon are still the same Tyre and Sidon, and God is still the same God. Possibilities always occur within a context where some things are assumed to remain the same. And Jesus is speaking here with prophetic authority. He also speaks with divine authority backed up ultimately by divine knowledge, which includes knowledge of all possi-

---

[3] In the city of Sodom, the angels staying with Lot did strike the attackers with blindness (Gen. 19:11). That in itself should have been enough to awaken them to their peril. But they were a stubborn, hard-hearted lot—just not as hard-hearted as Capernaum.

bilities. We ourselves, as finite human beings, must frequently admit that we do not know what is possible. Would Tyre and Sidon have repented? If Jesus had not told us, would we be able to be sure? I do not think so.

Undefined Symbols

So how does modal logic proceed? How does it define what "possibility" and "necessity" mean? In one sense, the formal side of modal logic avoids definition completely. The symbols are treated from a completely *formal* point of view, the point of view of formal language. They are just undefined symbols. And then we add rules for constructing well-formed formulas, and we add axioms. These axioms are not given a real-world meaning either, but are just well-formed formulas without any "extra" meaning. Then we follow the rules for manipulating the symbols and come up with formal proofs. We are playing the game of symbol manipulation. And, for those who like it, it can be a game that is "fun."

But the game has a human interest primarily because we eventually will establish a correlation—a translation—between the so-called "meaningless" symbols of the formal system and the language and thinking that we use about the world. When we do that, we have to ask whether the correlation is assuming or denying the Creator-creature distinction, and whether it is showing awareness of all the complexities.

Making the correlation with the world is a big task. And it cannot be avoided. The unavoidability of the task seriously decreases the value of what logicians may hope to achieve by symbol manipulation. People frequently hope that formalization will give us power over the world and over reality. Maybe it will give us power even over the Logos. But, rightly understood, it does not. As in the case of propositional logic and quantificational logic, so here, the formal manipulations have to be sifted and tested in relation to everything we know about God and the world, not just blindly applied. The Logos judges us, and not the other way around. We cannot avoid responsibility through formalism.

An analogy may be helpful. A child can build a miniature town with Legos. Or an adult can play a simulation game like SimCity on a computer, and build an imaginary city. The imaginary city may have streets, railroads, energy supplies, businesses, residential areas, and so on. Both the child and the adult are playing with a small model of a town or a city. The model is interesting because it has correspondences with a real town. And the correspondences can be an occasion for insights. A child playing with Legos or a person playing SimCity might grow in appreciation of the complexities that go into the construction of a real town. But the child or the adult who is wise also recognizes that there are limitations. Being successful at building a Lego town does not qualify you either to be a construction engineer or to be the mayor of a real town.

In a parallel manner, the construction of a formal logic that imitates possibility and necessity can have real value. It may be fun. It may be fascinating. It may suggest insights. It may help now and then to make distinctions. But we have to be like the child or the adult playing with a model town. We have to recognize that we are not learning all the complexities and all the abilities. The model deliberately leaves out a lot of worrisome complexity, so that it will be manageable. When a person starts interacting with the real town in which he lives, he has to make informed judgments as to when and where the model is inadequate. And these judgments depend on many factors—a huge context with many dimensions. He cannot avoid his obligations to be wise. He cannot pretend that the Logos is captured by his model.

For Further Reflection

1. Discuss in what senses it was possible or impossible for Peter not to deny Christ.
2. In what way do different conceptions of possibility and necessity have a foundation in God?
3. What does Jesus's statement about Tyre and Sidon show about the nature of possibility?
4. How is it possible for us to discuss events that never actually take place, and to imagine "worlds" differing from the present world? What are our limitations when we do so?
5. How is the idea of a possible world similar to a town built of Legos?

Chapter 67

Models for Modal Logic

Let us consider the idea of making models. Modal logic offers a kind of model for reasoning about possibility and necessity in the real world. But logicians have considered modeling in a second sense. We can build a *formal model* that corresponds to a formal system. A formal model is a simplified, stripped-down representation of what a formal system stands for or is intended to refer to. We had an earlier discussion of formal models when we considered models for classical logic (chapter 60). Now we will do the same thing for modal logic.

Syntax and Reference

In modal logic, we can distinguish between syntax and semantics. Because of analogies with natural language, this distinction makes sense. The *syntax* for modal logic is the formal system, with the special symbols ◊ and □. Within the *formal language* that includes them, these symbols are "meaningless." But then we give them meaning by constructing reference points. This part is the *semantics*. The semantics consists in models for modal logic, that is, models with specific correspondences to the elements in the formal language of modal logic.

So we now look at some models that have been constructed to represent modal logic. We can only begin an exploration, and give readers an idea of what such models attempt to represent. As is usual in formal logic, these models will be "stripped-down," bare-bones models. They are nevertheless valuable for drawing our attention to one dimension of the character of God and his purposes for the world.

Constructing a Model

In a model for ordinary classical logic, we have to correlate between propositional symbols p and true or false values in the model. In addition, if we include quantification theory, the model has to have individuals belonging to some set U.

We have to use propositional logic when we deal with modal logic, because modal logic is intended to be an extension of propositional logic. Modal logic has all the capabilities of propositional logic, and in addition has extra symbols for possibility and necessity.

When we make a model for modal logic, we have to represent the formal symbols $\Diamond$ and $\Box$ in some manner within the model. That is, the formal symbols $\Diamond$ and $\Box$ have to be correlated with something in the model. What? Model theory for modal logic starts with the models used for propositional logic (chapter 60). It then multiplies the number of these models, and specifies that each model represents a *possible world*. A model for modal logic consists in a whole collection of these models of possible worlds. The ideas of possibility and necessity can then be represented by means of the idea of possible worlds.

Now let us carry out the process of construction. Suppose W is a model for classical propositional logic. W includes a set $S = \{T,F\}$ for the truth values that will be assigned to propositions. It also includes a function f that establishes a correlation between each propositional symbol in the formal language on the one hand, and one of the two elements T and F on the other hand (see chapter 60). For instance, if our formal language includes the elementary symbols P_1, P_2, P_3, etc., we may have the function f assign a truth value to each of these symbols: $f(P_1) = T$, $f(P_2) = F$, $f(P_3) = F$, and so on. On the basis of these assignments, we can then calculate the truth value of compound propositions such as $\sim(\sim P_1 \vee P_3)$. If $f(P_1) = T$, $f(\sim P_1) = F$. If also $f(P_3) = F$, $f((\sim P_1 \vee P_3)) = F$, and $f(\sim(\sim P_1 \vee P_3)) = T$. And so on. As a result of this correlation function f, we find that some formulas can be said to "come out true" in the model W. For any such formula p, that comes out being interpreted as true ($f(p) = T$), we say that W *satisfies* p and write

$$W \vDash p$$

So far, we have a model W without any reference to possibility or necessity.

Now we take the crucial step. We multiply the number of models W. Each model W represents a "world." Make any number of worlds, and collect them into a set U of "all possible worlds." Each member W within U is a model for classical propositional logic. U as a whole is a model for modal logic.

We also have to have some unique world W that will represent the actual world that we are in. Let us call this one world E (E stands for "earth"). E is one among many possible worlds W, each of which is a member of the set

U of all possible worlds. *E* is "actualized," while the other worlds that are members of *U* are not actualized. They are only possible.

Now we have to define how we work out the relationship of "satisfaction," which is the key part of making a model. We consider formulas *p* within the formal language of modal logic. We have to specify when these formulas come out true in the world *E* within the model *U*. For formulas *p* with no symbol for possibility or necessity, the relation of satisfaction is the same as before:

> *E* ⊨ *p* ("*E* satisfies *p*", or "*p* comes out true in *E*") if and only if *p* comes
> out true when interpreted by the correlation function *f* that the model *E*
> sets up between *p* and {T,F}.

Next, how do we interpret what is the meaning of ◊*p*?

> *E* ⊨ ◊*p* if and only if *W* ⊨ *p* for some world *W* in *U*.

That is to say, *E* satisfies ◊*p* if and only if there is some possible world *W* that satisfies *p*. Or, still more simply: ◊*p* is true in *E* if and only if *p* is true is some possible world *W*. Or: "possibly *p*" is true in *E* if and only if *p* is true in some possible world.

Now, how do we interpret the necessity operator □?

> *E* ⊨ □*p* if and only if *W* ⊨ *p* for *all* possible worlds *W* in *U*.

The meaning can be re-expressed. *E* satisfies □*p* if and only if, for all possible worlds *W*, *W* satisfies *p*. Or we can say, "necessarily *p*" is true in *E* if and only if *p* is true in all possible worlds.

Let us consider a simple example. Suppose we have two elementary propositional symbols *P* and *Q*. Let us also suppose that, in world *E*, *P* is T and *Q* is F (that is, *f*(*P*) = T and *f*(*Q*) = F). So the world *E* satisfies *P*. In the special notation for satisfaction, *E* ⊨ *P*. Also, *E* ⊨ ~*Q*. Now let *X* be a second possible world. In world *X*, let us suppose that *P* is F and *Q* is T. Since *P* is T in at least one world (namely *E*), *P* is possibly true (◊*P*). That is, *E* satisfies ◊*P* (*E* ⊨ ◊*P*). Since *Q* is true in at least one world, namely *X*, *Q* is possibly true (◊*Q*). *E* satisfies ◊*Q* (*E* ⊨ ◊*Q*). Since *P* fails to be true in *X*, □*P* ("necessarily *P*") is F in *E*. ~□*P* is T in *E*. *E* satisfies ~□*P* (*E* ⊨ ~□*P*). Since *Q* fails to be true in at least one world, namely *E*, □*Q* is F. However, (*P* ∨ *Q*) is true in both *E* and *X*. If *E* and *X* are the only possible worlds in *U*, (*P* ∨ *Q*) is true in all possible worlds, and so $\Box(P \lor Q)$ is T. $E \vDash \Box(P \lor Q)$. If, on the other hand, there is a third possible world Y, in which P is F and Q is F, $(P \lor Q)$ is F in Y. So $\Box(P \lor Q)$ is false in E.

Necessity and Quantification

With these specifications, we can see a clear relationship between ordinary quantification with the words *all* and *some* and the ideas of necessity and possibility. A proposition is "necessary" if it is true in *all* possible worlds. It is possible if it is true in *some* possible world. We can write it symbolically if we like:

$E \vDash \Diamond p$ if and only $(\exists W)$ $W \vDash p$
$E \vDash \Box p$ if and only if $(\forall W)$ $W \vDash p$

But we must make a clarification. We must understand that the symbols $(\exists W)$ and $(\forall W)$ are used in our metalanguage, in which we are talking about the worlds. They are not part of the formal language that has the operators $\Diamond$ and $\Box$.

If we wish, we can enhance the possible worlds W by adding a set of individuals to each world, and allowing formulas that use quantification over the individuals. A difficulty arises because there are two main ways to do it. In what is called the "fixed domain" approach, individual variables x range over all *possible* individuals belonging to any of the worlds. $(\forall x)$ is interpreted as meaning, "for all individuals x in the fixed domain comprised by the individuals in *all the worlds together*." In the "world-relative" or "actualist" approach, an individual variable x ranges only over the individuals that actually exist within the world W on which we are focusing at the time.

There are difficulties with both routes.[1] These difficulties stem partly from a more fundamental difficulty over the scope of ordinary quantification over "individuals." What counts as an "individual" is not precisely defined. The difficulties are compounded in modal logic, because our human finiteness limits our ability to specify what it might mean for God to contemplate worlds other than our own.

Variations in Modal Logic

So far, we have depicted in a model U only the commonest form of modal logic, a kind of modal logic that has been given the label $S5$. This common

---

[1] James Garson, "Modal Logic," *Stanford Encyclopedia of Philosophy (Winter 2009 Edition)*, ed. Edward N. Zalta, http://plato.stanford.edu/archives/win2009/entries/logic-modal/, accessed Aug. 24, 2012, §13.

form is often considered adequate for representing the idea of alethic or logical necessity. But it is not suitable for the logic of future possibilities or some
other meanings of possibility and necessity.

Logicians have considered more complex cases, by using what is called
an *accessibility* relation. A world Y (within some set U of all possible worlds)
is *accessible* from a second world X if, when we stand in world X, world Y
is conceivable as a possible world. Accessibility is a relation between two
worlds, X and Y. It can be written as a relation A(X, Y). It means, "world
Y is accessible, as a possible world, from the standpoint of world X." The
relation A is true for some combinations X and Y, but it may not be true for
some other combinations. In other words, some worlds Y may *not* be accessible from world X.

If we start in world X, the possible worlds Y are exactly the worlds such
that A(X,Y). If no world is accessible from X except X itself, X is, from the
point of view of X, the only possible world. That is not very interesting. In
such a world, possibility and necessity collapse into actuality. This situation
is an extreme case. But the logicians find it fascinating to explore the different possibilities for models, including such extreme cases.

Another possibility would be that a world Y is accessible from world X,
and a third world Z is accessible from Y, but that Z is not directly accessible
from X (see figure 67.1):

Fig. 67.1: Nontransitive Accessibility

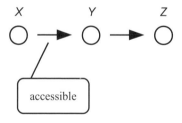

Going from world X to world Y allows its inhabitants, as it were, to con-
ceive of a possible world Z beyond the ken of inhabitants of X. In this case,
A(X,Y) ("Y is accessible from X") and A(Y,Z), but it is not the case that
A(X,Z). The possible worlds from the standpoint of X include Y but not Z.

Within this more complicated system, the properties of necessity and
possibility have to be more carefully defined.

$E \vDash \Diamond p$ if and only if $W \vDash p$ for some world W that is possible from E, i.e., such that $A(E,W)$.

$E \vDash \Box p$ if and only if $W \vDash p$ for *all* worlds W that are possible from E, i.e., such that $A(E,W)$.

The accessibility relation A may or may not have various desirable properties. One such possibility is what we have just seen denied with the example of worlds X, Y, and Z above. The relation A is called *transitive* if $A(X,Y)$ and $A(Y,Z)$ together imply $A(X,Z)$. The property of transitivity means, in more ordinary language, than any world Z accessible from a world Y, where Y is a possible world from X, is already accessible directly from the world X from which we start (see figure 67.2):

Fig. 67.2: Transitive Accessibility

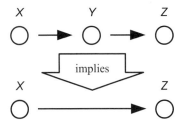

A second desirable property is being *symmetric*. A relation $A(X,Y)$ is *symmetric* if $A(X,Y)$ implies $A(Y,X)$. This property means that, if Y is a possible world from the standpoint of our starting world X, it is also the case that our starting world X is a possible world from the point of view of world Y (see figure 67.3):

Fig. 67.3: Symmetric Accessibility

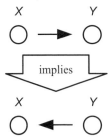

A final desirable property is being *reflexive*. A relation A is reflexive if A(X,X) for all X. This property means that each world is a possible world from its own viewpoint (see figure 67.4):

Fig. 67.4: Reflexive Accessibility

Each of these additional properties, in turns out, corresponds to distinctive axioms that we could add. The property of reflexivity is expressed with the axiom

$$\Box p \supset p$$

Likewise, symmetry gets expressed as

$$p \supset \Box \Diamond p$$

Transitivity means

$$\Box p \supset \Box \Box p$$

If all three of these axioms hold, the system of modal logic is called an *S5* system. This system is the strongest system in terms of the power of its axioms. It corresponds to our initial example, in which we had only the set *U* of possible worlds, and every world was accessible from every other.[2]

If we drop one of these axioms, we "weaken" the system of modal logic. The label *S4* designates the system that does not have the axiom of symmetry ($p \supset \Box \Diamond p$), but does have the other two. The label *M* designates the system that has the axiom of reflexivity as its only extra axiom. A system with none of the extra axioms is the weakest system, and is conventionally labeled *K*.

---

[2] Technically, the axioms still allow a case in which a subset of possible worlds could all be accessible to one another, but totally inaccessible in relation to another subset. This other subset would then be like an alternate universe that was beyond our conception of possibility.

Godlike Vision

All of these systems are innocent, if we treat them as games we play with symbols and with models. It is as if we were playing SimCity or making a miniature town out of Legos. We can play the game just for the enjoyment. Or we can try to gain appreciation of the complexities of real towns. The latter purpose involves interpretations and judgments about the world.

The same holds for models of modal logic. We can look at them as games, or we can look at them as aids for insight. And we can indeed sometimes get insight. In fact, models for modal logic have fruitful connections in fields outside their original interpretation as "possible worlds," in the theory of provability and computation. Both provability and computation present logical connections similar to modal logic.[3]

But what value does modal logic have in dealing with questions of necessity and possibility in ordinary life? When we think of the systems and their models as representing possible worlds, the advantage is that we draw attention to the fact that possibility goes beyond actuality. We ourselves, made in the image of God, can think God's thoughts after him in the realm of possibility as well as actuality. We can imagine what God might have done as well as what he has done in the working of his plan.

But we can easily fall into temptation. The models might tempt us to imagine that we can actually "get above" the world in a fundamental sense and envision possible "worlds" *at the same level* as God. We imagine that we know what he could and could not do. We imagine ourselves at that point virtually to be God. We make ourselves idolaters, whose god is ourselves. Instead, the wise course is simply to recognize both the limitations of the model and our own limitations. We cannot be the mayor or the construction engineer for the real town, that is, for the universe. We cannot be God.

This feeling of getting above the limitations of the world is particularly visible when we do not have the property of transitivity for the accessibility relation A. We are in world E, let us say. The possible world Y is accessible from E, $A(E,Y)$. And from Y we could access still another world, let us say Z. Let us further suppose that Z is *not* accessible directly from E. We can nevertheless access it indirectly, by means of two successive steps. We go first to Y, and then from there to Z.

I have said, "we." But who is this "we"? We began by considering ourselves to be inhabiting world E. And from that world "we" can envision

---

[3] Garson, "Modal Logic," §§10–12.

only the possibilities *Y* that are accessible from *E*. Yet eventually we also envision world *Z*, which is *not* accessible directly from *E*, but only from *Y*. And we envision still more worlds, accessible from *Z*, but not from either *X* or *Y* directly.

We are flying high, so to speak. We envision what we ourselves have postulated that we cannot envision as long as we are inhabiting *E*. That is to become godlike—unless, of course, we realize that it is all a little game, imagining what it would be like to look down from infinity on poor finite creatures like ourselves inhabiting a world *E* and being limited in their imaginations by their location. It is as if we were building several different Lego towns with different architectures. We populate the towns with little Lego pieces shaped to look like human beings. We look down on them with godlike powers. We can do it with Legos because we are subcreators who can make little miniature towns.

These Lego towns may even have real applications in some specialized field of study, such as the theory of provability or computation theory, because we can in fact "stand above" a limited sphere that we have precisely delineated.

We can also imagine what it might be like to stand transcendently above whole physical worlds or whole universes. This powerful imagination reflects the fact that we are made in the image of God. We can imagine much. We can imitatively transcend the limitations of a formal system or a system of artificial mini-worlds *W* that we have constructed in our imagination. But we remain finite. Possibility and necessity remain mysteries. We must be in awe of God, not pretend that we understand possibility in the same way that he does.

For Further Reflection

1. What is the difference between a "simple" model for possible worlds and one that uses an accessibility relation? What properties must the accessibility relation have in order for the more complex model to mirror exactly the simpler model?
2. Show that the reflexive property of the accessibility relation can be deduced from the properties of symmetry and transitivity, provided we make the additional assumption that any starting world *E* can access at least one possible world.
3. What are potential advantages and liabilities of the possible-worlds model for modal logic?
4. What does modal logic and its models display about the glory of God?

Chapter 68

Conclusion

Let us reflect on what we have seen about logic and neighboring fields.

Beauty and Wonder

Even in the midst of a world marred by sin and its effects, a world corrupted by human suffering and cruelty and death, God has left imprints of his beauty. We admire the beauty of clouds, or mountains, or cheetahs, or contemplate with awe the intricacy of a ladybug or an ant.

> O Lord, how manifold are your works!
>> In wisdom have you made them all;
>> the earth is full of your creatures.
> Here is the sea, great and wide,
>> which teems with creatures innumerable,
>> living things both small and great.
> There go the ships,
>> and Leviathan, which you formed to play in it. (Ps. 104:24–26)

The beauty and wonder and magnificence of creation lie around us and even in us, inviting us to praise God.

Logical Wonders

Not least among these wonders are the wonders of logic and related fields. Not everyone is sensitive to the beauty in these fields, but there is beauty in abundance for those who enter. The harmonies between various fields, including the perspectival relations between them, derive from the harmony and self-consistency of God's own character. God ordained beautiful harmonies because he himself is beautiful.

We can also see reflections of God's glory in each of the individual fields on which we have touched. For example, syllogisms display the awesomeness of necessity and logical power. They reflect the glory of God and his character. He displays his eternity, omnipotence, omnipresence, immutability, transcendence, immanence, and truthfulness in the laws of logic.

Within the realm of logic, formal propositional logic is like a quiet pond, peaceful and elegant. It can be "mastered" in a sense. The validity or satisfiability of a proposition in propositional logic can be computationally decided. But even here there is a beautiful simplicity that the computer programmer, but not the computer, can appreciate. And proofs within a formal deductive system for propositional logic can still offer a challenge and a mental exercise. Proof theory waits before us, not only proof theory for propositional logic but also for quantification. Adding complexity also adds mystery. Surprises await.

Much remains to explore in set theory, computation theory, proof theory, model theory, and abstract algebra. Even in the natural numbers there are mysteries. We have seen one main mystery in Gödel's demonstration that a computable collection of axioms for arithmetic is necessarily incomplete.[1] Beyond that awaits the "arithmetic hierarchy," an infinite hierarchy of subsets of natural numbers, such that higher reaches are progressively more inaccessible to computation.

Or the would-be adventurer may explore the beauties and wonders of set theory. Set theory can be compared to seeing mountains in the foreground and then higher and more majestic mountains in the background. The adventurer who would "climb" these mountains may have delight: the "mountains" represented by infinite sets get progressively larger, with no end. An image of transcendence awaits.

In model theory, the *Löwenheim-Skolem theorems* await the venturesome with exhibitions of infinities. The theorems include the paradox that a model may satisfy all the rules and still not *be* what we thought we formulated the rules to describe uniquely. Behind that vista stand others: models for set theory, and "forcing" to produce models with desirable oddities.

Or go to abstract algebra, to enjoy a display of exhibitions for the visitor: vector spaces, groups, rings, fields, lattices, modules.

However far we go, we are living in God's world, with minds made by God. We and the world are governed by the decrees of God, subject to the Logos of God. We may rejoice in the works of his hands, in his beauty,

---

[1] Shawn Hedman, *A First Course in Logic: An Introduction to Model Theory, Proof Theory, Computability, and Complexity* (Oxford: Oxford University Press, 2004), 331, comments on David Hilbert's tenth problem (originally formulated in 1900): "[it] underestimates the complexity of the integers and reflects misconceptions that were commonly held at the time. . . . The First Incompleteness Theorem [by Gödel, 1931] shows that the integers are extraordinarily complex . . ."

power, majesty, and mystery. He takes pleasure in displaying, through the Spirit, the glory of his Son both in the heights and in the depths. He manifests himself in the grandeur of infinite sets and in the infinite number of tautologies, and in the ordinary facts, such as that Socrates is a man and that all collies are dogs. He manifests himself in the minutiae—a single character in a formal language.

May we grow in our ability to perceive his wonders and to praise him and enjoy him forever.

> Oh, the depth of the riches and wisdom and knowledge of God! How unsearchable are his judgments and how inscrutable his ways!
>
> "For who has known the mind of the Lord,
>   or who has been his counselor?"
> "Or who has given a gift to him that he might be repaid?"
>
> For from him and through him and to him are all things. To him be glory forever. Amen. (Rom. 11:33–36)

Part IV
Supplements

The supplements here include more examples and pieces that give more detail for some of the summary statements made in parts I-III. Part IV.F considers the relation of logic to some issues in philosophy.

Part IV.A

Supplements to Elementary Logic

Antinomies with Sets: The Set of All Sets and Russell's Paradox

As we indicated in chapter 18, human knowledge in practice involves the knowledge of unity in diversity and diversity in unity. Unity and diversity are entangled in the experience of learning. Our general concepts are colored by the particulars of the way in which we came to know them. God ordains both particulars and general categories, and plans for them to have a relation to one another.

But could we pretend? Could we pretend that we can have a "pure" universal, without worrying about the particulars? Could we thereby have "pure" reasoning about universals?

The attempt to make very general categories can lead to antinomies. We illustrate the difficulty by looking at the idea of a set of all sets.

More General Categories

We may start with a more prosaic level of observation. There are a large number of general categories like *horse*, *humanity*, *mortality*, and *carnivore*. Our ability to deal with these categories involves another use of the relation of unity to diversity. Each category like *horse* is a unity in relation to the diversity of different horses. By labeling the term *horse* a *category*, we also use the relation of the unity of the word *category* to the diversity of particular categories, *horse*, *humanity*, *carnivore*, and so on (see figure A1.1).

The top level, categories, is the most comprehensive and covers all the rest. Whether we have a special label for this top level or not, it seems to be implicit when we undertake to discuss syllogisms in general, because these would include syllogisms about horses, syllogisms about humanity, syllogisms about carnivores, and so on. We tacitly operate using our knowledge of the relation of particular categories like *horse* to the generality, namely, all categories.

Fig. A1.1: A Hierarchy of Categories

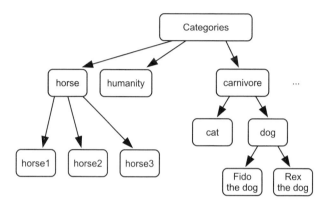

Sets

Let us shift our terminology slightly. Instead of speaking about categories, which suggest verbal labels and concepts, let us talk about *classes* or *sets*, terms that focus on the world rather than on language and thought. We can speak about the class of horses, a class whose members are all the horses. So it includes horse1, horse2, and so on.[1] In formal mathematical contexts, the word *set* is often used instead of the word *class*.[2] Roughly speaking, a set is a collection of members. So the class of all horses can be viewed as a set. But a collection that does match any natural class of creatures can also be a set. So, for example, the collection consisting of one horse named Sally, one human named Socrates, and one number, the number 2, is a set. This set can be described by listing its members. Customarily, the members are listed within braces. So the set {Sally, Socrates, 2} is the set consisting of the three members, Sally, Socrates, and 2.

We also need to introduce the idea of a subset. A subset of a set *H* is made up of some, but not necessarily all, the members in the original set *H*. Suppose a set *H* consists of three members, horse1, horse2, and horse3. The subsets are (1) the set {horse1} with only one member, namely, horse1; (2) the set {horse2} with only one member, namely, horse2; (3) the set

---

[1] The word *class* is here being used as a synonym for the mathematical concept of a "set"; not all versions of set theory use the terms in this way.
[2] The word *class* is also sometimes introduced as a technical term in the context of mathematical set theory, but this usage need not concern us.

{horse3}; (4) the set {horse1,horse2} with two members horse1 and horse2; (5) the set {horse1,horse3}; (6) the set {horse2,horse3}; and (7) the set {horse1,horse2,horse3} with all three members. This last set is identical to the original set. Mathematicians like, for the sake of completeness, to include also the "empty" set with no members at all: {}.

Now for any set H we define the *power set* of H as the set whose members are all the subsets of H. If H has three members, horse1, horse2, and horse3, the power set of H has as its members all the subsets that we have already mentioned above. An important theorem of set theory (see appendix E2) says that the power set of any set H always has more members than the original set. In this case, the original set has three members: horse1, horse2, and horse3. The power set has eight members in all.

Now consider the set consisting of all sets. It has as its members the set of horses, the set of human beings, the set of natural numbers, and so on. Call this set S. Then the power set of S is also a set. Each member of the power set of S is a set, and so it is also a member of S, by definition of S. Hence S contains all the members of the power set of S. This contradicts the theorem that says that the power set of H has more members than H.[3]

What has gone wrong? There has been much debate. But one possible source of difficulty lies in having conceived of a set of all sets without tying that conception to any particular members. The attempt to conceptualize a set of all sets does not reckon with the entanglement of unity (the set as a whole) and diversity (its members).

Imitative Transcendence in Sets

This paradox can also be viewed as a paradox due to transcendence. When we try to form a set of all sets, we practice standing back from the sets that we already have in hand. We take them all together and then form a single set whose members are the sets that we already have.

To this single set we can give the name S. We now stand back to transcend S, viewing it as a completed whole rather than still being in the process of analyzing its members and constructing it so that it includes all the members that we specify.

So we begin to construct another set, the power set of S, whose mem-

---

[3] The theorem about power sets can be extended even to sets with an infinite number of members, once we have adopted Georg Cantor's way of comparing sizes of infinite sets. See appendix E2 and Akihiro Kanamori, "Set Theory," in *Encyclopedia of Philosophy*, 2nd ed., ed. Donald M. Borchert, 10 vols. (Detroit/New York/ San Francisco, etc.: Thomson Gale, 2006), 8:833.

bers are all the subsets of S. Call the resulting set $P(S)$. If we were to describe S as the set of *all* sets, using the word *all*, we would seem to imply that the set $P(S)$ itself, as well as all its members, are already members of S. And this assumption leads to a contradiction (see above). But actually $P(S)$ was not really "available" when we constructed S. We had to *transcend* S first. Then we could construct $P(S)$. Likewise, we can transcend $P(S)$ and build another set, $P(P(S))$, the power set of $P(S)$, whose members are all the subsets of $P(S)$. We can transcend $P(P(S))$ and build $P(P(P(S)))$. And then $P(P(P(P(S))))$. This process is *recursive*. We never come to an end.

Infinity

We are imitating at each stage the transcendence and infinity of God. And the process of going through stages repeats itself indefinitely, imitating the infinity of God. The transcendence of God is infinite, and so is not identical with our ability momentarily to adopt a "transcendent" viewpoint toward a particular set S.

Infinity itself is a personal expression of God's character. Let us see one way in which this is so. We have indicated that the Son is the "image of the invisible God" (Col. 1:15). He is the archetypal image. But then there are subordinate images. Adam was made in the image of God (Gen. 1:26–27). The Father loves the Son (John 3:35). So the making of Adam, as a reflection of the Son the original, expresses the original love of the Father within this world, and reflects the glory of the eternal Son.

Adam fathered a son Seth after his image (Gen. 5:3). Adam was obviously imitating God. The glory of the Father and the Son in their love for each other was reflected. Seth fathered Enosh (v. 6). Enosh fathered Kenan (v. 9). And Kenan fathered a son in his turn. Genesis does not say it in so many words, but it is easy to infer that when Seth fathered Enosh, he imitated or imaged the pattern that took place when Adam fathered Seth.

All in all, there are multiple images, all deriving from the Son, who is the original image. These images go on indefinitely. The fathering of children will eventually come to an end, when we enter into the new heaven and the new earth. But we can understand in our minds the ideal of an indefinitely extended series of children. This pattern is a recursive pattern. Given the children resulting from one generation, we place the children into the same position as their parents, and we picture them producing children of their own, and so on *indefinitely*. This indefinite extension in the form of recursion is also imitated when we imitate transcendence. We transcend S with $P(S)$. And then we transcend $P(S)$ with $P(P(S))$. We construct each set by using the previous one and plugging back into the process recursively.

We are thinking God's thoughts after him. And in this case, we are imitating the pattern of recursion whose original we have found in a single relationship, the relation of the Son to the Father as his image, through the Spirit. The relationship is a personal, infinite, loving relationship. The personal character of God, his infinity, and his love are all expressed when he displays signs of his glory in the things that he has made (human children) and in the thoughts that he has given us (recursively building power sets).

Russell's Paradox

A second paradox was discovered by Bertrand Russell in about 1901, and has been named *Russell's paradox* in his honor.[4] It is again a paradox concerning sets. As we observed, a set can be described by listing its members. For example, the set $A = \{1, 2, 3\}$ is the set with exactly three members, 1, 2, and 3. Or a set can be specified by describing a property. For example, let us say that B is the set consisting of all points x on the line L. Since we cannot list all the points one by one, we use a general notation:

$B = \{x \mid x$ is a point on the line $L\}$.

The vertical bar symbol | stands for the English wording, "such that." The whole definition of B, translated into English, reads,

B equals the set that has as its members all x such that x is a point on the line L.

Now we are ready. Gottlob Frege's axioms for set theory imply that one can consider the set that has as its members all sets that do not contain themselves. Call this set C. Let the variable x range over all sets. By definition,

$C = \{x \mid x$ does not contain $x\,\}$,

that is,

$C = \{x \mid {\sim}(x \in x)\}$

---

[4] A. D. Irvine, "Russell's Paradox," *Stanford Encyclopedia of Philosophy (Summer 2010 Edition)*, ed. Edward N. Zalta, http://plato.stanford.edu/archives/sum2010/entries/russell-paradox/, accessed August 26, 2011.

where the symbol ∈ denotes membership of an element in a set, and the tilde symbol ~ means logical negation.

The key question is whether C contains itself or not. Is it the case that $C \in C$?

Assume that it does not contain itself. $\sim(C \in C)$. Then when $x = C$, x satisfies the property $\sim(x \in x)$. Therefore this x is one of the members of C. That is, $x \in C$, and so $C \in C$. We have derived a contradiction. So our starting assumption $\sim(C \in C)$ must be wrong. Therefore, the opposite is true. That is, $C \in C$. In order for C to be a member of C, it must satisfy the defining property of C, namely, $\sim(x \in x)$. Therefore $\sim(C \in C)$. Once again, we have a contradiction. Whether we assume that $\sim(C \in C)$ or that $C \in C$, either way we get a contradiction. By the law of excluded middle either $\sim p$ or p is true. So the system as a whole leads to contradiction.

The difficulty here is analogous to the difficulty with the set of all sets. In both cases the difficulty seems to be related to the entanglement of unity and diversity. A unity (a set) cannot be considered without having a conceptual grasp on the particulars that are its members.

For Further Reflection

1. Write out the power set of H by listing the subsets of H. Check that it has eight members.
2. Write out the power set of $B = \{1,2\}$. How many members does it have? (Do not forget the empty set.)
3. Write out the power set of $T = \{3\}$.
4. Would there be a conceptual difficulty in the idea of the power set of (the power set of H)? Why or why not? Can we "keep going," and consider the power set of (the power set of (the power set of H))?
5. What makes the hypothesis of a set of all sets different from the power sets in questions 1–4 above?

Deriving Syllogisms
of the First Figure

We can show other relationships between syllogisms of the first figure. All four syllogistic forms, Barbara, Celarent, Darii, and Ferio, have been described in chapters 26 and 28. All four types can be derived from Celarent or Darii if we use reasoning in the form of *reductio ad absurdum* (chapter 39; appendix B2).[1] These logical relationships show another way in which the different syllogistic forms offer perspectives on one another. Each one of the forms is derivable from another one.

Deriving Barbara from Darii

First, let us see how Barbara can be derived from Darii. We use a particular case to make the reasoning easier to follow. Here is an instance of the Barbara syllogism:

> All dogs are animals.
> All collies are dogs.
> Therefore, all collies are animals.

To derive its validity, we assume first that both premises are true:

> Premise 1: All dogs are animals.
> Premise 2: All collies are dogs.

To use the principle of *reductio ad absurdum*, we also assume that the conclusion is false. We then try to deduce a contradiction. If we succeed, the principle of *reductio ad absurdum* assures us that the initial assumption was false. And then we will have established the proper conclusion. The

---

[1] The earlier form of *reductio ad absurdum* said that if assuming the truth of a proposition p led to a deduction of its negation $\sim p$, the proposition must be false, i.e., $\sim p$ must be true. But the principle has a more general form (appendix B3). If assuming p leads to a contradiction of *any* kind, p must be false. Or if assuming that p is false leads to a contradiction, p must be true.

conclusion we want to establish is that all collies are animals. So we assume the contrary: assume some collie is not an animal (Assumption 1). We can rephrase it as saying that some collie is nonanimal, or there is something that is both a collie and a nonanimal. Or there is something that is both a nonanimal and a collie (Deduction 1).

Then some nonanimal is a collie (Deduction 2, from Deduction 1). We can arrange our results up to this point as follows:

> All collies are dogs. [Premise 2]
> Some nonanimal is a collie. [Deduction 2]

These two propositions conform to the pattern of Darii. Using Darii we deduce that some nonanimal is dog. Hence some dog is nonanimal, which contradicts Premise 1. Hence by *reductio ad absurdum* the initial assumption is wrong. Hence all collies are animals, which is the conclusion of Barbara. Hence we have derived Barbara from Darii.

Deriving Celarent from Darii

In a similar way we will now derive Celarent from Darii. Here is the example of Celarent with which we will work:

> No dogs are cats.
> All collies are dogs.
> Therefore, no collies are cats.

Once again, we use the principle of *reductio ad absurdum*. We assume that both premises are true:

> Premise 1: No dogs are cats.
> Premise 2: All collies are dogs.

We then assume that the conclusion is not true, and try to deduce a contradiction. That is, assume that it is not true that no collies are cats (Assumption 1). That is, some collie is a cat (Deduction 1, from Assumption 1). Then some cat is a collie (Deduction 2, from Deduction 1). We arrange our results in a pattern:

> All collies are dogs. [Premise 2]
> Some cat is a collie. [Deduction 2]

These two propositions conform to the pattern of Darii. Using Darii, we deduce that some cat is a dog. Hence some dog is a cat, which contradicts Premise 1. Hence, by *reductio ad absurdum*, the initial assumption is wrong when it said that it is not true that no collies are cats. Hence no collies are cats. This is the conclusion part of Celarent. Hence we have derived Celarent from Darii.

Deriving Darii from Celarent

Now we derive Darii from Celarent. We use a particular example of Darii:

> All mammals breathe air.
> Some sea creature is a mammal.
> Therefore, some sea creature breathes air.

Let us assume that both premises are true:

> Premise 1: All mammals breathe air.
> Premise 2: Some sea creature is a mammal.

We have to show that the conclusion is true: some sea creature breathes air. In the pattern of *reductio ad absurdum*, we assume the opposite. That is, we assume that no sea creature breathes air (Assumption 1). That is, nothing is both a sea creature and breathes air. Then it is also true that nothing that breathes air is a sea creature (Deduction 1, from Assumption 1). We can then arrange our results up to this point into a pattern:

> Nothing that breathes air is a sea creature. [Deduction 1]
> All mammals breathe air. [Premise 1]

These two premises conform to the pattern of Celarent. So it follows that no mammals are sea creatures. That is, nothing is both a mammal and a sea creature. Then it is also true that no sea creature is a mammal. This contradicts Premise 2, that some sea creature is a mammal. The initial assumption has led to a contradiction. It follows by the principle of *reductio ad absurdum* that the initial assumption is false. Therefore, some sea creature breathes air. Thus we have derived Darii using Celarent.

Deriving Ferio from Celarent

Now we derive Ferio from Celarent. We use a particular example of Ferio, as follows:

No reptiles are fish.
Some vertebrate is a reptile.
Therefore some vertebrate is not a fish.

We assume that both premises are true:

Premise 1: No reptiles are fish.
Premise 2: Some vertebrate is a reptile.

We also assume that the conclusion is false, and then try to deduce a contradiction. Assume: it is not true that some vertebrate is not a fish (Assumption 1). That is, all vertebrates are fish (Deduction 1, from Assumption 1). We also know from Premise 1 that no fish are reptiles (Deduction 2). We put our results into a pattern:

No fish are reptiles. [Deduction 2]
All vertebrates are fish. [Deduction 1]

These two propositions together conform to the pattern of Celarent. So using Celarent we draw the conclusion: No vertebrates are reptiles. This conclusion contradicts Premise 2. Hence the initial assumption is wrong. Hence some vertebrate is not a fish. We have thus derived the conclusion of Ferio, using Celarent.

Perspectives

All four types of syllogism, Barbara, Celarent, Darii, and Ferio, express or manifest in concrete form the logic and self-consistency of God. These expressions are in harmony with one another and lead to one another through forms of reasoning in conformity with God's harmony.

It is what we might expect, on the basis of what we have seen from the Gospel of John about the harmony in speech among the persons of the Trinity. This harmony can be expressed positively, as in John 12:50: "I [the Son] say as the Father has told me." It can be expressed negatively, as in John 12:49: "For I [the Son] have *not* spoken on my own authority." These two expressions in the context of John 12:49–50 support one another and represent two ways of expressing two sides of one comprehensive reality concerning the harmony among the persons of the Trinity. As we have seen before, so here also, God is the archetype, the original. Instances of logical coherence among affairs in this world reflect or mirror the original harmony in God. The other instances are "ectypes," which exist according to the pattern of the archetype.

The four syllogistic forms exhibit the pattern of one and many, in that we can use one, namely, Celarent, to derive all the rest, or use Darii to derive all the rest. In addition, using the observations from the previous chapter, we can view Celarent as a form of Barbara and Darii as a form of Ferio. The syllogistic patterns also exhibit the pattern of one and many in that each one is *one* form with many particular instances of application to dogs, cats, reptiles, and so on.

Syllogisms belonging to the second figure and others are treated in appendices A3 and A4.

For Further Reflection

1. How does the availability of multiple perspectives display the glory of God?
2. Is the conformity of vertebrates, fish, reptiles, collies, dogs, and other creatures to logic a necessity? How should it elicit praise to God?

Syllogisms of the Second Figure

Aristotle's list of kinds of syllogisms has a second grouping, called the *second figure*. The second figure contains syllogistic forms in which the middle term ("B" in our formulations) occurs as the predicate in both premises. We now consider the various syllogisms that belong to the second figure.

The First Type of Syllogism: Cesare

The first type of syllogism within the second figure is called *Cesare*.[1] It has the following form:

> No As are Bs.
> All Cs are Bs.
> Therefore, no Cs are As.

Here is an example:

> No cats are dogs.
> All collies are dogs.
> Therefore, no collies are cats.

Since "No cats are dogs" is equivalent to "No dogs are cats," we can reformulate the syllogism as follows:

> No dogs are cats.
> All collies are dogs.
> Therefore, no collies are cats.

This form is Celarent. So Cesare is equivalent to Celarent.

---

[1] For an explanation of the traditional names for the different types of syllogism, see chapter 28.

The Second Type of Syllogism: Camestres

A second type of syllogism is called *Camestres*. It has the following form:

> All As are Bs.
> No Cs are Bs.
> Therefore, no Cs are As.

Here is an example:

> All collies are dogs.
> No cats are dogs.
> Therefore, no cats are collies.

Since "No cats are collies" is equivalent to "No collies are cats," we can reformulate the syllogism as follows:

> No cats are dogs.
> All collies are dogs.
> Therefore, no collies are cats.

This form is Cesare. So Camestres is equivalent to Cesare, which we have seen is equivalent to Celarent.

The Third Type of Syllogism: Festino

A third type of syllogism is called *Festino*. It has the following form:

> No As are Bs.
> Some C is B.
> Therefore, some C is not A.

Here is an example:

> No fish are mammals.
> Some sea creature is a mammal.
> Therefore, some sea creature is not a fish.

"No fish are mammals" is equivalent to "No mammals are fish." So we can revise the arrangement as follows:

> No mammals are fish.
> Some sea creature is a mammal.
> Therefore some sea creature is not a fish.

We recognize this arrangement as *Ferio*. Hence Festino is equivalent to Ferio.

The Fourth Type of Syllogism: Baroco

A fourth type of syllogism, called *Baroco*, shows the following pattern:

> All As are Bs.
> Some C is not B.
> Therefore, some C is not A.

Here is an example:

> All fish are vertebrates.
> Some sea creature is not a vertebrate.
> Therefore, some sea creature is not a fish.

This syllogistic pattern has its own representation as a Venn diagram (figure A3.1):

Fig. A3.1: Venn Diagram of the Baroco Syllogism

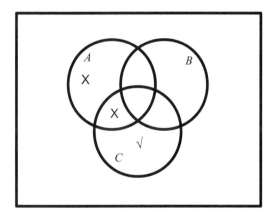

We can reformulate the pattern by restructuring the first premise:

> No fish are invertebrate [not vertebrate].
> Some sea creature is invertebrate.
> Therefore, some sea creature is not a fish.

With this reformulation, we can see that its pattern is the same as Festino. Accordingly, Festino and Baroco offer perspectives on each other.

We can also derive Baroco from Barbara by *reductio ad absurdum*. We assume the premises of Baroco:

Premise 1: All fish are vertebrates.
Premise 2: Some sea creature is not a vertebrate.

To prove that the conclusion follows, we assume the contrary. The conclusion is that some sea creature is not a fish. So the contrary is that all sea creatures are fish (Assumption 1). We can arrange our results in a pattern:

All fish are vertebrates. [Premise 1]
All sea creatures are fish. [Assumption 1]

Using Barbara, we deduce that all sea creatures are vertebrates. This conclusion contradicts Premise 2, that some sea creature is not a vertebrate. Therefore, by *reductio*, the initial assumption that all sea creatures are fish is false. Therefore some sea creature is not a fish, which is the conclusion that we wanted. We have shown that Baroco can be derived using Barbara.

Further Syllogisms

We can continue with syllogisms belonging to the third and fourth figures. The patterns are similar. (See the next appendix.)

For Further Reflection

1. Check the validity of the syllogisms Cesare, Camestres, and Festino using Venn diagrams.

Syllogisms of the Third and Fourth Figures

We consider how syllogisms of the third and fourth figures relate to others. Syllogisms of the third figure are those that have the middle term ("B") in the subject in both premises.

The First Syllogism of the Third Figure: Darapti

The first syllogism of the third figure is called *Darapti*.[1] It has the following pattern:

All Bs are As.
All Bs are Cs.
Therefore, some C is A.

Here is an example:

All artists are creative.
All artists are human.
Therefore, some human is creative.

The Darapti syllogism has its own Venn diagram (figure A4.1). Darapti and some of the other syllogisms (below) depend on assuming that a particular class is not empty. In the case of Darapti, the class represented by B must not be empty. If B is empty, we have a difficulty. Consider:

All unicorns have a horn.
All unicorns have the shape and build of a horse.
Therefore, something with the shape and build of a horse has a horn.

The class of unicorns is empty (in the real world). Since no unicorns exist, it is not true that "Something with the shape and build of a horse has a horn."

---

[1] For an explanation of the names for different types of syllogisms, see chapter 28.

Fig. A4.1: Venn Diagram of the Darapti Syllogism

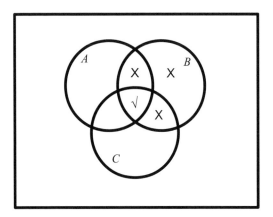

How do we deal with this difficulty? It is a general difficulty, which can crop up when one of the classes is empty. Aristotle's treatment of syllogisms includes the assumption that the classes about which it speaks are not empty. Thus, in the context of traditional Aristotelian logic, to say all As are Bs includes the assumption that at least one A exists. And so we can deduce that some A is a B.

But modern treatments of the logic of classes do not follow this route. There are situations in mathematics as well as in ordinary life when we may not know for sure whether a particular class B is empty. We want to have patterns of reasoning that do not necessarily commit us to one option or the other. So we have to say explicitly that Darapti is a valid form of reasoning only if we add the additional assumption that the class B is not empty.

We can derive Darapti from Celarent by *reductio ad absurdum*. As usual, we assume the truth of the premises of Darapti:

Premise 1: All artists are creative.
Premise 2: All artists are human.

We then assume the contradictory of the conclusion and try to deduce a contradiction. The desired conclusion is that some human is creative. So assume that no human is creative (Assumption 1). We have

No human is creative. [Assumption 1]
All artists are human. [Premise 2]

Using Celarent, we deduce that no artists are creative. This result contradicts Premise 1, that all artists are creative.[2] Hence the initial assumption was wrong. Hence some human is creative. So we have derived Darapti from Celarent.

The Second Syllogism of the Third Figure: Disamis

A second syllogism in the third figure, called *Disamis*, has the following pattern:

> Some B is A.
> All Bs are Cs.
> Therefore, some C is A.

Here is an example:

> Some mammal is a sea creature.
> All mammals breathe air.
> Therefore, some air-breathing thing is a sea creature.

"Some mammal is a sea creature" is equivalent to "some sea creature is a mammal." Likewise, "some air-breathing thing is a sea creature" is equivalent to "some sea creature breathes air." So we can restructure the pattern to read:

> All mammals breathe air.
> Some sea creature is a mammal.
> Therefore, some sea creature breathes air.

This pattern is an instance of Darii. So Disamis follows from Darii.

The Third Syllogism of the Third Figure: Datisi

A third syllogism of the third figure, called *Datisi*, has the following pattern:

> All Bs are As.
> Some B is C.
> Therefore, some C is A.

Here is an example:

> All mammals breathe air.
> Some mammal is a sea creature.
> Therefore, some sea creature breathes air.

---

[2] Note that we have to assume that the class of artists is not empty.

"Some mammal is a sea creature" is equivalent to "Some sea creature is a mammal." So we can get:

> All mammals breathe air.
> Some sea creature is a mammal.
> Therefore, some sea creature breathes air.

This pattern represents Darii. Or by another rearrangement we can obtain Disamis.

The Fourth Syllogism of the Third Figure: Felapton

A fourth syllogism of the third figure, named *Felapton*, has the following pattern:

> No Bs are As.
> All Bs are Cs.
> Therefore, some C is not A.

For this pattern Felapton, we have to assume that the class B is not empty.

Here is an example:

> No dogs are cats.
> All dogs are animals.
> Therefore, some animal is not a cat.

This pattern has a Venn diagram given in figure A4.2:

Fig. A4.2: Venn Diagram of the Felapton Syllogism

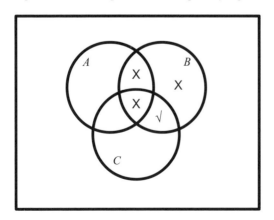

We can attempt to derive Felapton by *reductio*. Assume the premises:

Premise 1: No dogs are cats.
Premise 2: All dogs are animals.

The desired conclusion is that some animal is not a cat. Assume the contrary. No animal is not a cat. That is, all animals are cats (Assumption 1). We have the results:

All animals are cats. [Assumption 1]
All dogs are animals. [Premise 2]

Using Barbara, we deduce that all dogs are cats. This conclusion contradicts Premise 1.[3] Therefore the assumption is false. Therefore some animal is not a cat. We have derived Felapton from Barbara.

The Fifth Syllogism of the Third Figure: Bocardo

A fifth syllogism of the third figure, named *Bocardo*, has the following pattern:

Some B is not A.
All Bs are Cs.
Therefore, some C is not A.

Here is an example:

Some mammal is not a land animal.
All mammals breathe air.
Therefore, some air-breathing thing is not a land animal.

Again we can make a derivation by *reductio*. Assume that the conclusion is false. No air-breathing thing is not a land animal (Assumption 1). That is, all air-breathing things are land animals (Deduction 1). We have

All air-breathing things are land animals. [Deduction 1]
All mammals breathe air. [Premise 1]

Using Barbara, we deduce that all mammals are land animals.
That conclusion contradicts Premise 1, that some mammal is not a land

---
[3] We have to assume that the class of dogs is not empty.

animal. Therefore the assumption is false, and we have derived Bocardo from Barbara.

The Sixth Syllogism of the Third Figure: Ferison

A sixth syllogism of the third figure, called *Ferison*, has the following pattern:

> No B is A.
> Some B is C.
> Therefore, some C is not A.

Here is an example:

> No mammals are fish.
> Some mammal is a sea creature.
> Therefore, some sea creature is not a fish.

We can alter the formulation to obtain:

> No mammals are fish.
> Some sea creature is a mammal.
> Therefore some sea creature is not a fish.

The resulting pattern is an instance of Ferio.

The First Syllogism of the Fourth Figure: Bramantip

The fourth figure[4] is characterized by a pattern in which the middle term B is in the predicate in the first premise and in the subject in the second premise, while the subject in the first premise is used as the predicate in the conclusion and the predicate in the second premise is used as the subject in the conclusion. The first syllogism *Bramantip* belonging to the fourth figure has the following pattern:

> All As are Bs.
> All Bs are Cs.
> Therefore, some C is A.

---

[4] In the *Prior Analytics* (Aristotle, *Prior Analytics*, trans. Hugh Tredennick [Cambridge, MA: Harvard University Press, 1973], bound together with *The Categories* and *On Interpretation* in the Loeb Library) Aristotle discusses only three figures. The fourth figure and its syllogistic forms were added later.

(We have to assume that the class A is not empty.)

Here is an example:

All collies are dogs.
All dogs are animals.
Therefore some animal is a collie.

Rearranging, we have

All dogs are animals.
All collies are dogs.
Therefore, all collies are animals.

That deduction is Barbara. Since we have deduced that all collies are animals, it also follows that some collie is an animal.[5] And so some animal is a collie. We can deduce Bramantip from Barbara.

The Second Syllogism of the Fourth Figure: Camenes

A second syllogism of the fourth figure, named *Camenes*, has the following pattern:

All As are Bs.
No Bs are Cs.
Therefore no Cs are As.

Here is an example:

All collies are dogs.
No dogs are cats.
Therefore no cats are collies.

We can rearrange:

No dogs are cats.
All collies are dogs.
Therefore, no collies are cats.

This rearrangement is the pattern of Celarent. So Camenes is equivalent to Celarent.

---

[5] We must assume that the class of collies is not empty.

The Third Syllogism of the Fourth Figure: Dimaris

A third syllogism of the fourth figure, named *Dimaris*, has the following pattern:

> Some A is B.
> All Bs are Cs.
> Therefore, some C is A.

Here is an example:

> Some bird is an ostrich.
> All ostriches are flightless.
> Therefore, some flightless entities are birds.

By rearrangement we get:

> All ostriches are flightless.
> Some bird is an ostrich.
> Therefore, some bird is flightless.

The rearrangement is the pattern of Darii. Therefore Dimaris is equivalent to Darii.

The Fourth Syllogism of the Fourth Figure: Fesapo

A fourth syllogism of the fourth figure, named *Fesapo*, has the following pattern:

> No As are Bs.
> All Bs are Cs.
> Therefore, some C is not A.

(We have to assume that the class B is not empty.)
> Here is an example:

> No dogs are cats.
> All cats are animals.
> Therefore, some animal is not a dog.

Rearranging, we obtain:

> No cats are dogs.

All cats are animals.
Therefore, some animal is not a dog.

This rearrangement is an instance of Felapton. So Fesapo and Felapton are equivalent.

The Fifth Syllogism of the Fourth Figure: Fresison

A fifth syllogism of the fourth figure, named *Fresison*, has the following pattern:

No As are Bs.
Some B is C.
Therefore, some C is not A.

Here is an example:

No fish are mammals.
Some mammal is a sea creature.
Therefore, some sea creature is not a fish.

Rearranging, we obtain:

No mammals are fish.
Some sea creature is a mammal.
Therefore some sea creature is not a fish.

The rearrangement is an instance of Ferio. So Fresison is equivalent to Ferio.

Other Syllogistic Forms

There are other syllogistic forms in which a particular conclusion ("some") is drawn when a general conclusion ("all") is warranted. For example, Barbara has the pattern:

All dogs are animals.
All collies are dogs.
Therefore, all collies are animals.

But we can also have an alternate, particular conclusion:

All dogs are animals.
All collies are dogs.

Therefore, some collie is an animal.

This syllogistic form is called *Barbari*. It depends on the additional assumption that the class of collies is not empty. All syllogisms of this kind derive from the corresponding syllogisms with universal conclusions (provided we assume the class described in the subject of the conclusion is not empty). We list them for convenience:

Barbari (derived from Barbara, first figure)

> All dogs are animals.
> All collies are dogs.
> Therefore, some collie is an animal.
> (Compare with the conclusion "all collies are animals" for Barbara.)

Celaront (derived from Celarent, first figure)

> No dogs are cats.
> All collies are dogs.
> Therefore, some collie is not a cat.
> (Compare with the conclusion "no collies are cats" for Celarent.)

Camestrop (derived from Camestres, second figure)

> All collies are dogs.
> No cats are dogs.
> Therefore, some cat is not a collie.
> (Compare with the conclusion "no cats are collies" for Camestres.)

Cesaro (derived from Cesare, second figure)

> No cats are dogs.
> All collies are dogs.
> Therefore, some collie is not a cat.
> (Compare with the conclusion "no collies are cats" for Cesare.)

Camenop (derived from Camenes, fourth figure)

> All collies are dogs.
> No dogs are cats.
> Therefore, some cat is not a collie.
> (Compare with the conclusion "no cats are collies" for Camenes.)

For Further Reflection

1. Show that the pattern of Datisi can be rearranged so that it is an instance of Disamis.
2. What are the general forms (laid out with As, Bs, and Cs) for Barbari, Celaront, Camestrop, Cesaro, and Camestrop?
3. Draw Venn diagrams to test the following inferences.[6]
   a. No children are patient; no impatient person can sit still. Hence, no children can sit still.
   b. All pigs are fat; no skeletons are fat. Hence, no skeletons are pigs.
   c. Some days are rainy; rainy days are tiresome. Hence, some days are tiresome.
   d. No fat creatures run well; some greyhounds run well. Hence, some greyhounds are not fat.
4. Show by Venn diagrams that the following are fallacious.
   a. No muffins are wholesome; all buns are unwholesome. Hence, no buns are muffins.
   b. No misers are generous; some old men are ungenerous. Hence some old men are misers.

---

[6] Examples are taken (sometimes with modification) from Lewis Carroll, *The Game of Logic* (London/New York: Macmillan, 1886), available in reprint from (New York: Dover, 1958). (This is same Lewis Carroll who wrote *Alice in Wonderland* and *Through the Looking Glass*. He was a versatile individual!)

Part IV.B

Supplementary Proofs
for Propositional Logic

Some Proofs for Boolean Algebra

We offer some proofs of additional properties that hold in any Boolean algebra. These proofs also provide an example of how proofs in general work.

The Axioms for Boolean Algebra

In chapter 35 we presented the following standard axioms for Boolean algebra.

1. The operation $\oplus$ is a binary operation.
2. The operation $\oplus$ is commutative:

   $a \oplus b = b \oplus a$

3. The operation $\oplus$ is associative:

   $a \oplus (b \oplus c) = (a \oplus b) \oplus c$

4. The operation $\otimes$ is a binary operation.
5. The operation $\otimes$ is commutative:

   $a \otimes b = b \otimes a$

6. The operation $\otimes$ is associative:

   $a \otimes (b \otimes c) = (a \otimes b) \otimes c$

7. The operations $\oplus$ and $\otimes$ are distributive with respect to each other:

   7a: $a \otimes (b \oplus c) = (a \otimes b) \oplus (a \otimes c)$
   7b: $a \oplus (b \otimes c) = (a \oplus b) \otimes (a \oplus c)$

8. The rule of absorption describes conditions in which an element a can "absorb" an element b:

8a: $a = a \otimes (a \oplus b)$
8b: $a = a \oplus (a \otimes b)$

9. The operation $\ominus$ is a unary operation.
10. There are extremal elements, normally denoted '1' and '0', which have the following properties:

10a: $(\ominus a) \oplus a = 1$ (for any a)
10b: $(\ominus a) \otimes a = 0$ (for any a)

The Distributive Laws for Boolean Algebra

Let us first show that one of the forms of the distributive rule 7 can be derived from the other. Assume that we know that

7a: $a \otimes (b \oplus c) = (a \otimes b) \oplus (a \otimes c)$

We will establish that

7b: $a \oplus (b \otimes c) = (a \oplus b) \otimes (a \oplus c)$

We start with 7a, and substitute into it $(a \oplus b)$ for a and a for b. We get

$$(a \oplus b) \otimes (a \oplus c) = ((a \oplus b) \otimes a) \oplus ((a \oplus b) \otimes c)$$

This formula is the first step in the proof. We continue as follows:

$(a \oplus b) \otimes (a \oplus c) = ((a \oplus b) \otimes a) \oplus ((a \oplus b) \otimes c)$ (by distributivity 7a)
$= (a \otimes (a \oplus b)) \oplus (c \otimes (a \oplus b))$ (by commutativity 5)
$= a \oplus (c \otimes (a \oplus b))$ (by absorption 8a)
$= a \oplus ((c \otimes a) \oplus (c \otimes b))$ (by distributivity 7a)
$= a \oplus ((a \otimes c) \oplus (b \otimes c))$ (by commutativity 5)
$= (a \oplus (a \otimes c)) \oplus (b \otimes c)$ (by associativity 3)
$= a \oplus (b \otimes c)$ (by absorption 8b)

If we exchange the symbols $\oplus$ and $\otimes$ in the proof, we get the *dual*, which is a proof that 7a can be derived from 7b. Here it is:

$(a \otimes b) \oplus (a \otimes c) = ((a \otimes b) \oplus a) \otimes ((a \otimes b) \oplus c)$ (by distributivity 7b)
$= (a \oplus (a \otimes b)) \otimes (c \oplus (a \otimes b))$ (by commutativity 2)

$= a \otimes (c \oplus (a \otimes b))$ (by absorption 8b)
$= a \otimes ((c \oplus a) \otimes (c \oplus b))$ (by distributivity 7b)
$= a \otimes ((a \oplus c) \otimes (b \oplus c))$ (by commutativity 2)
$= (a \otimes (a \oplus c)) \otimes (b \oplus c)$ (by associativity 6)
$= a \otimes (b \oplus c)$ (by absorption 8a)

More Implications for Boolean Algebra

In chapter 35, we already deduced:

11. $a \oplus (\ominus a) = 1$
12. $a \otimes (\ominus a) = 0$
13. $a \oplus 0 = a$
14. $0 \oplus a = a$

In a manner similar to the proof of rules 13 and 14, we can prove:

15. $a \otimes 1 = a = 1 \otimes a$

In fact, this theorem is the *dual* of rules 13 and 14. It can be proved by repeating the derivation of rules 13 and 14, but exchanging the symbols $\oplus$ for $\otimes$ and '1' for '0'. Let us proceed to do it. Rule 8a says that $a = a \otimes (a \oplus b)$. Substitute $\ominus a$ for b. $a = a \otimes (a \oplus (\ominus a))$. By rule 11, $a \oplus (\ominus a) = 1$. So $a = a \otimes (a \oplus (\ominus a))$ simplifies to $a = a \otimes 1$, which is half of what we wanted to prove. $1 \otimes a = a \otimes 1$ by commutativity (5). So the other half follows.

Now let us prove:

16. $a \oplus a = a$

Start with 8b, the rule of absorption:

$a = a \oplus (a \otimes b)$

Let b be 1.

$a = a \oplus (a \otimes 1)$
$= a \oplus a$ (by 15)

Now prove:

17. $a \otimes a = a$

The proof is the dual of the previous proof:

$a = a \otimes (a \oplus 0)$ (absorption, 8a)
$= a \otimes a$ (by 13)

Now prove that

18. $a \oplus 1 = 1 = 1 \oplus a$

$a \oplus 1 = a \oplus (a \oplus \ominus a)$ (by 11)
$= (a \oplus a) \oplus \ominus a$ (by associativity 3)
$= a \oplus \ominus a$ (by 16)
$= 1$ (by 11)

By commutativity (2), we therefore also have $1 \oplus a = 1$.

19. $a \otimes 0 = 0 = 0 \otimes a$

This is the dual of 18.

To establish the remaining results, it is convenient to have an intermediate result (often called a *lemma*).

Lemma B.1: if $x \oplus a = 1$ and $x \otimes a = 0$, then $x = \ominus a$.

This lemma says that if x behaves like the complement $\ominus a$ of a, it is $\ominus a$. Here is the proof:

Assume that $x \oplus a = 1$ and $x \otimes a = 0$.
$x = x \oplus 0$ (by 13)
$= x \oplus (a \otimes \ominus a)$ (by 12)
$= (x \oplus a) \otimes (x \oplus \ominus a)$ (by distributive rule 7b)
$= 1 \otimes (x \oplus \ominus a)$ (by assumption that $x \oplus a = 1$)
$= (\ominus a \oplus x) \otimes 1$ (by commutativity, 2 and 5)
$= (\ominus a \oplus x) \otimes (\ominus a \oplus a)$ (by 10a)
$= \ominus a \oplus (x \otimes a)$ (by distributive rule 7b)
$= \ominus a \oplus 0$ (by assumption)
$= \ominus a$ (by 13).

Now let us show that

20. $\ominus \ominus a = a$

We use the lemma B.1, with $\ominus a$ substituted for a. The lemma says that if $x \oplus \ominus a = 1$ and $x \otimes \ominus a = 0$, then $x = \ominus\ominus a$. Substituting a for x, the result is immediate.

Now let us prove that:

21. $\ominus(a \otimes b) = (\ominus a) \otimes (\ominus b)$

We have to show that $(\ominus a) \otimes (\ominus b)$ is the complement of $a \oplus b$. Again, we use the lemma, this time with $a \oplus b$ substituting for a and $(\ominus a) \otimes (\ominus b)$ for x. The lemma says that we need to demonstrate that $(\ominus a) \otimes (\ominus b)$ acts like the complement of $a \oplus b$. That is, we need to show that $(\ominus a \otimes \ominus b) \oplus (a \oplus b) = 1$ and $(\ominus a \otimes \ominus b) \otimes (a \oplus b) = 0$.

$(\ominus a \otimes \ominus b) \oplus (a \oplus b)$
$= (a \oplus b) \oplus (\ominus a \otimes \ominus b)$ (by commutativity 2)
$= ((a \oplus b) \oplus \ominus a) \otimes ((a \oplus b) \oplus \ominus b)$ (by distributive rule 7b)
$= (\ominus a \oplus (a \oplus b)) \otimes ((a \oplus b) \oplus \ominus b)$ (by commutativity rule 2)
$= ((\ominus a \oplus a) \oplus b) \otimes (a \oplus (b \oplus \ominus b))$ (by associativity rule 3)
$= (1 \oplus b) \otimes (a \oplus (b \oplus \ominus b))$ (by 10a)
$= (1 \oplus b) \otimes (a \oplus 1)$ (by 11)
$= 1 \otimes 1$ (by 18)
$= 1$ (by 15).

Now we proceed to prove the second half, namely, that $(\ominus a \otimes \ominus b) \otimes (a \oplus b) = 0$.

$(\ominus a \otimes \ominus b) \otimes (a \oplus b) = ((\ominus a \otimes \ominus b) \otimes a) \oplus ((\ominus a \otimes \ominus b) \otimes b)$ (by 7a)
$= (\ominus a \otimes (\ominus b \otimes a)) \oplus (\ominus a \otimes (\ominus b \otimes b))$ (by associativity 6)
$= (\ominus a \otimes (a \otimes \ominus b)) \oplus (\ominus a \otimes (\ominus b \otimes b))$ (by commutativity 5)
$= ((\ominus a \otimes a) \otimes \ominus b) \oplus (\ominus a \otimes (\ominus b \otimes b))$ (by associativity 6)
$= (0 \otimes \ominus b) \oplus (\ominus a \otimes 0)$ (by 10b)
$= 0 \oplus 0$ (by 19)
$= 0$ (by 13).

Since both halves are established, the lemma applies to $(\ominus a \otimes \ominus b)$, showing that it is the complement of $a \oplus b$.

22. $\ominus(a \otimes b) = (\ominus a) \oplus (\ominus b)$

This rule is the dual of 18. The proof is exactly analogous.

Verifying the Rule of *modus ponens*

We can "translate" logical truths about propositions into Boolean algebra in a natural way. Logical disjunction $\vee$ corresponds to the symbol $\oplus$; logical conjunction $\wedge$ corresponds to the symbol $\otimes$. Logical negation $\sim$ corresponds to the symbol $\ominus$. Material implication $p \supset q$ corresponds to $\sim p \vee q$, which translates as $(\ominus p) \oplus q$. The claim that a composite proposition p is true translates as $p = 1$. With these translations, we can verify *modus ponens*.

If p is true and $p \supset q$ is true, is it always the case that q is true? Within Boolean algebra, the corresponding question is whether, if $p = 1$ and $(\ominus p) \oplus q = 1$, does $q = 1$? Here is the proof:

$q = q \oplus 0$ (by rule 13)
$= q \oplus (p \otimes (\ominus p))$ (by rule 12)
$= (q \oplus p) \otimes (q \oplus (\ominus p))$ (by distributivity 7b)
$= (q \oplus 1) \otimes (q \oplus (\ominus p))$ (by assumption that $p = 1$)
$= 1 \otimes (q \oplus (\ominus p))$ (by rule 18)
$= 1 \otimes ((\ominus p) \oplus q)$ (by commutativity 2)
$= 1 \otimes 1$ (by assumption that $(\ominus p) \oplus q = 1$)
$= 1$ (by rule 15 or 17).

Testimony to God

The coherence of rules and the tightly knit character of proofs in Boolean algebra reflect, as usual, the self-consistency of God. The unity and diversity in different kinds of binary operations in different kinds of fields reflect the wisdom and beauty of God.

For Further Reflection

1. Write out a proof of the rule #22.
2. Prove that $\ominus 1 = 0$ and $\ominus 0 = 1$. [Hint: use Lemma B.1 to prove $\ominus 1 = 0$. Then to prove $\ominus 0 = 1$, use rule 20 above.]
3. Use rules 20, 21, and 22 repeatedly to "push down" the occurrences of the symbol $\ominus$ in compound expressions, so that each remaining occurrence of the symbol $\ominus$ immediately precedes a letter a, b, c, ... , standing for an element. Do this with
   a. $\ominus\ominus\ominus(\ominus a \otimes (\ominus b)) = a \oplus b$
   b. $\ominus(a \otimes (b \oplus \ominus c)) = \ominus a \oplus (\ominus b \otimes c)$
   c. $\ominus\ominus((\ominus a \otimes (\ominus(b \oplus \ominus c))) \oplus \ominus((\ominus b \otimes c) \oplus (b \oplus \ominus c)))$
4. Use the distributive law 7a to "push down" the occurrences of the symbol $\otimes$ in compound expressions, so that all the operations with the symbol $\oplus$ can be performed after all the operations with the symbol $\otimes$.
5. Example: a. $(a \otimes (b \oplus c)) \oplus (b \otimes (b \oplus c)) = ((a \otimes b) \oplus (a \otimes c)) \oplus ((b \otimes b) \oplus (b \otimes c))$
   b. $(a \oplus b) \otimes (b \oplus c) = ?$

Deriving Whitehead and Russell's Axioms

We now derive the remaining axioms of propositional logic that are part of Whitehead and Russell's system. We use the deduction rules introduced in chapter 42 to derive the principle of permutation, the associative principle, and the principle of summation.[1]

The Principle of Permutation

Let us deduce the principle of permutation, $(p \lor q) \supset (q \lor p)$.

(1) $q \supset (p \lor q)$ (by the principle of addition, already proved in chapter 42 as a theorem)

(2) $p \supset (q \lor p)$ (by substituting p for q and q for p in (1))

(3) $p \supset (p \lor q)$ (a form of the principle of addition, already proved)

(4) $q \supset (q \lor p)$ (by substituting p for q and q for p in (3))

(5) Assume $p \lor q$.

    (6) $q \lor p$ (by the rule of disjunction elimination, applied to lines (5) (2), and (4))

(7) $(p \lor q) \supset (q \lor p)$ (by the rule of conditional proof, applied to lines (5)-(6))

In general, if we have to prove a particular proposition using natural deduction rules, we can take a clue from the structure of the proposition that we are being asked to prove. In this case, the proposition to be proved is

$$(p \lor q) \supset (q \lor p)$$

In any such proposition, let us call the logical truth function that is least enclosed in parentheses the *highest-order* truth function within the proposition. In this case, the highest-order truth function is $\supset$. The other truth

---

[1] Alfred North Whitehead and Bertrand Russell, *Principia Mathematica*, 2nd ed., 3 vols. (Cambridge: Cambridge University Press, 1927), 1:96–97, propositions 1.4, 1.5, and 1.6.

functions ∨ are enclosed within parentheses, whereas ⊃ is outside the parentheses. This highest-order truth function often offers the best clue as to how to go about proving the proposition. If the highest-order truth function is material implication ⊃, it is best to proceed by the method of conditional proof. Assume the antecedent $(p \lor q)$ as an extra assumption, and then try to derive the consequent $(q \lor p)$. That is what we have done in lines (5)-(7) in the proof above.

Now how do we get from the antecedent to the consequent? Look at the highest-order truth function, namely, $(p \lor q)$, in the antecedent. The structure of this proposition, with disjunction as the highest-order truth function, suggests that we should try to use disjunction elimination. The pattern for disjunction elimination says that, if you have an assumption $(p \lor q)$, you try to see whether you can derive the conclusion both with the assumption p and with the assumption q. If you can derive the conclusion from both starting points, then the conclusion will follow from assuming only $(p \lor q)$. Such a patterning of reasoning explains how we arrived at the proof given above.

The Associative Principle

The fourth axiom of Whitehead and Russell, the associative principle, says that $(p \lor (q \lor r)) \supset (q \lor (p \lor r))$. It takes more work to derive it, but we use the same kinds of procedures as before.

The highest-order truth function is material implication ⊃. So try a conditional proof in which we assume that $(p \lor (q \lor r))$. If we assume it, can we derive $(q \lor (p \lor r))$? We should be able to, using enough instances of disjunction elimination on $(p \lor (q \lor r))$.

The plan would be to see if we can derive $(q \lor (p \lor r))$ from p and also derive it from $(q \lor r)$. Deriving $(q \lor (p \lor r))$ from p is relatively easy. We mostly use the rule of addition.

    (1) $q \supset (p \lor q)$ (by the principle of addition, already proved)
    (2) $(p \lor r) \supset (q \lor (p \lor r))$ (by substituting q for p and $(p \lor r)$ for q in (1))
    (3) Assume p.
       (4) $p \lor r$ (by the rule of addition applied to (3))
       (5) $(q \lor (p \lor r))$ (by the rule of *modus ponens* applied to (4) and (2))
    (6) $p \supset (q \lor (p \lor r))$ (by the rule of conditional proof applied to lines (3)-(5))

Now we have to see if we can derive $(q \lor (p \lor r))$ from $(q \lor r)$. How do we it? The form of $(q \lor r)$ suggests that we do it by another instance of disjunction elimination. If q implies $(q \lor (p \lor r))$ and r implies $(q \lor (p \lor r))$, then $(q \lor r)$ implies $(q \lor (p \lor r))$ according to the principle of disjunction elimination. That is the plan for the rest of our proof, which continues as follows:

(7) Assume r.

    (8) $p \lor r$ (by the rule of addition applied to (7))

    (9) $q \lor (p \lor r)$ (by the rule of addition applied to (8))

(10) $r \supset (q \lor (p \lor r))$ (by the rule of conditional proof applied to (7)-(9))

(11) $p \supset (p \lor q)$ (a form of the principle of addition, already proved)

(12) $q \supset (q \lor (p \lor r))$ (by substituting q for p and $p \lor r$ for q in (11))

(13) Assume $q \lor r$.

    (14) $q \lor (p \lor r)$ (by the rule of disjunction elimination on (13), (12), and (10))

(15) $(q \lor r) \supset (q \lor (p \lor r))$ (by the rule of conditional proof applied to (13)-(14))

Now that we have the partial results from lines (6) and (15), we are ready to put them together with a final application of the rule of disjunction elimination.

(16) Assume $p \lor (q \lor r)$.

    (17) $q \lor (p \lor r)$ (by the rule of disjunction elimination on (16), (6), and (15))

(18) $(p \lor (q \lor r)) \supset (q \lor (p \lor r))$ (by the rule of conditional proof applied to (16)-(17))

The Principle of Summation

The fifth axiom of Whitehead and Russell says that $(q \supset r) \supset ((p \lor q) \supset (p \lor r))$. Let us deduce it. Once again, we follow clues given by the highest-order truth function. The highest-order truth function in the whole proposition is material implication $\supset$, linking an antecedent $(q \supset r)$ and a consequent $((p \lor q) \supset (p \lor r))$. The occurrence of the symbol $\supset$ at the highest order suggests using the method of conditional proof. We assume $(q \supset r)$. Then, to prove the consequent $((p \lor q) \supset (p \lor r))$, we use another conditional proof, assuming that $(p \lor q)$. We have to embed an assumption within an assumption.

(1) Assume $(q \supset r)$.

    (2) Assume $(p \lor q)$.

Given these two assumptions, we have to prove that $(p \lor r)$. How will we do it? We can use the assumption $(p \lor q)$ effectively if we apply the rule of disjunction elimination. This rule suggests that we try to prove $(p \lor r)$ from p separately, and then from q separately.

To prove that p implies $(p \lor r)$ is easy:

> (3) $p \supset (p \lor q)$ (a form of the principle of addition, already proved)
> (4) $p \supset (p \lor r)$ (by substituting r for q in (3))

(Technically, substitution is not allowed inside a conditional proof, but this particular substitution works even if (3) is placed earlier, outside the conditional assumptions. Once we rearrange the position of (3), we can see that (4) is valid.)

> (5) Assume q.
>> (6) r (by *modus ponens* from (5) and (1))
>> (7) $p \lor r$ (by addition from (6))
>> (8) $q \supset (p \lor r)$ (by conditional proof from (5)-(7))
>> (9) $p \lor r$ (by disjunction elimination on (2), (4), and (8))
> (10) $(p \lor q) \supset (p \lor r)$ (by conditional proof from (2)-(9))
> (11) $(q \supset r) \supset ((p \lor q) \supset (p \lor r))$ (by conditional proof from (1)-(10))

Line (11) is the principle of summation.

Using the Rules

The proofs of Whitehead and Russell's system may seem complex to a beginner. But the availability of the extra rules for deduction helps in making the construction of a new proof more manageable. For those who are interested, we provide in appendix B3 more experience in constructing proofs. We also show in appendix D3 that one of the axioms from Whitehead and Russell, namely, the associative principle (axiom 4) can be derived from the rest.

For Further Reflection

1. Use natural deduction to derive
   a. $p \supset (q \supset p)$
   b. $p \supset (q \supset (r \supset p))$
   c. $(p \lor q) \supset (q \lor (r \lor p))$
2. What makes the method of natural deduction easier than a proof with just the rule of substitution and *modus ponens*?

Practice in Proofs

In chapter 42 we introduced extra rules for deduction. These extra rules enabled us in appendix B2 to prove the axioms of Whitehead and Russell's system. The extra rules also make it intuitively simpler to construct a new proof.

Discovering a Proof

Suppose, for example, that we want to prove theorem 2.04 in Whitehead and Russell: $(p \supset (q \supset r)) \supset (q \supset (p \supset r))$.[1] How do we do it? It is not obvious, given Whitehead and Russell's starting axioms (explained in chapter 40). Here is how Whitehead and Russell do it:[2]

(1) $(p \lor (q \lor r)) \supset (q \lor (p \lor r))$ (axiom 4, the associative principle)
(2) $(\sim p \lor (\sim q \lor r)) \supset (\sim q \lor (\sim p \lor r))$ (by substituting $\sim p$ for p and $\sim q$ for q in (1))
(3) $(p \supset (q \supset r)) \supset (q \supset (p \supset r))$ (from (2) by definition of $\supset$)

The proof above is also satisfactory as a proof in our new system without axioms. The only difference is that in our new system line (1) is a theorem previously proved (appendix B2), rather than an axiom.

But how could we have thought up this proof for ourselves? The result that we want to prove, namely, $(p \supset (q \supset r)) \supset (q \supset (p \supset r))$, does not contain on the surface any obvious hints as to how we might proceed.

Within our new system, which has the additional rules for deduction, we have a more obvious way of proceeding. The result that we want to prove has the form $A \supset B$, where A and B are composite propositions (A is $(p \supset (q \supset r))$ and B is $(q \supset (p \supset r))$). The highest-order logical truth function $\supset$ between the parts A and B gives us our clue. We can try to prove $A \supset B$ by a conditional proof, in which we first assume that A is true. Then we try to deduce B in a conditional proof. Here is how we begin:

---

[1] Alfred North Whitehead and Bertrand Russell, *Principia Mathematica*, 2nd ed., 3 vols. (Cambridge: Cambridge University Press, 1927), 1:100.
[2] We have taken the liberty of slightly altering their proof in order to make it conform to our conventions for notation and our explanation of the rule of substitution.

(1) Assume $p \supset (q \supset r)$.

What do we do next? Given the assumption that we have made, we now have to deduce B. That is, we have to deduce $q \supset (p \supset r)$. How do we do it? We use the same hint as before. The highest-order logical function in $q \supset (p \supset r)$ is $\supset$. It suggests that we attempt to prove $q \supset (p \supset r)$ by a conditional proof. We assume q and try to prove that $(p \supset r)$. The assumption that q is true is now embedded in a context where we have already assumed on line (1) that $p \supset (q \supset r)$. Here is how it looks:

(1)Assume $p \supset (q \supset r)$.
   (2) Assume q.

We know that we are aiming to prove (as a conditional proof) that $(p \supset r)$. How do we do it? By a conditional proof in which we assume p. So here is what we have:

(1)Assume $p \supset (q \supset r)$.
   (2) Assume q.
      (3) Assume p.

Now our way forward is relatively clear.

(1)Assume $p \supset (q \supset r)$.
   (2) Assume q.
      (3) Assume p.
         (4) $q \supset r$ (by *modus ponens* from (3) and (1))
         (5) r (by *modus ponens* from (2) and (4))
      (6) $p \supset r$ (by conditional proof from (3)-(5))
   (7) $q \supset (p \supset r)$ (by conditional proof from (2)-(6))
(8) $(p \supset (q \supset r)) \supset (q \supset (p \supset r))$ (by conditional proof from (1)-(7))

We are done!

It is also convenient to have the rule of hypothetical syllogism:

From $q \supset r$ and $p \supset q$ deduce $p \supset r$.

Here is how we can deduce this rule.

(1) $q \supset r$ (assumption)
(2) $p \supset q$ (assumption)

(3) Assume p.
    (4) q (by *modus ponens* from (3) and (2))
    (5) r (by *modus ponens* from (4) and (1))
    (6) $p \supset r$ (by conditional proof from (3) and (5))

In the same way that conditional proof offers us a promising route for producing a proof of a proposition involving the symbol $\supset$ at a key point, the rules for addition and for disjunction elimination offer a promising route for producing a proof of a proposition involving disjunction $\vee$ ("or").

Dealing with Negation

For dealing with logical negation ($\sim$), it is useful to add some more rules of deduction. But first, let us use our existing rules to obtain some theorems to help to justify new rules.

$$(p \supset \sim p) \supset \sim p$$

If p implies not-p, then not-p. This is a form of the principle of *reductio ad absurdum*, already mentioned in chapter 41.

We know that $(p \vee p) \supset p$. (axiom 1 of Whitehead and Russell, proved in chapter 42.) Substitute $\sim p$ for p. $(\sim p \vee \sim p) \supset \sim p$. By definition of the symbol $\supset$, this is the same as $(p \supset \sim p) \supset \sim p$.

Having established this theorem, we can propose a new rule of deduction:

The rule of *reductio* (also called the rule of indirect proof): If by assuming p we can deduce its negation $\sim p$, we may conclude that $\sim p$ is true.

Strictly speaking, this rule is not necessary, since any result that we can achieve by using it can also be achieved by combining a conditional proof with the *reductio ad absurdum* theorem $(p \supset \sim p) \supset \sim p$. Let us see how:

(1) Assume p.
    (2) additional steps.
    ... [here we take the steps to deduce $\sim p$.]
    (6) $\sim p$.
(7) $p \supset \sim p$ (by conditional proof from (1)-(6))
(8) $(p \supset \sim p) \supset \sim p$ (*reductio* theorem, already proved)
(9) $\sim p$ (by *modus ponens* from (7) and (8))

It is convenient to add this extra rule of indirect proof, because it is a reminder of one way we may try to construct a proof when we are attempting to prove a negative proposition of the form ~p.

For handling negation we can also use some other convenient theorems. Let us start with the following:

Prove ~$p \lor p$. This is called the law of excluded middle. It is not so obvious how to prove it:

    (1) $p \supset p$ (previous theorem from chapter 42)
    (2) ~$p \lor p$ ((from (1) by definition of $\supset$)

Now prove $p \lor$ ~p. This is a second form of the law of excluded middle. We use the principle of permutation:

    (1) ~$p \lor p$ (just proved)
    (2) $(p \lor q) \supset (q \lor p)$ (axiom permutation; proved in the previous appendix)
    (3) $($~$p \lor p) \supset (p \lor$ ~$p)$ (by substituting ~p for p and p for q in (2))
    (4) $p \lor$ ~p (by *modus ponens* from (1) and (3))

We can also add the following results from Whitehead and Russell:

$$p \supset \,\sim(\sim p)$$
$$\sim(\sim p) \supset p^3$$

These theorems together assure us that a double negation is equivalent to the original proposition (p).

    Also, consider:

$$(\sim p \supset p) \supset p^4$$

---

[3] Whitehead and Russell, Principia Mathematica, 1:101–102, propositions 2.12 and 2.14. Here are proofs in our new system of natural deduction:

    (1) $p \lor$ ~p (law of excluded middle, proved above)
    (2) ~$p \lor$ ~$(\sim p)$ (substitution from (1))
    (3) $p \supset$ ~$(\sim p)$ (definition of $\supset$ from (2))

Now to show that ~$(\sim p) \supset p$.

    (4) ~$p \supset$ ~~$(\sim p)$ (substitution, from (3) above)
    (5) $($~$p \supset$ ~~$(\sim p)) \supset (($~$p \lor$ ~$p) \supset (p \lor$ ~~$(\sim p)))$ (axiom 5, principle of summation)
    (6) $(p \lor$ ~$p) \supset (p \lor$ ~~$(\sim p))$ (modus ponens from (4) and (5))
    (7) $p \lor$ ~~$(\sim p)$ (modus ponens from (1) and (6))
    (8) $(p \lor$ ~~$(\sim p)) \supset ($~~$(\sim p) \lor p)$ (principle of permutation)
    (9) ~~$(\sim p) \lor p$ (modus ponens from (7) and (8))
    (10) ~$(\sim p) \supset p$ (definition of $\supset$ from (9))

[4] Ibid., 1:103, proposition 2.18.

It represents a second form of the principle of *reductio ad absurdum*. It says that if assuming not-*p* leads to a deduction of *p*, *p* is in fact true. Using the preceding principles, we may prove this latter form of the principle of *reductio ad absurdum* by a conditional proof:

(1) Assume $\sim p \supset p$.
   (2) Assume $\sim p$.
      (3) p (by *modus ponens* from (2) and (1))
      (4) $p \supset \sim(\sim p)$ (previous theorem)
      (5) $\sim(\sim p)$ (by *modus ponens* from (3) and (4))
   (6) $\sim(\sim p)$ (by the rule of *reductio* in the form already established)
   (7) $\sim(\sim p) \supset p$ (previous theorem)
   (8) p (by *modus ponens* from (6) and (7))
(9) $(\sim p \supset p) \supset p$ (by conditional proof from (1)-(8))

Several more theorems are very convenient.

$\sim p \supset (p \supset q)$[5]

This theorem, a form of the principle of falsehood, is like Łukasiewicz's third axiom. It says that if one can infer the contradictory of a starting proposition, one can infer anything whatsoever.

Here is a proof:

(1) $p \supset (p \vee q)$ (proved in chapter 42)
(2) $\sim p \supset (\sim p \vee q)$ (by substituting $\sim p$ for p in (1))
(3) $\sim p \supset (p \supset q)$ (from (2) by definition of $\supset$)

Earlier in this chapter we proved what Whitehead and Russell call the commutative principle:

$(p \supset (q \supset r)) \supset (q \supset (p \supset r))$[6]

We can apply this principle to the result $\sim p \supset (p \supset q)$ and "commute" the positions of $\sim p$ and p.

(1) $\sim p \supset (p \supset q)$ (from a previous theorem)
(2) $(p \supset (q \supset r)) \supset (q \supset (p \supset r))$ (from a previous theorem, the commutative principle)

---

[5] Ibid., 1:104, proposition 2.21.
[6] Ibid., 1:99–100, proposition 2.04.

(3) $(\sim p \supset (p \supset q)) \supset (p \supset (\sim p \supset q))$ (by substituting $\sim p$ for p, p for q, and
    q for r in (2))

(4) $p \supset (\sim p \supset q)$ (by *modus ponens* from (1) and (3))

Expanded Rule of *reductio* (Indirect Proof)

With the help of the principle of falsehood, just proved, we may expand the principle of *reductio*, also called the principle of indirect proof.

> Expanded rule of indirect proof: if assuming q leads to a contradiction (both p and $\sim p$ for some proposition p), we may conclude that q is false, i.e., $\sim q$ is true.

Here is how it works:

(1) $p \supset (\sim p \supset q)$ (principle of falsehood, already proved)

(2) $p \supset (\sim p \supset \sim q)$ (by substituting $\sim q$ for q in (1))

(3) Assume q.

    [Now suppose that through a series of steps we can deduce both
        p and $\sim p$.]

    … [additional steps]

    (6) p

    (7) $\sim p$

    (8) $\sim p \supset \sim q$ (by *modus ponens* from (6) and (2))

    (9) $\sim q$ (by *modus ponens* from (7) and (8))

(10) $\sim q$ (by the rule of *reductio*)

In short, if a key assumption leads to a contradiction of any kind, that assumption must be wrong.

The rule of indirect proof also involves an exercise of imagination. We make an assumption, and try to imagine a world in which the assumption is true. As we observed with the rule of conditional proof, so also here, the imagination has its basis in the creativity of the human mind, which rests on the creativity of God. But creativity is bounded by the self-consistency of God. Nothing alien to self-consistency can actually work. So the attempt to make it work tests the truthfulness of the initial assumption.

More Proofs

Now let us try to construct some further proofs, guided by the rules of deduction that we have added.

Prove that $(p \supset q) \supset (\sim q \supset \sim p)$.[7] Because logical implication $\supset$ is the highest-order truth function in the desired result, let us try to use a conditional proof. Assume what? Assume the first half:

(1) Assume $p \supset q$.

We have to deduce the second half, $\sim q \supset \sim p$. To deduce it, begin by assuming $\sim q$:

(1) Assume $p \supset q$.
  (2) Assume $\sim q$.

Now what are we trying to reach, assuming that $\sim q$? We are trying to reach $\sim p$. Try to reach it by assuming the contrary and doing an indirect proof:

(1) Assume $p \supset q$.
  (2) Assume $\sim q$.
    (3) Assume p.
      (4) q (by *modus ponens* from (3) and (1))
      (5) $\sim q \supset (q \supset \sim p)$ (the principle of falsehood, already proved)
      (6) $q \supset \sim p$ (by *modus ponens* from (2) and (5))
      (7) $\sim p$ (by *modus ponens* from (4) and (6))
    (8) $\sim p$ (by indirect proof from (3) and (7))
  (9) $\sim q \supset \sim p$ (by conditional proof from (2)-(8))
(10) $(p \supset q) \supset (\sim q \supset \sim p)$ (by conditional proof from (1)-(9))

In a similar manner we may prove:

$(p \supset \sim q) \supset (q \supset \sim p)$
$(\sim p \supset q) \supset (\sim q \supset p)$
$(\sim p \supset \sim q) \supset (q \supset p)$[8]

Try to prove $p \supset ((p \supset q) \supset q)$:

(1) Assume p.
  (2) Assume $p \supset q$.
    (3) q (by *modus ponens* from (1) and (2))
  (4) $(p \supset q) \supset q$ (by conditional proof from (2)-(3))
(5) $p \supset ((p \supset q) \supset q)$ (by conditional proof from (1)-(4))

---

[7] Ibid., 1:103, proposition 2.16.
[8] Ibid., 1:100, proposition 2.03; 1:102, proposition 2.15; and 1:103, proposition 2.17, respectively.

Logical Conjunction ("And")

We can also produce theorems related to the conjunction operation "and" (∧). We have chosen in our approach to start with only two basic logical connectives, ∨ and ~. Other choices (which are possible) produce other perspectives but the same results in the form of theorems. If we start with only two connectives ∨ and ~, the other operations have to be defined as shorthand for formulas using ∨ and ~. The symbol ⊃ has already been defined by saying:

$p \supset q$ is interpreted to be short for $\sim p \vee q$.

Logical conjunction ∧ is defined by saying:

$p \wedge q$ is interpreted to be short for $\sim(\sim p \vee \sim q)$.

As the most fundamental results, we want to show that

$(p \wedge q) \supset p$
$(p \wedge q) \supset q$

Let us see if we can do it.

(1) Assume $(p \wedge q)$.
  (2) $\sim(\sim p \vee \sim q)$ (from (1) by definition of ∧)
  (3) Assume $\sim p$.
    (4) $\sim p \vee \sim q$ (by rule of addition from (3))
    [Note that (4) contradicts (2). So:]
  (5) p (by rule of *reductio* from (3), (2), and (4))
(6) $(p \wedge q) \supset p$ (by rule of conditional proof, from (1)-(5))

In the same way we may prove that $(p \wedge q) \supset q$.

So if we like, we may introduce the rule of conjunction elimination:

If $p \wedge q$ then we may infer p and we may infer q.

Now let us prove that $(p \wedge (p \supset q)) \supset q$. It is not that hard, given the previous results for logical conjunction ∧:

(1) Assume $p \wedge (p \supset q)$.
  (2) p (rule of conjunction elimination from (1))
  (3) $p \supset q$ (rule of conjunction elimination from (1))

(4) q (*modus ponens* from (2) and (3))

(5) $(p \land (p \supset q)) \supset q$ (rule of conditional proof from (1)-(4))

Prove that $p \supset (q \supset p \land q)$.

(1) Assume p.

 (2) Assume q.

  (3) Assume $\sim p \lor \sim q$.

   (4) $p \supset \sim q$ (from (3) by definition of $\supset$)

   (5) $\sim q$ (*modus ponens* from (1) and (4))

  (6) $\sim(\sim p \lor \sim q)$ (*reductio* from (3), (2), and (5))

  (7) $p \land q$ (from (6) by definition of $\land$)

 (8) $q \supset (p \land q)$ (conditional proof from (2)-(7))

(9) $p \supset (q \supset p \land q)$ (conditional proof from (1)-(8))

By virtue of this result, we may also introduce a rule of conjunction introduction:

If we know that p and that q are true, we may infer that $(p \land q)$

Now prove $((p \land q) \supset r) \supset (p \supset (q \supset r))$ and $(p \supset (q \supset r)) \supset ((p \land q) \supset r)$. First let us undertake to prove that $((p \land q) \supset r) \supset (p \supset (q \supset r))$.

(1) Assume $(p \land q) \supset r$.

 (2) Assume p.

  (3) Assume q.

   (4) $p \land q$ (rule of conjunction introduction from (2) and (3))

   (5) r (*modus ponens* from (4) and (1))

  (6) $q \supset r$ (conditional proof, from (3)-(5))

 (7) $p \supset (q \supset r)$ (conditional proof, from (2)-(6))

(8) $((p \land q) \supset r) \supset (p \supset (q \supset r))$ (conditional proof, from (1)-(7))

Now prove that $(p \supset (q \supset r)) \supset ((p \land q) \supset r)$.

(1) Assume $p \supset (q \supset r)$.

 (2) Assume $p \land q$.

  (3) p (conjunction elimination from (2))

  (4) $q \supset r$ (*modus ponens* from (3) and (1))

  (5) q (conjunction elimination from (2))

  (6) r (*modus ponens* from (5) and (4))

 (7) $(p \land q) \supset r$ (conditional proof from (2)-(6))

(8) $(p \supset (q \supset r)) \supset ((p \land q) \supset r)$ (conditional proof from (1)-(7))

Here are some other tautologies that could be proved using our rules:

$p \supset (q \supset (p \wedge q))$
$q \supset (p \supset (p \wedge q))$
$(p \wedge q) \supset (q \wedge p)$
$((p \wedge q) \supset r) \supset ((p \wedge \mathord{\sim} r) \supset \mathord{\sim} q)$

The Rule of Disjunctive Syllogism

It is useful also to have the rule of disjunctive syllogism, which says that from $p \vee q$ together with $\mathord{\sim} p$, one may infer q. In terms of truth functions, this makes sense. If p is not true, the only way for $p \vee q$ to be true is if q is true. In terms of lines of proof, the rule of disjunctive syllogism uses three lines:

Premise 1: $p \vee q$
Premise 2: $\mathord{\sim} p$
Therefore q (by disjunctive syllogism, applied to (1) and (2))

Or we can express it in terms of a single principle of implication:

$((p \vee q) \wedge \mathord{\sim} p) \supset q$

Here is a derivation:

(1) Assume $(p \vee q) \wedge \mathord{\sim} p$.
   (2) $p \vee q$ (conjunction elimination from (1))
   (3) $\mathord{\sim} p$ (conjunction elimination from (1))
   (4) Assume p.
      (5) $\mathord{\sim} p \supset (p \supset q)$ (already proved)
      (6) $p \supset q$ (*modus ponens* from (3) and (5))
      (7) q (*modus ponens* from (4) and (6))
   (8) $p \supset q$ (conditional proof from (4) and (7))
   (9) $q \supset q$ (already proved)
   (10) q (disjunction elimination from (2), (8), and (9))
(11) $((p \vee q) \wedge \mathord{\sim} p) \supset q$ (conditional proof from (1)-(10))

Likewise, $(q \vee p) \wedge \mathord{\sim} p) \supset q$, by a similar argument. From $q \vee p$ and $\mathord{\sim} p$ you may infer q.

The Rule of *modus tollens*

We have mentioned before the principle of *modus tollens*. It is useful to add it as a rule:

Modus tollens: From $p \supset q$ and $\sim q$ you may infer $\sim p$.

Proof:

> (1) $p \supset q$ (given as an assumption)
> (2) $\sim q$ (given as an assumption)
> (3) Assume p
> > (4) q (*modus ponens* from (3) and (1))
> (5) $\sim p$ (indirect proof from (3), (4), and (2))

We may also prove it by using a definition:

> (3) $\sim p \lor q$ (from (1) by definition of $\supset$)
> (4) $\sim p$ (from (3) and (2) by disjunctive syllogism)

The Rule of Replacement

We may also add the *rule of replacement*, which says that, with a compound proposition, any embedded component proposition may be replaced by one to which it is logically equivalent. This rule is discussed and verified in the next appendix.

The Law of Noncontradiction

The proposition $\sim(p \land \sim p)$ says that it is not the case that both p and $(\land)$ $\sim p$. This is known as the *law of noncontradiction*. It is not too hard to prove:

> (1) Assume $p \land \sim p$.
> > (2) p (conjunction elimination from (1))
> > (3) $\sim p$ (conjunction elimination from (1))
> (4) $\sim(p \land \sim p)$ (indirect proof from (1), (2), and (3))

Some people have said that the law of noncontradiction is the most basic law of logic. If it is basic, how can we prove it? In a sense we are assuming it in our informal reasoning before we even get to the study of logic. We are assuming it informally whenever we deal with a particular proposition p and trust that it is distinct from its opposite. In this assumption we are relying on God, who is consistent with himself and who does not contradict himself.

But we also rely on God for many other things, and do so all the time. God's self-consistency has many aspects, all of which can be seen as implications of the Father's love for the Son. Each of these aspects is in everlasting harmony with the rest. We can start from any of them, because they all testify to and point to and manifest the goodness of the One who is their origin. No one of the laws of logic is "basic" in itself, independent of God. Their basis is in God. When we recognize the personal character of the laws of logic, we also can see that any can be used as a perspective on the rest. We can start with the law of noncontradiction as "basic." Or we can start with rules of deduction as "basic," which is what we have done above.

For Further Reflection

1. Use the rules of natural deduction to confirm the validity of the following inferences:
   a. Assuming $A \wedge B$, deduce $A \vee C$.
   b. Assuming $A \wedge B$, deduce $C \supset B$.
   c. Assuming $A \supset B$, and $\sim B$, deduce $\sim A \wedge \sim B$.
   d. Assuming $A \supset \sim B$, $(C \vee D) \supset A$, and D, deduce $\sim B \vee E$.
   e. Assuming: $\sim A \wedge B$ and $A \vee C$, deduce C.
   f. Assuming $A \supset (B \wedge C)$, $\sim D \vee A$, and $D \wedge \sim E$, deduce $A \wedge C$.
2. Use the rules of natural deduction to derive:
   a. $p \supset (q \supset (p \wedge q))$
   b. $q \supset (p \supset (p \wedge q))$
   c. $(p \wedge q) \supset (q \wedge p)$
   d. $((p \wedge q) \supset r) \supset ((p \wedge \sim r) \supset \sim q)$.

Appendix B4

The Rule of Replacement

For a system of natural deduction, it is helpful in addition to the rules we have already discussed to have *the rule of replacement*. This rule says that, if two expressions R and S have already been proved to be logically equivalent, one expression can replace the other in any more complicated truth-functional formula in which they are embedded, and still preserve the truth value of the formula as a whole. For example, since p is equivalent to $\sim\sim p$, p can replace $\sim\sim p$ or vice versa in an expression such as

$$q \supset (\sim\sim p \wedge (\sim p \vee r) \supset \sim\sim p)$$

So we have the equivalences:

$$\{q \supset (\sim\sim p \wedge (\sim p \vee r) \supset \sim\sim p)\} \equiv \{q \supset (p \wedge (\sim p \vee r) \supset \sim\sim p)\}$$
$$\equiv \{q \supset (p \wedge (\sim p \vee r) \supset p)\} \equiv \{q \supset (p \wedge (\sim\sim\sim p \vee r) \supset p)\}$$

The ability to replace one expression by another can be very helpful when we are trying to prove some new result.

By the definition of logical equivalence, R and S always have the same truth value. So their truth value will be transmitted "upward" into the formulas in which they are embedded. It seems obvious, then, that the rule of replacement is a valid rule for deduction. But we can confirm it by a series of more careful steps.

The basic idea is first to verify that replacement can take place for simple compound expressions that use either of the two truth-functional symbols $\sim$ and $\vee$, the two original symbols (not defined in terms of other symbols) in Whitehead and Russell's system. Then we progress from there to more complicated compound expressions, using mathematical induction.

First, show that replacement can take place with the expression $\sim R$, which uses the symbol $\sim$.

Lemma 1: if $R \equiv S$, $\sim R \equiv \sim S$.

Proof:

By definition, $p \equiv q$ is shorthand for $(p \supset q) \wedge (q \supset p)$. So we can proceed:

(1) $R \equiv S$ (assumption)
(2) $(R \supset S) \wedge (S \supset R)$ (definition from (1))
(3) $(R \supset S)$ (conjunction elimination from (2))
(4) $(R \supset S) \supset (\sim S \supset \sim R)$ (proved in the preceding appendix)
(5) $(\sim S \supset \sim R)$ (*modus ponens* from (3) and (4))
(6) $(S \supset R)$ (conjunction elimination from (2))
(7) $(S \supset R) \supset (\sim R \supset \sim S)$ (proved in the preceding appendix)
(8) $(\sim R \supset \sim S)$ (*modus ponens* from (6) and (7))
(9) $(\sim R \supset \sim S) \wedge (\sim S \supset \sim R)$ (conjunction introduction from (8) and (5))
(10) $\sim R \equiv \sim S$ (definition of equivalence from (9))

Now, for simple expressions involving the symbol $\vee$:

Lemma 2: if $R \equiv S$, $(p \vee R) \equiv (p \vee S)$.

(1) $R \equiv S$ (assumption)
(2) $(R \supset S) \wedge (S \supset R)$ (definition from (1))
(3) $(R \supset S)$ (conjunction elimination from (2))
(4) $(R \supset S) \supset ((p \vee R) \supset (p \vee S))$ (Whitehead and Russell axiom 5)
(5) $(p \vee R) \supset (p \vee S)$ (*modus ponens* from (3) and (4))
(6) $(S \supset R)$ (conjunction elimination from (2))
(7) $(S \supset R) \supset ((p \vee S) \supset (p \vee R))$ (Whitehead and Russell axiom 5)
(8) $(p \vee S) \supset (p \vee R)$ (*modus ponens* from (6) and (7))
(9) $((p \vee R) \supset (p \vee S)) \wedge ((p \vee S) \supset (p \vee R))$ (conjunction introduction from (5) and (8))
(10) $(p \vee R) \equiv (p \vee S)$ (definition of equivalence from (9))

Lemma 3: if $R \equiv S$, $(R \vee p) \equiv (S \vee p)$.

We use Lemma 2 and Whitehead and Russell's axiom 3, $(p \vee q) \supset (q \vee p)$:

(1) $R \equiv S$ (assumption)
(2) $(p \vee R) \equiv (p \vee S)$ (Lemma 2, from (1))
(3) $((p \vee R) \supset (p \vee S)) \wedge ((p \vee S) \supset (p \vee R))$ (definition from (2))
(4) $(p \vee R) \supset (p \vee S)$ (conjunction elimination from (3))
(5) $(p \vee S) \supset (S \vee p)$ (axiom 3)
(6) $(R \vee p) \supset (p \vee R)$ (axiom 3)
(7) $(R \vee p) \supset (S \vee p)$ (hypothetical syllogism from (6), (4), and (5))
(8) $(p \vee S) \supset (p \vee R)$ (conjunction elimination from (3))

(9) $(S \lor p) \supset (R \lor p)$ (repeat steps (5) through (7) with the symbols R and S reversed)

(10) $((R \lor p) \supset (S \lor p)) \land ((S \lor p) \supset (R \lor p))$ (conjunction introduction from (7) and (9))

(11) $(R \lor p) \equiv (S \lor p)$ (definition of $\equiv$ from (10))

Theorem: if $R \equiv S$, and T' is the result of replacing R with S once in T, then $T \equiv T'$.

We will do the proof by mathematical induction on the number of symbols in T.

First, write T with no abbreviations, that is, only using the original symbols $\sim$ and $\lor$.

(1) If T has one symbol, T must be identical to R. So T' is S, and $T \equiv T'$.

(2) Suppose the theorem is true for all R and S, with the restriction that T has less than n symbols. We will show it is also true for T with exactly n symbols. T may still be R, if R has n symbols. But in that case the argument is the same as in stage (1).

If T is not R, T has one of two forms, $\sim U$ or $U \lor V$. Take these one at a time.

(2a) T has the form $\sim U$. Then since U has less than n symbols, $U \equiv U'$, where U' is the result of replacing R by S in U. By Lemma 1, $\sim U \equiv \sim U'$. But T is $\sim U$ and T' is U'. So $T \equiv T'$.

(2b) T has the form $U \lor V$. (2ba) If R is replaced by S in the U part of T, U has less than n symbols, and so $U \equiv U'$ by the inductive assumption at the beginning of (2). By Lemma 3, $(U \lor V) \equiv (U' \lor V)$. So $T = (U \lor V) \equiv (U' \lor V) = T'$. Likewise, (2bb), if R is replaced by S in the V part of T, V has less than n symbols, and so $V \equiv V'$. By Lemma 2, $(U \lor V) \equiv (U \lor V')$. So $T = (U \lor V) \equiv (U \lor V') = T'$. So for all cases, the theorem has now been shown to be true for any T with n symbols. Hence by induction it is true for all T.

By another induction on the number of replacements, one can show that, if $R \equiv S$, and T' is the result of replacing R with S *any number of times* in T, then $T \equiv T'$.

For Further Reflection

1. Use the rule of replacement to show that
   a. $(p \supset (p \land q)) \equiv (p \supset \sim(\sim p \lor \sim q))$
   b. $(\sim\sim r \lor (p \supset \sim q)) \equiv (r \lor (\sim p \lor \sim q))$
   c. $(\sim\sim r \lor (p \supset \sim q)) \equiv (r \lor \sim(p \land q))$

Reasoning toward the Completeness of Propositional Logic

In chapter 44 we considered whether the logical system of Whitehead and Russell for propositional logic, or the natural deduction system of chapter 42, was complete. Here we undertake to sketch one kind of reasoning that can confirm its completeness.[1]

Representing the Logic of Truth Tables

We will show completeness by trying to represent the logic of truth tables in Whitehead and Russell's notation. For convenience, we will refer also to the natural deduction system of chapter 42, which is more intuitive to use than Whitehead and Russell's original system.

For concreteness, let us suppose that we are dealing with the proposition $(p \lor q) \supset (q \lor p)$ (which happens to be Whitehead and Russell's third axiom). We want to show that this is a theorem, that is, that it can be proved in our natural deduction system. And we want to establish this result by a method that would apply not only to this one proposition but to any proposition that is a tautology. We first "translate" the symbol $\supset$ using its definition within Whitehead and Russell's system. $(p \lor q) \supset (q \lor p)$ becomes $\sim(p \lor q) \lor (q \lor p)$. We proceed to check that it is a tautology using truth tables (table B5.1; see next page).

There are four possible options for p and q: TT, TF, FT, and FF. Each option generates a row in the truth table. Together, these options exhaust the possibilities.

---

[1] For a more rigorous but less digestible discussion of this process, see Irving M. Copi, *Symbolic Logic*, 5th ed. (New York: Macmillan, 1979), 250–258. Copi is examining a different system, developed by J. Barkley Rosser. But the process of proof is essentially the same as with Whitehead and Russell's system.

TABLE B5.1: Checking a Tautology

p	q	$p \vee q$	$q \vee p$	$\sim(p \vee q)$	$\sim(p \vee q) \vee (q \vee p)$
T	T	T	T	F	T
T	F	T	T	F	T
F	T	T	T	F	T
F	F	F	F	T	T

The Plan for a Proof

We have completed the demonstration using truth tables. Now we want to mimic the same demonstration using the resources of our deductive system rather than directly using the resources of the truth table. Our goal is to prove within our deductive system that the formula in the right-most column always comes out true. We do it by splitting the process of proof into pieces. Each piece corresponds to one row in the truth table. First, attack the row TT (p is T and q is T). We will prove that the final column is true if we make the assumption that p is true and that q is true, using a method of conditional proof. Then we will do the same thing for the next row. When we are through, we will have established that the final column is true for any row whatsoever. Since together the rows exhaust all the possibilities, the final column is true without any conditions.

Doing One Row

We can represent the assumption made in any one row as a conjunctive proposition. In the row TT, where p and q are both T, we represent the starting assumption in our logical system as $p \wedge q$. This proposition mimics the first two columns in the row TT.

Given the assumption that $p \wedge q$, we proceed to deduce the truth values in all the columns of row TT. The entries in the first two columns follow immediately. If we want, we can write it out as a series of lines in a deduction:

(1) Assume $p \wedge q$.
    (2) p (conjunction elimination from (1))
    (3) q (conjunction elimination from (1))

Next, can we deduce the result in column 3, namely, that $p \vee q$ is true?

Yes, it follows from knowing that p is true. It follows from the rule of addition (chapter 42).

Similarly, we deduce that $q \lor p$ is true. Can we deduce $\sim(p \lor q)$ is false? We represent the information that $\sim(p \lor q)$ is false as the truth of its negation: $\sim\sim(p \lor q)$ is true. Can we deduce it? Yes, from the properties of negation ($\sim$). Then can we deduce the truth of the final column? We have already established in column 4 that $q \lor p$. By the rule of addition, the final column is also true. Our overall result is that, given the truth of $p \land q$, we can deduce $\sim(p \lor q) \lor (q \lor p)$.

This relationship is a conditional relationship. We have been saying that, if we assume that $p \land q$, we can deduce $\sim(p \lor q) \lor (q \lor p)$. As lines of a proof, it would look like this:

(1) Assume $p \land q$.
   (2) p (conjunction elimination from (1))
   (3) q (conjunction elimination from (1))
   ...
   ...
(10) $\sim(p \lor q) \lor (q \lor p)$

By the rule of conditional proof developed in chapter 42, we can write this as

(11) $(p \land q) \supset (\sim(p \lor q) \lor (q \lor p))$ (conditional proof from (1) and (10))

It takes work to move through all these steps. But the result follows "mechanically," because the value T or F in each column can be inferred from the previous columns. The only truths that we have to use are truths with respect to the properties of logical negation $\sim$ and logical disjunction $\lor$. For instance, for logical disjunction, we have to know all the inferences to use to go from the truth or falsehood of p and q to the truth or falsehood of $p \lor q$. We need to know that if p is true then $p \lor q$ is true: $p \supset (p \lor q)$. Also $q \supset (p \lor q)$. We also need to know that, if $\sim p$ and $\sim q$, then we may infer that $p \lor q$ is not true: $\sim(p \lor q)$. So we need to know $(\sim p \land \sim q) \supset \sim(p \lor q)$. These truths taken together are what we need to know to move from the columns establishing the values of p and q to the column establishing the value of $p \lor q$. To move from a column establishing the value of p to a column establishing the value of $\sim p$, we also need to know that $p \supset \sim\sim p$. Also, $\sim\sim p \supset p$. All these propositions can be deduced within Whitehead and Russell's system or our system of natural deduction. So in the end, for the row with p as T and q as T, we prove that

$(p \wedge q) \supset (\sim(p \vee q) \vee (q \vee p))$

Now we go to the next row. In the next row, p is T and q is F. This row corresponds to the assumption that $p \wedge \sim q$. Given this assumption, we once again make our way through the remaining columns, proceeding to prove each result. We once again obtain for the last column the result $\sim(p \vee q) \vee (q \vee p)$. This is again a result depending on a condition, in this case the condition $p \wedge \sim q$. So we conclude, by the method of conditional proof:

$(p \wedge \sim q) \supset (\sim(p \vee q) \vee (q \vee p))$

We go on to the next row, where p is F and q is T. This row corresponds to the assumption that $\sim p \wedge q$. By the end of the row, we have deduced again that $(\sim(p \vee q) \vee (q \vee p))$, given the assumption that $\sim p \wedge q$. Thus, we have

$(\sim p \wedge q) \supset (\sim(p \vee q) \vee (q \vee p))$

From the final row, we deduce

$(\sim p \wedge \sim q) \supset (\sim(p \vee q) \vee (q \vee p))$

Now, let us stand back from the process. Altogether, we have four distinct assumptions that we have used:

$(p \wedge q), (p \wedge \sim q), (\sim p \wedge q), (\sim p \wedge \sim q).$

By the nature of truth tables, these four assumptions exhaust the field. These are the only possibilities. But this means that we should be able to prove that at least one is true:

$(p \wedge q) \vee (p \wedge \sim q) \vee (\sim p \wedge q) \vee (\sim p \wedge \sim q)$?

Can we? Remember that our logical operations mimic Boolean algebra. By the associative laws of Boolean algebra, we do not have to worry about how we group the operations $\vee$. Thus

$(p \wedge q) \vee (p \wedge \sim q) \vee (\sim p \wedge q) \vee (\sim p \wedge \sim q)$

is equivalent to any of the following:

$$\{[(p \wedge q) \vee (p \wedge {\sim}q)] \vee ({\sim}p \wedge q)\} \vee ({\sim}p \wedge {\sim}q)$$
$$[(p \wedge q) \vee (p \wedge {\sim}q)] \vee [({\sim}p \wedge q) \vee ({\sim}p \wedge {\sim}q)]$$
$$\{(p \wedge q) \vee [(p \wedge {\sim}q) \vee ({\sim}p \wedge q)]\} \vee ({\sim}p \wedge {\sim}q)$$
$$(p \wedge q) \vee \{[(p \wedge {\sim}q) \vee ({\sim}p \wedge q)] \vee ({\sim}p \wedge {\sim}q)\}$$
$$(p \wedge q) \vee \{(p \wedge {\sim}q) \vee [({\sim}p \wedge q) \vee ({\sim}p \wedge {\sim}q)]\}$$

We have for simplicity written it without any extra parentheses.

Now consider the first two pieces that are linked together with disjunctions, namely

$$(p \wedge q) \vee (p \wedge {\sim}q)$$

These two pieces correspond to the first two rows, TT and TF. By the distributive law in Boolean algebra,

$$[(p \wedge q) \vee (p \wedge {\sim}q)] \equiv [p \wedge (q \vee {\sim}q)]$$

$(q \vee {\sim}q)$ is always true, and can be proved to be true. So

$$[p \wedge (q \vee {\sim}q)] \equiv p \, .$$

So the first two pieces reduce to p.

Likewise, look at the next two pieces, namely,

$$({\sim}p \wedge q) \vee ({\sim}p \wedge {\sim}q)$$

By the distributive law,

$$[({\sim}p \wedge q) \vee ({\sim}p \wedge {\sim}q)] \equiv [{\sim}p \wedge (q \vee {\sim}q)]$$

and

$$[{\sim}p \wedge (q \vee {\sim}q)] \equiv {\sim}p \, .$$

So these two pieces reduce to ${\sim}p$. The total number of alternatives for p and q has now been reduced to the two alternatives for p, namely, p or ${\sim}p$.

$$[(p \wedge q) \vee (p \wedge {\sim}q) \vee ({\sim}p \wedge q) \vee ({\sim}p \wedge {\sim}q)] \equiv (p \vee {\sim}p)$$

$(p \lor \sim p)$ is always true, and can be proved to be so. The equivalences that we laid out can also be proved. So the disjunction of all the alternatives is always true, and can be proved to be so. That is, we can prove

$(p \land q) \lor (p \land \sim q) \lor (\sim p \land q) \lor (\sim p \land \sim q)$

Each of the alternatives $(p \land q)$, $(p \land \sim q)$, $(\sim p \land q)$, $(\sim p \land \sim q)$ implies the sought-for conclusion, $\sim(p \lor q) \lor (q \lor p)$. So by repeated disjunction elimination the conclusion follows.

Dealing with More than Two Starting Propositions

Now suppose that we have a complex proposition that contains not two propositional symbols p and q, but multiple symbols, p, q, r, s, … . We can repeat the same procedure, except that it becomes more tedious and more elaborate. If we have four propositional symbols p, q, r, s, we have a total of 16 rows, one for each possible alternative.

p, q, r, s, can take on any of the following possibilities:

T T T T
T T T F
T T F T
T T F F
T F T T
T F T F
T F F T
T F F F
F T T T
F T T F
F T F T
F T F F
F F T T
F F T F
F F F T
F F F F.

The process of reasoning is nevertheless the same in principle. So we have a fixed recipe by which we can go from truth tables to a deduction within our natural deduction system. This recipe guarantees that every tautology can be proved.

For Further Reflection

1. Suppose we want to use the technique explained in this appendix to produce a proof of a tautology involving three propositional symbols, *p*, *q*, and *r*. Write out (in standard formal notation with the symbols ~ and ∧) the eight conditional assumptions that have to be used, one corresponding to each row of the truth table for *p*, *q*, and *r*. (Hint: the first such conditional assumption is (*p* ∧ *q*) ∧ *r*, corresponding to the first row of the truth table, where *p*, *q*, and *r* are all T.) Must at least one of the eight possibilities be true?

2. In this chapter, what field of study are we using as a perspective on truth tables?

Part IV.C

Proofs for Quantification

Appendix C1

Deductions of Rules for Quantification

We now use rules of natural deduction to show the validity of some of the rules introduced in chapter 50.

    We must first understand that the earlier rules for natural deduction are now being extended to include the same patterns for deduction, now newly applied to propositional functions as well as to propositions with no variables.

Deducing Quantification Movement

Can we deduce the rule of quantification movement, namely,

$$\{(\forall x)(q \lor \varphi(x))\} \supset (q \lor (\forall x)\,\varphi(x))\ ?$$

Here is how we do the proof:

    (1) Assume $(\forall x)(q \lor \varphi(x))$.
        (2) $(q \lor \varphi(y))$ (principle of universal instantiation, from (1))
        (3) $q \lor {\sim}q$ (principle of excluded middle; proved earlier)
        (4) Assume q.
            (5) $q \lor (\forall x)\,\varphi(x)$ (rule of addition, from (4))
        (6) $q \supset q \lor (\forall x)\,\varphi(x)$ (rule of conditional proof, from (4) and (5))
        (7) Assume ${\sim}q$.
            (8) $\varphi(y)$ (disjunctive syllogism [appendix B3] from (7) and (2))
            (9) $(\forall x)\,\varphi(x)$ (universal generalization, from (8))
            (10) $q \lor (\forall x)\,\varphi(x)$ (rule of addition, from (9))
        (11) ${\sim}q \supset (q \lor (\forall x)\,\varphi(x))$ (conditional proof, from (7) and (10))
        (12) $q \lor (\forall x)\,\varphi(x)$ (rule of disjunction elimination, from (3), (6), and (11))
    (13) $\{(\forall x)(q \lor \varphi(x))\} \supset (q \lor (\forall x)\,\varphi(x))$ (conditional proof, from (1) and (12))

Line (13) is the rule of quantification movement, which was to be established.

Existential Generalization

Now we establish the rule of existential generalization, namely

$\varphi(k) \supset (\exists x)\, \varphi(x)$

(1) Assume $\varphi(k)$
    (2) Assume $\sim (\exists x)\, \varphi(x)$ [we are assuming the contrary and endeavoring to produce an indirect proof]
        (3) $\sim\sim (\forall x) \sim\varphi(x)$ (definition of $\exists$)
        (4) $\sim\sim p \supset p$ (tautology, already proved)
        (5) $\sim\sim (\forall x) \sim\varphi(x) \supset (\forall x) \sim\varphi(x)$ (substitution into (4))
        (6) $(\forall x) \sim\varphi(x)$ (*modus ponens* from (3) and (5))
        (7) $\sim\varphi(k)$ (universal instantiation from (6))
    (8) $(\exists x)\, \varphi(x)$ (indirect proof, from (2), (1) and (7))
(9) $\varphi(k) \supset (\exists x)\, \varphi(x)$ (conditional proof, from (1) and (8))

For Further Reflection

1. How does the introduction of quantifiers and predicates increase the capability of the system of formal logic?

Natural Deduction of Syllogisms

We now show how to deduce a few of Aristotle's syllogistic forms using the system of natural deduction developed in chapter 42 and enhanced in chapter 50 to include quantification.

Deducing the Barbara Syllogism

First consider the Barbara syllogism. Our example is

> All dogs are animals.
> All collies are dogs.
> Therefore, all collies are animals.

We convert to modern notation, with $A(x)$ standing for "x is an animal," $D(x)$ standing for "x is a dog," and $C(x)$ standing for "x is a collie." The trio of propositions is

> $(\forall x)\, (D(x) \supset A(x))$
> $(\forall x)\, (C(x) \supset D(x))$
> Therefore, $(\forall x)\, (C(x) \supset A(x))$

Now we use the natural deduction system. We begin by assuming the premises.

> (1) $(\forall x)\, (D(x) \supset A(x))$
> (2) $(\forall x)\, (C(x) \supset D(x))$

The natural way of proceeding is to remove the quantification $(\forall x)$ by the rule of universal instantiation. Then we can see what is true for an arbitrary element y.

> (3) $D(y) \supset A(y)$ (universal instantiation from (1))
> (4) $C(y) \supset D(y)$ (universal instantiation from (2))

Now what? As usual, we try to see hints of how to proceed by looking at the goal for which we aim. The goal is to deduce $(\forall x)\,(C(x) \supset A(x))$. We can get there if we can establish that $C(y) \supset A(y)$ for arbitrary y. To establish a conclusion with the symbol $\supset$ as the uppermost truth function, it is natural to assume the antecedent, in this case $C(y)$.

   (5) Assume $C(y)$
      (6) $D(y)$ (*modus ponens* from (5) and (4))
      (7) $A(y)$ (*modus ponens* from (6) and (3))
   (8) $C(y) \supset A(y)$ (conditional proof, from (5) and (7))
   (9) $(\forall x)(C(x) \supset A(x))$ (universal generalization from (8))

Deducing the Celarent Syllogism

We now undertake to deduce Celarent. Our example is

   No dogs are cats.
   All collies are dogs.
   Therefore, no collies are cats.

In logical notation,

   $(\forall x)\,(D(x) \supset {\sim}\mathrm{Cat}(x))$
   $(\forall x)\,(\mathrm{Collie}(x) \supset D(x))$
   Therefore, $(\forall x)\,(\mathrm{Collie}(x) \supset {\sim}\mathrm{Cat}(x))$

This form is an instance of Barbara, already proved, when we substitute ${\sim}\mathrm{Cat}()$ for $A()$. The proof is the same as for Barbara.

Deducing the Darii Syllogism

How do we deduce Darii? Our example is

   All mammals breathe air.
   Some sea creature is a mammal.
   Therefore, some sea creature breathes air.

In logical notation,

   $(\forall x)\,(M(x) \supset B(x))$
   $(\exists x)\,(S(x) \wedge M(x))$
   Therefore, $(\exists x)\,(S(x) \wedge B(x))$

How do we proceed? Again, look at the conclusion that we have to establish. The uppermost element in the conclusion is an existential quantifier. For such propositions, it is natural to try to establish them by the principle of existential generalization. Try to find a particular x for which $(S(x) \land B(x)$ is true. The particular x might come from premise 2.

(1) $(\forall x) (M(x) \supset B(x))$ (premise)
(2) $(\exists x) (S(x) \land M(x))$ (premise)
(3) $S(c) \land M(c)$ (existential instantiation from (2))
    (4) $M(c) \supset B(c)$ (universal instantiation from (1))
    (5) $M(c)$ (conjunction elimination from (3))
    (6) $B(c)$ (*modus ponens* from (5) and (4))
    (7) $S(c)$ (conjunction elimination from (3))
    (8) $S(c) \land B(c)$ (conjunction introduction from (7) and (6))
(9) $(\exists x) (S(x) \land B(x))$ (existential generalization from (8))

We have chosen to indent lines (4)-(8) because they are under the "scope" of the special individual constant c introduced by existential instantiation. This constant produces special constraints, until it is eliminated in line (9).

We may also produce the same result, even without the principle of existential instantiation, by using a method of indirect proof. We first eliminate the existential quantifiers in the syllogism by using the definition that the quantifier $(\exists x)$ is short for $\sim(\forall x)\sim$. The syllogism is then:

$(\forall x) (M(x) \supset B(x))$
$\sim(\forall x)\sim (S(x) \land M(x))$
Therefore, $\sim(\forall x)\sim (S(x) \land B(x))$

How do we proceed? Again, look at the conclusion that we have to establish. The uppermost truth function in the conclusion is the symbol $\sim$. For such propositions, it is natural to try to establish them by the method of indirect proof. We assume that both premises are true, and then assume the opposite of the conclusion. We try to deduce a contradiction.

(1) $(\forall x) (M(x) \supset B(x))$
(2) $\sim(\forall x)\sim (S(x) \land M(x))$
(3) Assume $(\forall x)\sim (S(x) \land B(x))$.

Now what? To get to the "meat" of propositions (1) and (3), it is natural to use universal instantiation.

(4) $M(y) \supset B(y)$ (universal instantiation from (1))

(5) $\sim (S(y) \wedge B(y))$ (universal instantiation from (3))

We get to the "meat" of a negation applied to a logical conjunction $\wedge$ by using De Morgan's theorems:

(6) $\sim (S(y) \wedge B(y)) \supset (\sim S(y) \vee \sim B(y))$ (tautology, De Morgan's theorem)

(7) $\sim S(y) \vee \sim B(y)$ (*modus ponens* from (5) and (6))

(8) $(\sim S(y) \vee \sim B(y)) \supset (\sim B(y) \vee \sim S(y))$ (tautology, axiom of permutation)

(9) $\sim B(y) \vee \sim S(y)$ (*modus ponens* from (7) and (8))

We also want somehow to use the information from premise 2, in the process of deducing a contradiction. Can we deduce that $(\forall x) \sim (S(x) \wedge M(x))$? We could if we could first establish $\sim (S(y) \wedge M(y))$ for arbitrary y. As usual, we translate the negation of a conjunction by De Morgan's theorems into $\sim S(y) \vee \sim M(y)$. That proposition is our proximate goal. That gives us a hint by which we can move forward.

(10) $B(y) \supset \sim S(y)$ (definition of $\supset$ from (9))

We have now both $M(y) \supset B(y)$ (from (4)) and $B(y) \supset \sim S(y)$ (from (10)). We can deduce $M(y) \supset \sim S(y)$.

(11) Assume $M(y)$

    (12) $B(y)$ (*modus ponens* from (11) and (4))

    (13) $\sim S(y)$ (*modus ponens* from (12) and (10))

(14) $M(y) \supset \sim S(y)$ (conditional proof from (11 and (13))

(15) $\sim M(y) \vee \sim S(y)$ (definition of $\supset$ from (14))

(16) $(\sim M(y) \vee \sim S(y)) \supset (\sim S(y) \vee \sim M(y))$ (tautology, permutation)

(17) $\sim S(y) \vee \sim M(y)$ (*modus ponens* from (15) and (16))

(18) $(\sim S(y) \vee \sim M(y)) \supset \sim (S(y) \wedge M(y))$ (tautology, De Morgan's theorems)

(19) $\sim (S(y) \wedge M(y))$ (*modus ponens* from (17) and (18))

(20) $(\forall x) \sim (S(x) \wedge M(x))$ (universal generalization from (19))

(21) $\sim (\forall x) \sim (S(x) \wedge B(x))$ (*reductio* from (3), (2), and (20))

The last line is the conclusion of the syllogism.

For Further Reflection

1. Try to derive the Ferio syllogism using natural deduction. Use the example:

   No reptiles are fish.
   Some vertebrate is a reptile.
   Therefore some vertebrate is not a fish.

2. Try to derive the Cesare syllogism using natural deduction Use the example:

   No cats are dogs.
   All collies are dogs.
   Therefore, no collies are cats.

3. Try to derive the Baroco syllogism using natural deduction. Use the example:

   All fish are vertebrates.
   Some sea creature is not a vertebrate.
   Therefore, some sea creature is not a fish.

Part IV.D

Proofs for Formal Systems

Introducing Gödel's First Incompleteness Theorem

Gödel's First Incompleteness Theorem[1] is difficult to digest without simplified introductions. We offer one such simplification, which, for the sake of digestibility, alters some details in Gödel's original plan.

For clarity, we must distinguish between the logical system under study and the language that we use in studying it. Gödel studied a logical system that was a variant of Whitehead and Russell's system. It is a *formal system*. The language in which we talk about it and study it is our *metalanguage*.

The Starting Logical Symbols

Gödel considered a formal system, which has two logical symbols ∨ and ~. (Remember that the other truth-functional symbols, like ⊃ and ∧, can be defined in terms of these two.) He specified that the "language" of the system, the *formal language*, would have symbols for individual variables x_1, x_2, x_3, ... , which are intended to range over the nonnegative integers. He included more variables intended to range over classes of integers and classes of classes of integers, but we need not focus on these. He included the quantification symbol ∀. He did not have to include the symbol ∃, because it can be defined in terms of ∀. The expression ∃x is shorthand for ~∀x~ (plus suitable extra parentheses) within the logical system he studied.

He also added parentheses, '(' , ')', as symbols, because these are needed to distinguish different groupings of logical functions. He included as axioms for the formal system all of Whitehead and Russell's axioms for propositional logic and ordinary (first-order) quantification. In addition to all this, he included in the formal language an individual constant symbol '0' for zero, the lowest number, and a successor function S(x). It is intended that S(0) will stand for 1, S(S(0)) will stand for 2, S(S(S(0))) will stand for 3, and

---

[1] Kurt Gödel, *On Formally Undecidable Propositions of* Principia Mathematica *and Related Systems*, trans. B. Meltzer (New York: Dover, 1992).

so on. That system of notation assures us that we can in principle represent all the nonnegative integers with only a few starting symbols. It is convenient also to add the symbol = for numerical equality, which Gödel took care of in another way. Gödel also included Peano's axioms for arithmetic, but the details of these need not concern us.

Numerical Encoding of Logical Symbols

Gödel then established a recipe for moving from logical symbols to numbers. The symbol '0' within the formal language will be associated with the number 1 in our metalanguage. The symbol S is associated with the number 3. The symbol ~ is associated with 5. Here is the complete list:

$$
\begin{array}{ccc}
\text{Language} & \leftrightarrow & \text{Metalanguage} \\
0 & \leftrightarrow & 1 \\
S & \leftrightarrow & 3 \\
\sim & \leftrightarrow & 5 \\
\vee & \leftrightarrow & 7 \\
\forall & \leftrightarrow & 9 \\
(& \leftrightarrow & 11 \\
) & \leftrightarrow & 13 \\
= & \leftrightarrow & 15
\end{array}
$$

The individual variables $x_1, x_2, x_3, \ldots$ also have to be assigned to numbers. They are assigned to prime numbers greater than 15. x_1 is assigned to the prime number 17, x_2 to the prime number 19, x_3 to the prime number 23, x_4 to the prime number 29, and so on. There are an infinite number of primes, so there are enough to assign one to each of the individual variables $x_1, x_2, x_3, \ldots$.

In this way, a number is assigned to every symbol within the formal language that Gödel was studying. Using this assignment, we can easily move in either direction. Given the symbol in the formal language we can determine the number in the metalanguage, and given the number in the metalanguage we can reconstruct the symbol from which it came.

Numerical Encoding of Propositional Functions

Now we go to a second stage, and associate a number with each propositional function in the formal language. Any propositional function can be treated merely as a series of symbols. For example, consider

$\sim(S(0)=0)$

It is a simple series of symbols: ~, (, S, (, 0,), =, 0, and). The order must be preserved. We encode each symbol as before:

~ $\leftrightarrow$ 5
($\leftrightarrow$ 11
S $\leftrightarrow$ 3
($\leftrightarrow$ 11
0 $\leftrightarrow$ 1
) $\leftrightarrow$ 13
= $\leftrightarrow$ 15
0 $\leftrightarrow$ 1
) $\leftrightarrow$ 13

Then we take the resulting sequence of numbers, 5, 11, 3, 11, 1, 13, 15, 1, 13, and attach these numbers as exponents to prime numbers, starting with the lowest prime number 2. We get

$$G = 2^5 \times 3^{11} \times 5^3 \times 7^{11} \times 11^1 \times 13^{13} \times 17^{15} \times 19^1 \times 23^{13}$$

2^5 means 2 multiplied by itself 5 times. The resulting number G contains 5 factors of 2, 11 factors of 3, 3 factors of 5, and so on. G is the Gödel number corresponding to the starting formula ~(S(0)=0). It is known from the theory of numbers that given any number, its factorization into prime numbers is unique. Given a number, we can break it up into prime factors in only one way. That means that if we start with a number n, we can write it in a form like what is given above:

$$n = 2^9 \times 3^{11} \times 5^9 \times 7^3 \times 11^1 \times 13^{13} \times 17^1 \times 19^1$$

Then we can read off a specific sequence a numbers, namely, the sequence given by the exponents of each prime. We obtain:

9, 11, 9, 3, 1, 13, 1, 1

Not all numbers n encode propositional functions. But if a number G is the number encoded from a propositional function, we can reconstruct exactly the same propositional function from its number. We can move in either direction.

Any sequence of the starting symbols, such as the sequence S))0~S, can be encoded in a number. But many of these sequences are not "well-formed"; that is, they do not represent a proposition or a propositional function within the system.

Call any sequence of the basic symbols in the formal language a *formula*. Only some of the formulas are well-formed. We can "translate" the meaning of being well-formed into a property of Gödel numbers. A formula is well-formed only if its Gödel number has certain numerical properties. We can also describe the axioms as well. A well-formed formula is an axiom only if its Gödel number n has some additional property, let us say $Ax(n)$. This numerical property can be written out explicitly, though it is tedious to do so.

Encoding Proofs

Next, we can encode proofs numerically. A proof consists in a series of lines, each of which is either an axiom or is derivable from previous lines by *modus ponens*. Suppose the lines of one particular proof are as follows:

$$Q_1$$
$$Q_2$$
$$Q_3$$
$$Q_4$$
$$Q_5$$

Each of the Q's is a propositional function. So each line separately can be encoded into its Gödel number. Suppose the Gödel numbers are, g_1, g_2, g_3, g_4, g_5.

$$Q_1 \leftrightarrow g_1$$
$$Q_2 \leftrightarrow g_2$$
$$Q_3 \leftrightarrow g_3$$
$$Q_4 \leftrightarrow g_4$$
$$Q_5 \leftrightarrow g_5$$

Now we use the same technique to convert from a series of numbers to a single number that encodes them all. The Gödel number of the proof is

$$2^{g_1} \times 3^{g_2} \times 5^{g_3} \times 7^{g_4} \times 11^{g_5}$$

This encoding allows us to reconstruct any proof if we are given its Gödel number, and to construct a unique Gödel number if we are presented with the proof.

Expressing Provability

In the next stage, we translate the idea of provability from the formal system to the Gödel numbers that represent formulas and proofs within the system.

Let z represent the Gödel number of a series of lines that is being offered as a possible proof. Let x represent the Gödel number of a proposition P. Then the proffered proof is a proof of P if and only if Prove(z, x), where "Prove" represents some very complicated numerical property relating z and x. The property "Prove" depends, of course, on what are the starting axioms of the system that Gödel examined.

The logical proposition or formula encoded by x is provable if and only if there is some proof: $(\exists z)$Prove(z, x). This property too is some complicated numerical property of x. Let us abbreviate it as Provable(x), which is the same as $(\exists z)$Prove(z, x). The formula encoded by x is *not* provable if and only if $\sim$(Provable(x)).

What Gödel achieved here was to mimic proofs using numbers and complicated properties of numbers. By careful reasoning, Gödel was able to show that the property $\sim$(Provable(x)) could itself be expressed as a propositional function using only the resources *within* the formal logical system he was studying, provided the system has sufficient axioms to sustain a reasonable amount of arithmetic. Let this representation of $\sim$(Provable(x)) within the formal system be designated $\sim$(ProvableF(x)), to distinguish it from the representation outside, in Gödel's metalanguage talking about the system. Actually, we need to write it as $\sim$(ProvableF(x_1)), so that the individual variable x_1 is one of the symbols within the formal system. The extra letter F stands for "Formal," reminding us that the whole thing resides within the formal system. Provable(x) is a property in Gödel's metalanguage. ProvableF(x_1) is a formula within the formal system that Gödel is studying. The two are not the same, and may differ in notation. But the *meaning* is the same, once we interpret the meaning of ProvableF(x_1) by looking at it from outside the system, that is, from the point of view of our superior position and our metalanguage.

So let n be the Gödel number of the specific propositional function $\sim$(ProvableF(x_1)), which is a propositional function within the formal system. Can we produce Gödel's paradoxical result by plugging n into $\sim$(ProvableF(x_1)) and getting $\sim$(ProvableF(n))? Actually, that will not work, because n is the Gödel number of the propositional function $\sim$(ProvableF(x_1))

rather than the Gödel number of ~(ProvableF(n)) itself. These two are not identical, because x_1 is not the same symbol as n within the formal language. And, once we think about it, we realize that n may or may not be part of the "language" of the logical system, depending on how we represent it. Any number n is represented in simplest fashion *within* the language by a formula S(S(S(S ... (0) ...))), in which there are n copies (counted within our metalanguage) of the symbol S. To calculate the Gödel number of the formula ~(ProvableF(n)), where n is represented within the symbolism of the formal language, we would already have to have known n to start the calculation. But we need the calculation in order to obtain n. We seem to be in a circle. We are like a dog chasing its tail, and we can never find n.

Expressing Self-Reference

So let us take an indirect way around. First, we must have a clear way of representing any number n within the formal language. We do it by specifying that, for any nonnegative integer n in our metalanguage, formalizednumber(n) is the formula S(S(S(... S(0)...))) with n copies of the symbol S. If n is 0, formalizednumber(0) is simply '0'. Next, we construct a numerical property that allows a formula K in the formal language to use its own Gödel number as input. Suppose that $K(x_1)$ is a propositional function in the formal language, with a free variable x_1. Suppose its Gödel number is k. Let Subst(k, n) be a numerical function that produces as its output the Gödel number of the formula $K(n)$, where $K(n)$ is the formula *in the formal language* that results from replacing each free occurrence of x_1 in K with formalizednumber(n).

As before, ~Provable(x) expresses the numerical property that says there is no formal proof (within the formal system) for the formula with Gödel number x. Consider now ~Provable(Subst(k, n)). Its meaning is that there is no proof for the formal formula $K(n)$, where k is the Gödel number of K.

Now consider the propositional function ~Provable(Subst(x, x)). Translate this propositional function back into the formal language, using the variable x_1 that belongs to the formal language. Let the formal representation within the formal language be

UnProvableF(x_1, x_1))

Let its Gödel number be n. Is UnprovableF(formalizednumber(n),formalizednumber(n)) provable? When we translate the *meaning* of the formal formula back into the metalanguage, it says exactly the same thing as ~Provable(Subst(x, x)), with now n substituted for x. That is, its meaning is the same as ~Provable(Subst(n, n)). And this expression in turn says that what is not provable is the formula whose Gödel number is Subst(n, n). Which formula is that? It is the formula $K(n)$ that results from substituting formalizednumber(n) for each occurrence of x_1 in the formula whose Gödel number is n. The formula with Gödel number n is UnProvableF(x_1, x_1)), by the definition of n given above. The result of the substitution of formalizednumber(n) is UnprovableF(formalizednumber(n),formalizednumber(n)). Thus, the meaning of the formula, when translated into the metalanguage, is that it asserts it is unprovable *within* the formal language. If we did discover a proof, it would mean that the formula is untrue. The formal system has proved an untruth. If, on the other hand, the formal system cannot prove it, it is true.

Metalanguage

We can see again the importance of preserving a distinction between the formal language and the metalanguage in which we discuss it. Truth and meaning belong to the metalanguage. The formal system just plays with the symbols and constructs formal proofs. The metalanguage studies the rules leading to proofs and formulates an arithmetical expression of what it means to be provable.

The two distinct correspondences make it possible, without any contradiction or lapse in logic, to construct a formula within the system whose meaning outside the system is to assert its own unprovability.

For Further Reflection

1. What personal human resources do we use in following the steps in Gödel's proof?
2. How does Gödel's proof avoid producing a direct contradiction?
3. Why is this proof important for our thinking about mathematics?

Simple Proofs within a Formal System

We may now illustrate the study of a formal system by beginning to develop a study of Whitehead and Russell's propositional logic, treated as a formal system.

The Starting System

We start with the formal language and the deduction rule explained in chapter 56. The possible formulas that we might use as axioms include A1, A2, A3, A4, and A5, each being actually an axiom *schema*, which describes an indefinite number of axioms. The deduction rule is *modus ponens*.

To start with, we assume no axioms. If we have no axioms, we have no way of producing the start for a proof. So this system does not appear to be interesting.

But we can make things interesting if we watch what happens when we *temporarily* permit the use of extra assumptions or postulates in proofs. We will not call them "axioms," because we do not want to suggest that they are being regarded as permanent parts of the logical system. (Modern symbolic logic sometimes treats "axioms" and "postulates" as synonyms; we are using "postulate" more in the sense of "temporary axiom.")

So what can be proved if we assume as postulates only the well-formed formulas of the form A2? Then, in one line, we can prove

(1) $(q \supset (p \vee q))$

because line (1) is a postulate from A2. Now we introduce a special notation in our metalanguage in order to describe the relation between postulates like A2 and what can be proved when we assume such postulates. We write:

$A2 \vdash (q \supset (p \vee q))$

The added special symbol is the symbol ⊢. The symbol means that what follows this symbol is provable once we assume the postulates that precede the symbol. (This usage is slightly different from the "plain" use of the symbol ⊢, with no preceding postulates, to assert the truth of the following proposition.)

In this case, it says that we can prove $(q \supset (p \lor q))$ as a theorem once we have A2 as a assumption. We can translate, "Assuming A2 makes provable $(q \supset (p \lor q))$." This is a statement in our metalanguage, in which we are studying what is provable in the formal system. Substituting $\sim p$ for p, we get

A2 ⊢ $(q \supset (\sim p \lor q))$

Since $(\sim p \lor q)$ is the same as $(p \supset q)$, we can also write

Metatheorem 1: A2 ⊢ $(q \supset (p \supset q))$

We call this a *metatheorem* because it is a theorem in our metalanguage. We label it with a number (1) because we will have occasion to use it later on.

Now consider A5 as a postulate.

A5: $((q \supset r) \supset ((p \lor q) \supset (p \lor r)))$

Substituting $\sim p$ for p in the schema, we get instances of A5. So,

A5 ⊢ $((q \supset r) \supset ((\sim p \lor q) \supset (\sim p \lor r)))$

By the definition of ⊃,

Metatheorem 2: A5 ⊢ $((q \supset r) \supset ((p \supset q) \supset (p \supset r)))$

This theorem is a form of the principle of the *hypothetical syllogism*. If we know that p implies q and that q implies r, we can infer that p implies r. We can express it this way:

Corollary 2.1: A5, $(q \supset r)$ ⊢ $((p \supset q) \supset (p \supset r))$ (hypothetical syllogism)
Corollary 2.2: A5, $(p \supset q)$, $(q \supset r)$ ⊢ $(p \supset r)$ (hypothetical syllogism)

These are called *corollaries* of Metatheorem 2 because they are implications closely related to Metatheorem 2. We give them numbers because we want to be able to use them later on.

We verify the truth of these claims by constructing a proof using any of assumptions that we need from the left-hand side of the symbol ⊢.

(1) $(q \supset r)$ (postulate)
(2) $((q \supset r) \supset ((p \supset q) \supset (p \supset r)))$ (Metatheorem 2)
(3) $((p \supset q) \supset (p \supset r))$ (*modus ponens* from (1) and (2)) [this proves Corollary 2.1]
(4) $(p \supset q)$ (postulate)
(5) $(p \supset r)$ (*modus ponens* from (4) and (3)) [this proves Corollary 2.2]

We can, if we wish, string together several instances of implications of this kind:

Corollary 2.3: A5, $(p \supset q)$, $(q \supset r)$, $(r \supset s)$ ⊢ $(p \supset s)$
             A5, $(p \supset q)$, $(q \supset r)$, $(r \supset s)$, $(s \supset t)$ ⊢ $(p \supset t)$

This result follows immediately from repeated applications of Corollary 2.2.

Now let us assume A1, A2, and A5 together. We have

A2 ⊢ $(p \supset (p \lor p))$ (substituting p for q in the general form of A2)

Since we are assuming A2, we can use $(p \supset (p \lor p))$ as one line of our proof.

(1) $(p \supset (p \lor p))$ (from A2)
(2) $((p \lor p) \supset p)$ (A1)
(3) $(p \supset p)$ (hypothetical syllogism from A5, (1), and (2))

The last line follows from the general principle of the hypothetical syllogism. We substitute $(p \lor p)$ for q and p for r in the general principle of the hypothetical syllogism that we formulated above. "Hypothetical syllogism" is a kind of abbreviation for a fully spelled out proof, which can be obtained by going through exactly the same steps that we used to establish the principle of hypothetical syllogism in the first place. If we do not want to invoke the principle, we have to insert all the steps, as follows:

(1) $(p \supset (p \lor p))$ (from A2)
(2) $((p \lor p) \supset p)$ (A1)
(3) $(((p \lor p) \supset p) \supset ((p \supset (p \lor p)) \supset (p \supset p)))$ (from Metatheorem 2)

(4) $((p \supset (p \lor p)) \supset (p \supset p))$ (*modus ponens* from (2) and (3))

(5) $(p \supset p)$ (*modus ponens* from (1) and (4))

The recipe for hypothetical syllogism allows us to dispense with inserting these extra steps (3) and (4) every time. We have shown once and for all that we can do it wherever we have a situation within a proof in which we have established both that $(p \supset q)$ and that $(q \supset r)$ (for any wffs p, q, and r).

So now we have established:

Metatheorem 3: A1, A2, A5 ⊢ $(p \supset p)$

This metatheorem says that if we have A1, A2, and A5 as postulates, we may construct a valid proof that $(p \supset p)$.

Generalizations

We can also make some general observations about proofs. To begin with, let F, G, and H be *sets* of wffs. The notation G ⊢ H will mean that all the wffs in H can be proved using the postulates in G.

Metatheorem 4: F ⊢ F

All the wffs in F can be proved immediately if they are postulates.

Let F ∪ G denote the set union of F and G, the set having as members all members of F and all members of G.

Metatheorem 5: If F ⊢ H, then F ∪ G ⊢ H.

Adding more postulates G to F still leaves old proofs of H valid.

Metatheorem 6: If F ⊢ G, then F ⊢ S for any subset S of G.

Suppose F ⊢ G. Let s be a wff in S. Then s is also in G. Since every g in G is provable from F, s is provable from F. So F ⊢ S.

Metatheorem 7: If F ⊢ G, and F ⊢ H, then F ⊢ G ∪ H.

This follows directly from the meaning of provability. If all wffs in G are provable and all in H are provable, all wffs in the set union are provable.

Metatheorem 8: If F ⊢ G and G ⊢ H, then F ⊢ H.

This is a little more difficult to see. But once you think about its meaning, it is clear that it is true. If *h* is a wff in H, then *h* has a proof using some set S from the postulates in G (because G ⊢ H). Since the proof of *h* has only a finite number of lines, it can use only a finite number of postulates. So the set S is finite. Take each postulate *s* in S, and prove it using postulates from F. (This can be done because F ⊢ G.) Stitch these proofs together, one after the other, and you have a proof in which every wff in S appears at the end of one section of the proof. Append to the end of the collection the proof of *h* from S. You then have a proof of *h* using only postulates from F.

Metatheorem 9: If F ⊢ G and F ∪ G ⊢ H, then F ⊢ H.

We can prove this as a metatheorem from the previous metatheorems.

(1) F ⊢ G (assumption)
(2) F ∪ G ⊢ H (assumption)
(3) F ⊢ F (Metatheorem 4)
(4) F ⊢ F ∪ G (Metatheorem 7 from (3) and (1))
(5) F ⊢ H (Metatheorem 8 from (4) and (2))

Metatheorem 9 is significant. It says that if you can establish results G on the basis of postulates F, you do not need to add as extra postulates any of the members of G. Anything that can be deduced using the extra postulates can already be deduced using F alone as postulates.

This principle is relevant to Whitehead and Russell's system. It has axioms A1, A2, A3, A4, and A5. It turns out that A4 can be proved using the remaining axioms. So A4 is dispensable. Any theorem that can be proved from all five axioms can be proved without using A4.

Strictly speaking, our notation "F ⊢ G" applies only when F and G are sets, and where all the members of these sets are wffs. But for simplicity we will sometimes just list postulates and sets of postulates rather than use set notation. Thus we can write F,H ⊢ G when we mean F ∪ H ⊢ G. Or we write F,$(p \supset q)$ ⊢ G when we mean F ∪ {$(p \supset q)$} ⊢ G. The last notation, F ∪ {$(p \supset q)$} ⊢ G, means that every wff in G is provable using the postulates on the left-hand side, including not only all the postulates in the set F but also the postulate $(p \supset q)$. Strictly speaking, the placeholders *p* and *q* need to be filled with specific wffs. But we will allow such placeholders both on the left and on the right of the symbol ⊢ for provability. It is understood that in the end, when we apply our results to the formal system, p and q must be replaced by specific wffs.

Metatheorem 10: If F ⊢ $(p \supset q)$ then F,p ⊢ q

This result follows simply:

(1) F ⊢ $(p \supset q)$ (assumed)
(2) F,p ⊢ $(p \supset q)$ (Metatheorem 5)
(3) F,p ⊢ F,p (Metatheorem 4)
(4) F,p ⊢ p (Metatheorem 6, from (3))
(5) F,p ⊢ q (*modus ponens* from (4) and (2))

We already used a form of this theorem in proving Corollaries 2.1 and 2.2.

For Further Reflection

1. Why does adding more postulates sometimes not result in being able to prove any more theorems?
2. Show that, if F ⊢ G, G ⊢ H, and H ⊢ K, then F ⊢ K.
3. Generalize the principle given in question #2 to a series F, G, H, K, L. (You need not prove it.)
4. Show that, if F ⊢ G, F ∪ G ⊢ H, and F ∪ G ∪ H ⊢ K, then F ⊢ K.

Deriving Natural Deduction and the Associative Axiom

Now let us turn back again to the specific features of the axioms A1, A2, A3, A4, and A5. We will endeavor to show that A4 and the rules for natural deduction developed in chapter 42 are derivable from A1, A2, A3, and A5.

All the statements of the form F ⊢ G are somewhat like rules for natural deduction. They say, "If you know F, you can deduce G." So this new notation enables us to discuss rigorously the ideas about natural deduction developed in chapter 42.

Disjunction Elimination

We first establish, within our metalanguage, a rule akin to the rule of disjunction elimination. It is needed if we are to prove A4, which involves a number of disjunctions. We will establish it in the form of the following metatheorem:

Metatheorem 11: A1, A3, A5, $(a \supset c)$, $(b \supset c)$ ⊢ $((a \lor b) \supset c)$

How will we go about such a proof? The most important key is A5.

A5: $((q \supset r) \supset ((p \lor q) \supset (p \lor r)))$

If we have a valid implication of the form $(q \supset r)$, A5 allows us to add a disjunction with p on the front end of q and r. So, looking at what we can assume in Metatheorem 11, we see $(b \supset c)$ is one of the postulates, and we can add a to the left:

$((a \lor b) \supset (a \lor c))$

If we do this much, we are partway there. Can we also show that $((a \lor c) \supset c)$? If we knew that too, then by hypothetical syllogism (Corollaries 2.2 and

2.3) we could get all the way to the desired conclusion $((a \lor b) \supset c)$. Perhaps we cannot get to the conclusion $((a \lor c) \supset c)$ directly, but if we get from $(a \lor c)$ to $(c \lor a)$, we can treat the c disjunct as "added on" to $(a \supset c)$, just as we earlier treated the a disjunct as added on to $(b \supset c)$. Taken all together, this suggests a series of steps by which we might arrive at our final result. To do the complete reasoning, it is useful first to establish two preliminary results, which are called *lemmas*.

Lemma 1: $p, (p \supset q) \vdash q$.

This lemma is just a restatement of *modus ponens*.

Proof:

(1) p (postulate)
(2) $(p \supset q)$ (postulate)
(3) q (*modus ponens* from (1) and (2))

Lemma 2: A5, $(q \supset r) \vdash ((p \lor q) \supset (p \lor r))$

Proof: immediate application of Lemma 1 with $(q \supset r)$ substituted for p and $((p \lor q) \supset (p \lor r))$ substituted for q in Lemma 1.

Now for the proof of the Metatheorem 11: A1, A3, A5, $(a \supset c)$, $(b \supset c)$ $\vdash ((a \lor b) \supset c)$.

(1) $(a \supset c)$ (postulate)
(2) $(b \supset c)$ (postulate)
(3) $((a \lor b) \supset (a \lor c))$ (Lemma 2 applied to (2))
(4) $((a \lor c) \supset (c \lor a))$ (A3)
(5) $((c \lor a) \supset (c \lor c))$ (Lemma 2 applied to (1))
(6) $((c \lor c) \supset c)$ (A1)
(7) $((a \lor b) \supset c)$ (Corollary 2.3: hypothetical syllogism on (3), (4), (5), and (6))

So the rule for disjunction elimination can be mimicked using A1, A3, and A5.

Deducing A4

With this much in place, we can deduce A4 if we "mimic" the way in which we deduced A4 by natural deduction (appendix B2). To construct the proof, we try to get hints by working backward from the endpoint, which is

A4: $((p \lor (q \lor r)) \supset (q \lor (p \lor r)))$

The antecedent $(p \lor (q \lor r))$ consists of two parts, p and $(q \lor r)$, which we can treat like the a and b in Metatheorem 11. If we can establish that p implies the consequent $(q \lor (p \lor r))$ and that $(q \lor r)$ implies the consequent, we can apply Metatheorem 11. But these are comparatively easy results to establish using A2 (and sometimes A3).

First, can we see that $(q \lor r)$ implies $(q \lor (p \lor r))$?

>   Lemma 3: A2, A5 $\vdash ((q \lor r) \supset (q \lor (p \lor r)))$

This is a more complicated application of the rule of addition, related to A2.

Proof:

>   (1) $(r \supset (p \lor r))$ (A2)
>   (2) $((q \lor r) \supset (q \lor (p \lor r)))$ (by applying Lemma 2 to (1))

Can we also establish that $(p \supset (q \lor (p \lor r)))$?

>   Lemma 4: A2, A3, A5 $\vdash (p \supset (q \lor (p \lor r)))$

Again, this can be established using primarily A2.

Proof:

>   (1) $(p \supset (r \lor p))$ (A2)
>   (2) $((r \lor p) \supset (p \lor r))$ (A3)
>   (3) $((p \lor r) \supset (q \lor (p \lor r)))$ (A2)
>   (4) $(p \supset (q \lor (p \lor r)))$ (hypothetical syllogism from (1), (2), and (3))

Now we complete the proof of A4:

>   Metatheorem 12: A1,A2,A3,A5 $\vdash$ A4, that is
>   A1,A2,A3,A5 $\vdash ((p \lor (q \lor r)) \supset (q \lor (p \lor r)))$

Proof:

In Metatheorem 11, substitute p for a, $(q \lor r)$ for b, and $(q \lor (p \lor r))$ for c. We get

A1, A3, A5, $(p \supset (q \lor (p \lor r)))$, $((q \lor r) \supset (q \lor (p \lor r))) \vdash ((p \lor (q \lor r)) \supset (q \lor (p \lor r)))$.

Lemma 3 and Lemma 4 have established that the two extra postulates, $((q \lor r) \supset (q \lor (p \lor r)))$ and $(p \supset (q \lor (p \lor r)))$, are provable using A2, A3, and A5. So by Metatheorem 9 these two extra postulates are dispensable. We need only the postulate A1, A2, A3, and A5 in order to prove A4.

Conditional Proof: The "Deduction Theorem"

Next, we want to deduce the validity of the method of conditional proof that we used in our system of natural deduction. We state it as a metatheorem:

> Metatheorem 13: If A1,A2,A3,A5, $p \vdash q$, then A1,A2,A3,A5, $\vdash (p \supset q)$

This metatheorem says that, within a system with Whitehead and Russell's axioms (minus A4, which we showed in Metatheorem 12 that we do not need), you can temporarily make an additional assumption p, which is the "condition" in the conditional proof. Then at the end, when you have deduced q, you may "close off" the extra condition p, and conclude that $\vdash (p \supset q)$ with no conditions (other than the normal axioms).

How shall we go about establishing Metatheorem 13? Let us think about what it requires. It begins by taking A1,A2,A3,A5, p as postulates. If the fact that p is a postulate is never used in the proof of q, then the proof shows that q can be proved using A1 A1,A2,A3,A5 alone: A1,A2,A3,A5, $\vdash q$. In addition, $(q \supset (p \supset q))$ is an instance of A2 (Metatheorem 1). So A1,A2,A3,A5, $\vdash (p \supset q)$ by *modus ponens*. So the metatheorem proves to be true in this kind of case.

Now suppose that p is in fact used as a postulate somewhere in the proof of q. At the point where p is introduced, we have a line:

...
(20) p.

Then further lines follow, culminating in the conclusion q:

(20) p.
(21) r_1
(22) r_2
(23) r_3

...
(29) r_9
(30) q

This arrangement is like what we did with conditional proofs in natural deduction. We have not really proved the intermediate lines or the conclusion q in absolute terms. We have only deduced them *conditionally*. It is as if, in our minds, we preceded each of the lines with the qualification, "if p holds true." So what does the series of deductions look like if we actually insert this extra supposition into the notation? We would have:

[(20) p] [this line can be deleted]
(21) $(p \supset r_1)$
(22) $(p \supset r_2)$
(23) $(p \supset r_3)$
...
(29) $(p \supset r_9)$
(30) $(p \supset q)$

With this alteration, we have a suggestion as to how to construct a proof within Whitehead and Russell's system. But we have to verify that it is a proof, or that it can be made into a proof by adding some extra lines.

So let us think it through. Let us say that we are on the line $(p \supset r_3)$. Within the system of natural deduction, which uses conditional proofs, the line formerly read r_3. According to the rules for producing proofs, r_3 must either be a postulate or be deduced by *modus ponens* from preceding lines. If r_3 is a postulate from A1, A2, A3, A5, it is still a postulate in the new setting. So we add a line to the *new proof* that just says r_3. Then by Metatheorem 1, $(r_3 \supset (p \supset r_3))$. Add this too as a new line, and then by *modus ponens* we deduce $(p \supset r_3)$. So $(p \supset r_3)$ can still be deduced in the new proof, which is not supposed to use p as an extra postulate.

The second case is where r_3 follows by *modus ponens* in the old proof. *Modus ponens* appeals to two preceding lines. One line will have the form s, while the other will have the form $(s \supset r_3)$. There are four cases, depending on whether these lines lie inside or outside the scope of the condition p in the old proof.

Case (1). Both lines lie outside the scope of the condition p (line 20 in the example above). Then the lines still exist intact in the new proof. *Modus ponens* still holds, and we can deduce r_3. Hence by Metatheorem 1 $(p \supset r_3)$.

Case (2). Both lines lie inside the scope of the condition p. Then in the new proof they take the form $(p \supset s)$ and $(p \supset (s \supset r_3))$. We have to deduce that $(p \supset r_3)$. So this is a new result that we will need, prior to proving Metatheorem 13. We will have to make it a lemma:

Lemma 5: $A1, A2, A3, A5, (p \supset s), (p \supset (s \supset r)) \vdash (p \supset r)$

The proof is available in Whitehead and Russell's volume[1] and in appendix D4.

Case (3). The line s lies inside the scope of the condition p, while the line $(s \supset r_3)$ lies outside. Then $(p \supset (s \supset r_3))$ by Metatheorem 1. So this situation reduces to case (2).

Case (4). The line $(s \supset r_3)$ lies inside the scope of the condition p, while the line s lies outside. By Metatheorem 1 we can deduce from s that $(p \supset s)$. So again this case reduces to case 2.

The result is that we can always find a way to make a valid proof after eliminating the condition p, provided that we introduce each subsequent line with the prefix $(p \supset \ldots)$.

Proof of the Deduction Theorem by Mathematical Induction

Now let us provide a more rigorous metaproof of the same Metatheorem 13. Here is the same metatheorem:

Metatheorem 13: If $A1, A2, A3, A5, p \vdash q$, then $A1, A2, A3, A5, \vdash (p \supset q)$

We use induction on the number of lines in the proof that is used to prove q from p.

Step 1: show that Metatheorem 13 holds for all wffs p and q for which q can be proved using a one-line proof.

A one-line proof must have as its one line either a postulate of $A1, A2, A3, A5$ or p itself. If it is a postulate of $A1, A2, A3, A5$, q is proved even without using p. That is,

$A1, A2, A3, A5, \vdash q$

We now proceed with a metaproof:

[1] Alfred North Whitehead and Bertrand Russell, *Principia Mathematica*, 2nd ed., 3 vols. (Cambridge: Cambridge University Press, 1927), 1:108, proposition 2.77.

(1) A1,A2,A3,A5, ⊢ q (postulate)
(2) A2 ⊢ $(q \supset (p \supset q))$ (by Metatheorem 1)
(3) $q, (q \supset (p \supset q)) \vdash (p \supset q)$ (by Lemma 1)
(4) A1,A2,A3,A5 ⊢ $(q \supset (p \supset q))$ (from (2) by Metatheorem 5)
(5) A1,A2,A3,A5 ⊢ $q, (q \supset (p \supset q))$ (from (1) and (4) by Metatheorem 7)
(6) A1,A2,A3,A5 ⊢ $(p \supset q)$ (from (5) and (3) by Metatheorem 8)

The other alternative is that q is derived from the postulate p. The only way that can happen with a one-line proof is if q is identical with p. Now we know that

A1,A2,A5 ⊢ $(p \supset p)$ from Metatheorem 3.

Hence by Metatheorem 5

A1, A2, A3, A5 ⊢ $(p \supset p)$

Hence Metatheorem 13 holds for proofs of one line.

Step 2. Now we assume that Metatheorem 13 holds for all wffs q that can be proved, using p as an additional postulate, in proofs of n lines long or less. In the inductive step, we have to show that Metatheorem 13 holds true for a proof of q—any q—when the proof of q is $n + 1$ lines long.

So consider a proof of q that is exactly $n + 1$ lines long.

The last line of this proof is q. By the rules for proofs, q must either be a postulate or be deduced by *modus ponens* from preceding lines. If q is p itself, then

A1, A2, A3, A5 ⊢ $(p \supset p)$

as we already showed.

If q is one of the other postulates, it is immediately deducible without using p. That is,

A1, A2, A3, A5 ⊢ q—in a one-line proof.

We have already shown that Metatheorem 13 holds for all q provable in one line.

So now we are left with the difficult case, where q has been deduced by *modus ponens* from two preceding lines. One of these lines is $(s \supset q)$ and the other is s, for some wff s.

Because these are lines in a proof with postulates A1,A2,A3,A5, and p, we know immediately that

A1, A2, A3, A5, $p \vdash s$, $(s \supset q)$

Since the Metatheorem 13 holds for all proofs of lengths less than or equal to n, we can apply the metatheorem to both of these cases, and obtain:

A1, A2, A3, A5, $\vdash (p \supset s)$, $(p \supset (s \supset q))$

By Lemma 5, A1, A2, A3, A5, $\vdash (p \supset q)$

Hence Metatheorem 13 holds for proofs $n + 1$ lines long. By mathematical induction, Metatheorem 13 holds in general.

Proof Theory Illustrating Imitative Transcendence

The distinction between the formal system and the metalanguage analysis of the system operates all the way through the discussion. This distinction is a manifestation of our ability to transcend an earlier viewpoint. We look down on a field of study from above, and at the same time make correlations between the field and our analysis of it. In our actions we are created imitators of the transcendence of God, in whose image we are made. (See the discussion in chapter 57.)

For Further Reflection

1. How does the notation $F \vdash G$ help us to think about proofs?
2. What formulation using the symbol $\vdash$ expresses the principle of conditional proof?

Helping Lemmas

In this appendix we establish a key lemma used in the previous appendix for establishing the method of conditional proof. The lemma is

> Lemma 5: A1,A2,A3,A5, $(p \supset s)$, $(p \supset (s \supset r)) \vdash (p \supset r)$

According to the definition of the symbol $\supset$, $(p \supset (s \supset r))$ can be rewritten as $(\sim p \vee (s \supset r))$. This rewriting suggests that we try using disjunction elimination (Metatheorem 11) on the disjunction $(\sim p \vee (s \supset r))$. Substitute $\sim p$ for a, $(s \supset r)$ for b, and $(p \supset r)$ for c in Metatheorem 11. We get

> A1, A3, A5, $(\sim p \supset (p \supset r))$, $((s \supset r) \supset (p \supset r)) \vdash ((\sim p \vee (s \supset r)) \supset (p \supset r))$.

Can we arrive at $(p \supset r)$ from either of these two starting points a (that is, $\sim p$) or b (that is, $(p \supset r)$)?

First, can we show that $(\sim p \supset (p \supset r))$? $(\sim p \supset (p \supset r))$ means $(\sim p \supset (\sim p \vee r))$ by the definition of $\supset$. That is close to a form of A2. So we have a first part of the proof suggested as follows:

(1) $(\sim p \supset (r \vee \sim p))$ (A2)
(2) $((r \vee \sim p) \supset (\sim p \vee r))$ (A3)
(3) $(\sim p \supset (\sim p \vee r))$ (hypothetical syllogism from (1) and (2)
(4) $(\sim p \supset (p \supset r))$ (definition from (3))

The other part, establishing $(b \supset c)$, when b is $(s \supset r)$ and c is $(p \supset r)$, means showing that $((s \supset r) \supset (p \supset r))$. This result looks similar to Metatheorem 2 and Corollary 2.1 for hypothetical syllogism. So it suggests that we add a line:

$((p \supset s) \supset ((s \supset r) \supset (p \supset r)))$.

This line is like Metatheorem 2, except that the role of two items in the antecedents to the implications is reversed. It would be useful to have another Lemma 4.5:

Lemma 4.5: A4 $\vdash ((p \supset (q \supset r)) \supset (q \supset (p \supset r)))$

Proof:

A4 (which follows from A1,A2,A3,A5) says $((p \lor (q \lor r)) \supset (q \lor (p \lor r)))$. Substituting $\sim p$ for p and $\sim q$ for q,

$((\sim p \lor (\sim q \lor r)) \supset (\sim q \lor (\sim p \lor r)))$

By definition of $\supset$, this is

$((p \supset (q \supset r)) \supset (q \supset (p \supset r)))$

which was to be established.

Corollary 4.5: A4,$(p \supset (q \supset r)) \vdash (q \supset (p \supset r))$

This corollary follows from applying Metatheorem 10 to Lemma 4.5.

Now we are ready for Lemma 5.

Proof:

(1) $(\sim p \supset (r \lor \sim p))$ (A2)
(2) $((r \lor \sim p) \supset (\sim p \lor r))$ (A3)
(3) $(\sim p \supset (\sim p \lor r))$ (hypothetical syllogism from (1) and (2))
(4) $(\sim p \supset (p \supset r))$ (definition from (3))
(5) $((s \supset r) \supset ((p \supset s) \supset (p \supset r)))$ (Metatheorem 2)
(6) $((p \supset s) \supset ((s \supset r) \supset (p \supset r)))$ (Corollary 4.5 from (5))
(7) $(p \supset s)$ (postulate)
(8) $((s \supset r) \supset (p \supset r))$ (*modus ponens* from (7) and (6))
(9) $((\sim p \lor (s \supset r)) \supset (p \supset r))$ (Metatheorem 11 applied to (4) and (8))
(10) $((p \supset (s \supset r)) \supset (p \supset r))$ (definition from (9))
(11) $(p \supset (s \supset r))$ (postulate)
(12) $(p \supset r)$ (*modus ponens* from (11) and (10))

Conclusion

The formal system hangs together. Natural deduction can be derived from the formal system with only *modus ponens*, or vice versa. God's harmony is displayed in human reasoning, at the levels of informal reasoning, semi-formal logic, and fully formalized formal systems. His glory, wisdom, and beauty are to be praised.

Part IV.E

Other Proofs

The Halting Problem for Computer Programs

Here we sketch how one can show that the halting problem cannot be solved.

As a first step, suppose that we have a computer into which we have loaded a specific program. Call the program P. In Turing's conception, the ability of the computer to perform a calculation specified by P is represented abstractly by a Turing machine. A Turing machine is chosen as the object of study so that there can be a way of mapping back and forth between a computer program P and an encoding number e.

Program $P \leftrightarrow$ encoding number e

A Program to Perform a Calculation

The computer program P is embodied in a Turing machine by writing a specific set of rules for the states of the Turing machine. The rules constitute its program. These rules are encoded in the single encoding number e. P is correlated with e in a specific, calculable way. As a result, a fixed set of rules in P leads by way of a specific numerical recipe to a number e; conversely, given a number e that encodes a computer program, the program P itself can be reconstructed exactly by decoding e. (The encoding and decoding is akin to what Gödel did to encode and decode formulas as proofs; see appendix D1.)

When the computer program P starts its calculation, it is also presented with an input. The input is a number n with which it will begin its calculation. Maybe it will calculate what is the double of n: $2 \times n$. Maybe it will calculate the square of n: n^2. There are many possible calculations, each represented by its own program. The output, which we may write as $P(n)$, depends in a typical case on which number n we use as input as well as on the specific program P that we have chosen.

A Mimicking Computer

As a second step, suppose we have a computer program that calculates the behavior of any other computer that has a specific program in it. Such a "universal" program does exist, and Turing showed how we might construct one. The program corresponds to what has been called a *universal Turing machine*. It is *universal* because it can accomplish anything that can be accomplished by any other Turing machine. General purpose computers, as opposed to electronic calculators and TV controllers, have this capability. Call this computer program that mimics any other program M.

To mimic the behavior of a computer program P, the program M must have two inputs. One input is the encoding number e for the computer program P that it is supposed to mimic, and the other number is the number n that is to be used as the starting input that is presented to the computer being mimicked. $M(e, n)$ represents the result when e and n are the two inputs.

A Hypothetical Program to Calculate Halting

Now suppose that H is a hypothetical computer program that calculates whether other programs halt. H needs two inputs, which we can represent as $H(e, n)$. e is the encoding number for some specific computer program P_e. n is a number that will be fed as the input into P_e. Let us suppose that if e is not the encoding number of a computer program, $H(e, n)$ produces the output 0 and halts. If e is an encoding number, $H(e, n)$ produces the output 1 if P_e eventually halts when n is its input. $H(e, n)$ produces the output 2 if P_e does not halt.

Now construct a second program $H_2(n)$ that produces the same results as $H(n, n)$. That is, it uses a single number n as input. It treats this number n as the encoding number of some program P_n and takes the same number n and uses it as input to the program P_n. Finally, construct a third program $H_3(n)$ that does exactly the same calculations as $H_2(n)$. After it finishes these calculations, if $H_2(n)$ produces the output 1, $H_3(n)$ puts itself into an endless loop (in other words, it enters a loop that guarantees that it will never halt). If on the other hand $H_2(n)$ produces the output 0 or 2, $H_3(n)$ produces the same output, and then halts. This construction of the program $H_3(n)$ is clearly possible, given the blueprint from $H_2(n)$. Now, calculate the encoding number E for H_3. H_3 expects only *one* input. So we have overcome the obstacle presented by the difference between mimicking computers and the computers being mimicked.

Consider $H_3(E)$. When we are presented with the input E, H_3 goes through the same computation and produces the same results as $H(E,E)$, because it was constructed for precisely this purpose. Now what does the program H accomplish? According to its definition, $H(E,E)$ produces an output 1 if and only if the program with encoding number E halts when E is fed in as input. But the program with encoding number E is precisely H_3, according to the definition of E. If $H_3(E)$ halts, then according to the definition of H_3 it is because $H(E,E)$ has output 0 or 2. Since E is an encoding number, the output 0 is excluded. So $H(E,E)$ has an output of 2. According to the way in which we have defined H, the output 2 occurs for $H(E,E)$ because the program with encoding number E (i.e., H_3) does not halt with input E. That is, $H_3(E)$ does not halt. But we began by assuming that it does. We have reached a contradiction, so that the initial assumption that $H_3(E)$ halts must be false.

Assume on the other hand that $H_3(E)$ does not halt. It must be because it has entered its endless loop. That means that $H(E,E)$ has output 1. According to the definition of H, that means that the program with encoding number E does halt when given the input E. I.e., by definition of E, $H_3(E)$ halts. Again we have reached a contradiction. Since the assumption that $H_3(E)$ halts and the assumption that it does not halt both lead to a contradiction, the program H_3 does not exist. Neither does the program H exist from which it was constructed. Then there is no program that can solve the halting problem.

Comparison of this argument with Gödel's argument for incompleteness (appendix D1) shows fascinating similarities.

A Specific Program for Which Halting Can Be Calculated

The argument just given says that there are some programs whose halting cannot be calculated according to a general procedure. But we can still give definite answers for *some* programs. For example, a program designed to produce a rule-defined numerical calculation like $2 \times n$ will always be able to come to a halt, no matter what is the input n. And a program that simply goes into an endless loop between states A and B can be shown never to halt.

Can we find one particular program for which the halting problem is unsolvable? Yes. The program M for the universal Turing machine will do. But again we must be careful, because M, as we defined it above, expects two inputs e and n. We can eliminate the obstacle by encoding e and n in a single number in some agreed upon way, let us say as powers of two distinct prime numbers:

$$N = 2^e \times 3^n$$

We then produce a second program M_2 that takes numbers N as input, and does the same thing as the program M does with the two numbers e and n.

Can we produce a program $H_4(N)$ that will tell us whether or not M_2 will halt when it has the input N? M_2 is capable of mimicking the behavior of any program whatsoever. If H_4 can tell us when M_2 halts, it can also tell us when any program whatsoever halts, and it is therefore a solution to the general halting problem. Since, as we have shown, the general halting problem has no solution, neither does the specific halting problem for the program M_2.

For Further Reflection

1. What does the result for the halting problem imply about the limitations of computer programming?
2. What does the halting problem imply for the mysteries still left in computer programming?
3. Name a specific computer program for which the halting problem is solvable. For what specific computer program is the halting problem known to be unsolvable?

Diagonalization

Let us explore *diagonalization*, a technique used in particular ways in Gödel's incompleteness theorem (appendix D1) and in the halting problem (appendix E1). A form of diagonalization is used in some simpler cases in set theory. We begin with these simpler instances of diagonalization.

Introducing Infinite Sets

We first have to understand some things about the behavior of sets. A set is simply an abstract object with certain fixed members. $S = \{2, 5, 9\}$ is a set whose members are 2, 5, and 9. A finite set S is a set with a finite number of members. If there are only a few members, we typically just list them one by one. We can also consider sets with an infinite number of members. The set of natural numbers N, with all positive integers as members, is such a set.

$$N = \{1, 2, 3, 4, \ldots\} = \{n \mid n \text{ is a natural number}\}$$

(The symbol $\mid$ means "such that.")

Here is the set of even numbers:

$$E = \{2, 4, 6, 8, 10, \ldots\} = \{n \mid n \text{ is a natural number and } n \text{ is evenly divisible by 2}\}$$

If we have a finite set $S = \{2, 5, 9\}$, and we add one or more extra members, we increase its size. S has 3 members. If we add 1 and 3 as additional members, we get $S \cup \{1, 3\} = \{1, 2, 3, 5, 9\}$, which has 5 members.

But with infinite sets, the same is not quite true. Suppose we have N, the set of natural numbers, and we add to it the extra member 0:

$$N' = N \cup \{0\} = \{0, 1, 2, 3, 4, \ldots\} = \{n \mid n \text{ is a nonnegative integer}\}$$

Does N' have more members than N? In a sense, yes, because it has the extra member 0. Is N' larger than N? In a sense, yes, because it is "enlarged" by having 0. But in another sense, no, because both sets have an infinite number of members. We do not enlarge infinity by adding one more member to N. We can show that the two sets are in a sense the same size by setting up a one-to-one correlation between their members (table E2.1):

TABLE E2.1: One-to-one Matching of Infinite Sets

N:	1	2	3	4	5	...
N':	0	1	2	3	4	...

Each number n in N is mapped into the number $n - 1$ in N'.

Georg Cantor, who first explored the issue of the size of infinite sets, decided to specify that two infinite sets were "the same size" if one could find just such a one-to-one correlation between their members. If not, set B was *bigger* than A if A could be put into correspondence with some part of B, but B could not be put into correspondence with a part of A. By this definition, the two sets N and N' are "the same size," even though one (N) is a proper subset of the other (N').

The set of even numbers E is clearly a subset of N. Is it smaller in size? No, because we can find a one-to-one correspondence between E and N, namely, by mapping each number n in N into $2 \times n$ in E (table E2.2):

TABLE E2.2: Matching Even Numbers with Whole Numbers

N:	1	2	3	4	5	...
E:	2	4	6	8	10	...

Suppose now we consider the set of positive rational numbers R:

$R = \{1/1, 1/2, 2/1, 1/3, 2/3, 3/1, 3/2, 1/4, ...\} = \{a/b \mid a$ and b are natural numbers$\}$

We might naively think that surely there are a lot more rational numbers than natural numbers. But if we are clever enough, we can set up a one-to-one correspondence. We do it by arranging all the rational numbers in a two-dimensional pattern (table E2.3):

TABLE E2.3: A List of Rational Numbers (with Duplicates)

1/1	2/1	3/1	4/1	5/1	6/1
1/2	2/2	3/2	4/2	5/2	6/2
1/3	2/3	3/3	4/3	5/3	6/3
1/4	2/4	3/4	4/4	5/4	6/4

Next, we cross out duplicates. 2/2 is the same number as 1/1, and 4/2 is the same number as 2/1 (table E2.4):

TABLE E2.4: Rational Numbers with Duplicates Eliminated

1/1	2/1	3/1	4/1	5/1	6/1
1/2	~~2/2~~	3/2	~~4/2~~	5/2	~~6/2~~
1/3	2/3	~~3/3~~	4/3	5/3	~~6/3~~
1/4	~~2/4~~	3/4	~~4/4~~	5/4	~~6/4~~

Next, we draw a "snaking line" through the remaining numbers, starting from 1/1 and zigzagging back and forth so that we gradually cover the whole array (table E2.5):

TABLE E2.5: Enumerating the Rationals

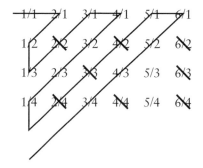

The snaking line gives us a way of numbering the whole set of rational numbers. The first rational is 1/1, the second is 2/1, the third is 1/2, the fourth is 1/3, and so on. No rational number will be left out. Hence, by Cantor's criterion, the set of rational numbers is the same size as the set of natural numbers.

Cantor's Diagonalization for Real Numbers

Now consider the set of real numbers. Each real number can be represented as a decimal expansion. For example, *pi* is 3.1415926535 … . A number like 1/2 is 0.5. 1/3 is 0.33333 … . Is the set of real numbers larger than the set of natural numbers? In an intuitive sense, there are many more real numbers than rationals. But intuition is not enough. Maybe, by some clever pattern, we could rearrange all the real numbers so that they could be enumerated one by one. How do we know?

We can show that there can be no possible way of enumerating the real numbers one by one, that is, of producing a one-to-one correlation with the natural numbers. We use the method of *reductio ad absurdum* or indirect proof. We assume the contrary.

Suppose we found a way to produce a one-to-one correlation. Let us picture a situation in which each of the real numbers is arranged into a list, in one-to-one correspondence with a natural number (table E2.6):

TABLE E2.6: Trying to Enumerate Real Numbers

```
1 ↔ 3.05618590544 …
2 ↔ 0.50000000000 …
3 ↔ 2.24444033055 …
4 ↔ 0.20020020002 …
5 ↔ 0.33456789002 …
6 ↔ 0.34555565555 …
7 ↔ 0.22223333444 …
  ↔ 0.22350998631 …
…
```

Any real numbers like 1/2 that can be written as a terminating decimal 0.5 are expanded by adding an unending number of 0's.

Cantor's decisive contribution begins with the next step. Draw a diagonal through the numbers at successive decimal places (table E2.7):

TABLE E2.7: Real Numbers with a Diagonal

```
1 ↔ 3.05618590544 ...
2 ↔ 0.50000000000 ...
3 ↔ 2.24444033055 ...
4 ↔ 0.20020020002 ...
5 ↔ 0.33456789002 ...
6 ↔ 0.34555565555 ...
7 ↔ 0.22223333444 ...
  ↔ 0.22350998631 ...
...
```

Now create a new real number. The new real number will have no whole number part, that is, it will begin with '0.' as its decimal expansion. Its first decimal place after the decimal point will be filled with a number from 1–8 differing from the first decimal place of the first number in our list. For our sample list, the first decimal place must not be 0. Make it 1. So we now have the beginning of a new real number: '0.1'.

The second decimal place of the new real number must differ from the second decimal place of the second number on our list. On our sample list, this decimal is 0. So for the new real number, make the second decimal place 1. We now have 0.11 for the new number.

For the third decimal place, we look at the third decimal place in the third number on our list. It is 4. So the third decimal place in our new real number must be something other than 4. Make it 5. We now have 0.115 for our new number. We can clearly continue this procedure. The result is a new real number with an unending decimal expansion: 0.11537641 ... .

Now we are about to produce our contradiction. What about this real number? By assumption, this real number, like all other real numbers, must appear somewhere on our list. But we have forced it to be different from every number on the list. So we have a contradiction. Therefore the initial assumption was wrong. Therefore, there is no one-to-one correspondence between the natural numbers and the reals. Therefore, the set of all real numbers is bigger than the set of all natural numbers. This result was first set forth by Georg Cantor.

The method used to arrive at this result is called *diagonalization*. It is named after the diagonal line used in the argument.

Diagonalization in Gödel's Incompleteness Theorem

Gödel's incompleteness theorem uses a kind of approach similar to diagonalization. Gödel's proof depends on having numbers that encode the various formulas in the formal system he is studying. They are the Gödel numbers of formulas. These numbers, considered in terms of their meaning in designating formulas, are like one "axis" for analysis—let us say the horizontal axis. Gödel also considers numbers as "bare" numbers that can be plugged into a formula with one free variable x_1. They are just numbers without meaning attached. This kind of bare number constitutes the vertical axis in our analogy. Gödel then presents us with a two-dimensional array, with Gödel numbers on the horizontal axis and bare numbers to substitute for the variable x_1 on the vertical axis. The entry at the intersection of one row and one column is supposed to be the answer to whether formula $K(x_1)$ with Gödel number k is provable when the formal representation for the number n is substituted for the free variable in $K(x_1)$. This information represents an encoding of the information about provability (see table E2.8.):

TABLE E2.8: Diagonalization with Gödel Numbers

numbers n to plug into a formula:	Gödel numbers for formulas $K(x_1)$:			
	k_1	k_2	k_3	k_4
1	$K_1(1)$	$K_2(1)$	$K_3(1)$	$K_4(1)$
2	$K_1(2)$	$K_2(2)$	$K_3(2)$	$K_4(2)$
3	$K_1(3)$	$K_2(3)$	$K_3(3)$	$K_4(3)$
4	$K_1(4)$	$K_2(4)$	$K_3(4)$	$K_4(4)$

Then Gödel's approach "diagonalizes." He forces the number n for the vertical axis to be the same as the number k enumerating the horizontal axis. For a general n, the information along the diagonal is supposed to say that the formula with Gödel number n is unprovable when the formalized expression for the number n is entered into the formula. If the Gödel number for this very formula is entered into the formula, we reach the conclusion that it is true but unprovable, or else provable but untrue (which would make the system as a whole unsound).

Diagonalization for the Halting Problem

The approach to the halting problem also uses a kind of diagonalization. In this case, the horizontal axis consists of numbers that encode the programs of Turing machines. The vertical axis consists of bare numbers that will be provided as inputs to each Turing machine. The intersection of a row and a column gives the information as to whether Turing machine e halts when presented with the input n. Diagonalization, where $e = n$, shows that the halting problem is unsolvable.

Possible General Principle

The details in each diagonalization have technical details. But there does seem to be something like a general pattern in them. Each involves looking for a diagonal running askew to two distinct axes x and n. The two axes have different meanings. One is the axis involving what we have called bare numbers—numbers that will be plugged into some formula without worrying about whether the numbers encode some special meaning. The other axis is the axis of meaning. In fact, the numbers encode the structure of formulas or the structure of state transitions in Turing machines. And they can be assigned another level of meaning still, where we look at the meaning of the formulas or the meaning of the calculations carried out by a particular Turing machine. The diagonalization procedure works its magic because its two axes are related to two distinct translations between formal structures on the one side and the meaning or interpretation assigned to those structures in a metalanguage on the other side.

Cantor's diagonalization for the real numbers shows some similarities. Clearly Cantor's diagonalization depends on having two axes, horizontal and vertical. The horizontal axis looks at one kind of internal meaning for each real number, namely, the value of its decimal expansion at position x. The vertical axis, on the other hand, has no meaning. It is just a list that we imagine having drawn up. Now by going along the diagonal and negating each entry, we assure ourselves that the new real number produced must contradict any attempt to identify it with any of the numbers in the list. Likewise in Gödel's proof of incompleteness and in the halting problem, we negate at a crucial point the information contained in the diagonal, about proofs in the one case and about halting in the other. We produce a formula whose meaning is that it is unprovable rather than provable. We produce a computer program that does the opposite of the program it is mimicking.

Theistic Foundations

These diagonalization arguments are interesting in their own right. But they also illustrate what we have called *imitative transcendence*, the ability of human beings in the image of God to stand back and transcend the reasoning in which they have temporarily been engaged. To do the diagonalization, we must stand back from the two axes and the meaning of any one point of intersection of the rows and columns. Knowing the meaning, we must deliberately create a new meaning that will violate the old. In having before us the two axes, we also have before us two "translations" between numbers and meaning. The one is "meaningless," just numbers to plug into a formula, while the other is meaningful, numbers representing something about the real numbers or formulas or computer programs that we want to study.

Diagonalization in Power Sets

We can give another illustration of diagonalization in the case of power sets. If S is a set, the *power set* of S, sometimes written P(S), is the set of all subsets of S. That is, it is the set whose members are exactly the subsets of S. If S has three elements 1, 2, and 3, the power set of S has $2 \times 2 \times 2$ elements. Here is how it works. To form any particular subset of S, we make choices for each successive element in S. First, choose whether or not 1 will be in the new subset. There are two possible choices: either we put it in, or we do not. Next, make a choice about whether 2 will be in the new subset. Again there are two choices, to put it in or not. Since there are two choices for 2 when we have already chosen for 1 to be in the subset, and two more choices when we have chosen for 1 not to be in, we have a total of $2 \times 2 = 4$ choices. Finally, make a choice about whether 3 will be in the new subset. Again, there are two choices. There are two choices, that is, corresponding to each of the 4 choices that we have already made. So we have a grand total of $2 \times 2 \times 2$ choices, making $2 \times 2 \times 2 = 8$ different subsets. In general, for a starting set with n elements, the number of distinct subsets is 2^n.

2^n is always greater than n.[1] There are always more subsets than there are elements in the original set S with which we started. In other words, P(S), the power set of S, is always bigger than S.

But now suppose we consider infinite sets, like the set N of all natural

---

[1] For $n = 0$, 2^0 is defined as 1. So the inequality holds in this case as well.

numbers. Is P(N) bigger than N? We cannot any longer rely on a numerical calculation, because the number of elements is infinite in both cases. Perhaps P(N) is actually the same size as N, the way the set of rational numbers is the same size as N. Or perhaps P(N) is bigger than N, in the way that the set of real numbers is bigger than the set N of natural numbers. How do we know?

Cantor found a way of showing that P(S) must be bigger than S, even if S is infinite. His proof actually works for finite sets S as well. It is a method of diagonalization.

We achieve the result by means of indirect proof. We assume the contrary. That is, we assume as a hypothesis that P(S) is not bigger than S. According to Cantor's definition of size, this means that we can find some one-to-one correspondence between S and P(S). Let this correlation be denoted by f. For each element x in S, $f(x)$ will be the corresponding element in P(S). That is, for each x, $f(x)$ will be a subset of S.

Given the information available from f, we are going to build *another* subset of S, a new subset. And we are going to build it in such a way that we will force it not to be in the list that f purports to give us, a list that allegedly correlates each and every subset of S with an element of S.

Our new subset T will be composed of precisely those elements x of S such that x is not an element of $f(x)$.

$$T = \{ x \in S \mid \sim(x \in f(x))\}$$

T is a subset of S. So T is in P(S). So, by assumption, f correlates T with some element a in S, in such a way that $f(a) = T$. Let us now ask whether a is a member of T itself. Is it or is it not true that $a \in T$? Suppose that it is in T. $T = f(a)$ by definition of a. So $a \in f(a)$. So a does not satisfy the defining property for members of T. So a is not in T after all. But if a is not in T, and $T = f(a)$, a does satisfy the defining property for T, namely, that $\sim(x \in f(x))$. So a is in T. Assuming either that a is in T or that it is not in T leads to a contradiction. Therefore, the initial assumption that the one-to-one correspondence f exists must be false. So P(S) is always bigger than S.

In this proof we have had to use simultaneously two translations between S and P(S). One is the translation f, which does not inspect the meanings of the elements x or the subsets $f(x)$ with which they are correlated. The other translation is the translation in terms of the meaning of membership. Either an element x is in a subset, or it is not. Along a horizontal axis, as it were, we have a list of elements of S, taking into account their properties of membership. Along a vertical axis we have a list of subsets, which, someone alleges, correspond in a one-to-one fashion with elements y of S through the function $f(y)$. At the intersection of the rows and the columns, we include the information as to whether the element x from column x is a member of the subset $f(y)$ from row y. Along the diagonal we force the condition $\sim(x \in f(y))$ for the case when $x = y$. We create a new subset T that we force not to be in the alleged list. It cannot be in the list, because for each $f(y)$ in the list, T has the opposite property from what we find on the diagonal (table E2.9).

TABLE E2.9: Diagonalizing for a Power Set

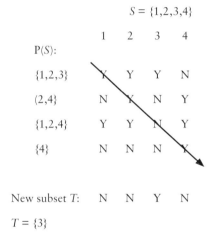

$S = \{1,2,3,4\}$

P(S):	1	2	3	4
{1,2,3}	Y	Y	Y	N
{2,4}	N	Y	N	Y
{1,2,4}	Y	Y	N	Y
{4}	N	N	N	Y

New subset T:	N	N	Y	N

$T = \{3\}$

To succeed, we have to transcend the correlations in the total two-dimensional array, and construct a new subset based on the information from the diagonal.

Building New Sets

The fact that the power set of S is bigger than S implies that we can perform repeated acts of transcendence and construct bigger and bigger sets indefinitely. If we start with a finite set S, we get only larger and larger finite sets. S, P(S), P(P(S)), P(P(P(S))), … . But if we take the set union of all the products, we get an infinite set. If we start with an infinite set, let us say N, we get a "bigger infinite" set P(N). P(N), it happens, is the same size as the set of all real numbers. P(P(N)) is the same size as the set of all subsets of real numbers. If we go up the ladder, we can imagine $P(P(P(N)))$, $P(P(P(P(N))))$, and so on. We can abbreviate the n-th iteration as $P^n(N)$.

We can imagine for ourselves the union of all these sets, written $N \cup P^1(N) \cup P^2(N) \cup P^3(N) \cup \ldots$, or $P^\omega(N)$ for short. It is bigger than any of the earlier sets. Then we can produce the power set of $P^\omega(N)$, namely, $P(P^\omega(N))$, which must be bigger than $P^\omega(N)$. And so on. Each step constitutes an imitative transcendence. And we can transcend the whole sequence $P^\omega(N)$, $P(P^\omega(N))$, $P(P(P^\omega(N)))$, $P(P(P(P^\omega(N))))$, $\ldots$, if we want. Modern set theory studies these ladders. The ladders reflect the glory of God, who is transcendent. They reflect the original imaging and creativity in the Father eternally begetting the Son.

Russell's Paradox

Russell's paradox (appendix A1) concerns the set of all sets that do not contain themselves. The paradox arises from "diagonalizing" the relation between sets and their members. It illustrates the fact that we cannot really transcend all particular sets to observe the set of all sets, nor the set of all sets that do not contain themselves.

Part IV.F

Philosophy and Logic

Kantian Subjectivism

The philosopher Immanuel Kant (1724–1804) produced subtle and complex works. Professionals continue to debate their meaning within their historical context. We cannot enter into such a complex discussion. We focus rather on what might be called *Kantianism*, that is, what Kant has been taken to mean or imply. And within Kantianism we consider only a few leading ideas that may influence how people think about logic. Experts in philosophy will have to bear with many simplifications.

Things and Their Appearances

Kantianism says that there is a world out there, and there are things in the world. Kantianism provides a label for it: "The thing in itself." But, says Kantianism, what we perceive depends on our minds and the natural framework of our thinking and our perceiving, not just on what is out there. What we perceive are *appearances*, *phenomena*. The *phenomenal world* is the kind of thing that we see, hear, smell, and feel. It contains apples, houses, roads, books, and so on. The apples and houses are *appearances*. The apple has a round shape and red color. We can also touch an apple, smell it, or taste it. We can hear the crunch when we bite into it. All five of our senses supply us with *phenomena*. We interact with apples in the context of how they appear to us.

We experience these phenomena in time and in space. And we experience phenomena in terms of causality. That is, one phenomenon leads to or causes another. Time, space, and causality are conditions under which we receive all the particulars of our experience.

Kantianism says that we receive the phenomena in time and space and in causal sequences because time and space and causality are part of the mental framework under which we organize raw input. We cannot imagine what it would be like *not* to have time and space and causality. Our mental equipment provides structure for whatever we experience, and time and space and causality are aspects of this structure. They are aspects of human rationality. They are categories of the mind.

That means that we cannot get beyond them or behind them. It also means that we cannot get beyond them in the direction of the thing-in-itself. We cannot leap out of our minds in order to have "direct" contact with a thing-in-itself. Hypothetically, a thing-in-itself might have features of time and space and causality, but then it might not. We cannot tell, since what we are receiving within phenomenal experience reflects our own built-in categories.

Ideas Beyond Phenomena

Kantianism also says that we can have ideas that attempt to reach beyond the phenomena. We have ideas about things, things as they might be in themselves. We have ideas about God and about morality. The realm of these ideas is called the *noumenal* (from Greek *nous*, meaning "mind").

Limits of Reason

According to Kantianism, our rationality works properly on phenomena in time and space and in causal connections, because these phenomena conform naturally to the categories of time and space and causality that our human mental equipment supplies. This rationality is the basis for scientific achievements. Scientists describe causal relationships in time and space. But, says Kantianism, if we try to apply our rationality to the realm of the noumenal, such as ideas about God, we produce paradoxes, because we are stretching rationality beyond its proper sphere, the sphere of the phenomena.

Logic in Kantianism

Now where does logic fit into this picture? Immanuel Kant wrote long after Aristotle founded the discipline of logic through his study of syllogisms. But Kant wrote *before* the development of formal symbolic logic in the nineteenth and twentieth centuries. He spoke about *reason*. And reason is a broader category. For Kantianism reason in a broad sense encompasses not only the character of arguments but the categories of the mind, that is, time and space and causality.

We might conclude that logic should be included as one aspect among the categories of the mind. Or if this conclusion is disputed, we can *extend* the framework of Kantianism to encompass logic. Under this extension, logic gets treated in the same way as Kantianism treats time and space and causality. One way or another, Kantianism can include logic in its account.

According to this account, logic becomes an aspect of our mental furniture, just as the categories of time, space, and causality are part of our mental furniture. Logic is part of what reason and the mind bring to the table when they interact with the world.

According to these assumptions, it would follow that we can apply logic to the world of phenomena because logic has already been *imposed* on the world of phenomena in the process of its becoming phenomena. Time and space and causality get imposed by the human mind on the thing-in-itself, in the process of the thing-in-itself becoming phenomena and being part of our experience. In just the same way, logic gets imposed by the human mind on the thing-in-itself.

Science studies the phenomena and achieves results. These results conform to the regularities of time, space, and cause. They also conform to the regularities of logic. They *must* conform, because all these regularities are built into the world of phenomena from the start, by the fact that these phenomena have already submitted to our mental categories in order to become phenomena at all, that is, part of our actual conscious experience.

According to Kantianism, it is a mistake to infer that the thing-in-itself must necessarily exist in time and space and in causal relations. Just so, it is a mistake to infer that the thing-in-itself must be subject to logic. We cannot know the thing-in-itself.

In this way, Kantianism traces the origins of logic to the human mind, not to the world. In this sense, Kantianism has a *subjectivist* view of logic. Logic originates in the "subject," the mind of a person. That is why we have titled this appendix "Kantian subjectivism." But in some modern contexts the word "subjectivism" can connote skepticism or relativism. Kantianism attempts to avoid both. Kantianism affirms science rather than being skeptical of it in the way that David Hume was. The achievements of science are real in their own sphere. The key phrase is "in their own sphere." That sphere is the sphere of phenomena, a sphere that exists only by virtue of the contribution of two inputs, the input from the things-in-themselves and the input from subjects, from perceivers and their mental categories.

In addition, Kantianism would claim not to be relativist. In a sense, logic is "relative" to the world of phenomena. But all rational minds experience essentially the same type of world. Among human beings logic is universal, as is rationality.

Attractiveness of Kantianism

Superficially, Kantianism might seem to have much plausibility to it. It seems to explain the successes of science. It seems to explain why we confront paradoxes if we have too exalted a view of the power of reason. It seems to explain the origins of very basic aspects of the world, namely time, space, causality, and logic. It seems to answer skeptics like David Hume who managed to doubt whether our perception of causal connections was real, rather than merely the product of habit and the chance perception of repeated instances.

It seems also to take seriously the role of human perceptual apparatus. It is friendly to phenomena like optical illusions, in which our perception differs demonstrably from what is actually "out there." It is friendly to phenomena like color-blindness, where a person has diminished perception of color. Is color as we perceive it actually "out there," or is it rather a phenomenon produced by nerves receiving signals from cone cells in the retina that are tuned to three different parts of the visual spectrum of light?[1]

Partly because of its plausibility, Kantianism has had enormous influence on the Western world, not only within the realm of professional philosophy, but gradually more and more within modern worldviews of people who have never read Kant. Kantianism says that science is sound, while real knowledge of God is problematic, because God belongs to the noumenal. Religion becomes a matter of opinion.

Philosophers subsequent to Kant have sometimes taken over pieces of Kant while altering the system as a whole. "Kantianism" is pretty diffuse. Kantianism can move in a more objective direction by emphasizing the reality and objectivity of science. Science gives us solid knowledge, while religion and morality become subjective.

Or Kantianism can become more subjective, by suppressing the thing-in-itself. If the thing-in-itself is inaccessible in itself, we cannot really talk about it without paradox. So let us stop talking about it. *Everything* becomes phenomena already processed by the categories of the mind. It is all mental.

Difficulties with Kantianism

If Kantianism is so plausible, why are we not all Kantians? Are there difficulties? There are.[2] We cannot enter into a thorough discussion. We con-

---

[1] On what is real, see Vern S. Poythress, *Redeeming Science: A God-Centered Approach* (Wheaton, IL: Crossway, 2006), chapters 15 and 16.
[2] For a start, see Cornelius Van Til, *A Survey of Christian Epistemology*, volume 2 of the series *In Defense of Biblical Christianity* (n.l.: den Dulk Christian Foundation, 1969), 106–115.

centrate on one element, namely, Kantianism's explanation for logic. Its explanation differs markedly from what we have expounded in this book. Yet a Kantian explanation remains plausible to many people in the modern world. So it is fitting for us to indicate, in a short compass, a few of the main difficulties.

Relying on God

The number one difficulty for Kantianism is that it suppresses the knowledge of God, not only in the realm of logic but in every other realm of the phenomena. We have been concerned for this difficulty all the way through this book, so we will not repeat all the arguments here. We can at least note that Kantianism relies on God.

Kantianism builds a philosophy through reasoning. It uses arguments. It uses logic, at least at an informal level. In doing so, it relies on God covertly. It relies on the attributes of God: his faithfulness, his self-consistency, his eternity, his immutability, his omnipotence (chapter 7). It does so because in the process of using logic it relies on these attributes as they are displayed in the rules of logic. It relies on the Logos, on the absolute reason of God. This reason is constantly and unavoidably reflected in our minds in human reasoning.

At the same time, Kantianism claims that God does *not* reveal himself in the world, that is, the world of phenomena. It relies on God's revelation of himself and at the same time denies that there is such revelation. Its foundations are rotten. One effect of this book, I hope, may be to make it clearer just how rotten the foundations are when people attempt to use reasoning to evade the God of the Bible.

Second, let us ask what kind of conception Kantianism has concerning reason and logic when it proceeds with arguments to build up its system. It presupposes a non-Christian view of transcendence and immanence, in the sense of chapter 14. In particular, it presupposes non-Christian immanence, in that it assumes that our minds at present are normal, rather than abnormal because of sinful rebellion. It assumes that we can use our standards for rationality and logic without consulting God.

Third, Kantianism implicitly presupposes that it is all right to engage in the kind of reasonings in which it engages in order to build itself as a philosophical system. With this sense of being "all right," it presupposes a moral standard. And what is the moral standard? Kantianism is saying that we should go forward with reasonings that seek to answer some of the most basic questions about the nature of the world, the nature of our knowledge, and the nature of our minds without consulting God's special revelation in Scripture. Scripture is available in the Western world. Kantianism systematically refuses to be instructed by it in the process of laying its foundations. That is a moral decision and a religious decision. Unfortunately, it is the wrong one.

My point here is not to dispute these assumptions in detail. It is rather to lay bare the fact that Kantianism in its beginnings is not religiously neutral. It has already taken a stance, implicitly. The religious conclusions are not so surprising, given the starting religious commitments. In particular, it has a commitment to the *autonomy* of the human mind in its reasonings. *Autonomy* connotes that we are to be a law to ourselves, rather than submitting meekly to God's law, that is, his instruction.

We can see further difficulties by zeroing in on inconsistencies within the point of view of Kantianism itself. We now proceed in this direction.[3]

Exceeding Reason

Let us ask ourselves what sort of documents Kant and Kantianism have produced. What do they do to produce arguments in favor of their philosophical viewpoint? They produce *arguments*. They use *reason*. At the same time, Kantianism has very particular things to say about the limits of reason. Pure reason, allegedly, works satisfactorily when applied to the realm of phenomena, but only there. In the realm of the noumenal it generates paradoxes.

And what, we may ask, is the subject matter when we proceed to read works on Kantian philosophy? Is the subject matter only phenomena? Then we would be reading works of science or works concerning everyday phenomenal observations. No, Kantian philosophy discusses everything under the sun, including God, including morality, including the noumenal realm, and proceeds to tell us what we can and cannot expect to know about the noumenal realm, and why. An impressive scope, would you not say? A scope far larger than the scope that Kantian philosophy assigns as the limits of reason. Kantianism uses reason to build a system that sets the limits of reason.

---

[3] We are here following the procedure of Van Til's presuppositional apologetics. We discuss other systems partly by showing their contrasts with a Christian viewpoint or Christian presuppositions. Then, as a separate project, we look inside the other systems and show the inner difficulties that they generate, on the basis of their presuppositions.

To do so, it has to survey the field. It has to transcend the phenomena and look at the noumenal realm as well. It has to take a God's-eye view. This view, once achieved, afterwards allows it to tell you and me the narrower limits in which our reason can safely operate.

The God's-eye view is Kantianism's secret, and simultaneously its weakest point. Kantianism is self-destructive. In its results, it tells us what are the limitations of reason. If we take those results seriously, we have to apply them to Kantianism's own reasonings about philosophy. Those reasonings go beyond the limits, and so we conclude that they are not sound. And so the whole philosophy is unsound. And so the limits have not been established. And so we are back to the beginning. We have gotten nowhere. Except now we know not to follow Kantianism.

In addition, Kantian philosophy testifies unwittingly to the reality of human ability to transcend the immediate. We can stand back from the immediacy of experience and survey what we have been doing. And then we can stand back from that and survey the meaning of our more abstract meditations. We have the capacity, as we have observed earlier in this book, for a miniature transcendence, because our minds imitate the mind of God. We can imagine what it would be like to look at everything from God's point of view.

But Kantian philosophy engages in this whole process of transcendence *autonomously*. By its act of attempting transcendence, it testifies to God who made the human mind. By its autonomy, it defies God's instruction in Scripture and refuses to give him thanks (Rom. 1:21). Not only that, but in effect it tries to be God. Having achieved what it hopes is a godlike transcendence, it can then dictate as a god what limits we poor mortals must have for our reasoning.

In a sense, the Kantian philosophers are the godlike beings, because they can dictate to poor mortals the limits of their experience and their reason. But in another sense Kantianism allows all human beings to be godlike. Each of us becomes in his own person a kind of godlike creator of the world. We "create" the whole world of phenomena, including all the structures of time and space and causality and logic and reason, by imposing structure through our mental categories. We become gods. Can you see how such a conception has a covert *religious* appeal for people—really all of us in our sinfulness—who desire autonomy?

The World Talking Back

The passage of time and the changes in science since the time of Kant have created difficulties. We might call them empirical difficulties. There are several.

Kantianism up through the end of the nineteenth century said that the categories of time and space and causality were innate categories of the human mind. These categories are the same in principle for all human beings and for all times. But twentieth-century physics has created difficulties for this claim by disrupting earlier scientific theories in a way that Kantians—as well as everyone else—thought was impossible. This disruption has changed the scientific understanding of time and space.

The Theory of Relativity

Albert Einstein's special theory of relativity (1905) set forth a theory in which time and space do not exist as purely independent "axes" or "dimensions" in scientific measurement. Time and space are in a sense entangled with one another in a way that depends on the relative movement of observers. This theory is counterintuitive, at least by the standards of the normal intuitions of ordinary people concerning time and space.

Kantianism claims that time and space are categories imposed on things by the human mind. If so, they are so basic that our intuitions can never be disrupted. And in 1905, here they are being disrupted anyway! The experiments and the phenomena of physics are, as it were, "talking back" to us. Our categories, it appears, are not so powerful after all. The thing-in-itself has ideas of its own. And it may make us uncomfortable and push us to reorganize our intuitions or our categories.

Over the course of the twentieth century, things got worse rather than better for Kantianism. In 1915 Einstein published the general theory of relativity. This theory proposes a four-dimensional geometry, which includes one dimension of time and three of space.[4] In this theory, time and space together can be *curved* rather than flat, and Euclid's parallel postulate no longer holds. Up until this point, Kantians would have said that our minds imposed the category of space on phenomena, and such an imposition explained why space was experienced as it was, including its *flatness*. Again, the world talked back through the physicists.

This shift in physics is significant because it does more than poke one

---

[4] As in the special theory of relativity, there is no clear separation as to what is a time dimension and what is a space dimension in some absolute, observer-independent sense.

or two holes in the Kantian system. It destroys a large amount of the over-all appeal of the system. Kantianism was appealing because it appeared to explain the success of science and the rationality of science. It said that science comes out of our own minds, by rational imposition that organizes the things, thus making them *phenomena*. Twentieth-century physics makes it painfully plain that lawfulness exists "out there," not just in our minds. It has to be out there first, and it has to differ from standard intuitions, if it is going to challenge those intuitions. By contrast, Kantianism places the origin of science in the mind. One of its main attractions is that it can then seamlessly explain science. The laws that science discovers, according to Kantianism, have to be there because the mind generates them.

But if the laws pertain to the things-in-themselves, and not just to our minds, we are back into a situation of having no explanation for the coherence between the laws and our minds—unless, of course, we say that God ordained both the law and our minds. And philosophy does not want God intruding and disrupting autonomous thought.

The twentieth century can still admit a grain of truth in Kantianism. It can observe that people's previous intuitions make it easy to accept Newtonian physics, with flat space and time, while intuitions make it difficult to accept Einsteinian physics, with curved space and time. Intuitions have an influence. But to say this much is miles away from saying that intuitions generate laws, as if by themselves.

Quantum Theory

Later developments in the twentieth century have not been kind to Kantianism. Kantianism until the nineteenth century would have said that the perception of time and space as smooth continua was also an aspect of the mind. The phenomena appear continuous in time and space because that is how our minds necessarily organize them. Necessarily. That is the key claim, which gives Kantianism some of its superficial attractiveness.

Quantum theory has cast doubt on this assumption. Developments in quantum theory appear to indicate that it is not possible to divide up space or time into smaller and smaller pieces indefinitely. Physicists wonder whether it is meaningful to consider a length much smaller than the so-called Planck length, 1.6×10^{-35} meters. Similarly, it may not be meaningful to consider a time smaller than the Planck time, the time it takes for light to cross the Planck length, 5.4×10^{-44} seconds. These are incredibly small lengths, so they do not directly affect ordinary life. The issue is rather in the Kantian principle. Kantianism claims our intuitions of time and space are necessary. They virtually create the world. Unfortunately, the world talks back, and disrupts our intuitions, which demonstrates that our intuitions are not in fact the source of the world. We are not gods.

Laws of Physics

In fact, even science at the time of Kant creates difficulties for Kantianism, if people pause to think about it. Let us consider a particular case. In 1687, before Kant was born, Isaac Newton proposed a universal law of gravitation. The law says that any two small bodies of masses M and m exert a gravitational force F on each other according to the formula

$$F = GMm/r^2$$

where r is the distance between the two bodies[5] and G is the universal gravitational constant. Modern measurements indicate that G is about 6.7×10^{-11} in modern units of N m^2 kg^{-2}.

Newton's laws and other developments in science were one of the motivations behind building Kantianism. How do we explain the existence of such precise and impressive regularities, and their universal scope? Kantianism hoped to produce an explanation by the principle of *causality*. If we grant that time and space are projected from categories in the human mind, we still need to deal with causes such as the force of gravity. Newton's theory says that one body *causes* another to deviate from motion in a straight line. Why does such causality exist? In answer to this challenge, Kantianism said that causality was like time and space. The world of phenomena is characterized by consistent causality because our minds organize it that way. Our minds project or impose causality on the world, and that is how the world rises to the status of becoming phenomena.

It sounds plausible to a nonscientist. But science in practice has to deal with a world that talks back. Newton knew this, and so did the scientists before him like Kepler, Galileo, and Copernicus on whom he built. Newton did assume that the world that he observed acted according to causal prin-

---

[5] Technically, we need to specify that the diameter of each of the two bodies must be much less than the distance r. For large bodies like the earth and the moon, the total gravitational attraction must be calculated by summing (integrating) over the amount of attraction produced by all the smaller bits that make up the earth and the smaller bits that make up the moon. Fortunately, for a spherically shaped body of uniform density, the result is the same as if all the mass were concentrated at the center of the sphere.

ciples. But when he began his investigations he did not know exactly what those principles were. He could not just impose a law on the world. He had to discover what laws were "out there." The law of gravitation, as well as the three laws of motion that go together with it, were all formulated in response to the need to account for the phenomena, phenomena that, for all Newton knew, could have been different.

Another way of putting it is this: why does gravitation exist as one *kind* of cause? And why *this* law of gravitation? And why does the gravitational constant G have the exact value that it has? The law of gravitation is not just "causality" in some vague, philosophical sense. It is a very specific law. Why this law? We are not asking why there are causal connections at all. Rather, granted that some causal connections are there, we are asking why they are precisely *what* they are.

A general philosophical principle of causality says much too little. It says only that there will be causes of some sort. That is not enough to account for science. If causality originates in the mind and is projected onto the world, then the mind, in order to do its job, has to project *particular* causalities such as Newton's law of gravitation. But the mind obviously does not do this. Newton has to go to the world. He goes, to be sure, with some assumptions that there will be causes. In addition, he has to find out from data which formula works. That additional part, coming from the data, has no basis in Kantianism. If we say that the additional part comes from the thing-in-itself, we destroy the reason for Kantianism by admitting that there are not only causes in the things-in-themselves, but very *particular* causes, namely, Newton's law of gravitation with all its particularity, and the gravitational constant G with all its particularity.

Ordinary Life

We can also see difficulties for Kantian subjectivism by returning to our example (chapter 6) of a practical syllogism:

> All pedestrians can be killed by rapidly moving buses.
> I am a pedestrian.
> Therefore I can be killed by rapidly moving buses.

What does Kantianism have to say about this practical syllogism and about buses? Kantian subjectivism suggests that this practical syllogism is merely the projection of the mind's propensity to organize the world according to its innate categories. Logic is our projection onto the phenomena.

If so, the thing-in-itself, the thing *behind* the phenomena of rapidly moving buses, need not have any connection to our logic. Can we believe that the thing-in-itself behind the buses has no logic? The Kantian would say we cannot subjectively do so because it is outside our categories. Very well. But what about the buses? Is my mind *making* them not run me over by its logical "impositions"? Am I really a god? Does anyone really believe this?

Multicultural Objections

As if Kantianism did not have troubles enough, multiculturalism produces additional difficulties. Old-fashioned Kantianism assumed the uniformity of human reason and the human mind. So it assumed also the uniformity of logic. But how do we know that all human beings are in fact alike in the ways that Kantianism claims? According to the multiculturalist, we do not. Reason itself varies from culture to culture. Therefore, says the multiculturalist, Kantianism is a Western system that has no necessary claim to universal cultural validity.

From a Christian point of view, from outside the Kantian system, we know that all human beings are made in the image of God. We know there is commonality. We know also that there is diversity, so we can take cultural differences seriously without falling into relativism.[6] But within Kantianism, the issue of cultural differences becomes painfully threatening. How can you know, by just inspecting your own individual rationality, that what you see is culturally universal? You cannot.[7] So Kantianism condemns itself as culturally imperialistic. Kantians are simply attempting to impose their cultural ideas on the rest of the world.

Returning to Logic

Where do these reasonings about Kantianism leave us when it comes to the status of logic? Kantianism tempts people to say that logic is subjectivistic, that is, to say that it is a projection of the rationality of the human mind. But this subjectivist view will not work for logic any more than it works for science and for multicultural objections. Logic is found in the world of science.

---

[6] See Vern S. Poythress, *In the Beginning Was the Word: Language—A God-Centered Approach* (Wheaton, IL: Crossway, 2009), chapters 16–18.

[7] At least you cannot without appealing to God's revelation; on the other hand, if you do appeal to God, he can tell you about the universalities of human nature without your having to be a god yourself.

The things-in-themselves talk back to us, indicating that they conform to logic even *before* they become phenomena processed by our categories. Nor will Kantian subjectivism explain the cultural universality of logic, which is demonstrated by the CPUs in computers and cell phones spreading through the cultures of the world (chapter 13).

For Further Reflection

1. What is the Kantian view of space, time, and causality? What does such an approach seem to suggest for how we view logic?
2. Why does a Kantian view have plausibility?
3. What difficulties does Kantianism generate for itself? How has the progress of science created further difficulties?
4. In what way does the general principle of causality not explain Newton's law of gravitation?

The Role of Logic in Philosophy

Our reflections on logic have implications for philosophy.

The word *philosophy* comes from the Greek word *philosophia*, which etymologically means love of wisdom. The Greek philosophers wanted wisdom, and pursued it with vigor. They pursued it using reason. Some became skeptical in the process, and despaired of finding ultimate truth. Others, like Socrates, Plato, and Aristotle, placed confidence in human rational processes. They hoped that rational reflection combined with diligence could lead to truth. Socrates, Plato, and Aristotle were remarkably gifted men, and they have left a legacy that the Western world has sifted through ever since. As we have stressed in discussing common grace, they left valuable insights. But their insights were also contaminated by sin.

We cannot here take time to sift through their legacy, or the legacy of later philosophers. But we can ask how they used logic.

Socrates

Plato's dialogue *Euthyphro* provides a revealing window into Greek philosophy. The dialogue asks what is piety and what is holiness. Much goes on in this dialogue. But Socrates brings one key question: "Is that which is holy loved by the gods because it is holy, or is it holy because it is loved by the gods?"[1] The dialogue then proceeds. The participants, Euthyphro and Socrates, are able to agree that the first alternative is correct: holiness is loved by the gods because it is holy.

Given the flow of the dialogue, the conclusion seems reasonable. But there is a price to pay. Holiness is understood as essentially independent of the gods. In the language of Plato, holiness is a rational form—an impersonal form to be grasped by reason.

---

[1] Plato, *Euthyphro*, trans. Harold N. Fowler (London: Heinemann; Cambridge, MA: Harvard University Press, 1966), 12A.

The Gods versus Reason

Socrates has uncovered a challenge similar to what we saw earlier in considering the foundation of logic. If logic is superior to God, it is more absolute than God himself. If logic is inferior to him, God is essentially irrational. Similarly, if holiness is an abstract form superior to God, holiness (and not God) is the true absolute. On the other hand, if holiness is inferior to God, then God is not essentially holy.

The solution can be found by rooting holiness and logic in the character of God. This approach is a third alternative. When the dialogue offers us the choice between the two alternatives for holiness, it has succumbed to the fallacy of bifurcation, by presuming that there are no other alternatives.

Socrates makes a second significant move. He says, ". . . tell me what holiness is, no matter whether it is loved by the gods or anything else happens to it."[2] Given the context of the dialogue, the request seems reasonable, because the previous dialogue has already decided that holiness is independent of the gods' preferences.

The dialogue ends inconclusively. But it has still achieved something. At the beginning Euthyphro was confident that his own actions were holy and that he knew what holiness was. By the end, Socrates has shown that he does not know.

The Gods versus the True God

The gods in question are the Greek gods, each of whom is limited in relation to the others. Euthyphro admits that the gods quarrel with one another, and that they may sometimes differ in their views of right and wrong. They are clearly incapable of being an ultimate source of wisdom. Socrates is right that, even if these gods existed, their opinion would not settle the question. The dialogue also contains a grain of truth in its endpoint. Euthyphro did not know what he was talking about, and the participants are better off confessing their ignorance. At least by the end they know that they do not know.

The dialogue makes interesting reading, and it is always a pleasure to have human arrogance and folly defeated (in the person of Euthyphro). If the dialogue only had the effect of questioning dependence on the Greek gods, it could be seen as potentially valuable in opening the way to pre-

---

[2] Plato, *Euthyphro*, 13B.

senting the message of the true God and his plan of redemption. But the dialogue contains other elements that can have less beneficial consequences.

Rational Autonomy

Socrates moves the dialogue away from focusing on the gods' preferences. He asks what holiness is ". . . no matter whether it is loved by the gods." The movement away from the gods can tempt readers to pursue wisdom through autonomous reason.[3] The temptation works out in a one-level conception of rationality. To achieve human rational mastery of a concept, we must eliminate mystery through reasoning on one level only. Human reason must be made into a master that—at least in theory—governs and determines truth rather than receiving it imitatively from God's transcendence. We have here a manifestation of a non-Christian view of immanence.

The dialogue also tempts us to involve ourselves in the fallacy of equivocation with respect to the term *holiness*. The term owes its meaning to God. The meaning of holiness in the mind of God is superior to the meaning of holiness in the mind of man (though the two meanings are intimately related). The word *holiness* has two levels to its meaning, corresponding to the Creator and the creature. But the dialogue does not reckon with the Creator-creature distinction. One-level logic seems reasonable, given the non-ultimacy of the Greek gods.

An Alternative

If the gods cannot give us a final resting point, Plato's dialogue tempts us to assume that the only viable alternative is to settle the question through human reason. Human reason, if rightly used, may access a realm of truth superior to the gods. What alternative has been left out? The alternative of the true God, the God of Israel. God, not human reason, is the source of truth and wisdom. God makes himself known in the created world, but people suppress that knowledge, and need redemption in Christ.

The Bible as the word of God then comes to show us the way of salvation, and to instruct us in God's own wisdom:

. . . Christ, in whom are hidden all the treasures of *wisdom* and knowledge. (Col. 2:2–3)

---

[3] The issue is made more complex by the fact that Socrates sees himself as receiving "the divine monitor" (Plato, *Euthyphro*, 2B). But when analyzed, the practical effect of the divine influence is to deify human reason. In practice, human reason becomes the standard (non-Christian immanence).

> And because of him you are in Christ Jesus, who became to us *wisdom* from God, righteousness and sanctification and redemption, so that, as it is written, "Let the one who boasts, boast in the Lord." (1 Cor. 1:30–31)

> The fear of the LORD is the beginning of *wisdom*. (Ps. 111:10)

The Bible notices that Greeks seek wisdom, but in the wrong way:

> For Jews demand signs and Greeks seek *wisdom*, but we preach Christ crucified, a stumbling block to Jews and folly to Gentiles, but to those who are called, both Jews and Greeks, Christ the power of God and the *wisdom* of God. For the foolishness of God is wiser than men, and the weakness of God is stronger than men. (1 Cor. 1:22–25)

Western Philosophy

Socrates, and then Plato and Aristotle after him, inaugurated a long history of Western philosophy. They set the tone by seeking wisdom through human reason.

There is a paradox in the whole endeavor. In reality, human reason and logic reveal divine rationality and logic. They require us to give God thanks and conduct our lives in communion with God. But Greek philosophy hoped to use reason without giving thanks. It substituted an impersonalist concept of reason and logic, in which reason and logic are just "there"—superior to the gods—rather than revealing the Creator. Philosophers rely not on the instruction of divine revelation but on human reason. In principle, they hope, human reason has the power to grasp holiness or justice or goodness or other important concepts in their essentiality, which is above the gods.

This reasoning rejects the true God. And in the process, it violates reason. True reason is the personal rationality of the Logos. The philosophers are in rebellion. And it should not be surprising that, in the foundations of philosophy, they commit two interlocking fallacies. They commit the fallacy of bifurcation, by presuming that autonomous use of reason is the only viable alternative to submission to unreliable gods (or unreliable "revelations"). They commit a fallacy of meaning by failing to acknowledge the infinite superiority of God's meanings and God's logic to their own use. They violate their own most essential principles by committing fallacies and thereby being irrational at the foundations.

Make no mistake. Philosophers through the centuries have often been very clever, gifted people. They have many insights through common grace.

But the project of seeking wisdom and acquiring it apart from communion with Christ is deep folly.

And what has been the result? René Descartes (1596–1650), a famous philosopher in his own time, did not speak optimistically about the successes of the project:

> As to philosophy, I shall say only this: that when I noted that it has been cultivated for many centuries by men of the most outstanding ability, and that none the less there is not a single thing of which it treats which is not still in dispute, and nothing, therefore, which is free from doubt, I was not so presuming as to expect that I should succeed where they had failed.[4]

> Already in my college days I had been brought to recognise that there is no opinion, however strange, and however difficult of belief, which has not been upheld by one or other of the philosophers.[5]

Philosophy in the Twentieth Century

Despite Descartes's discouraging words, Descartes himself endeavored to achieve a decisive breakthrough in the methods of reason. Philosophy, as a work of would-be autonomous reason, has continued actively into the twenty-first century. But people have become restless about it. Philosophy so far has failed to obtain assured answers to the big questions—questions about the nature of the world, the nature of the good, the nature of beauty, the nature of knowledge, the nature of reason, and the meaning of life and death. Individual philosophers do claim to offer abundant answers for our reflection. But there are multiple alternate answers from multiple philosophers, and no guarantee of a definitive resolution.

In the late twentieth century and early twenty-first century, many people have in practice turned away from philosophy. By and large, prestigious and powerful cultural leaders no longer look primarily to philosophy for guidance. Science seems to many people to be a better source, because it offers in a number of areas clear and well-supported results. It appears to be cumulative. It goes from strength to strength, rather than continually returning to the beginning to start over with a fresh plowing of the ground of reason.

---

[4]René Descartes, *Discourse on the Method of Rightly Conducting the Reason and of Seeking for Truth in the Sciences*, trans. Norman Kemp Smith, in *Descartes' Philosophical Writings* (London: Macmillan, 1952), 121.
[5]Ibid., 127.

Physical and biological science are limited in their scope by their starting focus to the material aspect of the world. But that has not prevented people like Richard Dawkins from blowing them up into a materialist worldview that is in fact a philosophy only loosely related to rigorous science. Others look to the social sciences, psychology, sociology, anthropology, political science, and economics, in the hope that these fields of study may gradually be able to provide guidance more reliable and more well-grounded than philosophy.

Parting Ways

Philosophy proper does still receive energetic engagement in some quarters, especially in university departments of philosophy, literature, and cultural criticism. To some extent, the study of philosophy has split in two in the twentieth century. To speak of a split is an oversimplification, but it is still useful to distinguish two main directions.

The first direction, associated more with continental (European) thought, has continued to ask the big questions about the nature of God, man, morality, and the world, and has offered its products in elaborate prose form, in continuity with previous generations of philosophy. Heidegger and the French existentialists, for example, meditated on the meaning of human existence, finiteness, and death.

The other stream, analytic philosophy, associated more with the Anglo-Saxon world, has tried to incorporate into its tradition the tight, rigorous, formal logic that has blossomed especially in the twentieth century. Whitehead and Russell's work *Principia Mathematica* became an inspiration for greater rigor not only in mathematics but beyond mathematics, in the discussion of much broader philosophical questions.

In my judgment, the first route, concerned with big questions, has run aground on postmodernism. The title of Alasdair MacIntyre's book *Whose Justice? Which Rationality?*[6] is symptomatic. Reason among human beings is culturally *situated*. It is *contextually* qualified. Everyone brings assumptions to the table. This reality tends to destroy hope of any final unity in producing human answers to big questions. Some postmodernists would say that we must "muddle through," as it were, doing the best we can to pick up clues within our limited cultural perspective. This chastening of

---

[6] Alasdair C. MacIntyre, *Whose Justice? Which Rationality?* (Notre Dame, IN: University of Notre Dame Press, 1988).

reason is a far cry from Euthyphro's initial confidence that he knows what holiness is.

Some postmodernists may still hope to stake out a more modest scope for human knowledge, and to promote peace and understanding by encouraging others to imitate their modesty. But there is a difficulty. The situated nature of reason will, I think, infect their endeavor as well as previous ones. Just as culturally generated variations in the operations of reason frustrate the project of getting "big answers" to big questions, so similar variations will frustrate the endeavor to get agreements on the nature of cultural modesty. Variations will infect the project to stake out "reasonable" boundaries for reason, and reasonable boundaries for cultural variation. Reason with no roots does not achieve permanent answers. The rational critique of reason devours not only its own foundations but all its fruits.

Yet the postmodernist concern about limitations to reason has a grain of truth. A Christian can readily agree that human reason on its own will not reach definitive answers. It will not, partly, because we are finite and God never designed us to operate successfully with autonomy. It will not, more fundamentally, because the gospel is "folly to Gentiles" (1 Cor. 1:23):

> For since, in the wisdom of God, the world did not know God through wisdom, it pleased God through the folly of what we preach to save those who believe. (1 Cor. 1:21)

Analytic Philosophy

What about analytic philosophy? Can philosophy rescue us by using the more rigorous methods of logic developed in the twentieth century, some of which we have explored in this book (parts II and III)? One movement within the early history of analytic philosophy hoped to purify language. According to its thinking, the fault that made philosophy fail was partly the slippage in natural language, which might be cured by constructing more formalized or perfected languages. These purified languages might, perhaps, match the rigorous language of physical science and its methods.

Logical positivism, also called logical empiricism, was one such attempt. A. J. Ayer[7] thought that the speculative philosophy of metaphysics was hopelessly muddled, because it was not empirically testable. People just went on speculating and speculating, and no one could test by any scientific

---

[7] A. J. Ayer, *Language, Truth, and Logic* (London: Gollancz, 1936).

means what claims were true. In fact, the lack of testability made the speculations "cognitively meaningless."

Hopes ran high, fueled by the successes of science in comparison with the failure of philosophical speculation. But logical positivism failed to secure its own foundation.

Logical positivism put forward the central thesis that only two kinds of propositions had cognitive meaning, namely, tautologies and empirically verifiable statements. All other propositions had only "emotive" significance. Speculative philosophy was consigned to the dustbin of history as merely "emotive." But positivism's own thesis about what was cognitively meaningful was neither tautologous nor empirically verifiable. So its thesis was not cognitively meaningful. Using its own criterion, logical positivism issued its own death-warrant.[8]

Other, less extreme currents within analytic philosophy still want to purify language. And, as we have seen in discussing formal logic, formal logic and formal symbolism do reduce ambiguity and offer some insight, *if we as human observers also recognize their limitations and their one-dimensionality*. Formal logic can be seen as a special supplement and enhancement to ordinary language, rather than as a replacement for it.

If formal logic is considered in this light, we can advocate an approach in which human beings with their full capabilities still play the decisive role. Human beings oversee the judgments as to what insights formalism offers in particular cases where it partly corresponds to one dimension of natural language. Human beings offer discerning judgments about the nature and the appropriateness of the partial correspondences—and those contextual judgments cannot themselves be formalized.

But now consider an alternative. Do we give *wholesale* commitment to the alleged superiority of formalization? The claim for superiority needs a foundation, and it cannot be provided. An attempt to do so within a formalized system is a circular argument. It uses formalism to establish formalism. Gödel's incompleteness theorems also stand in the way, in that they use formalism to demonstrate the limitations of formalism.

Moreover, God by his use of ordinary language in the Bible shows that ordinary language is usable. On that sort of basic level, there is nothing

---

[8] See Vern S. Poythress, *In the Beginning Was the Word: Language—A God-Centered Approach* (Wheaton, IL: Crossway, 2009), 351–352. But there were attempts at resuscitation. See Richard Creath, "Logical Empiricism," *Stanford Encyclopedia of Philosophy (Winter 2011 Edition)*, ed. Edward N. Zalta, http://plato.stanford.edu/archives/win2011/entries/logical-empiricism/, accessed October 15, 2012.

"wrong" with it, though there is plenty wrong with human misuse of language to lie, cheat, and deceive. We have a responsibility to grow in communion with God and in holiness. That responsibility cannot be evaded. And it is being evaded if we think that formalization will relieve us of responsibility by solving our problems of truth by purely formal means. At the end of the day *we* still have to make the judgment as to how a formalized or semi-formalized argument relates to the real world. How does a formalized logic, deliberately constructed to confine the focus to one dimension of language and truth, relate to the fullness of language and truth in God and in human beings made in the image of God?

The judgment of superiority given to formalized argument may neglect what can be learned by opening our eyes to the rich, multidimensional character of natural language. And people sometimes rate formalized argument as superior because they are influenced by a religious motive. People want to escape God and escape responsibility by creating a sphere that they can perfectly master and control. The desire for human autonomy underlies the process. By common grace, many fascinating achievements have come about in the fields of formalization. But the achievements do not overthrow the reality of the overall situation, that we in fact deal in a world of many dimensions using language with many dimensions.

The fallacies of meaning and of presumption and of relevance can creep in when people make the transition from formalized argument to the world at large. Are the meanings exactly the same in the two spheres? No. So we commit the fallacy of equivocation. Do the arguments transfer in a perfectly reliable fashion from one sphere to the other? The correspondences between a tightly controlled formal logical system and a rigorous metalanguage discussion of that system may be reliable, as Gödel's incompleteness results showed. But when we talk about correlation between formal systems and the richness of language and the world in which we live, the answer is no.

If we assume that the correlations are exact, we commit the fallacy of presumption. Is the formal sphere relevant to the world at large? Perhaps in some way. But the lack of perfect correspondence means that we can commit the fallacy of relevance when we appeal to a formal argument. The formal argument *looks* the same as reasoning about the world at large, but in fact it is not the same. Context makes a difference. Context is always there, and we as full human beings are always embedded in a context. We are responsible to be wise in the presence of God.

Formalization within formal logical systems, and the lesser formalization in philosophical attempts to clarify and purify language, have taken place partly out of human curiosity and out of a desire to explore small models imitating human reasoning. Like children, we construct our Lego towns. Much that can be admired has come out of the attempts. They display the ingenuity of the investigators and the beauty and wonder of what is investigated. But formalization has also had in mind the purpose of avoiding fallacies, to which ordinary human beings are prone. Ironically, the very process of formalization produces potential fallacies lurking in its context, ready to seize us when we assume that our specially shaped formal world has the power to dominate and dictate what can logically be the case in the real world. The desire for autonomous mastery betrays us into fallacies.

Ordinary Language Philosophy

In addition to the philosophical tradition that attempts to purify language, analytic philosophy includes a second tradition, called *ordinary language philosophy*. The tradition begins with Ludwig Wittgenstein. In the early part of his career, shortly before the rise of logical positivism, Wittgenstein anticipated some of the concerns of logical positivism by exploring the possibility of purifying language.[9] But he later gave it up. He decided that ordinary language was richer than his early formulation. He began to reflect on language and its context when used in human action. His followers developed his ideas further. Their contributions have been called "ordinary language philosophy," because they mainly analyze ordinary language rather than trying to purify it. At root, ordinary language philosophy proposes to gain insight from studying language as it is. And it proposes to leave language as it is rather than to purify it. The philosophical program has the conviction that language is already in good working order.

But ordinary language philosophy is in a bit of a dilemma.[10] If language is to be left as it is, we have, on the basis of human autonomy, no normative basis for judging some language to be defective and other language to be in working order. If, on the other hand, we criticize some language as defective, what grounds do we have to do so? Logic? But whose logic? "Which rationality?" as Alasdair MacIntyre asked. Wittgenstein appealed

---

[9] Ludwig Wittgenstein, *Tractatus Logico-philosophicus* (London: Routledge & Kegan Paul; New York: Humanities, 1963).
[10] I owe this insight to John Frame, who spoke of it in oral lectures on Wittgenstein.

to what he called a "form of life." Human life, social life in particular, was the context for understanding and evaluating language. But which form of life among many cultures? We can see how Wittgenstein's seminal reflections could lead to forms of multicultural postmodernism, where truth is in danger of being relativized to a cultural "form of life."

Moreover, the attempt to evaluate language leads in one way or another to a purification motif. If we are not careful, we are soon back into the dilemma of logical positivism, which wants purification but cannot purify its own foundations.

Fallacies also await us. The fallacy of meaning crops up if we equate meanings in pre-purified language and post-purified language. The fallacy of presumption awaits us if we assume that there is no third way in addition to the alternatives of (1) leaving everything the same (multi-cultural "tolerance") and (2) self-purifying (bootstrapping from an unfounded origin to a new purified language and world).

As usual, the Christian faith offers a third way. The fundamental "purification" comes from outside us, from God through Christ. That leads to a different conception of what it means to grow in wisdom in how to use language or logic or reason.

The history of philosophy, though it has many benefits from common grace, is a history of fallacies. The fundamental fallacy of meaning lies in the assumption that we can control meanings in a single-level universe without an absolute Creator. The fundamental fallacy of presumption is the presumption that autonomous reason will lead to truth rather than to fragments of truth inwardly corrupted by autonomous desire.

The use of logic in philosophy runs the danger of falling into a fallacy in another way. It is easy to assume that every participant in the discussion has the same conception of logic, rigor, and truth. Every participant should also have the same view of the relation between formalized and unformalized reasoning. As we have indicated in parts I and II, the Christian conception is distinct. The assumption of commonality therefore runs the danger of falling into the fallacy of presumption. And the assumption of common meaning between Christian and non-Christian runs the danger of falling into the fallacy of equivocation. Philosophers often do not discuss these difficulties. But it seems to me that the direction that they take tacitly suggests or assumes the validity of one-level reasoning, and therefore excludes a Christian view from the outset.

Autonomous philosophy, pretending to love wisdom, corrupts wisdom. Pretending to itself that it loves logic, it commits fallacies in the very foundations of its stance, its stance toward God and toward the world:

> Claiming to be wise, they became fools, and exchanged the glory of the immortal God for images . . . (Rom. 1:22–23)

Autonomous philosophy hates true logic, the Logos of God.

There is a true philosophy, that is, a true love of wisdom. The wisdom of God has become incarnate in Christ: "" ". . . Christ Jesus, who became to us wisdom from God" (1 Cor. 1:30). To love wisdom is to love Christ, "with all your heart and with all your soul and with all your mind" (Matt. 22:37).

For Further Reflection

1. How does Socrates's dialogue with Euthyphro illustrate both positive potential for uncovering unfounded autonomous confidence, and negative potential for encouraging autonomy?
2. What are the similarities and differences between the quest for wisdom in Western philosophy and the path of wisdom in 1 Corinthians 1 and Proverbs 1?
3. In the twentieth century, what cultural institutions have in part displaced the key role that philosophy once played in intellectual life?
4. What characterizes the distinction between Continental and Anglo-Saxon philosophy in the twentieth century?
5. In the twentieth century, what different courses have philosophical movements followed in their relation to logic and language?
6. What difficulties beset (a) ordinary language philosophy and (b) analytic philosophy that aspires to refine ordinary language?

A View of Modern Logic

The previous appendix shows some of the historical ties between logic and philosophy. Does logic today show influence from the philosophical tradition that seeks human autonomy in thought?

An Introduction to Logic

Let us consider a particular example. The textbook *Introduction to Logic* (2011) notes in the preface to its 14th edition that it is "the world's most widely used book in the study of logic."[1] In chapter 1, subsection 1.1, "What Logic Is," it introduces the subject with the following claim:

> Reasoning is not the only way in which people support assertions they make or accept. They may appeal to authority or to emotion, which can be very persuasive, or they may rely, without reflection, simply on habits. However, when someone wants to make judgments that can be completely relied upon, their only solid foundation will be correct reasoning. Using the methods and techniques of logic—the subject of this book—one can distinguish reliably between sound and faulty reasoning.[2]

This key paragraph introduces a notable contrast. On the one side stand authority, emotion, and reliance on habit. On the other side stands "correct reasoning." The authors commend logic as a worthy area of study because it enables people to "distinguish reliably between sound and faulty reasoning."

If we understand the distinction between strict deductive reasoning and other, looser forms of reasoning, we might want to interpret these claims generously. Perhaps the paragraph is merely saying that rigorous deduction results in conclusions that are certain, while induction and analogical reasoning typically do not. Unfortunately, the key paragraph does not contrast deduction with induction or analogy, but contrasts "correct reasoning" with

---

[1] Irving M. Copi, Carl Cohen, and Kenneth McMahon, *Introduction to Logic*, 14th ed. (Boston . . . : Prentice Hall, 2011), xvi.
[2] Ibid., 2.

authority, emotion, and habit.[3] By implication, authority cannot "be completely relied upon."

Authority

It is true that human authorities cannot "be completely relied upon." But what about divine authority? Has the paragraph accidentally overlooked divine authority? Or has it assumed that divine authority does not actually exist, or has it conflated divine authority with the authority of false religious claims to authority? Or is there some other explanation? It is hard to say.

In the medieval period in the Western world, the Bible enjoyed great authority. Then this authority was challenged, especially in the Enlightenment, by people who thought that human reason could and ought to sift through all religious claims. It is not plausible to think that the textbook *Introduction to Logic* is merely ignorant of this history, especially because it contains a number of short biographical notes on figures in the history of logic. Some of these figures, like Peter Abelard and William of Ockham, interacted strongly with the Christian religion and the Bible.[4]

For whatever reason, the paragraph has simply passed over the possibility of divine authority that would belong to a divinely authorized text, such as the Bible claims to be. The Bible as well as other authorities are, by implication, inferior in reliability to "sound . . . reasoning." If we want results that "can be completely relied upon," we cannot trust ourselves to anything except the "only solid foundation," namely, "correct reasoning."

This claim sounds similar to the discussion in Plato's *Euthyphro*, as to whether we can find out the real nature of holiness by inquiring what the gods prefer (see preceding appendix). Socrates requests, ". . . tell me what holiness is, no matter whether it is loved by the gods or anything else happens to it."[5] Interpreted in the context of Plato's writings, and in the context of the history of philosophy, this request of Socrates opens the way for a program of *rational autonomy*. It pointedly refuses to be instructed by revelation, but wants to know the truth by the operation of reason independent

---

[3] In addition, a supposed contrast between deductive and inductive reasoning does not work well in the context of the book as a whole, which has not only a part 2 on "Deduction" but also a part 3 on "Induction," and under induction includes a chapter on "Analogical Reasoning" (chapter 11). The claim for complete reliability, when taken strictly, applies at most only to part 2. Part 3 has on its first page the acknowledgment, "Induction [which cannot provide complete "demonstrative certainty"] thus provides the starting points—the foundation—for the reasoning that concerns us most" (ibid., 444).

[4] Copi, Cohen, and McMahon, *Introduction to Logic*, 35, 48.

[5] Plato, *Euthyphro*, trans. Harold N. Fowler (London: Heinemann; Cambridge, MA: Harvard University Press, 1966), 13B.

of revelation. Socrates, speaking around 400 BC, wants truths that can be relied upon *independent* of any external authority. Our modern logic book, speaking in 2011, similarly appears to champion complete reliability independent of any external authority. Apparently, the tradition of autonomy continues into the present.

We cannot be sure of all the meanings or implications that the authors intended in this key paragraph. We do not want to impose an ungenerous interpretation. Maybe there was some accidental oversight. But we also want to consider how the paragraph *will be read*—whether or not it was intended to be so read.[6] It will be read as a reinforcement of autonomous reasoning. It is not so surprising that it will be read this way, because autonomy has a strong influence in the West. In the modern world, autonomy is in some ways the cultural atmosphere that we breathe, particularly in intellectual circles and in most colleges and universities where logic is taught. It goes without saying in many circles that "we modern people" reject claims of divine authority.

Irony of Using What You Reject

Why is it so easy for modern readers to pass by the possibility of divine authority when they read a paragraph like the one we have quoted? First, divine authority as a source for certainty and reliability is being rejected partly by *habit*. In many people's lives, there is no discussion, no careful weighing of options, no argument concerning alternatives. The passing over of divine authority is part of our cultural atmosphere. Second, divine authority is rejected partly by tacit use of *authority*, namely, the authority that belongs to a tradition of autonomy and the authority invested in universities and schools that follow this tradition. The university says, "This, and not otherwise, is how we conduct our analysis."

Third, at least for some readers, rejection of divine authority also takes place on the basis of *emotional* factors. Some people find it convenient to reject divine authority because it is emotionally painful to have to deal with the possibility that they may be guilty in the presence of a holy God. They are indeed guilty because of sin; at the same time, their emotional response arises from sin.

---

[6] I would like to allow leeway here. But Copi, Cohen, and McMahon, *Introduction to Logic*, in section 3.3, section 3.6 rule 6, and section 4.6 (pp. 75–76, 97, 140–142), make a point of targeting ambiguity, and pointing out that it represents a hazard in argument. By the criteria that the book champions, it is not ideal to have crucial unanswered questions about meaning in the very paragraph that introduces the nature of logic. The ambiguities threaten to infect one's conception of logic, and thereby contaminate the whole book.

Thus, the three rejected sources for judgment, namely authority, emotion, and habit, all tend to play a significant role in the acceptance of the very paragraph in which they are said to be rejected. To crown the irony, people may uncritically accept the claims of the paragraph partly because, if they learn to use "correct reasoning," they can feel superior to those who follow authority, emotion, and habit. They are being swayed by their own emotional desire for superiority.

Ground to Stand

Consider another kind of difficulty. Correct reasoning is not enough. As all textbooks on logic recognize, deductive reasoning must have premises. And the premises cannot be guaranteed by deduction except on the basis of other, earlier premises. These premises in turn need still earlier premises. Where do we get a secure starting point?

Some premises, like $2 + 2 = 4$, or axioms of propositional logic, might be accepted as "secure." But in many matters of importance, the premises cannot be secured in a manner that "can be completely relied upon," at least if we apply the criteria for deductive rigor that professional logicians themselves bring to the process. Hence, conclusions that depend on the premises cannot produce "judgments that can be completely relied upon." The logic book cannot deliver what the naive reader expects on the basis of its opening invitation.

We might attempt to rescue the cogency of our key paragraph by proposing that the "judgments" in question are judgments *only* about the validity of the reasoning *process*, not judgments about the truth of the conclusions. But on page 2 of the logic textbook, readers can hardly be expected to produce such a sophisticated and nonobvious interpretation. To a naive reader, "judgments" must include judgments with respect to issues of life and issues of importance—political, ethical, religious, personal, scientific. So the book promises more than it can deliver.

And now, another irony: such "judgments that can be completely relied upon" *can* be attained by relying on the Bible. Authority—divine authority—will do what our key paragraph falsely implies that logic can do. Here is one reliable judgment: "God so loved the world that he gave his only Son, that whoever believes him should not perish but have eternal life" (John 3:16). There are many others. These judgments "can be completely relied upon" not because we can, through autonomous reasoning, make them completely transparent and see to their deepest foundations, and not because we can deductively establish them from premises even more secure, but because we can trust God whose speech is reliable.

Even if an unbeliever dismisses the Bible, he cannot dismiss either authority or habit. He relies on the authority of his parents or guardians or other parental substitutes who were instrumental in teaching him language and social skills. He relies on the habits of language and social skills that he has now internalized. Thus, he must presuppose authority and habit in the form of skill if he is going to start reading the key paragraph in *Introduction to Logic*. The paragraph says, "their only solid foundation will be correct reasoning." Strictly speaking, that is an illusion even when we deal with logic textbooks, because the solidity of language and habit must first be in place before it is possible even to build solidity in one's understanding of the subject matter in the textbooks. If we lose confidence in language and habit, we fall into total skepticism or into insanity. What sense does it make to trust the language in the logic textbook if we cannot trust our knowledge of language and our habits of reading?

Fallacies

Our key paragraph exhibits a further irony. Given the concerns that we have mentioned, the paragraph seems to contain fallacies. One is the fallacy of bifurcation. The paragraph tacitly assumes that the only alternative to autonomous reasoning is some kind of unreliability. It also commits another fallacy of presumption by (apparently) assuming that correct reasoning is the *only* solid foundation, when in fact we have to supplement it in practice with authority, emotion, and habit. It also commits a fallacy of presumption when it overlooks the fact that judgments have to depend on premises as well as correct reasoning from premises to conclusions.

The paragraph is also in danger of a fallacy of equivocation, because some of the key terms can be used in more than one way. We have seen that the word "judgment" can describe either a narrow judgment about the validity of a piece of deductive reasoning from premises, or a much broader judgment about the truth of a conclusion, based both on evaluating the truth of the premises and on reasoning from the premises. The word "authority" can include or exclude divine authority. The expression "completely relied upon" can refer to the special standards of rigor that apply to formal deductive arguments, or, for the naive reader, can refer to the kind of reliability that we would like to have in making major life decisions.

But perhaps our key paragraph is not an argument at all. Is it just an explanation or a series of observations, intended to speak loosely? Again, we cannot say for sure what may have been the exact configuration of intentions on the part of the authors. The paragraph is looser than many of the more explicit arguments later in the book. But the book provides in chapter 1 a subsection that explicitly discusses "Recognizing Arguments."[7] Quite insightfully, it indicates that arguments may not always be wholly explicit. By its own loose criteria, the key paragraph on page 2 does seem to be an argument. It is designed to persuade people that it is worthwhile to study logic. We can even construct some of the additional unstated propositions:

1. You ought to want to make judgments that can be completely relied upon.
2. If someone wants to make judgments that can be completely relied upon, he must use correct reasoning.
3. If someone learns logic, he can distinguish correct reasoning.
4. If someone can distinguish correct reasoning, he can use correct reasoning.
5. If someone must use correct reasoning, he ought to study all the means that give him that ability.
6. Conclusion: you ought to learn logic.

The above argument is still not completely "tight," by the tight standards of syllogistic deduction, but it suggests that the key paragraph does present an argument. And this argument may contain hidden fallacies.

In principle, fallacies in a recommendation for learning logic need not affect the substance of logic. But there is still a difficulty. This particular recommendation has force partly because of its implications about the nature of logic, as something worthy of being pursued. Logic, it appears, functions as part of the way of autonomy: logic is one key to the "only solid foundation," namely, "correct reasoning" in distinction from authority. The reader is invited to understand logic as logic that is being pursued as part of the program for human autonomy in reasoning. And so the paragraph (as we interpret it) invites readers to treat logic itself as an aspect of autonomous reasoning.

Since the book's invitation depends on fallacies, this conception of logic remains without rational foundation. Such a situation is not an ideal starting point for readers to build sound knowledge of logic.

---

[7] Copi, Cohen, and McMahon, *Introduction to Logic*, section 1.3, p. 11.

For Further Reflection

1. Why is the issue of authority significant? Explain the possible ambiguity in the term.
2. Why is a sound reasoning *process* insufficient for reliable knowledge?
3. What significance can be found in the idea of a starting point for reliability? Is there more than one conception of a starting point, and if so what are they?
4. Can the key paragraph in the textbook be "rescued" by reconstruing it?
5. How might the full participation of human users of logic as persons influence the ability of a logic textbook to establish secure foundations for what it claims to do?
6. What kinds of reliance ("completely relied upon") may be in view by various parties, including professional logicians, students of logic, and potential readers with broader interests?
7. How do the questions that surface in this appendix relate to questions about the nature of logic in part I.B?

Modal Ontological Argument

As an example of the use of logic in arguments concerning God, we focus on modal ontological argument for the existence of God. Kurt Gödel wrote up one such argument, which was not published until after his death. It has been refined and reworked by a number of others. Alvin Plantinga offered another argument, which we choose because of its relative simplicity:

> There is a possible world in which there is an entity which possesses maximal greatness.
> (Hence) There is an entity which possesses maximal greatness.[1]

The language about "a possible world" takes us into the field of models for modal logic (chapter 67).

How does this argument move from possibility to actual existence? It builds the concept of necessity into the meaning of "maximal greatness." Earlier, Plantinga has specified its meaning: "An entity possesses 'maximal greatness' if and only if . . . it is necessarily existent and necessarily maximally excellent."[2]

Let G stand for the proposition that an entity exists that is maximally excellent (not maximally great). Then to say there is a maximally great entity is to say that it is necessary that G is true. In the formal notation of modal logic, $\Box G$. So the first premise says that it is possible that it is necessary that G is true. In formal notation, this premise comes out

$$\Diamond \Box G$$

---

[1] Cited in Graham Oppy, "Ontological Arguments," *Stanford Encyclopedia of Philosophy (Fall 2011 Edition)*, ed. Edward N. Zalta, http://plato.stanford.edu/archives/fall2011/entries/ontological-arguments/, accessed August 24, 2012, §7.
[2] Ibid.

The conclusion is

□G

The conclusion does follow in the S5 version of modal logic, where every possible world is accessible from every other.[3]

The argument is formally valid, given the version (S5) for modal logic that we have set up. Some people might, of course, dispute the choice of the S5 version, which is stronger than some other forms of modal logic.

But there is another difficulty. Alvin Plantinga himself admits that the argument may not be convincing, even if it is sound. The same is true of virtually any deductive argument whose premises and conclusions address the actual world. Suppose we present such an argument. "All men are mortal. Socrates is a man. Therefore Socrates is mortal." One person might be convinced of the conclusion because he already accepts the premises. Another person might be already convinced that the conclusion is false. Maybe he thinks that Socrates has come to him in a dream and asserted his own immortality. By *modus tollens* (a valid form of argument), he concludes that one of the premises is false. Maybe Socrates is not really a man. Or maybe Socrates is man, but constitutes an exception to the claim that all men are mortal. A person's firm conviction that Socrates is not mortal leads to his reexamining the premises, and denying one or both of them.

In the case of Plantinga's argument for the existence of a "maximally great" entity, there is only one premise. So an atheist will deduce that ◊□G must be false.

Modal Logic as Revealing God

Since we have tried to examine some of the ways in which God's glory is revealed in logic in general and in modal logic in particular, we can make some other observations about this argument. It is an interesting argument, and it has some correlations with the real world. It is subject to the nor-

---

[3] As usual, universal accessibility means that every possible world that is accessible at all, or from which our world is accessible, is accessible directly. But the postulates of S5 cannot exclude a model where there are other universes of worlds, all of which are inaccessible to our local group of possible worlds and from which there is no access to our local group.

   Here is the reasoning that establishes the conclusion □G. Assume the premise, namely, ◊□G. Let the initial world be E. By definition of the symbol ◊ in the model, there exists a possible world W in which □G. By definition of the symbol □, G is true in all possible worlds (in the subset of mutually accessible worlds). Therefore, back in E, G is true. Moreover, G is true in all the other worlds accessible from E. Hence □G in E.

mal limitations that we saw in discussing possibility and possible worlds in modal logic (chapters 65–67).

Since modal logic as a whole reveals God, so does this particular argument. Since models in modal logic reveal God, so does the model of possible worlds in this particular argument. The argument would reveal God even if the subject of the argument were something other than the existence of God. The difficulty with the atheist or agnostic starts before the argument gets moving, because he is suppressing the truth that he knows from the world around him (Rom. 1:18) and from the revelation of God's character in logic itself.

A Finite God?

Plantinga's argument has an additional difficulty because God is the infinite Creator. God is not an "entity" *within* a possible world. Maybe the language concerning possible worlds does not intend to say that God is finite, but the idea that "an entity which possesses maximal greatness" can be described as related to "a possible world *in which* there is an entity . . ." invites us to have a picture in which God is *confined* to a world—in other words, it invites a picture in which an entity "with maximal greatness" is finite.

A similar difficulty arises on a more general level when we consider having possible worlds and modal logic, both of which seem to operate independent of whether there is a God. By so doing, they might allegedly enable us to come later to the conclusion that there is (or is not) a God. The logic ruling over the possible worlds, and the idea of possibility that enables us to conceptualize these worlds, can easily be taken to be an impersonal absolute above God who is supposed to be a personal absolute. So the formulation of this argument produces temptations to violate the absoluteness of God and to ignore the dependence of logic and worlds on God.

One way of patching up the argument would be to say that the "worlds" in question are not to be construed as physical universes, but as maximal "states of affairs," that is, descriptions that would include all possible facts not only about the created world but about God as well. One difficulty here is that a "maximal" description of God can be achieved only by God himself, because of God's incomprehensibility. A second, minor difficulty is that if the description includes God, it must describe God's thoughts, not only about this world but also about possible worlds that he imagines but does not create. These other worlds can still be distinguished from the actual world by the fact that God knows them as possibilities rather than actualities. Still, the presence of these worlds within the description makes less "clean" the characterization of this world as "actual." Finally, a danger arises that we would then treat all facts about all states of affairs as facts on a single "level," thereby threatening to undermine the Creator-creature distinction. All in all, the language that "includes" God *within* one or more possible worlds does not appear to work well with the Creator-creature distinction.

Views of Logic

Next, we must as usual confront the issue of whether there is a distinctively Christian logic. It is quite possible for the argument to be interpreted within a framework of personal commitments, where the recipient of the argument already presupposes a non-Christian view of logic. Then it will not prove the existence of God. If, as a non-Christian view presupposes, logic is one-level logic, with no Creator-creature distinction, then the word "entity" represents a variable that can in theory range only over creatures. If we prove the existence of an entity, it must be a finite entity on the same level as other finite entities. If, on the other hand, we maintain a Creator-creature distinction, the argument has built into it an *analogical* rather than univocal meaning for "entity." A non-Christian may not accept that an analogical argument is sound because it is no longer formal.

Because the argument is formalized at least to some extent, we must as persons use the full context of our own humanity, and our relationship to God and to his truth, when we assess in what ways the formalized argument correlates with arguments in the larger world of ordinary language. The meanings do not correlate in a one-to-one fashion, precisely because on the one side we have formalization that reduces meaning from the richness of human experience to a one-dimensional precision. If the meanings do not correlate perfectly, the non-Christian could object that we are being equivocal.

In a Christian view, by contrast, analogy is built into all meaning because man is made in the image of God. All sound logic admits the presence of analogical thinking in the contextual background. Analogical thinking, and the personal involvement and commitments that go with it, provide the indispensable context for understanding the meaning of formalization.

Formalization gives us a kind of one-dimensional scale model for full-blown human reasoning, just as the child's town built out of Legos gives us a model for a town. A model town can teach us and draw attention to features in real towns. It can be helpful. But we enter a world of confused thinking if we do not admit to ourselves that we must always be ready to assess, as full persons, in what ways the model town does teach us, and in what ways it may be misleading us.

If we confuse the model with the town, we have fallen into error. Likewise, if we confuse formalized argument with substantive reasoning by human beings, we have fallen into error. If we evade the responsibility to do assessment of the relationships on the basis of full knowledge of context, including the context of our fellowship with God (or alienation from God), we have fallen into rebellious confusion. In a sense, then, formalization when viewed as the substance of an argument presents more of an illusion of argument than a genuine argument. It hides some of the essential ingredients for sound logic. And such hiding can tempt human beings into autonomous stances toward logic, toward theistic arguments, and toward their moral responsibility before God.

It is wise to surrender and to give God thanks, not only for his majesty revealed in logic, but for his mercy in not immediately condemning us for our sins. Not the least of those sins is the desire for human autonomy in logic. *Every* formalized argument that is alleged to be relevant to genuine human issues includes also the possibility of this temptation.

For Further Reflection

1. What common difficulties does Plantinga's ontological argument share with other arguments for the existence of God?
2. What are the strengths and weaknesses of the route that Plantinga has set forth?
3. What dependencies on God operate in the argument?
4. How might Christian and non-Christian concepts of transcendence and immanence (chapter 14) be applied to the issue of whether God exists in some possible world?
5. What is one difficulty with the idea that a supreme being resides within a possible world?

Reforming Ontology and Logic

[The following article by Vern Poythress, originally entitled "Reforming Ontology and Logic in the Light of the Trinity: An Application of Van Til's Idea of Analogy," was published in the *Westminster Theological Journal* 57/1 (1995): 187–219. Used with permission. A few formatting changes have been made to conform the style to the rest of this book.]

ABSTRACT

Reflection on John 1:1 can lead us in reforming our conceptions of fundamental philosophical categories and logic.

John 1:1 shows that understanding the Trinity involves three aspects inextricably. First, there is *classification*. Each Person of the Trinity is classified as God. Second, there is *instantiation*. Each Person is particular, an "instantiation" of God, distinct from the other Persons. Third, there is an *associational* aspect. Each Person exists in association and communion with the other Persons ("the Word was with God").

The language describing these aspects of the Trinity works by analogy with language used in describing the classificational, instantiational, and associational aspects of creaturely things. Since the Trinity is ontologically ultimate, the aspects of creatures derive from and depend on the aspects of the Trinity.

In contrast to the coinherence of classificational, instantiational, and associational aspects, philosophical realism postulates that universals or fundamental categories exist with a classificational aspect alone, independent of instantiational and associational aspects. This approach is therefore covertly unitarian rather than Trinitarian in its roots. Analogous problems belong to philosophical nominalism and to the fundamental categories of Platonic and Aristotelian philosophy.

Since modern conceptions of syllogism and logic depend on the Aristotelian framework of categories, we must undertake a fundamental reform of logic as well as of metaphysical categories.

God is the all-sufficient Creator and King of the universe (Ps. 103:19). We are creatures made in the image of God (Gen. 1:26–28). What are the implications of these fundamental biblical ideas for ontology and logic?

Beginning with the Basics

Let us begin with the basics. According to the Bible, the Creator-creature distinction is fundamental (Genesis 1; Isaiah 40; 1 Cor. 8:6; Col. 1:15–17). There are two levels of being, two levels of existence: the self-sufficient, original existence of God the Creator, and the dependent, derivative existence of creatures.[1]

By contrast, non-Christian philosophy pretends that there is only one universal level of being.[2] Then within this universal being one may differentiate different types of being, such as trees, horses, human beings, or perhaps even gods. A god might be more powerful and more knowledgeable than human beings, but nevertheless exists in conformity with universal principles with respect to "being itself." Philosophy pretends to uncover these principles. On the basis of such philosophical insight, philosophers then dictate to the gods what is and is not possible. According to the Bible all such thinking is inherently self-deifying and idolatrous (2 Cor. 10:5; Isaiah 40).

The ontological distinction between Creator and creature has implications for epistemology.[3] God's knowledge must be differentiated from the knowledge that creatures have (Isa. 40:28). God's knowledge is original and self-sufficient (Isa. 40:13–14). Our knowledge is derivative and dependent (Ps. 94:10).[4]

But we do have true knowledge (John 17:3). God is not the unknown god of some philosophers, but the God and Father of Jesus Christ, who has revealed himself through Jesus Christ, through the word of God in Scripture, and through general revelation (Rom. 1:18–21; Psalm 19). Ontologically, human beings are created in the image of God (Gen. 1:26–28). They are thus "analogical" to God.[5] Likewise, epistemologically,

---

[1] Cornelius Van Til, *An Introduction to Systematic Theology* (Phillipsburg, NJ: Presbyterian & Reformed, 1974), 12: "Christians believe in two levels of existence, the level of God's existence as self-contained and the level of man's existence as derived from the level of God's existence"; cf. Cornelius Van Til, *The Defense of the Faith*, 2nd ed. (Philadelphia: Presbyterian & Reformed, 1963), 29.

[2] Van Til, *Systematic Theology*, 21.

[3] Ibid., 12.

[4] Ibid., 14–20; Van Til, *Defense*, 39–41.

[5] Throughout our reflections we use "analogy" and "analogical" in the sense that Cornelius Van Til did, namely, to express the derivative, dependent, and genuine character of our human knowledge. In talking this way we do not make any specific pronouncement on whether any particular statement about God is literal

their knowledge is analogically related to God's knowledge.[6]

The Word as Standard

Now let us turn to a specific word of God, namely, "In the beginning was the Word, and the Word was with God, and the Word was God" (John 1:1). Let us consistently apply theistic reasoning, that is, analogical reasoning, to this passage. When we do so, we find that it destroys all would-be autonomous human thinking.

The Word is the Second Person of the Trinity, who became incarnate in the fullness of time (John 1:14). What does it mean that he is called "the Word"? In the context of John 1:1–18 there are several allusions to the account of creation in Genesis 1. The contextual allusions to creation make it clear that we are to relate what is said in John 1:1 to the words that God spoke in creating the heavens and earth, as recorded in Genesis 1. According to Genesis 1, God spoke. God *said*, "Let there be light" (Gen. 1:3). As Psalm 33:6 summarizes it, "By the *word* of the LORD were the heavens made, their starry host by the breath of his mouth." God later spoke to human beings, as in Genesis 1:28–30.

By calling the Second Person of the Trinity "the Word," God invites us to see a relation between the Second Person of the Trinity and the speech of God at creation. The two are analogous. God alone fully knows the character of the analogy. But we can understand that he is saying that the two are analogous. We can even see some aspects of the analogy. In both cases the word of God has divine power and divine wisdom. In both cases God expresses who he is in what he says.

The speech of God at creation is striking. We might be tempted to call it unusual, because there is no obvious human addressee involved. Genesis 1 nevertheless represents God as *saying* something. God invites us to understand *this* saying as somehow similar to the saying in which God addresses human beings. The two kinds of sayings are analogous, else there is no point in representing God as "saying" in Genesis 1. But here we sense that the two kinds of sayings are analogous rather than identical in every respect. God normally addresses human beings in human languages that they already

---

or figurative. See John M. Frame, *The Doctrine of the Knowledge of God* (Phillipsburg, NJ: Presbyterian & Reformed, 1987), 36.

[6] Van Til, *Defense*, 39–46. We focus primarily on what is true by virtue of creation. But subsequent to the fall, we make a radical distinction between non-Christians, who suppress the knowledge of God (Rom. 1:18–21), and Christians, who welcome such knowledge and grow in it (John 17:3).

know. But when God speaks without a human addressee, what language does he speak? It is not clear. It is mysterious. The Bible nevertheless teaches us to believe that this other kind of speaking is genuinely analogous to the instances when God speaks to us.

Now we may consider how we understand the instances when God speaks to us. He speaks to us in a human language. (In the canon of Scripture God uses the languages Hebrew, Greek, and Aramaic.) We understand the human language and the particular words partly by reference to what those words mean in other circumstances, including circumstances when human beings speak to one another. We all learn our native tongue from human beings who speak to us. The upshot is that we understand God's speaking to us by analogy with human beings who speak to us and who speak to other human beings as well.

God is master of all these analogies, whereas we are not. But we do recognize that they *are* analogies. God himself has told us so, through the way he has spoken to us in Scripture! If there were no analogy, we would not be able to understand the description of the Second Person of the Trinity as the "Word."

We also know from Scripture that God, not we, is the standard and origin for these analogies. The Word, the Second Person of the Trinity, is the standard for the analogically related word of God to us. The word to us is the standard for the analogically related words of human beings to one another.

Naming

We may observe a similar pattern with respect to the area of names and naming. God names himself (Gen. 17:1; 26:24; 49:24; Ex. 3:13–14). God gives names to created things (Gen. 1:5, 8, 10). Adam gave names to the animals (Gen. 2:19–20). Later human beings also bestow names (Gen. 25:25–26; 17:5 [in this case, God is renaming Abraham]). We use names that have already been bestowed by others.

This truth already suggests that *every* name or term in human language is ultimately mysterious. We understand any term whatsoever only by analogy with God's understanding of the term. And we understand God's understanding of the term only by analogy with his understanding of his own name. God's name is ultimately mysterious because he is self-sufficient and self-defining (Ex. 3:13–14; Judges 13:18; Ex. 34:5–6; 33:19–20).

Yet God has not left us in complete ignorance of his name. When Jesus commands us to make disciples, he talks about ". . . baptizing them in the *name* of the Father and of the Son and of the Holy Spirit" (Matt. 28:19). God's name, revealed climactically through Christ, is Trinitarian.

Aspects of God's Self-revelation in John 1:1

Let us pursue this mystery a little further, by returning to John 1:1. We focus particularly on some of the features of this text that offer a foundation for our thinking about particulars and universals, or better, things and the larger groups to which they belong.

"In the beginning was the Word." The Word "was." The Word existed. How can we possibly understand this language? We understand the language because we know of other instances of similar uses of the word *was*. The temple of Solomon once "was." We are working with an analogy between the existence of created things and the existence of the Word.

Created things exist for a time, temporally. The Word exists eternally. He always "was." Created things exist in a dependent way (Acts 17:28; Heb. 1:3; Col. 1:17; Rom. 11:36). God exists independently, *a se*. There is a distinction between two types of existence.

But there is also, unavoidably, an analogy. We can use this language, with the words *was*, *exists*, and so on, because there is an analogy between the existence of the Creator and the existence of creatures. Apart from some analogy, there is no reason why these words of John 1:1 should be used instead of any other words, or instead of no words at all (mere silence).

The Word exists in his specific particularity. He is a particular Person. By analogy, created things are particular things. They remain, even in their dependent existence, self-identical through time.

"And the Word was with God." The Word is who he is not only in his particularity but in fellowship with God. As John 1:18 says, the One and Only "is at the Father's side." There is a fellowship of love and communion between the Father and Son. This relation is expressed in a rich multitude of ways elsewhere in the Gospel of John. "The Father loves the Son" (John 3:35). They share in glory "before the world began" (John 17:5). They indwell one another (John 17:21).

Again, we understand this language by analogy. We have experience of loving other human beings, of being beside them and with them, and so on. The relation of the Father to the Son is described by analogy with human relations. Jesus even makes the analogy explicit when he prays that his people may be one "*just as* you are in me and I am in you" (John 17:21).

As usual, in this analogical relation, the being of God has the primacy. People exist in association with other people because first of all and primarily, the Word exists in association with God the Father. Human words exist in association with other words because, first of all, the eternal Word exists in association with God.

"And the Word was God." In view of the testimony elsewhere in John and elsewhere in the rest of the Bible, we know that this assertion does not mean that the Word is to be identified with the Father, in a modalistic or mathematical sense. According to the Bible as well as later orthodoxy, the Father is God, and the Word is God. But the Word is distinct from the Father, as the preceding clause already reminds us, "The Word was with God."

Hence, in the assertion, "The Word was God," the Word is classified as God. Likewise the Father and the Spirit, though distinct from the Word, are classified as God. We understand such statements by analogy with other statements in human language. For example, when we say, "This liquid is water," we do not mean that this liquid is the only thing that is water. We may also say, "That other liquid is water." By analogy, we say that the Word is God and the Father is God.

Nevertheless, as usual, the relation here involves analogy rather than identity. Distinctions must be made as well. Any particular piece of water is a part of all the water in the world. But the Word is not a "part" of God. The mutual indwelling of the Father and the Son assures us that "in Christ all the *fullness* of the Deity lives in bodily form" (Col. 2:9).

There is then an analogy between the plurality of Persons in the Trinity and the plurality of created things of the same kind. In this analogy, the Creator has primacy. There is a plurality of things that are water, a plurality of apple trees, and a plurality of human beings because first of all, preeminently, there is a plurality of Persons in the Trinity.

A Triad of Attributes

The revelation of God in John 1:1 is mysterious and never exhaustively analyzable by us. But we can conveniently summarize our results so far in terms of three attributes or perfections belonging to God and to the Persons of the Godhead. First, there is particularity or individuality. God is particular. The Word is particular. Each Person of the Godhead is particular. Let us call this particularity the *instantiational* aspect. Each Person is an instantiation of God.

Second, God exists in fellowship and communion. The Persons of the Godhead exist in association with other Persons, in context of fellowship with other Persons. We may call this aspect the *associational* aspect.

Third, the Persons of the Godhead are all God. They are classified using the category "God." We may call this aspect the *classificational*.[7]

The *classificational* aspect expresses the fact that the three Persons share common attributes and are all God. Thus it is closely related to the *unity* of the three Persons in one God. The *instantiational* aspect expresses the particularity of each Person, and in this way is closely related to the *plurality* of Persons in the Godhead. But of course each Person is one Person, with unity. And the one God is three Persons, with diversity. Unity and diversity are "equally ultimate," as Van Til reminds us.[8]

We understand these three aspects only through God's revelation to us. God speaks John 1:1 and other words of the Bible to us in order that we may understand. In this process of revelation, we understand analogically.

For example, we understand the associational aspect of mutual fellowship and indwelling within the Trinity, because God consents to have fellowship with us through the work of Christ and the Holy Spirit. Preeminently, God the Father sends the Holy Spirit to us to dwell in us (Rom. 8:9–11). Through the Spirit Christ dwells in us (Rom. 8:10) and the Father as well (John 14:23). The indwelling of the Father and the Son is analogically related to the indwelling of the Holy Spirit in us (John 17:23). Thus, the associational aspect is closely related to the work of the Holy Spirit.

We also understand instantiation analogically. The Word is eternally the instantiation of God. By analogy, the Word became flesh and "instanti-

---

[7] These three categories, classificational, instantiational, and associational, are closely related to my earlier categories of contrast, variation, and distribution, respectively. The earlier labels are used in Vern S. Poythress, *Philosophy, Science and the Sovereignty of God* (Nutley, NJ: Presbyterian & Reformed, 1976), 123; and Vern S. Poythress, "A Framework for Discourse Analysis: The Components of a Discourse, from a Tagmemic Viewpoint," *Semiotica* 38/3–4 (1982): 277–298. The earlier categories derive from Kenneth L. Pike's feature mode, manifestation mode, and distribution mode, in Pike, *Language in Relation to a Unified Theory of the Structure of Human Behavior*, 2nd rev. ed. (The Hague/Paris: Mouton, 1967), 84–93; see also Kenneth L. Pike, *Linguistic Concepts: An Introduction to Tagmemics* (Lincoln: University of Nebraska Press, 1982), 41–65. I employ a new terminology here in order to make my meaning more transparent, to emphasize the basis for the categories in Trinitarian revelation in John 1:1, and to expand the potential range of application of the categories. My newer terms express aspects of God, and analogically they pertain to anything in creation. They have the generality of Pike's earlier terminology of three "modes." By contrast, the terms *contrast, variation,* and *distribution* are customarily narrower: they denote three aspects of descriptions of linguistic units. They are thus the expression of classificational, instantiational, and associational aspects in a particular area, namely, in the description of a single linguistic unit.

[8] Van Til, *Defense*, 25.

ated" God in time and space (John 1:14). We understand the eternal instantiation by analogy with the temporal one. The instantiational aspect is related to the Second Person of the Trinity.

We understand classification analogically. God the Father, God the Son, and God the Holy Spirit are God. But in the revelation in time, God the Father is preeminently the one called "God." He is the one who first represents the attributes of God. Moreover, the classificational aspect focuses on what is the same or common to all instantiations. All instantiations are instantiations belonging to the *same* one class. The Son becomes incarnate, and the Holy Spirit is sent, both of which are dynamic actions in relation to the *sameness* of the eternal plan of the Father (Acts 2:22–23, 32–36). Hence, the classificational aspect is especially expressed in God the Father.

We should not think that this situation is strange. Because God is self-sufficient, the revelation of God comes from the supply of his self-sufficiency. The process of revelation is inherently Trinitarian because God is the Trinitarian God. The classificational, instantiational, and associational aspects of revelation reflect the character of God as Father, Son, and Spirit. The classificational aspect reflects the character of God the Father, who is the same through all the dynamicity of God's historical actions. The instantiational aspect reflects the character of God the Son, who became flesh for us. The associational aspect of mutual fellowship and indwelling reflects the character of God the Holy Spirit, who indwells us.

By virtue of the coinherence of the Persons of the Trinity, God's revelation of himself is also coinherent. Hence we may also note that each Person of the Trinity is eternally God. Each possesses the attributes of God and thus manifests the classificational aspect. Each Person of the Trinity is a particular Person, an "instantiation," thus manifesting the instantiational aspect. Each Person of the Trinity is with the other Persons, thus manifesting the associational aspect.

In addition, we can appreciate an analogy between the coinherence of the Persons of the Trinity and the coinherence of the classificational, instantiational, and associational aspects. Coinherence of these aspects follows from the fact that all three aspects derive from God, who is one.

First, consider the instantiational aspect, as expressed in John 1:1a, "In the beginning was the Word." The assertion of the eternality of the Word implies his deity. That is, the Word is "classified" as God. Thus the instantiational aspect implicates the classificational. Moreover, the designation "Word" indicates that he is the Word spoken by Someone. In the context, that Someone must be the Father. Hence the Word is already in association with the Father. The instantiational aspect thus implicates the associational aspect.

Now consider John 1:1b, "the Word was with God." The word *God* refers to the Father, and in that reference already presupposes the classification of the Father as God. Hence, the associational statement in 1b implicates the classificational aspect. Moreover, the Word must remain the Word in his particularity in all three clauses of John 1:1. Hence, he is involved in his instantiational aspect in 1:1b. Hence the associational presupposes the instantiational.

In like manner, in 1:1c, the mention of the Word presupposes his instantiational identity. Hence the classificational aspect, as expressed in 1:1c, presupposes the instantiational.

In order not to collapse 1c into modalistic heresy, we assert that the Word is not mathematically identical with the entirety of the Godhead—in particular, that he is distinct from the Father. To be classified as God, in the particular sense of John 1:1c, demands that there be simultaneously other instantiations, namely, the Father and the Spirit. Hence, the classificational aspect presupposes the associational aspect.

All three of these aspects, classificational, instantiational, and associational, are incomprehensible. The classificational aspect is an expression of God's distinctiveness as God, and of the distinctive work of the Father, which is incomprehensible. The instantiational aspect is an expression of the plurality of Persons in the Godhead and of the unique work of the Son in the incarnation, which is incomprehensible. The associational aspect is an expression of the mutual indwelling and coinherence of Persons of the Trinity, and of the unique work of the Holy Spirit, which is incomprehensible. The relation among the three aspects is incomprehensible, since it analogically represents the relation among the Persons of the Trinity.

The incomprehensibility can be evaded only by denying analogy. We might pretend that the language of John 1:1 is not analogical. That is, we claim that it does *not* invite us to understand its assertions by analogy with creaturely things, and by analogy with the work of God in the incarnation and at Pentecost. But if we drop our reliance on analogy, we fail to relate the language of John 1:1 to other instances of human language and to instances of God's action in the world. We then do not understand John 1:1 at all.

We lapse into the theory of the unknown god of pagan philosophy. Pagan philosophy ends with an unknown god precisely because it is unwilling to accept analogy as a mode of knowledge appropriate to creatures. Pagan philosophers principally deny that they are created and that their thinking is dependent and derivative.

Terms

We earlier discussed names. God's name identifies himself. By analogy, God gives names to creatures and to aspects of creation. We understand the names and the terms for creatures by analogy with the name of God himself. Since the name of God is Trinitarian (Matt. 28:19), we expect other names to be dependent on God the Triune Lord.

To put it another way, human words are ontologically dependent on the eternal Word, revealed in John 1:1. Human words exist according to the pattern of the eternal Word. Hence human words show classificational, instantiational, and associational aspects.

For example, consider the word *camel*.

First, *camel* has an instantiational aspect. The word *camel* occurs in various instances. It may be pronounced rapidly or slowly. It may be used to refer to any of a number of different creatures in the camel class, both one-humped dromedaries and two-humped Bactrian camels.

We learn the word *camel* through instances of its occurrence in certain contexts and associations. Perhaps we see some pictures of camels. Or we just hear a verbal description. Either way, the particular pictures or the particular verbal descriptions are instances. The particularity of these instances or "instantiations" is necessary for learning.

Frequently if not always the particularities color our subsequent knowledge. Immediately after we have learned the meaning of the word *camel*, it means for us "an animal like the ones I saw in the pictures," or "an animal matching the description that I heard and the impression that I formed in my mind concerning what are the salient features." Our knowledge may of course be modified by further experiences in which we see camels, smell them, or have them mentioned to us. But these later experiences involve more instantiations. The further instantiations modify the impact of the initial instantiation. We never simply dispense with instantiations.

Second, *camel* has a classificational aspect. Every instance of occurrence of the word *camel* belongs to the *class camel*. We classify a particular occurrence as an instance of the word *camel*. There is a unity belonging to all such instances, namely, the unity of the *one* word *camel*. That *one* word is recognizable as one in and through all the individuality of its particular occurrences.

As an expression of this classificational unity, we recognize this word as distinct from other words in English. It is distinct in pronunciation. It is identifiable as a certain sequence of sounds or letters (c + a + m + e + l) in contrast with other possible sequences. It is distinct in meaning. It singles out large mammals of the genus *Camelus*, with their characteristic features, in contrast with other kinds of animal. It contrasts with other words, *dog*, *horse*, *pig*, etc. *Contrast* is an integral feature of the classificational aspect of words.

Third, *camel* has an associational aspect. The word *camel* occurs in association, in contexts of other words that occur before and after, and contexts of human situations that may help to make plain what camel is being referred to, contexts of human communication in which we speak, listen, and think. It occurs in the context of the English language and speakers of English. We learn the word *camel* as children by observing contexts in which it is used.

Our word *camel* presupposes God's word governing the creation of camels. The word *camel* is one in all its occurrences because God is stable and self-consistent; his word concerning camels is one. The human word *camel* has a diversity of particular occurrences because God in his creativity and fecundity ordains a diversity of occurrences. There is an associational context of human words because any particular word of God has an associated context in a whole plan, according to the unity of God's wisdom.

The three aspects, namely, the classificational, instantiational, and associational, coinhere. Any particular instance of the word *camel* must be identified as an occurrence of this word, *camel*, rather than some other word. Hence the instantiational presupposes the classificational aspect. We can only talk about the class *camel* if we are able to produce particular occurrences or instances of the word. Hence the classificational aspect requires the instantiational. And so on.

In principle, we could conduct a similar analysis of any word in any human language. All words have classificational, instantiational, and associational aspects. This situation derives from the fact that human language and human words are dependent on God's language. Trinitarian speech is necessarily Trinitarian, trimodal, and coinherent. Human speech is dependent. Since it provides access to real knowledge of God, it is necessarily trimodal and coinherent by analogy.

We can see similar effects when we look not at words and language but at earthly creatures. Camels themselves, as creatures, were created through a Trinitarian operation of God. The Father is Creator (1 Cor. 8:6), the Son is Creator (1 Cor. 8:6; John 1:3; Col. 1:16), and the Spirit is Creator (Gen. 1:2; note Ps. 104:30, where there is a providential action analogically related to the original creating activity of God). What are some of the implications?

First, in accordance with the classificational aspect, all camels are camels. According to Genesis 1:24, they reproduce "according to their kinds." In accordance with the faithfulness of God, they hold to a common pattern fixed by the word of God, the pattern of "being a camel." Camels in their commonness display the faithfulness, the self-consistency, and the unchangeability of God, as Romans 1:20 indicates. The Word is who he is from all eternity (John 1:1a). So derivatively, analogically, camels are what they are in constant conformity to the pattern specified in the constant word.

Second, in accordance with the instantiational aspect, each camel is particular. It is this camel and no other. Each camel is an instantiation. It is a particular being, not simply camelness, not simply a camel, but *this* camel.

The Word is himself particular, in relation to the category of God. Derivatively, analogically, the Word calls forth particular creatures (Ps. 104:30; 147:15). These creatures exist and are sustained in conformity with the word that creates them (John 1:3; Heb. 1:3). Each camel displays the control of God over details, and each camel displays the creativity of God through its creational uniqueness in being what it is.

Third, in accordance with the associational aspect, all camels exist in contextual associations. Camels live in certain ways, eat certain foods, are used by human beings for certain purposes. The eternal personal association of the Word is the original to which all creational associations analogically relate. The existence of a camel in association with other things displays the universal presence of God by which he holds all things together (Col. 1:17).

Word and Thought

So far we have focused almost wholly on words and expressed language rather than on thought. Do the same considerations apply to thought as well as to language?

In God there is a close relation between thought and word. "I make known the end from the beginning, from ancient times, what is still to come. I say: My purpose will stand, and I will do all that I please" (Isa. 46:10). In the clause "I make known . . ." God speaks of what he is making known to human beings, and hence he includes his words to them. In the later clauses, "My purpose will stand," and "I will do all that I please," he speaks of his will, his inward thought if you will. Clearly his word is in conformity with his thought.

We might infer the same conclusion from John 1:1. The Word of God is an expression of his thought, in analogy with the fact that the words of human beings express their thoughts. In this close relation between thought and word, the thought belongs preeminently to the Father, while the Son is his Word. On a human level, we may say that the relation between human thought and human word is analogical to the relation between the Father and the Word. In consequence, the same fundamental mysteries confront us with respect to both thought and word.

Ontological Trinity and Economic Trinity

We should recognize that much of the Bible focuses on God's relations to us and the historical outworking of redemption. God's Trinitarian character stands forth most fully and eloquently in the redemptive events where the Persons of the Trinity have a distinct role (e.g., Matt. 3:16–17; Acts 2:33; Rom. 8:11; 1:4; John 16:13–15). God reveals himself to us through the "economy" of redemption. We understand the Trinity through the economic relations of the Persons of the Trinity in their functions in creation, redemption, and consummation.

In John 1:1 and elsewhere, the Bible does sometimes focus more directly on aspects of the *ontological* Trinity, that is, on God as he is in his own existence before creation and independent of creation. But even here we recognize that the language is crafted for the purposes of nourishing our faith, enlarging our understanding, and promoting our redemption. Hence the language as a whole is tied in with "functional" or "economic" purposes.

Since God is our standard and his word is our standard, there is nothing more ultimate than this revelation of himself. We believe that God is true. He truly reveals himself, not a substitute. We believe it because God says so. Hence we believe that God is in conformity with what he reveals. The Trinity in economic operations reveals the ontological Trinity. Hence,

I have not tried to separate in any strict or exhaustive way between functional (economic) and ontological statements. Such separation on the part of a creature would itself be a repudiation of creaturehood.

The Destruction of Would-be Autonomous Categories

Now what are the implications for ontology? First, consider the medieval controversy between realism and nominalism. Realism maintained that universals had a "real" existence, whereas nominalism contended that universals were simply humanly convenient names for collections of individuals. Realism tended to exalt the unity of the universal, the class, at the expense of diversity. Nominalism tended to exalt the diversity of particulars, the individual things, at the expense of unity (the universal).

This dichotomy is in fact a false one. Unity and diversity are equally ultimate. Unity of the universal, that is, the class or "kind," is an expression of the classificational aspect, while diversity of the particulars is an expression of the instantiational aspect. Both presuppose each other and neither is more fundamental than the other. There is no such thing as a "pure" universal graspable apart from particularities of instances. There is no such thing as a "pure" particular apart from the (universal-like) features that it possesses according to the plan of God. The unity of class and the diversity of particularity both rest on the ontologically ultimate unity and diversity of God, as expressed in the classificational and instantiational aspects, respectively.

Our analysis has still broader implications, applicable to Western philosophy as a whole. Since before the days of Plato and Aristotle, Western philosophy has concerned itself with fundamental ontology. What is the fundamental ontological character of things? Philosophy has endeavored to explore this ontology through human thought and human language. Philosophers produce systems of categories. These categories supposedly enable us to obtain insight into the systematic character of the world. For example, in Plato, the categories of "form" and "good" and "idea" play a key role. In other philosophies the categories may be different. But some particular categories always play a key role. The philosopher holds forth these categories as particularly promising for understanding the world.

In the time of Descartes and Kant, philosophy came to focus largely on epistemology rather than simply on ontology. In the twentieth century, it has focused on language. Through all these variations, fundamental categories have played an important role.

Now what do these categories look like under close inspection? We have to do with words. These words belong to human language. And as we have seen, human language is not autonomous or self-sufficient. Every single term or category of human language is dependent on divine language. Classificational, instantiational, and associational aspects belong together—they enjoy a mysterious coinherence testifying to God's Trinitarian character. Yet pagan philosophers do not want to acknowledge that dependence. They prefer to walk in darkness rather than light (John 3:19–20).

Characteristically, within the system of rationalist philosophers, philosophical categories pretend self-sufficiency. The categories simply are what they are. They pretend to identify themselves not in the mystery of the Trinity, but in the supposed exhaustive clarity of self-sufficiency.[9]

Typically, philosophers exalt the classificational aspect of categories at the expense of the associational and the instantiational aspects. The categories of classical philosophy supposedly need no associations or instantiation for understanding. In fact, if they *were* needed, association and instantiation would potentially bring in "impurities." The categories are grasped by pure reason or pure insight, independent of ordinary life and personal idiosyncrasies.

To be sure, the categories may typically apply to various instances, but the instances are not necessary for the being of the categories. That is, no instantiation is really needed. The essence of a category remains completely independent of the grubby instantiations through which, in actual life, the categories may have been learned by real human beings. In Plato, the instantiations of the forms actually contaminate the forms and confuse knowledge by bringing in matter. In other cases, with more debt to Aristotle, the forms may exist only "in" their instantiations, but human reason still suffices in principle to distinguish the form from the particularity of its instantiation. The self-identity of what is really common to the instances is still unproblematic.

The rationalist philosopher claims deity by being able to master language in one divine vision. If not all language can be mastered, at least the philosopher masters that crucial piece of language that he needs in order to make the systematic assertions and the universal claims. In the philosophic

---

[9] For a similar dissatisfaction with the use of formal modal logic in metaphysics, see James F. Ross, "The Crash of Modal Metaphysics," *Review of Metaphysics* 43 (1989): 251–279. From a Thomistic point of view Ross raises many objections to the attempt to have abstract universals or predicates independent of instantiations (actual individuals to which they may apply). But insofar as Thomism conforms to an Aristotelian view of categories, it is still deficient.

vision the philosopher triumphs over the mystery of coinherence by reducing everything to the pure identity of a class (the identity of the category). Thus philosophers think that they can manipulate their categories without reference to an associational aspect or an instantiational aspect. The categories are supposedly association-free and instance-free.

Philosophers are in fact human beings. Hence, they have themselves learned language from associations and instances. Their present knowledge is not in fact free from the "contamination" of their past learning, as well as their present bodily existence. They themselves are *instantiations* of humanity. Their own thoughts and words are *instantiations* of human thoughts and words. They themselves live within social and historical *associations*, in the context of their own bodies.

But philosophical reflection is idealized. Philosophers project their reflection out toward an ideal that is association-free and instance-free. If they are candid and alert, they may admit that this projection is somewhat idealized. But the idealization is useful, if not necessary, to provide the sort of results that they desire.

But we can now see that the particular type of idealization that characterizes traditional rationalist Western philosophy is intrinsically and irreducibly idolatrous. According to this approach, the ideal category is a self-identical classification, but with no instantiational or associational aspect. Or if it has such instantiational or associational aspects, they are trivial and can safely be ignored in philosophical reflection. This view of categories is intrinsically monist or unitarian.

Sometimes philosophers may admit that differentiation exists. But it still comes in at a subordinate, applicational level. Each category is intrinsically an undifferentiable monadic classificational universal; but it does somehow differentiate itself into instances when applied to the real world in practical terms.

This differentiation is analogous to the kind of differentiation postulated in a modalistic view of God. Modalistic heresy says that God in himself is one, in a pure undifferentiated manner. God reveals himself in three persons as three modes of revelation or three modes of action of the one original. Threeness (differentiation) occurs in God's contact with his creation, but not in God as he is in himself. Thus, rationalistic philosophy recapitulates a unitarian view or at best a modalistic view of God in its approach to fundamental categories.

If philosophical rationalism is a false trail, what about empiricism? For empiricists the event, the datum, the percept, or the particular instance is fundamental. (Thus modern empiricism is akin to medieval nominalism.) In essence empiricists begin by exalting the instantiational aspect at the expense of the classificational and the associational. At its root, this approach is just as unitarian and just as idolatrous as is the rationalistic approach. The main difference is that the instantiational rather than the classificational aspect is deified.

Moreover, when empiricists *talk* about their views, they talk using categories that are viewed as unproblematic, universal, and self-identical. The categories of "sense data" or "physical objects" or "sense experience" function in the same deified role that belonged to the categories of rationalistic philosophy. Such a result is inevitable. If there is only one level of being and one level of knowledge, one's own analysis, to be correct, must have virtually divine status. It must make universal assertions, and at the same time be exhaustively grasped by the human philosopher.

Subjectivistic or personalistically oriented philosophies have analogous difficulties. Here the ultimate starting point is with the associational aspect. Specifically, we deal not with just any kind of association, but its personal dimension. In the Trinity there is personal interaction between the Word and the Father, according to John 1:1b. Analogously, among creatures, there is personal interaction between persons and their environment. Subjectivistic philosophies advocate unitarianism or modalism by collapsing the classificational and the instantiational into the personal. The classificational aspect comes into being when persons produce the classes that they use to classify their "world"; the instantiational aspect comes into being when persons perceive instances.

Subjectivistic philosophy has the same difficulty as does all pagan philosophy when it attempts to state itself. The statements come out in language claiming universality in a de-associationalized and de-instantiationalized fashion. Theoretical formulation falls victim to the same difficulties that beset rationalistic philosophy.

Human language and human categories are in actual fact dependent on our Trinitarian God. They display God's "eternal power and divine nature" (Rom. 1:20). In fact, since God's nature is Trinitarian, human language reflects this Trinitarian nature. But non-Christians do not want to submit themselves to the Trinitarian God. They substitute idols, whether idols made of wood or idols of thought. They wish to be autonomous. So they make their idols, in order to govern them as well as to worship them. Their idolatry is manifest in their would-be autonomous approach to fundamental categories.

Idolatry cannot succeed, because there is only one God and God rules the world in righteousness (Ps. 97:1–2). Rationalism, empiricism, and subjectivism falsify the very nature of the language that they use. Yet rationalism, empiricism, and subjectivism remain plausible. They appear to give us powerful insights. Why?

They are plausible precisely because the classificational, instantiational, and associational aspects coinhere. Each is presupposed by the others, as we have seen. But each also involves the others. Each in a sense encompasses the others. The classificational aspect always involves the identification of instances in association. Properly understood, it tacitly includes the instantiational and associational as inevitable aspects of its being.

This structure of things is, of course, dependent on the nature of the Trinity. The Persons of the Trinity coinhere. To know Christ is also to know the Father (John 14:9). The indwelling of one Person also involves the indwelling of the others (John 14:17, 23; Rom. 8:9–10). Properly understood, each Person offers us a "perspective" on the whole Trinity. Analogously, within the triad of classificational, instantiational, and associational aspects, each one offers us a perspective on everything.

Rationalism exploits the perspectival character of the classificational aspect in order to view all of reality through it. Similarly, empiricism uses an instantiational perspective and subjectivism uses an associational perspective. All three are parasitic on coinherence. All three fail because they worship their own unitarian corruption rather than the Trinitarian God.

Expressive, Informational, Productive Perspectives

We can arrive at a similar result by considering John 1:1 from another standpoint, the standpoint of communication. We are familiar with instances of human communication. One persons speaks to another, in order to produce some effect. By calling the Second Person of the Trinity "the Word," John 1:1 invites us to understand the Second Person of the Trinity by analogy with human utterance. The Second Person of the Trinity is the Word spoken by a Person. Clearly, the speaker is preeminently the Father.

To whom is this Word spoken, and with what effect? John 1:1 does not say explicitly. But since the speaking takes place from all eternity (John 1:1a), it is not merely a matter of God speaking to human beings or speaking to some other created thing or even to the created world as a whole. In the beginning there was God alone. Hence, we infer that God speaks to himself and finds satisfaction in himself.

Remember now that the eternal speaking of John 1:1a is analogous to God's speaking at the creation of the world in Genesis 1. This speaking in creation is in turn analogous to God's speaking to human beings. God speaks to us through Christ, who accomplishes our redemption. In the realm of redemptive re-creation, the Spirit of God is operative, as in John 3 and Ezekiel 36–37. In 2 Corinthians 3:3, the Spirit is instrumental in the impact of the word on our hearts: he writes the word on our hearts.

To engage in all these operations, the Spirit must himself understand the purpose of God. And so we find places in the Bible that represent the Spirit not only as active and initiating, but as receptive of the truth of God. "He [the Spirit] will speak only what he *hears*" (John 16:13). "The Spirit *searches* all things, even the deep things of God" (1 Cor. 2:10).

All these things are true concerning the work of the Holy Spirit in our *redemption*. Since redemption takes the form of re-creation, we are led to expect that the Holy Spirit is similarly operative in the creation of the world. Thus, in Genesis 1 the Spirit of God is present, presumably in making effective the speech of God. The work of the Spirit is also alluded to in Psalm 33:6, "the breath of his mouth," and Psalm 104:30, "When you send your Spirit, they are created." The Spirit empowers and makes effective the speech of God. The Spirit produces the effectiveness of the word.

In sum, we may say that the eternal Word is the archetypal speech of God. This archetypal speech enjoys three aspects: in its *expressive* aspect, it is the speech of God the Father; in its *informational* aspect, its specific content is God the Son; in its *productive* aspect, it is "searched" and carried into effect in God the Holy Spirit.

By analogy, God's speech to us displays these three aspects. It is expressive of who God is, and in it we meet God himself; it is informational and contains specific statements and commands; it is productive in us in blessing or curse—in sanctification, or in punishment, or in judgment.

These three aspects are coinherent and presuppose one another, as we would expect. Each is a perspective on the whole. Together they form a perspectival triad analogically related to the Trinitarian character of God.

Note that this new triad, which focuses on communicative *purpose*, is not identical with the former "categorial" triad, consisting of classificational, instantiational, and associational aspects. In fact, the two triads "intersect," so that we could consider, for example, how the classificational aspect displays both expressive, informational, and productive purposes of God.

We can use the new triad of communicative purposes to produce a new form of critique of philosophical rationalism, empiricism, and subjectivism.

Rationalism projects the idea of absolute rationality or absolute truth. This projection utilizes the informational perspective. But the ideal is unitarian rather than Trinitarian. Rationalism denies that the truth of God is personal (the expressive aspect). And it denies that the truth of God is eternally productive (the productive aspect). Instead, it conceives of truth as a rationalist abstraction independent of its practical effects. Hence the truth so conceived is not ultimately God's truth, but the rationalist's own human idea of truth.

Empiricism projects the idea of absolute data, that is absolute effects. It thus utilizes the productive perspective. But again the ideal is unitarian, denying expressive and informational aspects. (The informational aspect is denied in that the data exist prior to and essentially independent of all language.) Note that the result idolizes an aspect of the creation (data) rather than the Creator.

Finally, subjectivism projects the idea of absolute personality, absolute personal expression. It twists the expressive perspective into a unitarian counterfeit. It idolizes human personality instead of the Creator.[10]

---

[10] John M. Frame already arrived at the same conclusion using his triad of perspectives, the normative, situational, and existential perspectives. See John M. Frame, *Doctrine of the Knowledge of God*, 73–75, 89–90, 109–122.

Frame observes that rationalism tries to reduce everything to rules, thus deifying a normative perspective. Empiricism tries to reduce everything to data, thus deifying a situational perspective. Subjectivism tries to reduce everything to the personal subject, thus deifying the existential perspective. Non-Christian category systems are most often rationalistic, in that the categories have no necessary attachment to the data that instantiate them (situational perspective) or the persons who formulate and understand in a personal context (existential perspective).

Alert readers will perceive that expressive, informational, and productive perspectives are analogous to Frame's existential, normative, and situational perspectives, respectively. But the two sets of perspectives are not completely the same. My triad of perspectives applies archetypally to God and ectypally to creatures. By contrast, Frame's triad is asymmetric (as he himself recognizes, ibid., 63). The normative perspective is focally oriented toward the law, which is divine (ibid.). The existential and situational perspectives are oriented toward creatures, namely, human persons and the world.

Frame's triad is then an analogical image of mine. I believe that Frame's approach remains useful in emphasizing the interrelatedness of norm, world, and self in people's practical, concrete reception of the word of God.

Reforming Logic

A Trinitarian understanding of language requires also a Trinitarian reform of logic. How shall we think about logic? Logic deals with reasoning. Reasoning is a kind of processing of language or thought or both. Shall we focus on language or on thought? As we have already seen, language and thought are analogically related. The same fundamental truths hold for both. But because language is in a sense more "accessible" for public discussion, we continue our focus on language. All the conclusions apply to thought as well as language.

Logic, then, works on pieces of language. Our conception of language thus influences our conception of logic. The supposed character of the pieces of language forms the basis on which logic must work. Hence, pagan misconceptions concerning language and categories are bound to affect pagan conceptions of logic.

Sure enough, the influence is perceptible with Aristotle. Aristotle undertook to analyze and expound syllogistic logic especially in the *Prior Analytics*. Aristotle recognized that a syllogism is invalidated if there is equivocation in the use of terms. For example, consider the syllogistic form

> All lions are dangerous.
> This stone statue is a lion.
> Therefore this stone statue is dangerous.

Within Aristotle's system of classification, this particular syllogistic form conforms to the normal structure of "Darii," a valid syllogism of the first figure. But there is an equivocation in the word *lion*. The word *lion* in the first premise includes real lions but not statuary. The *lion* in the second premise includes all statues of lions. The equivocation invalidates the syllogism.

The proper operation of syllogisms thus requires the use of univocal terms. A univocal term must cover a perfectly fixed kind of thing, belonging to one or another of Aristotle's basic categories (see Aristotle, *The Categories*). These categories are the fundamental categories of ontology, the beginnings of Aristotle's metaphysics. For the operation of the syllogism Aristotle needs categories that are perfectly fixed and whose boundaries of definition are perfectly sharp. If perfection fails, equivocation enters.

Now such perfection and such absoluteness of knowledge belong only to God. Aristotle tacitly tries to take a divine viewpoint when he uses categories. Each category is an idealization of the actual character of human language.

The idealization pushes for a pure classificational aspect, with no need for instantiational and associational aspects. Like the abstract reasoning of Euclid, it aspires to dispense with the knowledge of particular cases (instantiational) and the interaction of persons with knowledge (associational). Moreover, it attempts to arrive at a language of pure information, without an expressive or productive aspect. The syllogistic premises and the syllogistic structures must exist as formulas independent of the personal involvement and influence of persons who are practitioners of logic—thus the expressive aspect is excised. The syllogistic structure must also exist independent of any concrete application, for the sake of its absolute universality and necessary truthfulness. Only in this way can the reasoning be purely abstract.

Hence, Aristotle's categories presuppose the unitarian ontology that we have already analyzed. The categories must collapse instantiation and association into pure classification. They must also collapse expressive and productive aspects into pure information.

The syllogistic premises must be association-free to guarantee that meaning is not influenced by association or context. The syllogistic premises must also be instantiation-free, in order that the purity of the categories may not be contaminated by the grubbiness of particular instantiations. The syllogism must be what it is independent of the expressivity and productivity of God. Associations, instantiations, expressivity of persons, or the particulars of productivity all threaten to introduce equivocation.

Thus, within Aristotle's system, syllogisms can operate *only* with unitarian ontology. Hence syllogistic reasoning is itself tacitly unitarian. Only so can one claim that the reasoning is mechanically valid.

The nineteenth and twentieth centuries have seen the rise of alternative accounts of logic, by Frege, Russell and Whitehead, C. I. Lewis, and Arend Heyting, among others. There are considerable variations. But all formalized logics retain the fundamental Aristotelian approach to categories. In order for the logics to work, the categories must be perfectly stable, in the unitarian sense.[11]

Do we then throw out logic, and become pure irrationalists? Certainly

---

[11] Superficially, the fuzzy logic of Lotfi Zadeh, growing out of Łukasiewicz's work on multivalued logic, might seem to be an exception (see, e.g., Lotfi Zadeh, "Fuzzy Sets," *Information and Control* 8 [1956]: 338–353; Zadeh, "Quantitative Fuzzy Semantics," *Information Science* 3 [1971]: 159–176; Bart Kosko, *Neural Networks and Fuzzy Systems: A Dynamical Systems Approach to Machine Intelligence* [New York: Prentice Hall, 1991]). Zadeh's concept of fuzziness produces an interesting analogue to the phenomena of fuzziness in the classificational aspect of words and categories in natural human language. But it still does not include in any integral way the instantiational and associational aspects.

not. God is faithful and does not lie (Num. 23:19). Jesus Christ is the truth (John 14:6) and opposes lying (John 8:44–45). God's loyalty to himself forms the only foundation for logical consistency. Pagan logics are attractive and plausible because, for all their idolatry, they are parasitic on the self-consistency of God.

Hence, we do not eliminate logic, but we reform it. God's self-consistency is the foundation for all human consistency. God's self-consistency is intrinsically Trinitarian in character. Hence reformed logic will be analogically Trinitarian. In this article we can only sketch the basic directions that such a reform may take.

Substitution in John 5:19-26

First, all human thinking and our categories as well are intrinsically analogical. They are imitative of God—though sinners attempt to twist this relation.[12] All categories are analogical rather than univocal. Recall that Aristotelian syllogisms require univocal terms. Hence, there is no such thing as a valid syllogism in the Aristotelian sense.

Second, God is self-consistent and is faithful to himself (2 Tim. 2:13). His reliability and consistency offer the only firm foundation for logic in all its aspects. We know as a matter of broad, general principle that God is the foundation. But we can also explore some particular instances.

As a first instance, let us consider how God's self-consistency applies to phenomena of substitution in formal logic. We may start with John 5:19, 21, and 26.

> . . . whatever the Father does the Son also does. . . . For just as the Father raises the dead and gives them life, even so the Son gives life to whom he is pleased to give it.
> . . . For as the Father has life in himself, so he has granted the Son to have life in himself.

John 5:19–26 exhibits some logical reasoning. We might compare the reasoning to formal logic in several ways. Verse 19 is analogous to a formal implication, namely, (x)(the Father does x $\rightarrow$ the Son does x), where x ranges over predicates and "$\rightarrow$" is the symbol for formal implication. In type theory, x would be a "second-order" variable.

---

[12] Even fallen human beings do not cease imitating God, though they do so with the twist that they attempt to imitate his autonomy by making themselves gods (cf. Gen. 3:22)!

In verse 21 we can single out two propositions, namely, that the Father gives life and that the Son gives life. If b represents the predicate "gives life," then we can obtain a deduction as follows:

(x)(the Father does x → the Son does x)
The Father does b → the Son does b.
The Father does b.
Hence the Son does b.

The first step in the deductive pattern above is the substitution of a particular instance b for the variable x. The substitution of b yields an instantiation in line 2 of the general principle expressed in line 1. The kind of instantiation here is *analogous* to the instantiation that we earlier saw in John 1:1, where the Word is an "instantiation" of God. The Word manifests all the attributes of deity. Analogously, line 2 manifests an instance of the truth in line 1. The Word is faithful to what God is. Analogously, line 2 is faithful to what line 1 is.

As a general *formal* pattern, the relation between line 1 and line 2 is a matter explored in formal derivations in formal logic. It is analogically related to the way in which the Word is an instantiation of God. In virtue of the Creator/creature distinction, the Trinitarian relations are basic and the formal patterns derivative. The formal patterns thus depend ultimately on the self-consistency of God and the faithfulness of the Persons of the Trinity to one another and to the perfections of deity.

It is worth noting that formal expression of the derivation, in the way that we have stated it in lines 1 and 2, is not of the essence. There are several ways in which the dynamics of derivation are rich, complex, and mysterious. First, the truth relations hold when they are expressed more informally and tacitly, as in John 5:19–26. The formal summary is secondary to this meaning that can be expressed in a variety of informal ways.

Second, the derivation holds only if the instantiation is appropriate. In order for the derivation to be proper, we must know that instance b is genuinely within the range of the quantifier in line 1, namely "(x)." b must be an *appropriate* substitute. What is appropriate? We earlier specified that x is a "second-order" variable, a variable over predicates. Hence b must be a second-order instance, a particular predicate. It works to say, "If the Father loves, the Son loves," or "If the Father has life, the Son has life." It does not work to say, "If the Father apple, the Son apple," because an apple is a first-order instance; it is a thing rather than a predicate.

In fact, the situation is even more complicated, because there are still exceptions. If we mechanically substitute for b the words "begets the Son," we obtain "If the Father begets the Son, the Son begets the Son." Such a substitution is obviously not an appropriate instance within the intended range of (x). The universality of "(x)" extends over all the usual attributes of God, but does not include actions unique to one Person of the Trinity. Since God is incomprehensible, we cannot specify beforehand exhaustively all the instances that will or will not be within the range of (x), though we have a general idea.

In general, we may say that b must be a genuine instantiation of the generality expressed in line 1. A genuine instantiation of something (in this case, of the variable x) is what it is by virtue of being in analogical relation to the archetypal instantiation, namely, the Word as an instantiation of God in John 1:1. Hence the derivation depends on the being of the Word.

Third, the derivation holds only if the occurrences of b have a stability and self-identity. We need to be confident that the various occurrences of b in line 2 have analogous functions, else we may be actually dealing with several distinct entities b_1, b_2, b_3, etc. The instances of *b* have a stability, classificational identity, and distinctiveness only in analogical relation to the archetypal classificational self-identical stability of God the Father. Hence, the derivation depends on the being of the Father and the self-identity of the entire Godhead.

Fourth, the derivation holds only if the statement in line 2 is viewed as interpreted with associations and context similar to the context for understanding line 1. (Otherwise, we may be dealing with equivocal use of terms.) The sharing of associations is what it is in analogical relation to the sharing of association in John 1:1b, where the Word was with God in the association with the sharing of the Holy Spirit. Hence the derivation depends analogically on the being of the Spirit.

The point of these observations is that derivation by substitution is never the merely mechanical process that many specialists in logic imagine it to be. Derivation always depends on the support of concepts of instantiation, classification, and association. We must always judge whether a given case has the right sorts of instantiation, classification, and association. The judgment relies on appeal to a standard. And the ultimate standard is no other than God himself, in his Triunal character.

We may make analogous observations using the informational, expressive, and productive perspectives. When we inquire concerning the correctness of the form of the substitution in line 2, we focus on the informational perspective. Thus, we ask ultimately whether the substitution conforms with the character of the Word of God, as the standard for all human language patterning. But the informativity of the Word coinheres with the personal expressivity of the Father as the speaker and the productivity of the Spirit as the one who searches divine meaning.

Hence, in particular, we cannot ultimately evaluate the informational aspect of a syllogism without taking into account *who* is speaking (the expressive perspective). Who is making the substitution and setting forth the result? If an unbeliever makes the substitution, the result looks "formally" correct—it appears to be the same result that we as believers would obtain. But what person's understanding of the result is decisive? The unbeliever understands the result and the process as well in a distorted fashion, since in the bondage of idolatry he does not relate it properly to the archetypal knowledge in God. And would-be knowledge not properly related to the archetype is in fact defective. The associational relations are different for the believer and the unbeliever. Only by denying the relevance of the associational aspect (and thus falling into unitarianism) do we avoid the conclusion that believer and unbeliever do not do exactly the same thing when they go through a process of substitution.

Similarly, the productive perspective is an irreducible aspect in evaluating the informational aspect of the process of substitution. We must ask what is being referred to. In this case, we refer to the Father and the Son, and once again the unbeliever is incapable of understanding the referent in the same way that the believer does.

Modus ponens in John 5:19–26

As another case, consider the derivation of line 4 from lines 2 and 3. The formal pattern here is the pattern of *modus ponens*. Supposing that p is true and that p implies q, we may deduce that q is true. In this derivation, it is crucial that we understand the nature of the premise "p implies q" or symbolically $p \rightarrow q$. What is being connoted by the word *imply* in such a context?

Our starting point is the fact that "*as* the Father has life in himself, *so* he has granted the Son to have life in himself" (John 5:26). We are dealing with an intimate relation between the Father and the Son. Elsewhere John speaks analogously of the fact that "the Father loves the Son and has placed everything in his hands" (John 3:35). This giving of the Father to the Son involves the Spirit, who is the Spirit of love (John 3:34). We have seen above that the intimacy between the Father and the Son takes place through the Spirit's capacity of indwelling. Hence, the "implication" involved in the Son's imitation of the Father is an implication from the dynamic of the Spirit.

When we say that "the Father has life in himself," we focus on the Father. When we say that "the Son has life in himself," we focus on the Son. When we say that "if the Father has life in himself, so does the Son," we focus on the relation between the Father and the Son, and thereby we tacitly involve ourselves with the Spirit. Thus, in the total derivation we involve all three Persons of the Trinity. In the initial premise of line 3 we have the Father; in the implicational premise of line 2 we have the Spirit, and in the conclusion of line 4 we have the Son.

It is customary to regard such an derivational process as a particular application or particular instance of a general, abstract, impersonal principle, namely, the abstract principle of *modus ponens*. But what is the standard by which the operation of *modus ponens* in human reasoning is to be judged? Clearly, God is the Original to which human reasoning must conform. Hence, the derivation in John 5:19–26 is not "an" application of a higher and more exalted principle that is just "out there" independent of God. Rather, the derivation is an instance of personal Trinitarian communion, and this communion is the standard for all human application of *modus ponens*. To put it provocatively, the *Original modus ponens* is not an abstract principle, but God himself in the mystery of his Triunity. Human instances of use of *modus ponens* are to be evaluated according to whether they show appropriate analogical relation to the Original.

From this understanding of the ontological roots of *modus ponens*, we can see many ways in which the operation of *modus ponens* involves something other than pure Platonic abstraction. To begin with, in the archetypal *modus ponens* of God, the movement "*p* implies *q*" involves the giving or "granting" by the Father. "He has *granted* the Son to have life in himself" (John 5:26). This granting takes place in connection with the granting of the Spirit, who is the heart of the bond of love between the Father and the Son: "For the one whom God has sent speaks the words of God, for

God gives the Spirit without limit. The Father loves the Son and has placed everything in his hands" (John 3:34–35). Without the Spirit and without the granting of the Father, there is no such thing as *modus ponens*. It is inconceivable that the Father would *not* love the Son and would *not* give him the Spirit. Hence we can rely on *modus ponens*. But note that *modus ponens* rests not on abstract impersonal law, but on the love of God and the character of God.[13]

More broadly, use of *modus ponens* involves dependence on classificational, instantiational, and associational aspects. Consider *modus ponens* in the schematic form

p.
p implies q.
Therefore, q.

For *modus ponens* to work properly, the p in the two premises must be classificationally the same. The q in the conclusion must be classificationally the same as the q in the premise "p implies q." This classificational sameness is analogically derivative from the sameness of the Father and the Son in the archetypal *modus ponens*.

Next, the whole argument must be an instance or instantiation, a genuine analogue of the archetypal *modus ponens* in John 5:19–26. Formal correspondence is not enough, unless we know that the meanings of "implies" and of the total structures are genuinely analogous to the archetype.

Third, the whole argument depends on personal associations for its interpretation and application. Marks on paper mean little unless there is a language in which to interpret them. Likewise for abstract mathematical symbols like p and q.

We can specify still other ways in which *modus ponens* interacts with contexts. For example, using the informational, expressive, and productive perspectives, we may stress that any given example of the use of *modus ponens* involves all three perspectives inextricably. According to the informational perspective, the use of *modus ponens* must be an expression of language in conformity with the divine archetype. This conformity means that we can cast the use into the formal structure: p; p implies q; therefore

---

[13] The operation of logic rests ultimately on the eternal, ontological Trinitarian character of God. But human beings come to know of logic through the economic operations of God in creation, providence, and revelation. As usual, God acts economically in accord with who he is ontologically.

q. But in addition to the informational perspective, we may use the expressive perspective and the productive perspective. In most real, practical uses of *modus ponens* we need to know that *p* is true and that "*p* implies *q*" is true. We obtain these premises from other sources, including observations about the world (a creational productive focus). Having obtained the conclusion *q*, we also use it by reckoning with what it says about the world (productive focus). In every step of this process, our interaction with the world ought be in conformity with the Spirit's archetypal productivity in the world.

At the same time, in all these reflections it is *we* who do the operations. The focus on *us* is expressive. Our own persons must be in conformity with the original expressivity of the Father. For the operations to be of any use to us, we must in some way know what we are doing and be convinced that it is true or valid or useful.

If we had time, we could explore the divine origin of other logical rules. For example, we could see how in John 16:13 the law of excluded middle has its archetype in the distinction between the Spirit and the Father. In John 16:14–15 we see operation of various aspects of predicate logic. The distinction between truth and falsehood derives from the loyalty of love between the Father and the Son (John 14:30–31; 16:13).

The Nature of Formal Logic

Modern formal logic or mathematical logic may appear to evaporate all personal and associational factors in reasoning, including the presence of the Trinitarian God. Apparently, reasoning means just pushing around abstract symbols. But the evaporation of association is illusory. The logician has ideas about how the symbols are going to be applied; but such ideas reside in the logician's mind rather than on paper. Or they come out on paper in the natural language explanations that introduce and frame the formal symbolic material.

The formal symbolic material "works" to bring impressive results partly because it is controlled by a personal logician who imparts significance. But more ultimately, it "works" because the symbolism is analogous to the formal structure or grammatical structure of parts of natural human language. The symbolism provides a kind of picture (analogy) of certain regular classificational features belonging to practical derivations in human language. These practical derivations "work" because they are analogical instantiations of the archetypal divine *modus ponens* and other aspects of divine self-consistency.

Modus ponens is *intrinsically* an analogical concept. So is the law of excluded middle and other laws of logic, because all such laws are intelligible only through analogical relations to a divine, Trinitarian archetype.

Formalized logic "works," in a certain sense, if we regard it as a convenient summary and schematic representation of regular structural features in reasoning that honors God and images God's self-consistency. But not every instantiation that formally conforms to a syllogistic pattern or other formal logic pattern actually has the necessary traction. Not every instantiation enjoys an analogical relation to God such that it is in fact actually valid.

Even within an Aristotelian framework, Aristotle has to admit that equivocation destroys the validity of a syllogism. Within a Christian framework, the analogical character of categories makes it necessary to check on the content or meaning of each statement, and to evaluate it within a larger network of contexts, including the context of persons who are reasoning, the situation being reasoned about, and ultimately the context of God himself.

In other words, we take into account not only classification but association and instantiation, not only the informational but expressive and productive perspectives.

First, we take association into account. The interpretation of a particular premise inevitably involves a context of persons and world, leading to the ultimate context of God himself in his Trinitarian fellowship. Apart from this interpretation, there is no assurance that p and q are what they are and that the terms are sufficiently stable in classification to avoid the fallacy of equivocation.

Second, we take instantiation into account. As human beings, we have always come to understand *through* instances. Moreover, all instances are instantiated witnesses to God's creative power and his presence in the world (Rom. 1:19–21). To interpret the premises we utilize the background of instances through which we understand each premise. We also know that the total structure is one *instance* of *modus ponens*, an instance expressed in language by a particular person, at in a particular time, and through a particular medium. Without such interpretation, again there is no stability.

Validation in reasoning also depends on God. Validity and truth in human reasoning depend on the original self-validating and self-confirming character of God, whose word is truth (John 17:17). Christ is the Word of the Father (John 1:1), the truth (John 14:6), and the wisdom of God (Col. 2:3; cf. Matt. 11:28–30). The self-validation, self-confirmation, and truthfulness of God are not unitarian but Trinitarian in character. The Father testifies to the Son and the Son testifies to the Father, in order that validation may have two witnesses (John 5:36–37; 8:17–18; 7:18; 8:54; 13:31–32; 17:1–5). The Holy Spirit is also witness (John 15:26; 16:9–10).

Hence validity and truth depend on the personal presence of God in his Triunity. Validity in reasoning is never self-sufficient, but dependent on the validation of God through the giving of the Spirit of truth.

Within a biblical worldview, logic is personalist. Or better, it is Trinitarian. It is Trinitarian in origin, in the sense that the being of God, in his self-consistency, is the Origin for the creation of human beings and their reasonings. It is Trinitarian as to standard, in that Trinitarian commitment in love is the archetypal standard to which human reasoning must be compared. It is Trinitarian in purpose, in that the glorification of the Persons of the Trinity is the goal of logical consistency.

Let us now explore briefly some ways in which our reformed understanding of logic impacts evaluation of theological "paradoxes."

Theological Paradox: The Trinity

Is the doctrine of the Trinity a "paradox"? It is a paradox according to the common opinion of human beings. But of course the common opinion of human beings is not the ultimate standard by which we measure real truth or the intractability of problems.

Within a biblical worldview, the doctrine of the Trinity is not a kind of inexplicable surd that violates known logic. Rather, God is the very foundation of logic, and so of course logic properly understood confirms rather than challenges the doctrine.

How does this kind of logic work in practice? Consider the argument of Jehovah's Witnesses from John 1:1. In John 1:1b, the Word is with God. Hence, according to Jehovah's Witnesses, the Word is distinct from God. Word ≠ God. In John 1:1c, either Word = a god or Word = God. Hence Word = a god.

We might bring various exegetical objections to bear on this piece of spurious reasoning. But we may best illustrate the functioning of Trinitarian logic by examining the reasoning process itself.

Consider first the premise, "Word ≠ God." Distinction or classificational nonidentity in this premise is derivative from the archetypal distinction or nonidentity of the Persons of the Trinity. This distinction coinheres with instantiational and associational aspects relating to the Persons of the Trinity. The Word is nonidentical with the Father only in the instantiatedness of the Word as being God. The first premise cannot be true unless we set it in the context of the archetypal divine being. Once we do so, it is clear that the Jehovah's Witnesses' understanding of the premise is false.

Consider the identification of the word "God" used in the premises. For checking the validity of the argument, we must understand this word in terms of its classificational, instantiational, and associational aspects. Reflection on these aspects once again destroys the argument, because "God" in the first premise most naturally refers to the Father, while "God" in the second refers to the Godhead, with the classificational aspect in prominence.

Consider also the derivational process from the premises to the conclusion. Since the conclusion is dishonoring to the Son, the Spirit refuses to honor it (John 16:14). The derivation does not conform to the divine archetype, and therefore is illicit.

Logic, properly understood, depends on the Trinity. Hence Jehovah's Witnesses cannot disprove the Trinity using logic (properly understood).

Logical Circularity

Our observations involve circularity, of course. We rely on our knowledge of the Trinity to arrive at a form of logic that prevents people from attacking the Trinity. But what do we expect? We are creatures. Circularity expresses our status as dependent on God. We must rely on God in order to praise God and in order to reason about him.

The archetypal knowledge of God is also "circular" in a sense. The Father knows the Son and the Son knows the Father (Matt. 11:27). The Father testifies to the Son and the Son to the Father (John 5:36–37; 8:18; 17:6–8). Circular reasoning is licit when it is validly dependent on the archetypal knowledge of the Father and the Son. It is illicit when it sets up idolatrous substitutes. Hence, the idea that all "circular reasoning" is fallacious is itself fallacious. It is not only fallacious, but idolatrously fallacious, since it is in tension with who God is as ultimate standard.

Theological Paradox: Divine Sovereignty and Human Responsibility

We may note briefly how this reformed approach to logic affects arguments concerning divine sovereignty and human responsibility. Consider the following argument.

1. Human beings are ethically responsible in many of their actions.
2. If a human being is ethically responsible for a particular action, that action is unconstrained.
3. If God causes an action, that action is constrained by him.
4. Hence, the actions in which human beings are ethically responsible are not caused by God.
5. If God does not cause an action, he is not sovereign over that action.
6. Hence God is not sovereign over many human actions, namely, those actions that are ethically responsible.

How do we evaluate this sort of argument? Typically, people follow one of four options. First, they may claim that the argument is substantially correct, and use it as one argument against the existence of God. Second, they may claim that the argument is substantially correct, and therefore conclude that Arminians or Pelagians are right: a god of some kind exists, but he does not sovereignly control many free human actions. Third, they may think that the argument is technically incorrect by conventional Aristotelian standards. Some of the premises are untrue, or there is an equivocation, or there are still hidden premises that are incorrect. Fourth, people may substantially accept the argument, but claim that the relation of God to human beings involves paradoxes that are insuperable.

Along with the fourth category of people, I believe that God is incomprehensible, and his relation to human beings is incomprehensible. We know God truly, but there are impenetrable mysteries in our understanding. But I would also challenge the correctness of the argumentation on another ground, namely, that it does not conform to divine standards of validity.

In particular, the categories of "cause," "responsibility," "constraint," and "sovereignty" are analogical rather than univocal. Reasoning using these categories is valid when it relates in a proper analogical fashion to God's standard. When we reflect on the divine standard, we find that the Father causes the resurrection of the Son (Rom. 8:11) and the Son causes his own resurrection (John 10:18). The Son is responsible to obey the command of the Father (John 12:49–50) and the Father is responsible to fulfill his promise to the Son (John 17:1–2; Ps. 2:8–9). The Son is constrained so that "the Son can do nothing by himself; he can do only what he sees his Father doing" (John 5:19). At the same time, the Son is free (John 8:35–36) and saves whomever he chooses (Matt. 11:27).

It follows that human beings are responsible, free, and constrained, respectively, by analogy with the responsibilities, freedom, and constraint of the eternal Son. There is no "logical paradox" in these truths because logic and paradox alike are defined and determined by the Son's relation to the Father, through the Spirit.[14]

Logic as Conditioned by Redemptive History

Modern people commonly conceive of logic as independent of history and the particularities of human beings. But it should now be clear that this conception is confused. God is unchangeable. Hence the divine archetypal logic is unchangeable. But human understanding undergoes development.

Human reasoning and human use of logic are dependent on knowledge of God and are guided by it. This truth should be obvious from the very character of human thought, which should "think God's thoughts after him." But this dependence becomes more obvious when we root logic in the Trinitarian character of God. God in his Triunity decisively reveals him-

---

[14] At this point I seem to be in tension with Van Til, since Van Til repeatedly asserted that Christian teaching is irreducibly paradoxical (Van Til, *Defense*, 44–46; Van Til, *Common Grace and the Gospel* [n.p.: Presbyterian & Reformed, 1972], 9; see the discussion in John M. Frame, *Van Til: The Theologian* [Phillipsburg, NJ: Pilgrim, 1976], 13–37). But the tension is more apparent than real. Since the Trinity is incomprehensible, I insist as much as Van Til does on the mystery and nonexhaustiveness of all human knowledge, including human knowledge of logic. The one and many of the Trinity and the question of divine sovereignty and human responsibility are not resolvable by human formulation or logical analysis in any way that would dispense with the analogical character of human knowledge.

My statements do, however, differ from Van Til's in their *terminology*. I resort to a new formulation in order to provoke people to think further along the very lines that Van Til laid down. In particular, apparent contradictions appear to be contradictions only against a standard for what is a contradiction. Since the standard is God himself, there can be no real contradiction. Since our *knowledge* of the standard is derivative and analogical, we cannot exhaustively penetrate situations where, by Aristotelian standards or other autonomous standards, there appear to be contradictions.

In particular, precisely because God is God, the Creator, there are *disanalogies* as well as analogies between him and his creatures. God is both one and three, in a manner that is disanalogous to oneness and threeness among creatures. If we insist that logical rules be made perfectly abstract, mechanical, and impersonal, we naturally will formulate rules about oneness and threeness that we claim must apply to all being without discrimination; but such a move betrays a remaining rebellion against the Trinitarian character of true logic.

Nevertheless, if there are no logical "tensions" for God, there still may be for us, even when we are Christians. We are called to grow in knowledge in all these areas, and within this life there always remain areas of tension in our understanding. Intellectual growth is a struggle against the principalities and powers (Eph. 6:10–20).

Van Til emphasizes paradox and apparent contradiction in order to point to the permanent limitations and qualifications of human knowledge; conversely I emphasize that when we feel that so-called paradoxes are a problem, the real problem is our pretended autonomy, not creatureliness. These emphases are complementary.

self through the redemptive work of Christ in the New Testament. The full revelation of the character of God, the being of God, and the logical self-consistency of God comes in the form of a climax of redemption in the person and work of Christ.

Before the coming of New Testament redemption, human beings knew God less fully. This deficiency is not an incidental fact arising merely from some mental or moral deficiency in the individual or the society. It is an inevitable consequence of the very structure of history and the structure of redemption. Human knowledge of God can grow only in step with the redemptive operations that work out God's plan.

Consequently, God's Trinitarian character is only dimly revealed and dimly understood in the Old Testament. Trinitarian theology in its full form rests on New Testament revelation.

Hence, the human development of Trinitarian logic requires New Testament revelation. The fullness of logical understanding requires a fullness in development of redemptive history. Human logic is redemptive-historically conditioned. It is not the same before and after the coming of Christ. Redemption in Christ includes the redemptive reformation of human logic. That reform takes place once and for all in the resurrection of Christ. As the last Adam, the spiritual man (1 Cor. 15:45–49), seated at God's right hand, he is the human pattern and exemplar for all redeemed human logic. On the basis of this one climactic event, reformation of human logic takes place in the church through the progressive renewal of our minds (Rom. 12:2).

It goes without saying that categories and category-systems are also redemptive-historically conditioned. Understanding categories in their classificational, instantiational, and associational aspects grows with the fuller revelation of the Trinity in Christ. Human categories are not univocal, not only because of their analogical relation to God's knowledge, but because of the fact that they undergo change in the course of redemptive history.

The Antibiblical Character of Common Alternatives

We have already examined the common pagan philosophical ideal of univocal categories. Plato and Aristotle both share this ideal, though in variant forms.[15] Pieces of this ideal were adopted into Christian theology at an

---

[15] Note also Van Til's analysis of non-Christian philosophy in terms of the problem of the one and the many and rationalist-irrationalist dialectic (e.g., Van Til, *A Survey of Christian Epistemology* [n.p.: den Dulk Christian Foundation, 1969], 47; *Defense* 123–128).

early point—at least as soon as the second century apologists. The apologists and others after them tried to Christianize ideas from the philosophy of Plato, Aristotle, and the Stoics. But Christian critique never went nearly far enough. In particular, the pagan unitarian ideal for categories was never decisively rejected.

One way of Christianizing Plato is to suppose that Plato's forms, which are his fundamental categories, are not independent of God or above God, but are ideas in God's mind (so Augustine). Nevertheless, in their "inward structure" and character the categories remain more or less as they were conceived before within the framework of pagan philosophy. It is only their location that is changed. This kind of Christianizing is in fact superficial and inadequate.

Let us see some of the difficulties. The first difficulty, of course, is that the categories in God's mind are still conceived in an essentially unitarian fashion. They have a classificational aspect, but not an instantiational or associational aspect.

We may be modest enough to admit that human ideas about God's categories are not identical with God's categories. Our human ideas always require associations and instantiations for their learning. But the projection or idealization into God's mind sloughs off these deficiencies and inelegancies. This idea of projection gives rise to a second difficulty: how do we know that we have projected correctly? The existence of an alternative (such as mine) shows that hidden assumptions about the nature of God are coming in. What is the source of these assumptions? How do we justify our view as the *correct* view rather than a view that we imagine to be possible?

A third difficulty is that the categories in God's mind are still being conceived as univocal rather than analogical in their meaning and application. How do we avoid abolishing the Creator-creature distinction? For example, the Second Person of the Trinity is the Son. I am a son of a human father. I have also been made a son of God through Christ. What is the relation among these three occurrences of *son*? If we say that there is only one univocal category here, we deny the unique Sonship of the divine Son. On the other hand, if we have here three distinct categories, with no relation to one another, we destroy knowledge. We know the meaning of the divine Son only by analogy with our experience of human sonship, and conversely we know the meaning of human sonship only because there is a divine Son who offers us the archetype for that meaning.

So we may try another alternative. We may say that there are three categories sustaining an intimate relation to one another. Perhaps there are three subcategories, divine-Son, human-son-of-God, and human-son-of-human-father. All these are subdivisions within the larger category generic-son. But now the divine Son has apparently become only a differentiation within the wider category generic-son. How do we understand this differentiation or instantiation? And if the differentiation differentiates the divine Son from human sons, then is the association of other possibilities (e.g., human sons) necessary for understanding the distinctiveness of the divine Son? Both instantiations and association have been introduced here. Are they essential to the picture or not? It appears that in this theory we have begun to destroy the association-free and instantiation-free character of divine categories. Hence the initial model is fundamentally flawed.

In addition, when we attempt to patch up the theory, it becomes more speculative. How do we know what is the organization of God's mind? The presumption that we can correctly guess the details of God's mind is arrogant, and God punishes such arrogance through darkening the understanding.

Finally, the picture of abstract categories in God's mind is in fundamental tension with the revelation of the Second Person of the Trinity as the Word. The Word is himself the archetype. He is personal, not an impersonal abstraction. He is one Person, not a string of disconnected monadic categories.

In a second approach, we may postulate that categories are created by God. Their origin is simultaneous with the origin of the created universe, as described in Genesis 1. The difficulty here is that placing of categories purely on the side of the creature leads to the denial of the divine authority of the Bible. The message of the Bible is written in human languages and as such uses created categories. Hence, by this reasoning, the message belongs wholly on the side of the creature. Hence it has no divine authority and power. Moreover, it is hard to see how we can speak truly of God. How can we say that "God is light," when both "God" and "light" are created categories?

The fundamental flaw with all these approaches is the virtual denial of the Creator-creature distinction and the accompanying presumption of human autonomy. Rather than thoroughly submitting themselves to the revelation of God in Christ, we project an idolatrous unitarian ideal back onto God.

Implications for the History of Theology

Corrupt ontology and logic from Plato and Aristotle has deeply influenced the entire history of Western theology. We have already touched on the Platonic influence on the apologists and Augustine. Augustine became the dominant source for medieval theology, so the influence continued until the revival of Aristotle in the late middle ages.

Petrus Ramus was one of the few who attempted to reform logic and move away from Aristotle. But his alternative was just as much a victim of the unitarian ideal as was the Aristotelian system. It should be evident, then, that it is necessary to reform the whole of theology in the light of the Trinity.

The development of the doctrine of the Trinity in the first four centuries was itself not free from the influence of pagan philosophy! But in the struggle to develop the doctrine, philosophical terminology was reformed in order to express truths fundamentally incompatible with the substance-accidence schema as well as the category schema of Aristotle. The Trinitarian teaching of the Fathers and the great creeds uses the language of essence and hypostasis, substance and person. These words can of course be understood in the univocal framework of pagan philosophy. But they are best understood as analogical terms, used in conformity with the Creator-creature distinction to summarize the teaching of the Bible itself and to warn against crucial deviations.

The best theological work of all ages must be similarly understood. The theologians knew God, as he is revealed in Christ. Hence, time after time, their theology came out better than what a purely Aristotelian or Platonic framework would have dictated. We need to learn from them, especially since we are doubtless trapped in deceptions and idolatries of our own, tempted by the fads and follies of our own age and culture.

What I say, then, is simply this: in the long run, theology needs radical recasting in the light of Trinitarian ontology and logic. In view of the unitarian character of the deductive systems of Aristotle and later formal logics, we must move away from the ideal of theology by formal deduction, which would mean ultimately impersonal, mechanical, association-free and instantiation-free deduction.

How are we to evaluate my own reasoning in this article? I strive to use reasoning analogically consistent with the Trinitarian being of God, and with the logic that I have expounded here. The argument of this article is circular, in the sense that I use Trinitarian logic in order to argue for Trinitarian logic. Such circularity is inevitable, but not vicious.

Implications for Apologetics

The reform of ontology and logic has direct implications for the practice of apologetics. Apologetic reasoning with unbelievers requires, at the very outset of reasoning, the use of categories and the use of logic for reasoning with the categories. To be consistent Christians must adopt a Trinitarian view of categories and Trinitarian logic. Non-Christians are created in God's image and live in God's world. Hence in spite of themselves they depend on God and on God's standards for categories and logic. Nevertheless, they constantly try to rebel and escape God in this area as in other areas. Hence there is no prospect of neutral reasoning. The realities of sinfulness and rebellion confront us in the midst of every attempt at intellectual endeavor.[16]

Implications for Other Fields

The view that I have sketched here results in a new approach to language and linguistics. Linguistics requires reform, inasmuch as almost all the major linguistic theories, in their technical linguistic terms, attempt to approximate the unitarian philosophical ideal.[17]

This new approach to categories also entails a fundamental reinspection of the sciences, of all academic subjects, and of the use of language in

---

[16] My reform of logic helps to highlight the uniqueness of Van Til's "transcendental" presuppositional approach to apologetics. According to Van Til's understanding of biblical theism, God in his Triunity is foundational for every category (classificational), for every particular (instantiational), and for every relation (associational), as well as for every step in logic. Hence in the actual practice of apologetic discussion with unbelievers we must presuppose God before we even begin any argument whatsoever.

In particular, Van Til's position should not be confused with an approach that seeks to show by a classic *reductio* that all non-Christian thought systems are contradictory according to supposedly neutral, Aristotelian standards, and that therefore Christianity is true. Such a *reductio* operates *within the already-accepted framework of classical logic*. Logic would then exist in unitarian fashion whether or not God exists. Van Til's conviction about the pervasiveness of creational dependence is much more radical. We do not start with "neutral" logic. Rather, we as Christians confess loyalty to God as the foundation for the very categories that underlie the logic that we develop.

[17] However, as noted above, Kenneth Pike's tagmemics is a radical exception. My own approach to language attempts to deepen Pike's work through explicit theological reflection.

ordinary communication. The fundamental technical and metatheoretical categories used in the various academic subjects all depend on God. But because of the drive toward secularization, this dependence on God is radically suppressed (Rom. 1:18–21). Thankfulness to God must be restored, and this goal requires radical desecularization.[18]

---

[18] Herman Dooyeweerd's work in *New Critique of Theoretical Thought*, 4 vols. (Philadelphia: Presbyterian & Reformed, 1969), attempted to begin a critique of categories and concept-formation in theoretical thought. The goal was laudable. But in my opinion Dooyeweerd's decision to isolate theology as a special science alongside other sciences greatly suppressed the power of the Bible to reform philosophy. There are also difficulties with Dooyeweerd's fundamental philosophical categories. These categories looks suspiciously "abstract" and unitarian, apparently following the model of the fundamentally unitarian Western philosophical tradition.

There are other problems as well. I am disturbed, as was Van Til, by the way that discussion of God enters at a certain third "stage" of Dooyeweerd's transcendental critique (cf. E. R. Geehan, ed., *Jerusalem and Athens* [n.l.: Presbyterian & Reformed, 1971], 74–127). Apparently, Dooyeweerd hopes that his reasoning will carry non-Christian people along with him, at least until this third stage (p. 76). But unless more is said, Dooyeweerd's followers may naively hold to an unanalyzed assumption that the standards of reasoning are common to Christians and non-Christians. The development of Trinitarian logic shows that it is impossible to agree with non-Christians about standards for reasoning and truth.

Dirk Hendrik Theodoor Vollenhoven represented concerns similar to Dooyeweerd in his attempt to reform Christian thought. He gave attention specifically to the area of logic: *De noodzakelijkheid eener christelijke logica* (Amsterdam: H. J. Paris, 1932); "Hoofdlijnen der logica," *Philosophia Reformata* 13 (1948): 59–118; Nicolaas Theodor Van der Merwe, "Op weg na 'n christelike logika: 'n studie van enkele vraagstukke in die logika met besondere aandag aan D. H. Th. Vollenhoven se visie van 'n christelike logika," M.A. thesis, University of Potchefstroom, 1958. Unfortunately, in a manner similar to Dooyeweerd, Vollenhoven's fundamental categories remain unitarian.

Bibliography

Anderson, James N., and Greg Welty. "The Lord of Non-Contradiction: An Argument for God from Logic." *Philosophia Christi* 13/2 (2011): 321–338.

Anderson, Stephen R. *Doctor Dolittle's Delusion: Animals and the Uniqueness of Human Language.* New Haven, CT: Yale University Press, 2004.

Aristotle. *The Categories* and *On Interpretation.* Translated by Harold P. Cooke. *Prior Analytics.* Translated by Hugh Tredennick. Loeb Classical Library. Cambridge, MA: Harvard University Press, 1973.

Ayer, A. J. *Language, Truth, and Logic.* London: Gollancz, 1936.

Bahnsen, Greg L. *Van Til's Apologetic: Readings and Analysis.* Phillipsburg, NJ: Presbyterian & Reformed, 1998.

Birkhoff, Garrett. *Lattice Theory.* 2nd ed. New York: American Mathematical Society, 1948.

Birkhoff, Garrett, and John von Neumann. "The Logic of Quantum Mechanics." *Annals of Mathematics* 37 (1936): 823–843.

Borchert, Donald M., ed. *Encyclopedia of Philosophy.* 2nd ed. 10 vols. Detroit/New York/San Francisco/ . . . : Thomson Gale, 2006.

Bromiley, Geoffrey W. et al., eds. *The International Standard Bible Encyclopedia.* Rev. ed. 4 vols. Grand Rapids, MI: Eerdmans, 1988.

Brouwer, L. E. J. *Collected Works 1. Philosophy and Foundations of Mathematics.* Edited by Arend Heyting. Amsterdam: North-Holland, 1975.

Carroll, Lewis. *Symbolic Logic and the Game of Logic.* New York: Dover, 1958.

Church, Alonzo. *Introduction to Mathematical Logic.* Princeton, NJ: Princeton University Press, 1956. 10th printing, 1996.

Clark, Gordon H. *Logic.* 2nd ed. Jefferson, MD: Trinity Foundation, 1988.

Cohen, S. Marc. "Aristotle's Metaphysics," *Stanford Encyclopedia of Philosophy (Spring 2009 Edition).* Edited by Edward N. Zalta. http://plato .stanford.edu/archives/spr2009/entries/aristotle-metaphysics/. Accessed October 11, 2011.

Collins, C. John. *Science and Faith: Friends or Foes?* Wheaton, IL: Crossway, 2003.

Copeland, B. Jack. "The Church-Turing Thesis." In *The Stanford Encyclopedia of Philosophy (Summer 2010 Edition).* Edited by Edward N. Zalta. http://plato.stanford.edu/archives/sum2010/entries/church-turing/. Accessed August 26, 2011.

Copi, Irving M. *Symbolic Logic.* 5th ed. New York: Macmillan, 1979.

Copi, Irving M., Carl Cohen, and Kenneth McMahon. *Introduction to Logic.* 14th ed. Boston . . . : Prentice Hall, 2011.

Cothran, Martin. *Traditional Logic: Introduction to Formal Logic: Book I.* Classical Trivium Core Series. Louisville, KY: Memoria, 2000.

———. *Traditional Logic: Advanced Formal Logic: Book II.* Classical Trivium Core Series. Louisville, KY: Memoria, 2000.

Creath, Richard. "Logical Empiricism." In *The Stanford Encyclopedia of Philosophy (Winter 2011 Edition).* Edited by Edward N. Zalta. http://plato.stanford.edu/archives/win2011/entries/logical-empiricism/. Accessed October 15, 2012.

de Saussure, Ferdinand. *Course in General Linguistics.* New York/Toronto/London: McGraw-Hill, 1959.

Descartes, René. *Discourse on the Method of Rightly Conducting the Reason and of Seeking for Truth in the Sciences.* Translated by Norman Kemp Smith. In *Descartes' Philosophical Writings.* London: Macmillan, 1952.

Dooyeweerd, Herman. *New Critique of Theoretical Thought.* 4 vols. Philadelphia: Presbyterian & Reformed, 1969.

Engel, S. Morris. *With Good Reason: An Introduction to Informal Fallacies.* 2nd ed. New York: St. Martin's, 1982.

Euclid. *Euclid's Elements.* Edited by Dana Densmore. Translated by T. L. Heath. Santa Fe, NM: Green Lion, 2002.

Frame, John M. *Apologetics to the Glory of God: An Introduction.* Phillipsburg, NJ: Presbyterian & Reformed, 1994.

———. *Cornelius Van Til: An Analysis of His Thought.* Phillipsburg, NJ: Presbyterian & Reformed, 1995.

———. *The Doctrine of God.* Phillipsburg, NJ: Presbyterian & Reformed, 2002.

———. *The Doctrine of the Christian Life.* Phillipsburg, NJ: Presbyterian & Reformed, 2008.

———. *The Doctrine of the Knowledge of God.* Phillipsburg, NJ: Presbyterian & Reformed, 1987.

———. *The Doctrine of the Word of God.* Phillipsburg, NJ: Presbyterian & Reformed, 2010.

———. "Greeks Bearing Gifts." In *Understanding the Flow of Western Thought.* Edited by W. Andrew Hoffecker. Phillipsburg, NJ: Presbyterian & Reformed, 2007. 1–36.

———. *Perspectives on the Word of God: An Introduction to Christian Ethics.* Eugene, OR: Wipf & Stock, 1999.

———. *Van Til: The Theologian*. Phillipsburg, NJ: Pilgrim, 1976.

Galavotti, Maria Carla. *Philosophical Introduction to Probability*. Stanford, CA: Center for the Study of Language and Information, 2005.

Garson, James. "Modal Logic." In *The Stanford Encyclopedia of Philosophy (Winter 2009 Edition)*. Edited by Edward N. Zalta. http://plato.stanford.edu/archives/win2009/entries/logic-modal/. Accessed August 24, 2012.

Geehan, E. R., ed. *Jerusalem and Athens*. N.l.: Presbyterian & Reformed, 1971.

Gensler, Harold J. *Introduction to Logic*. London/New York: Routledge, 2002.

Gillon, Brendan S. "Logic and Inference in Indian Philosophy." In *Encyclopedia of Philosophy*. 2nd ed. Edited by Donald M. Borchert. 10 vols. Detroit/New York/San Francisco/ . . . : Thomson Gale, 2006. 5:410–414.

Gödel, Kurt. *On Formally Undecidable Propositions of* Principia Mathematica *and Related Systems*. Translated by B. Meltzer. New York: Dover, 1992.

———. "On Formally Undecidable Propositions of *Principia Mathematica* and Related Systems." Translated by Martin Hirzel. http://www.research.ibm.com/people/h/hirzel/papers/canon00-goedel.pdf. Accessed January 18, 2011.

———. "Über formal unentscheidbare Sätze der *Principia Mathematica* und verwandter Systeme, I." *Monatshefte für Mathematik und Physik* 38 (1931): 173–198.

Graham, A. C. "Chinese Logic." In *Encyclopedia of Philosophy*. 2nd ed. Edited by Donald M. Borchert. 10 vols. Detroit/New York/San Francisco/ . . . : Thomson Gale, 2006. 5:414–417.

Grätzer, George. *Lattice Theory: First Concepts and Distributive Lattices*. Reprint. Mineola, NY: Dover, 2009.

Hansen, Chad. *Language and Logic in Ancient China*. Michigan Studies on China. Ann Arbor, MI: University of Michigan Press, 1983.

Hedman, Shawn. *A First Course in Logic: An Introduction to Model Theory, Proof Theory, Computability, and Complexity*. Oxford: Oxford University Press, 2004.

Hilbert, David. *The Foundations of Geometry*. Translated by E. J. Townsend. Reprint. La Salle, IL: Open Court, 1950. http://www.gutenberg.org/files/17384/17384-pdf.pdf. Accessed August 25, 2011.

Iemhoff, Rosalie. "Intuitionism in the Philosophy of Mathematics." In *The Stanford Encyclopedia of Philosophy (Summer 2010 Edition)*. Edited by Edward N. Zalta. http://plato.stanford.edu/archives/sum2010/entries/intuitionism/. Accessed August 29, 2012.

Irvine, A. D. "Russell's Paradox." In *The Stanford Encyclopedia of Philosophy (Summer 2010 Edition)*. Edited by Edward N. Zalta. http://plato.stanford.edu/archives/sum2010/entries/russell-paradox/. Accessed August 26, 2011.

Kanamori, Akihiro. "Set Theory." In *Encyclopedia of Philosophy*. 2nd ed. Edited by Donald M. Borchert. 10 vols. Detroit/New York/San Francisco, . . . : Thomson Gale, 2006. 8:831–847.

Keller, Timothy J. *The Reason for God: Belief in an Age of Skepticism*. New York: Dutton, 2008.

Kline, Meredith G. *Images of the Spirit*. Grand Rapids, MI: Baker, 1980.

Kosko, Bart. *Neural Networks and Fuzzy Systems: A Dynamical Systems Approach to Machine Intelligence*. New York: Prentice Hall, 1991.

Kuyper, Abraham. *Lectures on Calvinism*. Grand Rapids, MI: Eerdmans, 1931.

——. *Principles of Sacred Theology*. Grand Rapids, MI: Eerdmans, 1968.

Lewis, C. S. *Out of the Silent Planet*. New York: Macmillan, 1943.

——. *The Pilgrim's Regress: An Allegorical Apology for Christianity, Reason, and Romanticism*. 3rd ed. Grand Rapids, MI: Eerdmans, 1943.

Longacre, Robert E. *An Anatomy of Speech Notions*. Lisse, Belgium: De Ridder, 1976.

——. *The Grammar of Discourse*. New York/London: Plenum, 1983.

MacIntyre, Alasdair C. *Whose Justice? Which Rationality?* Notre Dame, IN: University of Notre Dame Press, 1988.

Mackey, George W. *Mathematical Foundations of Quantum Mechanics*. New York/Amsterdam: Benjamin, 1963.

Milbank, John. *The Word Made Strange: Theology, Language, Culture*. Oxford: Blackwell, 1997.

Moschovakis, Joan. "Intuitionistic Logic." In *The Stanford Encyclopedia of Philosophy (Summer 2010 Edition)*. Edited by Edward N. Zalta. http://plato.stanford.edu/archive/sum2010/entries/logic-intuitionistic/. Accessed August 26, 2011.

Murray, John. "The Attestation of Scripture." In *The Infallible Word: A Symposium By Members of the Faculty of Westminster Theological Seminary*. 3rd revised printing. Philadelphia: Presbyterian & Reformed, 1967.

Negri, Sara, and Jan von Plato. *Structural Proof Theory*. Cambridge: Cambridge University Press, 2001.

Nicod, Jean. "A Reduction in the Number of Primitive Propositions of Logic." *Proceedings of the Cambridge Philosophical Society* 19 (1917): 32–41.

Oliphint, K. Scott. *The Battle Belongs to the Lord: The Power of Scripture for Defending Our Faith.* Phillipsburg, NJ: Presbyterian & Reformed, 2003.

―――. *Reasons for Faith: Philosophy in the Service of Theology.* Phillipsburg, NJ: Presbyterian & Reformed, 2006.

Oppy, Graham. "Ontological Arguments." In *The Stanford Encyclopedia of Philosophy (Fall 2011 Edition).* Edited by Edward N. Zalta. http://plato.stanford.edu/archives/fall2011/entries/ontological-arguments/. Accessed August 24, 2012.

Packer, J. I. "The Adequacy of Human Language." In *Inerrancy.* Edited by Norman L. Geisler. Grand Rapids, MI: Zondervan, 1980. 195–226.

Pike, Kenneth L. *Language in Relation to a Unified Theory of the Structure of Human Behavior.* 2nd ed. The Hague/Paris: Mouton, 1967.

―――. *Linguistic Concepts: An Introduction to Tagmemics.* Lincoln/London: University of Nebraska Press, 1982.

Plato. *Euthyphro.* Translated by Harold N. Fowler. London: Heinemann; Cambridge, MA: Harvard University Press, 1966.

Pohlers, Wolfram. *Proof Theory: An Introduction.* New York: Springer, 1989.

Poythress, Vern S. "A Framework for Discourse Analysis: The Components of a Discourse, from a Tagmemic Viewpoint." *Semiotica* 38/3–4 (1982): 277–298.

―――. *God-Centered Biblical Interpretation.* Phillipsburg, NJ: Presbyterian & Reformed, 1999.

―――. *In the Beginning Was the Word: Language—A God-Centered Approach.* Wheaton, IL: Crossway, 2009.

―――. *Philosophy, Science and the Sovereignty of God.* Nutley, NJ: Presbyterian & Reformed, 1976.

―――. *Redeeming Science: A God-Centered Approach.* Wheaton, IL: Crossway, 2006.

―――. *Redeeming Sociology: A God-Centered Approach.* Wheaton, IL: Crossway, 2011.

―――. "Reforming Ontology and Logic in the Light of the Trinity: An Application of Van Til's Idea of Analogy." *Westminster Theological Journal* 57/1 (1995): 187–219.

―――. *The Returning King: A Guide to the Book of Revelation.* Phillipsburg, NJ: Presbyterian & Reformed, 2000.

―――. "Science as Allegory." *Journal of the American Scientific Affiliation* 35/2 (1983): 65–71.

———. *Symphonic Theology: The Validity of Multiple Perspectives in Theology.* Reprint. Phillipsburg, NJ: Presbyterian & Reformed, 2001.

———. "Tagmemic Analysis of Elementary Algebra." *Semiotica* 17/2 (1976): 131–151.

———. "The Quest for Wisdom." In *Resurrection and Eschatology: Theology in Service of the Church: Essays in Honor of Richard B. Gaffin, Jr.* Edited by Lane G. Tipton and Jeffrey C. Waddington. Phillipsburg, NJ: Presbyterian & Reformed, 2008. 86–114.

Poythress, Vern S., and Hugo Sun. "A Method to Construct Convex, Connected Venn Diagrams for Any Finite Number of Sets." *The Pentagon* 31/2 (1972): 80–82.

Pratt, Richard L. *Every Thought Captive: A Study Manual for the Defense of Christian Truth.* Phillipsburg, NJ: Presbyterian & Reformed, 1979.

Prior, A. N. "Logic, Traditional." In *Encyclopedia of Philosophy.* 2nd ed. Edited by Donald M. Borchert. 10 vols. Detroit/New York/San Francisco/ . . . : Thomson Gale, 2006. 5:493–506.

Rescher, Nicholas. "Logic in the Islamic World." In *Encyclopedia of Philosophy.* 2nd ed. Edited by Donald M. Borchert. 10 vols. Detroit/New York/San Francisco/ . . . : Thomson Gale, 2006. 5:417–420.

Ronning, John. *The Jewish Targums and John's Logos Theology.* Peabody, MA: Hendrickson, 2010.

Ross, James F. "The Crash of Modal Metaphysics." *Review of Metaphysics* 43 (1989): 251–279.

Sayers, Dorothy. *The Mind of the Maker.* New York: Harcourt, Brace, 1941.

Smullyan, Raymond M. *Godel's Incompleteness Theorems.* Oxford: Oxford University Press, 1992.

Torretti, Roberto. "Geometry." In *Encyclopedia of Philosophy.* 2nd ed. Edited by Donald M. Borchert. 10 vols. Detroit/New York/San Francisco/ . . . : Thomson Gale, 2006. 4:53–64.

———. "Nineteenth Century Geometry." In *The Stanford Encyclopedia of Philosophy (Summer 2010 Edition).* Edited by Edward N. Zalta. http://plato.stanford.edu/archives/sum2010/entries/geometry-19th/. Accessed August 26, 2011.

Turing, Alan M. "On Computable Numbers, with an Application to the *Entscheidungsproblem.*" *Proceedings of the London Mathematical Society* 2.42 (1936): 230–265.

van Atten, Mark. "Luitzen Egbertus Jan Brouwer." In *The Stanford Encyclopedia of Philosophy (Summer 2010 Edition).* Edited by Edward N. Zalta. http://plato.stanford.edu/archives/sum2010/entries/brouwer/. Accessed August 26, 2011.

van Dalen, Dirk. "Intuitionism and Intuitionistic Logic." In *Encyclopedia of Philosophy*. 2nd ed. Edited by Donald M. Borchert. 10 vols. Detroit/ . . . : Thomson Gale, 2006. 4:737–743.

Van der Merwe, Nicolaas Theodor. "Op weg na 'n christelike logika: 'n studie van enkele vraagstukke in die logika met besondere aandag aan D. H. Th. Vollenhoven se visie van 'n christelike logika." M.A. thesis, University of Potchefstroom, 1958.

van Heijenoort, Jean, ed. *From Frege to Gödel: A Source Book on Mathematical Logic 1879–1931*. Cambridge, MA: Harvard University Press, 1967.

Van Til, Cornelius. *Christian Apologetics*. Phillipsburg, NJ: Presbyterian & Reformed, 2003.

———. *Common Grace and the Gospel*. n.l.: Presbyterian & Reformed, 1973.

———. *The Defense of the Faith*. 2nd ed. Philadelphia: Presbyterian & Reformed, 1963.

———. *An Introduction to Systematic Theology*. Phillipsburg, NJ: Presbyterian & Reformed, 1974.

———. "Response." [to Herman Dooyeweerd, "Cornelius Van Til and the Transcendental Critique of Theoretical Thought."] *Jerusalem and Athens: Critical Discussions on the Theology and Apologetics of Cornelius Van Til*. Edited by E. R. Geehan. n.l.: Presbyterian & Reformed, 1971. 89–127.

———. *A Survey of Christian Epistemology*. Volume 2 of the series *In Defense of Biblical Christianity*. n.l.: den Dulk Christian Foundation, 1969.

———. *Why I Believe in God*. Philadelphia: Commission on Christian Education, Orthodox Presbyterian Church, n.d.

Vidyabhusana, Satis Chandra. *A History of Indian Logic: Ancient, Mediaeval, and Modern Schools*. Delhi: Motilal Banarsidass, 1971.

Vollenhoven, Dirk Hendrik Theodoor. "Hoofdlijnen der logica." *Philosophia Reformata* 13 (1948): 58–118.

———. *De noodzakelijkheid eener christelijke logica*. Amsterdam: H. J. Paris, 1932.

von Plato, Jan. "The Development of Proof Theory." *The Stanford Encyclopedia of Philosophy (Summer 2010 Edition)*. Edited by Edward N. Zalta. http://plato.stanford.edu/archives/sum2010/entries/proof-theory-development/. Accessed August 26, 2011.

Warfield, Benjamin B. *The Inspiration and Authority of the Bible*. Reprint. Philadelphia: Presbyterian & Reformed, 1967.

Watts, Isaac. *Logic; or, the Right Use of Reason in the Enquiry after Truth: With a Variety of Rules to Guard against Error, in the Affairs of Religion and Human Life, as Well as in the Sciences.* [Many editions.] London: Tegg, 1811.

Whitehead, Alfred North, and Bertrand Russell. *Principia Mathematica.* 2nd ed. 3 vols. Cambridge: Cambridge University Press, 1927.

Wittgenstein, Ludwig. *Tractatus Logico-philosophicus.* London: Routledge & Kegan Paul; New York: Humanities, 1963.

Zadeh, Lotfi. "Fuzzy Sets." *Information and Control* 8 (1956): 338–353

———. "Quantitative Fuzzy Semantics." *Information Science* 3 (1971): 159–176.

General Index

Scripture Index

Vern Poythress Answers
Modern Challenges
to the Bible

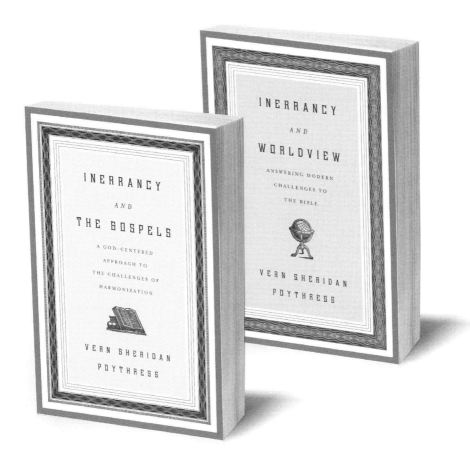

Accomplished scholar and author Vern Poythress brings his expertise to bear on the Synoptic Gospel problem and the question of worldview.